The Biblical Foundations
of Christian Worship

THE COMPLETE LIBRARY
OF
CHRISTIAN WORSHIP

THE COMPLETE LIBRARY
OF
CHRISTIAN WORSHIP

Volume 1, The Biblical Foundations of Christian Worship

ROBERT E. WEBBER, EDITOR

StarSong
PUBLISHING GROUP

Nashville, Tennessee

Unless otherwise indicated, all Scripture quotations taken from the HOLY BIBLE, NEW INTERNATIONAL VERSION. Copyright © 1973, 1978, 1984 by International Bible Society. Used by permission of Zondervan Publishing House.

Scripture quotations marked (KJV) are from the HOLY BIBLE, KING JAMES VERSION.

Scripture quotations marked (NASB) are taken from the NEW AMERICAN STANDARD BIBLE. Copyright © 1960, 1962, 1963, 1968, 1971, 1972, 1973, 1975, 1977, the Lockman Foundation. Used by permission.

Scripture quotations marked (RSV) are taken from the REVISED STANDARD VERSION of the Bible. Copyright © 1946, 1952, 1971, 1973, the division of the Christian Education of the National Council of Churches of Christ in the U.S.A. Used by permission.

Scripture quotations marked (NRSV) are taken from THE HOLY BIBLE: NEW REVISED STANDARD VERSION. Copyright © 1989 by Division of the Christian Education of the National Council of Churches of Christ in the United Stated of America. Used by permission.

Scripture quotations marked (TEV) are taken from TODAY'S ENGLISH VERSION of the Bible, Third Edition. Copyright © 1966, 1971 American Bible Society. Used by permission.

Star Song Publishing Group, a division of Jubilee Communications, Inc.
2325 Crestmoor, Nashville, Tennessee 37215.

Library of Congress Cataloging-in-Publication Data

The Biblical Foundations of Christian worship / Robert E. Webber, editor.—1st ed.
   p. cm.—(The Complete library of Christian worship : v. 1)
  Includes bibliographical references and index.
  ISBN 1-56233-011-X
  1. Public worship—Biblical teaching. I. Webber, Robert.
  II. Series.
  BS680.W78B53 1993
  264′.009′01—dc20   93-33585
                                               CIP

Printed in the United States of America
1 2 3 4 5 6 7 8 9 — 98 97 96 95 94 93

CONTENTS

Part 4: MUSIC AND THE ARTS IN BIBLICAL WORSHIP

Part 5: THE BIBLICAL FOUNDATIONS OF CHRISTIAN WORSHIP

List of Illustrations and Tables

Board of Editorial Consultants

The Board of Editorial Consultants is made up of leaders in worship renewal from major Christian denominations. They have functioned as advisors, often through letter and telephone. Every attempt has been made to include material on worship representing the whole church. For this reason, different viewpoints are presented without any attempt to express a particular point of view or bias. A special word of thanks is due to the executive and consulting editors for their helpful input. Their ideas, suggestions, and contributions have strengthened the *Complete Library of Christian Worship*. Omissions and weaknesses in all seven volumes are the sole responsibility of the compiler and editor.

Paul Bassett
Nazarene Theological Seminary, Kansas City, Missouri

Robert J. Batastini
GIA Publications, Chicago, Illinois

Kevin G. Bausman
First Presbyterian Church of Southport, Indianapolis, Indiana

Patricia Beal
South Park Community, Surrey, Australia

John Bell
Iona Community, Scotland

W. Wilson Benton, Jr.
Kirk of the Hills Presbyterian, St. Louis, Missouri

Philip Berggrov Peter
Associate Professor Emeritus, University of Michigan, Dearborn, Michigan

Jerome W. Berryman
Christ Church Cathedral, Houston, Texas

Harold M. Best
Wheaton College Conservatory of Music, Wheaton, Illinois

Perry H. Biddle, Jr.
First Presbyterian Church, Old Hickory, Tennessee

Warren Bird
Charles E. Fuller Institute, Suffern, New York

Richard Bishop
Evangel College, Springfield, Missouri

Robert Black
Central Wesleyan College, Central, South Carolina

Donald Bloesch
University of Dubuque Theological Seminary, Dubuque, Iowa

Edith Blumhoffer
Wheaton College, Wheaton, Illinois

Markus Bockmuehl
Cambridge University, Cambridge, England

Richard Allen Bodey
Trinity Evangelical Divinity School

Nick Boone
Madison Church of Christ, Madison, Tennessee

P. Wayne Boosahda
St. Barnabas the Encourager, Tulsa, Oklahoma

Deena Borchers
Overland Park, Kansas

Gordon Borrow
Western Theological Seminary, Portland, Oregon

Lamar Boschman
Lamar Boschman Ministries, Bedford, Texas

Walter Bouman
Trinity Lutheran Seminary, Columbus, Ohio

Paul Bradshaw
University of Notre Dame, Notre Dame, Indiana

Vincent Branick
University of Dayton, Dayton, Ohio

James Brauer
Concordia Theological Seminary, St. Louis, Missouri

Emily Brink
***Reformed Worship**, Grand Rapids, Michigan*

John Brooks-Leonard
Center for Pastoral Liturgy, Univeristy of Notre Dame, Notre Dame, Indiana

Geoffrey Bromily
Fuller Theological Seminary, Pasadena, California

Wayne Brouwer
First Christian Reformed Church, London, Ontario, Canada

Donald Bruggink
Western Theological Seminary, Holland, Michigan

Steve Burdan
Willow Creek Community Church, South Barrington, Illinois

Eileen C. Burke-Sullivan
All Saints Parish, Dallas, Texas

John E. Burkhart
McCormick Theological Seminary, Chicago, Illinois

David Buttrick
Vanderbilt Divinity School, Nashville, Tennessee

William Caldaroni
Holy Transfiguration Orthodox Mission, Carol Stream, Illinois

Gerald Calhoun
Jesuit Novitiate, Jamaica Plains, Massachusetts

Alkiviadis C. Calivas
Holy Cross Greek Orthodox School of Theology, Brookline, Massachusetts

Melvin Campbell
La Sierra University, La Sierra, California

Lorene Carlson
Women's Aglow International, Seattle, Washington

Richard Carlson
North Park Theological Seminary, Chicago, Illinois

James A. Carr
San Antonio, Texas

Carole J. Carter
First Presbyterian Church, Charleston, West Virginia

List of Cooperating Publishers

BOOK PUBLISHERS

Abbott-Martyn Press
2325 Crestmoor Road
Nashville, TN 37215

Abingdon Press
201 8th Avenue South
Nashville, TN 37202

Agape
Hope Publishing
Carol Stream, IL 60187

Alba House
2187 Victory Boulevard
Staten Island, NY 10314

**American Choral
Directors Association**
502 Southwest 38th
Lawton, Oklahoma 73505

**Asian Institute for
Liturgy & Music**
P.O. Box 3167
Manila 1099 Philippines

Augsburg/Fortress Press
426 S. Fifth Street
Box 1209
Minneapolis, MN 55440

Ave Maria Press
Notre Dame, IN 46556

Baker Book House
P.O. Box 6287
Grand Rapids, MI 49516-6287

Beacon Hill Press
Box 419527
Kansas City, MO 64141

Bethany House Publishers
6820 Auto Club Road
Minneapolis, MN 55438

The Brethren Press
1451 Dundee Avenue
Elgin, IL 60120

Bridge Publishing, Inc.
200 Hamilton Blvd.
South Plainfield, NJ 07080

Broadman Press
127 Ninth Avenue, North
Nashville, TN 37234

C.S.S. Publishing Company
628 South Main Street
Lima, OH 45804

Cathedral Music Press
P.O. Box 66
Pacific, MO 63069

**Catholic Book
Publishing Company**
257 W. 17th Street
New York, NY 10011

CBP Press
Box 179
St. Louis, MO 63166

Celebration
P.O. Box 309
Aliquippa, PA 15001

Channing L. Bete Company
South Deerfield, MA 01373

Choristers Guild
2834 W. Kingsley Road
Garland, TX 75041

Christian Literature Crusade
701 Pennsylvania Avenue
Box 1449
Ft. Washington, PA 19034

Christian Publications
3825 Hartzdale Drive
Camp Hill, PA 17011

**The Church
Hymnal Corporation**
800 Second Avenue
New York, NY 10017

The Columba Press
93 Merise
Mount Merrion
Blackrock, Dublin

Concordia Publishing House
3558 S. Jefferson Avenue
St. Louis, MO 63118

Covenant Publications
3200 West Foster Avenue
Chicago, IL 60625

Cowley Publications
980 Memorial Drive
Cambridge, MA 02138

CRC Publications
2850 Kalamazoo SE
Grand Rapids, MI 49560

**Creative Communications
for the Parish**
10300 Watson Road
St. Louis, MO 63127

**Crossroad Publishing
Company**
575 Lexington Avenue
New York, NY 10022

Crossroad/Continuum
370 Lexington Avenue
New York, NY 10017

Dominion Press
7112 Burns Street
Ft. Worth, TX 76118

Duke Univesity Press
Box 6697 College Station
Durham, NC 27708

Faith and Life Press
724 Main Street
Box 347
Newton, KS 67114

The Faith Press, Ltd.
7 Tufton Street
Westminster, S.W. 1
England

Fleming H. Revell Company
184 Central Avenue
Old Tappen, N.J. 07675

Folk Music Ministry
P.O. Box 3443
Annapolis, MD 21403

Franciscan Communications
1229 South Santee Street
Los Angeles, CA 90015

Georgetown University Press
111 Intercultural Center
Washington, D.C. 20057

GIA Publications
7404 S. Mason Avenue
Chicago, IL 60638

Great Commission Publications
7401 Old York Road
Philadelphia, PA 19126

Grove Books
Bramcote Notts
England

Harper & Row Publishers
Icehouse One-401
151 Union Street
San Francisco, CA 94111-1299

Harvard University Press
79 Garden Street
Cambridge, MA 02138

Harvest Publications
Baptist General Conference
2002 S. Arlington Heights Road
Arlington Heights, IL 60005

Hendrickson Publishers, Inc.
P.O. Box 3473
Peabody, MA 01961-3473

Herald Press
616 Walnut Avenue
Scottdale, PA 15683

Hinshaw Music Incorporated
P.O. Box 470
Chapel Hill, NC 27514

Holt, Rinehart & Winston
111 5th Avenue
New York, NY 10175

Hope Publishing Company
Carol Stream, IL 60188

Hymn Society of America
Texas Christian University
P.O. Box 30854
Ft. Worth, TX 76129

Indiana University Press
10th & Morton
Bloomington, IN 47405

Integrity Music
P.O. Box 16813
Mobile, AL 36616

J.S. Paluch Company, Inc.
3825 Willow Road
P.O. Box 2703
Schiller Park, IL 60176

**The Jewish Publication
Society of America**
1930 Chestnut Street
Philadelphia, PA 19103

Judson Press
P.O. Box 851
Valley Forge, PA 19482-0851

**Light and Life Publishing
Company**
P.O. Box 26421
Minneapolis, MN 55426

Liguori Publications
One Liguori Drive
Liguori, MO 63057

Lillenas Publishing Company
Box 419527
Kansas City, MO 64141

The Liturgical Conference
1017 Twelfth Street, N.W.
Washington, D.C. 20005-4091

The Liturgical Press
St. John's Abbey
Collegeville, MN 56321

Liturgy Training Publications
1800 North Heritage Avenue
Chicago, IL 60622-1101

**Macmillan Publishing
Company**
866 Third Avenue
New York, NY 10022

Maranatha! Music
25411 Cabot Road
Suite 203
Laguna Hills, CA 92653

Mel Bay Publications
Pacific, MO 63969-0066

Meriwether Publishing, Ltd.
885 Elkton Drive
Colorado Springs, CO 80907

Michael Glazier, Inc.
1723 Delaware Avenue
Wilmington, Delaware 19806

Morehouse-Barlow
78 Danbury Road
Wilton, CT 06897

Multnomah Press
10209 SE Division Street
Portland, OR 97266

**National Association
of Pastoral Musicians**
25 Sheridan Street, NW
Washington, DC 20011

NavPress
P.O. Box 6000
Colorado Springs, CO 80934

New Skete
Cambridge, NY 12816

**North American
Liturgical Resources**
1802 N. 23rd Avenue
Phoenix, AZ 85029

Oxford University Press
16-00 Pollitt Drive
Fair Lawn, NJ 07410

The Pastoral Press
225 Sheridan Street, NW
Washington, D.C. 20011

Paulist Press
997 MacArthur Boulevard
Mahwah, NJ 07430

The Pilgrim Press
132 West 31st Street
New York, NY 10001

Psalmist Resources
9820 E. Watson Road
St. Louis, MO 63126

Pueblo Publishing Company
100 West 32nd Street
New York, NY 1001-3210

Regal Books
A Division of Gospel Light
    Publications
Ventura, CA 93006

Resource Publications, Inc.
160 E. Virginia Street #290
San Jose, CA 95112

The Scarecrow Press
52 Liberty Street
Box 416
Metuchen, NJ 08840

Schocken Books
62 Cooper Square
New York, NY 10003

**Schuyler Institute for
Worship & The Arts**
2757 Melandy Drive, Suite 15
San Carlos, CA 94070

SCM Press Ltd.
c/o Trinity Press International
3725 Chestnut Street
Philadelphia, PA 19104

Servant Publications
P.O. Box 8617
Petersham, MA 01366-0545

The Sharing Company
P.O. Box 2224
Austin, TX 78768-2224

Sheed & Ward
115 E. Armour Boulevard
P.O. Box 414292
Kansas City, MO 64141-0281

Shofar Publications, Inc
P.O. Box 88711
Carol Stream, IL 60188

SPCK
Holy Trinity Church
Marylebone Road
London, N.W. 4D4

St. Anthony Messenger Press
1615 Republic Street
Cincinnati, OH 45210

St. Bede's Publications
P.O. Box 545
Petersham, MA 01366-0545

St. Mary's Press
Terrace Heights
Winona, MN 55987

St. Vladimir Seminary Press
575 Scarsdale Road
Crestwood, NY 10707-1699

Thomas Nelson Publishers
P.O. Box 141000
Nashville, TN 37214

Twenty Third Publications
P.O. Box 180
Mystic, CT 06355

Tyndale House Publishers
351 Executive Drive
Carol Stream, IL 60188

United Church of Christ
Office of Church Life and
    Leadership
700 Prospect
Cleveland, OH 44115

United Church Press
132 West 31st Street
New York, NY 10001

**The United Methodist
Publishing House**
P.O. Box 801
Nashville, TN 37202

**United States
Catholic Conference**
Office of Publishing and
    Promotion Services
1312 Massachusetts Avenue, NW
Washington, DC 20005-4105

University of California Press
1010 Westward Blvd.
Los Angeles, CA 90024

**University of Notre
Dame Press**
Notre Dame, IN 46556

The Upper Room
1908 Grand Avenue
P.O. Box 189
Nashville, TN 37202

Victory House Publishers
P.O. Box 700238
Tulsa, OK 74170

Westminster John Knox Press
100 Witherspoon Street
Louisville, KY 40202-1396

**William B. Eerdmans
Publishing Company**
255 Jefferson S.E.
Grand Rapids, MI 49503

**William C. Brown
Publishing Company**
2460 Kerper Boulevard
P.O. Box 539
Dubuque, IA 52001

William H. Sadlier, Inc.
11 Park Place
New York, NY 10007

Winston Press
P.O. Box 1630
Hagerstown, MD 21741

Word Books
Tower-Williams Square
5221 N. O'Conner Blvd. Suite
    1000
Irving, TX 75039

**World Council of
Churches Publications**
P.O. Box 66
150 Route de Ferney
1211 Geneva 20, Switzerland

**World Library
Publications, Inc.**
3815 N. Willow Road
P.O. Box 2701
Schiller Park, IL 60176

**The World
Publishing Company**
Meridian Books
110 E. 59th Street
New York, NY 10022

Yale University Press
302 Temple Street
New Haven, CN 06510

Zion Fellowship
236 Gorham Street
Canadagina, NY 14424

**Zondervan Publishing
Company**
1415 Lake Drive S.E.
Grand Rapids, MI 49506

PERIODICAL PUBLISHERS

The American Center for Church Music Newsletter
3339 Burbank Drive
Ann Arbor, MI 48105

American Organist
475 Riverside Drive, Suite 1260
New York, NY 10115

ARTS: The Arts in Religious and Theological Studies
United Theological Seminary of the Twin Cities
3000 5th Street, NW
New Brighton, MN 55112

Arts Advocate
The United Church of Christ Fellowship in the Arts
73 S. Palvuse
Walla Walla, WA 99362

The Choral Journal
American Choral Directors Association
P.O. Box 6310
Lawton, OK 73506

Choristers Guild Letters
2834 W. Kingsley Road
Garland, TX 75041

Christians in the Visual Arts
(newsletter)
P.O. Box 10247
Arlington, VA 22210

Church Music Quarterly
Royal School of Church Music
Addington Palace
Croyden, England CR9 5AD

The Church Musician
Southern Baptist Convention
127 9th Avenue N.
Nashville, TN 37234

Contemporary Christian Music
CCM Publications
P.O. Box 6300
Laguna Hills, CA 92654

Diapason
380 E. Northwest Highway
Des Plaines, IL 60016

Doxology
Journal of the Order of St. Luke in the United Methodist Church

1872 Sweet Home Road
Buffalo, NY 14221

Environment and Art Letter
Liturgy Training Publications
1800 N. Hermitage Avenue
Chicago, IL 60622

GIA Quarterly
7404 S. Mason Avenue
Chicago, IL 60638

Grace Notes
Association of Lutheran Church Musicians
4807 Idaho Circle
Ames, IA 50010

The Hymn
Hymn Society of the United States and Canada
P.O. Box 30854
Fort Worth, TX 76129

Journal
Sacred Dance Guild
Joyce Smillie, Resource Director
10 Edge Court
Woodbury, CT 06798

Journal of Ritual Studies
Department of Religious Studies
University of Pittsburgh
Pittsburgh, PA 15260

Let the People Worship
Schuyler Institute for Worship and the Arts
2757 Melendy Drive, Suite 15
San Carlos, CA 94070

Liturgy
The Liturgical Conference
8750 Georgia Avenue, S., Suite 123
Silver Spring, MD 20910

Liturgy 90
Liturgy Training Publications
1800 N. Hermitage Avenue
Chicago, IL 60622

Modern Liturgy
Resource Publications
160 E. Virginia Street, Suite 290
San Jose, CA 95112

Music in Worship
Selah Publishing Company
P.O. Box 103
Accord, NY 12404

Newsnotes
The Fellowship of United Methodists in Worship, Music, and Other Arts
P.O. Box 54367
Atlanta, GA 30308

Pastoral Music
225 Sheridian Street, NW
Washington, D.C. 20011

PRISM
Yale Institute of Sacred Music
409 Prospect Street
New Haven, CT 06510

The Psalmist
9820 E. Watson Road
St. Louis, MO 63124

Reformed Liturgy and Music
Worship and Ministry Unit
100 Witherspoon Street
Louisville, KY 40202

Reformed Music Journal
Brookside Publishing
3911 Mt. Lehman Road
Abbotsford, BC V2S 6A9

Reformed Worship
CRC Publications
2850 Kalamazoo Avenue, SE
Grand Rapids, MI 49560

Rite Reasons
Biblical Horizons
P.O. Box 1096
Niceville, FL 32588

St. Vladimirs Theological Quarterly
757 Scarsdale Road
Crestwood, NY 10707

Studia Liturgica
Department of Theology
University of Notre Dame
Notre Dame, IN 46556

Today's Liturgy
Oregon Catholic Press
5536 NE Hassalo
Portland, OR 97213

Worship
The Liturgical Press
St. John's Abbey
Collegeville, MN 56321

Worship Leader
CCM Communications, Inc.
107 Kenner Avenue
Nashville, TN 37205

Worship Today
600 Rinehard Road
Lake Mary, FL 32746

Preface to Volume 1

In 1985 I envisioned a medium-sized book for pastors, ministers of music, and other leaders of worship, entitled *The Worship Resource Book*. As I began to gather and classify the materials for this book, it soon became obvious that a single volume could not begin to contain all the information and resources available on the subject of worship. The one volume expanded to five, then to six, and finally to seven.

The purpose of the original vision has been retained in the expanded version now known as *The Complete Library of Christian Worship*. The purpose is pastoral, and grows out of the urgent desire to serve those who lead worship in the local church. For this reason the *Library* is not primarily intended for the scholarly community.

Nevertheless *The Complete Library of Christian Worship* is compiled out of the conviction that the purposes of the local church are best served by taking advantage of the best in biblical, historical, and theological research. Consequently, the *Library* is an attempt to unite academic studies in worship with the day-to-day and week-to-week practice of worship in the local church.

Volume 1, *The Biblical Foundations of Christian Worship,* addresses worship themes developed in biblical literature. The editors and contributors have not attempted to show how these themes are further developed in the history, theology, and practice of worship. This is the task of the next six volumes.

The phrase *complete library* in the title is not used in the sense that these volumes represent an exhaustive treatment of the subject. While every effort has been made to provide a comprehensive survey of issues and themes relevant to Christian worship, many other excellent resources exist which offer in-depth examinations of specific subjects.

Moreover, it is appropriate to say that the Bible itself is a liturgical book, the book of the church's worship. Most of the entries in Volume 1, *The Biblical Foundations of Christian Worship,* avoid the critical issues that occupy the attention of scholars in favor of a treatment of the biblical text as it stands. This is in keeping with the pastoral orientation of *The Complete Library of Christian Worship*.

It is my hope that this volume, as well as those which follow, will serve the church in its educational task of understanding the theory and practice of worship and in its renewing task of allowing the fresh winds of the Spirit to revitalize the immediate experience of Christian worship.

Robert E. Webber, Editor

Introduction

The *Complete Library of Christian Worship* has been designed to meet a need in the church. Christian leaders and congregations are becoming increasingly interested in the subjects of worship and worship renewal in the local church. Often, however, they lack adequate biblical and historical perspective or the necessary materials and resources to engage in the renewal process.

To fulfill the demand for worship resources, publishing houses, particularly those of specific denominations, have been producing materials for the local church. While these materials may find use within the constituency of a particular denomination, only a few break across denominational barriers and become known throughout the church at large.

The Complete Library of Christian Worship draws from more than one hundred publishing houses and the major Christian denominations of the world in order to bring those resources together in a seven-volume work and make them readily available to all.

The purpose of this introductory material is to acquaint the reader with *The Complete Library of Christian Worship* and to help him or her to use its information and resources in the local church. First, the reader needs to have some sense of the scope of worship studies and renewal that are addressed by *The Complete Library of Christian Worship* (see section 101 below). Second, it is important to learn how to use the *Library* (see section 102). Finally, there is a need to understand the precise content of Volume 1, *Biblical Foundations of Christian Worship.*

These three introductory entries are a key to the whole concept of the *Library,* a concept that brings together instruction in worship and vital resources for use in worship. The *Library* also directs the reader to a vast array of books, audio tapes, videotapes, model services, and resources in music and the arts. It seeks to provide direction and inspiration for everything the church does in worship.

101 • Introduction to *The Complete Library of Christian Worship*

The word *library* implies a collection of resources, together with a system of organization that makes them accessible to the user. Specifically, *The Complete Library of Christian Worship* is a comprehensive compilation of information pertaining to the worship of the Christian church. It draws from a large pool of scholars and practitioners in the field, and from more than two thousand books and media resources in print.

The purpose of *The Complete Library of Christian Worship* is to make biblical, historical, and contemporary resources on worship available to pastors, music ministers, worship committees, and the motivated individual worshiper. The *Library* contains biblical and historical information on all aspects of worship and numerous resource materials, as well as suggested resource books, audio tapes, and video instructional material for every worship act in the local church.

The twentieth century, more than any century in the history of Christianity, has been the century for research and study in the origins, history, theology, and practice of Christian worship. Consequently there are seven broad areas in which worship studies are taking place. These are:

1. the biblical foundations of worship;
2. historical and theological development;
3. resources for worship and preaching;
4. resources for music and the arts in worship;
5. resources for the services of the Christian year;
6. resources for sacraments, ordinances, and other sacred acts; and
7. resources for worship and related ministries.

The Complete Library of Christian Worship is organized around these seven areas of worship renewal. In these seven volumes one will find a wide variety of resources for every worship act in the church, and a select but broad bibliography for additional resources.

102 • HOW TO USE *THE COMPLETE LIBRARY OF CHRISTIAN WORSHIP*

The Complete Library of Christian Worship differs from an encyclopedia, which is often organized alphabetically, with information about a particular subject scattered throughout the book. The *Library* does not follow this pattern, because it is a work that intends to educate as well as to provide resources. Consequently, all the material in the *Library* is organized under a particular theme or issue of worship.

The difference between the *Library* and an encyclopedia may be illustrated by examining the topic of environmental art in worship. Some of the themes essential to environmental art are banners, candles, stained glass windows, lighting, pulpit hangings, table coverings, and Communion ware. In a typical encyclopedia these entries would be scattered in the B, C, L, P, S, and T sections. Although this is not a problem for people who know what environmental art is, and what needs to be addressed in environmental art, it is a problem for the person whose knowledge about the subject is limited. For this reason *The Complete Library of Christian Worship* has been organized—like a textbook—into chapters dealing with particular issues. Therefore, all the matters dealing with environmental art may be found under the chapter on environmental art (see Volume 4, *Music and the Arts in Christian Worship*). In this way a reader becomes educated on environmental art while at the same time having the advantage of encyclopedia information on the various matters pertaining to this aspect of worship.

Therefore, the first unique feature of *The Complete Library of Christian Worship* is that each volume can be read and studied like a book.

The second unique feature of the *Library* is that the materials have been organized to follow the actual *sequence in which worship happens.*

For example, Volume 1, *The Biblical Foundations of Christian Worship,* looks at the roots of Christian worship in the biblical tradition, while Volume 2, *Twenty Centuries of Christian Worship,* presents the development of various historical models of worship along with an examination of the theology of worship. Next, Volumes 3 through 7 provide resources for the various acts of worship: Volume 3, *The Renewal of Sunday Worship,* provides resources for the various parts of worship; Volume 4, *Music and the Arts in Christian Worship,* presents resources from music and the arts for the different aspects of worship. Volume 5, *The Services of the Christian Year,* branches out to the services of Advent, Christmas, Epiphany, Lent, Holy Week, Easter, and Pentecost, providing resources for those special services that celebrate the saving acts of God in Jesus Christ. Volume 6, *The Sacred Actions of Christian Worship,* deals with communion, baptism, funerals, weddings, and other special or occasional acts or worship. Finally, Volume 7, *The Ministries of Christian Worship* deals with evangelism, spirituality, education, social action, children's worship, and other matters impacted by Christian celebration.

Each volume contains an alphabetical index to the material in the book. This index makes desired information readily available for the reader.

The resources in these volumes are intended for use in every denomination and among all groups of Christians: liturgical, traditional Protestant, those using creative styles, and those in the "praise and worship" tradition. Resources from each of these communities may be found in the various volumes.

It is difficult to find material from the "free" churches (those not following a historic order of worship) and from the charismatic traditions. These communities function with an oral tradition of worship, and therefore do not preserve their material through written texts. Nevertheless, a considerable amount of information has been gathered from these oral traditions. Recently, leaders in these communities have been teaching their worship practices through audio tapes and videotapes. Information on the availability of these materials has been included in the appropriate volumes.

The written texts have been the easiest to obtain. Because of this, *The Complete Library of Christian Worship* may give the appearance of favoring liturgical worship. Due to the very nature of written texts, the appearance of a strong liturgical bent in unavoidable. Nevertheless the goal of the *Library* is not to make free churches liturgical. Rather, it is to expand the perspective of Christians across a wide range of worship traditions. In this way, liturgical resources may serve as guides and sources of inspiration and creativity for free churches, while insights from free traditions may also enrich the practices and understanding of the more liturgical communities.

In sum, the way to use *The Complete Library of Christian Worship* is as follows:

1. *Read each volume as you would read a book.* Each volume is full of biblical, historical, and theological information—a veritable feast for the curious, and for all worshipers motivated to expand their horizons.
2. *Use the alphabetical index for quick and easy access to a particular aspect of worship.* The index for each volume is as thorough as the listings for an encyclopedia.
3. *For further information and resources, order books and materials listed in the bibliography of resources.* Addresses of publishers may be found in your library's copy of *Books in Print.*
4. *Adapt the liturgical materials to the setting and worship style of your congregation.* The worship materials in *The Complete Library of Christian Worship* have been intentionally published without adaptation. Most pastors, worship ministers, and worship committee members are capable of adapting the material to a style suitable to their congregations, with effective results.

103 • INTRODUCTION TO VOLUME 1: *THE BIBLICAL FOUNDATIONS OF CHRISTIAN WORSHIP*

Volume 1, *The Biblical Foundations of Christian Worship,* has been compiled in the conviction that a congregation cannot approach the renewal of worship in a superficial way. Because worship is the primary calling of the church and a key to all the ministries of the church, both within the body and to the world, worship renewal is to be approached in a thorough and comprehensive manner through a solid grounding in what the Bible has to say about worship.

The material and resources of Volume 1, *The Biblical Foundations of Christian Worship,* introduce the reader to pertinent and helpful entries that present the practice of worship in both the Hebrew tradition and the early Christian church.

First the entries in Volume 1 provide an introduction to biblical worship. Here the reader is introduced to the vocabulary of worship and to major themes that underlie biblical worship, such as the covenant, sacrifice, and the numinous, as well as symbolism in biblical worship.

Next, Volume 1 introduces the reader to the history of worship in both testaments and to the various Israelite and Christian institutions of worship, such as the tabernacle, temple and synagogue, and house church worship in the New Testament. Surveys of worship leadership in Scripture also appear.

In successive sections, Volume 1 presents the place and use of festivals and the arts in biblical worship. Festivals of Israelite worship receive treatment, and the church festivals are placed in scriptural perspective. Music, the Psalms, and the worship arts in general discussed.

Finally, Volume 1 addresses the biblical foundations for practices of Christian worship, such as the exercise of charismatic gifts, acts of traditional worship, and the sacraments and ordinances of the church.

PART ONE

Introduction to Biblical Worship

Old Testament Vocabulary of Worship

The Hebrew Scriptures, especially the Psalms, employ a rich vocabulary of words denoting acts and features of worship. These words may apply to expressions of speech or music, to movements and gestures, to offering and sacrifice, to the general attitude of worship, and to festivals and places of worship. In the Psalms these terms are often strung together in extended calls to worship (Pss. 9:1-2; 33:1-3; 68:3-4; 81:1-4; 92:1-4; 98:4-6; 100:1-4; and others) or narratives of the worshiper's activity (Ps. 63:1-5).

The following survey discusses most of these terms, referring them to their Hebrew equivalents and citing examples of usage. Expressions associated with worship in the Hebrew Scriptures may be broken down into eight major categories: (a) general expressions for worship, (b) words for assemblies and festivals, (c) terms of movement and gesture, (d) words for expressions of praise and acclamation, (e) terms of declaration and meditation, (f) musical terms, (g) words for offering and sacrifice, and (h) terms for the place of worship. Some of these terms apply to the activities of all worshipers of Yahweh, while others apply more specifically to the activity of priests, who perform the service ("*vodah*, Neh. 10:32) of the house of God and minister (*sheret*, Deut. 10:8; 1 Chron. 16:4; Neh. 10:39; Ps. 101:6) before the Lord as representatives of the covenant community.

Note: Hebrew verbs may exist in a number of forms or "constructions," and a verbal root may have a different meaning in its various constructions. For example, the verb *shavar*, "break," in the intensive construction *shibber*, would mean "shatter." This discussion will refer to the applicable form. Verse numbers for the Psalms cite the English translation; Hebrew verse numbers often differ, because in the Hebrew text the Psalm superscription, if any, is verse 1.

104 • GENERAL EXPRESSIONS FOR WORSHIP

There is no general term for "worship" in the Old Testament. Instead, many words are used to describe the actions of worshiping the Lord.

The Hebrew word usually translated "worship" in English means, literally, to bow down (see section 106 below). Worship is an expression of loyalty to the God of the covenant. The phrase "give thanks" (*hodah*) commonly applied to worship means to "make confession" of Yahweh as Lord and King. The worshiper "knows" the Lord, that he is God (*yada'*, Pss. 46:10; 100:3; Hos. 6:3), and trusts (*batah*, Pss. 13:5; 31:6; 56:3-4; 115:9-11) in him and in his *hesed* or covenant love. The awesome Lord is to be feared (*yare'*, Pss. 34:9; 67:7; 96:4), and those who worship him are called fearers of the Lord (Ps. 135:20). Israel is bidden to be in dread or awe of him (*gur*, Ps. 22:23); the land is summoned to be agitated or tremble (*ragaz*, Ps. 99:1) before him. Israelite worship frequently envisions all peoples coming under the covenant, as the nations are summoned to serve the Lord (*'avad*, Pss. 100:2; 102:22) in worship.

The worshiper seeks the Lord and his presence (*biqqesh*, Pss. 24:6; 27:8; *darash*, Ps. 34:4) or seeks him early or eagerly (*shihar*, Ps. 63:1). He or she calls on the Lord or on his name (*qara'*, Pss. 18:3;

50:15; 105:1). Thus the worshiper "appears" before the Lord (*nir'ah*, Exod. 23:17; Ps. 42:2; Isa. 1:12) to confront him or come before his presence (*qiddem*, Ps. 95:2; Mic. 6:6). In the sanctuary may Yahweh "make his face shine" or give light (*ha'er*, Pss. 67:1; 80:3); worshipers behold (*hazah*, Pss. 17:15; 63:2) the Lord's presence, lift up (*nasa'*) to him their eyes (Ps. 123:1) or soul (Ps. 25:1). Thus they set the Lord (*shavah*, Ps. 16:8) before them.

In the holy place the worshiper "waits" for the Lord (*qavah*, Pss. 27:14; 37:34; Isa. 40:31; *hikkah*, Ps. 33:20). The worshiper sojourns (*gur*, Ps. 15:1) in the Lord's tent, or dwells (*yashav*, Pss. 23:6; 84:4; 91:1) in his house or in the shelter of the Most High. The Lord brings him or her near to dwell (*shakhan*, Ps. 65:4) in his courts. In the presence of the ark of the covenant, with its winged guardian cherubim, the worshiper of the Lord takes refuge in the shadow of his wings (Pss. 36:7; 57:1; 91:4). In prayer, he or she implores the Lord's favor (*hithannen*, 1 Kings 8:33; Ps. 30:8; related nouns *tehinnah*, "supplication," 1 Kings 8:38; Ps. 55:1; *tahanun*, Ps. 143:1). The worshiper intercedes with the Lord (*hitpallel*, 1 Sam. 2:1; 1 Kings 8:42), offering prayer or intercession (*tefillah*, 1 Kings 8:38; 2 Chron. 6:19; Ps. 80:4; Isa. 1:15). The first half of the book of Psalms is called the "prayers of David" (Ps. 72:20). On penitential occasions, the worshipers might "make confession" (*hitvaddah*, Neh. 9:2-3).

105 • WORDS FOR ASSEMBLIES AND FESTIVALS

Biblical worship is corporate. The worshiper comes to God as a part of a larger community bound to the Lord in covenant and celebrating in festal assembly.

The Israelite worshiper is a member of the congregation (*'edah*, Num. 1:2; 27:13) or assembly (*qahal*, Num. 16:3; 20:4) of those called to serve Yahweh. These terms refer both to the general body of all Israelites and more specifically to the community assembled for worship (*'edah*, Ps. 1:5; *'adat 'El*, "congregation of God," Ps. 82:1, NASB; *'adat Yisra'el*, "congregation of Israel," 2 Chron. 5:6, NASB; *qahal*, 2 Chron. 30:25; Neh. 5:13; Pss. 22:25; 149:1; Joel 2:16; *qehal Yahveh*, "assembly of Yahweh," Deut. 23:2; *qehal Yisra'el*, "assembly of Israel," 1 Kings 8:14). For worship, the leaders assemble the people (*hiqhil*, "cause to assemble," Exod. 35:1; Num. 10:7; passive form *niqhal*, "be assembled," Lev. 8:3; Num. 20:8; 1 Kings 8:2) or gather them

(*'asaf*, Ps. 50:5; Joel 2:16; passive form *ne'esaf*, "be gathered," 2 Chron. 30:3; Neh. 8:1; *qabatz*, "collect," 1 Kings 18:19; passive form *niqbatz*, Ps. 102:22).

The Pentateuch lays out a sequence of three major annual observances (Exod. 23:14-17; Lev. 23; Deut. 16:1-17), the "appointed times" (*mo'adim*, Lev. 23:4; Num. 29:39; Isa. 1:14) of the Lord, when the people would gather at the sanctuary in a holy convocation or assembly (*miqra' qodesh*, Lev. 23:4). Beginning in the spring, the festivals include Passover (*pesah*), the Feast of Unleavened Bread (*hag hammatztzot*), the Feast of Weeks (*hag shavu'ot*), the Feast of Harvest (*hag haqqatzir*), the observance of Bread of the Firstfruits (*lehem habbikkurim*), the Day of Atonement or Covering (*yom hakkippurim*), the Feast of Shelters or Booths (*hag hassukkot*), and the Feast of Ingathering (*hag ha'asif*); some of these terms overlap one another and describe various aspects of the same major festival. Some scholars have suggested that the Day of Yahweh (*yom Yahveh*, Amos 5:18) may have been an annual festival of the enthronement and kingship of the Lord, perhaps coinciding with the observance of the new year. The remark in Nehemiah 8:17 suggests that the Feast of Shelters was not regularly celebrated during the period of the Israelite kingdoms.

Thus Israelite worship centered in the pilgrimage feast (*hag*, Deut. 16:14; Ezek. 46:11; Amos 8:10), as the worshipers would "keep festival" (*hagag*, Exod. 23:14; Ps. 42:4; Nah. 1:15). In connection with festivals, several terms are translated "observe" or "celebrate": to "keep" (*shamar*, Exod. 23:15; Deut. 16:1), to "commemorate" (*hizkir*, 1 Chron. 16:4), or to "do" (*'asah*, Deut. 16:1; 2 Kings 23:21-23) them. The expression "celebrate a festival" (*la'asot simhah*, 2 Chron. 30:23; Neh. 8:12) literally means "make joy"; other terms for a festival are *miqra'* and *'atzarah* (Deut. 16:8; Isa. 1:13), both meaning "assembly." The Sabbath (*shabbat*), though primarily a day of rest, was also a day of convocation when sacrifices were brought in addition to the daily offerings. Special sacrifices were offered on the first day of the month, called the "new [moon]" (*hodesh*, Num. 28:11; Isa. 1:13-14).

106 • TERMS OF MOVEMENT AND GESTURE

Biblical worship is active worship, involving movements of the body as well as of the lips, to express both submission to the covenant God and exultation in his presence.

An example of prostration taken from the Black Obelisk of Shalmaneser III. "Jehu, Son of Omri" presents his tribute to the King. Worship is described as a prostration before the Lord.

The word usually translated "worship" (*shaḥah,* in the reflexive form *hishtaḥᵃvah*) means "to bend down or prostrate oneself" (Gen. 22:5; 1 Sam. 1:3; 1 Chron. 29:20; Pss. 66:4; 99:9; 138:2; Isa. 66:23). Worshipers are invited to bow down (*kara',* Ps. 95:6; Isa. 45:23) to the Lord, to kneel or bend the knee (*berekh,* Ps. 95:6) before him; or they might "bow low" (*qadad,* Gen. 24:26; Exod. 12:27; 2 Chron. 29:30; Neh. 8:6) or "bow [themselves]" (*nikkaf,* Mic. 6:6). Having done so, they may rise up (*qum,* Ps. 24:3; Neh. 9:5) and stand (*'amad,* Pss. 122:2; 135:2) within Zion's gates or in the Lord's house, lifting up their hands (*nasa',* Pss. 63:4; 134:2) to the name of the Lord or spreading out their hands (*peras,* 2 Chron. 6:13; Ps. 143:6) in prayer. As we have seen, the verb *hodah,* "give thanks," has the basic meaning of confessing Yahweh as Lord. It is derived from the root *yadah,* which signifies the extending of the hand (*yad*), and refers to the lifting of the hand in the oath of covenant loyalty.

On festal occasions, the worshipers may join in dance (*maḥol,* Pss. 149:3; 150:4). The word often translated "rejoice" indicates a type of circle dancing (*gil,* Pss. 9:14; 35:9; 53:6; 118:24; 149:2). All the land is urged to "tremble," actually to writhe or twist before the Lord (*ḥul,* Ps. 96:9). Additional words for dancing occur in the accounts of David's bringing the ark to Zion; before the ark, David was leaping (*pazaz,* 2 Sam. 6:16), dancing around (*kirker,* 2 Sam. 6:16), skipping or springing (*roqed,* 1 Chron. 15:29), and the people were celebrating (*siḥaq,* dance or play to music, 1 Chron. 13:8).

To observe the festivals of the Lord, one must "go up" or ascend (*'alah,* Isa. 2:3; Pss. 24:3; 122:4) to the sanctuary of Yahweh, enter his gates or courts, or go to his altar (*bo',* Isa. 1:12; Pss. 43:4; 96:8; 100:4; 118:19-20). In the sacred courts worshipers might be seen "walking around" Zion or its altar (*savav,* Ps. 48:12; intensive form *sovev,* Ps. 26:6; *hithalekh,* Ps. 56:13). Processions into the sanctuary (*halikhot,* Ps. 68:24) may have featured movements of the ark, as the symbol of the Lord's "going up" (*'alah,* Ps. 47:5) to ascend his throne in Zion, the King of Glory "coming in" to his sanctuary (*bo',* Ps. 24:7-10). At such times of victory, worshipers would clap their hands (*taqa',* Ps. 47:1), and even the rivers are urged to clap (*maḥa',* Ps. 98:8) their figurative hands. It was an honor for tribal dignitaries to lead a procession (*hiddaddah,* "cause to move slowly," Ps. 42:4; *radah,* "rule, govern," Ps. 68:27). The celebrants might wear special adornment or vesture (*hadarah,* Pss. 29:2; 96:9), perhaps a reference to the fine linen garments of the priests (Exod. 39:27-29; 1 Chron. 15:27; 2 Chron. 5:12).

There is a time for activity and a time to cease from activity. Along with praise, there is repose or silence in Zion (*dumiyyah,* Ps. 65:1). God urges those who fear him to relax or be still (*hirpah,* Ps. 46:10) and know that he is God. Because the Lord is in his holy temple, all the land is hushed into silence (*has!,* Hab. 2:20).

107 • WORDS FOR EXPRESSIONS OF PRAISE AND ACCLAMATION

Vocal expressions of praise abound in the Scripture; many of these terms apply to musical as well as spoken celebration. The biblical worshiper expresses praise to God aloud.

A verb frequently used is *halal,* in the intensive form *hillel,* meaning "praise" or "boast about" (1 Chron. 29:13; Pss. 44:8; 56:4; 84:4; 99:3; 111:1; 150:1-6). The expression "Hallelujah!" means "Praise the Lord!" and is a combination of *hillel* and a short form of the Lord's personal name, *Yahweh.* The reflexive construction *hithallel* (Pss. 34:2; 105:3) means "to make one's boast in the Lord." The related noun *tehillah,* "praise," also occurs (Pss. 33:1; 102:21) and, in the plural form, *tehillim* is the Hebrew name for the book of Psalms. An often-associated term is the verb *yadah,* in the causative form *hodah,* meaning "to confess allegiance to Yahweh," but generally translated "give thanks" (Pss. 9:1; 67:3; 92:1; 100:4; 111:1; 136:1). *Yadah* also yields the noun *todah,* thanksgiving (1 Chron. 29:13; Pss. 95:2; 100:4). David appointed Asaph and his family specifically to celebrate by praising and giving thanks (*hillel, hodah,* 1 Chron. 16:4-7).

Equally common is the expression "bless [or praise] the Lord" (*berekh,* Neh. 9:5; Pss. 103:1; 104:1; 134:1-2); although this is the same word as "kneel" (see section 106), in most cases it no longer has that meaning, since God may also bless his people (Ps. 67:1). Another verb for praise is *shibbah* (Pss. 63:6; 96:3; 145:4). The worshiper desires to "make high," to extol or exalt the Lord (*romem,* Pss. 34:3; 99:9; 118:28; 145:1); the related noun (*romemot,* Ps. 149:6) indicates "high praises"; he or she seeks to glorify the Lord (*kibbed,* Ps. 22:23) and magnify him (*giddel,* Ps. 34:3). All are summoned to give or ascribe (*yahav*) to God greatness (Deut. 32:3) and glory (Ps. 29:1-2).

The vocal praise of Yahweh is characterized by abandon and even tumult. Often the invitation goes forth to raise a shout (*rua',* in the causative construction *heria',* Pss. 47:1; 66:1; 95:1-2; 100:1); the related noun (*teru'ah,* Pss. 33:3; 47:5; 89:15) means a shout like a war cry. The worshipers may "make a ringing cry" (*rinnen,* Pss. 33:1; 71:23; 98:4-6; 145:7; noun *rinnah,* Pss. 30:4; 47:1); this term can indicate joyful shouting or singing and is sometimes combined with the verb *patzah* (Ps. 98:4; Isa. 49:13), meaning "break out into joyful celebration." In the Lord's presence, his people must be joyful or glad (*samea h,* Pss. 9:2; 53:6; 97:12; 118:24; Joel 2:23). There is complete joy or gladness (*simhah*) in serving him (Pss. 16:11; 100:2); indeed, he is the worshiper's joy (Ps. 43:4). Therefore the Lord's people exult (*'alatz,* Ps. 68:3; *'alaz,* Pss. 96:12; 149:5; *sis,* Ps. 68:3) and rejoice (*gil,* see 106) before him.

108 • TERMS OF DECLARATION AND MEDITATION

The worshiper is called on to praise God specifically for his great deeds of salvation. The biblical worshiper offers praise both because of the Lord's character and because of his saving action in history.

Hand in hand with the praise of the Lord goes testimony to his great deeds. The Psalms, for example, often alternate between expressions of direct praise to the Lord and declarations of his acts of salvation. Frequently, the psalmists speak of proclaiming or showing forth the Lord's covenant love, faithfulness, and gracious deeds (*higgid,* "bring out, reveal," Pss. 19:1; 51:15; 92:2; 145:4). Another often-used expression is *sipper,* "to tell or recount" the praise, glory, righteousness, and mighty deeds of Yahweh (Pss. 19:1; 26:7; 71:15; 96:3; 102:21). The worshiper may speak of (*'amar,* Ps. 9:1; 40:10) the Lord's faithfulness and salvation or utter (*hagah,* Pss. 35:28; 63:5) his praise. Worshipers are encouraged to make known (*hodia',* Ps. 89:1) his faithfulness, cause his praise to be heard (*hishmia',* Ps. 106:2), or bear good news (*bissar,* Ps. 96:2) of his salvation.

The worship of Israel was a continual representation and declaration of the covenant granted by the Lord. The biblical history records several special events of covenant renewal under Joshua (Josh. 24:24-25), Asa (2 Chron. 15:14), and Josiah (2 Kings 23:3). In the second example, the people "made an oath" (*nishba'*) to the Lord with celebration and music; the same word is used by Isaiah in declaring that every tongue will swear allegiance to the Lord (Isa. 45:23). The worshiper's attitude of declaring covenant loyalty is expressed in Psalm 31:14: "I trust in you, O LORD; I say 'You are my God.'" Festival worship may have included the ceremonial recitation of the covenant commandments. Psalm 50:16 refers to taking up the covenant (_nasa' b^erit_) on the lips of the worshipers; Psalm 81:10 quotes the beginning of the commandments, "I am the LORD your God, . . . Open wide [_hirhiv_] your mouth and I will fill it," probably with the remainder of the Decalogue. In worship on Zion, Israel always stood figuratively at Mount Sinai, renewing and confirming the covenant made there; as Moses had told the post-Sinai generation, "It was not with our fathers that the LORD made this covenant, but with us . . ." (Deut. 5:3).

Consideration of the Lord's greatness and faithfulness to the covenant also has its contemplative aspect. In his temple, the worshipers of Yahweh inquire or meditate (_biqqer,_ Ps. 27:4). They converse with themselves, or meditate, concerning the Lord (_si^ah,_ Ps. 77:6; intensive form _sohe^ah,_ Ps. 143:5; noun _si^ah,_ "meditation," Ps. 104:34). They think of, or "compare" (_dimmah,_ Ps. 48:9), his covenant love.

109 ✦ MUSICAL TERMS IN WORSHIP

Music, both vocal and instrumental, played a central role in the worship of Israel. Many Hebrew words refer to musical activity in the praise of the Lord.

Some of the terms for spoken praise, such as _hodah_ or _hillel,_ apply equally to musical expression. The verb _rinnen,_ "cry joyfully," can mean "sing for joy" and is often found parallel with words specifically associated with singing (Pss. 33:1; 81:1; 98:4). The most common terms for sung praise are _zimmer_ and _shir,_ which frequently occur together (Pss. 101:1; 104:33). The worshiper of Yahweh often "makes melody" or "sings praise" (_zimmer,_ Pss. 47:6; 66:2; 92:1; 149:3). This term seems to indicate singing accompanied by an instrument; related nouns are _zimrah,_ "singing" (Pss. 81:2; 98:5) and _mizmor,_ "psalm" (Ps. 95:2, and the superscriptions of several psalms such as Pss. 92 and 98). Worshipers frequently declare their intention to sing (_shir,_ Pss. 13:6; 57:7; 89:1; 101:1) or speak of their song (_shir,_ Ps. 28:7). Another term for song is _maskil,_ perhaps "skillful song" (Ps. 47:7, and the superscriptions of

a number of psalms such as Ps. 42). The verb _'anah_ (Ps. 147:7), translated "sing," means "to pronounce with a loud voice" or "to answer." When the ark was brought into the newly completed temple, the musicians "lifted up sound" (_herim qol_) with voices and instruments (2 Chron. 5:12-13).

The congregation of the Lord is often invited to sing "a new song" (_shir hadash,_ Pss. 33:3; 40:3; 96:1; Isa. 42:10); perhaps this was spontaneous song under prophetic anointing. Free-flowing singing with instruments may also be indicated by the term _selah,_ occurring in thirty-nine psalms and in Habakkuk 3, usually at the end of stanzas; the meaning of the term is obscure, but Psalm 68:4, which uses the related verb _salal,_ "lift up" a song, suggests that it may indicate an interlude of vocal and instrumental praise. In Israelite worship, music accompanies prophecy. In 1 Samuel 10:5, we see prophets coming down from a "high place" or sanctuary, prophesying (_hitnabbe'_) to instrumental accompaniment. David appointed the sons of Asaph, Heman, and Jeduthun to prophesy (_nibba'_) with instruments (1 Chron. 25:1). Even at a much later time, prophets and musicians were so closely associated that Ezekiel complained that people thought of him as just another performer (Ezek. 33:32).

Additional expressions refer to the use of instruments in worship. In the praise of the Lord, one might "lift up the horn" (_herim qeren,_ 1 Chron. 25:6), play the flute (_halal,_ Ps. 87:7), or play a stringed instrument (_niggen,_ Ps. 33:3; noun _nogen,_ "player of a stringed instrument," Ps. 68:25). Scripture contains abundant references to the various instruments used in worship, especially in the Psalms (Pss. 81:2; 98:5-6; 150:3-5).

110 ✦ WORDS FOR OFFERING AND SACRIFICE

Sacrifice and offering were a part of Israelite worship, and extensive portions of the Pentateuch are devoted to the regulation of these activities (Lev. 1–7; 22–23; Num. 18; 28–29; and others). This brief survey can only mention the major terms associated with the sacrificial cultus.

All sacrifices were to be offered to Yahweh by the priest (_kohen_), who would "draw near" (_hiqriv_) to the altar (_mizbe^ah_) to sacrifice (_zavah_) in the worshiper's behalf. The worshipers might bring an offering of meal or grain (_minhah_) or an animal for a sacrifice (_zevah_); individuals bringing an animal for sacrifice usually killed and dressed it themselves.

Depending on the particular need, the worshipers could bring a sin offering (*hatta't*), a guilt or trespass offering (*'asham*), or a peace offering (*shelem* or *zevah shelamim*).

The officiating priest might present the offering as a burnt offering (*'olah*, literally an offering "going up"") or as an offering made by fire (*'ishsheh*); he might wave it (*henif*) as a wave offering (*tenufah*) or pour out a drink offering (*nesekh*). Regular offerings and sacrifices were mandated for the various festivals and the daily and monthly observances, but the individual worshiper might also bring a voluntary offering (*nedavah*), or a votive offering, that is, one brought to pay or fulfill (*shillem*) a vow (*neder*) he or she had made (Num. 30). Any offering or gift brought to the Lord might be called a "holy thing" (*qodesh*), that is, something set apart, or a "dedicated thing" (*qorban*).

It is a striking phenomenon that the Psalms, the hymnody of the sanctuary, so seldom refer to the sacrificial cultus. When the Psalms refer to sacrifice, it is almost always the sacrifice made by praise and thanksgiving. A prophetic voice speaks in Psalm 50:14, 23 declaring the Lord's preference that the worshiper "sacrifice thanksgiving" (*zavah todah*) to him, rather than sacrifice animals. The worshiper of Psalm 27:6 indicates his intention to "sacrifice with shouts of joy" (*zivhei teru'ah*). Vows are paid by praise and thanksgiving (Pss. 22:25; 50:14; 65:1). When the offerings and sacrifices of the Mosaic cultus are mentioned, it is often in a derogatory way (Pss. 40:6; 50:8-13; 51:16).

This situation is not as strange as it may seem. When David brought the ark to Zion, he established worship there without the sacrificial altar, which remained with the Mosaic sanctuary at Gibeon (1 Chron. 21:29). Many of the Psalms had their origin in this prophetic worship of the "tent of David" and were composed by David himself or by Levitical musicians who did not officiate at sacrifices. Indeed, sacrificial terminology is largely missing from their literature.

III • TERMS FOR THE PLACE OF WORSHIP

The places where the Lord's people met to celebrate the presence of their God are designated by a special vocabulary relating to the sacredness of the place and the actions performed there.

Yahweh's worshipers were acutely aware of the sacredness of the place where they would meet with God. It is called the holy place (*maqom qodesh*, Ps. 24:3) or the sanctuary (*miqdash*, Exod. 25:8; Lev. 19:30; Num. 18:1; 1 Chron. 22:19; Ezek. 47:12) or simply the "holy" (*qodesh*, Exod. 29:30; Ps. 20:2); these terms are derived from the root *qadash*, which designates a thing set apart from common use. A frequent term for the place of worship is *bet Yahveh*, "house of Yahweh," or "house of the Lord" (Exod. 23:19; 1 Sam. 1:7; 2 Kings 12:4; 1 Chron. 26:12; Pss. 23:6; 122:1; Isa. 2:2; Jer. 26:2; and others); sometimes we find the phrase "house of God" (*bet 'Elohim*, Gen. 28:17; Ps. 42:4; *bet ha'Elohim*, Judg. 18:31; 2 Chron. 5:14) or "house of our God" (*bet 'Eloheinu*, Neh. 10:34), or sometimes just "house" (Ezek. 47:1, NASB).

Both the temple erected by Solomon and the Mosaic sanctuary, which preceded it, could be designated as the house of *Yahweh*. The Mosaic sanctuary was called the tabernacle or dwelling (*mishkan*, Exod. 26:1; 36:8; 40:34-35; Num. 9:15), or sometimes "dwelling of the testimony" (*mishkan ha'edut*, Exod. 38:21; Num. 1:50), because it contained the ark. The *mishkan* was covered by the tent (*'ohel*, Exod. 35:11), sometimes called the tent of meeting or "tent of appointment" (*'ohel mo'ed*, Exod. 40:34-35; Lev 1:1; Num. 4:30), also "tent of the testimony" (*'ohel ha'edut*, Num. 9:15; 18:2), so that both terms can refer to the movable sanctuary. The altar was in the court, or outer enclosure, of the dwelling (*hatzer hammishkan*, Exod. 27:9).

The sanctuary might also be referred to simply as the Lord's tent (*'ohel*, Pss. 15:1; 27:5-6), his dwelling (*ma'on*, Ps. 76:2), his "secret place" (*seter*, Pss. 27:5; 91:1), or his shelter (*sukkah*, Pss. 27:5; 76:2). After the building of Solomon's temple, the sanctuary building proper was called the temple or palace (*heikhal*, Ps. 27:4; Isa. 6:1). However, the older terms continued in use. Zion, the site of the sanctuary from the time of David, was called the hill of the Lord (*har Yahveh*, Ps. 24:3) or his holy hill (*har qodesh*, Ps. 99:9). The psalmists speak poetically of the entire sacred precincts as the courts (*hatzerot*, Pss. 84:2, 10; 100:4) or gates (*sha'arim*, Pss. 87:2; 100:4) of the Lord.

The inner area of the sanctuary, where the ark was placed, was called the Holy of Holies, or Most Holy Place (*qodesh haqqodashim*, Exod. 26:33-34); after the construction of the temple, it was also known as the *devir* (1 Kings 6:19; Ps. 28:2), "innermost room" or throne room. The ark (*'aron*) itself was a movable chest containing the covenant commandments; while not a place of worship, it was thought of as the throne or footstool of *Yahweh,* and therefore represented the Lord's dwelling in the midst of his people. It is variously termed the ark of the covenant (*'aron habbᵉrit,* Num. 10:35; 2 Sam. 15:24), the ark of the testimony (*'aron ha'edut,* Exod. 26:34), the ark of Yahweh (*'aron Yahveh,* Josh. 7:6; 1 Sam. 4:6), the ark of the Lord Yahweh (*'aron 'Adonai Yahveh,* 1 Kings 2:26), the ark of God (*'aron ha'Elohim,* 1 Sam. 4:11), and the ark of the covenant of God (*'aron bᵉrit ha'Elohim,* 2 Sam. 15:24-25). The lid or cover (*kapporet,* sometimes translated "mercy seat") of the ark was more specifically the throne of *Yahweh,* who spoke to Moses from between the cherubim on either end of the cover (Exod. 25:17-22).

The Pentateuch mandates the centralization of the sacrificial and festive worship of the Lord in one place (Deut. 12:1-18). Eventually this place was identified as Jerusalem and Mount Zion, but prior to that time the sanctuary was periodically relocated to various local shrines. The local sanctuaries (*bamah,* high place) continued to be the site of regional festivals even after the erection of the temple, and the kings of Israel and Judah were taken to task for not removing them (1 Kings 15:14; 2 Kings 15:35; and others).

Conclusion

The Old Testament vocabulary of worship presents a rich panorama of acts and features of the service of almighty God. The wealth of expression described here forms a vital background for Christian worship and for the Christian understanding of the person and work of Jesus Christ.

Richard C. Leonard

TWO

New Testament
Vocabulary of Worship

Like the Old Testament, the New Testament contains many terms that refer to acts or features of worship. To a degree, however, there is a difference in the way the New Testament presents these terms. There is less specific worship material, proportionately, in the New Testament—nothing, for example, having the scope of the book of Psalms or the extended directives for festivals, offering, and sacrifice that are found in the Hebrew Scriptures.

The explanation for this is found in the cultural position of the New Testament church, which in most localities was regarded, by the authorities and by the populace in general, as a sectarian movement within Judaism, but which was violently opposed by the traditional Jewish community. The desires of the apostles and the local assemblies of Christians notwithstanding, there was little opportunity for Christians to conduct large-scale public worship of the type that forms the background for the worship terminology of the Old Testament. Distinctively Christian worship usually had to be carried on in private gatherings, limited in size and scope. The remarkable thing is that, given these practical restraints, the New Testament writers are able to develop such a magnificent vision of the universal worship of the Father and the Son.

References to acts and features of worship in the New Testament may be summarized under four main categories: (a) terms from Old Testament worship used to interpret Christ; (b) references to the practice of Jewish worship; (c) terms referring to the practice of Christian worship; and (d) words relating to visionary worship. This discussion will cite Greek terms from the New Testament, with the caveat that Jesus and the earliest Christians would have used some equivalent Aramaic or even Hebrew words.

112 • TERMS FROM OLD TESTAMENT WORSHIP USED TO INTERPRET CHRIST

It is significant that the New Testament authors apply words and images from Israelite worship to Jesus Christ. In so doing, they show how the church sought to interpret Jesus, whom it recognized to be the Christ.

Jesus Christ, in his appearance as the incarnate Word of God, displayed a personal presence and power that moved people to an awed and worshipful response. When Jesus directed the Galilean fishermen to a miraculous catch, Peter fell at his feet, crying, "Go away from me, Lord; I am a sinful man!" (Luke 5:8). As a woman suffering from a hemorrhage touched the hem of his garment and was healed, Jesus sensed that power had gone out from him; in fear and trembling the woman fell down before him (Mark 5:25-34). The soldiers who came to arrest Jesus "drew back and fell to the ground" when he spoke (John 18:6). The resurrection of Christ further verified his identity as the one appointed by God to fulfill his purpose in the redemption of his people. This left the apostles with the task of explaining the crucifixion as a part of the divine plan. To do this, they drew on the work of the prophets of Israel, especially the portrait of the "servant" of the Lord found in the later chapters of Isaiah; they also drew on the imagery and terminology associated with the festal and sacrificial cultus of the

Hebrew sanctuary, including the concept of atonement.

Atonement Terminology

The idea of atonement relates to the need to be shielded from the wrath of a holy God, yet not in the moral sense alone (that God is good and man is evil); rather it is because God is God, the Creator, and the worshiper is a finite creature that the gap between them must be bridged by some atoning act. The Creator is of surpassing worth; in contrast, the worshiper is as nothing before him. Atonement is a "covering" (the basic meaning of the Hebrew *kafar*) that provides a cleansing or consecration for the worshiper, enabling him or her to enter the presence of God and to have fellowship with him. Thus, by sacrifice atonement is made for priests, the people, and even for the sanctuary and the altar (for example, Lev. 16) that the profane might venture to approach the sacred and serve God's purposes. In another connection, a leper who is cleansed must have atonement made through the slaughter of a male lamb (Lev. 14:1-20). The concept of atonement defies rational explanation but belongs to the realm of the "numinous," or suprarational, intuitively experienced aspects of the holy.

The word *atonement* is not found in the New Testament, although a suggestion of its basic meaning is found in Peter's statement that "love *covers* over a multitude of sins" (1 Pet. 4:8). But the concept of atonement underlies the apostolic proclamation that "Christ died for our sins according to the Scriptures" (1 Cor. 15:3), and the New Testament theologians approach the mystery of the atonement using symbols drawn from Israelite worship. In this respect the apostles were following the example of Jesus himself, who had told them that the Son of Man had come "to give his life as a ransom for many" (Mark 10:45). The term *lutron,* "ransom," relates to the Israelite concept of the redemption of the firstborn. The firstborn of clean animals were to be offered on the altar (Num. 18:17), but the firstborn of humans and of unclean animals were to be redeemed by a payment (Num. 18:15-16). As understood by the early Christians, however, the concept of ransom goes deeper, as a symbol interpreting the atonement of Christ.

Thus, in the New Testament, Christ's death is called an offering or sacrifice; Hebrews calls his death "for all time one sacrifice [*thusia*] for sins"

(Heb. 10:12), and Paul says that Christ "gave himself up for us as a fragrant offering [*prosphora,* something brought forward or presented] and sacrifice [*thusia*] to God" (Eph. 5:2), introducing also symbolism from the incense offerings of the Hebrew sanctuary. Paul's declaration that God made Christ "who had no sin to be sin for us" (2 Cor. 5:21) also relates to the sacrificial rites; as applied to Christ, the word *sin* (*hamartia*) should be understood as "sin offering," equivalent to the Hebrew *ḥaṭṭa't,* the sacrifice that rehabilitates the worshiper after transgression. Hebrews elaborates on the concept of sacrifice as applied to the obedient death (under the figure of the "blood") of Christ (Heb. 10:1-22) and also refers to our sanctification "through the offering [*prosphora*] of the body of Jesus Christ once for all" (Heb. 10:10, NASB); Christ is not only the sacrifice, but also the High Priest who offers it (Heb. 7:26-27).

The furnishings of the sanctuary also provide an image used to interpret the atoning death of Christ. In Romans 3:25, Paul refers to the redemption in Christ Jesus, "whom God displayed publicly as a propitiation in His blood through faith" (NASB). The word translated "propitiation" or "means of expiation" is *hilastērion;* the Septuagint (the Greek version of the Old Testament) uses this term for the lid of the ark of the covenant (Exod. 25:16-22), on which the blood of the sin offering was sprinkled on the Day of Atonement (Lev. 16:14). The apostle John employs a related term in declaring that if anyone sins, Jesus Christ, our Advocate with the Father, is himself "the propitiation [*hilasmos*] for our sins" (1 John 2:2; 4:10, NASB); the Septuagint uses this word in the sense of "sin offering" or "atonement" (Num. 5:8; Ezek. 44:27).

Imagery of the Lamb

The idea of atonement for sin is only part of the Old Testament worship symbolism the early Christians used to interpret the death of Christ. In the context of a discussion of judgment of immorality within the church, Paul compares Christ to the Passover lamb (1 Cor. 5:7-8). The Passover lamb was not a sin offering but the meal signifying the Lord's covenant with the people he was about to deliver in the Exodus from Egypt; the blood of the Passover lamb marks the household of the people of the Lord for their protection during the time of divine judgment (Exod. 12:1-13). Thus, Paul urges the Christian community to separate itself from the "leaven" of unrighteousness, for "Christ our Passover [*pascha*] also has been sacrificed. Let us therefore celebrate the feast [*heortazō*] . . . with the unleavened bread of sincerity and truth" (1 Cor. 5:7-8, NASB). The crucified Christ is the Lamb whose blood identifies the true covenant community in the face of the wrath about to fall on the unfaithful.

The writings of the apostle John also use the slain lamb of Israelite worship as a symbol interpreting the crucified Christ; uniquely in the Johannine writings, Jesus is directly called "the Lamb." In the gospel of John, John the Baptizer testifies to Jesus as "the Lamb of God [*ho amnos tou theou*], who takes away the sin of the world!" (John 1:29). However, the concept underlying this phrase does not seem to be atonement and sacrifice. It is noteworthy that in the Old Testament it was not a male lamb, but typically a bull, a ram, or a goat that was offered for sin (or, in the case of the scapegoat, driven away bearing the residual sin of the people, Lev. 16:20-22), yet the New Testament never likens Christ to any of these animals, but only to the lamb. How, then, does he "take away the sin of the world"? The thought seems to be that he does so through his *victory over sin,* in the utter obedience of his death on the cross. Christ's obedience "to the point of death" is an important aspect of Paul's Christology, but in Philippians 2:8 he relates it to Christ's exaltation as Lord rather than to atonement for sin, just as the author of Hebrews relates Jesus' endurance of the cross to his exaltation to the right hand of God (Heb. 12:2). In the same manner, the Revelation exclaims: "Worthy is the Lamb [*arnion*], who was slain, to receive power and wealth and wisdom and strength and honor and glory and praise!" (Rev. 5:12). Here Christ appears as the victorious Lamb, reigning with the Father as "KING OF KINGS AND LORD OF LORDS" (Rev. 19:16). He takes away sin, not only by his offering of himself, but by his victory and dominion over evil as the "great King" who delivers his covenant people from their enemies. He takes away sin through the power of his life, dwelling as God himself in the midst of his people, the new Jerusalem (Rev. 21:1-8). He takes away sin through the radiance of his presence, as the temple of the holy city and its light: "I did not see a temple in the city, because the Lord God Almighty and the Lamb are its temple [*naos*]. The city does not need the sun or the moon to shine on it, for the glory of God gives it light, and the Lamb is its lamp [*luchnos*]" (Rev. 21:22-23). Here, through the figure of the Lamb, Christ is compared also to the lamp of the sanctuary.

Light and Glory

Imagery of light or radiance, so familiar from Israel's worship of the Lord, is applied also to Jesus Christ in the New Testament. Jesus is the "light of the world" (*to phōs tou kosmou,* John 8:12), the "radiance [*apaugasma*] of God's glory [*doxa*]" (Heb. 1:3). The apostles witness Jesus transfigured in brightness like the sun (Matt. 17:2); John beholds his face "like the sun shining in all its brilliance" (Rev. 1:16). New Testament witnesses affirm that in Christ we behold "the light of the knowledge of the glory [*doxa*] of God in the face of Christ" (2 Cor. 4:6, RSV), that "we have seen his glory [*doxa*], the glory of the One and Only, who came from the Father" (John 1:14). As the glory of God, Christ is also "the image [*eikōn*] of the invisible God" (Col. 1:15, RSV), the "exact representation [*charaktēr*] of his being" (Heb. 1:3). This language originates in the festal worship of Israel, which centered in the theophany or manifestation of the Lord, as his glory [*kavod*] appeared to his people or filled the holy place. In the Sinai covenant, Yahweh descended on the mountain in fire (Exod. 19:18). In Israel's subsequent worship of the Lord, which was a continual renewal of the covenant, his glory manifested itself, so that "from Zion, perfect in beauty, God shines forth" (Ps. 50:2). No image could be made of Yahweh, but his "glory," the radiant envelope of his presence, was understood to be enthroned over the ark of the covenant. This concept further illuminates the application of the term *hilastērion,* "mercy seat," to Jesus Christ, for the mercy seat was the place where Yahweh was to meet with his people, speaking to them "from between the two cherubim that are upon the ark of the testimony" (Exod. 25:22, RSV). As the triumphant Passover Lamb and as the representation of God's glory, Christ maintains and defends the covenant between the Lord and his faithful people and is the Word (*logos*) through whom God speaks to his people (John 1:1, 14; 1 John 1:1; Rev. 19:13).

The Curse of the Covenant

Understanding the covenantal foundation of Israelite, and Christian, worship sheds light on another expression used by the apostle Paul, who declares, "Christ redeemed us from the curse of the law by becoming a curse [*katara*] for us, for it is written:

'Cursed is everyone who is hung on a tree'" (Gal. 3:13). The biblical covenant is modeled on the ancient treaty, which included both stipulations and sanctions in the form of blessings if the covenant is maintained and curses that take effect if it is broken. In the Bible, the clearest example is Moses' farewell sermon in Deuteronomy (Paul was quoting from Deut. 21:23 in the Galatians passage), a description of a covenant liturgy that closes with an extended ceremony of blessing and, especially, cursing (Deut. 27–28; 32–33). The curse element in the covenant liturgy was what generated the pronouncements of the prophets of Israel and Judah; in their declarations of judgment against the nation, they were announcing the outworking of the curse of the covenant as the consequence of its violation by an unfaithful people. Paul sees Christ, who died on the "tree," as having borne this curse so that the covenant, broken by its original grantees, may now be renewed with the new "Israel of God" (Gal. 6:16) made up of both Jew and Gentile. Jesus understood his own death in this way, as is clear from his prayer in Gethsemane, when he asks the Father to "take this cup from me" (Luke 22:42). The cup of poison was one of the curses traditionally administered to covenant breakers; in his death, Jesus is to bear this curse on behalf of the unfaithful, that others might be set free to enter the kingdom of God. In the Revelation, John sees that in the new Jerusalem "no longer will there be any curse" (Rev. 22:3), for the Lamb receives the homage of the community of the new covenant.

Imagery Relating to Gentile Inclusion

The inclusion of Gentiles in the covenant, through the death of Christ, is the great "mystery" or now-revealed truth Paul celebrates (Eph. 3:3-7). In explaining this mystery, Paul uses additional terminology drawn from Old Testament worship. "He [Christ] himself is our peace [_eirēnē_], who has made the two one" (Eph. 2:14). In the Bible, peace (_shalom_) is that state of blessing and salvation which is the purpose and effect of the covenant, but one gets the impression here that, in speaking of Christ as our "peace," Paul is thinking specifically of the _peace offering_ (_shelem_), which in Israelite worship was a sacrifice that restored and maintained fellowship between the worshiper and the Lord. Both Jew and Gentile were condemned as "objects of wrath"

under the old covenant (Eph. 2:3), the Gentiles as "foreigners to the covenants of the promise" (Eph. 2:12) and the Jews as disobedient (Eph. 2:3). But Christ in his death has reconciled both groups to God (Eph. 2:16), building them together into "a holy temple [_naos_]," "a dwelling of God in the Spirit" (Eph. 2:21-22, NASB). The image of the Israelite sanctuary as emblematic of the union of Jew and Gentile in Christ also occurs in the statement of James during the apostolic council recorded in Acts 15. Here the inclusion of Gentiles in the people of God is viewed as the fulfillment of Amos's prophecy concerning the restoration of the booth, or tent (_skēnē_), of David (Acts 15:16-17; Amos 9:11); the tabernacle was the original tent that housed the ark after David had it brought to Zion and for which he directed continual prophetic, nonsacrificial worship as reflected throughout the book of Psalms (1 Chron. 15–16).

Sabbath Imagery

The epistle to the Hebrews employs the imagery of the Sabbath in interpreting the event of Jesus Christ. Whereas the disobedient and unbelieving are excluded from entering God's rest (Heb. 3:18-19), "there remains a sabbath rest for the people of God" (Heb. 4:9, RSV). The thought seems to be that by his sacrifice of himself, Jesus the "Great High Priest" has become the Sabbath rest of the believer, who "rests from his own work, just as God did from his" (Heb. 4:10).

Conclusion

The New Testament thus applies much of the worship vocabulary of the Old Testament to its understanding of Jesus Christ and his new covenant community. But there is a new spirituality to the use of these terms; they are employed not to describe external acts or features of worship, but as a means of grasping the inward significance of the event of Jesus Christ. As the writer of Hebrews says, "You have not come to a mountain that can be touched. . . . But you have come to Mount Zion, to the heavenly Jerusalem, the city of the living God . . . to Jesus the mediator of a new covenant" (Heb. 12:18, 22, 24). The same spirituality that infuses the Christians' use of the terminology of Hebrew worship is now to transform their worship as well. In Jesus' words to the woman of Samaria, the Father is to be worshiped "neither on this mountain nor in Jerusalem" (John 4:21) but by genuine worshipers who "will worship the Father in spirit and truth" (John 4:23).

113 ✦ REFERENCES TO THE PRACTICE OF JEWISH WORSHIP

The New Testament records a number of occasions on which Jesus, the apostles, or the early Christians are found taking part in Jewish festivals or other acts of worship. The accounts of these events involve terminology descriptive of Jewish worship.

———— Jesus and Jewish Worship ————

As an infant, Jesus was presented in the temple; since he was the first child of Mary and Joseph, they offered the mandatory sacrifice (*thusia*) to redeem the firstborn (Luke 2:21-24). As a young man, Jesus went with his family in pilgrimage to Jerusalem for the Feast of the Passover (*hē heortē tou pascha*), as was their annual custom (Luke 2:41-42). At the beginning of his public ministry, he would teach in synagogues (*sunagōgē*, "assembly"), including the ones in his hometown of Nazareth (Luke 4:14-16) and in Capernaum (John 6:59), where he later seems to have made his home. The synagogue was an institution not primarily for worship but for prayer and instruction in the Scriptures. But on one occasion, at least, Jesus also attended the Jewish Feast of Booths or Tabernacles (*hē heortē tōn Ioudaiōn hē skēnopēgia*) in Jerusalem; Jesus sent his brothers on without him but later went up privately and began to teach in the temple in the middle of the feast (John 7:2-14). On the last day of the feast ("the great day of the feast," *tē megalē tēs heortēs*), Jesus spoke of the river of living water, the Holy Spirit, which was to flow from those believing in him (John 7:37-39). His imagery may have been drawn from the ceremony of the "drawing of water," a post-Mosaic addition to the Feast of Tabernacles in which the priest at the altar poured out a pitcher of water drawn from the pool of Siloam.

———— Jesus and the Passover ————

The best-known of Jesus' observances of the feasts of Israel is, of course, his participation in the Passover (Greek *pascha*, cognate to Hebrew *pesaḥ*) with his disciples on the night of his arrest (Matt. 26:17-30; Mark 14:12-26; Luke 22:7-38). As head of the "family" of his followers, Jesus gave instructions for preparation of the meal on the first day of the Feast of Unleavened Bread (*hē prōtē tōn azumōn*, Matt. 26:17), when the Passover lamb was to be sacrificed (Mark 14:12). At the end of the meal, Jesus and his disciples sang a hymn (*humneō*, "sing a hymn," Matt. 26:30), no doubt the "Egyptian Hallel," Psalms 113–118, an act of praise that was traditionally sung at Passover and on other festive occasions. Within this outward framework of the meal celebrating the old covenant, Christ instituted the sacred meal of the new covenant, transforming the bread and wine of the feast into the symbols of his body broken and his blood shed for the forgiven people of the kingdom of God (Matt. 26:26-29).

———— Jesus and Mosaic Institutions ————

During his ministry, Jesus evidenced a respect for the institutions of Mosaic worship, though he often criticized the Pharisees and their scribes for their superficial and casuistic approach to the Torah. After healing a leper, Jesus instructed him to follow the Mosaic procedure outlined in Leviticus 14:1-32, showing himself to the priest and making the required offering (Mark 1:44). In the Sermon on the Mount, Jesus spoke of the need to be reconciled with a "brother" member of the covenant community before offering worship. "Leave your gift there in front of the altar [*thusiastērion*]. . . . First go and be reconciled to your brother; then come and offer your gift [*prosphere to dōron sou*]" (Matt. 5:24). Jesus told of the respected Pharisee and the despised publican, who collected taxes for the Roman administration, both of whom entered the temple to pray; he commended the publican, who threw himself upon the mercies of God, rather than the Pharisee, who saw himself as spiritually superior (Luke 18:9-14). In an extended diatribe against the Pharisees, Jesus utters a remarkable statement concerning temple and its altar. The Pharisees had taught that the *worshiper's gift* is more important than the sanctuary, so that one is obligated if he swears by the gold contributed to the temple or by the gift on the altar; to the contrary, Jesus declares it is the temple (*naos*) that makes the gold holy and the altar (*thusiastērion*) that sanctifies the gift (Matt. 23:16-22). Jesus' high view of the Israelite sanctuary—the destruction of which he nevertheless predicted—is foundational to an appreciation of the depth of temple symbolism in the New Testament's picture of the body of Christ as the temple of the Holy Spirit (2 Cor. 6:16) or of the Lord God and the Lamb as the temple in the midst of the people of the new covenant (Rev. 21:22).

The Early Church and Jewish Worship

Luke concludes his gospel by mentioning that, after the resurrection, the followers of Christ "were continually in the temple blessing [_eulogeō_] God" (Luke 24:53 RSV) and continues this theme into the book of Acts in recording that the earliest Christians of Jerusalem frequented the temple for prayer (Acts 2:46). This attendance in the temple was not participation in the sacrificial rites conducted by the Jewish priesthood. Christians understood that the crucifixion of Christ had fulfilled these and brought them to an end. However, a number of synagogues met within the precincts of the temple for study and prayer; these were the assemblies in which the Christians participated. According to Acts 2:42, the early Christians of Jerusalem applied themselves "to the apostles' teaching and to the fellowship, to the breaking of bread and to prayer," literally "the prayers" (_hai proseuchai_); these were probably the traditional public prayers of the Jewish assembly, since Acts 3:1 records that Peter and John were going up to the temple "at the ninth hour, the hour of prayer" (NASB). The importance the early believers attached to participation in the worship of the Jewish community is signified by the fact that it was on the day of Pentecost, one of the three annual feasts mandated in the Torah (Lev. 23:16; Deut. 16:10), that the apostles were filled with the Holy Spirit and for the first time publicly proclaimed the crucified and risen Jesus as "both Lord and Christ" (Acts 2:36). The Greek term for the Hebrew "Feast of Weeks," _hē pentēkostē,_ literally means "the fiftieth," as it falls fifty days after Passover.

Separation from Jewish Institutions

As time went on, the participation of Christians in Jewish worship decreased. In the early stages of Christian missionary expansion, the apostles used the synagogues of the Jewish diaspora as forums for the preaching of Jesus as the Christ (Acts 9:20; 13:5; 13:14-43; 14:1; 17:1-4). As opposition developed within the Jewish community, however, Christian involvement in the synagogues became a less attractive proposition. Theological factors, of course, played their part in the separation, along with persecution. In time the radical departure of the new covenant faith from the traditions of institutional Judaism became more readily apparent to Christian thinkers. In the teaching of Paul, Christian faith is the true and free "Jerusalem that is above" (Gal. 4:26), whereas "the present city of Jerusalem . . . is in slavery with her children" (v. 25) and is persecuting those born "by the power of the Spirit" (v. 29). The book of Acts (Acts 21:23-28) records that Paul undertook a Jewish vow of purification and paid the expenses of four other Jerusalem Christians who were under an oath or vow (_euchē_). Paul thus showed his willingness to please the Jerusalem church by participating in strict observance of the Law. Some Asian Jews, however, seeing Paul in the temple and knowing of his affiliation with Gentiles, led an attack on Paul for defiling the temple, which resulted in Paul's final imprisonment. Troubled relations with synagogues persisted in the first century and, in places like Smyrna, generated great ill-feeling (Rev. 2:9).

114 ✦ TERMS REFERRING TO THE PRACTICE OF CHRISTIAN WORSHIP

The New Testament also contains a vocabulary of terms that reflect the worship of the new covenant community, a worship that was anticipated before the formation of the Christian church by the awed and worshipful response of many to the person of Jesus himself and by Jesus' own worship of the Father.

General Terms for Worship

There is no New Testament term that exactly corresponds to our English word _worship_. The biblical expressions are concrete, whereas the word _worship,_ etymologically, conveys the more abstract idea of "ascribing worth." A common term in the New Testament (though seldom found in the Epistles) is the verb _proskuneō,_ which means literally to "fall to the knee before," to bow down or prostrate oneself; the Septuagint uses this term often as a translation of the equivalent Hebrew term _hishtaḥªvah._ The term _latreuō,_ "serve," is employed in the Greek Old Testament to translate the Hebrew _'avad,_ as applied to the cultic service of priests. In the New Testament, this word sometimes refers to serving the Lord through the devout and upright life (Rom. 1:9;

2 Tim. 1:3; noun *latreia,* Rom. 12:1), but can also refer, more specifically, to worshiping. Paul declares that the church is the true circumcision, the faithful covenant people, "who worship [*latreuō*] by the Spirit of God, who glory [*kauchaomai,* 'boast'] in Christ Jesus" (Phil. 3:3). The author of Hebrews also places the term in a context of worship when he urges his readers to exhibit thanksgiving (*charis*) "and so worship [*latreuō*] God acceptably with reverence and awe" (Heb. 12:28). In the New Testament, the word *leitourgia* (verb *leitourgeō*), the root of the English word *liturgy,* refers to the service or ministry of priests (Luke 1:23; Heb. 8:6; 9:21) and to the church's corporate ministry to the Lord (Acts 13:2), but also to Christian service in general (Rom. 15:27; 2 Cor. 9:12; Phil. 2:7), as an act of sacrificial devotion both to God and to fellow believers.

Worship at the Birth of Christ

Acts of worship accompanied the incarnation of the Son of God, as the gospel accounts of the birth of Christ in both Matthew and Luke demonstrate. Luke's narrative is especially rich in worship materials; he incorporates several early Christian hymns, which later came to be known by their opening words in Latin: the *Magnificat* of Mary (Luke 1:46-55), the *Benedictus* of Zacharias (Luke 1:68-79), the *Gloria in Excelsis* of the heavenly host (Luke 2:14), and the *Nunc Dimittis* of Simeon (Luke 2:29-32). Without denying that these hymnic utterances could have come forth from those to whom Luke's account originally ascribes them, one cannot help but observe that his gospel narrative has much the character of a modern nativity pageant with traditional Christmas carols interspersed at appropriate points. These hymns owe much to their Old Testament antecedents in the Psalms, and in the case of Mary's hymn, to the song of thanksgiving uttered by Hannah at the birth of Samuel (1 Sam. 2:1-10). All these hymns have a common theme: the ascription of glory (*doxa*) to God for his new and gracious act in the deliverance of his people, an act that not only fulfills the promise made to the patriarchs and prophets of Israel, but also extends the covenant blessing of peace and salvation to the Gentiles and to all "on whom his favor rests" (*anthrōpois eudokias,* Luke 2:14). (The hymn of the heavenly host finds an echo later in the third gospel, in the acclamation of the disciples at Jesus' entry into Jerusalem, "Peace in heaven and glory in the highest!"

[Luke 19:38].) Other acts of praise in the Lucan infancy narrative include the rejoicing of the shepherds, who returned from Bethlehem "glorifying and praising God" (*doxazontes kai ainountes ton theon,* Luke 2:20) and of the prophetess Anna, who on seeing the infant Jesus, "gave thanks to God" (*anthomologeito tō theō,* Luke 2:38, RSV).

As for Matthew's account of the Nativity (Matt. 2:1-12), his narrative stresses the homage paid to the child Jesus by the Magi, who "bowed down and worshiped him" (Matt. 2:11) as they offered their gifts. This passage uses the term *worship* (*proskuneō*) three times (Matt. 2:2, 8, 11). As with Luke, who stressed the salvation to come to the Gentiles through the appearance of the Christ, so with Matthew the worshipful Magi are not Jews but Gentiles, in fact Persian astrologers.

Homage to Christ During His Ministry

During the years of his earthly ministry, Jesus Christ frequently received the worship of those whose lives he touched. In some instances, people bowed down to him as a gesture of entreaty, asking to be cleansed from leprosy (Matt. 8:2) or for the healing of a family member (Matt. 9:18; 15:25). At other times, people worshiped Jesus because they recognized in him the presence of God. Those in the boat acclaimed him as the Son of God when he came to them upon the water (Matt. 14:33); even the demons in the man from the Gerasene tombs were constrained to worship Jesus as "Son of the Most High God" (Mark 5:7). (In all these instances the verb is *proskuneō*.) At his entry into Jerusalem, Jesus received the praise of those going in procession with him, who were acclaiming him as Son of David with shouts of "Hosanna!" (*hōsanna,* from a Hebrew phrase meaning "Save, Lord!") and "Blessed [*eulogēmenos*] is he who comes in the name of the Lord!" (Matt. 21:9), a quotation from Psalm 118:26. But the disciples' worship of Jesus reached a climax of awestruck amazement at his resurrection, as they fell to their knees before him (Matt. 28:9, 17), rejoiced (*chairō*) to behold him (John 20:20), or like Thomas, exclaimed, "My Lord and my God!" (John 20:28).

Jesus' Worship of the Father

Jesus set the example for his disciples as a worshiper of the Father. He instructed them to approach the Lord of the covenant with praise and adoration:

> hallowed be your name,
> your kingdom come,
> your will be done
> on earth as it is in heaven.
> (Matt. 6:9-10)

Yet Jesus' worship was not a dignified formality but a joyous abandon before his Father (Luke 10:21). Upon the return of the seventy from their mission of proclaiming the kingdom of God, Jesus danced in the Holy Spirit (the basic meaning of the verb *agalliaō,* often translated "exult, greatly rejoice") and praised the Lord of heaven and earth (*exōmologeō,* to praise in the sense of acknowledging the mighty deeds of God).

In praying to the Father, Jesus frequently gave thanks (*eucharisteō*), as in distributing the loaves and fish (John 6:11, 23) or in preparing to raise Lazarus (John 11:41), but most memorably at the Last Supper with his disciples when he blessed (*eulogeō*) the bread and gave thanks (*eucharisteō*) over the cup, the meal solemnizing the new covenant of the kingdom of God (Mark 14:22-25; 1 Cor. 11:23-25). In the church's later celebration of the Lord's Supper, this act of thanksgiving was of such importance that it supplied one of the terms, *Eucharist,* traditionally designating this basic act of Christian worship.

Thanksgiving and Rejoicing

Moreover, the *attitude* of constant thanksgiving became the hallmark of the life of the worshiping Christian. In Paul's view, to fail to give thanks is to refuse to acknowledge God (Rom. 1:21). Expressions of gratitude abound in his epistles, whether giving thanks for the faithful church (Eph. 1:16) or uttering thanks (*charis*) to God for the victory of the Resurrection (1 Cor. 15:57); repeatedly he commends thanksgiving (verb *eucharisteō,* noun *eucharistia*) to his readers: "Give thanks in all circumstances" (1 Thess. 5:18); be filled with the Spirit, continuously giving thanks (Eph. 5:18, 20); walk in Christ, overflowing with thanksgiving (Col. 2:7); include thanksgiving in making your requests to God (Phil. 4:6). For Paul, the primary purpose of the use of tongues in worship is for thanksgiving, hence his directive in 1 Corinthians 14:13-17 to the effect that utterances in a tongue need to be interpreted for the "ungifted" so that they may "say 'Amen' to your thanksgiving [*eucharistia*]." The author of Hebrews likewise commends thanksgiving

(*charis*) for the eternal kingdom as the reverential service of God (Heb. 12:28). He urges the church to offer up a continual "sacrifice of praise" (*thusian aineseōs*), confessing (*homologeō*) the name of God (Heb. 13:15); that he has thanksgiving primarily in mind is evident from the fact that his words echo those of Psalm 50, which invites the worshiper to "sacrifice thanksgiving" (*zavaḥ todah*) to the Lord (Ps. 50:14, 23, NASB).

Hand in hand with thanksgiving goes continual rejoicing; Paul's oft-quoted dictum comes to mind: "Rejoice [*chairō*] in the Lord always. I will say it again: Rejoice!" (Phil. 4:4; cf. 1 Thess. 5:16). This rejoicing is a response to the new life of the kingdom of God, but also an anticipation of redemption to come despite adverse conditions in the present. As Paul said, "we rejoice [*kauchaomai,* literally 'boast'] in the hope of the glory of God," and even "rejoice in our sufferings" (Rom. 5:2-3), words reminiscent of those of Jesus to his disciples (Luke 6:22-23) when he commanded them to rejoice (*chairō*) in the day of persecution and "leap for joy" (*skirtaō*). "Do not rejoice [*chairō*] that the spirits submit to you," he told them, "but rejoice that your names are written in heaven" (Luke 10:20).

Christian Worship As Corporate

New Testament worship was not simply a matter of inward attitude or individual expression. It was a corporate experience of the gathered church celebrating its existence as a covenant people before the Lord, who had called it into being. Whereas in Israelite religion the priesthood was the special vocation of the few, the church collectively is "a royal priesthood [*basileion hierateuma*], a holy nation, a people belonging to God," called forth to proclaim the excellencies of a redeeming God (1 Pet. 2:9). The church is created for worship, "being built into a spiritual house to be a holy priesthood, offering spiritual sacrifices [*pneumatikas thusias*] acceptable to God through Jesus Christ" (1 Pet. 2:5). The church is *ekklēsia,* a people "called out" from the unfaithful and from the world, set apart for the Lord as "the saints" or "holy ones" (*hoi hagioi,* never used in the New Testament to refer to an individual Christian but applied only to the church as a whole). To be a Christian is to be a part of the body of Christ (*sōma christou,* 1 Cor. 12:27; cf. Eph. 4:12), a favorite metaphor of the apostle Paul for the corporate gathering of the new covenant. Worship takes place in the assembling together (*episunagōgē,* Heb.

10:25) of the community of faith; describing the spontaneous worship of the Corinthian church, Paul indicates that it occurs when the people "come together" (*sunerchomai*, 1 Cor. 11:18; 14:23, 26).

Spiritual Gifts in Worship

In his directives to the Corinthians for the conduct of corporate worship (1 Cor. 12–14), Paul includes prophesying (noun *prophēteia*, 1 Cor. 12:10; verb *prophēteuō*, 1 Cor. 14:1, 39, and others), speaking with tongues (noun *glōssai*, 1 Cor. 12:10; verb *lalein glōssais*, 1 Cor. 14:39), interpretation of tongues (*hermēneia*, 1 Cor. 12:10; verb *diermēneuō*, 1 Cor. 14:27), as well as (1 Cor. 12:8) the "word of wisdom" (*logos sophias*) and the "word of knowledge" (*logos gnōseōs*). In the Bible, the prophet is the spokesman for the Lord, uttering the inspired word; Paul, however, specifically describes the function of the prophet in the assembly as speaking to men "for their strengthening, encouragement and comfort" (1 Cor. 14:3). The function of tongues appears to be addressing God to bless him and give thanks (1 Cor. 14:3, 16). Paul's words in 1 Corinthians 14:18 should probably be translated, "I thank God, speaking in tongues, more than you all"; the usual translation ascribes to him a spiritual arrogance worthy of the Pharisee in the temple (Luke 18:11). Other worshipers may enter into this act of praise, adding their "Amen!" only if someone interprets the thanksgiving (1 Cor. 14:16). Understanding tongues as praise and thanksgiving is consistent with what is said about them in the account of the day of Pentecost, when visitors to Jerusalem from other parts of the ancient world understood the apostles to be "declaring the wonders of God" in their own languages (Acts 2:11). (The modern practice in some churches of following an utterance in tongues with an interpretation in the form of a message *from* the Lord is unknown in the New Testament.) These "vocal gifts" are enumerated among the *pneumatika* or "spiritual things," such as gifts of healing or the effecting of miracles.

Music in Christian Worship

Music played an important role in early Christian worship. Paul lists "psalms and hymns and spiritual songs, singing and making melody with your heart to the Lord" as the outflow of the filling of the Holy Spirit and the word of God whereby believers express their thanksgiving to God (Eph. 5:18-20; Col. 3:16). "When you assemble," he says, "each one has

a psalm" (1 Cor. 14:26, NASB); even in prison in Philippi, Paul and Silas were "praying and singing hymns (*humneō*) to God" (Acts 16:25). By *psalm* (*psalmos*), we should probably understand the biblical Psalms as used in Israelite and Jewish worship. The meaning of *hymn* (*humnos*) is less certain and might include not only the biblical Psalms but also other hymnic material, such as prophetic songs in the Scriptures, the Christian hymns of Luke 1–2 and the Revelation to John, and several other New Testament passages of a hymnlike character (John 1:1-18; Phil. 2:5-11; and the acclamation of 1 Tim. 3:16). No doubt there was much early Christian hymnody that has not been preserved. As to "spiritual songs" (*ōdai pneumatikai*), perhaps this term refers to spontaneous, free-flowing song, including singing in tongues.

Prayer and Instruction

The worship of the New Testament church also included times of prayer and instruction. Prayer, as an act of worship, was both personal and corporate. Encouraging the church in spiritual warfare, Paul admonishes the Ephesians, "Pray in the Spirit on all occasions with all kinds of prayers and requests" (*proseuchēs kai deēsōs*, Eph. 6:18). He urges the Thessalonians to "pray continually" (1 Thess. 5:17); he seems to have corporate prayer in mind, since he sets it within a context of rejoicing (1 Thess. 4:16) and thanksgiving (1 Thess. 5:18) and associates it with prophetic utterance (1 Thess. 5:20). Writing to Timothy, a pastoral leader, Paul urges the church to offer "requests, prayers, intercession and thanksgiving" (*deēseis, proseuchas, enteuxeis, eucharistias*) in behalf of all people (1 Tim. 2:1). The ministry of prayer was one function in which women could lead the assembly in worship; in his discussion of headship (1 Cor. 11:3-16) Paul assumes that a woman may pray or prophesy in the assembly, the only issue being whether her head should be covered, as a reflection of the headship of Christ.

Instruction also took place in the assembly. Acts 2:42 records that the early Christians of Jerusalem "devoted themselves to the apostles' teaching [*didachē*]," and the Epistles, especially the Pastorals, contain abundant references to the need for accurate instruction in the church. Paul indicates that in the gathering of the church some came with "a word of instruction" (1 Cor. 14:26). The role of the pastor or "shepherd" (*poimēn*) was primarily that of teacher (*didaskalos*) of the assembly. Paul seems to equate the two offices in his list of the ministry gifts of the ascended Christ (Eph. 4:11) and indicates to Titus that the special task of the superintendent, or "overseer" (*episkopos*), is "to exhort in sound doctrine" (Titus 1:9).

The New Testament is not explicit about the order of service that combined prayer with instruction in the Scriptures (although some have found the suggestion of a sequence of events in 1 Cor. 14:26). It is widely held that early Christian worship was derived in part from the form of worship developing in the synagogue during the New Testament period, which combined prayers or blessings with the reading of the Scripture. But the biblical prayers of the Psalms and the various Old Testament accounts of the reading of the covenant laws supply the underlying scriptural model for this form of worship in both synagogue and church.

The Lord's Supper

In any event, the most distinctive act of Christian worship in the New Testament church, as in the contemporary church, was the Lord's Supper. The term *Lord's Supper,* or perhaps more accurately, "imperial banquet" (*kuriakon deipnon*) occurs in Paul's discussion of the ceremony in 1 Corinthians 11:20-34. In 1 Corinthians 10:16, he calls the cup "a participation [*koinōnia*] in the blood of Christ," while the bread or loaf is called "a participation in the body of Christ." This concept of *koinōnia* is difficult to translate; it embraces a deep and intense participation, sharing, fellowship, and mutual identification as one body in and with Christ (1 Cor. 10:17), and so underlies the theme of *communion* associated with this act of worship, although the modern term *Holy Communion* is not applied to it in the New Testament. Another New Testament expression that may refer to the Lord's Supper is "the breaking of the bread" or loaf (*klasis tou artou*), especially since in Acts 2:42 it is associated with the *koinōnia* of the apostles as one of the distinctive features of the Jerusalem church in the days immediately after Pentecost. If John's account of Jesus' feeding of the multitude is understood as his method of interpreting the Lord's Supper (since, when he comes to the account of the final meal with the disciples in Chapter 13, he omits the institution of the Lord's Supper), then perhaps John 6:11 and 6:23 are a reference to the term *Eucharist,* or giving of thanks, as applied to this act.

During the New Testament period, the Lord's Supper appears to have been not a liturgy in the modern sense, but an actual meal, or a portion of one, shared by members of the Christian community. As such, it was the covenant meal, the ceremonial enactment of the bond created between God and his new people through Jesus Christ, a parallel to the covenant meal shared by Moses and the elders of Israel as they ate and drank before the Lord on Mount Sinai (Exod. 24:11). In his institution of the ordinance, Jesus had given the loaf and the cup as the representations of his body and blood, declaring the cup to be "my blood of the covenant" (Matt. 26:28; Mark 14:24) or "the new covenant [*hē kainē diathēkē*] in my blood" (Luke 22:20). As the Passover, which Jesus and the disciples were observing, was a re-presentation of Yahweh's deliverance of Israel in the Exodus and his creation of a covenanted people, so the Lord's Supper was also an anticipation of Jesus' impending death on the cross, under the figure of his body broken and his blood poured out, and also of the victory of the enactment of the judgments and kingdom of God through his death and resurrection—events that were to bring into being the renewed people of the covenant. Thus, offering the cup to his disciples, Jesus told them he would "drink it anew with you in my Father's kingdom" (Matt. 26:29), just as Paul later stated that in sharing the bread and the cup "you proclaim the Lord's death until he comes" (1 Cor. 11:26). It seems clear that the "imperial banquet" was not the somber and introspective rite practiced in many churches of today, but a solemn yet festive and triumphant celebration.

Worship As Active and Visible

Although Jesus had spoken of genuine worship of the Father as worship "in spirit and truth" (*en pneumati kai alētheia,* John 4:23), this did not mean that Christian worship was so spiritual that it was invisible. The Lord's Supper itself is an outward action—consuming a sacred meal—which conforms to an inward reality—the creation of the people of the new covenant. In other words, it has a "sacramental" character as a visible expression of the invisible. The great celebrations of Israelite worship, with their pilgrimages, public festivity, processions, dancing, shouting, and tumultuous praise, were not possible for the New Testament church, which had to maintain a low profile in a hostile environment. Nevertheless, within the assembly of believers, acts of worship were visible acts. The word translated "worship," as noted above, means to kneel, bow, or prostrate oneself, and such actions must have accompanied the vocal expressions of praise or supplication. Paul, for one, expressly states in prayer "I kneel before the Father" (Eph. 3:14); to Timothy he expresses his desire "I want men everywhere to lift up holy hands in prayer" (1 Tim. 2:8). The author of Hebrews describes the church using the word *panēguris*, "festal gathering" (Heb. 12:22); the elements of the Greek word (related to the English *panegyric*) originally pictured a group of people celebrating with festive circle dancing.

Sacred Exclamations and Outbursts of Praise

New Testament worship was also marked by the use of certain terms that might be described as "sacred exclamations." One such is the word *Hallelujah!* (*hallēlouia*, Rev. 19:1, 3-4, 6), taken directly from the Psalms of Israelite and Jewish worship, many of which begin and end with *hallelu-Yah*, "praise Yah," a shortened form of the name Yahweh (Pss. 112–117; 146–150). Another exclamation is "Amen!" (Rom. 1:25; 1 Cor. 14:16; Rev. 5:14; 19:4; 22:20-21), also taken from the benedictions that close the first four books of the Psalms (Pss. 41:13; 72:19; 89:52; 106:48). "Amen" does not literally mean "so be it," but is derived from the Hebrew root signifying truth, in the sense of dependability or reliability, and its use as a sacred exclamation has something of the character of the contemporary English colloquialisms "Right on!" and "You said it!" In the gospel of John, Jesus uses the term *amen* to introduce an especially pointed utterance, as in "*Amēn, amēn,* I say to you . . ." (John 1:51, and others); the word is used in twenty-four places and, as usually in the Psalms, is always doubled. "Amen" also concludes the doxology of the prayer Jesus gave as a model for his disciples (Matt. 6:13, NASB), although the doxology does not appear in the earliest manuscripts. Another sacred exclamation is "Maranatha" (1 Cor. 16:22, NASB), an Aramaic phrase meaning either "Come, our Lord!" or "Our Lord has come!" In favor of the latter interpretation is the use of *maranatha* to conclude the thanksgiving after the Lord's Supper in the second century order described in the *Didachē*, or *Teaching of the Twelve Apostles*. The expression "Hosanna!" described above, also occurs in the same context (*Didachē*, 10). The fact that such sacred exclamations were left

untranslated from the Hebrew or Aramaic, even in a Greek-speaking church, shows that they conveyed their meaning not through their rational content, but through their spiritual quality as bearers of a sense of awe and mystery in the presence of the holy Lord, in much the same manner as thanksgiving in tongues.

It is possible that some of the doxological outbursts in the Epistles (Rom. 11:33-36; Gal. 1:4-5; 1 Tim. 6:15-16; Jude 25) had their origin in spontaneous exclamations within the corporate worship of the church. Another type of outburst is the blessing, similar to the blessing or *berakhah* of Hebraic worship. Such expressions as Paul's great blessing of Ephesians 1:3-23, which begins, "Blessed be [*eulogētos*] the God and Father of our Lord Jesus Christ," the blessing at the beginning of his second letter to the church in Corinth (2 Cor. 1:3, NASB), or the interjection in Romans 1:25 when he speaks of "the Creator, who is blessed forever. Amen" (NASB) belong to this category.

Later Development of Calendar and Liturgy

The New Testament does not directly stipulate the times of worship, though it seems clear that the church customarily assembled on the first day of the week (Acts 20:7; 1 Cor. 16:2), which may be equated with "the Lord's Day" (*hē kuriakē hēmera*, Rev. 1:10), on which John received from Christ the revelation of "what must soon take place" (Rev. 1:1). Second-century sources provide more details; the *Didachē* (14) directs the church to "assemble and break bread and give thanks" on the Lord's Day, and Justin Martyr (*Apology*, I, 67) explains that Sunday was chosen because the first day was both the day of the Creation and the day of the resurrection of Christ. Neither does the New Testament provide any calendar of distinctively Christian festivals; there is no mention, for example, of special annual celebrations of the birth or the resurrection of Christ.

Second-century Christian sources indicate that Christian worship had become differentiated into the "service [*leitourgia*, liturgy] of the word," a time of prayer and instruction similar to the synagogue service, and the "service of the Lord's table" or the observance of the Lord's Supper. Worshipers who were not fully instructed, such as new converts, were dismissed before the Lord's Supper. The New Testament, however, does not give any details about this differentiation. It appears that unbelievers might come into the assembly (1 Cor. 14:24), but there are no instructions to exclude them from the covenant meal and no rubrics that provide clues to an order of service.

115 ✦ WORDS RELATING TO VISIONARY WORSHIP

In addition to the vocabulary of worship actually being offered in the church, the New Testament contains references to worship that may be described as "visionary"; that is, worship is described in images that seem to transcend the actual practice of the nascent church and which place its worship in an eternal and glorious context.

—— Visionary Worship in the Epistles ——

Paul, commending to the Philippians Christ's attitude of humility, declares that his obedience even to death on the cross has led to his exaltation; God "gave him the name that is above every name, that at the name of Jesus every knee should bow . . . and every tongue confess that Jesus Christ is Lord, to the glory of God the Father" (Phil. 2:9-11). Here, in words partially borrowed from Isaiah (Isa. 45:23), Paul portrays the universal sweep of the covenant as all people swear allegiance to the Lord Jesus Christ; the word _confess (exōmologeō)_ translates Isaiah's _nishba'_, which means to swear an oath of covenant faithfulness. In 2 Corinthians 3:12-18 Paul speaks of the veil of Moses, which conceals the glory _(doxa)_ of God. But when a person turns to Christ, the Spirit of the Lord removes that veil, so that "we, who with unveiled faces all reflect the Lord's glory, are being transformed into his likeness with ever-increasing glory . . ." (2 Cor. 3:18). Paul goes on to refer to the Christian's inward experience of "the light of the knowledge of the glory of God in the face of Christ" (2 Cor. 4:6). That worship is the background for this thought is clear when we recall that the manifestation of the glory of the Lord was a high point in Israelite worship, reflected in many of the psalms and in other passages, such as the account of the dedication of Solomon's temple; the Sinai covenant was initiated by just such a manifestation or "theophany."

The writer to the Hebrews also carries covenant worship into the visionary realm, declaring that his readers have come not to an earthly place of meeting with God but to the true and spiritual Mount Zion, "and to the city of the living God, the heavenly Jerusalem, and to myriads of angels, to the general assembly and church of the first-born who are enrolled in heaven, and to God, the Judge of all, and to the spirits of righteous men made perfect, and to Jesus, the mediator of a new covenant . . ." (Heb. 12:22-24, NASB). In such language the distinction between the earthly assembly (_panēguris,_ "festival gathering") or worshiping church (_ekklēsia_) and the heavenly city of God, the angelic Jerusalem, is lost; the concepts merge as one and the same new covenant reality.

—— Worship in the Revelation ——

It is the Revelation to John that is the supreme worship book of the New Testament. Composed in the form of a great drama of the victory of Christ, it begins with letters addressed to Christian assemblies in seven cities of Asia Minor and ends with a vision of the new Jerusalem in which God himself dwells among his people (Rev. 21:3), in fulfillment of the Israelite prophets' capsule formulation of the covenant, "I will be their God, and they will be my people" (Jer. 31:33). This new Jerusalem is a spiritual reality, described in rich symbolism drawing on themes from the Old Testament; for example, there is no temple in the city, for "the Lord God Almighty and the Lamb are its temple" (Rev. 21:22); the foundation stones of the city are precious stones corresponding to those that adorned the breastpiece of the high priest, which in turn stood for the twelve tribes of Israel (Exod. 28:15-21). It seems clear that a statement is being made about the church as the embodiment of the true worshiping Israel; it is, as Hebrews says, the "heavenly Jerusalem" to which Christian believers have already come (Heb. 12:22), the free "Jerusalem above," which Paul calls "our mother" in contrast to the present Jerusalem with its temple (Gal. 4:25-26, alluding to Ps. 87:5-6). This worshiping church is the bride of the Lamb (Rev. 21:9), who joins the Spirit in the invitation to genuine life: "the Spirit and the bride say, 'Come!'" (Rev. 22:17).

Setting the pattern for the worship of the Creator are the twenty-four elders (_presbuteroi_); their number combines the twelve tribes with the twelve apostles, a representation of the fullness of the worshiping Israel of both old and new covenants. Like the chorus of a Greek drama, the elders, and the larger choir of which they are a part, appear at strategic points in the unfolding drama of the gospel. As the judgments of the Lamb against the unfaithful are revealed, they interject their commentary in the form of powerful declarations of praise, falling down to worship God (*proskuneō*, Rev. 5:14; 11:16; 19:4) and singing hymns (Rev. 4:8b, 11; 5:9-10, 12, 13b; 11:15b, 17; 15:3-4; 19:6-7), which seem to press the vocabulary of worship to its very limits. The elders sing antiphonally with four "living creatures," an image drawn from Ezekiel's vision of the glory of the Lord (Ezek. 1) and whose number may signify the universal adoration of the Creator by the created order, the earth or land. At the outset, the living creatures take up the seraphic hymn of Isaiah, "Holy [*hagios*], holy, holy, is the Lord God, Almighty" (Rev. 4:8). The elders echo with a similar-sounding word: "You are worthy [*axios*], our Lord and God . . ." (Rev. 4:11), also uttered three times, as the elders' acclamation is taken up by a widening chorus, first of angelic beings ("You are worthy . . ." Rev. 5:9) and then of all creatures ("Worthy is the Lamb . . ." Rev. 5:12). These anthems pile declaration upon declaration, with ascriptions of "glory and honor and power" (*hē doxa kai hē timē kai hē dunamis,* Rev. 4:11), "praise and honor and glory and power" (*hē eulogia kai hē timē kai hē doxa kai to kratos,* Rev. 5:13b) to the Lamb.

At that point in the drama that narrates the crucifixion and resurrection of Jesus (under the figure of the two witnesses; Jesus is the "faithful witness" [Rev. 1:5]), the chorus joins in a massive declaration of the kingship and dominion of the Lord and of his Christ (Rev. 11:15b), to which the elders respond, "We give thanks" (*eucharisteō,* Rev. 11:17b). Significantly, it is here that "God's temple in heaven was opened, and within his temple was seen the ark of his covenant" (Rev. 11:19); this corresponds to the gospel narrative of the Crucifixion, when the veil of the temple was torn, with similar theophanic manifestations (Matt. 27:51), to reveal the emptiness of the earthly sanctuary. In Israelite worship, the ark was the symbolic throne of Yahweh the King and played an important part in the covenant cult of Israel. With this imagery, as with so much else, the Revelation takes us into the realm of covenant worship, making the point that the covenant is renewed through the death and resurrection of Christ.

At the dramatic climax, when the seven final plagues of judgment are about to be released, the chorus of the overcomers sings "the song [*ōdē*] of Moses the servant of God, and the song of the Lamb 'Great and marvelous are your deeds, Lord God Almighty. . . . For you alone are holy. . . . for your righteous acts have been revealed'" (Rev. 15:3-4). In the Old Testament, the Song of Moses (Deut. 32) is the conclusion of a curse liturgy invoking the sanctions of the covenant against an unfaithful people. In the Revelation, the "song of Moses and of the Lamb" stands in a similar place, preceding the outpouring of judgment against the apostate harlot "Babylon," the persecutor of the prophets and saints (Rev. 18:24)—a description that fits Jerusalem far better than it fits Rome. Finally, after the destruction of the city, come the "Hallelujahs!" of chapter 19, culminating in the great affirmation, "For our Lord God Almighty reigns" (Rev. 19:6b).

The Revelation to John is a work of dramatic and liturgical art, based on symbolism drawn from the Hebrew Scriptures. How far the worship in the Revelation corresponds to actual worship in the New Testament church is an open question, but the book was written to first-century Christians who may be expected to have had a definite frame of reference by which to interpret the symbolism of the events narrated, including the descriptions of the worship of the Lord God and of the Lamb. Although "visionary," in the sense that John includes it with the transcendent imagery of his drama, it is not heavenly worship, as is often claimed, but the worship of the "new creation" (2 Cor. 5:17), a "new heaven and a new earth" (Rev. 21:1), the new Jerusalem created "for rejoicing, and her people for gladness" (Isa. 65:18, NASB).

Richard C. Leonard

THREE

The Names of God in Worship

The following entries deal with the most important biblical names or titles for God the Father, God the Son, and God the Holy Spirit. Some of the concepts referring to God the Father in the Old Testament are applied also to God the Son in the New Testament, and this usage is dealt with in the most convenient place. The study does not attempt to describe every metaphor or simile used for God in the Scriptures, which contain a rich variety of such terms.

116 ◆ BIBLICAL CONCEPT OF "NAME"

The concept of the "name" is an important one in biblical worship. In fact, a synonym for "worship" in the Scriptures is the expression "call upon the name of the Lord" (Gen. 26:25; Pss. 80:18; 99:6; 105:1; 116:13, 17). Often we hear the summons to praise, bless, or exalt his name (Pss. 34:3; 96:2; 100:4; 135:3; 148:13; 149:3) or to ascribe glory to his name (Pss. 29:2; 66:2; 96:8; 115:1). The worshiper may speak of lifting his or her hands to the name of the Lord (Ps. 63:4) in the universal ancient gesture of homage.

Importance of the Name

In biblical thought, a name is more than a designation differentiating persons or things. A person's name encompasses his complete identity, reputation, and character and refers to his whole self or person. In the Scripture, the phrase "my name" is often used in place of "I" or "me," and "his name" means "him." Thus, the Lord assures Moses that his name will be in the angel who goes before Israel, meaning that the Lord himself will be present (Exod. 23:20-21). When God's people are commanded to praise the name of the Lord, they are in fact being told to praise the Lord himself. The sanctuary is the place where the Lord causes his name to dwell (Deut. 12:11), or establishes his name (Deut. 16:6; 26:2), which is to say that his people may worship there in his presence.

Name and Character

One's character is known by one's name. Nabal's reputation with his wife was reflected in his name, which meant "fool" (1 Sam. 25:25). Jacob's name, "supplanter," was descriptive of a life-style (Gen. 27:36), until the Lord changed his name with the idea that his behavior would be modified accordingly. Even much later, in New Testament times, a person's name might be changed at a significant turn in his or her life. Jesus gave Simon the new name of Cephas (Aramaic) or Peter (Greek), meaning "rock," when he first met him (John 1:42) and again when he became the first to acclaim Jesus as the Christ (Matt. 16:13-20). Saul became Paul, exchanging his Jewish for his Roman name, when he changed from a persecutor to a preacher of the gospel. In making a covenant with Israel, Yahweh first revealed his name to Moses as an indicator of his character in the covenant relationship. The term *God* is not really a name but a title, describing the "office" that Yahweh holds.

Covenant Significance of a Name Change

Covenant ceremonies often included changes of name. A great king who was granting a covenant to a subject king and his people was said to "form" or "create" the vassal nation. In the ancient world an object was not thought to exist until it was named, so the king who "created" the people would usually name them as well, sometimes calling them by his own name as a sign of ownership. Abram became Abraham when the Lord established a covenant with him. Jacob's name was changed to Israel, which means "God rules" (Gen. 32:28), a name which later came to refer to Jacob's descendants, the people God had created for himself. Aaron the priest put the Lord's name on the covenant people (Num. 6:27); God has named Israel (Isa. 43:1), calling them by his own name (2 Chron. 7:14). His name is on the sanctuary where they are to worship him (Neh. 1:9) and the city in which it is located (Jer. 7:12).

117 ♦ NAMES OF GOD THE FATHER

Biblical worshipers reverenced the name of the Lord, but the terminology they used varied depending on the worshipers' needs, preference, or customary usage within the community. Included here are some of the major names or titles applied to God the Father in worship.

God (*'El*)

'El was the original supreme god of the Semitic pantheon; the title is associated with the idea of strength or might. By the time the Israelite tribes settled in Canaan, the principal god was Baʻal ("husband" or "lord"), the divinity of popular worship, especially fertility rites. *'El* had receded into the background, and his name had become a generic term for "god." Hence the name *'El* could be applied to Yahweh, usually in combination with a qualifier. The following are the major compound names with *'El* found in the Scripture.

Almighty God (*'El shaddai*). *Shaddai* is sometimes used alone. It comes from a Hebrew word meaning "mountain" and carries the meaning of "mountain God," as well as the sense of strength and majesty. The thought, though not the name, is suggested in Psalm 121:1. As a title for God, *'El shaddai* is largely associated with the patriarchal period; it is used often in the book of Job, which is set in that period, and it is as *'El shaddai* that God changes the names of both Abram (Gen. 17:5) and Jacob (Gen. 35:10-12), in reaffirming his promise of land and descendants.

God Most High (*'El 'elyon*). The root is probably *'alah* which means "to go up." The name seems to have been associated with Salem (Gen. 14:18-20), a pre-Israelite designation for Jerusalem, where the Israelite sanctuary would eventually be located, and quite possibly came into use in Israel through Jebusites who converted to the worship of Yahweh. In the Psalms, the name is usually associated with Zion, either as *'El 'elyon* or simply *'Elyon* (Pss. 46:4, 50:14; 91:1; 92:1).

Mighty God (*'El gibbor*). The term *gibbor,* which describes a military man or warrior (1 Chron. 27:6), is frequently applied to God (Isa. 9:6; 10:21; Hab. 1:12). Psalm 24:8 celebrates "The LORD strong and mighty, the LORD mighty in battle."

Eternal God (*'El 'olam*). In Beersheba, Abraham called on the name of Yahweh, the everlasting or "Eternal God" (Gen. 21:33). The word *'olam* refers to continuous existence or long duration, both past and future. Eternity is ascribed to God as the sustainer of the creation, and more significantly, as the guarantor of the stability and enduring quality of the covenant with his people; the expression "everlasting covenant" occurs a number of times in Scripture (*bᵉrit 'olam,* Gen. 9:16; Isa. 61:8; Jer. 50:5; Ezek. 37:26; Ps. 105:10; *diathēkē aiōniou,* Heb. 13:20). The "Song of Moses" (Deut. 32:40) presents a picture of the Lord taking a covenant oath, lifting his hand and swearing, "as I live forever [*lᵉ'olam*]." The phrase "eternal God" occurs also in Isaiah 40:28, using another Hebrew word for God (*'Elohei 'olam*).

The Living God (*'El ḥai, Theos zontos*). The expression "living God" describes Yahweh as a God of energy, vitality, and wrath. The name is associated with the ark (Josh. 3:10) and, in the longer form *'Elohim ḥayyim,* with the armies of Israel (1 Sam. 17:26, 36). The psalmists cry out for the presence of the living God in the sanctuary (*'El ḥai,* Pss. 42:2; 84:2). Moses refers to the living God speaking from the midst of the fire in the Sinai covenant, and Jeremiah speaks of the wrath of Yahweh, "the living God, the eternal King" (Jer. 10:10). These expressions (both *'Elohim ḥayyim*) form the background for the warning of the author of Hebrews, "It is a dreadful thing to fall into the hands of the living God" (*Theos zontos,* Heb. 10:31; *cf.* Rev. 7:2). Peter confessed Jesus as the Christ, "Son of the living God" (Matt. 16:16). Perhaps in allusion to the presence of the living God with the hosts of Israel, the New Testament church is called "the church of the living God, the pillar and foundation of the truth" (1 Tim. 3:15) and "Mount Zion . . . the city of the living God" (Heb. 12:22).

The Mighty One, God Yahweh (*'El 'Elohim Yahveh*). This expression occurs in Psalm 50:1; similar expressions are "great and mighty God" (*'El haggadol haggibbor,* Jer. 32:18) and "the God great and mighty and awesome" (*Ha'El haggadol haggibbor vᵉhannora',* Deut. 10:17; Neh. 9:32). These phrases are examples of the tendency of Semitic worshipers to pile up expressions in an attempt to convey the overpowering majesty of the Lord. The word *awesome* in Hebrew is *nora'*, literally, "to be feared." It communicates the worshiper's response of trembling or awe in the presence of the might and mystery of the Holy One; it is derived from the root *y-r-'*, the base for Hebrew words having to do with reverence and respect for God. Hebrew has no word for religion but conveys the idea through expressions such as "the fear of Yahweh" (Prov. 1:7; 9:10).

Deity (*'Elohim*)

Far more common than *'El*, as applied to Yahweh, is the term *'Elohim,* the plural of *'Eloah,* "god." The singular form is not found in the Hebrew Scriptures. In the New Testament, *Theos* translates both *'El* and *'Elohim* as a general term for God; usually it is preceded by the definite article, literally "the God."

God. *'Elohim* is the common Hebrew title for any divinity; since, for Israel, Yahweh is the only relevant divinity, he is called *'Elohim* by his people, frequently with no qualifiers. In Scripture, the word *'Elohim* can refer to pagan gods (Josh. 24:2; Ps. 96:4-5), to angelic beings (Ps. 8:5), or even to prominent or powerful people such as judges or princes (Ps. 82:6). As applied to Yahveh, the plural *'Elohim* always takes a singular verb or modifier. Use of the plural conveys the idea of importance or majesty, a common practice in Semitic languages. It does not have implications for the doctrine of the Trinity, as is sometimes suggested. In a group of the Psalms found in Books II and III, *'Elohim* appears to have been substituted by scribes for an original *Yahveh;* scholars occasionally refer to this part of the Psalms as the "Elohistic Psalter."

God of Jacob (*'Elohei Ya'aqov*); God of Israel (*'Elohei Yisra'el*). Since Jacob and Israel are the same, these titles are equivalent. (Examples of the first are Isa. 2:3; Pss. 46:7; 81:1, 4; the second, which is more common, occurs in Exod. 24:10; Josh. 22:24; Isa. 45:3; Ruth 2:12; 1 Chron. 4:10; *Theos Israēl,* Matt. 15:31). Yahweh is the God who belongs specifically to Jacob, or Israel, by virtue of the covenant established at Mount Sinai. In pagan thought, gods ruled specific localities; thus Israel, when in Egypt, could have been expected to transfer its allegiance from the God who had met Abraham, Isaac, and Jacob in Canaan, to the gods of Goshen, where they were residing. At Sinai, however, they entered into covenant with one particular God whose name was Yahweh, in this case using the Hebrew construct form *'Elohei* or "God of" Jacob.

Lord (*'Adon*); My Lordship (*'Adonai*)

'Adonai is the plural form with the pronominal suffix. These are covenant titles for Yahweh; the plural form denotes majesty or increased status. Under ancient treaty structure the great king who entered into covenant with a lesser monarch was known as the "lord," while his vassal was the "servant." Because Israel, unlike the pagan nations around it, had entered into covenant with its God, they knew Yahweh as "the Lord" and regarded themselves as his servants (2 Chron. 6:22-23).

Jewish worshipers used *'adon* and *'adonai* as substitutes for the divine name *Yahveh.* The Hebrew alphabet does not have vowels, but in the early Christian centuries Jewish scholars known as Masoretes devised a system of vocalization, or "points," to show the vowel pronunciations in the biblical text. Devout Jews considered the name *Yahveh* too sacred to be pronounced, so when reading the Scriptures in worship they substituted the word *Lord.* In the text, scribes inserted the vowel points for *'Adonai* into the name *Yahveh* (written *YHWH*) as a reminder to the reader to use *'Adonai* instead. Translators of the seventeenth and eighteenth centuries did not understand this practice and sometimes combined the vowel sounds for *'Adonai* with the consonants for *Yahveh,* creating the name "Jehovah," which was unknown in ancient times. English versions usually substitute the term *the Lord* where the name *Yahveh* occurs in the Hebrew, often using capital letters to indicate the substitution (*the* Lord).

Yahweh (the Lord)

Yahveh (usually Yahweh in English texts) is the personal or covenant name of God. By this name the Lord introduced himself to Moses at the burning bush (Exod. 3:13-15). The biblical text relates it to the Hebrew verb "to be," and translates it "I am." Taken literally, the Lord's statement to Moses was, *'ehyeh 'asher 'ehyeh,* or "I will be who I will be." The name *Yahveh* seems to express his dynamic character, as the God who is revealed through events in history. He identifies himself in terms of the patriarchs who worshiped him, "the God of Abraham, the God of Isaac and the God of Jacob" (Exod. 3:15). Although the narrative suggests that Yahweh was unknown to Israel at the time he first appeared to Moses, the name was not a new one; the Bible relates that people began to call on the name of Yahweh in the time of Enosh, a grandson of Adam (Gen. 4:26). The original form of the name may have been *Yah,* which appears by itself several times in the Old Testament (Ps. 68:4) and as the ending of the exclamation *Hallelujah!* (praise *Yah!*). Another form may have been *Yahu,* as in the Hebrew forms of many names such as Isaiah (*Yᵉshaʿyahu,* "salvation of *Yahu*"), Jeremiah, Adonijah, Hilkiah, Hezekiah, Benaiah, and so on.

In Christian worship, the name of the Lord is sometimes combined with other terms that qualify his relationship to the worshiper. In the Bible, however, many of these are not actually names of Yahweh. They are often names given to *places* where he manifests himself in a special way to his people. The following is a discussion of the best-known phrases that belong in this category. (Because of its importance, the expression "Lord of hosts" is treated separately.)

The Lord Our Provider (*Yahveh yir'eh*). This expression, familiar in English as "Jehovah Jireh," literally means "Yahweh will see," in the sense of provide (just as we say, "I'll *see* to it"). Abraham gave this name to the place where the Lord provided a ram as the substitute for the sacrifice of Isaac (Gen. 22:14).

The Lord My Banner (*Yahveh nissi*). The banner, *nes,* was actually a standard or ensign used to rally an army in battle. After Israel's victory over the Amalekites, Moses built an altar and gave it this name (Exod. 17:15).

The Lord Your Healer (*Yahveh rof'ekha*). Following the Exodus from Egypt, the Israelites came to a place where the water was undrinkable. After providing sweet water for them, the Lord promised that if the people would obey him he would protect them from the diseases of Egypt as their healer (Exod. 15:26).

The Lord Our Righteousness (*Yahveh tzidqenu*). The prophet Jeremiah used this as a title, not for Yahweh, but for the ideal Davidic king who is to reign with justice (Jer. 23:6). In the New Testament the word *righteousness* (*dikaiosunē*) is applied to Jesus Christ, who fulfills this expectation (1 Cor. 1:30; cf. 2 Pet. 1:1; 1 John 2:1).

The Lord Is Peace (*Yahveh shalom*). Gideon gave this name to an altar he built after the messenger of

the Lord had appeared to him and called him to lead the Israelites against their Midianite oppressors. Because Gideon had seen a manifestation of God, he was afraid he would be struck dead (Judg. 6:11-24). But the messenger reassured him, saying, "Peace! Do not be afraid" (v. 23). From the context, it is obvious that the Lord's "peace" (*shalom*) is not the absence of war; Gideon was being summoned to *begin a war.* Rather, in the context of life under the condition of sin and conflict, "peace" in the Bible means wholeness, health, salvation, prosperity, blessing, success. The prophetic hope for the ultimate perfection of all things, however, envisions a peace that includes the cessation of war, conflict, and fear (Mic. 4:3; Isa. 2:4).

The Lord Is There (*Yahveh shammah*). Ezekiel, prophesying during the exile in Babylon, specified this name for the city where the sanctuary was to be restored (Ezek. 48:35). It is a wordplay on the name of Jerusalem in Hebrew (*Yᵉrushalayim*). Strictly speaking, it is not a name for the Lord. However, Christians understand that the Lord God himself is the temple in the new Jerusalem, the worshiping church (Rev. 21:22), and in that sense it is a name for God.

Lord of Hosts

We may derive the meanings of the names of God from the ways Israel used them in worship. *Yahveh,* as his covenant name, is associated with the ark of the covenant and often appears in combination with the term *tzᵉvaʿot,* "armies," as in "LORD of hosts" (*Yahveh tzᵉvaʿot,* 2 Sam. 7:26; Pss. 24:10; 84:1; Isa. 9:7), or "LORD of hosts" (*'Adonai Yahveh tzᵉvaʿot,* Jer. 32:18, NASB). (*Host* is an old English word meaning "army.") These expressions are the battle names of the Lord; as Israel's covenant Lord or King, Yahweh, symbolized by the ark, which was his throne and the place of his presence, led the nation into war (1 Sam. 4:1-11). The cry preserved in Numbers 10:35-36 and Psalm 132:8, "Arise, O LORD, and come to your resting place, you and the ark of your might," expressed this idea. The concept appears also in Psalm 24:7-10 when the Lord enters the gates of the sanctuary, probably reflecting a procession led by the ark, and in Psalm 10:12, when the psalmist asks the Lord to avenge his people. The title "Lord of hosts" appears also in the New Testament, the Hebrew word for *hosts* being taken over in transliteration (*Kurios sabaoth,* Rom. 9:29; James 5:4).

Other Names for God

In addition to the proper name *Yahveh* and the titles "God," "Deity," and "Lord," the Bible contains many other important names by which Yahweh's people know him.

Holy One (*Qadosh*); Holy One of Israel (*Qᵉdosh Yisra'el*). Yahweh is called "the Holy One" (Isa. 40:25; Hos. 11:9) or sometimes "the Holy One of Israel" (2 Kings 19:22; Ps. 89:18; Isa. 37:23) or *'Elohai Qᵉdoshi,* "my God, my Holy One" (Hab. 1:12). The root meaning of holiness is separation or being set apart; therefore the phrase "the Holy One of Israel" means "the God who is distinctively Israel's." By the same token, Israel is a people "holy to the Lord their God" (Deut. 7:6; 14:2, 21; 26:19; 28:9), set apart for him. The basic meaning of holiness, therefore, is not goodness, purity, or moral virtue, but the transcendent quality of being above and separated from the common or ordinary. The English words *sacred* and *sacrosanct* better convey the meaning. In worship, the concept of God as the Holy One is evident in such instances as the cry of the seraphim in Isaiah's temple vision: *qadosh qadosh qadosh 'Adonai Yahveh tzᵉva'ot,* "Holy, holy, holy is the LORD of hosts" (Isa. 6:3, NASB).

Mighty One of Israel (*'Avir Yisra'el*). An example of this usage is Isaiah 1:24. A variant is "Mighty One of Jacob" (*'Avir Yaʿaqov,* Isa. 49:26; 60:16; Ps. 132:2, 5). This is similar to *'Elohei Yaʿaqov,* with added stress on the superior power of Yahweh, who belonged to Jacob, or the nation of Israel.

King (*Melekh*). As the giver of the covenant, Yahweh stands in the position of King over his vassal subjects, the Creator of his people (Isa. 43:15). Although Israel and Judah had earthly kings, they could not rule with the same absolute authority enjoyed by kings of the surrounding peoples, because the ultimate kingship of the Israelite tribes was vested in the Lord. Kings in the ancient world were military leaders, and the ark of the covenant was the symbol of Yahweh's role as king in battle, the Lord of the hosts or armies of Israel (Isa. 6:5; Jer. 46:18; Mal. 1:14), the King in the midst of his people to defend them (Zeph. 3:15). As Lord of hosts, Yahweh is the "King of glory," who enters his sanctuary (Ps. 24:7-10) "enthroned upon the praises of Israel" (Ps.

22:3, NASB). The Psalms summon the people of God to rejoice with abandon before their King (Ps. 149:1-4), who is the great King or Lord of the covenant (Pss. 47:2; 95:3; Mal. 1:14; Matt. 5:35). The worship of the Lord in Zion is a celebration of his kingship, not only over Israel, but over the whole earth or land (Pss. 29; 47; 93; 95–99). Thus, even when Judah faced defeat and exile, God's true worshipers could praise him as King over all nations (Jer. 10:10), and even Nebuchadnezzar, the ruler of Babylon, is said to have honored him as King of heaven (Dan. 4:37).

In the New Testament, God is rarely called King (*Basileus,* 1 Tim. 1:17; Rev. 15:3), perhaps because the many Caesars and client kings of the Roman world rendered the title ambiguous for Christian usage. However, the concept of God's kingship underlies all that is involved in the other titles by which the church knew and worshiped him and is synonymous with the idea of the kingdom of God. The festive celebration of God's kingship is being increasingly recovered in many parts of today's church.

Judge (*Shofet*). The function of a "judge" in ancient Israel was not that of administering justice in the modern legal sense. Justice (*mishpat*) actually means the entire way of life that maintains the integrity of the covenant and binds the community together; another translation is "custom," referring to the conventional pattern of behavior that allows a society to function. The Lord is the maintainer and guardian of the covenant he has granted: "God himself is judge" (Ps. 50:6). As King, Yahweh is the Judge, or special guardian, of the weakest members of the covenant community, the orphaned and the oppressed (Pss. 10:18; 82:1-4). Thus, the worshiper who believes his position within the covenant has been compromised by the actions of others often cries out for the Lord to "judge" or vindicate him (Pss. 26:1; 43:1; 54:1). As Creator, Yahweh is also "the Judge of all the earth" (Gen. 18:25), the "judge of all men" (Heb. 12:23), deciding between peoples and nations (Judg. 11:27; Ps. 96:13). The Davidic king judges his people as God's vice-regent (Ps. 72:1-2), and thus the apostles proclaim Christ as the Judge of all people (Acts 10:42; 17:31) and the vindicator of his own (2 Tim. 4:8; Rev. 6:9-10).

Savior (*Moshiᵃ'*). This title occurs in Psalm 106:21 and often in Isaiah (Isa. 43:3, 11; 45:15; 49:26). In biblical usage, a savior was a national leader who delivered his people from their enemies by victory on the battlefield. In covenant terminology, "savior" is another title for the great king who fights the battles of his vassal. Yahweh was the King who protected Israel and won its military victories. His basic and most important act of deliverance, however, was the great emancipation of Israel from slavery to Pharaoh in Egypt. Because the death and resurrection of Christ effected a new exodus, calling forth a renewed covenant community, the title "Savior" is ascribed also to Jesus in the New Testament.

Redeemer (*Go'el*). This title is derived from the Hebrew root *ga'al,* literally "act as kinsman, do the part of the next of kin." Examples of its use are Isaiah 49:26 and Psalm 103:4. The *go'el* was the kinsman designated to protect the integrity of the family. It was he who took in a relative's widow, pursued the slayer of a family member to avenge his death, and bought back land or property that had been alienated from the family. In the Old Testament Yahweh is the Redeemer of Israel from Egyptian bondage (Exod. 15:3), from exile (Isa. 43:1, 14; 44:22-23), from enemies (Isa. 41:14), and from the pit (Ps. 103:4). In the New Testament the title "Redeemer" is not used. However, Paul says that Christ has redeemed, or bought back (*exagorazō,* Gal. 3:13; 4:5) his people, and speaks of the redemption (*apolutrōsis,* Rom. 3:24) that is in Christ, a concept that applies to the purchase of freedom for a slave.

Father (*'Av, Patēr, Abba*). God is called "Father" in the Old Testament (*'Av,* Jer. 31:9; 1 Chron. 29:10; Mal. 1:6), but far more often in the New Testament, in which the title is frequently on the lips of Jesus (*Patēr,* Matt. 6:9; John 4:23; 5:17-18; 17:1) and in the preaching and writings of the apostles (Acts 2:33; Eph. 1:2; Phil. 2:11). Jesus often spoke of "my Father," introducing a note of intimacy and intensity in the relationship between the Father and the Son. This intimacy was so characteristic of the kingdom of God, which Jesus proclaimed, that the Greek Gospels preserve the familiar Aramaic word *Abba,* which Jesus used (Mark 14:36), and Paul took it up even in a Greek-speaking church (Rom. 8:15; Gal. 4:6). *Abba* is always paired with its Greek equivalent, *Patēr;* the double usage does not simply translate the term, but intensifies it. *Abba, Patēr* probably became a liturgical expression quite early, since it

has covenant connotations. Ancient treaties sometimes refer to the great king who grants the covenant as "Father." When Jesus and the New Testament writers use the phrase "*Abba,* Father" they recognize not only a familial relationship between God and the church, but a covenant relationship as well.

Husband (*Ba'al, 'Ish, Anēr*). The Hebrew word *ba'al* means "lord, owner, husband"; *'ish* means "man, husband." As a title for Yahweh, *ba'al* is found in Israelite names from the period of the judges and the early kingdom (Jerubbaal, Judg. 7:1; Eshbaal, 1 Chron. 8:33; Meribaal, 1 Chron. 8:34). Because the title *Ba'al* was also associated with the prominent Canaanite fertility god, whose cult attracted many Israelites away from the undivided worship of Yahweh, Israelite worshipers abandoned its use for Yahweh in favor of *'ish* (Hos. 2:16). Biblical scribes sometimes substituted the word *bosheth,* "shame, shameful thing," in proper names that used *ba'al* (as in Mephibosheth for Meribaal). However, the Israelite prophets often compare the covenant between Yahweh and Israel to a marriage, especially in the portrayal of Israel and Judah as unfaithful wives (Hos. 2:1-13; Ezek. 23); in this sense Jeremiah applies the verbal form *ba'al,* "be a husband," to Yahweh (Jer. 31:32). In the New Testament, Paul uses the term *husband* (*anēr*) figuratively of Christ (2 Cor. 11:2), and the image of the church as the bride of Christ (Eph. 5:22-30; Rev. 21:2, 9) presupposes the concept.

Rock (*Tzur*). This word is sometimes translated "strength," "might," or "mighty," and refers to the power of the Lord to protect his people; examples are 2 Samuel 22:47; Psalm 18:46; and Habakkuk 1:12. *Tzur* also indicates faithfulness (Deut. 32:4) and can be used as a synonym for God, as in Deuteronomy 32:18: "You deserted the Rock, who fathered you; you forgot the God who gave you birth." The Lord calls himself a rock over which Israel will stumble (Isa. 8:14), and the New Testament sees Jesus as the embodiment of that rock of offense, who becomes the cornerstone of the new temple of God, the church (Luke 20:17-18; Rom. 9:33; Eph. 2:20; 1 Pet. 2:8). Paul also identifies Jesus as the Rock (*hē petra*) from which water gushed to quench the thirst of God's people during their wilderness wanderings (1 Cor. 10:4).

Shepherd (*Ro'eh*) or Shepherd of Israel (*Ro'eh Yisra'el*). The latter phrase occurs in Psalm 80:1. Ancient kings were often called shepherds of their people. As shepherd, a king's primary duty was to "feed the flock," which was the nation over which he reigned. God takes the shepherds of Israel to task for leading them into idolatry and sin and causing them to abandon the worship of Yahweh, a violation of their responsibility to feed their people the law of the Lord (Jer. 23:1-2; Ezek. 34:2-10). As King of Israel, Yahweh is its Shepherd. Speaking to Israel, God declares, "You my sheep, the sheep of my pasture, are people, and I am your God" (Ezek. 34:31). David calls the Lord his Shepherd (Ps. 23:1) and describes God's care and provision for him in terms of food (green pastures) and drink (quiet pools of water). Jesus identifies himself as the Good Shepherd, *poimēn,* who gives his life for the sheep (John 10:11). The writer of Hebrews calls him the "great Shepherd of the sheep" (13:20), and John pictures Jesus as the Lamb, who is the Shepherd in the midst of the worshiping church, feeding his flock and guiding them to living water (Rev. 7:16-17).

Ancient of Days (*'Attiq yomin*). This term is an idiomatic Aramaic expression that literally means "aged one." As it is used in Daniel 7:9, 13, and 22, it conveys the thought of the antiquity of God. Daniel's description of the Ancient of Days with hair like white wool is echoed in Revelation 1:14, in which John sees "one like a son of man" standing in the midst of the golden lampstands, his head and hair "white like wool." In using this language, John is identifying Jesus with Daniel's Ancient of Days, or Yahweh, as he also does when he writes that Jesus was "in the beginning . . . with God" (John 1:1) and "before Abraham" (John 8:58).

God of Gods (*'Elohei ha'elohim*). This phrase (Deut. 10:17) is an example of a Hebrew idiom that indicates a superlative. It does not mean there are other gods of whom Yahweh is the head but that he is the great and powerful God.

Lord of Lords (*'Adonai ha'adonim, Kurios kuriōn*). This is another example of a Hebrew idiom (Deut. 10:17) that indicates a superlative. The phrase means "great and lordly Lord." The idiom is carried over into the Greek (Rev. 19:16), although it is not idiomatic Greek, because the writers of the New Testament spoke and thought in a Semitic language. As a matter of fact, however, the covenant Lord *is* a Lord over other lords, since he is the great King in covenant with the priest-kings who make up the church (Rev. 1:6). As applied to Christ, the title is paired with "King of kings."

Glory (*Kavod*). The Hebrew word *kavod* denotes glory in the sense of "mass, weight." It refers to the radiant envelope or numinous aura of the manifest presence of the Lord. The Scriptures refer often to the glory of God, and occasionally the word *glory* stands for the Lord himself (Pss. 3:3; 89:17). This concept was more fully developed in the later Jewish Rabbinic writings, in which the word *shekhinah* (from the root *shakhan,* "dwell") became synonymous with God himself in the sense of his abiding glory. (*Shekhinah* is not used in the Bible.)

Power (*Dunamis*). The power of God is made known in his Creation, his acts of deliverance, his miracles and wonders, and especially in the resurrection of Christ and the administration of his kingdom. Jesus uses the term *Power* as a synonym for God in responding to the Jewish high priest at his trial: "You shall see the Son of Man sitting at the right hand of Power, and coming with the clouds of heaven" (Mark 14:62, NASB; cf. Luke 22:69).

Majesty (*Megalōsunē*). The august and majestic presence of the living God is expressed by this word, which literally means "greatness." The author of Hebrews uses it twice as a substitute for "God" (Heb. 1:3; 8:1).

Almighty (*Pantokratōr*). The title means "ruler of all things" and is used mainly in the Revelation to John (though also by Paul, 2 Cor. 6:18). The Greek Old Testament often employed this term to translate the phrase "Yahweh of hosts," and sometimes it appears in quotations from the Old Testament (Rev. 1:8; 4:8). As a title, "Almighty" is usually found in a context of judgment and wrath (Rev. 16:14; 19:15) and occurs several times in the majestic hymns of the Revelation (Rev. 11:17; 15:3; 16:7). In the renewed covenant of the new Jerusalem, "the Lord God Almighty and the Lamb" are the temple (Rev. 21:22).

118 • NAMES OF GOD THE SON

Paul encouraged his readers to "do all in the name of the Lord Jesus" (Col. 3:17). The Christian performs all aspects of his or her ministry and witness in the name of Jesus, and it is in his name that the church assembles for prayer and worship (1 Cor. 5:4) and offers thanksgiving to the Father (Eph.

5:20). The New Testament uses several titles to describe the meaning of God's action through his Son. Many of these expressions (such as "Son of Man," "Servant," and "Anointed") are applied in the Old Testament to significant leaders of the covenant people—prophets, priests, kings. As applied in the New Testament to the Lord Jesus, they are titles for God the Son.

Jesus

Jesus' name, which in Hebrew is *Yeshuᵃ'*, is equivalent to Joshua, and means "Yahweh is salvation." A messenger of the Lord revealed this name to Joseph (Matt. 1:21) and to Mary (Luke 1:31) before the birth of Jesus. It conveys the purpose for which he has come into the world: "for he will save his people from their sins." The biblical concept of salvation is not an abstract idea but a concrete image of God's action in behalf of his people. It means deliverance: the rescue of people from danger and from their enemies, and their release from that which enslaves and binds. Jesus' ministry, culminating in his death on the cross and his resurrection and exaltation, was not only a deliverance from the condemnation of sin and disobedience to God; it was also a release of the people from the strictures of a religious tradition that had lost sight of its foundations in the covenant granted by the Lord. Jesus, the Deliverer, taught a new ethic of the kingdom of God that was not new at all but went to the heart of the Hebrew Scriptures, "the law and the prophets" (Matt. 5:17; 7:12).

The name Jesus, then, has special significance in its own right. But it takes on infinitely more meaning when equated with the many titles by which he is known in the worship and proclamation of his church. The church confesses that "Jesus is Lord" (1 Cor. 12:3), its authority and head in the covenant. The apostles preach that "God has made this Jesus, both Lord and Christ" (Acts 2:36). They write of Jesus who, though humanly speaking a descendent of David, "was declared with power to be the Son of God by his resurrection from the dead" (Rom. 1:4). The gospel writers tell his story to the end "that you may believe that Jesus is the Christ, the Son of God" (John 20:31).

Jesus of Nazareth

This phrase differs from "Jesus" in being the name by which Jesus was known to the general public; New Testament evidence does not indicate that it was used within the church. Jesus is addressed in this way by demons (Mark 1:24); a blind man is told by the crowd that Jesus of Nazareth was passing by (Mark 10:46-47), and the crowds at Jesus' entry into Jerusalem describe him as "Jesus, the prophet from Nazareth in Galilee" (Matt. 21:11). After the crucifixion, two of Jesus' disciples refer to him as Jesus of Nazareth in speaking to a stranger on the Emmaus road, not realizing that Jesus has been raised from death and is, indeed, their traveling companion (Luke 24:19). In the period immediately following the resurrection, the apostles heal in the name of Jesus of Nazareth (Acts 3:6) and so identify him in preaching to the crowds (Acts 10:38; cf. 26:9). At the discovery of the resurrection, the women were told, "You are looking for Jesus the Nazarene, who was crucified. He has risen! He is not here" (Mark 16:6). Perhaps the messenger's words anticipate Paul's statement that although we once regarded Christ from a human point of view, we do so no longer (2 Cor. 5:16).

Christ (*Christos*)

The word is the Greek equivalent of the Hebrew *mashiᵃḥ,* or Messiah, meaning "anointed" or literally "oiled." In ancient Israel, olive oil was a staple of the economy and therefore a symbol of prosperity and blessing. Important leaders were commissioned by having special sanctifying oil poured over them. The high priest was anointed (Num. 35:25; cf. Ps. 133:2), and Elijah the prophet was told to anoint Elisha as his successor (1 Kings 19:16). Most importantly, the kings were anointed. Saul was so commissioned by Samuel the prophet (1 Sam. 10:1; 16:13) and David spoke of him as "the Lord's anointed" (*mᵉshiᵃḥ Yahveh,* 1 Sam. 24:10; 2 Sam. 1:14). David himself, anointed by Samuel while Saul was still reigning (1 Sam. 16:13), became the paradigm for the *Mashiᵃḥ,* and the concept of the enduring Davidic dynasty, first enunciated by Nathan (2 Sam. 7:12-16), was celebrated by prophets and psalmists. In theory, every descendant of David installed in Zion was a "David" and hence a "messiah." As the ruler ascended the Judean throne, he might be proclaimed the adopted son of Yahweh through a decree (Ps. 2:7), the Lord's vice-regent in the governing of his earthly dominion. Several of the prophets looked forward to the restoration of the ideal commonwealth symbolized by David's rule (Isa. 9:1-7; Jer. 30:1-9; Amos 9:11).

Such exalted language applied to the Judean ruler

forms the background for the messianic hope of Judaism at the time of the birth of Jesus. Although it is common to speak of the Jewish expectation of an ideal Davidic ruler who would restore the glory of Israel, delivering it from its foreign oppressors and governing it with justice, in truth there was great divergence in the eschatological expectancy of first-century Judaism, which was split into many sectarian movements. The scribes of the Dead Sea community, for example, wrote of *two* messiahs, the priestly "Messiah of Aaron" and the lay "Messiah of Israel," due to these sectarians' bad experience with the Maccabean rulers, who had united the priestly and kingly offices. It has been said that Jesus' own unique contribution to the concept of messiahship, and that of his apostles, was to combine the office of Messiah with that of the "suffering Servant" prefigured in the prophecy of Isaiah. Recent research involving the Dead Sea Scrolls, however, suggests that this idea was present in sectarian Judaism of the time.

When the New Testament writers call Jesus the "Christ," they make the claim that he is the fulfillment of Israel's messianic expectations: the instrument of God for their restoration as his people and their ultimate deliverance. But the exact nature of this restoration and deliverance did not conform to any one program in the contemporaneous Jewish scene. The *fact* of Jesus' messiahship preceded its *interpretation;* the crucifixion and resurrection verified that Jesus was the Anointed of the Lord (Acts 2:22-36; 10:34-43; 17:31), but what this meant was left largely for the apostles to develop under the guidance of the Holy Spirit. The central fact was that Jesus is the Christ, the Deliverer of the faithful; because of this, the title was attached to his name and became one with it, as "Jesus Christ" or "Christ Jesus."

Head (*Kephalē*)

The word *head* conveys not only the ideas of authority and summation, but also the concept of *source,* as in the expression "fountainhead." As "head of the body, the church" (Col. 1:18), Jesus is the Lord of his people and also the source of their life and growth (Eph. 4:16). Not only the church, but "all things" are summed up in Christ (Eph. 1:10). The apostolic proclamation is that, as head of the church, Christ is also "head over all things" (Eph. 1:22, NASB), the "head over every power and authority" (Col. 2:10). In this figure, Paul gives the church a powerful image of universal scope of Christ's dominion.

Lord (*Kurios*)

The earliest Christian confession is, "Jesus is Lord" (1 Cor. 12:3). The title "Lord" (*Kurios*) was the term substituted for the divine name *Yahveh* in the Greek version of the Old Testament, used in many communities of the Jewish diaspora. It is the Greek equivalent of *'Adonai,* with all the implications of this term for the understanding of covenant loyalty to the great King. The heart of the apostolic proclamation is that, in the resurrection from the dead, God has made Jesus "both Lord and Christ" (Acts 2:36). The title *Kurios,* when applied to Jesus, in effect equates him with God; the confession of Jesus' lordship, therefore, was what set the earliest Christians apart from their traditional Jewish contemporaries, who could abide no human claim to equality with God (John 5:18). In this, of course, they were quite correct. But, as Paul insisted, Jesus also made no such claim, even as the preincarnate Christ (Phil. 2:6); the Father exalted him to lordship because of his obedience to the point of death on the cross (Phil. 2:8-9). As Lord, Jesus will receive the oath of covenant allegiance from people of all times and places (Phil. 2:9-11), "from every tribe and language and people and nation" (Rev. 5:9).

The Christian confession, "Jesus Christ is Lord," means that for the believer and for the corporate church, Jesus is the sole authority in life. The Scriptures are the written authority, but the church receives them from the hand of the Lord and interprets them with a focus on God's action in Christ by the quickening guidance of the Spirit of Christ. Although it is through faith that a person is brought into the family of God (Eph. 2:8-9), this faith is accompanied by confession of the lordship of the risen Jesus (Rom. 10:9-10). Nor is this a vocal confession only (though it must be that), but a confession made with the whole of one's being in a life of obedience, as the New Testament makes clear throughout.

Son (*Huios*)

In classical Christian theology, the Son is the second person of the Trinity. In the Semitic languages of the Bible, the word *son* (Hebrew *ben,* Aramaic *bar*) has a wider meaning than in English. It indicates not only biological or genealogical descent, but also things belonging in a certain class or representing something. A Hebrew speaker expresses his age by using the term; if he is 30 years old, he says "I am a son of 30," that is, "I belong to the class of those who are 30 years old." In this way we understand expressions such as "sons of thunder," Jesus' epithet for James and John (Mark 3:17), perhaps because of their combative attitude (Luke 9:51-56); "sons of iniquity," (Hos. 10:9, NASB) describing a rebellious Israel; and "Son of Encouragement," the literal sense of the name Barnabas (Acts 4:36). The meaning of Jesus' sonship, as ascribed to him both by himself and by the New Testament authors, is clarified in relation to the various qualifiers that attach to the term *Son.*

Son of God (*Huios tou Theou*), Son of David (*Huios tou Dauid*). These titles of Jesus are interrelated, and also relate to the concept of the "Anointed." It is the idea of the covenant that imparts to them theological importance. In ancient treaties, a more powerful king would establish a treaty or covenant with a lesser one, who agreed to its terms as the representative of his people. Great kings were sometimes called "fathers," while their vassals were known as "sons." The Davidic ruler, as the anointed king, was the representative of Israel or Judah in the covenant with Yahweh and is thus termed the "son" (Pss. 2:7, 12; 72:1; Isa. 9:6). As a symbol of this mediatorial role in the covenant, when kings ascended the throne they were presented with the "Testimony," or Book of the Law, a statement of the covenant between the Lord and Israel (2 Kings 11:12). Although all the people of Israel were called "sons of God" (Exod. 4:22-23; Deut. 1:31; 8:5; Jer. 3:19; 31:9, 20; Hos. 11:1; Mal. 1:6; Ps. 80:15), the king was viewed as the son *par excellence* in his role as their representative. This mediatorial position was an inheritance from Moses, who also functioned as "king" and the one who maintained Israel's covenant relationship with Yahweh.

David was the symbol of the ideal royal son, whose appearance would bring a restoration of the covenant and the salvation of the people of the Lord. In identifying Jesus as the Son of David (Matt. 1:1; 21:9, 15; 22:42; Mark 11:10; John 7:42; Rom. 1:3; and others), the New Testament writers assert that he is also the Son of God, the agent and mediator of divine deliverance. Indeed, God declares Jesus' sonship before his birth (Luke 1:32-33), at his baptism (Mark 1:11), and on the Mount of Transfiguration (Matt. 17:5; Mark 9:7). At his crucifixion it is an awestruck centurion who says, "Surely he was the Son of God!" (Matt. 27:54b). In the gospel proclamation of the apostolic church, it is by his resurrection from the dead that Jesus is "declared with power to be the Son of God" (Rom. 1:4).

Son of Man (*Huios tou anthrōpou*). The phrase "Son of Man" (which some scholars translate as "the human being," taking "son" in the sense of "representative") is familiar from the prophecy of Ezekiel, whom the Lord repeatedly addresses in this way in imparting his visions. Its use in Daniel (Dan. 7:13-14) is more cosmic in scope, describing one who is to rule with "an everlasting dominion" granted by the Ancient of Days. It is at this more exalted level that the New Testament employs it as a title for Jesus Christ. As the Son of Man, Jesus is the representative of mankind, able to enter and maintain the covenant on behalf of all humanity. The title is not a reference to Jesus' ordinary human nature but to the extraordinary nature of his authority. Jesus healed the paralytic by forgiving his sins so the disciples would understand that he had that authority (Matt. 9:6; Luke 5:24). He declared that as Son of Man he was Lord of the Sabbath (Matt. 12:8; Luke 6:5), the keeping of which was a sign of the covenant (Exod. 31:13). In his prophecy of the destruction to come, Jesus borrows Daniel's imagery to speak of the coming of the Son of Man to judge the unfaithful and gather his elect from all over the earth (Mark 13:26-27).

The Son. John employs the expression "Son of God" somewhat differently from the other gospel writers, often using the unqualified title "the Son." In his interpretation, Jesus is the Son of God because he is one with the Father and therefore equal to him (John 5:18). In this sense, Jesus is not only the servant king who enters into covenant with the Lord as representative of the nation, maintaining its requirements in the nation's behalf. He is also one with the great King, and as such is the granter of the covenant who lays down its terms. In divine paradox, Jesus the Son becomes both sides of the relationship between God and the people of God; he *is* the covenant.

Savior (*Sōtēr*)

Luke records that Mary, the mother of Jesus, calls God her Savior (Luke 1:47). But at his birth, Jesus also assumes the title, as confirmed by the name given him by the angel (Luke 1:31; 2:11, 21). After the Resurrection, the apostles herald Jesus' exaltation as Savior (Acts 5:31; 13:23). The New Testament church looks forward to the appearance of its Savior, the Lord Jesus Christ (Phil. 3:20; Titus 2:13), but at the same time recognizes that he has already appeared (2 Tim. 1:10), delivering his people from bondage to the evil one through the mighty victory effected by his death and resurrection (Col. 2:15).

Servant (*'Eved, Pais*)

The word, as applied to Jesus, is not the usual word translated "servant" (*doulos*), which is often applied to Christian workers and means "slave" or "bond servant." Rather, it is the word *pais*, usually translated "child." In covenant terminology "servant" is another title given to a ruler who enters into covenant with the great King. It is a title not of servility but of authority, for the servant is his ruler's representative. Thus the Old Testament calls leaders such as Moses (Num. 12:7-8; 1 Chron. 6:49; Neh. 10:29), David (Ps. 89:20; Ezek. 34:23-24), and Zerubbabel (Hag. 2:23) the servant (*'eved*) of God. In the "servant songs" of Isaiah, the Lord's servant is sometimes an individual (Isa. 42:1-4; 50:4-9; 52:13–53:12; 61:1-2), sometimes Jacob or Israel (Isa. 44:1-2, 21), sometimes both (Isa. 49:1-6). The New Testament portrays Jesus as the suffering servant described by Isaiah (Matt. 12:18); Jesus himself inferred this identification in the synagogue of Nazareth at the beginning of his ministry (Luke 4:21). Jesus' designation as Yahweh's servant reinforces his role as covenant mediator on behalf of his people; he is the Servant-King. Peter, in his second sermon recorded in Acts (3:26), applies the title Servant (*Pais*) to Christ, as the one sent by God to turn the descendants of Abraham back to him, and the apostles in a prayer for God's protection refer to Jesus as God's "holy Servant" (*hagios Pais*, Acts 4:27, 30).

The Word (*Logos*)

Christ is directly called the Word only in the writings of John (John 1:1, 14; "the Word of Life," 1 John 1:1; "the Word of God," Rev. 19:13). In Hebrew culture, one's word is the extension of his person; it is the mechanism through which the "soul" or life force impacts others, so that in effect there is no distinction between one's word and one's being (Johannes Pedersen, *Israel: Its Life and Culture*, 2nd ed. [London: Oxford University Press, 1959], vol.

1–2, 166–168). Biblical theology builds on this idea; the word of the Lord extends the force of his being into all contexts. It is by his word that the Lord moves affairs of history, particularly the sacred history of his deeds of deliverance (cf. Ps. 107:20). In the saga of the Israelite kingdoms recounted in the books of Samuel and Kings, events occur according to the word of Yahweh through his prophets. In fact, the creation itself comes into being by the spoken word of God (Gen. 1:3; Ps. 33:6). Thus, in several passages of hymnlike or doxological character, the New Testament celebrates Christ as the Word through whom all things have been made and are sustained (John 1:3; Heb. 1:1-3; *cf.* also Col. 1:15-18, where the idea is present without use of the term *logos*).

But the concept of the word also has covenantal associations; in the Sinai covenant, Yahweh spoke "these words" of the Decalogue or Ten Commandments (Exod. 20:1). In the ancient treaty, the "word" was the text of the covenant, standing as a sanction against its violators. As the "Word of God," Christ appears at the head of the armies of heaven, executing the judgments of the Almighty against the rebellious (Rev. 19:14-15).

These two functions of Jesus as the Word—creation and covenant—are really one. Jesus, the incarnate Word, brings people into the family of God (John 1:12); through the "washing with water through the word" (Eph. 5:26) he prepares a church to be presented to God. By the word of Christ (Rom. 10:17), men and women enter into the new covenant, which is the "new creation" (2 Cor. 5:17).

Immanuel

After telling of Joseph's dream, in which an angel announces the coming birth of Jesus, Matthew's gospel indicates that his appearance was to be a fulfillment of the prophecy of Isaiah: "A virgin will be with child and will give birth to a son, and will call him Immanuel" (Isa. 7:14). The Hebrew phrase *'immanu-'El* means "with us is God." Isaiah used the imminent birth of a child as a sign for King Ahaz that the attacking enemies of Judah would soon cease to be a threat (Isa. 7:15-16); the expression occurs again in Isaiah 8:8. It is rooted in the very character of Yahweh, who had revealed his name to Moses (Exod. 3:13-15) as one known historically through his covenant with his people. As King, Yahweh often reassures Israel that he will be with them to protect and provide (for example, Josh. 1:9). Solomon's benediction at the dedication of the temple expresses the concept well: "May the LORD our God be with us ['*immanu*] as he was with our fathers; may he never leave us nor forsake us" (1 Kings 8:57).

Despite Matthew's citation of the Isaiah passage, Jesus is never actually called *Immanuel* in the New Testament. The name, however, is a powerful expression of the doctrine of the incarnation, consistent with such New Testament declarations as John's, that the Word, who is one with God (John 1:1), "became flesh and made his dwelling among us" (John 1:14), or Paul's statement that "God was reconciling the world to himself in Christ" (2 Cor. 5:19). Further, *Immanuel* aptly sums up the Christian's awareness of the presence of Christ with his church. Declaring his authority over all things, the risen Christ pledges his faithfulness to the covenant: "I am with you always, to the very end of the age" (Matt. 28:20). Jesus remains continuously with the church through the Spirit, "the Lord God Almighty and the Lamb" dwelling amid his people (Rev. 21:3; 22–23).

High Priest

The writer to the Hebrews consistently uses this title in reference to Jesus, calling him "the apostle and high priest whom we confess" (Heb. 3:1). The title "high priest" was a messianic one, having been applied to the Davidic ruler in Psalm 110:4, using Melchizedek, the priest-king of Salem, as the pattern (Gen. 14:18). The author uses this title as part of his demonstration of the superiority of the new covenant to the old. The Aaronic high priest of the old covenant, who was from the tribe of Levi, was subject to death. But Jesus is "a high priest forever, in the order of Melchizedek" (Heb. 6:20), whose priesthood came before the Mosaic priesthood, and who had received tithes from Abraham, the ancestor of the Israelite nation. The point is that Jesus came from the tribe of Judah, not Levi, and a change in priesthood means a change in the law (Heb. 7:12). Therefore a new covenant supersedes the old (Heb. 8:7, 13); God "sets aside the first to establish the second" (Heb. 10:9).

As the "great high priest" (Heb. 4:14), Jesus is the "mediator of a new covenant" through his own blood (Heb. 9:13-15), having offered the sacrifice of the heavenly sanctuary of which the earthly was only a copy (Heb. 9:23-24). Being the "great priest

over the house of God" (Heb. 10:21), Jesus lives forever to make intercession for those who approach God through him (Heb. 7:25). Believers have come, not to Sinai but to Zion, the place of celebration, to a "heavenly Jerusalem," which is not an ethereal and future reality but the worshiping church, "the general assembly [*panēguris,* 'festal gathering'] and church [*ekklēsia*] of the first-born" (Heb. 12:22-23, NASB). The theme of the high priesthood of Christ is therefore an incentive for the church to reflect in its worship the high celebration of the new covenant.

Rabbi; Teacher (*Didaskalos*)

In the Gospels, people sometimes address Jesus by the title "Rabbi," which means "great one," in the sense of master or teacher. These are usually people who are not yet believers (Nicodemus, John 6:25; a blind man, Mark 10:51; the crowds, John 6:25). However, Nathanael the disciple confesses his faith with the words, "Rabbi, you are the Son of God; you are the King of Israel" (John 1:49). At the empty tomb, Mary cries, "Rabboni!" when she recognizes the risen Christ (John 20:16), using a more honorific form of the title. Jesus applies the title "Teacher" (*Didaskalos*) to himself, telling his disciples, "One is your Teacher, and you are all brothers" (Matt. 23:8, NASB).

King (*Basileus*), King of Kings (*Basileus Basileōn*)

Although the kingship of Jesus is implicit in his role as Lord and Christ, the title "King" is not often ascribed to him in Scripture. Jesus is acclaimed King by his disciples at his entry into Jerusalem, according to Luke's account (Luke 19:38), and after Jesus' arrest Pilate scornfully calls him King (John 18:37; 19:15, 19). The phrase "King of kings," meaning "supreme king," is more common in the church's worship, as a title of the risen Christ. It is similar to the expression "Lord of lords," with which it is paired in all occurrences in Scripture. The title does not appear in the Old Testament but is attributed to Jesus Christ alone as the manifest Sovereign (1 Tim. 6:15, in the form *Basileus tōn basileuontōn*), as the Lamb (Rev. 17:14), and as the rider on the white horse (Rev. 19:16). As King, Jesus reigns as coregent with the Father; in the Resurrection, God exalted Jesus to his right hand (Acts 2:32-36); the kingdoms of the world have become the kingdom "of our Lord and of his Christ, and he will reign for ever and ever" (Rev. 11:15).

Prince of Peace (*Sar Shalom*)

The church worships Jesus as the Prince of Peace, although the title does not occur in the New Testament. The expression is one of the titles ascribed to the Davidic king in the familiar oracle of Isaiah (Isa. 9:2-7), which may have been composed for the coronation of an actual Judean ruler but later took on a messianic significance. Peace in the Bible is more than the absence of strife; it is *shalom,* a positive state of wholeness, prosperity, and blessing, which is the benefit of the covenant. The Prince of Peace is the one whose dominion brings this quality of life. In the New Testament, the peace of the covenant is extended beyond Israel to all people; in Christ, both Jew and Gentile have been united. Thus, Paul states, "He himself is our peace" (Eph. 2:14), having broken the dividing wall between cultural groups.

Ruler (*Arkhōn*)

As a synonym for "King," John the Revelator calls Jesus "the ruler of the kings of the earth" (Rev. 1:5).

Author, Originator (*Archēgos*)

This word has the meaning "ruler" but in the sense of one who begins or originates something. The apostolic preachers refer to Jesus as "the author of life" (Acts 3:15), for new life and forgiveness have been released in his resurrection (Acts 5:31).

119 • NAMES OF GOD THE HOLY SPIRIT

The Holy Spirit operates in association with the human spirit, motivating the worship of the Father and the Son. Jesus said of the Spirit, "He will bring glory to me" (John 16:14).

Spirit (*Ruᵃḥ, Pneuma*)

The most common designations for the Spirit in Scripture—Spirit (*Ruᵃḥ, Pneuma*); Spirit of God (*Ruᵃḥ 'Elohim*); Holy Spirit (*Pneuma Hagion*); Spirit of Truth (*Pneuma tēs Alētheias*)—describe the Spirit viewed in differing aspects, though it is really impossible to separate them. The Spirit of God, far greater in impact than any other, is often simply called "the Spirit." Because God is holy, set apart from the ordinary, the Spirit is the Holy Spirit and is thus distinguished from other spiritual forces. For the same purpose, John uses the expression "Spirit of truth," meaning the genuine or authentic Spirit. In the biblical languages, the same word (Hebrew *ruᵃḥ,* Greek *pneuma*) means "wind, breath, spirit";

often the correct English rendering is a matter of the translator's judgment. Sometimes the word may be used with deliberate ambiguity, as in Jesus' statement to Nicodemus that "the wind [or Spirit] blows wherever it pleases" (John 3:8).

In biblical psychology, the breath or "spirit" is the life force of a person, directed in a particular course of action. Thus a person's behavior may reveal a "spirit of infirmity," a "spirit of fear," a "spirit of meekness," a "spirit of wisdom," or the like. The life force of God, too, manifests itself in the breath or Spirit of God. In using this idiom, the Bible pictures God as dynamic, not static; there is a movement, a vitality within his being as he directs his energy toward the accomplishment of his objectives. Usually, these are purposes within the human scene. Although Scripture speaks of the Spirit of God moving over the surface of the primeval waters at the Creation (Gen. 1:2), most often it portrays the activity of the Spirit as it "comes upon" or "fills" some human instrument of his purpose.

Thus, to be filled or moved by the Spirit of God is to be equipped and directed in a certain way: to speak the Word of God (Acts 4:31), to proclaim the Lord's deliverance (Isa. 61:1), to be witnesses to the risen Christ (Acts 1:8), to extol the Lord in tongues (Acts 2:4), to give thanks in worship and song (Eph. 5:18-20). The Spirit imparts gifts for various functions of ministry and service (1 Cor. 12–14). The Scriptures themselves came into being as "men spoke from God as they were carried along by the Holy Spirit" (2 Pet. 1:21). As examples of the association of the Spirit with prophetic vision, we may cite Ezekiel (Ezek. 2:2; 3:12) and John the Revelator, who was "in the Spirit" when confronted by the glorified Christ (Rev. 1:10) and when given the vision of the throne of God and all that followed (Rev. 4:2). The Spirit of the Lord rests on his Anointed, the Davidic ruler (Isa. 11:2), to bring justice to the land.

The Spirit is a link between the divine and human personalities, for a human being, as a living creature, also has God-given spirit or breath (Gen. 2:7; Eccles. 12:7). By the Spirit or breath of God his people are given new life as the covenant community (Ezek. 37:1-14; 2 Cor. 3:5-6) and brought to life in the new birth (John 3:3-6; Rom. 8:10-11). The Spirit of God is intimately bound up with the spirit of the new covenant worshipers, who cry out, *"Abba,* Father!" as "the Spirit himself testifies with our spirit that we are God's children" (Rom. 8:16). By the Spirit the worshiper confesses that Jesus is Lord (1 Cor. 12:3). It is the Spirit who baptizes people of all backgrounds into one body (1 Cor. 12:13); the worshiping church's invitation to enter the covenant is also the invitation of the Spirit: "The Spirit and the bride say, 'Come!'" (Rev. 22:17). When the worshiper does not know how to pray in a situation, "the Spirit himself intercedes for us with groans that words cannot express" (Rom. 8:26). In the Bible it is sometimes difficult to separate the Holy Spirit from the spirit of people chosen for his purposes. The Lord may accomplish his ends by stirring up the spirit of such a person (the kings of the Medes, Jer. 51:11; Zerubbabel the governor and Joshua the high priest, Hag. 1:14; Paul, Acts 17:16).

Jesus proclaimed that the genuine worship of the Father would be worship "in spirit and in truth." As worship in truth, it is worship according to the principles of Scripture, the word of truth (John 17:17). As worship in spirit, it is worship motivated and directed by the Spirit of God, filled with the energy and vitality of his breath or life force. Thus, Jesus danced, or "rejoiced greatly in the Holy Spirit" (Luke 10:21, NASB), and Paul reminds us that the kingdom of God is "righteousness, peace and joy in the Holy Spirit" (Rom. 14:17).

—————— Helper (*Paraklētos*) ——————

Jesus used this title as another name for the Spirit of truth (John 16:7-15). It has the meaning of "one who is called alongside," in the sense of a counselor, comforter, or helper. As the Helper, the Spirit accompanies those who proclaim that Jesus is the Christ to bring conviction and a declaration of judgment upon those who refuse to believe in Jesus (John 16:8-10). The Helper or Counselor also discloses the truth of the Father and the Son to the followers of Jesus, including the course of things to come (John 16:13-14), and so brings glory to Christ.

120 • THE TRINITY

As a doctrine and a liturgical formula, the Trinity is not developed in the Bible, nor are the distinctions between the three "persons" always clearly articulated. Nevertheless, the concept of God as Father, Son, and Spirit is present.

The stress in Scripture is always on the unity of God. The Father and the Son are one (John 10:30; 17:21); they glorify one another (John 17:1). The Father and the Spirit are one, for the Spirit "searches all things, even the deep things of God," and knows his inward being (1 Cor. 2:10). The Son and the Spirit are one, since the Father sends the Spirit in the Son's "name" (John 14:26). The Word and the Spirit are one. When the psalmist declares, "By the word of the LORD were the heavens made, their starry host by the breath of his mouth" (Ps. 33:6), the principle of poetic parallelism suggests that the word of God and the Spirit (*ruᵃḥ*, "breath") of God are the same. Similarly in the New Testament, a comparison of the parallel passages, Ephesians 5:18-20 and Colossians 16, reveals the identity of the Spirit and the Word, and Paul says specifically that "the Lord is the Spirit" (2 Cor. 3:17). The apostolic church remained committed to the uncompromising monotheism of the Jewish faith, expressed in the *Shᵉma'* of synagogue worship: "Hear, O Israel: The LORD our God, the LORD is one" (Deut. 6:4), although the phrase is more accurately translated "Yahweh is our God, Yahweh alone." When the Trinitarian formulation, or an approximation thereof, appears in the New Testament, there is usually a strong suggestion that the different terms used express the same living reality.

The Trinitarian formula, so familiar in Christian worship, is found in Scripture only in Matthew 28:19, where the risen Christ commissions the apostles to make disciples of all people, baptizing them "in the name of the Father and of the Son and of the Holy Spirit." The use of the word *name* in the singular suggests that the unity of the three "persons," rather than their distinction, is in view, and in actual practice the early church usually baptized into Jesus Christ, or into his name (Acts 2:38; 8:12; 19:5; Rom. 6:3; 1 Cor. 1:13).

The Trinitarian formula is also implicit in certain expressions of the apostle Paul, although other words may be substituted for the classic terms *Father* and *Son*. Writing to the Corinthians, he mentions varieties of gifts (*charismata*) but the same Spirit, varieties of ministries or service (*diakoniai*) but the same Lord, and varieties of effects or workings (*energēmata*) but the same God (1 Cor. 12:4-6). Again, his wording suggests a stress on the oneness of the source of the church's power. In Ephesians 4:4-6 Paul proclaims "one body and one Spirit," the life or breath of the body; "one Lord, one faith, one baptism" into Jesus the Son; and "one God and Father of all." The Trinitarian pattern is repeated within the clause applying to the Father, who is "over all and through all and in all." Thinking in

Trinitarian terms, God is *over* all as Creator King, *through* all in the pervasive life-giving presence of the Spirit, and *in* all as Christ in the corporate church ("the hope of glory," Col. 1:27). Paul's familiar benediction of 2 Corinthians 13:14, often used in Christian worship, commends his readers to "the grace of the Lord Jesus Christ, and the love of God, and the fellowship [*koinōnia,* participation or communion] of the Holy Spirit."

In these expressions we see not the attempt to formulate a doctrine of God in three persons (the need for that was perceived later in the church's history) but the effort to convey, within the limitations of human language, something of the fullness of the workings of the divine in relation to his worshipers. In the Spirit he offers his people life, gifts, communion; in the Son he quickens in them service, obedience, and faith; in the Father he governs and provides for them in his authority, creative working, and steadfast love. In every way he moves toward them to dwell in their midst, the covenant Lord with his covenant people, that in the end "God may be all in all" (1 Cor. 15:28).

Janice and Richard Leonard

⚜ FOUR ⚜

Symbolism in Biblical Worship

Symbols are tokens or signs (Hebrew ʾot, Greek sēmeion) that point beyond themselves to another, often abstract, reality that is difficult or impossible to represent any other way. A symbol can be a person, object, place, or act—anything that conveys meaning about the concept it represents. The ability of human beings to communicate symbolically is one characteristic that sets humankind apart from all other creatures.

121 • INTRODUCTION TO SYMBOLISM IN WORSHIP

All worship is symbolic, even those intuitive encounters with the holy that seem to bypass the rational process, directly impacting the worshiper's consciousness. Symbolism must enter in once the worshiper begins to think about such an experience or to share it with others, for language and thought are symbolic processes.

—— Symbolic Character of Worship ——

Even in those churches that have opposed the use of traditional symbolism, especially visual symbols, worship remains highly symbolic. Such churches are oriented toward linguistic symbolism, with a heavy emphasis on the spoken word and a minimum of liturgical action. Moreover, the visual plainness of the auditoriums in such churches is itself a symbolic statement about the spiritual character of Christian faith. Regrettably, like all symbolism, these things can be misunderstood. The starkness of the meeting room can convey the impression that there is no compelling depth or mystery in the worship of God. The concentration on the spoken word creates a focus on the speaker and those who share the platform with him or her, resulting in a human-centered, rather than God-centered, worship experience. The lack of "liturgical" response, in whatever form, can reduce the involvement of the worshiper to that of a spectator. When these things happen, we are far removed from the biblical understanding of worship.

All language, including that of worship, is symbolic, for words are not the things they represent but communicable representations of them. Failure to understand this can create problems for the interpretation of Scripture. Many biblical expressions are *literally symbolic;* that is, they are word pictures rather than descriptions of something directly visualized. This applies to biblical accounts of the experience of worship, such as those of Isaiah (Isa. 6) or of the dedication of the temple. When we are told that "the glory of the LORD filled the house of the Lord" as the ark of the covenant was brought into the temple, so that "the priests could not stand to minister" (1 Kings 8:11, NASB), we should not take this for some sort of visual representation of the Lord's presence that we might wish to emulate in our worship today. The "glory" (*kavod*) of the Lord, although often associated with the imagery of radiance and light, is his "mass" or "weight"; it is a word picture for the overwhelming, "heavy" sense of the presence of God on this significant occasion, a presence that can be as powerful today in the worship of the new covenant community.

Symbols communicate because of the truths associated with them; what may be highly expressive for one community of worshipers may have another meaning, or none at all, for another community, where the associations are different or lacking altogether. A symbol does not serve its purpose unless its users share the same conventional framework of understanding. This is why an appreciation for covenant structure is so important for the interpretation of Scripture; the covenant provides the frame of reference that gives meaning to many of its symbols. For example, when Christians worship the Lord as King, this is not simply the ascription of dominion to him, but a pledge of loyalty in a covenant relationship, which has implications for the worshiper's behavior and for his or her faithfulness to other worshipers.

Biblical symbolism always directs to an action of God, especially God's action in establishing and maintaining the covenant. Humankind itself, in God's image, is a symbol of God's management of creation. Ancient kings often erected images of themselves at the borders of their territory to indicate that travelers were entering their dominion. God placed human beings on earth as images that declare to the principalities and powers his authority in the universe. Human beings, however, are not mere signposts of God's dominion; as living beings who have been given the "breath of life"—God's own breath—(Gen. 2:7) they participate in the reality to which they point. Thus the greatest and truest symbols have a universal validity because of the fulness with which they embody spiritual reality. "Let us make man in our image, in our likeness, and let them rule . . . over all the earth" (Gen. 1:26). This is especially true of the corporate gathering of people to worship the Lord; the very existence of such groups in the world is a powerful, symbolic statement of God's dominion and purpose.

Sometimes individuals in the Bible receive a new name as a symbolic statement about the Lord's intended action. Appearing to Abram in a renewal of his covenant promise to make him the father of many nations, God changed his name to Abraham (Gen. 17:5). Jacob was given the name Israel, "God rules," as a reminder of his struggle with the Lord at the brook Jabbok (Gen. 32:28). Both Isaiah and Hosea gave names to their children that were to be symbols or signs to Israel of the Lord's impending judgment on the nation (Isa. 8:3; Hos. 1:4-9). When Simon confessed his faith in Jesus as the Christ, Jesus gave him the name Peter (Cephas in the Aramaic version), saying, "On this rock I will build my church" (Matt. 16:18). In a sense, the renamed person became a walking symbol.

Symbol and Reality

Functionally, the symbol stands in the place of the symbolized reality as the worshiper responds to it. For this reason, it is easy to mistake the symbol for the reality. However, symbols that call attention to themselves defeat their own purpose. The most effective symbol is the least ambiguous, that is, the least likely to be confused with that to which it

points while still able to represent it. Thus, light might be a more effective symbol of the presence of the Lord than a physical object such as a temple. The temple may convey majesty and dignity, but one might confuse it with a confining, localized residence of God; light, on the other hand, while representing the energy and creative power of God, is not so easily localized. But all symbols have their drawbacks; light has no revelatory content, being only a medium, so it is only the association of light with the Lord in biblical worship and doctrine that fills it with symbolic content for the Christian.

Because Israel tended to focus on the symbol instead of the reality to which it pointed, many visual symbols used in the worship of the Lord were eventually lost. The bronze serpent, a reminder of God's intervention in behalf of his people in the wilderness, had to be destroyed (2 Kings 18:4). The ark of the covenant eventually disappeared, and the Solomonic temple itself, which the people came to regard as a talisman of God's protection (Jer. 7:4), was demolished. Symbolic expressions were often lost upon the Israelites. When Yahweh commanded that his words be written on their foreheads and right hands (Exod. 13:16; Deut. 6:8), they interpreted the directive literally and made phylacteries containing strips of parchment on which the passages containing this command were written to wear on their bodies. The prophets Isaiah (Isa. 44:12-19; 45:20) and Habakkuk (Hab. 2:18-19) ridicule the heathen practice of bowing down to inanimate objects of gold, silver, and wood fashioned by the worshiper himself. (An astute pagan might have responded that the idols were symbols of a mythological and demonic reality.) Paul understands this in his warning to the Corinthians about participating in pagan feasts and eating meat sacrificed to idols (1 Cor. 10:19-21).

When Aaron introduced his casting of a golden calf as the God who brought Israel up from Egypt (Exod. 32:4), he was not referring to the calf but to the invisible deity thought to be enthroned on the animal. The pagan god Ba'al was portrayed as riding a bull, and Aaron simply adapted this imagery to the worship of Yahweh. In the same manner, when Jeroboam cast two bulls and placed them in Bethel and Dan for Israel to worship (1 Kings 12:26-29), he intended to make thrones for Yahweh. The problem was that he used a ba'alistic image, which had a different frame of reference, and led the people into idolatrous worship. Yahweh's distinctive symbol was the ark of the covenant housed in the tabernacle and later the temple; as a rectangular box, it was less likely to be confused with the deity.

Dynamism of Biblical Symbolism

Symbolism can take the form of human action. Bowing before the Lord is a dynamic representation of the covenantal relationship between Yahweh and his people in which he is the great King and they are his vassals. Celebration of the feasts included such symbolic acts as building tabernacles from tree branches, waving sheaves before the Lord, and sending the scapegoat into the wilderness. The prophets also engaged in symbolic acts. Jeremiah, Ezekiel, and Hosea all had ministries characterized by pictorial representations of the content of their prophecies.

It is important to understand that Israel's symbolism was dynamic; it involved actions and words rather than static objects and required the context of human interaction. Words exist only when they are spoken, and actions when they are performed. Even the words of the book of the covenant were to be read aloud to the people. When he instituted the Lord's Supper, or Eucharist, Jesus said, "Do this," not, "Look at this" (1 Cor. 11:24-25). The eucharistic symbols point beyond themselves to the reality of God's action in Christ to redeem his people (1 Cor. 10:16-17; 11:26).

The cross is not only a visual symbol but has become a verbal symbol as well. Early Christians did not make physical representations of it, mounting it on buildings or wearing it around their necks, but proclaimed it. As a symbol, the cross represents the entire drama of the crucifixion, resurrection, ascension, and glorification of Christ. A visual symbol can become a verbal symbol. In the Old Testament blood was a visual symbol of sanctification as the priests sprinkled it on the furniture of the tabernacle and even on the people. However, in the New Testament the blood of Christ becomes a verbal symbol as it is used in the apostles' preaching and teaching to refer to the atoning sacrifice of the Cross.

122 • SYMBOLIC ACTS AND GESTURES

Biblical men and women experienced the Lord as a dynamic God known through his interaction with them in the course of history. It is fitting, therefore, that much of the symbolism of biblical worship consists of physical actions that direct people beyond themselves to spiritual realities.

Lifting of Hands

A common symbolic gesture is the lifting of hands. Still widely used in modern worship, it was a universal ancient symbol of covenant loyalty. A bas-relief contemporaneous with the reign of Hezekiah shows the Babylonian ruler Merodach-Baladan (2 Kings 20:12) making a grant to an official; each holds a staff in the left hand and has the right hand raised in oath (James B. Pritchard, *The Ancient Near East* [Princeton: Princeton University Press, 1958], plate 125). Covenants were sometimes signified by the scarring of the wrist; when the hand of the vassal was lifted to his monarch, the scar was a visible reminder of the great king's responsibility to defend and protect his servant. These traditions no doubt underlie the common practice of lifting hands in worship. The people of Israel made supplication with hands extended toward the sanctuary, the earthly dwelling of the great King (Pss. 28:2; 134:2); toward the ark of the covenant, which symbolized his throne (Lam. 2:19); or toward heaven (Lam. 3:41). As Solomon's prayer at the dedication of the temple indicates (1 Kings 8:28-30), by the lifting of hands prayer was directed toward the sanctuary, as part of the tribute offered to the great King (Meredith G. Kline, *The Structure of Biblical Authority* [Grand Rapids: Wm. B. Eerdmans Publishing Co.,

Lifting Hands in Covenant Oath

1972], p. 62). Moses stood with hands upraised while Joshua led Israel in war with the Amalekites. As long as his hands were up, Israel prevailed in the battle (Exod. 17:10-13).

David likens the lifting of his hands to the evening sacrifice (Ps. 141:2), a daily offering to Yahweh, which was specified in the covenant regulations. There was a meat offering at that time, but David's reference is to the offering of incense (Exod. 30:8). Incense, in turn, symbolizes the prayers of God's people (Rev. 8:3-4). In many churches this practice is preserved as worshipers in the new covenant lift their hands in praise, affirmation, or supplication toward the Lord. Paul expresses the desire that all believers should lift up holy hands (1 Tim. 2:8), that is, hands belonging to people set apart for the Lord through the covenant relationship.

Bowing, Kneeling, Falling Prostrate

Related to the lifting of hands are the gestures of bowing, kneeling, and falling prostrate, all of which were acts of obeisance and humility common throughout the ancient world. Usually these acts were carried out in the presence of a monarch or other powerful figure; thus they demonstrate respect and even a measure of fear. Moses fell down before the Lord in dread of his wrath because of Israel's rebellion (Deut. 9:18-19). A bas-relief from Nineveh depicts the siege of the Judean city of Lachish by the Assyrians; inhabitants of the city are shown kneeling before Sennacherib, the Assyrian ruler (Pritchard, plate 101). And the Black Obelisk of Shalmaneser III pictures Jehu, the king of Israel, kneeling with his face to the floor as he presents tribute to the monarch (Pritchard, plate 100A). Israel bowed before Yahweh because, as their God, he was their Lord or King (Ps. 95:6; Isa. 45:23). When the Magi bowed before the infant Jesus, they showed that they recognized his identity as King of Israel, despite the humble circumstances in which they found him.

Kneeling was a common posture assumed during prayer by saints of both the old and new covenants. At the consecration of the temple, Solomon knelt with his hands lifted to invoke the blessing of the Lord on the new sanctuary (2 Chron. 6:13). Daniel knelt to pray and give thanks three times every day (Dan. 6:10). Peter knelt to pray over the body of Dorcas (Acts 9:40). Paul and the elders from Ephesus knelt together to pray as Paul took his leave (Acts 20:36). And Jesus prayed on his knees in the Garden of Gethsemane (Luke 22:41).

Clapping the Hands

Israel worshiped the Lord also with the clapping of hands (Ps. 47:1); even the rivers (Ps. 98:8) and the trees of the open country (Isa. 55:12) are urged to clap their hands. Clapping was symbolic of a king's victory over his enemies; the people clapped their hands at the coronation of King Joash (2 Kings 11:12), which ended the heathen rule of the queen mother Athaliah. Hand clapping in Christian worship is more than the rhythmic beating of time; it is a declaration of the victory and dominion of the Lord.

Symbolic Drama

The prophets often engaged in symbolic acts. Jeremiah visited the house of a potter (Jer. 18:1-6), and broke a jar before the elders of the people (Jer. 19:1-11) to demonstrate that God planned to break Judah and Jerusalem. Later he bought a field at Anathoth, as a token of God's promise to restore Judah to the land (Jer. 32:6-44). Ezekiel drew a picture of Jerusalem on a brick and besieged it (Ezek. 4:1-3), among other actions, as a message to the nation of impending disaster. To picture the coming exile, he was told to dig a hole in the city wall and carry his belongings out through it (Ezek. 12:1-7). Hosea married a harlot (Hos. 1:2) as a symbol of Yahweh's relationship with idolatrous and unfaithful Israel. The dramatic actions of the prophets were not acts of worship, but some of them may have been performed during festival times, when large crowds would be gathered at the sanctuary. They were object lessons to illustrate the consequence of breaking the covenant.

The New Testament prophet Agabus engaged in symbolic action to picture the events that awaited the apostle Paul in Jerusalem (Acts 21:10-11). The Gospels record symbolic dramas performed by Jesus. The most colorful of these was his triumphal entry into Jerusalem to the acclamations of his disciples. Matthew (Matt. 21:5) explains the symbolism as the fulfillment of Isaiah's prophecy of the redemption of Jerusalem (Isa. 62:11-12) and Zechariah's announcement of the coming of the King to Zion (Zech. 9:9). According to Luke, this was not only a festive occasion, but one that dramatized the impending destruction of the city. Jesus wept over Jerusalem because of the people's blindness to the true deliverance of the Lord and went on to predict that the city would be leveled "because you did not recognize the time of God's coming to you" (Luke 19:41-44).

In the synoptic Gospels, another symbolic drama follows immediately. With a whip, Jesus drives the money changers from the temple (Mark 11:15-17), reminding them of the words of Isaiah and Jeremiah, "My house will be called a house of prayer for all nations" (Isa. 56:7), "Has this house . . . become a den of robbers to you?" (Jer. 7:11). Jesus' action dramatizes the change from the old covenant to the new, wherein God's "house" or kingdom will include not only believing Jews but all nations of the world.

Jesus' parables of the kingdom of God are word pictures that often take a dramatic turn. Through stories about such things as a vineyard rented out to wicked tenants (Matt. 21:33-46; Mark 12:1-11), a wedding feast to which the guests refuse to come (Matt. 22:1-14; Luke 14:16-24), and ten virgins waiting for a bridegroom (Matt. 25:1-13), Jesus illustrates the judgment that is soon to befall Jerusalem and the religious system it represents.

Symbolic Rituals

It can be said that the Israelite sanctuary with all its furnishings and the whole sacrificial system that accompanied it were one eloquent symbol. All the colors, the various metals, tables and lampstands, linen robes, fragrant incense, the ark with its cherubim, and the complicated rituals taken together pictured the salvation God would eventually enact, not to Israel alone, but to all the world in the person of his Son. Here we will consider a few of the more prominent symbolic actions in the worship of Israel and Judah.

Firstborn and Firstfruits. Because Israel was in covenant with Yahweh and recognized him as King, the people were required to bring him tribute. While all the sacrifices specified in the Law represented this tribute, the offering of first things carried a special symbolism of Yahweh's sovereignty over the nation. Thus Israel presented the firstborn to the Lord, sacrificed or redeemed the first of all animals to open the womb, and brought the offering of firstfruits at the harvest. In presenting these things, Israel acknowledged that all its possessions and indeed all its people belonged to the Lord of the covenant; these offerings were a token of the whole. Jesus, as the

firstborn, was presented to the Lord in the same manner (Luke 2:22-24).

The Day of Atonement. Once each year, on the Day of Atonement, which immediately preceded the Feast of Tabernacles, the high priest would enter the Most Holy Place of the sanctuary where the ark of the covenant was placed. He brought with him blood from the altar of sacrifice, where animals were being offered in behalf of Israel's sins, and sprinkled it on the *kapporet,* or cover of the ark, to represent God's cleansing of the people and his continued commitment to the covenant relationship.

On the same day two male goats were brought before the priests. One was offered for the sins of the priest and his household to prepare him ceremonially to offer sacrifices for the people. The other was presented live before the Lord; after the sin offering was completed, the high priest laid his hands on the goat's head, confessing the iniquities of the nation. Symbolically he transferred their sins to the goat, who was sent into the wilderness to take them away (Lev. 16:5-10, 20-22).

Living in Booths (Tabernacles). During the celebration of the Feast of Tabernacles the people were instructed to make temporary shelters (*sukkot*) for themselves from tree branches and to live in them for seven days. The act of dwelling in these shelters, called "booths" or "tabernacles" in English versions, symbolized the forty years of wandering in the wilderness when Israel had no permanent home (Lev. 23:40-43). During that period the people traveled about as the Lord led them in the movements of the ark of the covenant; thus the Feast of Tabernacles reminded the worshipers that their real leader and king was the Lord of hosts (Zech. 14:16-18).

Passover Symbolism. In the same way, the Feast of Unleavened Bread, which culminated in the Passover celebration, symbolically recalled the events through which Yahweh had delivered Israel from slavery in Egypt. The *matzah* was a reminder of the night they left Egypt in such haste that the bread did not have time to rise. The Passover supper included lamb as a symbol of the lamb killed and eaten by each family, whose blood, smeared over the doors of their homes, protected Israel's firstborn sons from the avenging angel of death. The bitter herbs that completed the menu symbolized the bitterness of the slavery they were leaving. Although these were visual objects, the focus was not on the various foods themselves but on the *act* of eating them in the setting of family and community.

Processions

Ceremonial processions, frequently including dance, were a feature of the festival worship of Israel. The festal march symbolized God's reign over Israel and presented the picture of an army following its King into war.

Processions in Israel's Worship. The procession around the walls of Jericho, which began the conquest of Canaan, was a ceremonial act that took place in the context of actual warfare (Josh. 6). Similarly, a company of musicians and worshipers led the armies of Jehoshaphat into battle (2 Chron. 20:21-22) and afterward marched back into Jerusalem carrying their instruments and rejoicing in the Lord's victory in their behalf (2 Chron. 20:27-28).

The most vivid biblical description of a festal procession is David's portrayal of the movement of the ark of God in Psalm 68. The psalm begins with the cry, "May God arise, may his enemies be scattered; may his foes flee before him" (Ps. 68:1). Moses used the same words whenever the ark was to move out before the congregation of Israel in their trek through the wilderness (Num. 10:35). David continues with an invitation to praise the Lord, "who rides through the deserts" (Ps. 68:4 NASB), and indeed the entire psalm appears to be a symbolic recalling of the wilderness wanderings of Israel. As such it may have been a liturgy for an annual festival such as the Feast of Tabernacles. David sings,

> When you went out before your people,
>   O God,
>   when you marched through the
>   wasteland,
> the earth shook,
> . . . before God, the One of Sinai,
>   before God, the God of Israel. . . .
> The Lord announced the word,
>   and great was the company of those who
>   proclaimed it. . . .
> When you ascended on high,
>   you led captives in your train. . . .
> Your procession has come into view, O God,
>   the procession of my God and King into
>   the sanctuary.
> In front are the singers, after them the
>   musicians;
>   with them are the maidens playing
>   tambourines. . . .

> There is the little tribe of Benjamin, leading
>   them,
>   there the great throng of Judah's princes,
>   and there the princes of Zebulun and of
>   Naphtali. (Ps. 68:7-8, 11, 18, 24-25, 27)

As the ark is returned to its place in the tabernacle David had erected for it, the musicians sing, "You are awesome, O God, in your sanctuary" (Ps. 68:35).

One is reminded of the festal procession that accompanied the bringing of the ark from Kiriath Jearim and three months later from the house of Obed-Edom up to David's tabernacle in Zion. In the former instance "David and the whole house of Israel were celebrating with all their might before the LORD, with songs and with harps, lyres, tambourines, sistrums and cymbals" (2 Sam. 6:5). In the latter, it is recorded that David, clad in a linen ephod like those worn by the priests, leaped and danced before Lord "with all his might" (2 Sam. 6:14, 16). Perhaps Psalm 68 was used in this procession since it is a Davidic psalm celebrating the movement of the ark into the sanctuary.

In Psalm 42, a Korahite psalm, the speaker, apparently detained away from the sanctuary (Ps. 42:6), expresses his longing for former days when "I used to go with the multitude, leading the procession to the house of God" (Ps. 42:4). At the dedication ceremonies for the rebuilt wall of Jerusalem, Nehemiah summoned the musicians, priests, Levites, and leading citizens of Judah for a procession of thanksgiving to the Lord (Neh. 12:27). Two great choirs led the marchers in opposite directions upon the wall until they met at the house of the Lord (Neh. 12:31-40). This was followed by rejoicing so boisterous that the sounds were heard far outside the city (Neh. 12:43).

Processions in the New Testament. The Gospels describe a procession similar to those found in the Old Testament, with one notable difference: instead of being led by the ark, the symbol of God's presence, this procession centers around Jesus Christ himself riding on a donkey, surrounded with throngs of worshipers, waving palm branches and shouting, "Hosanna!" or "Save us, Lord!" (Matt. 21:1-9; Mark 11:1-10; John 12:12-15). This celebration pictures the coronation of Christ as king of Israel. It is repeated in the Revelation as the great multitude of the redeemed stands before the throne with palm branches in their hands crying out, "Salvation belongs to our God, who sits on the throne, and to the Lamb" (Rev. 7:10). A similar procession pictures the Lamb on Mount Zion and 144,000 worshipers, symbolic of the faithful of both old and new covenants, following him wherever he goes, singing a new song (Rev. 14:1-4). Again, we see Christ wearing a robe dipped in blood, his eyes like fire and crowned with many crowns, leading an army of saints in white linen, who also ride white horses (Rev. 19:11-14). These visionary processions depict the spiritual reality of the victorious Christ as King over his worshiping people, which the Israelite processions symbolically anticipated. Like these biblical processions, those in the church's worship today dramatize the kingship of Christ.

Dance

Music and dancing of various kinds accompanied processions in Israel, whether liturgical or simply those that celebrated military victories or other joyous occasions. As used in the worship of the Lord, dance is a form of self-abandon by the creature made aware of the mystery and majesty of his Creator. It is thus a recognition of the presence of the holy. David's dance before the ark is an illustration of this abandon in worship. The orchestrated movement of group dancing involves the subordination of the individual to the corporate expression of praise and can therefore be a token of the covenant of the Lord with all his people.

Ceremonial dances were a feature of the feast of the Lord held at Shiloh each year (Judg. 21:19-21). Jephthah's only daughter greeted him with tambourines and dancing when he returned victorious from battle with the Ammonites (Judg. 11:32-34). Women danced in the streets of all the cities of Israel, singing and playing tambourines and other instruments, as King Saul and his young servant David returned from the slaying of Goliath (1 Sam. 18:6).

David cries out in exultation to the God of the covenant, "You turned my wailing into dancing . . . that my heart may sing to you" (Ps. 30:11-12). Other psalmists invite all God's people to praise him with dance: "Let the people of Zion be glad in their King. Let them praise his name with dancing" (Ps. 149:2; cf. Ps. 150:4).

For Jeremiah, the cessation of dancing is part of the curse visited upon Israel because it has broken the covenant. "Our dancing has turned to mourning . . ." he weeps. "Woe to us, for we have sinned!"

(Lam. 5:15-16). However, in his prophecy of the new covenant, he promises the restoration of dance as a symbol of the blessing of Yahweh on his people. "Again you will take up your tambourines and go out to dance with the joyful. . . . Then maidens will dance and be glad, young men and old as well. I will turn their mourning into gladness" (Jer. 31:4, 13).

123 ◆ Symbolic Structures

In the Bible, the primary aspect of God's character is that he is "holy," not only in the sense of being good and righteous, but in the sense of being "sacred, sacrosanct," set apart from the ordinary. The Lord's people, because they belong to him, participate in his holiness (Lev. 20:26). But not only are the Lord and his people holy; physical objects, including structures and the space they represent or enclose, can be separated to God for his exclusive use and thus serve a symbolic function as windows into sacred reality. This is true of the altar, the tent (tabernacle), and the temple.

The Altar

The Hebrew word *mizboaḥ*, "altar," means a place of sacrifice. Except for the altar of the tabernacle and temple, which was originally a portable altar of bronze, altars erected in the Bible were of stone. The Pentateuch (Exod. 20:24-26) stipulates that altars are to be constructed of earth (that is, brick) or of stone; if made of stone, the stones must not be cut with chisels because "you will defile it if you use a tool on it" (Exod. 20:25). The meaning seems to be that, as an instrument of sacrifice to the holy God, the altar and other material things "should be used for the service of God only in their natural condition before they have been interfered with in any way by man" (Roland de Vaux, *Ancient Israel: Its Life and Institutions* [London: Darton, Longman & Todd, 1961], p. 408). The prohibition of steps on the altar also served to separate it from anything profane. The Scriptures rarely speak of the altar of sacrifice as a "table" (Ezek. 44:16; Mal. 1:7, 12), since Israel rejected the pagan notion that what was placed on the altar was food for the gods. The biblical view is well expressed by Paul who, in preaching to the Athenians, rejects the idea that God can be literally served by human hands, "as if he needed anything" (Acts 17:25; cf. Ps. 50:12-13).

The altar is a sign of the presence of God. For this reason, in the period before the Israelite kingdoms,

Various Types of Altars

altars were often erected as memorials to a theophany, or appearance, of the Lord (by Abraham, Gen. 12:7; 26:24-25; by Jacob, Gen. 35:7, 14). As a structure commemorating a manifestation of God, an altar might be given a name, as with Jacob's altar at Bethel (*'El,* the God of Israel, Gen. 33:20) or the altar erected by Moses after Israel's defeat of the Amalekites (*Yahveh nissi,* "The LORD is my Banner," Exod. 17:15-16). Memorial altars were not necessarily used for sacrificial worship. The tribes that settled east of the Jordan built an altar, which they (when confronted by the rest of Israel) claimed was not for sacrifice but for "a witness between us and you" that they, too, were a part of Israel (Josh. 22:7-34).

As a token of the presence of the holy, the altar was sacrosanct, a "bearer of the holy." Jesus acknowledged this concept when he reminded the Pharisees that the gift offered on the altar is sanctified by the altar, not the other way around (Matt. 23:19). In the regular worship of Israel, as laid out in the Mosaic directives, only the priests, specially consecrated for the service of the altar, could "draw near" to officiate in sacrifice. Yet even the altar of the sanctuary was not inherently holy; it had to be purified each year on the Day of Atonement when atonement was made for the sin of the entire worshiping community. The sanctity of the altar is a reflection of the holiness of the God who receives the tribute of his people offered thereon.

In the Christian church there are no true altars, for the sacrifice has been offered once for all in Christ's death on the cross. Nor is the cross called an altar; as

the author of Hebrews makes clear, the sacrifice of Christ is offered in the heavenly sanctuary (Heb. 8–9), with the implication that Jesus himself is the altar as well as the sacrifice and the officiating priest (Heb. 13:10-13). In a sense the Christian "altar" is a "Communion table," although the Bible does not use that expression. The Israelite worshiper, having brought a sacrifice, was typically given back a portion of his offering to eat, becoming as it were a participant in a meal hosted by the Lord (cf. 1 Cor. 10:18). In the same manner, the Lord hosts his people in the Lord's Supper, the sacred meal of the new covenant. But the symbolism is in the action performed, not in the altar or table. In the Revelation to John, the martyrs cry out from "under the altar" (Rev. 6:9). The witness of the persecuted church, in its participation in Christ's suffering (Phil. 3:10) and its faithfulness to the true covenant, is the foundation for its sacrificial offering to God.

The Tent (Tabernacle)

The tent or tabernacle in Scripture is a picture of the Lord's presence with his people and of the true communion with the Lord which comes through faithfulness to his covenant.

The Tent in the Old Testament. The desert sanctuary established in the Mosaic covenant was called the tent, or tabernacle (*'ohel*). The tabernacle continued in use as the worship center after the settlement of Canaan, being stationed at a series of locations including Shiloh and Gibeon, until replaced by the temple. The tent stood within an enclosure, or court, which also contained the altar of sacrifice. The Pentateuch contains detailed instructions for the construction of the tabernacle (Exod. 26:1-30), which was made so that it could be easily disassembled, transported, and reassembled at a new site as the community moved about.

Tents were the dwelling places of Israel during the nomadic period of the wilderness; the tabernacle of the Lord is also called the *mishkan,* or "dwelling," representing his presence or "name" (Deut. 12:5) in the midst of his people. Like other dwellings of the period, the Lord's house had its hearth (the altar), its table (the table of shewbread), and its lamp, which burned continuously, there being no windows in most houses. In place of the bed, the inner sanctuary contained the ark, representing Yahweh's seat or throne. As a movable dwelling, the tent is an appropriate symbol of the dynamic character of Yahweh.

Even his name, given to Moses in the desert, is interpreted to reveal a God who is not stationary, but ever on the move: "I will be who I will be" (Exod. 3:14, AUTHOR'S TRANSLATION). When David proposed to erect a permanent temple as the house of the Lord, the prophet Nathan made it clear that Yahweh was satisfied to be "moving from place to place with a tent" (2 Sam. 7:5-7). The Israelite worshiper understood that the presence of the God who made heaven and earth could not be confined to one geographic location; this truth was more easily sustained through the symbolism of a simple tabernacle than that of a grand permanent structure, though Solomon attempted to do so in his prayer at the dedication of the temple (1 Kings 8:27). Many of the early psalms seem to have been composed for the worship David established in Jerusalem before the building of the temple; at this time the ark of the covenant stood in a tent of its own on Zion (1 Chron. 16:1), while the Mosaic tent remained at Gibeon (1 Chron. 21:29). As the Psalms passed into the worship of the temple, the words for the tabernacle came to stand for it as well.

After the settlement of Canaan, the Israelites began to live in permanent structures, houses built within villages or fortified cities. Israelite culture became influenced by that of Canaan, which included the polytheistic fertility cults and the political system of rule by kings instead of by tribal elders and family heads. Thus the tent became a symbol of the idealized Israel, its roots in the nomadic life of the desert where it had received the covenant and had faithfully served Yahweh. When Rehoboam refused to lighten the heavy burden of taxation and service that his father Solomon had levied on the nation for his grandiose court and construction projects, the northern tribes revolted with the cry, "To your tents, O Israel!" (1 Kings 12:16). In token of the nomadic ideal, the Rechabites (followers of Jonadab ben Rechab) refused to live in houses or cultivate the land but lived in tents; the prophet Jeremiah held them up as an example of faithfulness to the Lord (Jer. 35:5-10).

The Tent in the New Testament. Tent symbolism occurs in the New Testament also, where its meaning is dependent on Old Testament precedents. The letter to the Hebrews views the earthly institutions of Israelite religion as pictures of greater spiritual realities. Being the Great High Priest, Jesus "serves in the sanctuary, the true tabernacle set up by the Lord, not by man" (Heb. 8:1-2). This "greater and more perfect tabernacle" (Heb. 9:11) is a word picture of the heavenly and spiritual communion of the new covenant which the worshiper may enter in virtue of the atonement made by Jesus Christ.

But in another sense, Jesus himself is the tabernacle, as are those who belong to him. John introduces his Gospel with the statement, "The Word became flesh and made his dwelling among us" (John 1:14); the Greek word translated "made his dwelling" is *skēnoō,* literally "pitch a tent, tabernacle." The incarnation of the Word in Jesus fulfills the symbolism of the Israelite tabernacle, in which the Lord dwells in the midst of the community of his people to maintain the covenant. At the ascension of Christ, the Word in bodily form is succeeded by the Spirit of Christ, the Helper promised by Jesus (John 16:7), who dwells with the people who are his temple (1 Cor. 3:16-17; 6:19; 2 Cor. 6:16). The tabernacle (*skēnē*) is the worshiping church, the bride of the Lamb: "Behold, the tabernacle of God is among men" (Rev. 21:3, NASB).

Both Paul and Peter speak of the Christian's body as a "tent" (2 Cor. 5:1-2; 2 Pet. 1:13-14), a temporary residence to be replaced by an eternal one. This should not be misunderstood in an individualistic sense. The eternal "tabernacle" is not the believer's body, but the believer as the *body of the Spirit.* This is made clear by Paul's comparison of the "spiritual body" of the resurrection to Adam, who was filled with life by the Spirit or breath of God (1 Cor. 15:44-45). The life of the resurrection is corporate, since there is "one body and one Spirit" (Eph. 4:4).

The Temple As Sacred Space

The temple on Mount Zion epitomizes the concept of "sacred space." Like other sanctuaries, it was erected on a mountain or hill. Ancient peoples regarded such elevations as places where heaven and earth might intersect, as in Jacob's dream at Bethel in which he sees a ladder connecting heaven and earth with the angels of God ascending and descending on it. Upon awakening, Jacob is overcome with awe and exclaims, "This is none other than the house of God; this is the gate of heaven" (Gen. 28:11-18).

As the intersection of the cosmic and the earthly, the temple is also a picture of the universe in miniature, incorporating heaven, land, and sea within its confines. On Zion, sang the Israelite worshiper, the Lord "built his sanctuary like the heights, like the earth that he established forever" (Ps. 78:69). In the inner sanctuary, containing the ark of the covenant, the Lord is "enthroned between the cherubim" (Ps. 80:1; 99:1); he rides through the heavens on them to come to the aid of his anointed (Ps. 18:10). Ascending to the sanctuary in pilgrimage, the worshiper cries, "I lift up my eyes to you, to you whose throne is in heaven" (Ps. 123:1). "The LORD made the heavens," proclaims the psalmist, and in his next breath, "Splendor and majesty are before him; strength and glory are in his sanctuary" (Ps. 96:5-6). The heavenly majesty of the Lord, who covers himself "in light as with a garment," is depicted in psalmic imagery reminiscent of various features of the temple: its beams, its curtains, the fires and smoky cloud of the altar of incense (Ps. 104:2-4).

At the same time, the temple's sacred space is an architectural representation of the earth, its land and vegetation, its seas and rivers, and its inhabitants. The celebration of Yahweh's kingship in the sanctuary, as recorded in the Psalms, includes recognition that he sustains the physical creation: "The LORD reigns. The world is firmly established, it cannot be moved" (Ps. 96:10; cf. Ps. 93:1-2). Because of the overwhelming and beautiful presence of the Lord in his sanctuary, the field exults and the trees of the forest sing for joy before the judge of the earth (Ps. 96:12). Even the birds find a nest at the altars of the house of the Lord (Ps. 84:3). Through his covenant faithfulness, he preserves both "man and beast" in the place where "both high and low among men find refuge in the shadow of your wings" (Ps. 36:7), a reference to the wings of the cherubim overshadowing the ark. Here, encountering the radiant presence of the holy, "in your light we see light" (Ps. 36:9)—the first of God's creations (Gen. 1:3).

The sanctuary also represents the earth as the setting for Israel's "sacred history," the drama of the Lord's deliverance of his people from their enemies. "His tent is in Salem, his dwelling place in Zion. There he broke the flashing arrows, the shields and the swords, the weapons of war" (Ps. 76:2-3). Because God's dwelling place is in the midst of his city, attacking armies are defeated; the worshiper is invited to "come and see the works of the LORD, the desolations he has brought on the earth," destroying the enemy's armaments (Ps. 46:8).

A telling expression occurs in Psalm 24, which proclaims that "the earth is the LORD's, and all it contains, the world, and those who dwell in it. For He has founded it upon the seas, and established it

upon the rivers" (Ps. 24:1-2, NASB). Mention of seas and rivers seems out of place in landlocked Jerusalem, which has no stream except the intermittent brook of Kidron. But the sea and the river are in the temple! The metal "sea" cast by Solomon's craftsmen seems an oddity until we understand that the temple's sacred space also pictures the sea upon which the earth is established, "the floods," which "have lifted up their voice" to the mighty Lord (Ps. 93:3-4). In the sanctuary, "the sea roars" before the coming judge of the earth (Ps. 96:11-13). As to rivers, "there is a river whose streams make glad the city of God, the holy places where the Most High dwells" (Ps. 46:4). It is the sacred river, part of this symbolic microcosm, which Ezekiel sees flowing forth from the restored sanctuary to heal the land; "so where the river flows everything will live" (Ezek. 47:9).

In its architectural embrace of the creation, the sanctuary imparts to it a spiritual aspect; "in His temple everything says, 'Glory!'" (Ps. 29:9, NASB). We are reminded that heaven and earth were created as the setting in which the drama of human sin and divine redemption through the covenant is acted out and that they are witnesses to the covenant between the Lord and his worshipers (Deut. 4:26; 30:19).

As a pictorial microcosm of heaven and earth, the Israelite sanctuary proclaims the presence of the living God throughout all creation as he manifests his glory to his worshiping people. In thinking about the architectural needs of the church today, we do well to ponder the importance of "sacred space" as a symbol of the Lord's indwelling of his spiritual temple, the body of Christ.

124 ◆ SYMBOLIC OBJECTS

Together with symbolic actions and structures, biblical worship incorporates symbolic objects. Sometimes these are real objects, physically present in the place of worship. Sometimes they are verbal symbols of things not physically present. And sometimes they are both, either at the same time or at different times. Such objects include the ark of the covenant, books and scrolls, anointing oil, the lamp, incense, blood, the bread and cup, and the cross.

Ark of the Covenant

One of the most important and powerful symbols in the worship of Israel was the small, gold-covered box crowned with the fearsome cherubim. Beneath its golden cover were two stone tablets on which the Lord himself had written the covenant text, the Ten Commandments. These tablets were themselves symbols of the covenant and all that pertained to it—the stipulations and sanctions, the moral code by which it was lived out, and the system of sacrificial worship it required.

The Atonement Cover and Cherubim. The top of the ark was a lid or cover, sometimes called in English the "mercy seat," or atonement cover, because it played a role in the symbolic acts of the Day of Atonement. On either side of the atonement cover, and made of one piece with it, were cherubim, overlaid with gold, with wings outstretched and faces turned inward toward the ark. When the ark was moved to Solomon's temple it sat beneath a second pair of cherubim, making a total of four. These are the same living creatures that appear in Ezekiel's vision of the glory of the Lord (Ezek. 1:5-11) and in John's Revelation, in which they surround the throne of God (Rev. 4:6-7). Thus, although there were visual cherubim in the temple of Solomon, they became a verbal symbol in later worship.

In ancient sculpture, cherubim sometimes appear next to royal thrones; apparently these composite creatures symbolized the power of the king whose throne they guarded. For Israel, the ark of the covenant was the footstool of Yahweh's throne (1 Chron. 28:2; Pss. 99:5; 132:7); the throne itself was invisible, held aloft by the cherubim (Ezek. 10:1). The "glory" or weight of the Lord (another verbal symbol of his awesome presence) rested on it, between the wings of the cherubim (2 Sam. 6:2; Ps. 99:1); there he dwelt in the midst of his people and reigned over them.

Movements of the Ark. The ark, together with the manifestations of the Lord's glory, in cloud by day and fire by night, led the Israelites during their trek through the wilderness (Num. 10:33-36). The ark also led Israel's crossing of the Jordan into the land Yahweh had promised them (Josh. 3:8-17). When Israel went to war, the ark was sometimes carried into battle ahead of the military units (1 Sam. 4:3); symbolically, Yahweh as Israel's covenant king led his armies in warfare (1 Sam. 4:7-8). This practice ended after the ark was brought to Zion. However, scholars have theorized that the ark might sometimes have been carried in sacred procession at the festivals of Israel, as suggested by Psalms 24, 68, and 132.

The Heavenly Ark. Eventually the ark disappeared from the temple (Jer. 3:16). In Herod's temple the Holy of Holies was empty, although sacrifices were carried on as if the throne of Yahweh were still there. The rending of the temple veil at the crucifixion of Jesus exposed this emptiness; the presence of the Lord no longer graced the old institution, with its ceremonies, animal sacrifices, and symbolic cleansings. Jesus Christ, the Lamb of God and Great High Priest, was about to enter the heavenly sanctuary with his own blood to offer it before the throne of God once for all people (Heb. 9:11-14; 10:10). John describes the scene thus:

> Then God's temple in heaven was opened, and within his temple was seen the ark of his covenant. And there came flashes of lightning, rumblings, peals of thunder, an earthquake and a great hailstorm. (Rev. 11:19)

Thus the visible ark, which for centuries has symbolized the footstool of the throne of God in Israel's worship, has been replaced by a word picture conveying the greater reality of its heavenly pattern, now sprinkled with the blood of Jesus, which he presented on that final Day of Atonement to which all the annual observances looked forward (Heb. 9:11-12; 10:1-10). The Lord God and the Lamb dwell in the new temple, the church of the firstborn (Heb. 12:23), of which the old was a symbol (1 Cor. 3:16-17; 2 Cor. 6:16; Eph. 2:22). "The Word became flesh and made his dwelling among us" (John 1:14).

Books and Scrolls

In ancient times political agreements were inscribed on clay or stone tablets, or sometimes on papyrus, as a record of the treaty. These covenant texts were then deposited in the shrine of the god(s), whose duty it was to witness the oath and to enforce its stipulations. When Israel entered into a political treaty with Yahweh, Moses deposited a copy of the text at the shrine of Yahweh, the ark of the covenant. The ark in turn was housed first in the tabernacle of Moses, then in David's tent, and finally in the temple of Solomon.

The Book of the Covenant. Originally the text of the treaty between Yahweh and Israel was written on stone tablets, which Moses brought down from his encounter with the Lord on Mount Sinai. Later, however, the law, or covenant text, was recorded on a scroll. (Books in Scripture are always scrolls; the modern form of the book, known as the *codex,* was not used in the biblical period.) This book was known variously as the Book of the Covenant, the Book of the Law (or simply "the Law"), and the Book of the Testimony (or simply "the Testimony"). References to the "Book of Life" are probably to this document as well. The covenant was the structure through which Israel related to the Lord, and the written text was emblematic of that relationship. This explains Moses' breaking of the stone tablets on which the covenant was written when he witnessed Israel's idolatry; the action betokened what had happened to the covenant itself. The kings of Judah, like David, who had founded their dynasty, were considered mediators of the covenant on behalf of the people. In what may have been a typical coronation ceremony, the child king Joash was presented with the Book of the Law when he was enthroned (2 Kings 11:12). During the religious reforms under Josiah, the forgotten Book of the Law was found during temple renovations and was immediately brought to the king (2 Chron. 34:16).

The Book of Life. In ancient covenants, the "great king" granting the treaty was sometimes said to have "created" the servant nation, his treaty partner. Since a created thing was not thought to exist until it was named, the great king often renamed the servant people, sometimes giving them his own name as a sign of ownership. The covenant text, then, was the guarantee of the people's existence. When their names were inscribed in it, they had an identity. If the covenant were broken, however, their names were expunged and they no longer enjoyed the legal and military protection of the great king. Moses intercedes for wayward Israel saying: "Please forgive their sin—but if not, then blot me out of the book you have written" (Exod. 32:32). The Lord responds that he will blot out those who have sinned (Exod. 32:33-34). The result was death for the offenders, who could no longer remain among the covenant people whose names were recorded in the book. The same concept appears in the New Testament, where the symbolic "Book of Life" (Phil. 4:3; Rev. 3:5; 13:8; 17:8; 20:15; 21:27) contains the names of those who are in covenant with the Lord God and the Lamb.

Scrolls of Curse. Zechariah sees a flying scroll with curses written on both sides. The scroll is being sent to those who break the covenant by lying or by swearing falsely and will avenge these violations (Zech. 5:1-2). In a vision Ezekiel is given a book containing the covenant curses and told to eat it so the words will be in his mouth and he can speak them to the house of Israel (Ezek. 2:9–3:4). The book was as sweet as honey on his tongue because it was the covenant with Yahweh, but it became bitter in his stomach because he tasted the curses he was commissioned to announce to the unfaithful nation.

John relates a similar experience in his Revelation. He sees a book in the hand of the one sitting on the throne. This is also the book of the covenant curses, as the events that follow make clear. The scroll is sealed with seven seals and no one is found worthy to open it; only the slain but victorious Lamb, as mediator of the new covenant and redeemer of his people, is able to unseal it (Rev. 5:1-10). Later in his vision John is given the book to eat. Like Ezekiel, he experiences it as sweet in his mouth and bitter in his stomach; the covenant is his delight but the curses concerning which he is to prophesy leave an unpleasant aftertaste (Rev. 10:1-11).

Although the text of Yahweh's covenant with Israel includes stipulations for fulfilling the agreement and blessings for doing so, it appears that the pronouncement of curses on the unfaithful dominates in those biblical texts which refer to the Book or Scroll of the Covenant (Deut. 27:26; Gal. 3:10; cf. Rev. 22:18). Isaiah promises that when the new covenant is established those who have been deaf to the book will hear its words, and as a result their blind eyes will see. These afflicted "will rejoice in the LORD" (Isa. 29:19).

Anointing Oil

The land of Israel produced olive oil in abundance, reputed to have been the finest available in the ancient world. It was a staple of the economy and was sometimes used as a medium of exchange. When creditors threatened a widow of one of the prophets with selling her children as slaves, Elisha multiplied her last jar of oil so that she could pay her debts (2 Kings 4:1-7). Oil was valuable because it had many ordinary uses: it was burned in lamps to produce light, mixed with flour to produce bread, applied to the body as a cosmetic, and poured on wounds for healing. In addition to these pragmatic uses, oil was a part of the symbolic worship of Israel and is also mentioned in connection with practices in the New Testament church.

Oil in Israelite Worship. Jacob the patriarch poured oil over a stone to sanctify it as an altar, memorializing the place where God appeared to him in a dream (Gen. 28:10-19). The occasion was the Lord's affirmation that the covenant he had made with Abraham and Isaac was now being extended to include Jacob. At this point in his life Jacob probably did not realize the full significance of God's announcement, but to a young man who has deceived his father and has been sent away from home to escape an angry brother, the blessing of the Lord was an event of major importance.

The seven-branched lampstand that lit the sanctuary burned olive oil. As a part of the covenant worship instructions, Moses was told by the Lord to make a perfumed anointing oil using myrrh, cinnamon, cane, and cassia; this fragrant oil was sprinkled on the priests and their clothing and the tabernacle with all its furnishings to consecrate them and was not to be used for any other purpose. Pure olive oil was offered with flour as a part of some of the offerings made by fire to the Lord (Lev. 2:1, 4-6, 15; 14:10). When the offering was for cleansing from a disease, oil was also sprinkled before the Lord and put on the head of the diseased person "to make atonement for him before the LORD" (Lev. 14:29).

Oil and Commissioning. In the Old Testament, oil is a symbol of the special commission given by Yahweh to persons in public service. The high priest was consecrated with oil (Num. 35:25; Ps. 133:2). Prophets and kings were set apart for their special offices by anointing and were called "the LORD's anointed" or "oiled one" (*mashiaḥ,* 1 Sam. 16:6; 24:6, 10; 2 Sam. 23:1). In recognition that their commissioning was from the Lord, Samuel poured oil on the heads of both Saul (1 Sam. 10:1) and David (1 Sam. 16:1, 13) when the Lord chose them to be kings of Israel, but David testified that it was truly the Lord who had anointed him (Ps. 23:5). Jesus' very title "the Christ" (*Christos,* Acts 4:26) is the Greek equivalent of the Hebrew "messiah" (*mashiaḥ*), "the one anointed with oil." As Peter is praying after having been released by the Jewish religious leaders, he calls Jesus the holy Servant of God whom God had anointed (Acts 4:27).

Oil and the Holy Spirit. Elijah was told to anoint Elisha to succeed him as prophet (1 Kings 19:16); however, there is no record that he actually did so. Instead, Elijah's mantle or cloak fell upon the younger prophet when a flaming chariot of the Lord's presence separated the two men and Elijah was taken to heaven in a whirlwind. Elisha had requested a double portion of Elijah's spirit, which was, of course, the Spirit of the Lord empowering the prophet. Elisha's request was granted when Elijah's mantle fell to him (2 Kings 2:11-14). This incident provides one link between anointing with oil and empowerment or anointing by the Holy Spirit. In the New Testament, a connection between oil and the Holy Spirit is amplified; it is with the Spirit, rather than with actual oil, that the Lord commissions those whom he has called for his special purposes. While preaching to the household of Cornelius, Peter declares that God "anointed [Jesus] with the Holy Spirit and with power" (Acts 10:38). John writes that believers are also anointed with the Holy Spirit:

> As for you, the anointing you received from him [the Son] remains in you, and you do not need anyone to teach you. But as his anointing teaches you about all things and as that anointing is real, not counterfeit—just as it has taught you, remain in him. (1 John 2:27)

John is referring to Jesus' promise that he would send the Spirit to teach his disciples all things (John 14:26). Paul also refers to the believers' anointing and links it with the Holy Spirit (2 Cor. 1:21-22). Although the New Testament does not record anyone's being anointed with actual oil as an act of commissioning, the New Testament writers understand anointing with oil as a word picture of blessing and empowerment by the Holy Spirit, no doubt directly associated with the baptism or filling of the Spirit as described in Acts 2:1-4 and elsewhere.

Oil and Healing. Jesus tells of a Samaritan who finds a robbed and beaten man beside the road, whose wounds he treats with wine and oil (Luke 10:33-34). These two substances were commonly used medicinally: wine cleansed and reduced infection while oil promoted healing. In the New Testament wine often symbolizes the cleansing of God's people in the new covenant through the blood of Jesus, as in the institution of the Last Supper (Luke 22:20) and the marriage at Cana of Galilee (John 2:1-10). Oil speaks of God's blessing through the Holy Spirit; when James instructs Christians who are sick to be anointed with oil by elders of the church (James 5:14), he is combining the symbolism of physical healing and the Spirit's supernatural blessing.

The Lamp

In the sanctuary of Israel stood the golden lampstand with its seven lamps (Exod. 25:31-37), which were to burn continually (Lev. 24:2). The lampstand was not a "candlestick," as in older English versions, but used olive oil. The lamps served a practical function in the house of the Lord, as in other houses, where the lack of windows rendered the interior quite dark even in the daytime. However, the lamp also has a symbolic significance in the Bible.

When the Psalms associate light with the Lord's presence in the sanctuary, the image of the lampstand may be the background symbolism. Thus the psalmist cries out to the Lord to "send forth your light and your truth" to lead him to the house of God (Ps. 43:3). In the protective refuge of the holy place, "in your light we see light" (Ps. 36:9). Radiance, light, and shining are common scriptural images for the impact of the presence of the holy (Pss. 27:1; 50:2-3; 67:1; Matt. 17:2; 2 Cor. 4:6; 1 Tim. 6:16; Rev. 1:16). The lampstand, while not encompassing this imagery, is a part of it, especially as it is connected with the sanctuary.

The lamp is an element in the general biblical symbolism of light versus darkness, representing good versus evil, truth versus ignorance and falsehood. The Lord lights the lamp of the worshiper (Ps. 18:28; the variant in 2 Sam. 22:29 says, "You are my lamp, O Lord"). The lamp is a metaphor for the word of God, which gives direction to the faithful (Ps. 119:105). The spirit of man is called "the lamp of the Lord," which illuminates a person's inmost being (Prov 20:27; cf. John 1:4).

The lamp shares the association of olive oil with the Spirit of God, as in Zechariah's vision of the lampstand and the two anointed ones (Zech. 4:1-6) and Jesus' parable of the wise and foolish maidens (Matt. 25:1-13). This is most clearly seen in John's vision of the throne of God, in which "Before the throne, seven lamps were blazing. These are the seven spirits of God" (Rev. 4:5). In John's opening vision of the living Christ, he beholds him standing amid seven lampstands (Rev. 1:12-13), which represent the seven churches (Rev. 1:20). Since the number seven is symbolic of the covenant (being the root of the expression "swear an oath"), the seven lamps or lampstands are emblematic of the bond between the Lord and the people who are his witnesses. Thus Jesus compares the people of the kingdom of God to lamps, not hidden under baskets, but placed on stands, giving light to all the world (Matt. 5:14-16) as he supremely is the Light of the World (John 1:9; 8:12; 9:5).

Incense

The offering of incense in worship has its roots in antiquity. It was a common custom among the pagan peoples living in the vicinity of Israel, who burned incense to the moon, called the "queen of heaven," and to various other gods (1 Kings 11:8; Jer. 44:17, 25). Those ancient peoples that sacrificed animals and grain to their gods did so in order to provide them with food. However, the Lord made it clear to Israel that he did not need their offerings in order to satisfy his hunger (Ps. 50:12-13), but accepted them as a sweet smell (Exod. 29:18; Num. 15:13). Accordingly, he gave Moses instructions to add fragrant incense to some of the grain offerings (Lev. 2:1-2, 15-16; 6:15; Num. 7:14) and to burn incense morning and evening in the Holy Place within the tabernacle (Exod. 30:7-8). Pure frankincense was put with the twelve cakes known as the "shewbread" or "bread of the presence" (Num. 4:7), which was laid on the golden table in the Holy Place.

On the Day of Atonement the high priest brought a pan of burning coals from the bronze altar into the Holy Place and poured two handfuls of sweet incense on the coals. The cloud formed by the burning incense covered the ark of the covenant, preventing the priest from seeing the mercy seat when he presented the blood and from dying as a result of looking on the glory of the Lord (Lev. 16:12-13). Only a priest who was descended from Aaron was allowed to offer incense to the Lord (Lev. 2:2). Violation of this restriction brought death to Korah and his company and a plague upon the people (Num. 16).

Malachi prophesies that incense will be offered "from the rising to the setting of the sun. In every place" (Mal. 1:11) to honor the great name of the Lord. This offering symbolizes the prayers of God's people, which apparently accompanied it (Luke 1:10). David asks that the Lord will accept his prayer as the evening incense offering (Ps. 141:2), a symbol John repeats in his Revelation (Rev. 5:8; 8:3-4). In the early church, incense becomes a verbal symbol or word picture of prayer; Christian worship at this time does not include the literal offering of incense. In addition to prayer, the knowledge of Christ

(2 Cor. 2:14) and a gift given to Paul (Phil. 4:18) are likened to the offering of incense.

Blood

In the Scripture, blood is a symbol of life (Gen. 9:4). While the spirit or breath is the life force, blood is the life substance. For this reason the Lord forbade Israel to eat or drink the blood of animals; it was to be poured out into the ground, symbolically returning it to God, who had given them life (Lev. 17:10-14). Because blood represents life, it was used for sanctification ceremonies in Israel's rituals. Even before the law was given, while the Hebrews were still in Egypt, the Lord gave instructions for killing a lamb and smearing its blood over their doorways for protection. The blood "sanctified," or set apart, the family within; the messenger of death recognized that the occupants of the house belonged to Yahweh and refrained from killing their firstborn (Exod. 12:13).

This same symbolism is at the heart of the various sprinklings of blood required by the Mosaic Law. A sacrifice made to the Lord was holy, or set apart, for him. Whatever touched it also became holy (Exod. 30:29). When the various altars, tables, utensils, and the tabernacle itself were sprinkled with the blood of the sacrifice, they were sanctified (Lev. 16:11-20). The covenant theme underlies this practice; those persons entering into covenant typically kill an animal and either sprinkle the blood on themselves or drink it as a way of identifying with the animal. The idea is that they will share the fate of the slain beast if they break the stipulations of the treaty. As worshipers of Yahweh, the people of Israel were prohibited from drinking blood; when they offered sacrifices the priest sprinkled the animal's blood on them as an identification with the covenant, but they substituted drinking wine for drinking blood in the covenant meal. Being bound to Yahweh made Israel holy; since he is holy, all that belongs to him is holy as well (Lev. 11:44-45; Deut. 7:6, 14:2, 21; 26:19).

The author of Hebrews states that the blood of Jesus Christ is the blood of the new covenant. He is the Passover Lamb, sacrificed for the new covenant people. As the priest carried the blood of the sacrificed animal into the Most Holy Place on the Day of Atonement and sprinkled it on the cover of the ark, so Jesus, the High Priest and Mediator of the new covenant, entered the heavenly sanctuary with his own blood to make atonement for his people (Heb. 9:11-15; 10:29; 13:20).

Jesus said that those who eat his flesh and drink his blood will receive his life (John 6:54-56), a reference to the idea that blood is the life substance. When instituting the Lord's Supper, he used wine to symbolize the shedding of his blood. Wine was known to be a cleansing agent in the case of flesh wounds (Luke 10:34), while blood was the Old Testament agent for spiritual cleansing (Heb. 9:22). Under the new covenant it is Jesus' blood that provides cleansing for all who believe in him (1 Pet. 1:18-19; 1 John 1:7; Rev. 1:5), and that blood is symbolized by the wine of the Eucharist (Luke 22:20; 1 Cor. 11:25).

John visualizes the victorious Christ clothed in a "robe dipped in blood" (Rev. 19:13), while the great company of the redeemed are wearing garments that have been washed and made "white in the blood of the Lamb" (Rev. 7:14). Obviously the blood of Christ is a verbal, not a visual, symbol in New Testament usage; washing in literal blood would not make things white. Even the wine or grape juice of the Lord's Supper is not important as a visual symbol of Jesus' blood; it is the *corporate action* of partaking of the cup and the loaf that conveys the meaning of the ordinance as the covenant meal and the emblem of cleansing.

Bread and Cup

Both bread, or the loaf, and the cup are biblical symbols having several meanings. When combined, as the emblems of the Lord's Supper, they take on additional significance in Christian worship.

Bread and Life. Bread, which in the Bible often stands for all food, is a symbol for the Word of God, and by extension, for the covenant relationship it governs and the life that flows from the covenant. In the Lord's name, Isaiah appeals to Israel to "eat what is good," the true bread of the "everlasting covenant" (Isa. 55:2-3). Moses compared the Word of the Lord to bread as the true basis for life in the covenant (Deut. 8:3); his words are quoted by Jesus in resisting the tempter (Matt. 4:4). In speaking of bread, Moses was referring to the manna that fell during Israel's wanderings, by which the people were miraculously fed in a barren wilderness. Jesus also mentions the manna, contrasting it with himself as the "Bread of Life," or living bread (John

6:49-51). This discourse of Jesus is filled with overlapping symbols: the manna is a token of the "true bread out of heaven," yet the bread represents Jesus' flesh, which he gives in dying that the world might live (John 6:32-33, 51). The discourse is occasioned by the feeding of the multitude, in which Jesus "gave thanks"; John pointedly records this twice (John 6:11, 23), suggesting that the entire chapter is an interpretation of the Eucharist. (Mention of the impending Passover celebration in the introduction to the account [John 6:4] reinforces this hypothesis.) Yet, in the end, it is neither the manna, nor the bread, nor his flesh, nor any ceremonial act that Jesus has in mind, but a spiritual reality symbols can only suggest: "the words that I have spoken to you are spirit and they are life" (John 6:63).

Bread of the Presence (Shewbread). In the sanctuary, the "bread of the presence," or shewbread (*leḥem panim,* literally "bread of face"), was to be set out on a table before the Lord at all times (Exod. 25:30), being replaced each Sabbath. Since there were twelve loaves, placed with frankincense as a "memorial," the bread may have been symbolic of the continual covenant between Yahweh and Israel. The bread of the presence was sacrosanct, and only the priests could eat it (Lev. 24:9; 1 Sam. 21:4). However, David and his soldiers, being in a consecrated state, were allowed to eat it when no other food was available (1 Sam. 21:6). Jesus cites this incident to prove to the Pharisees that the institutions of Israel's religion, especially the Sabbath, were created to benefit the people of God and not to bind them (Mark 2:25-28).

Unleavened Bread. The unleavened bread eaten during the observance of the Passover (Exod. 12:15-30; 13:3-7) is a reminder of the Exodus from Egypt and especially of the haste in which the Israelites had to depart, there being no time on the journey to allow the dough to rise before baking (Exod. 12:39). As a memorial of the Lord's mighty act of deliverance, through which he created a people for himself (Exod. 19:4), the unleavened bread and the entire Passover are a covenant meal, celebrating the relationship God has decreed with his sons and daughters. The Lord's Supper transfers the same symbolism to the new covenant as Jesus relates the bread to his body given in death to enact it (Luke 22:19). Although some interpreters, in administering the Lord's Supper, have associated the striped appearance of modern commercial *matzah* with

Isaiah's words, "with his stripes we are healed" (Isa. 53:5, KJV), there is no scriptural evidence that the unleavened bread had this appearance or that the Lord's Supper was associated with physical healing.

The Bread of Communion. Paul, writing of the Lord's Supper, refers to the broken bread as "a *koinōnia* in the body of Christ" (1 Cor. 10:16). The term *koinōnia,* sometimes translated "fellowship" or "sharing," indicates mutual participation at a more than superficial level. The broken loaf symbolizes an inward communion in the body of Christ, both his body on the cross in death and his body the church: "we, who are many, are one body, for we all partake of the one loaf" (1 Cor. 10:17). Not only is the loaf an inadequate symbol of this communion, but the word *koinōnia* and its English equivalents cannot really encompass it; the unity of Christ's body, as energized by the Spirit of the living Lord, is a numinous reality that must be apprehended intuitively through corporate worship and the deeper bonding of covenanted lives.

The Cup of Wrath. Symbolism of the cup in Scripture includes the negative symbolism of God's wrath and judgment on the unfaithful; yet even this is relevant to worship, since biblical worship celebrates the covenant and employs its structure. The prophet Jeremiah is told to take from the Lord's hand the "cup filled with the wine of my wrath" and administer it to the disobedient nations of the world, including Jerusalem and Judah (Jer. 24:15-18). Ezekiel also proclaims the judgment of the Lord God against the harlot sister nations of Israel and Judah, using the figure of "the cup of ruin and desolation" (Ezek. 23:31-34). The background for such language is the use of cup symbolism in the sanctions of ancient treaties; one of the curses pronounced on the traitor is that he must drink the cup of poison (a practice with which we are familiar from Plato's account of the death of Socrates). As the Judge, God administers his poison cup to the wicked of the land (Ps. 75:8), the prideful who refuse to recognize his sovereignty (Ps. 75:4-5; cf. Ps. 11:6). When Jesus prays in the Garden of Gethsemane, "Father, if you are willing, take this cup from me" (Luke 22:42), he is referring to the penalty for unfaithfulness to the covenant that he himself is to bear on the cross that others might be released from its curse (cf. Gal. 3:13).

The Cup of Blessing. The cup is also, of course, a positive symbol of fellowship with the Lord and of his blessing. David celebrates the abundance of Yahweh his Shepherd in singing, "My cup overflows. Surely goodness and love [*ḥesed*] will follow me all the days of my life" (Ps. 23:5-6). In Psalm 16 he testifies, "LORD, you have assigned me my portion and my cup" (Ps. 16:5), perhaps in contrast to the libations, or drink offerings, of those who have exchanged Yahweh for another god (Ps. 16:4). Such a libation offered to Yahweh may be intended in Psalm 116:13, in which the speaker says, "I will lift up the cup of salvation and call on the name of the LORD," in fulfillment of a vow. In ancient Jewish custom, a meal was concluded by a prayer of thanksgiving over a cup of wine, called the "cup of blessing"; Paul borrows this phrase in describing the cup of the Lord's Supper: "Is not the cup of blessing which we bless a sharing [*koinōnia*] in the blood of Christ?" (1 Cor. 10:16, NASB). Like the common loaf, the cup of the Eucharist is a token of a deeper communion in the death of Christ, symbolized by his blood.

Eucharistic Symbols: The Bread and the Cup. The bread and the cup together are the visual tokens of the Lord's Supper, physical objects that do not stand in isolation but are part of a larger whole, a corporate act of worship that is the real sacramental symbol. It is significant that in the New Testament accounts of the institution of the Last Supper it is not the *wine* but the *cup* of which Jesus speaks. Had he spoken of the wine itself, the focus would be on the *substance,* a visual representation of his literal blood. In focusing on the cup, Jesus calls attention instead to the *action* by which his assembled worshipers are to memorialize and represent his death. The bread, which bore less resemblance to his physical body, could be mentioned directly without compromising the deeper symbolism intended. When the second-century church began to produce visual symbols, one of the favorite motifs in catacomb frescoes was the symbol of the Eucharist; typically it took the form, not of the loaf and cup, but of the *loaves and fish* of the feeding of the multitude (John 6:4-14), with the chalice of wine sometimes faintly visible in the background (Walter Lowrie, *Art in the Early Church,* 2nd ed. [New York: Harper Torchbooks, 1965], plate 13).

The Cross

The church did not use the cross as a visual symbol until around the fifth century A.D. In the New Testament, the cross is a physical object, the instrument of Jesus' execution. But it is also a word picture in apostolic teaching, and Jesus spoke of it symbolically.

Appearance of the Cross. The shape of the cross on which Jesus died is unknown. The Greek word *stauros* indicates the instrument of crucifixion but not necessarily the arrangement of "crossed" wooden beams that has become familiar from later Christian art, the so-called Latin cross. Although the Romans may have used crosses in this form, crucifixion was usually on a simple vertical stake without a cross arm. Several New Testament passages speak of Christ's death on a "tree" (*xulon,* Acts 5:30; Gal. 3:13; 1 Pet. 2:24) in fulfillment of Deuteronomy 21:22, suggesting a wooden stake.

Use of the cross as a visual symbol originated in paganism; it is found throughout the ancient world in cultures that preceded the Christian era. A common cross in the eastern Mediterranean world was that used in the worship of the god Tammuz. The symbol of Tammuz was the initial letter of his name, the Greek letter *tau,* shaped like a "T," with a circle over it representing the sun. Along with many pagan symbols and customs, the "T" cross and other cross symbols eventually passed into Christian usage, introducing the horizontal arm.

The Cross As Instrument of Execution. Roman officials used the cross as a means of execution in certain cases. An especially cruel method of torture and punishment, crucifixion was the penalty for acts of rebellion against authority, such as the revolt of slaves or of subject nations. The victim hung on the cross might linger for several days, alternating between periods of half-consciousness and agonizing pain. Josephus, the Jewish historian who deserted to the Romans during the revolt of A.D. 66-70, tells of encountering several of his friends, crucified, while traveling with the Roman commander; at his request the men were taken down, and some survived. The Jewish method of capital punishment was not crucifixion but stoning; however, the apostolic preaching of Acts holds the Jewish authorities ultimately responsible for the crucifixion of Jesus, with the Romans as their willing agents (Acts 2:23, 36; 3:13-15; 4:10).

Jesus' Use of the Symbolism of the Cross. In the discourse recorded in Matthew 16:21-28, Jesus predicted his own suffering at the hands of the religious establishment. When Peter protested, Jesus replied, "If anyone would come after me, he must deny himself and take up his cross and follow me" (Matt. 16:24). In this imagery, the "cross" does not mean trials and problems in general, but _persecution_ for the sake of the kingdom of God, as the context of Jesus' words makes clear. The cross is emblematic of the truth that one must "lose his life" in the present order of things in order to gain it in the new order to come (Matt. 16:25-26). Those entering the new order are considered traitors to the old institutions and are made the objects of abuse, a theme found elsewhere in Jesus' teaching (for example, Matt. 5:10-12; John 15:18-20) and throughout the New Testament. The author of Hebrews, for instance, reminds his readers that Jesus "suffered outside the city gate," adding, "let us, then, go out to him outside the camp, bearing the disgrace he bore" (Heb. 13:12-13). According to Jesus, the new kingdom is to make its appearance while some of those hearing his words are still living (Matt. 16:27-28), suggesting that the events of A.D. 70, the destruction of Jerusalem and its temple, are pivotal. At that time the victory of the one crucified will be manifest, and the persecuted of the new order will prevail over their persecutors of the old.

The Cross in Apostolic Teaching. Thus, in the proclamation and teaching of the apostles, the cross stands not only for Jesus' suffering, but also for his triumph over the forces opposed to the kingdom of God. Paul, in a remarkable turnabout of symbolism, declares that it is _Jesus_ who nails to the cross "the certificate of debt consisting of decrees against us and which was hostile to us"; in the cross, Jesus exposed and disarmed the "rulers and authorities" of the old system which had held people captive "through philosophy and empty deception, according to the tradition of men" (Col. 2:8-15, NASB). The powers of the old order, "the rulers of this age, who are passing away," were defeated when they "crucified the Lord of glory" (1 Cor. 2:6-8, NASB). It is not the cross, but the identity of the one crucified, which is the _crucial_ factor. In taking upon himself the curse of the old covenant (Gal. 3:13), the Son of God cancelled its effect, making it possible for both Jew and Gentile to enter the new covenant by faith (Gal. 3:22). "By making peace through his blood shed on the cross," Jesus has reconciled all people to God the Father (Col. 1:19-22). The cross of Christ, then, is his victory, one reality with his resurrection and exaltation, all summed up in Jesus' words: "But I, when I am _lifted up from the earth,_ will draw all men to myself" (John 12:32, italics added).

The preaching of the cross is an offense. The image of an instrument of torture is not a pretty one, nor is the message of the cross the clever and entertaining speech of the polished orator. To the world it is offensive and foolish (1 Cor. 1:17-23). But this is exactly the potency of the cross as a verbal image. As a mere image, the cross may degenerate into a decoration, a repetitive ornamental motif, or a magical talisman. In itself it is insignificant, unintelligible, even repulsive. As a true symbol, however, it can only direct _beyond itself_ to the reality it represents, and that is its power.

Janice and Richard Leonard

FIVE

The Concept of Covenant in Biblical Worship

Israel's worship was the celebration of a relationship between the Lord and his people, called the covenant. The biblical covenant was similar in form to treaties that were in common use in the ancient Near East and which were thus part of the cultural background for the Scriptures. A knowledge of the structure and terminology of the ancient treaty-covenant is, therefore, essential to the full understanding of biblical theology and worship.

125 • THE COVENANT BASIS OF BIBLICAL WORSHIP

Central to biblical worship is the covenant or agreement between God and the people of God. The covenant regulates worship and provides much of its structure, rationale, and vocabulary.

Function of the Covenant

The treaty or covenant was a political format for maintaining relationships without the use of force. It was used extensively in ancient Near Eastern culture to define acceptable modes of behavior among city-states and also between individuals. Although Israel's pagan neighbors were familiar with covenants as political treaties, they did not enter into covenant with their gods, who were undependable and treacherous and could not be held to any sort of agreement. A treaty between political states could be imposed by a strong ruler, known as the "lord" in covenant parlance, upon a weaker, known as the "servant"; or a weaker king might petition the stronger to grant a treaty for purposes of protection, since these pacts were primarily military agreements. Under the terms of such treaties, the lord is bound to protect the servant, and the servant is required to give allegiance to his lord alone; he must make no alliances with any other king and must fight together with his own lord against all his lord's enemies. He must also treat other client kings who are in covenant with his lord as brothers, and he cannot harm them or invade their territories. In addition, he must appear before his lord at specified times to bring tribute.

Israel's worship of Yahweh was based on this concept, which came to regulate and define its worship practices. This had been true for the patriarchs Abraham, Isaac, and Jacob, and it would eventually be true for the Christian church. It is the covenant that provides the basis for, and is the essence of, the relationship between the Lord God and his people. Through its framework they learn his ways, pledge their allegiance to him, and respond to him in worship. Worship at Sinai would take the form of the enactment of the covenant; the covenant would then provide regulations and a structure for worship.

Basic Covenant Structure

Political covenants, or treaties, were drawn up according to a specific pattern. They began with a *historical prologue,* in which the lord, or "great king," identified himself and often narrated the history of his relationship with the client king. He then indicated the boundaries of the *territory* he was granting to the servant king. This was followed by a statement of *stipulations* incumbent upon his partner and a listing of *sanctions:* blessing that would follow obedience to the stipulations and curses that would follow any violations of them. The servant king took an *oath;* the lord usually did not, for his reputation, or "name," was sufficient guarantee that he would honor the pact. *Witnesses* were invoked, not only to listen to the terms of the treaty, but also to carry out its sanctions. Witnesses always included the gods of both covenant partners and frequently heaven and earth, rocks, mountains, or other natural elements. Although Israel, like its pagan neighbors, had viewed the gods as being attached to specific territories, it came to understand Yahweh as the God of the whole land, whose territory was not localized and whose dominion extended to all nations (Josh. 3:11).

Covenants occasionally incorporated a *sign,* such as a physical scar, to remind the partners of their treaty obligations. For Israel the sign of circumcision was such an identifying mark, as were the keeping of the Sabbath and the observance of the Passover Feast (Josh. 5:2-5; Exod. 13:6-9; 31:13). The people of the servant king are viewed as having been *formed* by the lord through the covenant, and because the ancients customarily named whatever they made, the servant king or nation is often *renamed* by the lord as a sign of his ownership. Through the prophet Isaiah God says, "But now, thus says the LORD, your Creator, O Jacob, and He who formed you, O Israel, 'Do not fear, for I have redeemed you; I have called you by name; you are Mine!'" (Isa. 43:1, NASB).

Within the written text of the treaty itself, the granter laid down requirements for the periodic reading of its words to the servant people. This reading was to be done in the language with which they were familiar; there could be no plea of ignorance in the event of a violation. In addition, the covenant partners made provision for the document to be *permanently stored,* usually in the shrine of the most powerful god witness, as a reminder of its stipulations.

Ratifying the Covenant

The ceremony of ratification that usually accompanied the making of a covenant often included a blood *sacrifice.* Partners walked between the cut pieces of the animal (hence the Hebrew expression *karat bᵉrit,* "cut a covenant") or were sprinkled with its blood in order to identify with it. Implied in this exercise was the thought, "God do so to me, and more also, if I violate the terms of this treaty." A biblical example of this ceremony is the covenant God made with Abram (Gen. 15). Ratification could also be achieved with a *meal* shared by the covenant partners. Typically this involved drinking the blood of the sacrificed animal and eating its flesh. Since

the worshipers of Yahweh were prohibited from consuming blood, wine was substituted in their ceremonies. Again, identification with the sacrificial animal was the underlying theme of this ritual. A third ceremony appears in the covenant made between David and Jonathan and is alluded to in other biblical narratives (Isa. 22:21; 61:10; Ruth 3:9). Jonathan removes his *coat* and places it on David, identifying himself with his friend. He also gives David his *weapons* belt, as if to say, "Your enemies are my enemies; I obligate myself to fight for you" (1 Sam. 18:1-4).

Covenant Terminology

A number of technical terms that adhere to the covenant process are common in the Bible. The covenant *lord* is also the *king,* or frequently *the great king* (2 Kings 18:19), in contrast to the *servant,* who is also a king, albeit of lesser stature. The great king is sometimes called the *shepherd,* and his servants are known as *sheep.* The great king is a father and lord (Mal. 1:6), and all servants in covenant with the same king are known as *brothers.* The phrase *heaven and earth* refers to covenant witnesses; when biblical writers speak of their end or passing away (Isa. 34:4; Matt. 24:35; Rev. 6:14; 21:1, 4; cf. 2 Cor. 5:17), they are declaring that the covenant witnessed by them has been broken and will no longer be in effect.

Ancient treaties refer to the covenant stipulations and sanctions as the *words.* The Ten Commandments (Exod. 20:1-17), which constitute the text of the treaty between Yahweh and Israel, are known in Hebrew as "these words" (*dᵉvarim*). Therefore, keeping the words of the Lord, or hiding them in one's heart, means memorizing and giving attention to the text of the covenant. The *land ('eretz)* promised in Scripture to the patriarchs is the territory granted by Yahweh in his covenant with Israel. *'Eretz* can also be translated as "earth," meaning ground or soil, but rarely indicates the global earth, since the ancients had no such concept. To *know* (Jer. 10:25), to *follow after* (Deut. 13:4), and to *love* (Deut. 11:22-23) are all terms that describe loyalty to the lord of the covenant. *Mercy (ḥesed),* sometimes translated as "lovingkindness" or "steadfast love" in English versions, is favor based on the covenant, rather than a general attitude of benevolence. For the people of God, then, *ḥesed* is God's protection and care, based on his covenant relationship with them; the best translation is "covenant love."

Justice, faithfulness, and *righteousness* all indicate a fulfillment of covenant stipulations, whereas *judgment* is the taking effect of the sanctions (Deut. 6:25). References to *warfare* or to *deliverance,* or the use of the term *savior* (deliverer), all indicate that the writer has the covenant in mind, since it is the covenant lord who goes to war in the role of savior to deliver the servant people. *Peace* is a condition the granter promises in return for the servant's obedience. It is not defined as an absence of trouble *per se,* but is, specifically, the great king's protection of his servant from outside invaders or from attack by the lord himself. In a larger sense, peace is *salvation.* The word is *shalom* and connotes the blessing of the covenant granter and the resultant wholeness of the entire person or nation. *Shalom* is the essence of the covenant relationship.

Ancient Hittite and Egyptian treaties make extensive use of the number seven, as does the covenant between Yahweh and Israel. Significantly, the Hebrew word for "swear," *nishba',* literally translated is "to seven oneself." Thus, in Israel, a person could not take a covenant oath without using the number seven. This has important implications for the understanding of many parts of the biblical literature, such as the Revelation to John, as covenant documents.

126 • COVENANT WORSHIP IN ISRAEL

Although the Lord had granted the covenant to the patriarchs of Israel, the covenant at Mount Sinai was a new departure in the people's relationship to God. The covenant established the structure of the worship of Israel as a distinct people and formed the basis for the prophetic word and the ongoing religious life of the community.

Israel's History Begins with the Covenant

The children of Israel, who became the people of Yahweh, were essentially pagans. Although the Lord had appeared to their ancestors and entered into covenant with them, the nation of slaves in Egypt worshiped the same gods their heathen neighbors revered. This is not surprising, in view of the prevailing belief of the times that the jurisdiction of the various deities was confined to a specific geographic location. Those residing in Egypt, for example, paid tribute to whatever gods governed that territory.

The Pharaoh's objection is understandable, therefore, when Moses requested that the Hebrews be allowed to go into the desert to worship Yahweh, who was not an Egyptian god. The request had dangerous implications, for it revealed a conflict of interests. If the Hebrews were to declare allegiance to a god who reigned in the desert, they might decide it would be to their advantage to go to live in his territory. And whose god would ultimately be in charge—the God of the Hebrews or the gods of Egypt?

The idea was a novel one for the Hebrews as well. If the God of their fathers truly intended to break the yoke of Egypt from their backs, it might be in their best interests to follow Moses into the desert and sacrifice to this Yahweh. On the other hand, who could be sure that he was stronger than the gods of Egypt, especially on their own territory?

Convinced by the mighty miracles the Lord performed, the Hebrews and a large company of Egyptian converts began their trek to Mount Sinai to worship. But they soon discovered that the kind of worship Yahweh required differed from the pagan practices to which they were accustomed. The basis for the relationship was distinctively different. This new worship was to be a response to their God's mighty acts of deliverance on their behalf, not the placating of a capricious deity who could at any moment withhold his favor and do them harm. Although the covenant Yahweh was to make with them in the desert had its roots in his pact made with Abraham and affirmed with Isaac and Jacob, history for Israel as a worshiping community really begins with the Red Sea deliverance from Egyptian slavery and the subsequent act of worship at the mountain of God. In these events, the God who had entered into a covenant with their ancestor Abraham would now extend that covenant to the entire family of Abraham's descendants, and to others as well.

The Covenant at Sinai

The agreement the Lord granted Israel on Mount Sinai has the same essential structure as that of the ancient treaty, which described the previous relationship of the treaty partners and then laid down the requirements of the new relationship being enacted. Since, for Israel as a whole, the history of Yahweh's dealings with the nation really begins in the Exodus from Egypt, the *historical prologue* of the covenant also begins at that point; Yahweh, as the great King (Pss. 47:2; 95:3; Mal. 1:14; Matt. 5:35) granting the treaty, identifies himself as the one who has delivered his people from slavery (Exod. 19:4; 20:1-2). The *stipulations* are, of course, the ten *words* or commandments (Exod. 20:2-17), the basic requirement being total loyalty to Yahweh and a prohibition against alliances with any other authority. Covenant *sanctions,* in the form of *blessings* and *cursings,* do not appear as such in the Sinai narrative but are found in Leviticus (Lev. 26) and in Deuteronomy (Deut. 28–29), Moses' great reiteration of the covenant just before Israel enters the land of Canaan, the *territory* granted in the treaty.

These treaty formalities, however, do not obscure the fact that the Sinai covenant is in the first instance an act of *worship,* an act of reverent submission to one who reveals himself in majesty and power. The narrative introducing the actual granting of the covenant is filled with the imagery of theophany, the divine self-revelation of the Lord in thunder, lightning, smoke, the sound of the trumpet (Exod. 19:16-19). Yahweh has called his people to be his worshipers, a kingdom of priests (Exod. 19:6). The enactment and ratification of the covenant are acts of worship; the covenant is sealed as the people are sprinkled with the blood of the *sacrifice* and the elders ascend Sinai to eat and drink the *covenant meal* with Yahweh (Exod. 24:8-11). Instructions are given for the creation of the altar and the tabernacle, a sanctuary at which the covenant may be remembered and maintained through ongoing ceremonies (Exod. 25–27). The tablets containing the covenant *text* are deposited in the ark of witness and placed in the tabernacle's inner sanctuary, the shrine of Yahweh. Just as a "great king" granting a covenant to his vassal required the latter to appear in his courts at specified intervals to bring whatever tribute was agreed upon at the making of the covenant, so Israel is required to *appear before the Lord* for this purpose, to "bring an offering and come into his courts" (Ps. 96:8). These appearances are three annual festivals stipulated in the Pentateuch's festival calendars (Exod. 23:14-17; Lev. 23; Deut. 16:1-17), times of rejoicing and celebration in the presence of the Lord.

The Covenant Formulary

The covenant between God and Israel is frequently distilled into a short formulary—"I will be their God and they shall be my people" (Gen. 17:7; Lev. 26:12, 45; Deut. 29:10-13; and others). This phrase is found in various forms throughout the writings of the prophets (Isa. 51:15-16; Jer. 31:1, 33; Ezek. 11:20; 37:27; Zech. 8:8; 13:9) as they warn the people of Judah of the judgment that will surely follow their violation of the covenant stipulations. The formula is a basic definition of the relationship that was to exist between God and Israel. Henceforth, Yahweh would be identified with this particular nation—he would be known as their God, the God of Israel. His name would be upon them, as signified by the circumcision of their bodies. They, in turn, were to be exclusively his people. In response to his protection and blessing they must give him their undivided loyalty and complete obedience. They must love the Lord with all that they are and everything they possess (Deut. 6:4-5) and demonstrate that love through joyous and festive worship; they must also love one another as brothers (Lev. 19:18) because they are all in covenant with the same God.

Covenant Liturgics: Sacrifice, Festivals, Declamations

The worship through which Israel expressed its loyalty to the Lord took the form of sacrifice, festivals, and various forms of verbal expression or declamation. The Israelite worshiper brought sacrificial offerings to the designated sanctuary, where the priests offered them on the altar. Elements of the offering differed according to the purpose of the sacrifice. The daily sacrifices included an animal to be burned whole, grain or flour, and wine. Offerings brought to atone for violation of the law were always animals, with the blood used for ceremonial cleansing ceremonies. On festal occasions the major portion of the offering was given back to the worshiper after a certain amount was taken out for the use of the priest. On these occasions the people were viewed as receiving Yahweh's own food; thus, he hosted them at his table in a reaffirmation of the covenant relationship. The Passover sacrifice, in particular, was understood in this way, as it called to remembrance the miraculous Red Sea deliverance that had formed Israel into the people of God. In the same manner, the Christian covenant meal, the Lord's Supper, recalls God's deliverance of his own through the death and resurrection of Christ. The festivals were a fulfillment of Israel's obligation to enter the courts of the Lord to rejoice and give thanks to him.

Accompanying, and at times even displacing, the sacrifice of animals or grain was the "sacrifice of thanksgiving" or praise (Ps. 116:17; cf. Pss. 40:6-10; 50:7-15; 51:16-17). This outpouring of praise was principally a musical offering of tribute to the God of the covenant, and the Psalms are the literary deposit of this activity. In addition to sacrifice, other aspects of the covenant structure find expression in utterance associated with worship. At the offering of the firstfruits, for example, the Israelite worshipers are to confess their faith in the form of a historical recital of Yahweh's deliverance in the Exodus (Deut. 26:1-10). Joshua recited the history of Yahweh's deeds in behalf of Israel in leading the people in a renewal of the covenant at Shechem (Josh. 24:2-13). We often find such recitations in the Psalms (for example, Ps. 136).

The laws of the covenant were sometimes arranged in metrical groups, suitable for recitation in worship (Exod. 21:12, 15-17; 22:18-22; 23:1-9; 34:11-26; Lev. 18:7-18; Deut. 27:15-26), and the Psalms suggest that they were so used (Pss. 50:16; 81:10). The covenant sanctions could also be recited in worship, as with some of the material in the blessings and curses of Deuteronomy (Deut. 28:2-6, 15-19); Moses' final songs (Deut. 32:1-43; 33:2-29) are musical settings of such material. The prophets of Israel seem to have typically delivered their pronouncements of judgment at the sanctuaries (Isa. 6:1-13; Jer. 7:1-2; Amos 7:10-13), perhaps in association with the festivals when large groups of worshipers would be present (Isa. 1:10-15; Amos 5:21-24; Mic. 6:6-8); the speeches of the prophets are really an extension of the curse element of the covenant ceremony. Occasionally in the Psalms we hear the prophetic voice of judgment (Pss. 14; 50; 95:8-11).

The Covenant Lawsuit

This distinctive form of prophetic address deserves special attention because of its roots in the covenant worship of Israel. As the spokesmen (Hebrew *navi'*) for Yahweh, the prophets defended the covenant whenever Israel broke its vows of loyalty and drifted into idolatry. Acting as lawyers for Yahweh, the plaintiff, they brought formal charges against Israel for unfaithfulness, in what has been called the "covenant lawsuit" (Hebrew *riv*). Examples can be found in Deuteronomy 32:1-43; Isaiah 1:1-31; Micah 6:1-16; Jeremiah 2:1–3:5; 34:12-22; and Hosea 4:1-3. In these indictments the Lord, through the prophet, typically protests his own faithfulness to the covenant. He has brought the people of Israel out of bondage and established them in the land he promised them. He has protected them from curses and evil. Israel, however, has not kept the covenant. Yahweh lists their violations: the people have gone into idolatry and forgotten their King; they have oppressed the poor and enslaved their countrymen; they have not observed the Sabbath. The nation is called by the Lord to account for its sins before the covenant witnesses: mountains (Mic. 6:2), heaven (Deut. 32:1; Isa. 1:2; Jer. 2:12), and earth (Deut. 32:1; Isa. 1:2; Mic. 6:2). Because the covenant is legally binding, and the witnesses attest to its violation, Israel has no defense. Therefore, the prophets pronounce judgment on the unfaithful nation. Eventually they come to see the covenant as irrevocably broken. Only a small proportion of the people are faithful to Yahweh. Enactment of the curse of the covenant is inevitable: the nation will be invaded and taken captive to be resettled in other lands. As Micah says, "Her wound is incurable" (Mic. 1:9).

Covenant Renewal

A nation that refused to keep the terms of a covenant in the ancient world ran the risk of being invaded and punished by its lord. The gods were also expected to avenge covenant violations with poor crops, drought, famine, pestilence, and other punishments. God's covenant with Israel also incorporated a list of curses that would follow its violation, and it was he who would mete out the punishment. Throughout the history of Israel there were periods in which the covenant with Yahweh was neglected or forgotten entirely. Frequently these lapses resulted in God's judgment on the nation. Kings of both Israel and Judah, who set the religious standard for the nation, led the people into the worship of pagan deities. However, God raised up righteous prophets, priests, and kings who led the nation in a series of covenant renewals, reinstituting the worship of Yahweh according to the stated requirements of the covenant.

The book of Deuteronomy is an example of covenant renewal in the form of a farewell address given by Moses as he prepares to die and as the nation embarks on the conquest of Canaan under Joshua's leadership. Later, Joshua leads the people in an act of covenant renewal (Josh. 24:1-28) just before his own death. After consulting the Book of the Covenant to ascertain the "due order" for the worship of Yahweh (1 Chron. 15:13), King David appoints musicians to worship in Zion before the ark of the covenant in rotating shifts, twenty-four hours a day, to renew and maintain the covenant in the sacrifice of praise and thanksgiving; many of the psalms had their origin in this setting. At the dedication of the temple in Jerusalem, King Solomon led Israel in a festival of covenant renewal (1 Kings 8:1–9:9). Kings Josiah (2 Chron. 34:15–35:19) and Hezekiah (2 Chron. 29:1–31:21) also attempted to restore the covenant by reading its stipulations to the people and commanding that it be celebrated with a covenant meal. Ezra the priest and Nehemiah the governor renewed the covenant with the remnant of Israel who returned to the land from their captivity in Babylon (Ezra 9:1–10:19; Neh. 12:26–13:31).

The New Covenant

In the view of the prophets, the only possible remedy for Israel's dilemma is the cutting of a new covenant. Not with rebels will this new covenant be made, but only with a believing remnant, which will eventually be saved out of captivity and returned to the land. They will seek the Lord and remain faithful to him. In this way, the covenant people will survive and not be entirely cut off; the nation will have a future. To this remnant the law will be a delight; it will be written on their hearts, not just on stone tablets (Jer. 31:31-34). This people will show forth the glory of Yahweh in covenant worship.

The blessedness that God's people will experience under the new covenant is described by the prophets in typical covenant terms as a reverse of the curses (Jer. 32:42). Instead of famine there will be prosperity (Isa. 54:2); in place of invasion will be peace and joy (Isa. 55:12; Jer. 33:16); the voice of bridegroom and bride will be returned to the land (Jer. 33:11); wild animals will no longer be a threat but will become harmless (Isa. 11:6-8). The new covenant will come in the form of a person, whom Isaiah calls "the servant" (Isa. 42:1-3, 6-7) and describes as the one who suffers (Isa. 52:13-14; 53:1-6). In the end, Yahweh's covenant with Israel requires an obedience that only Jesus, the Servant of God, can fulfill (Matt. 12:18-21).

127 • COVENANT WORSHIP IN THE NEW TESTAMENT

In the New Testament, the concept of covenant is often subsumed under other metaphors that describe the relationship between the Lord and his people. The most important of these is the "kingdom of God," which was the primary theme of Jesus' teaching and preaching. The new Israel is also called God's temple (Eph. 2:21; 1 Cor. 3:16-17), Christ's body (Rom. 12:4; 1 Cor. 10:17; 12:12-27; Eph. 2:16; 4:15-16), and the city of God (Matt. 5:14; Rev. 21–22). The numerous references to God as Father, to believers as brothers, and to the church as a household portray the church in terms of a family. There are, however, many references to the covenant itself. The brief covenant formulary of the Old Testament—I will be their God and they shall be my people—is applied to the church by several New Testament writers (Heb. 11:16; 1 Pet. 2:10; Rev. 21:3).

Covenant in the Gospels and Acts

The Gospels narrate the coming of the Servant. In some cases they explicitly state that the stories they tell verify Jesus' fulfillment of prophecy; at other times, they simply recount events that make it obvious. In his teaching, Jesus appears as a spokesman for the covenant in much the same way as Moses is portrayed in the Pentateuch. For example, in response to a questioner he states the basic requirements of the covenant in language borrowed from Moses (Deut. 6:4; Lev. 19:18); the stipulations to love the Lord with one's entire being and to be loyal to one's brother servant of the Lord lie at the heart of the concept of the treaty-covenant (Mark 12:30-31).

The Gospels present the events of Jesus' passion and crucifixion in order to make the point that he fulfills the old covenant and institutes a new one. On the night of his arrest, Jesus offers the new covenant to his disciples in the upper room. The Lord's Supper, or Eucharist, is the Christian "Passover," or covenant meal (Matt. 26:26-29); it calls to the remembrance of the new Israel its deliverance by the sacrifice of Christ, the Passover Lamb (1 Cor. 5:7). As Christians eat the body and drink the blood of the sacrifice, they reaffirm their covenant relationship with the Lord in an act of worship.

At Jesus' death on the cross, the rending of the temple veil discloses the absence of the ark of the covenant in the temple; the Lord of hosts is no longer with the old institutions but with his new people of the kingdom. Clearly, the Gospel writers intend to emphasize that Jesus fulfills all the Old Testament prophecies that relate to the coming of the Messiah, or anointed Servant, in whom the covenant of the great King is fully realized. This theme is continued in the preaching of the apostolic church. In his sermon after the healing of the lame man, Peter tells the Jews gathered at the temple that all the prophecies from that of Samuel onward were fulfilled in the life, death, and resurrection of Jesus of Nazareth, the Servant of God (Acts 3:24).

——— Covenant in the Epistles of Paul ———

Paul's letters are replete with references to the covenant; indeed, his working out of the theology of salvation through Jesus Christ cannot be adequately understood apart from an understanding of covenant terminology.

Romans. From the outset, Paul's letter to the Romans has the covenant as its underlying theme. Worship, the acknowledgment of God's sovereignty over all things, is a requirement laid upon all people; those who refuse to give thanks to God are given up, or excluded from the covenant, becoming subject to its curses (Rom. 1:21-24). Paul picks up the imagery of marriage with Yahweh, which the Israelite prophets used as an analogy to the covenant, in order to explain the end of the old economy and the onset of the new. A marriage, he tells the Romans, is in force only as long as both partners are alive. If one dies, the other is free from his covenant and can legitimately marry another. A person who has acknowledged Jesus as Lord has identified with him in his death, becoming, as it were, dead along with Christ, in order to be raised with him into a new life. Thus Christian baptism, as an act of worship, has profound covenantal foundations. The death of the believer with Christ renders him free from the old covenant and places him within the new covenant nation, or bride of Christ (Rom. 7:4). The old covenant was not able to produce righteousness, being only a picture of the new, in which Jesus Christ, who embodies the covenant, becomes righteousness for the believer. This righteousness, the life that embodies the covenant, shines through the church to the world, as God's people "walk not after the flesh, but after the Spirit" (Rom. 8:4, KJV).

Paul uses the olive tree as a figure for the blending of the old and new covenants in Jesus. Gentiles who acknowledge Jesus as Lord are grafted into the tree alongside believing Jews. Together they make up the people of God under the new covenant. Blindness has come upon part of the Jewish people until the full proportion of Gentiles can be grafted into the olive tree. "And so [that is, 'in this way'] *all* Israel [both Jews and Gentiles] will be saved" (Rom. 11:26, italics added). Using an image taken from Old Testament symbolism of the exchange of clothing in a covenant, Paul urges his readers to "clothe yourselves with the Lord Jesus Christ," as one wears a garment (Rom. 13:14). He summarizes by admonishing both groups to receive one another and be like-minded in order to glorify God as one people (Rom. 15:5-12).

Corinthians. The remarkable passage in 2 Corinthians 6:14–7:1, which appears to break the continuity of thought in its context, may be a fragment from an earlier letter of Paul's, mentioned in 1 Corinthians 5:9. The thrust of this passage is that Christians are to separate from unbelievers. Paul presents this admonition in the form of a prophetic declaration of the covenant, in the name of "the Lord Almighty" (2 Cor. 6:16-18), which makes use of a chain of quotations from the Hebrew Scriptures. Here the Lord declares that he will dwell among his people, citing the covenant formulary—I will be their God, and they shall be my people (Lev. 26:12; Ezek. 37:27). He then summons his people to separate from uncleanness and to be gathered to him (Isa. 52:11). Extending the language of the Davidic covenant to all his people, the Lord declares that he will be their Father (2 Sam. 7:14), and they shall be his sons (Hos. 1:10) and daughters. Paul's Corinthian readers would have understood the covenant terminology underlying this passage, for (contrary to what is often said) the Corinthian church was mainly a Jewish congregation (cf. Acts 18:1-17).

Galatians. In his letter to the Galatians, Paul makes a particularly strong statement about the old and new covenants. Certain teachers who would require Christians to return to the old covenant were creating problems in Galatia, and Paul writes to address the subject. He uses the terms "the Law" and "Book of the Law" to refer to the old covenant and says that it cannot bring people into relationship with God. Even those who are born Jews, he asserts, cannot come to the Father except through Christ; how much less those who are Gentiles to begin with (Gal. 2:15-16).

Paul goes on to refer to Abraham, who was justified, or placed in a covenant relationship with the

Lord, through faith and not through observing regulations. The law that came later could not invalidate God's covenant with Abraham, which promised that in him all nations of the earth would be blessed (Gal. 3:17). The promise was made, Paul explains, to Abraham's "seed" and not his "seeds," and that "seed" (singular) is Jesus Christ. The old covenant was to serve only until the Seed came (Gal. 3:19), but it was not the promised blessing. The Seed comes to both Jews and Gentiles, because both are under sin and need the anointed Servant to be the covenant on their behalf. When a person is baptized into Christ, he or she is clothed with Christ (Gal. 3:27); here Paul again refers to the exchange of clothing in the enactment of a covenant. As a result of being clothed with Christ in the new relationship, no physical distinctions remain, whether of race, gender, or social status (Gal. 3:28-29). Paul uses the analogy of Hagar and Sarah to illustrate that the children of the promise are those who are born into the covenant relationship through faith, while the earthly Jerusalem and its old covenant inhabitants are children of the slave girl and will not inherit the promises (Gal. 4:21-31).

Ephesians and Colossians. Writing to the church in Ephesus, Paul adopts the style of the Hebraic blessing, a form of worship ascribing honor to the Lord; the hymnic quality of the opening passage is marked by the recurring refrain "to the praise of his glory" (Eph. 1:12, 14; cf. 1:6). He reminds the Ephesians that the people God has chosen to create and adopt are those redeemed by Jesus Christ, both Jews and Gentiles together. Both groups are in need of God's life-giving power. Jesus Christ himself has broken down the wall between Jew and Gentile and united them in a new creation. This created people is the mystery that Paul has been commissioned to make known; this was God's plan from the beginning, "his eternal purpose which [God] accomplished in Christ Jesus our Lord" (Eph. 3:11). The church, or "new man," is the culmination and crown of the new creation, just as mankind was in the old. It represents God's ultimate and eternal purpose in the earth. As he concludes, Paul uses the image of the exchange of weaponry between covenant partners; he presents his readers with a listing of the armor of God and admonishes them to wear it in their battles against the enemy (Eph. 6:10-17).

Paul assures the Colossians that they exhibit the sign of the covenant, a spiritual circumcision made

evident by water baptism (Col. 2:11-15). They should not submit to the regulations of the old covenant, which is only a shadow of the reality that is Christ (Col. 2:16-23).

Covenant in Hebrews

The letter to the Hebrews is dedicated almost entirely to a discussion of the new covenant (see especially Heb. 8:1-13). The writer identifies Jesus as the one who has appeared "in these last days" (Heb. 1:2) and has been appointed heir of all things. He is the "firstborn," or King (Heb. 1:6, 8), who has "provided purification for sins" (Heb. 1:3) as the covenant sacrifice and is the anointed Servant (Heb. 1:9) who was promised. He calls those in the new covenant "brothers" (Heb. 2:11-18); he is the seed of Abraham (Heb. 2:16) and the builder of God's house (Heb. 3:1-6). He embodies the Sabbath, the rest that is promised to God's people (Heb. 3:18–4:11). Jesus is our high priest (Heb. 5:1–8:6) who administers the new covenant (Heb. 8:6ff.). This new covenant is the one of which the prophets spoke, wherein all its adherents would know the Lord (Heb. 8:8-12). It takes the place of the old covenant, completely absorbing and superseding it (Heb. 8:13ff.). Christ is the covenant sacrifice (Heb. 9:24-28), removing by his death the need for animal sacrifices under the law (Heb. 10:1-22). Again and again the writer of Hebrews contrasts the two covenants, emphasizing that the new is far superior to the old and has taken its place; by it one enters "Mount Zion," the "heavenly Jerusalem, the city of the living God," to an assembly of angels and of one "firstborn," to God the judge, and to Jesus the mediator of the new covenant (Heb. 12:18-24). Neither are the sacrificial ceremonies of the Jewish sanctuary relevant (Heb. 13:10-14); in place of animals, new covenant people are to "offer to God a sacrifice of praise—the fruit of lips that confess his name" (Heb. 13:15).

Covenant in the Revelation

The Revelation to John is a covenant document of the first magnitude, a dramatic portrayal of the enactment of the curses inherent in the covenant against the unfaithful. The proliferation of *sevens* is a clue to the book's covenant content, a reminder of the taking of a covenant oath, which in Hebrew is literally "to seven oneself." The Revelation is also a picture of covenant worship in the response of God's new people to his mighty acts of deliverance on their behalf. John has given the church a pattern to follow in his descriptions of the twenty-four elders falling down before the Lamb, the white-robed saints playing harps, and the great congregation shouting, "Hallelujah! For our Lord God Almighty reigns. Let us rejoice and be glad and give him glory!" (Rev. 19:6-7). In the worshiping church, "the holy city, new Jerusalem," the covenant finds fulfillment: "Now the dwelling of God is with men, and he will live with them. They will be his people, and God himself will be with them" (Rev. 21:3).

Jesus Is the Covenant

Summarizing the witness of the New Testament authors, we see that Jesus himself takes on all the elements of the covenant in order to keep it for those who are "in him." He is Servant (Phil. 2:7), Lord (Phil. 2:11), and Shepherd (Heb. 13:20-21). He is the witness to the covenant (Rev. 1:4-5). He is the covenant sanctions, the blessing (Eph. 1:3) and the curse (Gal. 3:13). He is the Word made flesh (John 1:1, 14), the text of the new covenant in a language able to be understood, now deposited in the temple of God (1 Cor. 3:16; Eph. 2:19-22). He is the sacrifice (1 Cor. 5:7) and the covenant meal (John 6:48-54), which enact the covenant. He is the garment put on in token of the covenant (Gal. 3:27). He is the sign (Luke 2:34), our peace (Eph. 2:14), and our righteousness (1 Cor. 1:30). He has formed his people (Eph. 2:10) and named them in order to establish ownership (Eph. 3:15). In grateful recognition of God's covenant blessing in the person of Jesus Christ, the church as his royal priesthood is commanded to demonstrate loyalty to the covenant through worship that brings glory to the Lord (1 Pet. 2:9-10).

The Covenants Compared

From Genesis to Revelation, the covenant theme shines through the Bible, sending out a clear light for the believer's walk with God. The covenant is the basis of God's dealings with creation in general and with his created people in particular. The old covenant with its regulations was a guardian over God's chosen people until Jesus came. Christ, the "last Adam," entered into covenant with the Father and keeps it on behalf of those who trust in him. All who are identified with him are also in covenant with God, having Jesus' righteousness imputed to them.

Under the Israelite covenant it was Moses' faithfulness through which Israel had access to Yahweh. Moses was the one who entered the presence of God, spoke with him face to face, and interceded for his rebellious and unfaithful nation (Exod. 32:1-14). This picture is fulfilled in the ministry of Jesus as mediator of the new covenant. His faithfulness ensures the covenant for those who remain in him. As Moses interceded for Israel, so Jesus intercedes for his church, he himself being the sacrifice that makes the intercession acceptable (Heb. 10:1-10).

Response to the Covenant

The covenant people are called to acknowledge God's kingship and to respond with worship. When Israel violated the covenant by abandoning the worship of Yahweh and turning to idols, God rejected his treaty with them and abandoned them to defeat and captivity. Covenant blessings were withdrawn, and curses were released on the people (Ps. 78:21-22, 58-64). When they worshiped in song and dance before the Lord, he brought prosperity and victory over their enemies (2 Chron. 20:18-22).

In giving the covenant, the Lord delivered instructions for worship, which was to have been the chosen people's special ministry to him. In fact, it was his original intention that the whole nation and not the tribe of Levi alone be a worshiping priesthood (Exod. 19:3-6). Although they drew back out of fear (Exod. 20:18-21; Deut. 5:23-27), the Lord instituted for Israel a system of worship by which they maintained their identity as his covenant people and through which they were to reflect his glory to the nations.

As in the covenant of Israel, so in the Christian covenant it is incumbent upon the recipients of God's covenant love to worship him. In describing life under the new covenant, Isaiah declares, "For as the soil makes the sprout come up and a garden causes seeds to grow, so the Sovereign LORD will make righteousness and praise spring up before all nations" (Isa. 61:11). The first act of the newborn church on the day of Pentecost was a spontaneous outpouring of praise, with the disciples "declaring the wonders of God" (Acts 2:11). Jesus told the Samaritan woman that God seeks worshipers (John 4:23). As the people of Israel expressed their praise and thanksgiving to God through joyous festivals, the church celebrates in the Christian Eucharist, or "thanksgiving" feast. Peter writes that the body of believers has been made into a people for the express purpose of "[declaring] the praises of him who called [them] out of darkness into his wonderful light" (1 Pet. 2:9). The worship of the covenant people delights the Lord, as the psalmist writes:

> Praise the LORD.
> Sing to the LORD a new song,
>   his praise in the assembly of the saints.

> Let Israel rejoice in their Maker;
>   let the people of Zion be glad in their King.
> Let them praise his name with dancing
>   and make music to him with tambourine
>   and harp.
> For the LORD takes delight in his people;
>   he crowns the humble with salvation.
>   (Ps. 149:1-4)

Janice E. Leonard[1]

SIX

Sacrifice in Biblical Worship

From the dawn of history until the destruction of the Jerusalem temple in A.D. 70, human beings erected altars and offered sacrifice to the Lord in acts of worship. Since only descendants of Aaron were allowed to officiate at Jewish sacrifices, and genealogical records were destroyed in the siege of Jerusalem, even Judaism abandoned the sacrificial system at that time. Christians, of course, understood the death of Christ as the supreme sacrifice, rendering all others obsolete.

128 • SACRIFICE IN ISRAELITE WORSHIP

Sacrifices were a part of the tribute the Israelite worshiper offered to the God of the covenant. The Pentateuch goes into great detail concerning the altar and the sanctuary as the setting for sacrifice and the various types of sacrifices that were enacted in the worship of Israel.

Purposes of Sacrifice

In biblical times, sacrifice often accompanied the making of covenants, as in the cases of Noah (Gen. 8:20—9:17), Abram (Gen. 15:1-21), Isaac (Gen. 26:24-25), Jacob (Gen. 31:43-55; 35:6-12), and Moses on behalf of Israel (Exod. 24:1-8). Sacrifice was also a means of receiving direction from God; military leaders sometimes sacrificed to the Lord before inquiring whether they should go into battle, and Balaam offered a series of sacrifices to the Lord in order to determine whether he might pronounce a curse on Israel (Num. 23:1-30). Upon ascending the throne, Solomon offered extensive sacrifices at the tabernacle in Gibeon that he might receive the Lord's guidance and wisdom to rule over Israel (2 Chron. 1:5-13). People also brought sacrificial offerings for purposes of thanksgiving, supplication, and atonement. Job was said to have made sacrifices on behalf of his children in case they had sinned against the Lord (Job 1:5).

Although grain, wine, and other foodstuffs were used in some offerings, the primary sacrifice was an unblemished animal. This was the only acceptable offering if the sacrifice were to atone for sin and may explain why the Lord refused Cain's offering of produce but accepted the lamb brought by Abel (Gen.

4:3-4). Noah offered clean animals as burnt offerings after the Flood (Gen. 8:20); it is interesting that he differentiated between clean and unclean beasts even at this early period, before the law of Moses was given.

Sacrificial Altars

The altar, as the place where sacrifice was offered, occupied a focal position in Israelite worship. Abraham, Isaac, and Jacob built altars to the Lord and made sacrifices, at which times it is often said that they "called upon the name of the LORD" (Gen. 12:8; 13:4; 22:9; 26:25; 33:20; 35:1). An altar could be built of earth or stones, but if stones were used they were to be rough and uncut (Exod. 20:25; Josh. 8:31). An altar built on behalf of the entire nation, as in the case of Elijah's altar on Mount Carmel (1 Kings 18:30-32), was often constructed of twelve stones, representing the Israelite tribes. Unlike pagan altars of the same period, no altar used by Israel was to have steps up to it; the omission was to prevent the priest and worshiper from inadvertently exposing themselves to the altar as they approached it (Exod. 20:26).

The Mosaic Tabernacle

From the giving of the Sinai covenant, the tabernacle or tent (*'ohel*), also called the "dwelling" (*mishkan*), was the central place of sacrifice for Israel; its functions were transferred to the temple or "house of the Lord" after its construction under Solomon. Both tabernacle and temple featured a three-stage approach to the presence of the Lord: the

OLD TESTAMENT SACRIFICES

Sacrifice	OT References	Elements	Purpose
Burnt Offering	Lev 1; 6:8-13; 8:18-21; 16:24	Bull, ram, or male bird (dove or young pigeon for poor); wholly consumed; no defect	Voluntary act of worship; atonement for unintentional sin in general; expression of devotion, commitment, and complete surrender to God
Grain Offering	Lev 2; 6:14-23	Grain, fine flour, olive oil, incense, baked bread (cakes or wafers), salt; no yeast or honey; accompanied burnt offering and fellowship offering (along with drink offering)	Voluntary act of worship; recognition of God's goodness and provisions; devotion to God
Offering of Well-Being	Lev 3; 7:11-34	Any animal without defect from herd or flock; variety of breads	Voluntary act of worship; thanksgiving and fellowship (it included a communal meal)
Sin Offering	Lev 4:1—5:13; 6:24-30; 8:14-17; 16:3-22	1. Young bull: for high priest and congregation 2. Male goat: for leader 3. Female goat or lamb: for common person 4. Dove or pigeon: for the poor 5. Tenth of an ephah of fine flour: for the very poor	Mandatory atonement for specific unintentional sin; confession of sin; forgiveness of sin; cleansing from defilement
Guilt Offering	Lev 5:14—6:7; 7:1-6	Ram or lamb	Mandatory atonement for unintentional sin requiring restitution; cleansing from defilement; make restitution; pay 20 percent fine

When more than one kind of offering was presented (as in Num. 7:16-17), the procedure was usually as follows: (1) sin offering or guilt offering, (2) burnt offering, (3) fellowship offering and grain offering (along with a drink offering). This sequence furnishes part of the spiritual significance of the sacrificial system. First sin had to be dealt with (sin offering or guilt offering). Second, the worshiper committed himself completely to God (burnt offering and grain offering). Third, fellowship or communion between the Lord, the priest, and the worshiper (fellowship offering) was established.

Harold Lindsell

outer court surrounded the sanctuary proper, or Holy Place (*miqdash, qodesh*), which in turn led to the Holy of Holies, or inner sanctuary. (For a more extensive discussion of the Mosaic tabernacle and sacrifices, see Chapter 12: *The Tabernacle of Moses,* p. 154.)

The Altar. The altar of burnt offering stood just within the entrance to the tabernacle courtyard. It was seven and one-half feet square and four and one-half feet high, constructed of acacia wood covered with brass, with a protruding horn at each corner. On this altar the priests burned the atonement offerings prescribed in the law of Moses. The altar of burnt offering was the first object a worshiper encountered when coming to the tabernacle; its prominent position was a reminder that sin must be dealt with as a matter of first priority.

The Sanctuary and Its Furnishings. Beyond the altar of burnt offering stood the laver, where the priests, who alone were allowed access to the tabernacle proper, washed both hands and feet before entering. The tabernacle structure itself was divided by a heavy, embroidered curtain into two rooms, the Holy Place, or sanctuary, and the Most Holy Place, or Holy of Holies. The sanctuary contained a seven-branched lamp made of gold, a golden table that held the consecrated bread for the priests, and the altar of incense, smaller by far than the brass altar outside and made of acacia wood covered with gold. At specified hours each morning and evening a specially prepared incense was burned on this altar, symbolizing the prayers of the covenant people to Yahweh.

The Holy of Holies. On the other side of the curtain, in the Most Holy Place, the ark of the covenant resided. This small, gold-covered box, with two fierce-looking cherubim guarding its cover, was the place where Yahweh met with Israel, and it symbolized the throne from which he ruled. Entry into the Most Holy Place was restricted to the high priest, who went in only once each year on the Day of Atonement.

— Covenant Requirements of Sacrifice —

When Yahweh granted his covenant with Israel on Mount Sinai, he gave detailed instructions for the sacrifices that were to be a part of the nation's covenant responsibility as acts of tribute to the great King. These instructions included provisions for general sacrifices, sacrifices for consecration, and special festival sacrifices.

General Sacrifices. The law given to Moses mandated a variety of sacrifices. In *sin offerings* and *guilt offerings,* the blood of the slain animal was sprinkled on the altar to atone for the sin of the worshiper (Lev. 6:24-30; 7:1-6). *Peace offerings* were of either animals or grain; the worshiper brought these offerings on a voluntary basis as a thanksgiving or for other personal reasons (Lev. 5:14-17; 7:11-36). *Whole burnt offerings* were eaten by neither the priests nor the worshiper but were burned in their entirety on the altar (Lev. 3:1-17). Unlike pagan nations, which viewed sacrifices as food for the gods, Israel understood that Yahweh received only their "soothing aroma" (Num. 28:2, NASB). Offerings were brought in various combinations for the acts of cleansing required by the law, such as a woman's purification after childbirth, recovery from certain diseases, and contact with unclean objects or dead bodies. Other sacrifices made restitution for trespasses against one's fellow Israelites or for inadvertent legal infractions. A man who had completed a Nazirite vow was also to offer a sacrifice. The law specified that particular sacrifices, consisting of a burnt offering along with flour and wine, be made twice daily on behalf of the whole nation. These were doubled on the Sabbath and were always made in addition to sacrifices for special occasions.

Sacrifices for Consecration. The consecration of priests and holy objects also required sacrificing animals and applying the blood to the person or thing being sanctified. After the tabernacle had been completed, Aaron and his sons were cleansed and made holy in this way before assuming the priesthood. The tabernacle itself and all its furnishings were likewise sprinkled with blood before they were fit to be used in the worship of Yahweh.

Festival Sacrifices. The Mosaic laws established three major annual festivals, all of which involved the presentation of sacrifices: Passover, Pentecost, and the Feast of Tabernacles, which included the Feast of Trumpets and the Day of Atonement. Specified portions of the offerings of wine, grain, oil, and flesh were given to the priests; internal organs and fat were burned on the altar as a sweet odor to the Lord; and the rest was usually returned to the worshipers as food for themselves and their families. This was particularly true of Passover, the feast that commemorated Israel's deliverance from Egyptian slavery. Passover was essentially a covenant meal celebrating the event of the exodus from Egypt, which had established Israel as the Lord's covenant people. Hence, when the worshiper received back the sacrifice he had given, this was a picture of the Lord hosting his people at his own table and of their participation with him in a reaffirmation of the covenant.

——— Sacrifice and Atonement ———

In Israel's worship, the link between sacrifice and atonement for sin is most clearly seen in the ceremonies associated with the Day of Atonement. On this day each year, the high priest was to enter the inner sanctuary bearing the blood of the sacrifice from the brass altar outside. Sprinkling the blood on the lid of the ark of the covenant, he made atonement for the entire nation. *Kapporet,* the Hebrew word for the lid that covered the ark, also carries the meaning of atonement or propitiation, in the sense of "covering." The blood atoned for Israel's sin by symbolically covering the *kapporet* so the Lord could no longer see it. Yahweh's forgiveness was mediated; the sin did not cease to exist, but God refused to look at it or allow it to disrupt his relationship with the covenant nation. "Blessed is he whose transgressions are forgiven," writes David, "whose sins are covered'' (Ps. 32:1). When the principle of parallelism is applied to this verse it is clear that the two phrases are the same: one's transgression is forgiven when the sin is covered.

It is also true that under Mosaic law the worshipers, mindful of their sin, understood the sacrificed animal as a substitution for their own lives. Because all sin was a violation of God's law, any transgression was a sin against the Lord himself and punishable by death. Violators could be forgiven only if a death occurred, either their own or that of a substitute. From the Christian point of view, the sacrifices of the tabernacle and temple could not really take away sin (Heb. 10:4); the entire Mosaic sacrificial system is an extended picture of the true atonement that was to come in Jesus, the Lamb of God.

Local and Family Sacrifices

The concept of sacrifice extended beyond the centralized rituals of the Mosaic sanctuary. Apparently the building of altars as acts of personal or family devotion was an accepted practice in Israel, even when the tabernacle was in place with its complement of priests and Levites, who were designated to officiate at sacrificial rituals. Joshua sacrificed to the Lord after the unfortunate episode with Achan and the subsequent victory at Ai (Josh. 8:30-31). The men of Israel built an altar at Mizpah after punishing the tribe of Benjamin (Judg. 21:4). Samuel prepared a sacrifice for the people at Ramah (1 Sam. 7:17). David's family made sacrifice at the new moon, as did the court of Saul (1 Sam. 20:18-29), although new moon festivals were observed with special sacrificial offerings at the tabernacle site. Despite the Law's mandate of one sanctuary for the worship of Yahweh (Deut. 12:5; 16:16), these acts are not condemned, as is the continued worship at the various "high places" (1 Kings 22:43; 2 Kings 15:4; and others), probably because they did not pretend to be rites that rivaled those of the central sanctuary.

Davidic Worship and the Sacrifice of Praise

After David became king he installed the ark of the covenant in a tent in Zion. The tabernacle with its daily round of sacrifices was located several miles away in Gibeon, but the Most Holy Place was apparently empty for more than sixty years. The Bible does not tell us what the high priest did on the Day of Atonement when he carried the blood from the altar into the sanctuary, which no longer housed the ark. It does provide a description, however, of the worship activities that were carried on before the ark in David's tent. Except for the celebration at its initial installation, there is no reference to burnt offerings being made before the ark in Zion; instead the picture is of teams of worshipers singing, dancing, playing instruments, and prophesying in rotating shifts, day and night (1 Chron. 16:1-38; 25:1-8). This is apparently what both the psalmist and the writer of Hebrews have in mind when they speak of the sacrifice of praise or thanksgiving, the fruit of lips that give thanks to the name of the Lord (Pss. 107:22; 116:17; Heb. 13:15).

Neglect and Restoration of Sacrifice

After Solomon built the first temple in Jerusalem, the ark was returned to the inner sanctuary and the altar of burnt offering moved to the temple courtyard. Eventually this temple was destroyed and rebuilt and then destroyed again. During periods of apostasy in Israel the sacrifices to Yahweh were neglected; in times of reform they were reinstituted. At the time of the birth of Christ, Herod's temple was being built in Jerusalem, and it was to this structure that Jesus was carried when his mother brought sacrifices for her purification according to the law. There is no record that Jesus participated in sacrificial rituals, although he did attend more than one national feast in Jerusalem and ate the Passover lamb with his disciples.

129 • SACRIFICE AND ATONEMENT IN THE NEW TESTAMENT

New Testament Christianity stands in the tradition of Israelite sacrificial worship in viewing Jesus Christ as the ultimate and final sacrifice.

The Sacrifice of Christ

The earliest Christians of Jerusalem frequented the temple for prayer and considered themselves Jews, although they were aware that the sacrifice of Jesus on Calvary had put an end to the requirements of Moses' law. Luke records that Paul made a vow that involved a sacrifice at the temple in Jerusalem in order to appease the Jews (Acts 21:20-26). However, the writer of Hebrews is adamant in his argument that Jewish sacrificial ritual and all that pertained to the old covenant were made obsolete when Christ's death initiated the new covenant (Heb. 8:1-13; 10:1-18).

The Concept of Atonement

The concept of atonement, so prominent in the sacrificial theology of the worship of Israel, is also important in the New Testament. Jesus Christ is called the *hilastērion* (Rom. 3:25), literally "instrument of propitiation," the word used in the Greek Old Testament for the *kapporet* of the ark (Rom. 3:25). The word, also translated "expiation," identifies Christ as the one who stands between the Lord and the covenant people as their covering, or atonement. John pictures this mediating role of Christ in his description of the victorious Lamb who is *between* the throne and the twenty-four elders who represent the redeemed of all ages (Rev. 5:6).

In both Old and New Testaments, it is the Lord who initiates atonement, and not the people. Because God chooses to overlook sin and maintain the covenant relationship, he provides a covering: the blood of the sacrifice applied to the ark in the Old Testament and the blood of his Son applied to the heavenly ark in the New Testament (Heb. 9:11). It is also the Lord who provides a substitute by instituting the sacrificial system under the Mosaic law and by giving his own Son as a sacrifice in the new covenant (Heb. 9:12-14). The offering of Isaac by his father, Abraham, with the ram provided as a substitute sacrifice, is a poignant picture of the substitutionary death of Christ in behalf of his people (Gen. 22:1-14).

Some Bible expositors teach that the temple will eventually be rebuilt in Jerusalem and the sacrificial system reinstated. Whether this actually occurs is irrelevant, since the death of Christ has made all such offerings unnecessary and inappropriate. Jesus Christ stands between Yahweh and the covenant people as their atonement covering, having become the sacrifice for their sins. Sacrifices acceptable to God under the new covenant include praise and worship (Rom. 12:1-2; Heb. 13:15; 1 Pet. 2:5, 9), good works and sharing (Heb. 13:16), and material or financial gifts (Phil. 4:18).

Janice E. Leonard

❧ SEVEN ❧

The Numinous Aspect of Biblical Worship

Worship may serve many purposes in the life of the worshiper. It may be spiritual development, the cultivation of Christian graces, and the deepening of understanding. It may be an emotional release or catharsis, the healing of hurts through the touch of the divine. It may be a communion with God, the mystic identification with the source of life. It may be thanksgiving to God for benefits received and rejoicing in his presence. It may be an individual act of commitment to serve God or the corporate celebration of the identity of the people of God, the covenant community.

While worship may be all these things, biblical worship operates in an added dimension. For in all these things the focus is on the worshiper; in genuine biblical worship, the focus is always on the One who is worshiped. The biblical worshiper comes before the Creator with an overpowering sense of reverence, awe, even dread before the divine mystery. This aspect of worship is known as the numinous.

130 • THE SENSE OF AWE IN WORSHIP

When the Lord God is encountered in glory and majesty—high, holy, and lifted up—the worshiper is filled with a sense of awe and experiences an abandonment of self in the divine presence.

The biblical words for worship mean, literally, to bow, bend the knee, fall prostrate—gestures of awe and self-negation, the creature's recognition of the surpassing majesty and worth of his or her Creator. Worship ascribes glory to God; it occurs when the vision of his glory is conveyed to the worshiper, evoking the response of fear and trembling before the holy radiance. True worship lays bare the "great gulf fixed" between the divine and the human, the sacred and the profane, king and subject, covenant giver and covenant people—and then moves toward the bridging of that gap through the gracious initiative of the Holy One.

The Scriptures set the pattern for worship at this level of intensity in the covenant ceremony on Mt. Sinai; in the Psalms; and in the testimony of visionaries like Isaiah, Ezekiel, and John the Revelator. Indeed, Scripture is permeated with a reverential awe

before the majesty of God. He is high and lifted up; the splendor of his being fills the sanctuary, as the seraphim cry out, "Holy, holy, holy!" (Isa. 6:1-4). Ten thousand times ten thousand serve him, ascribing to him wisdom, blessing, power, honor, dominion (Rev. 5:11-13). The earth melts at the thunder of his voice (Ps. 46:6). The mighty wind rushes before him (Acts 2:2), the sea roars, the trees clap their hands at his coming (Ps. 96:11-13). "In His temple everything says, 'Glory!'" (Ps. 29:9, NASB). The worshiper trembles before God's judgments, confessing his or her nothingness before the consuming fire of God's wrath—then, paradoxically, receives absolution by means of that same devouring flame and, by that same thundering voice, his commission as the instrument of divine purpose (Isa. 6:5-10).

In these biblical examples of the worshiper's encounter with the living God, we see that the awesome manifestation of God's presence exposes the insignificance of the worshiper. Isaiah cries out, "Woe to me! . . . I am ruined!" at the manifestation of the Most High (Isa. 6:5). Moses is told, "Take off your sandals, for the place where you are standing is holy ground" (Exod. 3:5). Confronted with the miraculous revelation of the Son of God, Peter exclaims, "Go away from me, Lord; I am a sinful man!" (Luke 5:8). The apostle Paul was "caught up to paradise. He heard inexpressible things, things that man is not permitted to tell" (2 Cor. 12:4). John the Revelator turns suddenly about, to fall as a dead man before the Ancient of Days, whose eyes were flames of fire, whose face was radiant like the sun, who was dead and is alive forevermore (Rev. 1:12-18).

At the same time, there is an abandon in biblical worship, a reflection of the worshiper's overwhelming compulsion to respond to the holy. Miriam, with her timbrel, leads the women of Israel in dance at the joy of deliverance from their Egyptian pursuers (Exod. 15:20-21). King David loses his royal dignity dancing before the ark of God, to the disgust of his unresponsive wife Michal (2 Sam. 6:14-16). The Psalms describe tumultuous, exuberant worship, punctuated by shouting (Pss. 47:1; 100:1), clapping (Ps. 47:1), dancing (Pss. 149:3; 150:4), and festal processions (Ps. 68:24). Jesus "rejoices greatly," or literally dances, in the Spirit when his disciples report the results of their preaching of the kingdom of God (Luke 10:21, NASB); he tells his disciples to dance or leap for joy when persecution comes (Luke 6:23). Jesus himself receives the impulsive adoration of many, including the woman who breaks open a flask of expensive perfume and anoints his feet, kissing them and wiping them with her hair (Luke 7:36-38). Filled with the Holy Spirit on the Day of Pentecost, the assembled followers of Jesus break forth in other tongues (Acts 2:4), a practice continued in the worship of the New Testament church (1 Cor. 14). The elders of the Revelation to John fall impulsively on their faces and worship before the throne of God (Rev. 11:16; 19:4). Such abandon, a departure from the decorum of "normal" conduct, is the response of the worshiper to the compelling presence of that which is of supreme value and worth, the awesome presence of the Creator.

131 ✦ THE NUMINOUS AS THE HOLY ONE

The worshiper encounters God as the Holy One, who is beyond rational comprehension. There is a quality to this encounter that transcends revelation in terms of language, symbols, or concepts.

The Sense of the Numinous

The biblical worshiper experiences the *holiness* of God—holiness, not in the moralized sense of that which is perfectly good, but holiness in the primitive, generic sense of that which is "separated, set apart." This is the underlying meaning of the Hebrew root *q-d-sh* as the basis for *qodesh,* "holiness"; *qadosh,* "holy"; *qadash,* "be consecrated"; and *miqdash,* "sanctuary." As applied to the Lord, his holiness means that he is unlike anything pertaining to the common or mundane. He is overpowering, majestic, fascinating, mysterious. He is beyond the grasp of rational comprehension yet directly sensed in his dreadful and awesome aspect. His presence compels a spontaneous and intuitive response of worship.

For this original and basic element of the holy, in 1917 the historian of religion Rudolf Otto coined the term *the numinous,* from the Latin *numen* (*Das Heilige;* English translation, *The Idea of the Holy* [New York: Oxford University Press, 1923], pp. 5-7). Confronted by the numinous, the worshiper experiences the *mysterium tremendum,* the wonder, dread, or trepidation in the presence of the incomprehensible and the uncanny, the sense of creaturehood and nothingness before the Creator, who is all. The numinous overwhelms with its mass and unconditioned majesty; the Hebrew word translated "glory" (*kavod*) means "mass, weight." The holy pulsates with life and energy; it can break out in wrath or fury. Before its sublime radiance and commanding worth, the worshiper is rapt, in a state of transport.

The confrontation with the numinous is a direct apprehension in the inward being of the worshiper; the intellectual, moral, and even psychological categories that describe and define it are secondary to this intuitive encounter. Awareness of the numinous issues from the deepest level of apprehension in the human soul, transcending the rational mind. Otto writes that "though it of course comes into being in and amid the sensory data and empirical material of the natural world and cannot anticipate or dispense with those, yet it does not arise *out* of them, but only *by their means*" (Otto, p. 113). In other words, for the biblical worshiper, God is not an idea; he is a compelling reality encountered at the deepest level of being.

It is typical of biblical faith (in contrast to faith of other religions, such as Islam) that the numinous is usually qualified through the word of revelation, which makes it possible to speak of the Holy One and his purposes in rational terms. However, this is not always the case, even in the Scriptures.

The Numinous, Interpreted

When the numinous appears in Scripture, the awesome confrontation at the direct, intuitive level is almost always accompanied by some form of interpretation in categories that can be grasped by the mind and communicated in language. At Mount Sinai, the Lord appears not only in the compelling phenomena of thunder, lightning, smoke, fire, and the sound of the trumpet (Exod. 19:16-19), but also in the declaration of his identity—"I am the LORD your God, who brought you out of Egypt"—and in the declaration of his will—"You shall have no other gods before me" (Exod. 20:2-3).

Such interpretive revelation usually comes through the word of gifted prophetic voices, as "men spoke from God as they were carried along by the Holy Spirit" (2 Pet. 1:21). The person who has been overwhelmed and captivated by the holy, although perhaps brought to trembling silence during the encounter, frequently emerges from it as a speaker anointed with a message, a vision, a proclamation of judgment, a declaration of divine purpose. In Amos's words, "The lion has roared—who will not fear? The Sovereign LORD has spoken—who can but prophesy?" (Amos 3:8). If the more introspective Jeremiah is at all typical, the revelation is formed in the crucible of inner psychological processes, as the numinous impinges on the prophet "like a fire . . . shut up in my bones. I am weary of holding it in; indeed I cannot" (Jer. 20:9). The revelation that accompanies the manifestation of the holy forms the basis for the covenant relationship between the Lord and the worshiping community, which may be summarized in the prophetic formula, "I will be their God, and they will be my people" (Ezek. 37:27; Isa. 51:16; Jer. 31:33; Ezek. 11:20; Zech. 8:8). The covenant, with all its theological ramifications, forms the rational content of the encounter with the holy.

The Numinous, Noninterpreted

The rational content of the encounter with the Lord is secondary to the basic confrontation, which occurs at a deeper level. Hence the Bible records numinous encounters in which little or no interpretation is provided. One instance is found in the account of Jacob's night at Penuel, where "a man wrestled with him till daybreak" (Gen. 32:24). The identity of this presence remains an enigma; even when pressed, Jacob's mysterious adversary refuses to identify or explain himself in any way. It is left for Jacob and those who transmitted the story to infer the meaning of this event: "I saw God face to face, and yet my life was spared" (Gen. 32:22-32). Another such incident occurs in the account of Moses' return to Egypt, during which "the LORD met Moses and was about to kill him" (Exod. 4:24); his wife Zipporah's response in circumcising her son and touching Moses' "feet" (that is, his male member) with the foreskin does not really clarify what was happening here (Exod. 4:24-26).

The holy, in its aspect as the numinous, can break out in wrath on the careless worshiper. The priests on Mount Sinai are warned to "consecrate themselves, or the LORD will break out against them" (Exod. 19:22). In the incident recorded in Leviticus 10:1-3, Aaron's two eldest sons offer "strange" or unauthorized fire before the Lord; as a result, "fire came out from the presence of the LORD and consumed them, and they died before the LORD" (Lev. 10:2). Moses interprets their death as the consequence of their failure to regard the Lord as holy. The saga of the ark of the covenant also recounts outbreaks of the fury of the numinous resident in a holy object. When placed in a Philistine sanctuary, the ark causes the image of the god Dagon to fall over and shatter into fragments (1 Sam. 5:4); while the ark is being transported in an oxcart, an outburst of energy kills Uzzah as he reaches out to steady it (2 Sam. 6:6-7). These incidents depict the numinous almost as a kind of impersonal electricity, manifesting itself in wrath with no revelation of rational content.

Some relatively unexplained numinous encounters are described also in the New Testament. In particular, the Transfiguration of Christ (Matt. 17:1-8) is enigmatic. In the presence of Jesus' three closest associates, "His face shone like the sun, and his clothes became as white as the light" (Matt. 17:2). Obviously, this is a manifestation of the Son of God, perhaps as a confirmation of Peter's recent confession of Jesus as the Christ (Matt. 16:16). But except for the voice from heaven that repeats the declaration of divine sonship, no further explanation is provided; the disciples are left wondering about the meaning of what they have witnessed, including the appearance of Moses and Elijah with Jesus. Jesus orders them to say nothing about the incident until after the resurrection, a concept that also, for the moment, remains unexplained (Mark 9:9-10).

The Holy As the Unrevealed

Since the biblical confrontation with Yahweh as the Holy One is not confined within the rational, moral, or sentimental categories of the human mentality, to a great degree the holy always remains the unrevealed. There is always that quality in the encounter with God which transcends the ability to comprehend or communicate it in the symbolism of meaningful language. The experience of the prophet Elijah on Horeb (1 Kings 19:1-18) is a case in point. As the prophet stands upon the mountain, Yahweh passes by in the violent manifestations of wind, earthquake, and fire, similar to the phenomena that accompanied the Sinai covenant. Yet, the narrative states, Yahweh is not in any of these things. He is there, yet he is *not* there! But now the prophet senses something else: an eerie stillness, a silence so silent it could be heard, as though some tremendous pent-up energy were present, ready to burst forth again in overpowering force. And out of this stillness, Elijah hears the voice of the Lord of hosts, renewing his commission as the spokesman for the God of the covenant, the Holy One of Israel. No revelation of hidden truths about the Lord has taken place, yet in an experience of the numinous, Elijah has *met with God* with a life-changing impact.

There is ever the tendency to mistake the biblical revelation or the Christian system of knowledge that is theoretically based on it for a complete revelation of God. This is understandable, since Scripture speaks of Christ as the "Word of God" (John 1:1-14; Rev. 19:13), and throughout the Bible God's self-revelation is usually accompanied by a prophetic word of explanation or command, sometimes greatly extended. What is often forgotten, however, is that God's self-revelation is at the same time his *nonrevelation,* for there is that aspect of his being which surpasses our ability to grasp it in terms of human reason or communicate it in words. "Who has known the mind of the Lord," wrote Paul, "or who has been his counselor?" (Rom. 11:34, quoting Isa. 40:13). "For my thoughts are not your thoughts, neither are your ways my ways" (Isa. 55:8). Human language can only hint at the meaning of the divine encounter through the use of "ideograms" (Otto's

term), intellectual transforms of the divine self-revelation that can point to it and explore its implications but cannot encompass it. God is one, he is eternal, he is good, he is just, he is love, he is Spirit, he is light. The concept of the holy or sacred is itself one of these ideograms, an attempt to categorize the most fundamental and distinctive aspect of the divine presence as it impacts our consciousness. But not even the idea of the holy can fully convey the impact of the meeting with God. On the mountain Elijah received a word out of the "voice of stillness," whether inwardly or outwardly we cannot tell. But there was more. There was the stillness itself, a silence that spoke of that which cannot be expressed—a silence pregnant with the mystery of the unrevealed, a silence before which people must also keep silent in reverential dread, for the Holy is in his Holy Place (Hab. 2:20).

This appears to be the point of Job's extended dialogue with his three friends, together with the final interruption by Elihu and God's answer to Job. Initially, Job demanded an explanation of the ways of God in terms he could comprehend—a futile quest. What was to his credit, however, was his insistence on holding God personally to account and his refusal to be content with the secondhand arguments of God's defenders. Job did receive an answer from God, but when it came, it did not convert him with its logical coherence. As a rational argument, God's speech is not noticeably more impressive than that of Elihu, who spoke before him and of whom neither Job nor God seem to take any notice. What moves Job to repentance is a realization of quite another order. He and his friends have been exchanging their arguments, their "ideograms," as though these could somehow encircle God and tame him. But now God has spoken to Job, confronted him in his majestic mystery, and Job is brought to silence in the face of the holy. "Surely I spoke of things I did not understand, things too wonderful for me to know" (Job 42:3). Job's questions are not answered, but the unrevealed has met him, not in the sterility of intellectual arguments, but in the depth of direct encounter, and so purged the darkness from his soul.

132 • IMAGES ASSOCIATED WITH THE MANIFESTATION OF THE HOLY

The awesome experience of God cannot be reduced to scientific or even to conceptual language; it can only be suggested by word pictures. In Scripture the imagery of light, fire, earthquake, and storm are often associated with the manifestation of the holy. These are characteristic biblical features of divine "theophanies," or appearances of God.

------ Imagery of Light and the Holy ------

Light is a favorite biblical image of the presence of the Lord. The Psalms, for example, are filled with expressions such as "the LORD is my light" (Ps. 27:1), "in your light we see light" (Ps. 36:9), and "God . . . make his face shine upon us" (Ps. 67:1). Celebrating the covenant judgment of the Lord, the psalmist Asaph declares, "From Zion, perfect in beauty, God shines forth. . . . a fire devours before him" (Ps. 50:2-3). Such symbolism pervades the Old Testament. Expelling Adam from the garden, Yahweh stations a twisting, flaming sword to guard the way to the tree of life (Gen. 3:24). Making a covenant with Abraham, God appears to him in a flaming torch (Gen. 15:17). In the desert, Yahweh speaks to Moses from the midst of a bush glowing like fire (Exod. 3:2). At the dedication of Solomon's temple, the priests "could not stand to minister" but fell prostrate before the cloud of glory that manifested the Lord's presence (1 Kings 8:11, NASB). The prophet Amos warns the covenant people to seek the Lord, "lest he break out like fire in the house of Joseph" (Amos 5:6, RSV). Ezekiel beholds the court of the temple "full of the radiance of the glory of the LORD," the brilliant envelope of his presence (Ezek. 10:4). He sees the glory going up toward the east, deserting the temple and the city (Ezek. 11:23) because of their unfaithfulness and idolatry. Later, he envisions the return of the glory, as the Lord reestablishes his dwelling among the covenant people (Ezek. 43:1-9).

Similar imagery is found in the New Testament. At the Transfiguration, Jesus appears to the disciples in brilliant light (Matt. 17:2). At Pentecost, the Holy Spirit comes upon the apostolic church, accompanied by "tongues of fire" (Acts 2:3). Saul, persecutor of the church, is struck down by a blinding light on the road to Damascus and hears a voice he recognizes as the Lord's (Acts 9:3-4). Writing later to the Corinthians, he reminds them that the Creator of light "made his light shine in our hearts to give us the light of the knowledge of the glory of God in the face of Christ" (2 Cor. 4:6). The author of Hebrews, urging an approach of reverence and awe, quotes Deuteronomy 4:24, "Our God is a consuming fire" (Heb. 12:29). The apostle John, exiled to Patmos, upon being addressed by a loud voice, turns to see "one like a son of man," standing amid seven golden lampstands, a figure whose head glows whiter than wool or snow, whose eyes "were like a blazing fire," whose feet were like brass glowing in a furnace, whose face was "like the sun shining in all its brilliance" (Rev. 1:12-16).

Although "light" is a metaphor for intellectual understanding, light itself does not contain information. "God is light," wrote the apostle John, "in him there is no darkness at all" (1 John 1:5). But what is revealed by this light? The light does not reveal much about God, but it reveals much about the worshiper. "Everyone who does evil hates the light, and will not come into the light for fear that his deeds will be exposed. But whoever lives by the truth comes into the light, so that it may be seen plainly that what he has done has been done through God" (John 3:20-21). The radiance of the numinous exposes our sin, but it hides the Holy One. We do not stare at light bulbs, or at the sun, expecting to learn anything; but we receive information from what these sources illuminate. In the same way, the light of the holy reveals what it shines on, but it conceals its own source. The radiant and glorious God remains an impenetrable mystery, "the King of kings and Lord of lords, who alone is immortal and who lives in unapproachable light, whom no one has seen or can see" (1 Tim. 6:15-16).

"Show me your glory" Moses prayed on the holy mountain (Exod. 33:18). And the Lord answered, "I will cause all my goodness to pass in front of you, and I will proclaim my name, the LORD, in your presence. I will have mercy on whom I will have mercy, and I will have compassion on whom I will have compassion"—ideograms for his love and faithfulness in upholding the covenant—"but you cannot see my face, for no one may see me and live" (Exod. 33:19-20). Then the Lord offered to place Moses in a crevice in the rock, shielding him from his glory as he passed by. "Then I will remove my hand and you will see my back; but my face must not be seen" (Exod. 33:23). The God who is worshiped in Scripture gives the revelation of his truth at his own initiative but hides the workings of his own being behind the envelope of his radiance. The holy is the revealed yet the unrevealed.

Imagery of Theophany

Scholars use the term *theophany* to denote an appearance or manifestation of God. When the Holy One appears to his worshipers, symbolic language must be used to describe the experience. The Bible employs a conventional vocabulary to describe such events, incorporating symbolism drawn not only from light or fire (as discussed in the previous section), but also from other natural phenomena such as the earthquake or the electrical storm. The theophanic imagery of the Sinai covenant and of Elijah's confrontation with the Lord have already been mentioned. The same symbolism occurs often in the context of worship to convey the awesome and overpowering sense of the presence of the numinous. We encounter it, for example, in Isaiah's vision in the temple (Isa. 6:1-13)—the altar fires, the flaming seraphs (in Hebrew, literally "burning ones"), the sanctuary filled with smoke, the thunder of the Lord's voice, which shakes the foundations. Ezekiel beholds the Lord's throne coming in wind, cloud, fire, and glowing metal (Ezek. 1:4), and the prophet Joel's description of the "day of the Lord" incorporates the trumpet, clouds, darkness, and fire (Joel 2:1-3). The Psalms, especially, place theophany in the context of Israel's worship. An example is Psalm 97:2-5:

> Clouds and thick darkness surround him;
> righteousness and justice are the foundation of
> his throne.
> Fire goes before him and consumes his foes on
> every side.
> His lightning lights up the world;
> the earth sees and trembles.
> The mountains melt like wax before the LORD,
> before the Lord of all the earth.

Other psalms containing the same phenomena include Psalm 18:7-14 and Psalm 104:3-4, 32.

Theophanic imagery is also found in the New Testament, especially in the context of judgment. In Matthew 24:27-31, Jesus portrays the coming of the Son of Man with lightning, darkness, the shaking of the powers of heaven, clouds, and the sound of a great trumpet. John's vision of the throne of the Creator (Rev. 4:1-5) incorporates the trumpet, lightning, thunder, and fire. The revelation of the ark of the covenant in the temple of God is accompanied by lightning, thunder, earthquake, and hailstorm (Rev. 11:19), and John depicts the Lord's judgment on Babylon with lightning, thunder, and earthquake (Rev. 16:18). As in the Old Testament, aspects of the composite pictorialization (in addition to light and fire) sometimes appear by themselves. In John 12:29 a voice from heaven comes as thunder. Acts 4:23-31 records an assembly of the apostles, stating that when they prayed together "the place where they were meeting was shaken. And they were all filled with the Holy Spirit" (v. 31). Such biblical imagery is a conventional way of indicating that God has made his presence known to his gathered community in the accomplishment of some purpose such as instruction, deliverance, or especially judgment. The language of theophany is employed to point to that numinous experience of the presence of God which cannot be adequately conveyed in human speech. We should probably understand speaking in tongues, or unintelligible speech, as an attempt to accomplish the same end.

133 • HOLY PLACES, HOLY PEOPLE

Although holiness belongs to God, it may be imparted to objects, or even to people, which become the bearers of the holy.

The Holy Place

The men and women who first received the biblical revelation were acutely conscious of the ways ordinary things could take on an extraordinary, numinous quality as bearers of the sacred. The concept of the sanctuary, or holy place, comes readily to mind. The Old Testament records many occasions when the fathers of Israel worshiped at holy places. Some of these places were already sacred sites for the Canaanites, but they became Israelite sanctuaries as the result of a theophany of Yahweh God. When he appeared to one of the fathers to give or reaffirm the promise of the land, the patriarch would mark the site by erecting some holy object such as an altar or a memorial stone.

Altars. At Shechem Abraham "built an altar there to the LORD, who had appeared to him" (Gen. 12:7). This location continued to be a holy place where Joshua later led the people in the renewal of the covenant with the Lord, erecting a stone as a memorial to this event (Josh. 24:1-8). Thus, the Israelite sanctuary was "a token of the covenant and a guarantee of its blessing" (Johannes Pedersen, *Israel: Its Life and Culture,* 2nd ed. [1959], Vols. 3–4, p. 214). A classic expression of the significance of the holy place occurs in the account of Jacob's dream at Bethel, in which he sees a ladder reaching to heaven on which messengers of God are descending and ascending; the Lord appears and pronounces his promise of blessing, land, and descendants. Awakening, Jacob exclaims, trembling, "Surely the LORD is in this place. . . . This is none other than the house of God; this is the gate of heaven" (Gen. 28:16-17). Before leaving, Jacob sets up a sacred pillar, the stone on which he had been sleeping, and anoints it as a bearer of the holy, "God's house" (Gen. 28:10-22). The sanctuary is a place where earth and heaven meet, where "angels ascend and descend"; for this reason, ancient temples were usually erected on hills or, in flat country, on artificial elevations. Ascending Zion in pilgrimage, the later Israelite worshiper cries, "I lift up my eyes to you, to you whose throne is in heaven" (Ps. 123:1). The sanctuary is a place bearing a numinous aspect where the divine can break through into the ordinary, where man can sense the presence of the holy and communicate with him.

Mount Sinai. The archetype of the holy place in the biblical narrative is the desert sanctuary of Sinai. Here, the Lord appeared to his people in full and fearful theophany, in a presence of such intensity that only the specially consecrated could approach the mountain. After the Lord had set forth the stipulations of the Book of the Covenant (Exod. 20–23), Moses and the priests and elders of Israel went up the mountain to meet with Yahweh and to eat the covenant meal; there, in a further manifestation of the numinous, they "saw the God of Israel. Under his feet was something like a pavement made of sapphire, clear as the sky itself" (Exod. 24:10).

Ark and Tabernacle. These numinous aspects of the Sinai sanctuary were transferred to the ark of the covenant, where Yahweh was "enthroned between the cherubim" (Pss. 80:1; 99:1), and to the tent of meeting, as the place where Moses "entered the LORD's presence to speak with him" (Exod. 34:34). Not only the sanctuary structure with its altar, but all its furnishings and utensils, as well as the offerings presented there, were consecrated as "holy," set apart for the exclusive use and service of the Lord.

The Temple on Zion. Before Israel's entrance into Canaan, Moses spoke of "the place the LORD your God will choose from among all your tribes to put his Name there for his dwelling" (Deut. 12:5). This unnamed place turned out to be Jerusalem and Mount Zion, which David captured as a center for Israel's worship (2 Sam. 5:7). Zion had long been a Jebusite holy place, the "Salem" where Abraham had paid a tithe to Melchizedek, the king and "priest of God Most High" or 'El 'elyon (Gen. 14:18-20). But when David transferred the ark to Zion and when Solomon's temple assumed the role of the tabernacle, the sanctuary on Zion became, in effect, a continuation of Sinai, where the Lord "appeared" in theophanic majesty in the worship of Israel. Several of the psalms celebrate the numinous appearance of the Lord in his temple or in Zion with imagery that reminds us of the giving of the covenant on Mount Sinai (Ps. 50:1-6). Exactly how the Lord "appeared" in the worship of the temple is not clear, but there are indications in the Psalms that the liturgical recitation of the covenant Law, associated with a procession of the ark of the covenant, was a high moment when worshipers might experience the Lord's presence in an especially compelling way.

"Holiness adorns your house," sang the Israelite worshiper (Ps. 93:5). Israel's theologians understood, of course, that the sanctuary was inadequate as a bearer of the sacred. "But will God really dwell on earth?" asked Solomon. "The heavens, even the highest heaven cannot contain you. How much less this temple I have built!" (1 Kings 8:27; cf. Isa. 66:1). In the New Testament we meet with the concept of the heavenly sanctuary, of which the earthly one is but a copy (Heb. 8–9; cf. 2 Cor. 5:1; Rev. 11:19). No human edifice can convey the fullness of the presence of the holy. As Jesus explained to the Samaritan woman, the deepest and most authentic worship of the Father could occur "neither on this mountain [Gerizim] nor in Jerusalem" (John 4:21). Although Christ spoke of Jerusalem as "the city of the Great King" (Matt. 5:35), he foretold the impending desecration and violent destruction of its sanctuary (Matt. 24:2), a judgment on a religious establishment that had violated the Lord's covenant.

Jesus and the Holy Place. Nevertheless, Jesus understood and accepted the concept of the holy place in its deepest sense. He questioned the focus of the Pharisees, who swore by the _gold_ of the temple or by the _offering_ on the altar—in other words, by the products and symbols of man's religious commitment. To the contrary, said Jesus, it is the _temple_ that sanctifies the gold and the _altar_ that sanctifies the offering (Matt. 23:16-19). Jesus' language, incomprehensible as it may seem to us, was not incomprehensible to the early church, which continued to respect those places where God had manifested his presence in a numinous experience. Thus Peter speaks of that time when the apostles were with Christ "on the holy mountain," by which he meant not Sinai or Zion but the Mount of Transfiguration (2 Pet. 1:16-18). The proliferation of holy shrines in the Orthodox and Catholic traditions, however fanciful it may seem in Protestant perspective, is a witness to the persistence of this biblical concept.

The Numinous Aspect of the Church

When we appreciate the importance of the sanctuary in biblical worship, we can understand why the New Testament authors draw upon the imagery of Jerusalem and its temple to convey the significance of the church. Addressing Christian believers as a body, the apostle Paul asks, "Don't you know that you yourselves are God's temple and that God's Spirit lives in you? If anyone destroys God's temple, God will destroy him; for God's temple is sacred, and you are that temple" (1 Cor. 3:16-17). Again he declares, "we are the temple of the living God" (2 Cor. 6:16). (In both these passages he uses the plural form, speaking not to individuals but to the church collectively.) As a temple, the church of Jesus Christ is "a dwelling in which God lives by his Spirit" (Eph. 2:22). These are not simply moralistic expressions; they point to a reality that transcends the idea of the church as a mere human association.

John the Revelator most fully develops the picture of the church as "the Holy City, the new Jerusalem, coming down out of heaven from God" (Rev. 21:2). As the bride of the Lamb, the new sanctuary displaces the harlot "Babylon," the old temple, and its religious establishment. The appearance of the new holy place brings a renewal of the covenant, in the declaration that "the dwelling of God is with men, and he will live with them. They will be his people" (Rev. 21:3), words that echo the covenant formula of the Israelite prophets. The sanctuary is a picture of the covenant God living among his own, enthroned on the praises of his people (Ps. 22:3). As John takes the concept further, we are brought face to face with the numinous brilliance of the Holy City (Rev. 21:10-11), "for the glory of God gives it light, and the Lamb is its lamp" (Rev. 21:23). So overwhelmed is John by the vision that his description strains at the limitations of language. The Holy City is a temple yet not a temple: "I did not see a temple in the city, because the Lord God Almighty and the Lamb are its temple" (Rev. 21:22). There is a numinous, awesome aspect to the church as a bearer of the holy, a vehicle through which we may encounter the fearful presence of the King of kings.

Holy People

The mortal who would trespass into the territory of the sacred runs the risk of wrathful outburst and sudden destruction. It is paradoxical, then, that human beings can serve as bearers of the holy, vehicles through whom the numinous makes its presence felt. Study of the history of religions brings to light many instances of "holy" men and women, people whose presence is "larger than life," awesome, commanding, not to be trifled with. In such personages, the worshiper senses the workings of the divine. Biblical faith, too, is familiar with the concept of people as bearers of the holy.

Priests. The Pentateuch takes pains to spell out the procedures of vesture, sacrifice, anointing, and lifestyle by which a priest may become and remain consecrated, in order to enter the Lord's presence (Exod. 28–29; Lev. 8; 21). Through his consecration, some of the holiness of the Lord is imparted to the priest, enough to "inoculate" him against an outbreak of the wrath of the numinous. A special aura of holiness rested upon the high priest. He alone could enter the Holy of Holies, the inner sanctuary containing the ark of the covenant, on the Day of Atonement (Lev. 16). A person accused of manslaughter was protected from the avenger of the deceased, provided he remained in a city of refuge until the death of the high priest then in office (Num. 35:25-28).

Prophets. The Scripture often calls the prophet a "man of God"; the term is applied to Moses (Deut. 33:1), Samuel (1 Sam. 9:6), Shemaiah (1 Kings 12:22), Elijah (1 Kings 17:18), Elisha (2 Kings 4:40), David (2 Chron. 8:14), and to a number of unnamed prophets or messengers of the Lord (Judg. 13:6; 1 Sam. 2:27; 1 Kings 13:1). In these instances the term *man of God* (or woman of God) does not mean a *righteous* person but one of *special endowment,* a bearer of the numinous, even one to be feared. The people's reaction to Moses when he returned to them after speaking with the Lord was one of great fear because "his face was radiant" (Exod. 34:29); as a result, he had to wear a veil whenever he came out from before Yahweh. The biblical narrative ascribes miracles to prophets such as Elijah and Isaiah as the distinguishing mark of the "man of God" (1 Kings 17:24). Especially noteworthy is the numinous aura associated with the person of Elisha; he raises the dead son of the Shunammite woman by lying upon him, body member to member (2 Kings 4:32-37), and even after his death a corpse, thrown hastily into his grave, returns to life upon contact with Elisha's bones (2 Kings 13:20-21). The earlier prophets seem to have been distinguished by special appearance, having a tonsured head in a manner similar to later Christian monks (1 Kings 20:35-42; 2 Kings 2:23). A man or woman of God can make mistakes, disobey the Lord, and pay the penalty but still be known as a man or woman of God (1 Kings 13:26; 2 Kings 23:17). Samson was consecrated to God by the Nazirite vow (Judg. 13:7) and was moved by the Spirit of the Lord (Judg. 13:25); even when he turned away from the Lord, he remained an awesome man, capable of exploits larger than life.

The Apostles. Although the New Testament uses the expression "man of God" more in the sense of a godly person equipped for the service of the Lord (1 Tim. 6:11; 2 Tim. 3:16-17), it also portrays the apostles, like the prophets, as bearers of the numinous. People laid their sick friends in the street in the hope that Peter's shadow might fall on them (Acts 5:15); it was enough for Peter to confront Ananias and Sapphira with their duplicity, and they fell dead at his feet (Acts 5:1-11). The people of Lystra acclaimed Paul and Barnabas as gods and were prepared to sacrifice to them (Acts 14:11-13). Handkerchiefs or aprons from Paul's body were carried to the sick, and they were healed (Acts 19:11-12). In recording such incidents, Luke is not simply chronicling the ignorant superstition of ancient peoples. The awe-inspiring aspect of the apostles, despite their lack of formal education, is a recognizable quality in their lives, the result of the fact "that these men had been with Jesus" (Acts 4:13).

Jesus Christ. The powerful, wondrous impact of the holy is evident throughout the gospel portrait of Jesus Christ himself, from his birth to his resurrection and ascension, and requires no lengthy demonstration here. To those already mentioned, we would add only a few examples. As a woman, suffering from a persistent hemorrhage, touched the hem of Jesus' garment, Jesus immediately sensed that "virtue," or power (*dunamis*), had gone out from him (Mark 5:25-34). Led to the edge of a cliff at Nazareth by a mob angry at his indictment of their lack of response to the love of God, Jesus was able simply to pass through their midst and go on his way. When soldiers came asking for Jesus the Nazarene to arrest him, Jesus replied, "I am he," and "they drew back and fell to the ground" (John 18:6). The first preachers of the Resurrection referred to the miracles of Jesus, familiar to their audience, as acts that attested him as specially endowed and set apart by God (Acts 2:22). In his own preaching, Jesus spoke of the kingdom of God, a realm breaking into present time and space in supernatural manifestation. We can understand much about the principles and operation of the kingdom of God when we view it as another expression for God's covenant with his people. As to its inner dynamic, however, the kingdom is a mystery. It cannot be completely comprehended in rational argument and detail; its principles of growth can only be hinted at through picture and comparison, its power suggested through miracle and sign. Above all, it is present in the person of Jesus himself, as the bearer of the holy.

Like the prophets before him and the apostles afterward, Jesus was opposed, vilified, and persecuted by those who could not, or would not, look beyond the external to the reality of the unseen. Yet the final vindication of Jesus' identity as the incarnate revelation of the holy is that most awesome of all events, the Resurrection, which not only displays the workings of the Creator in the person of his Son, but releases in his worshipers some measure of that same quality of sacred and mysterious power. Thus, the New Testament frequently refers to the body of believers collectively as "the saints" or "the holy ones" (Greek *hagios,* equivalent to Hebrew *qadosh*). Scripture makes it clear that the entire covenant community is "a kingdom of priests" (Exod. 19:6), "a royal priesthood" (1 Pet. 2:9), consecrated to approach the Presence in worship. The awesome encounter with the living God is not the preserve of a spiritual elite but the inheritance of all who call on him.

Conclusion

This survey has attempted to demonstrate that in biblical worship there is a numinous dimension of awe, dread, majesty, transcendence in the presence of the Holy One. The worship of God is not confined to the flatness of the rational, the sentimental, or the moral. The error of much of both orthodox and modernistic Christianity is that it has tried, by default or by design, to constrain worship within these limits. Religion has been reduced, in the words of the nineteenth-century theologian Friedrich Schleiermacher, to a "feeling of dependence," or more crudely, to "morality tinged by emotion" (*On Religion: Speeches to its Cultured Despisers* [New York: Harper Torchbooks, 1958]). Or it has become a matter of words and statements, precise definitions, carefully crafted confessions. Or it has degenerated into a mere social ritual, an exercise in group identification. In such a domesticated form, it lacks the intensity, depth, mystery, and abandon of biblical worship and so fails to speak to the deepest instincts of the soul.

Richard C. Leonard

Biblical Worship as Response to Saving Events

==

Because it is God who always takes the initiative, Christian worship is best discussed in terms of response. In worship people are responding to God; this is true of the whole of the liturgy, whether it be praise, thanksgiving, supplication, repentance, Eucharist, baptism, liturgical prayer, or the celebration of the church's year. If this is so, worship must be seen in the context of saving history, which is the record of the divine initiative.

==

134 • ISRAELITE WORSHIP AS RESPONSE TO SALVATION HISTORY

The worship of the Israelites is a response to God's saving acts on their behalf, particularly the Lord's action of deliverance in the Exodus event. Through such events God spoke, calling the people to faith and commitment.

The history of salvation conventionally begins with the calling of Abraham, "our father in faith," though the liturgy includes in its scope the creation epic of Genesis 1 and 2, and like 1 Peter, sees the story of Noah as relevant to saving history (baptism). The whole of Old Testament history in a variety of ways is seen as preparation for the coming of the Messiah. He and his redeeming work of passion, death, and resurrection are the culmination of saving history, which is carried forward by the operation of the Holy Spirit in the church, which awaits the eschaton, the summing up of all things in Christ at the end. This pattern underlies the whole of the Christian liturgy. The proclamation of God's word in the Old Testament lessons prepares the way for the *kērugma* of the New Testament lessons, culminating in the reading of the Gospel. The Eucharist is set in the context of the Passover festival and of the making of the covenant in the desert. The paschal mystery of Christ's passion, death, and resurrection is the very heart of the Eucharist, which by *anamnēsis* recalls it and makes its power present to the people here and now. In its celebration, and in that of the other sacraments, the church looks and

reaches to the fulfillment of all things in Christ. The liturgical year from Advent to Pentecost follows the same course.

However, the history of salvation is not to be seen as a series of disparate events or as the mere record of what once happened. It is the record of God's self-disclosure, made in and through the events, the disclosure of a God who gives himself. This is the deepest meaning of salvation history. The whole record can be seen as the self-giving of God, who takes the initiative, who approaches humankind to bring people nearer to himself to make them his own people, and who binds them to himself by covenant, which is the expression of his love. In this perspective Abraham is a figure of crucial importance. God called him to make him the father of many peoples; he responded with faith, and in that faith entered an unknown destiny (cf. Heb. 11:8). It was this response of faith that made him pleasing to God (righteous), and it was on account of it that God made covenant with him (Gen. 17:19; cf. 22:17; Rom. 4:11). The same was true of all the great figures of the Old Testament (Heb. 11:11-40). It was by faith that Moses accepted his vocation to become the leader of his people, it was by faith that he led them out of Egypt, it was by faith that he kept the Passover, and above all it was by faith that he responded to the God who revealed to him that he is the God who acts, the God who saves.

The story can be briefly continued. God showed his love for his people in the saving events of the

Passover, in the rescue from Egypt, in the passage through the Red Sea, but above all, in the covenant, in which the people bound themselves to God, who is ever faithful to his promises. So close was this union intended to be that the later writers of the Old Testament could call the covenant the marriage union, or even the love match, between God and his people, thus foreshadowing the Pauline and Johannine teaching on the church as the bride of Christ (Eph. 5:22-32; Rev. 21:1-2). The role of the prophets was to recall to the people God's faithful love shown to them in the Exodus events, which for them meant "salvation," and to renew the response of faith of the people. But all was in vain. The response of faith that God sought, a response that would result in total commitment, was refused, and the divine purpose of salvation seemed to have been frustrated.

Then in the appointed time God sent his Son, "born of a woman, born under law, to redeem those under law" (Gal. 4:4-5). God had looked for the response of faith from his people, for their yes to his saving love. They were unable to give it, but Jesus, the second Adam, gave that radical assent to his Father's saving will: "In him it is always Yes. For all the promises of God find their Yes in him. That is why we utter the Amen through him, to the glory of God" (2 Cor. 1:19-20, RSV). The response of Jesus Christ is the correlative of the "faithful love" of his Father, or in other words, the whole meaning and intent of his life is to do the will of the Father, who sent him. But the radical change for the Christian is that now he is able to make the response of faith, to say yes to God in and through the response of Christ, whose yes we endorse with Amen "to the glory of God." Here we come very close to a definition of worship, for the glorifying of God, the response in faith that issues into praise, thanksgiving, and supplication, is exactly what we are doing in worship. This response is also prompted by the Holy Spirit (Rom. 8:27), so that through Christ in the Spirit we respond to the Father's love. This is the backdrop of all Christian worship.

In the Old Testament, as we have seen, God approached people in event and word, the word usually coming after the event to unfold its meaning. The Word of God is proclaimed in the Law; it is heard in the institution of the covenant. Above all, it is proclaimed by the prophets who recall to the people the primordial events by which they were made God's people and who, by so doing, attempt to deepen the people's understanding of these events

so they may turn or turn back to the God who has made himself known to them. But coming through all the words is God's Word, calling, inviting, urging the people to respond to him with the word of faith, to commit themselves totally to God. They respond to the Law by trying to keep it; they respond with a word of obedience at the institution of the covenant (Exod. 24:6-8); they respond with praise, blessing, and supplication in the psalms that were sung to accompany the sacrifices of the temple and the service of the word in the synagogue.

135 ✦ CHRISTIAN WORSHIP AS RESPONSE TO SALVATION HISTORY

The worship of Christians is in response to God's saving action in the living, dying, and rising again of Jesus Christ; it is patterned on the history of salvation, offered to the Father, through the Son, and in the Holy Spirit.

Through the centuries of the Old Testament, God was offering his love to the people, but they did not "know" him; he did not reveal his inner nature. Jesus came as the revelation of the Father (Matt. 11:25-27). The mystery of God, hidden for ages and generations, is now made manifest (Col.1:26), and the essence of that mystery is that God is love (1 John 4:8). This Jesus made plain by his life, his words, and his passion, death, and resurrection. That is why he has been called "the sacrament" of the Father, the showing forth of the Father, and the revelation of his saving purpose, adumbrated throughout the ages but now made known in Jesus Christ.

But Jesus is not only the revelation of the Father; he is in himself the communication of the Father's love, the primary and supreme gift of God to humankind. Christ makes God present to people with all his redeeming power and love, principally through his passion, death, and resurrection. In the terminology of St. Paul, Christ is the mystery (*mustērion*) "which is . . . in [*en*] you, the hope of glory" (Col. 1:27). Christ, then, makes effective in people the self-giving of God, who calls and urges them to respond to him in self-giving of faith and love through the word and sacrament of the liturgy. In the dialogue that is set up, in the exchange that takes place, we meet God and are able to enter into union with him, which is the end purpose of all worship.

The culmination, however, of God's self-revelation and self-giving in Christ were the passion, death, and resurrection, to which we must add, as the liturgies do, his ascension into heaven, the apparent end of the Lord's earthly work of redemption. All this has been called the paschal mystery, and the term is useful for putting Christ's redeeming work in the context of the Passover. The Passover of Christ fulfilled and transcended the Jewish Passover. It is in the Passover context that the Eucharist was instituted, thus indicating that it is through the Eucharist that the Passover of Christ, his redeeming work, is made available to all. It is of the Passover of Christ that the Eucharist is the _anamnēsis,_ or memorial. Just as the paschal mystery was the culmination of Christ's redeeming work, so the Eucharist becomes the culmination and center of Christian worship.

The liturgy, then, is the making present in word, symbol, and sacrament of the paschal mystery of Christ so that through its celebration the men and women of today may make a saving encounter with God. Stopping here, however, excludes a whole dimension of saving history as well as of Christian worship. If the Pentecost event has never formed part of the _anamnēsis_ of the Eucharist, the giving of the Spirit is always in view. In the liturgical context, the ascension (which has normally been one of the events mentioned in the _anamnēsis_) can be seen as the bridge between the paschal mystery of Christ and the giving of the Spirit. This is based on the New Testament perspective: Christ returns to his Father that he may send upon his church the Spirit he promised (Acts 2:33). But the presence of the Spirit in the liturgical celebration is not to be seen simply in terms of the _epiclēsis,_ as if he comes into the action only at a certain point. The liturgy is always celebrated in the power of the Holy Spirit. Just as prayer is made in the Spirit (Rom. 8:26-27), so is the celebration of the liturgy. If it looks back to Christ in his redeeming work, it looks to Christ as he now is, filled with the Spirit, as Lord (1 Tim. 3:16). It is possible to see that the historic Christian liturgy is patterned on the history of salvation. There is the original initiative of God, who throughout the ages offers humankind his love. The history is carried forward by the redeeming events of Christ, the Son of God, who on the cross gives himself totally to his Father and for the salvation of humankind. He ascends to the Father and sends upon his church the Holy Spirit so that his _ekklēsia_ may continue, in time and space and by the power of the Holy Spirit, his redeeming work. The church looks to the consummation of all things, when Christ will hand all

things to his Father so that he may be all in all things (1 Cor. 15:28). "To the Father, through the Son, and in the Holy Spirit" is the underlying pattern of the history of salvation and of the liturgy. In the eucharistic prayer we give praise and thanksgiving to the Father, through the Son, whose redeeming acts are recalled, and to the Holy Spirit, who is invoked on the offering (_epiclēsis_). The doxology at the end of the prayer expresses the whole truth succinctly but explicitly. Almost all collects begin with an ascription of praise to the Father, make petition through the Son, and conclude with a mention of the Holy Spirit. The phrase serves to remind us that the aim of the whole liturgy is entrance into communion with God, a communion in the divine life and love that constitute the Trinity.

136 • Worship as the Response of a Community

Worship is the action of a people made one body in Christ, the source of its life. Ultimately, then, worship is an act of Christ the High Priest.

In the liturgy there is a vertical movement, an out-going of human beings to God. But there is also a horizontal movement. Liturgy is celebrated with others, and the relationships between the members of the worshiping community are of the highest importance. "Private acts of public worship" is a phrase of contradictory terms.

The Pauline teaching on the church as "body" emphasizes at once the closeness of the relationship between Christ and the people—they are members, limbs, of the body—and the horizontal relationships between the members of the body (1 Cor. 12:8-31). In other words, perhaps more strongly than before, it is indicated that the priestly people is also a community, the community of Christ, with which he has a vital relationship. He is the source of all its life; it is totally dependent on him as the branches of a tree are on its trunk (John 15:1ff.). And the relationships of faith and love between its members are in the first instance created by Christ, though they are to be realized and strengthened by Eucharist, which is the sacramental sign of _koinōnia,_ of communion, the union of minds and hearts in faith and love. If the church can be said to "make" the Eucharist, in a much deeper sense the Eucharist makes the church. But the depth and richness of the relationship is best seen in Ephesians 5, where Christ is said to be the head of the church, of which he is also Savior; and this church is his bride (Eph. 5:25-26) which he brought into existence by the ''fragrant offering and sacrifice'' that he offered to his Father (Eph. 5:2).

It is this people, then, the priestly people, the body of Christ and the community of Christ, who are the ''subject'' of liturgical celebrations. In other words, it is they who celebrate the liturgy, and the form of the liturgy must be of such a sort as to make this possible. The Christian liturgy, by its nature, cannot be the monologue of a single participant. It is the action of a whole community. On the other hand, it is not an unstructured community. Each member, and indeed each group of members (for example, the choir), has a role to fulfill, and by fulfilling these functions all are exercising the priesthood they share with Christ and his ministers.

But neither they nor the ministerial priesthood act independently. By reason of their relationship to Christ, and because together they are the body of Christ, the whole liturgical action and every liturgical action is also the action of Christ, who is head and High Priest of the body. The closeness of the union between head and members, and the identity of the action of the church with that of Christ, is best illustrated by the saying ''When the church baptizes it is Christ who is baptizing,'' which is a paraphrase of a statement of Augustine, Bishop of Hippo and best known of the early church fathers, who said that the Lord baptizes through his ministers. The ultimate subject of the liturgical celebration, then, is neither the ordained ministry nor the people, nor indeed both together, but Christ, who acts in and through his church. Obviously his action is invisible, but the people of God, his body, is a visible and structured community, which over the whole range of its liturgical action, consisting of both Word and sacrament, manifests Christ's presence, shows forth the nature of his activity, which is redemptive, and by his power makes his redeeming work effectual and available to men and women of today.

Liturgy does not lend itself to definition, but if a definition is to be attempted it could be as follows: liturgy is the communal celebration of the paschal mystery by the church, which is Christ's body and in which he with the Holy Spirit is active. Through this celebration, which is by nature sacramental, Christ, the High Priest of the community, makes present and available to men and women of today the reality of his salvation.

J. D. Crichton[2]

NINE

Biblical Worship as Re-Presentation of Saving Events

Encounter with God in worship creates life as the worshiper's relationship to God is continuously sustained and renewed. In biblical worship this takes place as the saving events of God's action in history are made real again and again.

---

137 • ISRAELITE WORSHIP AS RE-PRESENTATION

The Israelite cultus, or worship pattern, is responsible primarily for the origin, preservation, and transmission of a large portion of the Old Testament.

Although Old Testament scholars continue to stress Israel's contributions in such areas as monotheism and ethical prophecy, not enough emphasis has been placed on Israel's achievement in worship. The purpose of this study is to explore the major lines of Israel's worship and to suggest the areas in which it can continue to enrich Christian worship.

The purpose of Israelite worship is to create life, that is, to maintain the ordered course of the world of nature and the world of humankind as it was created by God and as it is sustained by God. Encounter with God through worship sustains the world order, reaffirms the human relationship with God's creation, and maintains relationships among neighbors. Worship sustains, creates, and re-creates a relationship not magically, but sacramentally—a relationship initiated, sustained, and continually renewed by God himself.

In Israelite worship, the overriding purpose was the "re-presentation of history," the contemporizing of those creative, historical acts of salvation that had formed, nourished, and sustained Israelite existence. None will deny that the faith of Israel was historically oriented, based on the fact that God credeemed a people from Egyptian bondage, welded them into a covenant people through the Torah, and confirmed that salvation by the gift of the land. Whatever tribes or clans actually experienced

the Egyptian Exodus event, all Israel affirmed that God had acted in her behalf, that Yahweh had served Israel, and that this salvation was a continuing process in her existence. To be sure, the Exodus event occurred only once, at a particular point in human history, a unique and unrepeatable act. But Israel, uniquely conscious of history, could not allow this formative event to recede into timeless myth as her Near Eastern neighbors would have done. In no sense could the Exodus event be subject to annual repetition in the same way Marduk in Babylon annually defeated the chaotic Tiamat—the uniqueness of the Exodus event precluded annual cyclic recurrence. Nevertheless, Israel's worship sustained the faith that because God had acted once, he would continue to act for her salvation. Thus, Israel, freed from the reduction of her past to myth and assured of the continuation of redemptive history, "re-presented" in worship those historical acts that were determinative for her life.

These functions are primary to Israelite worship: to actualize, to re-present unrepeatable historical events, to bring the worshiper into an existential identification with these events, to bridge the time and space gap, and to participate in the original history. In Israelite worship, each generation vicariously entered into that original and nonrepeatable history through two patterns: (1) historical recital and (2) dramatic re-presentation.

138 • WORSHIP AND HISTORICAL RECITAL

The recitation of the history of Yahweh's redemptive acts forms the basis for creed, liturgy, and preaching in the Old

Testament. The Christian church took up the format of historical recital in its hymnic and creedal affirmation of God's actions in Christ.

Israel's Creedal Statements

Gerhard von Rad has isolated several creedal statements in the Old Testament which, he has argued, stand at the level of primary tradition. Among these confessions is the Deuteronomy passage:

> My father was a wandering Aramean, and he went down into Egypt with a few people and lived there and became a great nation, powerful and numerous. But the Egyptians mistreated us and made us suffer, putting us to hard labor. Then we cried out to the LORD, the God of our fathers, and the LORD heard our voice and saw our misery, toil and oppression. So the LORD brought us out of Egypt with a mighty hand and an outstretched arm, with great terror and with miraculous signs and wonders. He brought us to this place and gave us this land, a land flowing with milk and honey. (Deut. 26:5-9)

For this writer the creedal character of these verses cannot be denied. The emphasis of these creedal statements is historical: Egyptian bondage, salvation from that bondage by Yahweh, the occupation of the land. Moreover, one cannot escape the fact that these affirmations are in plural address—"we" were in Egyptian bondage, "we" were redeemed by Yahweh, "we" were given this fertile land. Each time this affirmation was recited, the worshiper bridged the time and space gap and became identified with that never-to-be-repeated salvation: he or she actualized, contemporized, re-presented history.

Another example of historical recitation is found in the antiphonal liturgies in Joshua 4:6-7 and 24:14-28. Although the liturgical form has been clouded by the context of historical narration, the liturgy may be easily reconstructed:

The priest: What do these stones mean?

The congregation: They mean that the waters of the Jordan were cut off before the ark of the covenant of Yahweh; when it passed over the Jordan, the waters were cut off.

The priest: So these stones shall be to the people of Israel a memorial forever.

Liturgical Affirmation of Yahweh's Kingship

H. J. Kraus has suggested that these liturgical foundations emanated from Gilgal, a center of worship that carefully preserved the Jordan crossing and the conquest traditions. In these liturgies the reader is in touch with historical recital of the re-creation of history, a means of allowing the existential involvement of later generations in those acts of Yahweh that effected salvation and that continue to effect salvation.

Or one may cite a central thrust of the Jerusalem worship community, namely the liturgical affirmation of the Psalter—Yahweh has become/is king. Despite the discussion this affirmation has evoked, no thought of a dying-rising Yahweh is intended; nor was the kingship of Yahweh predicated in an annual cultic renewal ceremony. Nevertheless, in the Jerusalem temple, this liturgical affirmation brought the worshiper face to face with the reality of Yahweh's kingship, not a theological abstraction, but an experiential and existential encounter that demanded a response. Indeed, one may posit that just such a worship encounter underlies the temple sequence in Isaiah 6, an encounter with the cultic reaffirmation of Yahweh's kingship, which redirected the prophet's life. Thus, in some sense, in the Jerusalem worship community, Yahweh's kingship was reactivated in worship, and he "became king" for those who entered into the experience. Cultic recital provokes existential identification.

Historical Recitation in Preaching

To be sure, Israel's worship was not limited to creedal and liturgical confessions—a flexibility developed within the cult, as witnessed by the book of Deuteronomy. In fact, Deuteronomy is a gigantic cultic actualization. Deuteronomy 5:3 reads: "It was not with our fathers that the LORD made this covenant, but with us, all of us who are alive here today." This passage perhaps originated between the eighth and the sixth centuries, a time far distant from the Sinai event; nevertheless, centuries later Israel could corporately and cultically confess that the present generation stood anew at the foot of the holy mountain. Moreover, historical recitation and re-presentation give way to preaching, a fact that explains Deuteronomy's homiletic or parenetic (that is, preaching) character. The creed is expanded into an injunction and a call for obedience as each generation is recalled to affirm Israel's ancient faith, to bridge the time and space gap, to participate existentially and creatively with those events that culminated in the covenant. Thus, Deuteronomy, with its pattern of creedal recitation and homiletic expansion, sets the pattern for Christian preaching.

Historical Recitation in Christian Hymn and Creed

These examples of Israelite historical recitation illustrate the means by which Israel sought to re-create her history by liturgical re-presentation. Small wonder that the early church also presented its message by historical re-presentation. The early Christian hymns and creeds contained in the Pauline corpus (1 Cor. 15:3-7; Phil. 2:6-11) are harmonious with the Israelite pattern of historical recitation and re-presentation, for their emphases are on the historical, concrete memories of our Lord's life and death. Even more illustrative is the creed in 1 Timothy 3:16:

> He appeared in a body,
> was vindicated by the Spirit,
> was seen by angels,
> was preached among the nations,
> was believed on in the world,
> was taken up into glory.

The death and resurrection of our Lord was a once-for-all, unique, unrepeatable historical event, and the early church, following the pattern of its spiritual ancestor, constructed similar historical recitations. In worship they stood again at the foot of the cross, by which they bridged the time and space gap, by which the Christ event continued in contemporaneity through cultic re-presentation.

And the church continued to formulate creeds. To be sure, such classic creeds as the so-called Apostles' Creed and Nicene Creed were formulated to preserve dogmatic integrity; nevertheless, the basic character of these creeds is rightly historical. Of course, Israel would not have opened her creeds with the theological abstraction of God's "almightiness," nor would she have spoken of the outset of creation. Nevertheless, when the Apostles' Creed begins the article of Jesus Christ, the Hebraic cultic

pattern is maintained: "born of the virgin Mary," "crucified under Pontius Pilate," "died, was buried, raised on the third day." To give audible expression to the Apostles' Creed in worship is not an intellectual exercise in dogmatic assertion; in this audible expression something should happen—the worshiper should encounter anew the historical elements of our faith, and in some sense, experience the sacramental contemporaneity of our Lord with the worshiper. If one is to take the Israelite worship community seriously, then one is confronted with the demand to reactivate the purpose of re-presentation by historical recital, to view creedal affirmations not as tests of theological soundness, but as a means of existential identification with the past, as a means of bridging the time and space gap, as a means of re-creating the original event and existentially participating in those events that have accomplished our salvation.

Undoubtedly, many Protestant evangelicals have eschewed creedal statements primarily because the basic purpose has been lost; nevertheless, from the example of Israel's worship community, such creedal re-presentations should be restored to Christian worship in order that the church may possess a more vital sense of its history, that it may become more aware of its corporate relationship with the church of all ages, and that it may participate in God's saving act in Jesus Christ and recognize the demands that event makes on the individual. The loss of historical identification undercuts the dynamism of the Christian faith; Israel's cultic pattern has pointed the way to a recovery of that historical involvement in Christian worship.

139 • WORSHIP AS DRAMATIC RE-PRESENTATION

Recent studies of the history of Israel's religion have demonstrated convincingly that the formative events of Israel's faith were dramatically acted out in worship. In fact, some of the Old Testament narratives have reached their present form as a result of the historicizing of cultic dramatic re-presentation.

The Exodus Narrative

The Exodus narrative in Exodus 1–19 is a re-clothed festal liturgy from which something of the ritual may be recovered. In Exodus 12:42, the "watch night" drama appears, a re-creating and a re-presenting of the drama in which the Hebrews anxiously awaited the intervention of Yahweh in

Egypt, a repeated cultic drama that bridged the gap of space and time and reestablished the saving relationship for each generation with Yahweh. In close connection is Exodus 12, the instructions for the Passover feast, said to be observed as "a memorial to all generations." The re-creation of the watch night, the blood on the doorposts and the lintel, the eating of unleavened bread and bitter herbs—these acts were re-created annually and physically in active worship. For Israel, no sterile symbolism is present, no more lifeless memory; by re-creating history through dramatic presentation, Israel re-presented her saving history, actualized her salvation, renewed her relationship to her God. Thus, historical recital has given way to historical re-creation.

Narratives of Joshua

The narratives of Joshua 2–6 are rehistoricized festal liturgies from the Gilgal cult. At Gilgal, through dramatic presentation, the crossing of the Jordan was re-created and the march around the ruins of Jericho reenacted, not in mere historical memory, but in contemporary actualization. The close connection of dramatic re-presentation with liturgical re-presentation as noted earlier is clearly evidenced in these passages from Joshua. Thus, the Gilgal cult, annually or periodically, re-presented the conquest story, dramatizing its history and making it sacramental.

The Jerusalem Worship Community

The greatest example of re-presentation of dramatic form is the Jerusalem worship community. Much has been written about the royal ritual in Jerusalem, with its interlocked themes of David and Zion. Despite those who find minimal cultic influence, one has little basis for doubting that the royal psalms have their setting in a royal Zion festival during which those events surrounding the Davidic dynasty were dramatically enacted at Jerusalem. The Psalms speak of the "night watch" at Gihon, of the procession through the streets of Jerusalem which preceded the entrance of the ark into the temple, and finally of the reactualization of the Davidic king as Yahweh's servant. The Psalms are primary testimony to historical re-presentation by dramatic actualization.

The Lord's Supper as Sacred Drama

Precisely at this point Christian worship has departed from the pattern of the Israelite cult, with particular reference to the Lord's Supper. If one will view the history of the Lord's Supper one will find few periods when the real drama of the Lord's Supper has been preserved. The theology of the Lord's Supper has moved from the extreme of the Roman church, with its doctrine of transubstantiation, to the barren symbolism of nonliturgical congregations. Both positions are in error. If Old Testament worship is correctly viewed, then an idea of the actual re-creation of the body and blood of our Lord in the Mass is incorrect. The suffering and death of Jesus were once-for-all, nonrepeatable, unique events in history; in no sense can the event be literally and physically re-created in worship. But on the other hand, the elements of the Lord's Supper transcend barren symbolism. In the celebration of the Lord's Supper something happens, not with the elements themselves, but in a dramatic re-presentation of history. To borrow the pattern of the Deuteronomic preachers, "it was not with our fathers that the LORD made this covenant, but with us, with all of us who are alive here today" (Deut. 5:3). The Lord's Supper is sacred art, a drama that manifests reality; it allows the worshiper to span the time and space gap of history and stand again with those who first experienced our Lord's death. In the mystery of dramatic presentation, the worshiper reenters original history; it is not a festal myth, but an actualization. "This is my body, broken for you," a brokenness that continues over and over again, a presentness of contemporary encounter. Thus, as one partakes of the elements, one becomes part of the original event, which was accomplished for our salvation.

The demand is to recover the true meaning of the Lord's Supper in Christian worship, a meaning that is patterned from Israelite worship with its motif of dramatic re-presentation. If the study of Israelite worship is taken seriously, the Lord's Supper must be rescued from its place as addendum in many congregations and restored to the central place of worship. The Lord's Supper is the reenactment of the Christian Exodus event, the historical beginning, which continues to give the church life. Jesus said, "Do this in remembrance of me" (1 Cor. 11:24). Yet to remember is not an intellectual discipline; "to re-member" is to re-create, "to re-member" is to re-present, "to re-member" is to respond. In Deuteronomy 16:3, the Feast of the Passover is said to be observed, "so that all the days of your life you may remember the time of your departure from Egypt."

Here is the annual re-presentation of history. Thus, "Do this in remembrance of me" must mean, "so that you may participate in the sufferings and death of our Lord and respond to them." For as Israel was redeemed from Egyptian bondage in the Exodus and annually actualized that redemption in the cult, the Christian church finds itself released from a similar bondage and must actualize that redemption by dramatic re-presentation. The Lord's Supper is truly sacramental in that by participating in the drama of our redemption, God himself reestablishes, maintains, and renews his relationship with us and we respond in obedience.

140 • ISRAELITE WORSHIP'S RELEVANCE FOR CHRISTIAN WORSHIP

Because the God of Israel and the God of the Christian church are the same God, it is not surprising that their patterns of worship have strong similarities. Christian worship has much to gain from the study and appreciation of the worship of ancient Israel.

Visual Impact

In worship, evangelicals in particular have tended to overemphasize the audible aspects of worship to the exclusion of the visible aspects. Primarily in the Lord's Supper the vitality of tangible and visible presentation has been retained. The Israelite cult is "sacred art." Only recently has the church begun to grasp the power of acted-out faith and worship in drama. Contemporary worship patterns need a new awareness of the impact of the visible, which is often more effective than the audible. Dramatic presentation of our faith offers a new and creative channel through which the re-presentation of history may be accomplished and the dynamism of the Christian faith may be preserved, so that we may bridge the time and space gap of two thousand years.

Symbolism

Closely related to the visual aspect of worship is the area of symbolism. The temple in Jerusalem was filled with symbolism, not merely as decorative art, but as a means of re-creating history. The ark of the covenant, the central cult object, stood in its semi-darkness as the throne of the invisible King Yahweh. The altar of incense, standing before the Holy of Holies, continually emitted sweet-smelling smoke to re-create the theophany of Sinai where Yahweh appeared "in a thick cloud." The great freestanding pillars outside the temple, at least according to one interpretation, served as mammoth incense burners so that the whole temple came to represent Sinai. The trumpets sounded in the liturgy were more than musical instruments; their sound re-created the thunder of the Sinaitic theophany. It is not necessary to install incense burners in sanctuaries, but an increased realization that cultic symbolism re-creates, re-presents, actualizes, and activates history is necessary. With the renewed emphasis on liturgy and worship, the church can learn much about the place and purpose of creative symbolism from the Israelite cult.

Participation

The Israelite cult was, as the Norwegian exegete Sigmund Mowinckel states, a place where something happened, a fact that is beginning to prompt renovations in church architecture. Renewed emphasis on worship as action and participation by the whole congregation has encouraged the construction of circular buildings with the Communion table at the center. Startlingly, a Northfield, Minnesota, architect has proposed that except for its size, the best analogy for church architecture is the Japanese tea room. The architect Edward Anders Sovik says, "Like a church, the tea room is not a place for private mediation, but for dialogue and certain actions in which human relationships are established." (cf. E. A. Sövik, *Architecture for Worship* [Minneapolis: Augsburg Publishing House, 1973], pp. 76-77). This statement is similar to the ideas of Mowinckel, who spoke of the cult as the "visible and audible expression of the relationship between congregation and deity" (Sigmund Mowinckel, *Religion and Kultus* [Göttingen: Vandenhoek & Ruprecht, 1953], p. 13). Thus, the recovery of the dynamism of Israel's cult may influence our traditional conceptions of sacred architecture with renewed emphasis on the worship as visible and audible, as expressions of relationships, as an event in which "something happens."

Flexibility

Insight into the Israelite cult grants Christian worship increased flexibility. Old Testament students know that many of Israel's worship patterns were adapted along the lines of Near Eastern culture, and even the Jerusalem cultus is a compromise between

Yahwistic and Jebusite cultic patterns. Israel could and did adopt forms from her contemporary culture, introduce them into her ancient patterns of worship, and baptize them into her distinctive Yahwism. This freedom to employ non-Christian elements in Christian worship must be recovered. While some have viewed attempts to introduce jazz and modern dance into worship as anathema, these experiments are harmonious with the Israelite point of view. The increased use and adaptation of twentieth-century art and music forms offer new and exciting challenges for creative revitalization of Christian worship.

Conclusion

If the God of Israel is the God and Father of our Lord Jesus Christ, as the church claims he is, then to contend that he chooses to be worshiped in similar patterns is not difficult to affirm. The central purpose of both Israelite and Christian worship is to re-present creative history by means of audible and visible expression, a re-presentation that culminates in active response. Perhaps one reason the Christian church has lost much of its vitality in the twentieth century is that it has lost the art of worship because it has divorced itself from the sense of the history that effected its salvation. Recovering that historical status is part and parcel with the revitalizing of the drama of worship.

Donald L. Williams[3]

141 ✦ BIBLIOGRAPHY: GENERAL OLD TESTAMENT THEMES

Childs, Brevard S. *Old Testament Theology in a Canonical Context.* Philadelphia: Fortress Press, 1985. This highly acclaimed book addresses worship subjects such as the role of the ritual and purity laws, the theological role of priesthood, the benefits of the covenant, and the life of Israel under promise.

Conner, Kevin J. *New Covenant Realities.* Portland, Oreg.: Bible Temple Books, 1990. This easy-to-read and clearly outlined study attempts to answer questions posed by the Bible student regarding the relationship between the Old and New Covenants. Special attention is paid to the teachings of Hebrews and Galatians.

_____. *The Name of God.* Portland, Oreg.: Bible Temple Publishing, 1975. This work addresses the significance of name and especially the name of God. The subject is covered both historically and topically. A special section deals with the use of the name in water baptism.

Conner, Kevin J., and Ken Malmin. *The Covenants.* Portland, Oreg.: Bible Temple Publishing, 1983. This work presents the covenant structure of Scripture and discusses the worship related to each of the covenants. It is clearly laid out for personal study and quick biblical references.

de Vaux, Roland, O.P. *Ancient Israel: Its Life and Institutions.* New York: McGraw-Hill, 1961. Called a classic of Old Testament sociology, this book includes a lengthy study of Israel's religious institutions, including sanctuaries, the priestly office, sacrificial ritual, and festivals.

Eichrodt, Walter. *Theology of the Old Testament.* 2 vols. Philadelphia: Westminster Press, 1961. This classic study approaches Israel's worship through the covenant motif. The entire cultus (worship) of Israel with its sacred sites, objects, seasons, and actions, as well as the whole history of Israel and its relation to God, is rooted in the covenant.

Herbert, S. J. *Worship in Ancient Israel.* Richmond: John Knox Press, 1959. This older but helpful work discusses the basis for Hebrew worship, presents the vocabulary of worship and the media of worship in cultic acts, ritual recitals, cultic objects and persons, and occasions of worship.

Hill, Andrew. *Enter His Courts with Praise.* Nashville: Abbott Martyn Press, 1993. This is the most clear and succinct presentation of Old Testament worship available. It covers vocabulary, matters dealing with a theology of worship, and all aspects of the cult such as sacrifices, the tabernacle, temple, and synagogue.

Hillers, Delbert R. *Covenant: The History of a Biblical Idea.* Baltimore: Johns Hopkins University Press, 1969. This study traces the development of the biblical theme of covenant in its various forms and relates it to the influence of ancient treaty structure.

Kaiser, Walter C., Jr. *Toward an Old Testament Theology.* Grand Rapids: Zondervan Publishing House, 1978. This standard evangelical work is written around the concept of the promise. It contains considerable material on Israel's worship as related to the covenant, to sacrifices, the tabernacle, the temple, the ark of the covenant, and the concept of God's blessing.

Kurtz, J. H. *Sacrificial Worship of the Old Testament.* Grand Rapids: Baker Book House, 1980. This reprint of a nineteenth-century classic presents the Old Testament sacrificial system in great detail. It discusses the basis of sacrificial works and details the rituals in both blood and bloodless sacrifices; it concludes with a treatment of the modification of sacrifices for the various seasons and feasts.

Martens, Elmer A. *God's Design: A Focus on Old Testament Theology.* Grand Rapids: Baker Book House, 1981. This evangelical author arranges the material of the Old Testament around the notion that God's design is to build his kingdom on earth as in heaven. Worship figures strongly in this approach. God's design is viewed as deliverance in history that results in the covenant community, a community which through worship comes to know God.

Ollenburger, Ben C., Elmer A. Martens, and Gerhard F. Hasel, eds. *The Flowering of Old Testament Theology.* (Grand Rapids: Wm. B. Eerdmans Publishing Co., 1992. This work contains a number of short excerpts from the writings of present-day Old Testament scholars. Among those articles that pertain to worship are Walter Eichrodt, "Covenant"; John L. McKenzie, "Cult," and Paul D. Hanson, "The Community of Faith."

Otto, Rudolf. *The Idea of the Holy,* New York: Oxford University Press, 1923. A modern classic study of the numinous aspect of the holy, this work deals with the nonrational elements in the communication of the Other. Special sections discuss the numinous in the Old Testament, the New Testament, and Luther.

Pedersen, Johannes. *Israel: Its Life and Culture.* 4 vols. New York: Oxford University Press, 1959. Originally published in Danish in 1920, this exhaustive treatment of Israelite institutions and cultural perspective deals with such themes as the soul, blessing, covenant, peace and salvation, and sin. The latter two volumes are devoted to holiness, holy places, holy offices such as warrior, priest and prophet, and the maintenance of holiness through sacrifice and festivals.

Peterson, David. *Engaging with God: A Biblical Theology of Worship.* Grand Rapids, Mich.: Eerdmans, 1992. This book attempts to cut through "custom and personal preference" and worship as feeling or spiritual self-gratification, to the touchstone of our worship, biblical revelation. Although parts of the argument of the book seem to suggest abandoning tradition, the picture of worship that finally emerges is selectively traditional within a free church structure.

Von Rad, Gerhard. *Old Testament Theology.* 2 vols. New York: Harper & Row, 1962. Volume 1 of this standard work deals with the theology of Israel's historical traditions. It covers worship issues such as the tent, the ark, the glory of God, cultic officials, the sacrifices, sin, and atonement.

Westermann, Claus. *Elements of Old Testament Theology.* Atlanta: John Knox Press, 1982. This classic work is written from the perspective of the covenant. That God rescued Israel from Egypt and entered into covenant is the central conviction of Israel's faith; its worship perpetuates the memory of this event.

PART TWO

History and Institutions of Biblical Worship

TEN

History of Israelite and Jewish Worship

From the beginning Israel's worship is a response to Yahweh for the acts he has performed in its history. Israel's whole history is a life of coexistence with God, a partnership in a historical drama. The emphasis is on Yahweh as the initiator, but Israel responds. The people address Yahweh in a personal way. They offer praise, ask questions, complain about suffering, and converse with him about all the issues of life. This conversation of worship is recorded throughout the Scriptures, binding Jewish history together in celebration of this relationship with the Creator God. In the New Testament church the emphasis falls on the historical acts of the triune God, with the central focus on the Incarnation, the Cross, and the exaltation of Jesus Christ the Lord, made real by the Holy Spirit (Eph. 1:3-14; 2:18).

142 ✦ WORSHIP IN THE PATRIARCHAL PERIOD

The central figure of patriarchal worship is Abraham, who received Yahweh's promise of land and descendants.

The book of Genesis records the history of Israel's ancestors from their nomadic beginnings. Abraham was called by Yahweh to leave his country and travel to a new land. A promise was given to Abraham that his name would be great and his family would become a mighty nation (Gen. 12). These themes originate in Genesis and weave throughout the whole of Israel's history. The fulfillment of these promises became the impetus for the people's response of worship and thanksgiving.

At Hebron, Abraham built the first altar to Yahweh in thanksgiving for the promise of the land (Gen. 13:18). Worship was offered to Yahweh after Abraham defeated the four kings (Gen. 14:17-24). The worship was "led" by Melchizedek, "the priest of God Most High." Bread and wine were part of the worship. Melchizedek pronounced a blessing on Abraham (cf. Heb. 7:1-3). Abraham responded by giving the high priest a tithe of everything he had. At this early offering of thankful worship to Yahweh, the basic elements of Israel's worship form were present. From its nomadic beginnings Israel's worship included theophanies, or appearances of the Lord, promises of the land, the practice of marking important places with an altar, the figure of a high priest, and a cultic celebration using bread and wine. The following chapter (Gen. 15) and the sacrifice of Isaac (Gen. 22) rooted the cultic practice of sacrifice in Israel's tradition, though as a protest against human sacrifice.

143 ✦ MOSAIC WORSHIP AND THE EXODUS

After the Exodus the worship of Israel became more formalized, characterized by the Mosaic institutions and regulations. The commitment to the law of the covenant became the central feature of Israelite worship.

Worship forms became more formalized in the book of Exodus. Yahweh's active intervention in Israel's history is characterized in the contest with Pharaoh. The deliverance from Egypt embodied the essence of Yahweh's relationship with his people; the "Song of Moses" (Exod. 15) enshrined deep-seated truths. One of Israel's great festivals looks back to this experience of liberation. The remembrance of the Passover incorporates Jews of every generation as actual participants in the Mosaic exodus.

Despite their murmurings through the desert wanderings, the Israelites learned to know Yahweh as he provided food for them and called them his own. The desert experience in later worship became symbolic of God's provision and care (Deut. 8:1-20). God's instructions for the building and arrangement of his dwelling in the tabernacle and the details pertaining to the priesthood, the sacrifices, and the worship service were very specific. Many chapters of the Pentateuch are dedicated to the details of the tabernacle's construction (Exod. 25–31). Worship and the manner in which worship was offered were evidently extremely important to Yahweh.

The tent of meeting illustrated the mobility of Yahweh. Unlike the pagan gods, who were deities of limited geographical areas, Yahweh went with his people as an ever-present reality through their wanderings. In the desert wanderings Yahweh led Moses and the people to Mt. Sinai. Here an encounter with Yahweh grounded Israelite worship in an event that would profoundly affect the rest of Judeo-Christian history. The covenant of Sinai bound the whole nation of Israel to Yahweh. The nation received the Law, that is, the Decalogue, and the Book of the Covenant, which would direct its future. The covenantal relationship and the commitment to the Law of Yahweh became the stamp of Judaism. Ironically, one of the historic high points of Yahweh's relationship with his people also revealed the sin and the alien worship that God's people were tempted to embrace later (Exod. 32). The golden calf became a reminder of the syncretistic nature of God's people. From this point forward *false* versus *true* worship would be a theme for the worshipers of Yahweh.

The Exodus was a fulfillment of God's promise to Abraham (Gen. 12:1-3). The book of Exodus is pivotal in describing the central experience of the Hebrew people. This story records the celebrations and ritual acts of Israel that arose in response to the liberation event that gave freedom to a nation. Exodus records the transformation of the old pagan notions into new forms, such as covenant and law, that brand Israel as unique among nations, with the Passover rite (Exod. 12) at the heart of all.

144 • THE DANGER OF CANAANITE RELIGIOUS INFLUENCE

In Canaan Israelite worship incorporated elements from pagan worship, especially that of Ba'al, and Israel went through periods of apostasy and reform.

Syncretism, the mixture of foreign elements with the Yahwism of Israelite worship, increasingly became a problem as the people of God moved from the wilderness to the Promised Land of Canaan. The religious procession to the land can also be seen as a military movement that collided with the cultures already existing in the area. Among other peoples, the Israelites encountered and settled near a Semitic people called the Canaanites. The Canaanite culture is thought to have existed in this area from perhaps as early as 3000 B.C. The Canaanite gods quickly became competitors for the loyalty and worship of the Israelites. The desert incident of the golden calf foreshadowed the problem of idolatry that would intensify during this period of settlement.

For the Old Testament writers the word *idolatry* meant veneration of an object other than the God of Abraham, Isaac, and Jacob. Since Scripture records Canaanite cultic centers at all the major cities and towns, including Dan, Gilgal, Shechem, Bethel, Shiloh, and Jerusalem, the temptation of idolatry for the Israelites was great. The difficulty for God's people was identifying what idolatry was. Syncretistic practices crept into the worship of the Israelites almost without their awareness. Scripture records examples of this pervasive and subtle cultural lure (Hos. 2:1-23).

One of the Canaanite deities was a god designated as *Ba'al* (see 1 Kings 18:21). The Hebrew word *ba'al* can mean "owner," "master," "lord," or "husband." Ba'al's power was over a particular locality. Thus Ba'al was the deity of a settled people. As the Israelites moved into a more settled life-style, they confronted the beliefs of Ba'al worship. The local ba'als were connected with the fertility cycles of human beings, animals, and agriculture. Ba'al power was closely linked with nature, particularly the bringing of rain to Palestine's parched landscape. The influence of the Ba'al cult led to extreme forms of worship such as child sacrifice (Jer. 19:5) and ritual prostitution (Judg. 2:17; Jer. 7:9; Amos 2:7).

The origins of Ba'al worship are uncertain, but evidence indicates that the Amorites brought their gods with them on their migration into Canaan in the second millennium B.C. Another Canaanite god, *'El*, is mentioned as the original head of the Canaanite gods in the Ras Shamrah texts. 'El, however, was the distant source, the "father of years" in the pantheon description. Ba'al symbolized the vigor and power behind the natural cycles of life-giving powers. *Asherah* became the feminine counterpart to Ba'al by the time of the judges (Judg. 3:7).

Ba'al was often depicted with some characteristics of a bull, which was the ancient symbol of strength and fertility. Ba'al statues exhibit helmets with horns of a bull or picture the god as riding a bull. The statues show Ba'al with a club in one hand, most likely representing thunder, and a spear with leaves in the other, depicting lightning and fertility.

Israelite worship was constantly threatened by the foreign aspects of Ba'al worship that conflicted with Yahweh's prescribed law. Syncretism was a serious issue for two major reasons. First, the Israelites settled in the land with the Canaanites and often intermarried with the Ba'al worshipers. This brought the seductive elements of the cult closer, even into the Israelites' homes. Second, the fact that Yahweh was viewed as the god of the wanderings posed a threat. The Ba'al worshipers' polytheistic background caused them to view the gods as having power along geographical lines. Since the Israelites were dependent on the land once they settled in Canaan, it might have seemed wise to pay homage to the god of that land, a feature recognized in David's confession (1 Sam. 26:19) and Naaman's request (2 Kings 5:17-19).

These syncretistic tendencies can be seen in Scripture (Judg. 3:5-7; 6:25-26). Many of the names in Scripture have elements of the Canaanite gods: Esh-baal, Meribaal (1 Chron. 8:33-34), and Beeliada (1 Chron.14:7). It is difficult to know whether these usages directly refer to the Canaanite deity or whether the term was used in reference to the Lord Yahweh as owner and master. In time the syncretistic tendency became so blurred that the Israelites banned the use of *ba'al* in reference to the lordship of Yahweh.

The syncretistic tendency was particularly prominent in the northern kingdom, according to the scriptural authors. This area was more exposed to pagan elements and more agricultural than was the south. The north was therefore more susceptible to elements of the Ba'al worship. In the northern kingdom the golden calves at Dan and Bethel horrified those who were seeking true worship of Yahweh. Even the southern kingdom eventually experienced the influence of Canaanite worship despite the reforms of Hezekiah and Josiah. Scripture indicates that even Jerusalem itself was influenced (2 Kings 21:7). One of the most blatant attempts at syncretism was a deliberate ploy by Queen Jezebel to make Ba'al the official god of the land. Scripture states that only seven thousand Israelites resisted her to follow the true religion of Yahweh (1 Kings 19:18). Throughout the eighth century the prophets constantly reminded the people of the syncretistic danger on all sides. It seems that the people of Yahweh did not recognize the apostasy in which they were involved (Jer. 2:23; Hos. 2:16-17).

145 • WORSHIP DURING THE DAVIDIC PERIOD

Under David's leadership, worship was established in Jerusalem. David organized the functions of the priesthood, placing special emphasis on the use of music in worship.

Although syncretism posed a threat and led to a struggle throughout Israel's history, periods existed in which Yahweh's place of centrality in the life of his people and their worship was stronger and clearer. One of these periods was that of the Davidic monarchy. David had been blessed by Yahweh from a young age and had been ordained to be Israel's king after an unstable period, when it was administered by the judges and then by Saul. David united the kingdom under a central government headquartered in Jerusalem (in place of Hebron). King David linked this political move to the center of cultic worship by bringing the ark of the covenant to Zion.

The worship of this period focused primarily on that of King David during a politically stable period in Israel's life. David is credited primarily as the one who organized Israel as a worshiping community. While the biblical narratives do not spare David's sinful side, they show a man who is willing to confess and be forgiven for his sin. In later literature this then became the biblical example of a true worshiper of Yahweh. Perfection of ethical and moral character was thus not indispensable for faith. Rather, Yahweh desired an honest worshiper who could confess and praise him in sincerity and truth (Mic. 6:6-8). David becomes the example par excellence of a true worshiper, the traditional author of "the psalms of David" that express cultic acts of worship (for example, Pss. 24; 150).

David's political strategies established a monarchy with its cultic center in Jerusalem. David brought revival to a people and a faith that had experienced a low period lacking unity and strength. The ark of the covenant had disappeared in the disaster at Aphek (Ps. 78:60), where the Israelites were defeated by the Philistines. David recovered the ark and had it brought to Zion, where it was placed in a tent. The ark reminded the people that Yahweh is not represented in wood or stone but that he is a living presence with his people. The whole practice of worship in Israel looked back for its basis to the covenantal relationship established in the Exodus and celebrated in the tabernacle, which had been the ark's previous dwelling place. The ark was also a reminder that worship alone is not enough. A broad requirement of service to Yahweh involves ethical implications of justice and mercy. In the reestablishment of the ark in a cultic center of worship, David laid a foundation for the royal ideology and the theme of a unique covenant established with David's lineage.

From the chronicler's viewpoint, David made a central contribution to Israel's worship. Jerusalem became the Holy City, the religious capital of the tribes of Israel. The temple began to take form and structure under David. This temple was completed and embellished around 950 B.C. by the king's successor and son, Solomon. David assigned to the Levites the official duties of leading the community in praise and prayer. The priesthood began to be a stratified hierarchy of functions. The priesthood would eventually be represented by the Zadokites (functioning in the sacrificial capacity), the high priests, the priests, and the Levites. While the major components of worship remained constant, according to the tradition, David instituted some changes, especially the addition of instrumental worship (1 Chron. 23–27).

David is said to have been skilled on the lyre. He is considered the composer of many songs and laments that were incorporated into the temple worship. From allusive indications, music guilds may have been established during this period (1 Chron. 25:6-8) and given a special role in the service. The collection of these Davidic compositions and other songs is known as the Psalter, with David as the traditional author.

146 ◆ WORSHIP FROM SOLOMON TO THE EXILE

Although Solomon completed and dedicated the temple, the foreign influences and faulty civil policy that set in during his reign eventually led to the demise of the Israelite commonwealth.

David's son and successor to the throne was Solomon. During his reign Solomon continued to focus on the cultic worship of the temple, adding to the edifice ornamentation of such glory and splendor that all who visited Israel marveled at its beauty. Solomon emphasized beautifying the temple not only because he was dedicated to the worship of Yahweh and desired to show his gratitude, but because he had also begun to be influenced by surrounding foreign powers. The temple and its ornamentation were a sign to foreigners of the wealth and cultural strength of Solomon's court. Scripture attests to these foreign influences during the reign of Solomon. This accentuated the syncretistic tendency that the Israelites had been dealing with since they first covenanted to be the people of Yahweh. Solomon often allowed civil policy to dictate ecclesiastical practices. He married foreign wives in order to establish alliances. These wives brought their alien gods into his courts (1 Kings 11:1-8).

The foreign influences from within the country cumulatively resulted in disaster. The northern kingdom's destruction (722 B.C.) and the demise of the southern kingdom, including Jerusalem and the temple (587 B.C.), were viewed by the postexilic writers in light of the corrupt worship practice that had infiltrated the practices ordained by Yahweh. The religion of Israel before the Exile is depicted as a headlong, spiraling decline leading to disaster. Ahab had allowed Jezebel's Sidonian influences to foster idolatry and despotism (1 Kings 16:32). Intermarriages between Jezebel's family and the southern kingdom continued to spread the destructive influences. The situation was so severe and irreversible that it necessitated the destruction of both kingdoms, the temple, and the city of Jerusalem to reestablish the pure remnant of Yahweh's chosen. The essentials of worship had been lost.

The Word of God, prayer, praise, confession, and forgiveness had become empty rituals that had lost the inner meaning and therefore impeded access to Yahweh.

147 ◆ WORSHIP DURING THE EXILE AND RESTORATION

The return of Israel after the Exile brought renewed interest in worship; the temple was rebuilt and sacrifices were reinstated. The synagogue, originated during the Exile, now became the focal point of a nonsacrificial worship.

The nature of worship in the exilic period is much debated. One theory postulates that the absence of the temple and the deportation to a new land forced the faithful to restructure worship to accommodate the new situation. The Psalms speak to the discouragement of those in exile and their longing for the land of Zion (Ps. 137:1-6). Historically it seems that not all Jews desired to return as earnestly as the author of Psalm 137, for not all Jews did return to Jerusalem when they were eventually allowed to do so by an edict of Cyrus (538 B.C.). It also appears that not all Jews were deported from the land in the Exile. Tension developed between the returning Babylonian Jews and the Jews who had remained behind and intermarried with other peoples.

The Persian armies under Cyrus swept across the eastern frontier of the Babylonian empire in 539 B.C. and reached as far as the Egyptian frontier. Cyrus was one of the most enlightened rulers of ancient times. His aim, as far as it was possible, was to allow subject nations to enjoy cultural autonomy within the framework of his empire. His successors tended to follow in his steps. By means of a complex civil and military bureaucracy, a firm control was established over the empire, but within this framework local customs were respected, established cults were fostered and protected, and responsibility was entrusted to native rulers. In the first year of his reign Cyrus issued a proclamation permitting the Israelites to return to their homeland, ordering the rebuilding of the temple, and inviting Jews remaining in Babylon to assist with contributions. Although this edict would seem to have been received with overwhelming gratitude, and a mass exodus back to Israel would have been expected, this did not happen.

Many of the Jews had become well established in Babylon and had no wish to leave, particularly on a long journey with uncertain goals. The initial wave of returnees was not large, and though it was reinforced by later immigrations, Jerusalem was still thinly populated and in a state of ruin seventy-five years after the edict. The inhabitants of the land, Judeans who had been left behind in the Exile, as well as Edomites who had moved to fill the vacant land, were not happy to have these returnees move back. The Samaritans to the north were antagonistic, claiming that they held fast to true worship while their exiled kin had become polluted with Babylonian influences. The Samaritans and Judeans who had remained in the land had absorbed pagan customs into their worship and began to affect some of the returnees. The leadership feared for the integrity of the community and sought to end all contact with the native population.

With the return of the exiles came a renewed interest in temple worship. The building of the second temple commenced around 520 B.C. and was completed in 515 B.C., overseen by the high commissioner Zerubbabel and the high priest Joshua. Nehemiah and Ezra the priest played important roles in the gradual return of the exiles and the rebuilding of the community of faith. Although the temple was rebuilt and worship, priestly sacrifices, and pilgrimages were reestablished at the cultic center, the enthusiasm was never to be of the same intensity. The frailty of a faith focused on a central location had been demonstrated in the fall and destruction of the temple one-half century earlier. The noncultic aspect of this faith, particularly as expressed through emerging synagogue worship, developed greater importance during the Exile, and Ezekiel and the prophet of Isaiah 40–55 had known God's presence in a strange land without the use of the temple.

Synagogue worship had a distinctive pattern. Wisdom and the study of the Torah became the goal and focus of the synagogue. A crisis existed in the faith of the Jews, who had been without a temple for the greater part of a century. A new form was needed to adapt to the new circumstances. The synagogue became the *ekklēsia,* that is, the assembly or congregation. The worship in the synagogue stressed reading and exposition of the Torah, prayer, recitation of the *Sh^ema'* (based on Deut. 6:4), and recitation of psalms.

Ezra's reorganization brought a fundamental change to Israel. No longer was Israel's identity centered on a national cult. Rather its identity from this point forward would be seen as that of a religious remnant who rallied around the Torah. Judaism did not change the basic elements of worship during the Exile and return; the focus and stress, however, were simply heightened to accent one feature of the tradition. The Law, or Torah, became the organizing principle.

148 • WORSHIP DURING THE INTERTESTAMENTAL PERIOD

Prior to the first Christian century, Judaism began to develop traditional interpretations of the Law that would eventually be written down to regulate Jewish life and worship. Judaism was influenced by Greek culture, resulting in the rise of a class of scribes and segments of the Jewish community which were more thoroughly hellenized. The groupings formed during this period set the stage for the various sectarian movements within Judaism of the early Christian era.

History

During this period Palestine came under the rule of Alexander the Great. Following the Exile, Cyrus had opened the way for the reestablishment of the Jews in Judah. The Persian rule under Cyrus had been positive for the Jews. Under imperial order Ezra and Nehemiah had reestablished the people in Jerusalem and made the Law of Moses the civil law of the Jews. Although many Jews did not live in Judah, those in the Diaspora accepted the Law of Moses as their law. The land continued to be an important part of Jewish identity and worship.

Jerusalem became the center for Jewish ritual life, despite the fact that a large number of writings were composed outside Israel. Jerusalem was the authoritative center for the Jews. The legal tradition developed under Ezra and Nehemiah, and the court of the law, known as the Sanhedrin, with its priests, elders, and scribes, had their roots in Jerusalem centered on the temple.

As a result of renewed interest in and tremendous value placed on the law of Moses, the arts of translation, interpretation, and study developed. The Pentateuch was translated into Aramaic, the language of the Persian empire. During this period the seeds were planted for the emergence of the *bet hammidrash,* "house of interpretation." These houses later became schools for studying Scripture and debating the traditions of the fathers. The synagogue was also taking structural shape during this period.

The Place of the Law in Worship

For the Israelite the giving of the Law was a cause for joyous celebration. The Torah was seen as a source of joy and life. The Law was Yahweh's way of expressing his love for his people. The boundaries and limits provided by the Law were a gift from God to prevent destruction and harm from coming to the lives of the Israelites. The importance of Torah interpretation was highly valued throughout Israel's history. The later *midrashim,* or commentaries and lengthy rabbinic debates over legal situations, illustrate the centrality of the Law. God's commands were examined and applied to life in a dynamic process of discovery. The Torah fenced the life of a Jew,

but it was not seen as a static, rigidly set boundary. Rather, the Jew viewed the Torah as a living Word, the pulse and heartbeat of life. The idea of "dancing with the Law" embodies the celebration and the joyous guidance that adherence to the Torah could bring. It was a gift from Yahweh, a gift of love. Jews rejoiced over the Law in a celebration they still practice each fall. The reading and exposition of the Torah became an increasingly important focus for worship. Nehemiah 9 illustrates the ceremony of covenant renewal that wed the remnant to Yahweh through his Word.

In time legalism developed. The rituals of worship tended to become empty forms that stifled the spirit of prophecy. Preoccupation with the letter of the law robbed the Torah of its beauty and grace (cf. 2 Cor. 3:6). The externalism of worship, which emphasized performance versus the examination of the inner spirit, was an abomination to Yahweh. The prophets saw this tendency and confronted the discrepancy between word and action, inner and outer commitment (1 Sam. 15:22; Amos 5:21). This critique is powerfully expressed in postexilic Judaism (for example, in Malachi).

The empty formalism, coupled with syncretism, was the major theme of these prophetic complaints. This hypocrisy was sin to the Israelites because it destroyed the covenantal relationship with Yahweh. The call was for joyful admission to the cult, not requirements of a ritual nature.

Hellenism

The Persians began to lose control of their empire during the latter part of the fourth century B.C. The great warrior from Macedonia, Alexander the Great, conquered the whole of the Persian empire. Alexander did not change the situation that the conquered peoples had experienced under Cyrus. He did, however, bring to the empire a new way of thinking. Alexander was a student of Aristotle and as such had been steeped in Greek thought. Alexander not only wanted to conquer the whole world, but he wanted to hellenize it and bring all the known world under a single ethos.

Hellenization influenced the Hebrew culture in many ways. Education, especially in science and anthropology, strongly influenced the formation of Jewish thought after Alexander. The Greek language became the *lingua franca,* replacing Aramaic as the language of trade and education in the empire. *Koinē,* or spoken Greek, emerged as a language used throughout the ancient world. Along with the language, Greek literature was introduced into the empire. Schools developed and were probably related to synagogues. Some suggest that many similarities existed between the method of teaching and even the pattern of argument within the synagogues and the institutions of Greek learning. The most important result of the Greek influence on Palestinian Judaism was the formation of a Jewish intelligentsia, different from the priesthood and not dependent on the sanctuary. The new class was known as "scribes."

The movement toward a literate public was strong in the Greek *polis,* or city, and although the Jews had already been a literate people as early as the Babylonian exile, the Greek ways of education, logic, and organizing left their mark. The Greek forms were accepted and gave Judaism a new vehicle for expressing its ideas.

The process of hellenization placed Israel in a position of surviving within a culture or syncretistically adopting the culture, which threatened the worship of Yahweh. This struggle between faith and culture can be seen in the divisions that emerged within this period. The Hasidim ("loyal" or "pious ones") emerged as a group determined to keep the Jewish faith pure and free of the negative impact of the Greek world.

Acculturation might have occurred gradually if not for Antiochus IV and his outlawing of Jewish worship in 167 B.C., which provoked the Maccabean revolt. After a period of years the Jews regained control of the land, securing the freedom to worship in their own ways. But hellenization had affected the Hasmonean dynasty, and Judaism was represented by a new order. The Sanhedrin became the governing body. Internal tensions developed during this period among the Sadducees, who sought tolerance and compromise; the Pharisees, who originated from the Hasidim and stood for legalism and separatism; and the Zealots, who were revolutionaries attempting to overthrow the politically oppressive structures. Into this arena a child was born in Bethlehem who would bring into being a new system of worship.

Jewish worship had been influenced by Persian customs, laws, purification rites, mythology, cosmology, angelology, and eschatology. The Greek influence, especially in education and thought forms, can be seen in the life of the synagogues. Although the cultures surrounding the Israelites had changed drastically, the central motif of the worship of Yahweh had allowed flexibility in a faith that sustained itself through crisis and domination by numerous foreign powers. Elements within the worship pattern grew to have more or less emphasis in differing situations, yet the praise and continuing echo of corporate and private worship express the soul of the people of Israel.

— Early Christians and Jewish Worship —

Christian worship originated in a Jewish setting. Although the early church developed its own worship forms, they reflect the worship of Judaism, especially that of the synagogue. Thus the lines between Jewish worship and Christian worship are not clearly distinguishable until late into the second century A.D.

The Gospels presuppose forms of worship that were native to Palestinian Judaism in the first century A.D. The temple was still important (cf. Zechariah in Luke 1:5; Joseph and Mary in Luke 2:21; and Jesus, who is said to have gone to the temple when he came of age at *bar mitzvah* time). Throughout the Gospels Jesus is shown as a Jew who participated in the feasts and lived within the framework of the life and practice of Israel (Luke 4:16-31). Jesus prophetically criticized aspects of the legalism and external show that prohibited true worship. But his goal was to fulfill the Law not to destroy it (Matt. 5:17; John 1:17). Yet his attitude toward the temple was ambivalent. He reverenced it but foretold its destruction (John 2:19).

In order to examine worship in the New Testament, one must see the intimate connection between Judaism and the early worship forms of the church. Acts 2:46 records that the earliest Christians attended the temple together and broke bread in their homes. The difference might have been expressed first in the communal meal. The sacrificial element of the temple was also eventually rejected by the Christians, for they viewed Jesus' self-offering as a once-for-all sacrifice for sins.

The synagogue, the local center of worship in postexilic Judaism, gave Christianity much of its worship form in the inheritance of Scripture reading, preaching, singing, and prayer. The service of the synagogue consisted of a service of the Word that proclaimed the creedal *Sh^ema'* (Deut. 6:4). This service included Scripture reading and exposition, prayer, and benedictions.

Ralph P. Martin[4]

149 ◆ BIBLIOGRAPHY: ISRAELITE AND JEWISH WORSHIP

Hoffman, Lawrence A. *Beyond the Text: A Holistic Approach to Liturgy.* Downers Grove, IL: Inter-Varsity Press, 1989. Although the author addresses Jewish liturgy, the material is applicable to all worshiping communities. It is a source of insight into how a religious consciousness is formed, nurtured, and lived through worship.

Idelsohn, A. Z. *Jewish Liturgy and Its Development.* New York: Schocken Books, 1975. A detailed treatment of the whole range of Jewish worship, this study discusses forms of worship and prayer in ancient Israel, daily public prayers, daily home prayers, services for the high holy days, and Jewish elements in the early Christian liturgy.

Kraus, Hans-Joachim. *Worship in Israel.* Richmond: John Knox Press, 1966. This work lays out the cultic calendars and festivals of Israel, cultic officials and the sacrificial system, and the traditions associated with Israelite sanctuaries, especially Jerusalem.

Millgram, Abraham. *Jewish Worship.* Philadelphia: Jewish Publication Society of America, 1971. This thorough introduction to Jewish worship presents the foundations of Jewish worship such as worship in the temple, the structure of Jewish worship, and the organization and contents of the services of Jewish worship, including the synagogue service, major festivals, the liturgy of high holy days, and minor festivals.

Rowley, Harold Henry. *Worship in Ancient Israel.* London: SPCK, 1967. This is a detailed study of the history of Jewish worship from the patriarchal age through the development of the synagogue in the post-exilic period.

ELEVEN

History of New Testament Worship

Early Christians continued to worship in the temple and in the synagogue. Gradually, however, they separated from the Jewish institutions of worship into their own assemblies. As to form, Christian worship involved prayer and praise but centered around the teaching of Scripture and the Lord's Supper. Christ was proclaimed in the Word and celebrated at the table.

---

150 • WORSHIP IN THE GOSPELS

The Gospels presuppose the forms of worship native to Palestinian Judaism in the early first century A.D. The Gospels record Jesus' involvement with both the temple and the synagogue and his example of individual piety.

——— The Temple in the Gospels ———

The temple still occupied an important place in primitive New Testament worship. Zechariah, father of John the Baptist, was a priest, and God's revelation came to him as he fulfilled his ritual ministry in the temple (Luke 1:5ff.). Joseph and Mary were careful to keep the law of circumcision and the law of purification (Luke 2:21ff.). When Jesus reached the appropriate age, he went up to the temple for the Passover. It is significant that his conversation on this occasion—a preview of his later ministry—took place among the doctors of Israel in the temple and that he gave to his parents a reply that at least carries the suggestion that the temple, the house of God, was his proper place (Luke 2:42-51). A noteworthy feature in Luke is that the beginnings of the gospel are thus set very plainly in the framework of the life and practices of Israel.

The temple maintains its importance throughout the incarnate life and ministry of Jesus. He attends the feasts of Passover, Tabernacles, and the Dedication. He also weaves the feasts into the pattern of his ministry. Teaching in the temple court, he shows at the Feast of Tabernacles that he is the true water of life. The Passover is the setting both of the institution of the Lord's Supper and also of the accomplishment of the new exodus by his self-offering on the cross as the Lamb that takes away the world's sin. The promised outpouring of the Holy Spirit takes place significantly at Pentecost.

If Jesus has words of criticism for temple worship, they are directed against those who corrupt and defile it rather than against the worship itself. His driving out of the merchants and overturning of the tables is an act of defense of the temple (cf. John 2:17) which arouses the hostility only of ecclesiastics and profiteers. Jesus foresees the overthrow of the temple, but he does so with the sadness of the true worshiper, not with the crazy zeal of the revolutionary.

Nevertheless, Jesus recognized that the temple had to be knocked down and that it could not be replaced in its familiar form. God never agreed to have a permanent dwelling built for himself, and the various temples had to perish. God did promise that he would build a house for himself from the lineage of David. This promise had now come to fulfillment in Jesus, the One in whom God tabernacled, in living presence, among men. Hence the temple had reached its end and goal in the person of the incarnate Son. Jesus could appreciate it because it had served as a type of the true and final presence God was to manifest in him. But he could not preserve it in its existing form; he could only "fulfill" it (John 1:14; 2:19-22).

The sacrifices and sacrificial ministry of the temple also served as precursors, or types, of a greater fulfillment. One may assume that as Joseph and Mary made their offerings, and as Jesus himself attended the feasts, so he and his disciples continued to participate in sacrificial worship. The life of Jesus, however, was oriented to making one sacrifice for sins forever (Heb. 10:12), which would fulfill the Passover, the regular offerings, and also the special ritual of the Day of Atonement. Hence, when the temple sacrifices ceased with the destruction of the sanctuary, there would be no need to restore them. They had already reached their consummation. The types had given way to the reality in the self-offering of the Lord. Similarly, Jesus accepted the ministry of the Aaronic priesthood during his incarnate life. Yet he came to fulfill the ministry of the eternal high priest after the order of Melchizedek (Heb. 7:1-3). He was concerned neither to restore nor to replace the sacerdotal service of the destroyed temple. If a newer form of Passover was set up when the Last Supper became the Lord's Supper, it should be noted that here, as in the Jewish modification, the core and center of the ancient ritual was removed with the necessary abandonment of the slaying of the Passover lamb. Jesus had offered himself as the final Passover (1 Cor. 5:7) of the new and definitive redemption.

The Synagogue in the Gospels

The synagogue is no less prominent than the temple in the Gospel records. The custom of Jesus was to attend the synagogue on the Sabbath (Luke 4:16). In the synagogue at Nazareth he read the prophetic passage and in answer to the people's expectation gave an (astonishing) exposition of it. In the first period of his ministry he went about all Galilee, teaching in the synagogues (Matt. 4:23; 9:35). He cast out the unclean spirit in the synagogue at Capernaum (Mark 1:21-28). He also faced the challenge of his opponents in the synagogue by healing the man with a withered arm on the Sabbath (Mark 3:1-5), and he warned his disciples that they would be scourged in the synagogues (Matt. 10:17). It seems that in the later stages of his ministry, although crowds still followed him (Matt. 19:2), he was no longer so welcome in the synagogues. Were not his followers put out of the synagogues (John 9:22; 12:42)? Nevertheless, there was no definitive break prior to the crucifixion, and even then the first

Christian missionaries were apparently still received in synagogues of the Dispersion.

Personal Piety in the Gospels

The Gospels give evidence of individual as well as public piety. One may refer again to saintly figures such as Anna and Simeon, whose lives were devoted to prayer and praise and expectation. John the Baptist continues an earlier stream; he is the dedicated prophet of the desert, pursuing a life of asceticism. The Lord himself, for all the contrast he draws between himself and John (Matt. 11:16-19), both commands and also practices an assiduous life of prayer. He wants no outward show (Matt. 6:1-5), but his disciples are told to engage in secret almsgiving, prayer, and fasting. He warns them that prayer and fasting are needed to perform certain works (Matt. 17:21). He insists that the disciples must live in an attitude of watchfulness (Matt. 24:42). He asks Peter, James, and John to watch with him in Gethsemane (Matt. 26:38). He tells them to watch and pray lest they enter into temptation (Matt. 26:41). He himself engages in a forty-day fast in the desert (Matt. 4:1-11). Time and again the Gospels record that he spent the early morning (Mark 1:35) or the evening (Mark 6:47) in solitary mediation and prayer. Before the final crisis he retired to the garden to find strength for obedience to the Father's will, which now meant such cruel pain and loss for himself. The prayers on the cross, from the cry of dereliction to the petition for his tormentors and the final committal, are a culminating testimony to the Savior's relationship with God. This is reflected also in his longer prayers, the cry of jubilation and thanksgiving (Luke 10:21), the beautiful high-priestly prayer (John 17), and the prayer he taught his disciples (Matt. 6:9-13). He refers, perhaps incidentally, to the *Sh*e*ma'* in basing the first and great commandment on the familiar passage from the Law (Mark 12:28-31).

In the true prophetic tradition, Jesus does not tolerate the perverting of true piety into empty formalism. He censures not only the display of prayer, but also the prayer that is merely vain repetition (Matt. 6:7). He also condemns the exaggerated emphasis on ritual practice that makes this a substitute for genuine righteousness (Mark 7:6-8). Nevertheless, he does not reject either form (cf. the Lord's Prayer and the new ritual of the Lord's Supper) or ritual observances (Matt. 23:23) as such. His call is the prophetic call for the inner walk, the true consecration, and the right conduct, which will naturally find expression in religious exercises and which alone give substance, reality, and power to the external motions.

151 • WORSHIP IN ACTS AND THE EPISTLES

The book of Acts and the Epistles reflect continuing involvement of Christians with the institutions of Jewish worship. However, with the Gentile mission and increasing separation from the temple and synagogues, the churches had to develop their own forms of common worship. Even Jewish Christians came under increasing pressure as persistent evangelism aroused the hostility of the ecclesiastical authorities.

The Temple and the Early Church

The temple figures prominently in the worship of the infant church. After the Ascension the disciples were continually in the temple praising and blessing God (Luke 24:51-53). Part of the fellowship of the Jerusalem church was daily attendance in the temple (Acts 2:46). Peter and John healed the lame man on their way to the temple at the hour of prayer (Acts 3:1-10). Like Jesus, the apostles stood in the temple and taught the people (Acts 5:25). Later, Paul was anxious to be in Jerusalem for the day of Pentecost (Acts 20:16). One of his first acts on reaching the city was to make his way to the temple and undergo ritual purification (Acts 21:23-26). When arrested and accused, Paul protested strongly that he had not offended in any way against either the law or the temple. The witness of Stephen shows that the early church had a strong sense of the transitoriness of the earthly temple (Acts 7:47-50). The problem of Judaizing was important at this very point, for those who attached greater importance to the temple naturally wanted the Gentiles to become Jews so they could worship there. The church, led by Stephen and Paul, came to see that this was neither possible nor right. Nevertheless, so long as the temple remained, it was for Jewish Christians a proper center of the true, divine worship, which is in faith, obedience, sincerity, and truth.

The Synagogue and the Early Church

The Christian's relationship to the synagogue was equally strong, though the opportunity of exposition soon made the synagogue a place of contention and separation. Stephen seems to have engaged in synagogue evangelism (Acts 6:9-10). Paul made the synagogue the starting point of his missionary work in the various cities (Acts 13). He preached in the synagogues at Pisidian Antioch and Iconium and found a house of prayer at Philippi. It was Paul's custom to attend the synagogue, and he reasoned for three Sabbaths in the synagogue at Thessalonica (Acts 17:1-2). As late as Acts 28:16 he called the Jewish leaders of Rome together—his detention probably prevented his worshiping at the synagogue—and sought to persuade them of the verity of the gospel. In most of the Pauline churches the first converts came from the synagogues, though in no instance did a whole synagogue become a Christian congregation.

The division that took place in the synagogues through the preaching of the gospel meant that Christians were forced to hold their own gatherings. They had been prepared for this by the special times of fellowship the first disciples had enjoyed with their Lord, whether formally at meals or more informally. The first church in Jerusalem met together in the upper room for prayer (Acts 1:14; 4:31; 12:12). The breaking of bread, whether in the form of common meals, the Lord's Supper, or both, played some part in the movement toward the church's independent worship. Outside Jerusalem Paul (and Barnabas) apparently took steps to bring believers together for their own gatherings, which in some instances might have been supplementary to synagogue services, though there was a definite separation at Ephesus (Acts 19:9). The comparative ease with which synagogues could be formed, the pattern of worship already provided, and the conversion of leading members (cf. Crispus, the ruler of the synagogue at Corinth, Acts 18:8) helped to make the formation of Christian congregations a smooth and simple process. Believers probably met in houses, due to the absence of church buildings, and so one reads of house churches (cf. Philem. 2). The apostles made provision for the supervision of the new assemblies (Acts 14:22). Somewhat after the pattern of the synagogue, the two chief ministers were the elder (bishop) and deacon, though it is perhaps a mistake to see too close an assimilation to synagogical forms.

What form of worship was pursued in the Christian assemblies? The New Testament gives little detailed information. From the first chapters of Acts it may be gathered that prayer and the breaking of bread were primary. The only other detailed sources are in Acts 20 and 1 Corinthians 11 and 14. Acts 20:7 records a meeting on the first day of the week at which the disciples broke bread and Paul preached; the meeting seems to have been in the evening. First Corinthians 11 also speaks of a common meal, which is plainly the Lord's Supper (1 Cor. 11:23-34), though probably in combination with an ordinary supper. First Corinthians 14 mentions a gathering at which members might contribute a psalm, a doctrine, a tongue, a revelation, or an interpretation, though with an emphasis on edifying and order. The injunction in 1 Corinthians 16:2 is perhaps a further hint that these assemblies were held on the first day of the week. Whether Corinth was typical cannot be decided, nor indeed whether the procedure in 1 Corinthians 14 is supplementary to more organized worship, such as at the Lord's Supper. Perhaps the Corinthian emphasis on tongues carried with it a more-than-customary drive for freedom.

The sources do not indicate that a recognized structure had emerged at this period. Nevertheless, even at Corinth the constituent features of worship—prayer, praise, exposition and perhaps reading of the Scriptures, and the Lord's Supper—are evident. The materials of liturgy are also present. The Psalms would be the Old Testament Psalter, and readings involved a fixed form of words. Paul gives a simple order for the Lord's Supper. Part of the general content of prayer is suggested in 1 Timothy 2:1-3. The prayer of Acts 4:24, though extemporaneous, uses liturgical phrases obviously drawn from the Old Testament. Even the sermons recorded in Acts are not without patent similarities of wording and structure. Since the primitive church is heir to the rich tradition of the Old Testament and Judaism, it would be strange if this were not so. The new spirit and power lie in the new understanding of the old forms, the fashioning of new forms out of the old, rather than in formlessness.

Personal Devotion and Piety of Early Christians

Individual piety finds no less expression in the life and teaching of the apostles than in that of the Lord. Paul is a good example. He practices (1 Thess. 2:1) and urges (1 Thess. 5:17) unceasing prayer. He calls for prayer in support of his ministry (Eph. 6:18). In many passages he indicates the content of his own prayers, which in the Epistles at least are largely intercessory in character (Phil. 1:4-11; Col. 1:9-12), though a passage like Philippians 3:8-11 becomes almost a prayer of aspiration, and his first Christian prayer (Acts 9:11) was almost certainly a prayer for forgiveness and enlightenment. The indication of content is even more extended in Ephesians 3:14-21, which seems to have been dictated by the apostle quite literally on his knees in the gesture of individual prayer (Dan. 6:10). This prayer of petition characteristically moves to a doxological climax that expresses the confidence of faith and that sees in all God's work a fulfillment of the first request of the Lord's Prayer. Steeped as he is in Old Testament and Jewish forms, Paul adopts quite naturally a liturgical language that is a free adaptation of existing phrases. The intensity of his faith and devotion, allied to extensive biblical knowledge, produces a perfect blend of dignity and fervor.

In addition to prayer, Paul commands a diligent study of the Scriptures, whether by reading or by committing to memory (cf. 2 Tim. 3:15-17; Eph. 6:17). He also calls for a life of self-discipline, which may include celibacy if this is the divine command (1 Cor. 7:1-8), but which certainly includes a subjection of the body for the sake of better service (1 Cor. 9:24). The discipline of fasting is not neglected (2 Cor. 11:27). Thanksgiving is also to be the constant attitude and exercise of the believer (1 Thess. 5:18). The grave and sober conduct expected of bishops and deacons (1 Tim. 3) does not specify a personal exercise of piety, but it is implied. Timothy, as a man of God, is exhorted to pursue godliness (1 Tim. 6:11). While the worship of the individual merges into that of the fellowship, and also into general uprightness of life and conduct, the personal exercise of religion is an important aspect of worship in the New Testament.

152 • ELEMENTS OF NEW TESTAMENT WORSHIP

Though the New Testament does not give any detailed information on the structure of the first Christian services, it leaves little room for doubt concerning the basic elements of primitive worship: prayer, praise, confession of sin, confession of faith, Scripture reading and preaching, the Lord's Supper, and the collection. Early descriptions of Christian worship, such as that in Justin's Apology, *reveal a close similarity to the practice of the synagogue. Even without the synagogue model, however, the fundamental elements would surely have found a place, and distinctive Christian features would have their own origin.*

Prayer

Prayer, in the more specific sense of petition, is a constituent element of worship. The first duty of the church between the Ascension and the outpouring of the Spirit was to wait in prayerful expectancy. Persecution quickly forced the Jerusalem church to its knees in common prayer. The needs of Christians, the needs of apostles, and the needs of the world all provided constant material for intercession. Common concern produced common petition. One cannot say exactly how the church prayed. Perhaps a leader prayed for the whole, perhaps individuals prayed in course, perhaps there was recitation of a form or forms of prayer. Rather surprisingly, there is no immediate reference to a congregational use of the Lord's Prayer; its use in the *Didachē,* or *Teaching of the Twelve Apostles* (an early Christian manual) is an individual usage (see Chapter 8). The *Amen,* having acquired a new and even deeper meaning from its use by Jesus (cf. 2 Cor. 1:20), occurs frequently in the New Testament and probably served as a congregational response, as in synagogue worship (cf. Justin, *Apology* I, 65-67). Stock phrases like *maranatha* might have been used also (1 Cor. 16:22; *cf.* Rev. 22:20; *Didachē* 10, 7); otherwise it is difficult to see why they should be preserved in Aramaic. Blessings, whether from the Old Testament or in the new Christian form of 2 Corinthians 13:14 or Revelation 22:21, probably came into rapid use. The Epistles especially testify to the emergence of distinctive vocabulary of Christian worship in the New Testament period. Whatever the forms, however, the essential element of prayer belongs to worship from the very outset, and a genuine Christian service without it is almost unthinkable.

Praise

Closely related to prayer is praise, the confession of God's nature and works. Indeed, prayer in the form of thanksgiving is itself praise. Almost all the prayers recorded in the New Testament contain an element of doxology. They recall God's acts and thus sound a note of assurance and triumph. Quite apart from prayer, however, the praise of God has its own place in New Testament worship. The infancy stories show how the life of Christ began with angelic and human canticles that ultimately served as new songs in the congregation. The cry of jubilation uttered by the Lord took quasi-hymnic form. Jesus and the disciples sang a hymn—probably the customary *Hallel*—at the Last Supper. Paul refers to a psalm at worship in Corinth and to hymns and spiritual songs in Ephesians 5:19. Scholars have discerned possible fragments of early Christian hymns in such passages as Philippians 2:5-11 and 1 Timothy 3:16. The hymns of Revelation show that songs are sung in heavenly as well as earthly worship, though some expositors think Revelation 4–5 might be based on the worship of the congregation. In the earliest period the Psalter was probably the hymnbook of the church, but if the reference in Pliny's letter to Trajan (*Letters* X, 96) is to Christological hymns, it seems that quite early new and more specifically Christian hymns found a place in the confession of praise.

Confession of Sin

The confession of sin is at the heart of worship, for as the worthiness of God is exalted, the unworthiness of man demands acknowledgment. The prayers and psalms of the Old Testament are full of the recognition of guilt, which obviously goes hand in hand with a plea for forgiveness and restitution, and with praise and thanks for the divine mercy and pardon. In the New Testament the gospel is by its very nature a divine word to sinners. The baptism of John is a summons to repentance and conversion. Jesus takes up the same call, followed by his apostles, in the first preaching of Acts. Peter, confronted by Jesus, confesses that he is a sinful man (Luke 5:8). The prayer God hears in the temple is the penitent prayer of the publican rather than the self-congratulatory prayer of the Pharisee (Luke 18:9-14). In the church's worship, the great occasion for the confession of sin is at baptism, when the old life of sin is renounced and the new life of faith and obedience is begun. In postapostolic days the public confession of specific faults was required when the excommunicated sought readmittance. It may be seen from 1 John 1:8-10, however, that confession of sins to God, whether individually or in concert, played a continuing role in the life of believers. Paul, in his letters, refers again and again to the utter dependence of himself and all believers on the divine mercy. Thus, although there is no great evidence of specific prayers of confession in New Testament worship, this element must be presupposed as the basis of all prayer and praise. Prayer itself has to be in the name of Jesus, since there is nothing in oneself or in one's own name that could constitute a valid ground of either access or answer (cf. the role of Jesus as high priest and intercessor in Heb. 7).

——— Confession of Faith (Baptism) ———

In the Old Testament the *Sh^ema'*, though primarily a commandment, served also as a confession of faith: "The Lord our God is one Lord." As such it had found its way into the worship of the synagogue. Though the Lord gave it added attention, it was not adopted by the early church. The main reason was not that this basic confession was abandoned but rather that there had now been added the distinctive Christian confession "Jesus is Lord." The faith of the primitive church is faith in Jesus as Savior and God. Peter makes this primary affirmation in Matthew 16:16. It is seen again in Thomas's confession (John 20:28). John's gospel was written with a view to the lordship of Jesus (John 20:31). The work of the Spirit is to induce in Christians the affirmation that Jesus is Lord (1 Cor. 12:3). All tongues will finally confess this (Phil. 2:11). On this belief rests the full confession of the triune God (Matt. 28:19). This confession is specifically made in the church at baptism, which is done in the name of Jesus (Acts 2:38). The eunuch professes belief in the Lord (Acts 8:37). Cornelius is baptized in Jesus' name (Acts 10:48). The Philippian jailer is baptized when he believes on the Lord and is saved (Acts 16:30-34). The evidence of the later church (Justin, *Apology* I, 61) is similar. The baptismal confession was often made in interrogatory form, and it was followed by baptism in the triune name (or triune immersion, as described in *Didachē* 7).

Whether there was also a specific confession of faith in ordinary worship is open to question; the New Testament offers no instance. Baptism itself, however, was also a normal part of the worship of the church. Taken over from John and continued and commanded by Jesus, it was required for admission to the church, and it included at its heart a confession of faith as well as repentance. Administered in various circumstances and with wide variations of wording, it retained its essential features through every change. The first service for the convert was of common concern to the whole congregation. Like the Lord's Supper, it had a primary declarative aspect, for the ultimate baptismal confession is confession of the saving act of God in the death and resurrection of Christ. Nevertheless, it also provided opportunity for the affirmation of faith, which was quickly seen to be a reaffirmation by existing believers. The later weekly confession is a fairly natural and not unbiblical development, which finds a regular place for this essential aspect of worship.

——— Reading of Scripture ———

Rather strangely, the New Testament does not refer to the reading of the Old Testament in the common worship of the church. Paul's epistles are publicly read (1 Thess. 5:27), and this might have formed the beginning of the later New Testament readings (cf. Justin's "Memoirs of the Apostles," *Apology* I, 66). The traditional texts relating to the Lord's Supper also seem to have been rehearsed (1 Cor. 11). In light of synagogue practice, the extensive use of the Old Testament in the New Testament, the later knowledge of the Old Testament displayed in the postapostolic period, and the early patristic references to Old Testament reading, it is virtually impossible to suppose that the New Testament church did not include Old Testament readings in common worship. The fact that there were sermons (for example, Paul at Troas) supports this. A sermon in the synagogue was primarily exposition. Early Christian preaching was especially concerned with showing the fulfillment of the Old Testament in Christ. Furthermore, the mention of an interpretation seems to presuppose reference to the Old Testament. The high estimation of Scripture (cf. 2 Tim. 3:15-17) is a further consideration. Great freedom was no doubt exercised—even the synagogue had, as yet, no prophetic lectionary. But the reading of God's written Word, first in the Old Testament and then increasingly in the New Testament, was surely a constituent part of worship from the very first, as it patently was in both temple and synagogue, and then again in the church of the second century.

——— Preaching ———

In contrast to reading, preaching is solidly attested. Paul preached at Troas. The prophesyings at Corinth also seem to be forms of Christian exhortation. The needs of evangelism and education as well as edification made it essential that the ministry of the Word be included in the early services. The synagogue provided a partial parallel; the teaching of Jesus was an example. The apostles were specifically called to the ministry of the Word (Acts 6). At a later time bishops were to be apt teachers (1 Tim. 3:2). Preaching combined several aspects of "worship": declaration of God's work, confession of faith, underlying prayer, and the climax of praise. Early preaching was particularly related to the Old Testament on the one side and to the life and work of Christ (later the New Testament) on the other. While not restricted to formal exposition, it had a strong expository content, judging from the sermons in Acts. Among Gentile Christians in particular, a good deal of information would have to be passed on in preaching, for the same level of biblical knowledge could not always be assumed as among Jewish Christians or the early "god fearers." Apollos, a man mighty in the Scriptures, exercised an important ministry in this field (Acts 18:24-28). Justin gives evidence of the secure position of preaching in the typical Christian service in the postapostolic period.

The Lord's Supper

If baptism was an addition to synagogue worship (though not without some parallel in proselyte baptism), this is even more true of the Lord's Supper. Both biblical and patristic evidence support the view that this was from the very first a constitutive part of weekly worship. Certainly in Justin's time there is no disjunction between ministry of word and ministry of sacrament, and the examples of Troas and Corinth suggest that, with variations of time and structure, the same applies in the New Testament period as well. The one gathering embraces not only prayer, praise, reading, and preaching, but also the holy meal, which was probably accompanied by blessings (cf. *Didachē* 9–10) after the manner of the Passover. The Lord's Supper took the place, not only of the Passover, but also of the temple offerings. This is why sacrificial language soon came to be used in respect to the Lord's Supper (cf. Mal. 1:11). Yet it was not strictly a replacement: the Lord's Supper shows forth the one sacrifice for sins forever. Christ as high priest has made a mediatorial and sacrificial ministry at the human level redundant. Hence the ministers of the Lord's Supper, whether apostles, bishops, presbyters, or deacons, are truly ministers, not priests. The focal point is declaration of the death and resurrection of Jesus Christ for mankind. This is the ground of the fellowship here enjoyed with God and with fellow believers. Ultimately, then, the Lord's Supper, like all else, is Christological rather than, in the narrower Old Testament sense, liturgical. To describe it as quintessentially liturgical is misleading. It is also to hold in disregard its real place and significance within the church's worship as a perpetual reminder that worship is possible only on the basis of the atonement that God himself has made by his self-offering in the Son.

The Collection

The reference to a weekly allocation in 1 Corinthians 16, the liturgical significance ascribed to alms in Philippians 4:18, and mention of an offering in patristic writings have lead to the view that a collection formed a basic element in Christian worship. Difficulties to this conclusion include the following: Paul does not speak of a church collection; like the Philippian gift, the Jerusalem collection was probably a special project (though rapidly succeeded by extensive relief for the poor); and Tertullian refers only to a chest for spontaneous gifts (*Apology* I, 39, 1-6). Furthermore, some scholars argue that Justin's offertory (*Apology* I, 65) is that of bread and wine for communion, though this was not an obvious part of the original institution. On the other side, one should consider that almsgiving had a long Old Testament history, and that the importance of liberality as part of serving God is beyond dispute. Thus, if it is too much to say that the collection is a constitutive part of the service, there are grounds for its later inclusion. The kiss of peace falls into a similar category.

Occasional Services

It has often been noted that there are no marriage or funeral services in the New Testament. It should be remembered, however, that such services are only an application of the basic elements of worship—prayer, praise, reading, exposition, and the Lord's Supper, where appropriate to specific situations. In fact, the New Testament mentions certain occasions—for example, confirming by the apostles, ordaining, and perhaps the anointing of the sick—when biblical signs (laying on of hands, anointing) were used along with other liturgical elements. This does not mean that there were developed special services for confirmation and other biblical signs. It shows that the basic elements can be rapidly adapted to particular needs, sometimes with a particular sign. The consecration of Paul and Barnabas to missionary service at Antioch offers an instructive example (Acts 13:2-3). Whether any given service can find a precedent in the New Testament, it offers the materials from which a genuinely biblical service may be constructed, and the injunction that all things are to be done in the Lord means that the introduction of elements of worship is never a misplaced or unwarranted intrusion.

153 ◆ THE ESSENCE OF NEW TESTAMENT WORSHIP

Though the elements of Christian worship are the same as those in the Old Testament, there are two new factors at the very heart of the New Testament that bring about a decisive reorientation. First, Christian worship is through God the Son; second, it is worship in the Holy Spirit.

——— Worship Through God the Son ———

The first of these new factors is that Christian worship is in its very core and essence the worship of God the Father through God the Son. The elements remain; the Christological orientation is new. If space allowed, one might easily work through the data afresh to show this truth. In this conclusion, a few indications must suffice. Worshipers now stand in a personal relation of sonship to God on the basis of adoption in Christ. They pray in the name of the Son (John 16:23). The works of God in the Son are the theme of their praise (Eph. 1:3-14). Their plea for forgiveness is that Christ gave himself as a perfect sacrifice for sin (1 John 1:7-9). Their confession is confession of Jesus as Lord (1 Cor. 12:3). The Scriptures, both the Old Testament and the New Testament, testify of Christ (John 5:39). Preaching is the setting forth of Christ in his revealing and reconciling work (2 Cor. 5:18-21). The Lord's Supper is the Passover of the new and final exodus, the showing forth of the one sacrifice for sin (1 Cor. 11:26). Christian almsgiving acquires a new ground and basis in the light of God's gift in Christ (2 Cor. 9:15) and of the giving of all gifts to him (Matt. 25:31-46). The suitability of worship at various points in life rests in the fact that all Christian life is life in the Lord (Rom. 14:8). The decisive point, then, is not that new forms are provided or new levels of devotion ensured, but that God has come in person and fulfilled his work of grace. With this focus worship is given a depth and content that it could hardly achieve in the time of Old Testament and Jewish expectation.

——— Worship in the Holy Spirit ———

The second of the new factors in Christian worship is that in its very core and essence it is worship of God the Father through God the Son and in and by God the Holy Spirit. True worship has always been both spiritual and in the Spirit, but as Jesus himself showed, his own ministry brought with it a specific coming of the Spirit that makes possible in fullness the worship that is in spirit and in truth. Prayer occurs with the assistance of the Spirit (Rom. 8:26-27). Praise is rejoicing in the Spirit (Eph. 5:18-20). Confession of sins is under conviction of the Spirit (John 16:8). Confession of faith is confession by the Spirit (1 Cor. 12:3). Holy Scripture, given by the Spirit, is illumined by the Spirit (2 Cor. 3:6-8). Preaching is a demonstration of the Spirit and of power (1 Cor. 2:4). The fellowship of the Lord's Table is a fellowship of the Spirit (cf. Acts 2). Liberality flows from the love that is a fruit of the Spirit (Gal. 5:22). Living life in a context of prayer and praise and proclamation is a walking in the Spirit (cf. Rom. 8:1-17). It is a question not of spiritual worship as distinct from liturgical worship, but rather of the inner ministry of the Spirit in regenerating and sanctifying power. The person who is born of the Spirit and led by the Spirit is one who even in outward expression offers to God through Christ fitting and acceptable worship.

Geoffrey W. Bromiley[5]

154 ◆ BIBLIOGRAPHY: NEW TESTAMENT WORSHIP

Attridge, Harold W. *A Commentary on the Epistle to the Hebrews.* Philadelphia: Fortress Press, 1989. This commentary gives special attention to the liturgical insights and materials of the book of Hebrews. Matters such as the development of a high priestly Christology, priesthood, and sonship, the veil and its symbolism, Melchizedek, the heavenly temple and its significance are a few of many subjects thoughtfully treated.

Branick, Vincent. *The House Church in the Writings of Paul.* Mahwah, N.J.: Paulist Press, 1991. This is an excellent treatment of the house church in general. Most important this book contains an extensive chapter on house-church worship in the Corinthian church.

Chilton, David. *Days of Vengeance.* Fort Worth: Dominion Press, 1987. This volume argues for the interpretation of the book of Revelation as a record of heavenly worship in progress.

Coleman, Robert E. *Songs of Heaven.* Tarrytown, N.Y.: Fleming H. Revell Co., 1980. The author explores the hymns of the Revelation and opens up a long-neglected aspect of the book.

Daniélou, Jean, S.J., *The Bible and the Liturgy.* Notre Dame: University of Notre Dame Press, 1956. This helpful work deals with the biblical images and metaphors in matters such as baptism, confirmation, the Eucharist, the paschal Lamb, canticles, the Lord's Day, Ascension, and Pentecost.

Deiss, Lucien. *Springtime of the Liturgy.* Collegeville, Minn.: Liturgical Press, 1979. This presentation of primary liturgical sources from the early church includes material from the *Didachē,* Clement of Rome, Hippolytus, the Apostolic Constitutions, and other works.

Delling, Gerhard. *Worship in the New Testament.* London: Darton, Longman & Todd; Philadelphia: Westminster Press, 1962. Reprint. A classic study of the origin and development of worship in the primitive church, deals with structure, fixed forms, creed and hymn, the Word, prayer, ceremonial acts, ministries, and the community.

Hahn, Ferdinand. *The Worship of the Early Church.* Philadelphia: Fortress Press, 1973. This is a scholarly investigation into Jesus' attitude toward worship and the foundations of early Christian worship. It deals with the worship of various groups, such as the Aramaic, Hellenistic, and early Gentile communities, and discusses worship in the sub-apostolic and apostolic fathers.

Martin, Ralph P. *Worship in the Early Church.* Grand Rapids: Wm. B. Eerdmans Publishing Co., 1964. In this standard work on early Christian worship, the author probes the Jewish inheritance in the temple and synagogue, prayers and praises of the New Testament, hymns and spiritual songs, early creeds and confessions of faith, the ministry of the Word, the collection, baptism, the Lord's Supper, and later developments in Christian worship.

Moule, C. F. D. *Worship in the New Testament.* 2 vols. Bramcote, Notts.: Grove Books, 1983. This is a standard treatment of New Testament liturgical issues; it deals with the roots of Christian worship in the synagogue, the breaking of the bread, baptism, and various forms of worship.

Shepherd, Massy H., Jr. *The Paschal Liturgy and the Apocalypse.* Richmond: John Knox Press, 1960. This study argues that the book of Revelation is structured according to the liturgy of the early church.

TWELVE

The Tabernacle

The tabernacle is the sacred house where God met with his people. It was a place of dwelling for God, a place for meeting, a place for revelation, and a place for sacrifice and atonement. The tabernacle is a symbol of God's dwelling with the people of the covenant and is the basis for the New Testament understanding of the incarnation of the Word in Jesus Christ (John 1:14) and of the presence of the Lord in the midst of the church.

155 ⬥ THE TABERNACLE OF MOSES

The central theme of the Mosaic tabernacle is the dwelling of God in the midst of Israel. The actualization of God's dwelling is expressed in every aspect of the tabernacle, including its structure, materials, courts, sanctuaries, and furnishings including the altars, the lampstand, and the ark of the covenant.

——— Terminology and References ———

A number of words and phrases are used in connection with the tabernacle.

(1) "The tent" occurs nineteen times; similar phrases include "tent of the LORD" (1 Kings 2:28-29); "the house of the tent" (1 Chron. 9:23); "the house of the LORD" (Exod. 23:19); and "the tabernacle of the house of God" (1 Chron. 6:48).

(2) "Tent of meeting," that is, of God and of Israel through Moses, indicates the tabernacle as a place of revelation. This name occurs over 125 times (Exod. 33:7; Num. 11:16; 12:4; Deut. 31:14). The place where the Lord met with Moses and Israel (Exod. 29:42-43; Num. 17:4) was for communication and revelation (Exod. 29:42; 33:11; Num. 7:89). It is equivalent to "tent of revelation," since here God declared his will for Israel. The rendering "the tabernacle of the congregation" is not exact.

(3) "Dwelling place" or "dwelling" indicates the place where God disclosed himself to his people and dwelt among them. The root is "to dwell." Exodus 25:8 uses the word to speak of the entire shrine; in Exodus 26:1 it is limited practically to the Holy of Holies.

(4) "The tabernacle of the testimony" also occurs (Exod. 38:21). Less frequently, we see "the tent of the testimony" (Num. 9:15, ASV).

(5) The general term *Holy Place,* or "sanctuary," appears in Exodus 25:8 and Leviticus 10:17-18. The root is the verb "to be separate, holy."

The principal passages dealing with the tabernacle are (1) Exodus 25–29; (2) Exodus 30–31; (3) Exodus 35–40; and (4) Numbers 3:25-26; 4:4-6; and 7:1-89.

——— The Structure of the Tabernacle ———

The purpose of the structure is stated in Exodus 25:8, 21-22. It was made after the pattern shown to Moses on the mount (Exod. 25:9; 26:30). The entrances to the court and to the structure were from the east. The altar of burnt offering was in the court, then the laver; inside the tabernacle, farthest west, stood the Holy of Holies, or Most Holy Place, which housed the ark of the covenant and was hidden by a veil, or curtain. The second division inside the tabernacle, the Holy Place, contained the table of shewbread, the golden lampstand, and the altar of incense.

In the development of Israelite religion, altars appeared before sanctuaries (Gen. 12:7-8). The tabernacle reflected the monotheism of Israel, and the later temples were modeled after it. The ground plan of the tabernacle is sufficiently clear, although there are various opinions concerning the details. It is customarily held that the shape of the structure was oblong with a flat roof and ornate coverings that hung

Artistic Re-creation of the Tabernacle in the Wilderness

down at each side and at the back. Another opinion is that the tabernacle had a sloping roof.

The outer court contained the altar of burnt offering and the bronze laver. The tabernacle structure consisted of two divisions: the Holy Place and the Holy of Holies, or Most Holy Place. In the former, which was on the north side, stood the table of shewbread (the structure was oriented toward the east); the golden lampstand was on the south; the golden altar of incense was on the west against the veil leading to the Most Holy Place. The innermost compartment held the ark of the covenant, in which were deposited the two tablets of the Law, the pot of manna, and the rod of Aaron that had budded. The ark's covering, a lid of pure gold, was the mercy seat, or propitiatory, overshadowed by two angelic figures called cherubim. At the mercy seat God met with his people in their need on the basis of shed blood.

Materials and Furniture

The tabernacle was made from the voluntary gifts of Israel. Materials are listed in Exodus 25:3-7 and 35:4-9: gold, silver, bronze; blue, purple, and scarlet material and fine, twined linen; goats' hair, dyed rams' skins, goatskins, acacia wood, oil for lamps, spices for anointing oil and fragrant incense, onyx stones, and stones for the ephod and the breastpiece. The three metals of ancient times—bronze, silver, and gold—were used in meaningful gradation from the outer court to the Most Holy Place. The most artistic use of the metals was found in the cherubim and the golden lampstand. The wood used throughout the structure was *shittim,* or acacia wood, known for its durability. The material employed was linen, also fine, twined linen, dyed blue, purple, and scarlet (Exod. 25:4). The yarn was spun by women in charge of the weaving (Exod. 35:25-35); the work included embroidery and tapestry.

Framework and Coverings

The framework of the tabernacle (Exod. 26:15-37; 36:20-38) was made of 48 wooden frames, fifteen feet high by 27 inches wide, with three vertical arms joined by three crosspieces. These were placed in wooden supports, and over them were hung two large curtains. Over all were spread three covers. The framework was constructed of uprights of acacia wood, making three sides of the oblong structure. The front was closed by an embroidered screen (Exod. 26:36-37). The boards, 48 in number, were overlaid with gold. The construction was divided into two compartments, separated by a veil hung from four pillars overlaid with gold and set in sockets of silver. The veil, like the covering of the tabernacle, was woven in blue, purple, and scarlet, with figures of cherubim. The Holy Place was thirty feet long by fifteen feet wide; the Most Holy Place was fifteen feet square. It has been suggested that the tabernacle proper was shaped like a tent, with a ridge pole and a sloping roof.

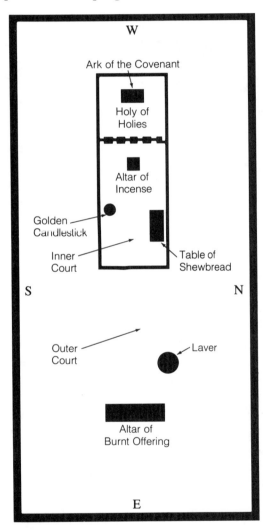

The Plan of the Tabernacle
(based on Exodus 40:16-34)

The coverings of the tabernacle are described in Exodus 26:1-14 and 36:8-9. The wooden framework of the tabernacle had three coverings: the total covering of the tabernacle itself, the covering of goats' hair, and the covering of ram's skins and goatskins spread over the entire structure. The first covering was made of ten curtains of fine, twined linen woven in blue, purple, and scarlet, with figures of

cherubim. The second covering was of eleven curtains of goats' hair. The top covering was made of rams' skins dyed red and goatskins.

Court of the Tabernacle

The court is described in Exodus 27:9-18 and 38:9-20. The court of the tabernacle was a rectangle on an east-to-west plan, one hundred cubits (about 150 feet) long and fifty cubits wide. To the west was the tabernacle proper and to the east, the altar. The court was screened from the camp by five white curtains five cubits high. It was an enclosure 150 feet long by 75 feet wide, with curtains of fine, twined linen, supported on bronze pillars and attached by silver hooks. In the court stood the altar of burnt offering and the laver, the latter being set between the altar and the tabernacle proper (Exod. 30:17-21). The entrance to the court was on the eastern side through a "gate" or "screen" with hangings.

The Altar

The altar of burnt offering is discussed in Exodus 27:1-8 and 38:1-7. It is called "the altar of bronze" for its appearance and "the altar of burnt offering" for its use. The fire on this altar was never to go out (Lev. 6:13). The most important of the contents of the outer court was the altar. It was a hollow chest of acacia wood covered with bronze, five cubits long, five cubits wide, and three cubits high, with a horn at each of the four corners. In the middle of the altar was a ledge (Lev. 9:22) and below it a grating. The altar was carried by bronze-covered poles in bronze rings. The horns of this altar were at times misused for asylum (1 Kings 1:50-51). They were sprinkled

An Artistic Conception of the Altar
(based on Exodus 27:1-8)

with blood at the consecration of the priests (Exod. 29:12), at the presentation of the sin offering (Lev. 4:18-34), and on the Day of Atonement (Lev. 16:18). The grating on the four sides at the foot of the altar permitted the blood of the sacrifices to be spilled at the base of the altar through the network. Laymen were permitted to approach the altar, for when they brought their sacrifices, they laid their hands on the victim (Lev. 1:4).

The Laver

The laver is described in Exodus 30:17-21. It was for the exclusive use of the priests as they ministered in the ritual of the tabernacle. They neglected this provision at the peril of their lives (Exod. 30:20-21). Made of bronze, the laver had a base, evidently for the washing of the feet of the priests. Some scholars believe the base was a part of the laver proper, whereas others with greater probability maintain that the base was a vessel separate from the laver itself. The record indicates that the bronze was contributed by the ministering women who were engaged in work about the tabernacle (Exod. 38:8).

The Sanctuary Proper

The tabernacle proper is described in Exodus 26:1-14 and 36:8-19. It appears that the curtains, rather than the boards, constituted the dwelling of the Lord (Exod. 26:1). The record of the wooden framework of the dwelling is in Exodus 26:15-30 and 36:20-34. At the inner portion of the court stood the tabernacle, an oblong structure 45 feet long by 15 feet wide, with two divisions, the Holy Place and the Most Holy (Exod. 26:33). These two divisions are found in the Solomonic temple as well (1 Kings 6:5). The area of the Most Holy Place was thirty feet square; the Holy Place measured sixty feet by thirty feet. The two were separated by a veil. On the Day of Atonement the high priest entered the veil, or curtain, at the open end, into the innermost sanctuary. The emphasis in Exodus 26 and 36 is on the tabernacle itself and its curtains, of which there were ten, each 28 cubits by 4 cubits. The ten curtains of colored fabric with woven cherubim were joined in two sets of five along the sides of the tabernacle. Fifty loops of violet thread were sewn onto the curtains, which were to be held together by fifty gold clasps, thus uniting the whole tabernacle (Exod. 26:6). Over all was placed a tent, one covering of goats' hair with five or six curtains coupled by hooks and clasps, amounting to a total size of fourty

cubits by thirty cubits, to make certain the tabernacle was completely covered. The covering overlapped the linen and permitted an extra fold at the front (Exod. 26:9). The tent had two coverings, one of rams' skins dyed red and another of goatskins (*cf.* Exod. 26:14; 40:19).

The curtains were held in place by forty-eight acacia frames. These frames consisted of two arms connected at the top, center, and bottom by rungs with two silver bases for each frame. The silver bases formed an unbroken foundation around the tabernacle. The frames were also held together by five bars. The frames and bars were gold plated. The front of the structure was enclosed by curtains. (Exodus 26:22-25 is difficult to interpret. It may speak of a pair of frames joined at each corner of the west or rear of the framework, sloping upward and inward from their bases to a point under the top bar.) The screen was the entrance to the Holy Place. The veil separated the Holy of Holies, or Most Holy Place, from the Holy Place. The veil was made of variegated material embroidered with cherubim, draped over four pillars of acacia wood, overlaid with gold, and supported by four silver bases. The screen was of the same material as the screen at the entrance to the outer court (Exod. 27:16). It was suspended from golden hooks on five pillars of acacia wood, overlaid with gold, and supported by bronze bases.

The Holy Place

The outer compartment, or Holy Place, contained three pieces of furniture: (1) the table of shewbread; (2) the golden lampstand; and (3) the golden altar of incense. The table was set on the north side of the Holy Place (Exod. 40:22); the lampstand on the south side (Exod. 40:24); and the altar of incense on the west side, before the veil. The table was made of acacia wood covered with fine gold and ornamented with gold molding. Rings and poles were used for carrying the table. A number of accessories were made for the table: gold plates to hold the loaves, dishes for frankincense (Lev. 24:7), and golden vessels for wine offerings. On this table were placed two piles of twelve loaves, or cakes, which were changed each week (Lev. 24:5-9). The dishes, spoons, and bowls were all of pure gold.

On the south side of the Holy Place stood the golden, seven-branched lampstand. It was the most ornate of all the furniture. Of pure gold, it had a central shaft (Exod. 25:32-35) from which sprouted six

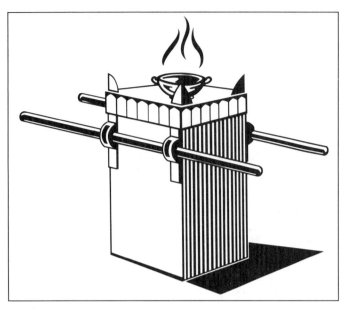

*An Artistic Conception of the Altar of Incense
(based on Exodus 30:1-10)*

golden branches, three on either side. The lampstand was adorned with almonds and flowers. Each branch supported a lamp that gave continuous (some say only nightly) illumination (Exod. 27:20; Lev. 24:2-3; 1 Sam. 3:3). Accessories of the lampstand, such as snuffers, snuff dishes, and oil vessels, were all of gold. The lampstand was made of a talent of pure gold (Exod. 25:38). In front of the veil was an altar of incense (Exod. 30:1-5; 37:25-28). Because it is not mentioned in Exodus 25, it is considered by some to be a later addition. It is not mentioned in the Septuagint translation of Exodus 37. It was a small altar, constructed of acacia wood and overlaid with gold, one cubit long, one cubit wide, and two cubits high. It was a miniature replica of the bronze altar (Exod. 30:1-10). Its fire was provided from the main altar. Horns, rings, poles, and a golden molding were made for it. Perpetual sweet-smelling incense was offered on it, and on the Day of Atonement expiation was made on its horns. On the basis of Hebrews 9:4, some believe Exodus 30:6 and 1 Kings 6:22 suggest that the altar of incense was inside the veil, in the Most Holy Place. The writer of Hebrews views the sanctuary and its ritual proleptically, that is, in light of future events: the rent veil and an accomplished redemption. Furthermore, the passages in Exodus and 1 Kings cannot be made to teach a condition contrary to the other passages on the Holy Place. Provision was made for replenishing the oil for the lampstand and the incense for the altar (Exod. 30:22-38).

The Holy of Holies

The smallest of all the parts of the sanctuary was the Holy of Holies, yet it was the most significant because of the ritual that was carried out there on the Day of Atonement and because of the reiterated declaration that God himself dwelt in the tabernacle in the Most Holy, a dwelling represented by the cloud of glory over the innermost sanctuary.

Exodus 25:10-40; 30:1-10; and 37 records the account of the tabernacle, beginning with the construction of the ark (Exod. 25:10). Its measurements were about 3¾ feet by 2¼ feet by 2¼ feet. It was the only furniture in the Holy of Holies. It contained the Ten Commandments (2 Kings 11:12; Ps. 132:12), the pot of manna (Exod. 16:33-34), and Aaron's rod, which had budded (Num. 17:10). It was covered within and without by pure gold and had golden moldings, rings, and staves. Resting on the ark of the covenant and held securely in place by the gold molding was a solid slab of gold called the mercy seat, or the propitiatory. Wrought on the ends of the covering, or lid, were cherubim of gold (Exod. 25:18; 37:7 8). They faced the mercy seat and their wings touched overhead. Between the cherubim the God of Israel dwelt visibly (Exod. 25:22; 30:6; Num. 7:89) and met with his people through their representatives—first Moses, then Aaron. The rendering "mercy seat" was first employed by William Tyndale, the first English translator of the Bible, who followed Martin Luther's translation, *Gnadenstuhl,* based on the Greek *hilastērion* and the Latin

*A Reconstruction of the Ark of the Covenant
(based on Exodus 25:10-22)*

propitiatorium. "Propitiatory" best conveys the concept intended, that is, that of making propitiation for sin; hence the place where God was rendered favorable to his people. The cherubim of pure gold were soldered to the propitiatory, making them "of one piece" with it (Exod. 25:19). They represented angelic ministers of the Lord who guarded the divine throne from all pollution. The ark was carried by poles through four golden rings at the sides of the ark. The ark was lost in the battle of Aphek (1 Sam. 4) but was later returned to Israel and eventually taken to Jerusalem. The second, or restoration, temple of Zerubbabel contained no ark with its propitiatory according to the apocryphal book of Baruch (cf. Bar. 6:7).

Construction and Consecration of the Tabernacle

The account of the construction and consecration of the tabernacle is in Exodus 25–29. Moses was instructed to erect the tabernacle on the first day of the first month in the second year of the Exodus, nine months after reaching Mount Sinai (Exod. 19:1). God revealed the pattern for his dwelling place (Exod. 25:8; 29:45). The many workmen were led by men of artistic skill who were empowered and illuminated by the Spirit of God: Bezalel the son of Uri and Oholiab the son of Ahisamach (Exod. 31:1-6). When the structure was completed and the furniture installed, the cloud symbolizing the presence of God filled the area. The cloud henceforth signaled to Israel when they were to camp and when to journey. When Israel was encamped, the tabernacle was at the center of the camp with Levites on three sides and Moses and Aaron and his sons on the fourth (east) side: Judah at the center of the east side; Ephraim at the center of the west side; Reuben on the south side. The number of Levites who ministered at the tabernacle was 8,580 (Num. 4:48). The tabernacle manifested what has been termed a "graduated holiness and perfection," that is, the metal in the Most Holy Place was solid gold; in the Holy Place, ordinary gold; in the court, bronze. The people were allowed in the court, the priests in the Holy Place, and only the high priest in the Most Holy Place (only one day a year). Only the altar is mentioned for consecration (Exod. 29:36-37), but later all the furniture of the sanctuary was included (Exod. 30–31).

The Tabernacle in the New Testament

John, in his prologue (John 1:14), makes much of the incarnation of the Lord Jesus Christ as the tabernacling among men. The testimony of Stephen (Acts 7:44) is unmistakable. Paul directly equates the cross of Calvary as God's mercy seat, or propitiatory, in finalizing the redemption of sinful man (Rom. 3:25). In speaking of regeneration (Titus 3:5) he had in mind the laver. The proper interpretation of Colossians 1:19 and 2:9 relates to the dwelling presence of God in the tabernacle of old. The Epistle to the Hebrews is inexplicable without the teaching of the worship of Israel and its priesthood residing in the tabernacle. Passages such as Revelation 8:3-4; 13:6; 15:5; and 21:3 are too clear to need comment.

Two extremes are discernible in discussions of the symbolism of the tabernacle. Some make little or nothing of the symbolism of the sanctuary, despite what has been shown of the New Testament references to that structure. On the other hand, some seek to draw some spiritual truth from every thread and piece of wood. Those somewhere in the middle do not deny symbolism in the colors, where white, blue, and scarlet predominate with their connotations of purity, heavenly character, and shedding of blood. Because some of the early church fathers imagined fanciful interpretations for the appointments of the tabernacle does not make it valid to posit that any figurative interpretations lack a solid basis in the Old Testament. Hebrews gives, at length, the Christian interpretation of the symbolism of the Mosaic tabernacle. The furniture symbolizes man's access to God. The tabernacle is patterned after a heavenly model (Heb. 8:5); there is a divine prototype (Heb. 8:2, 5; 9:11); it conveyed important spiritual truths in the first century A.D. (Heb. 9:9). Christ appeared and then entered after death into the heavens (Heb. 9:24).

The truth of the tabernacle is inseparably bound up with the fact of the Incarnation (Col. 1:19; 2:9). In fact, the tabernacle may rightly be considered, with its emphasis on the fact of God's dwelling with man, as the main foreshadowing in the Old Testament of the doctrine of the Incarnation. The tabernacle, rather than the later temples, is the basis of New Testament teaching. Hebrews (Heb. 9–10) refers not to any temple, but to the tabernacle. The tabernacle is the symbol of God's dwelling with his people (Exod. 25:8; 1 Kings 8:27). This concept progressed until it was fulfilled in the incarnation of God the Son (John 1:14). He is in the church (2 Cor. 6:16), in the individual believer (1 Cor. 6:19), and in the eternal state (Rev. 21:3). In Hebrews the central passages on the New Testament tabernacle represent the earthly and heavenly aspects of Christ's activity. The Old Testament was the shadow of which Christ is the substance (Heb. 8:5; 10:1). The tabernacle of Christ's ministry was pitched by the Lord, not by man (Heb. 8:2). He is the high priest of the more perfect tabernacle (Heb. 9:11). He is not in an earthly tabernacle, but appears now before "God for us" (Heb. 9:24). The writer of Hebrews draws his imagery from the ceremonies of the tabernacle and clothes his concepts in the priestly and sacrificial terminology of the sanctuary in the wilderness.

Paul refers to "the washing of regeneration" (Titus 3:5) and to Christ offering himself as a sacrifice to God (Eph. 5:2). The first three Gospels underscore the rending of the temple veil (Matt. 27:51; Mark 15:38; Luke 23:45) which the author of Hebrews indicates opened the way into the Holy of Holies (Heb. 9:8; 10:19-20).

The Significance of the Tabernacle

The tabernacle, with its priests and their ministry, was foundational to the religious life of Israel. The basic concept was that which underlay the theocracy itself: the Lord dwelling in visible glory in his sanctuary among his people (Exod. 25:8). Even if the tabernacle had no historical validity, which it assuredly had, it still may have value for the readers because of its embodiment of important religious and spiritual concepts. It reveals, first, the necessary conditions on which Israel could maintain fellowship in covenant relationship with the Lord. Second, it reveals the dominant truth of the presence of God in the midst of his people (Exod. 29:25), a dwelling that must conform in every detail with his divine character, that is, his unity and holiness. One God requires one sanctuary; the holy God demands a holy people (Lev. 19:2). Third, it reveals the perfection and harmony of the Lord's character, seen in the aesthetics of the tabernacle's architecture: the gradations in metals and materials; the degrees of sanctity exhibited in the court, the Holy Place, and the Most Holy Place; and the measurements of the tabernacle, for example, three, four, seven, and ten, with their fractions and multiples dominating and pervading every detail of furniture and material.

The tabernacle was the first sanctuary reared for the Lord at his command and was rendered glorious and effective by his actual indwelling. The dwelling of God with humanity is the dominant theme of the symphony of the tabernacle, pointing to the future, eternal communion with God. The ark of the covenant, with the propitiatory, was the symbol of God's meeting with his people on the basis of atonement (Rom. 3:25). The shewbread spoke of God's sustenance of spiritual life; the lampstand represented Israel as God's channel of light (Zech. 4); the incense was a symbol of prayer (Rev. 5:8; 8:3-4). The tabernacle was the authorized place of worship. It was the foundation of the theocracy. The mercy seat was the earthly seat of God's glory where he met with his people for his glory and their blessing. The tabernacle foreshadowed the time when God's kingdom would be fully realized and established on earth. Note the progress in the self-revelation of God to his people: first, his presence in the tabernacle; second, the incarnation of the Lord Jesus Christ; third, the indwelling of the Holy Spirit in believers; and fourth, the descent of the New Jerusalem to the glorified earth.

Charles L. Feinberg[6]

156 ◆ THE WORK OF THE PRIEST IN THE TABERNACLE

The legislation in the Pentateuch assigned numerous duties to the Hebrew priests and Levites. Chief among them were maintaining and transporting the tabernacle (Num. 3–4) and performing the rituals and liturgies associated with Israelite worship in the sanctuary (Exod. 28–29). It is likely that some of these duties were determined by lot and discharged on a rotating basis (cf. 1 Chron. 23–24).

Bronze Basin or Laver. The priests were to wash their hands and feet at the laver upon entering the tent of meeting (tabernacle proper) and before ministering at that altar of burnt offering (Exod. 30:17-21).

Altar of Burnt Offering. The national festival, daily, and individual sacrifices took place at the altar of burnt offering. Mosaic law instructed the priests to prepare and sacrifice a year-old lamb in the morning and evening each day. This burnt offering was to be accompanied by grain and drink offerings (Exod. 29:38-46; Num. 28:1-8).

The Mosaic legislation prescribing the five basic sacrifices offered to God by the people of Israel is found in Leviticus 1–7. Three types of sacrifices were required: offerings of expiation, offerings of consecration, and offerings of fellowship.

The offerings of expiation included a six-part ritual, three acts performed by the worshiper and three acts performed by the priest. The worshiper brought his offering to the gateway of the tabernacle (perhaps in the forecourt on the north side of the altar of burnt offering). He then laid his hands on the sacrificial victim and confessed his sin and guilt. Then the worshiper slaughtered the sacrificial animal. The priest cut the victim into pieces, arranged the sacrifice on the altar, and ignited the burnt offering. During this process the priest collected the blood of the victim in a basin and dashed it against the four sides of the altar. Then the priest and his family, or the priest and the worshiper, ate the remaining portions of the offering as a sacrificial meal.

Non-animal sacrifices were prepared by the worshiper; this preparation included anointing the offering with oil and frankincense, and in some cases baking without leaven. The worshiper brought the sacrifice to the entrance of the tabernacle. There the priest received the sacrifice and burned a portion of it on the altar of burnt offering. The priest was permitted to retain the remaining portion of the offering as a sacrificial meal for his family (Lev. 2:1-10).

Specific ritual sacrifice was also prescribed for the national and festival worship gatherings. Especially prominent were the Passover, the Feast of Firstfruits, Pentecost, and the Day of Atonement. Sacrificial instructions for these and other national and festival holy days are outlined in Exodus 12:3; 29; Leviticus 16; 23; and Numbers 28–29. The instructions to the priests for keeping the fire burning on the altar of burnt offering are in Leviticus 6:8-13.

Table of Shewbread and Lampstand. The priests were charged to keep the lampstand (Hebrew, mᵉnorah) burning during the hours of darkness (evening until morning) each day (Lev. 24:1-4). The priests also prepared twelve loaves of bread to be arranged on the table of shewbread in two rows of six loaves each. The loaves were to be garnished with frankincense and were replaced every Sabbath by the priests (Lev. 24:5-8).

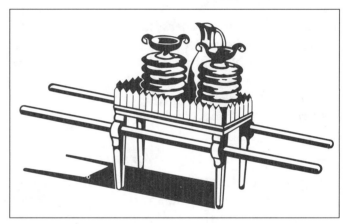

An Artistic Conception of the Table of Shewbread (based on Leviticus 24:5-19)

Altar of Incense. The priests were commanded to burn incense twice daily on the altar of incense, which stood before the curtain of the tabernacle separating the Most Holy Place from the sanctuary. The incense offerings coincided with the snuffing out of the lampstand in the morning and the lighting of the lampstand in the evening (Exod. 30:1-10).

Once a year sacrificial blood was sprinkled on the altar of incense to purify it as part of the Day of Atonement ceremony (Lev. 16:18-29).

Curtain or Veil of the Tabernacle. The curtain was made of wool, dyed blue, purple, and scarlet, and was embroidered with cherubim. The curtain divided the tent of meeting into two sections: the Holy Place and the Most Holy Place. Once a year, on the Day of Atonement, the high priest was permitted to go beyond the curtain into the Most Holy Place (Exod. 26:31-35).

An Artistic Re-creation of the Laver (based on Exodus 30:17-21)

Ark of the Covenant. The ark of the covenant was the visible symbol of God's holy presence and covenant relationship with Israel. The ark contained the tokens of Israel's redemption from slavery in Egypt: the stone tablets of God's law, a bowl of manna, and Aaron's rod. The ark of the covenant resided in the Most Holy Place. Annually, on the Day of Atonement, the high priest appeared before the ark to burn incense and sprinkle blood of the sacrifice on the mercy seat resting on the top of the ark. The ritual made atonement for the tabernacle, cleansing the sanctuary of Israel's uncleanness and transgressions (Lev. 16:11-19).

157 ✦ The Role of the Worshiper in Old Testament Sacrificial Ritual

The procedural order of sacrificial worship outlined in the following paragraphs is a reconstruction based on the prescriptions for the offerings and sacrifices set forth in Leviticus 1–5. Details may vary given the specific type of sacrifice being presented, whether offerings of expiation, offerings of consecration, or offerings of fellowship.

Tabernacle Worship

Step 1. The person offering the sacrifice must be ceremonially clean. Ritual purity was secured by washing one's clothes and bathing, and in some cases special offerings were presented to the priest (cf. Num. 19:17-21).

Step 2. The worshiper approached the tabernacle with his or her offering.

Step 3. The officiating priest received the worshiper, took the sacrificial (animal) victim, and led the worshiper to the altar of burnt offering in the tabernacle courtyard. The family of the worshiper may have watched from the gate or followed the two into the court area to observe from a better vantage point.

Step 4. After a statement of confession, a prayer, or praise (depending on the type of offering), the worshiper placed his hand on the (animal) victim's head and slit its throat with a knife. (Here the priest would collect the blood to be used in the sacrifice.)

Step 5. The worshiper, perhaps with the priest's help, would then skin the animal and cut it into quarters. (Once the sacrifice was brought into contact with the altar of burnt offering, the formal priestly duties commenced.)

Step 6. The worshiper witnessed the priestly activity, including burning the sacrifice on the altar. The worshiper may have responded to the priestly activity in some way, for instance with prayer, silent reflection and meditation, chanting, or singing of liturgical responses (depending on the nature of the sacrifice).

Step 7. After the sacrifice was consumed by fire on the altar, the priest formally dismissed the worshiper with some type of blessing or benediction. In some instances, the worshiper ate a fellowship meal with the priest from the remnant of the sacrificial animal upon completion of the burnt offering. In other cases the remainder of the sacrificial animal was taken home and eaten by the worshiper and his family. The remaining portions of the sacrifice were to be eaten within two days or destroyed by fire (cf. Lev. 19:5-8).

Andrew Hill

158 ✦ The Tabernacle of David

During the Davidic era the tabernacle of Moses and its worship were moved to Gibeon. In addition, David set up a worship center in Zion—a tent of meeting, also known as David's tabernacle—and instituted a nonsacrificial worship of praise and thanksgiving.

Historical Background of the Davidic Tabernacle

During the period when Eli was priest in Israel, the word of the Lord came through Samuel that judgment would soon fall on the priest and his household (1 Sam. 3:11-14). Unrestrained by their father, Eli's two sons had been perverting the sacrifices and committing adultery with the women who came to the tabernacle, which displeased the Lord (1 Sam. 2:22).

As a part of the prophesied judgment, Israel was engaged in a war they were losing to their perennial enemies the Philistines. After a particularly debilitating defeat, the elders brought out the ark of God from the tabernacle and carried it into battle with them. Traditionally, a nation's king led the armies into battle. Israel had no king but Yahweh; so when the ark, which was the symbol of God's presence with his people, was carried before the armies, it was as if the Lord himself went before them. However, the ark was of no help, since the presence of the Lord had been withdrawn, and not only was the battle lost, but Eli's two sons were killed and the ark of God was captured by the enemy (1 Sam. 4:2-10).

Months later, after the Philistines experienced plague and death wherever the ark went, they returned it to Israel on a cart pulled by two oxen. When the Israelites who found it were struck dead for looking inside it, the ark was not returned to its place in the tabernacle but was given over to the citizens of Kiriath Jearim, who housed it with a man named Abinadab and sanctified his son Eleazar to care for it. Samuel became judge of Israel and Saul followed as king, and still the ark of God was not returned to the tabernacle. Sometime during these years the tabernacle itself was moved from Shiloh to Gibeon (1 Sam. 6).

After David ascended the throne, he and the elders of Israel went to the house of Abinadab to retrieve the ark (2 Sam. 6:2-4). Surprisingly, however, they did not return it to the tabernacle in Gibeon but put it in a tent, sometimes called a tabernacle, that David constructed for it in the city of Zion, where he lived (2 Sam. 6:17). Priests and Levites were sanctified to carry on worship before it, but except for the initial dedication ceremonies, this worship did not involve burnt sacrifices.

Worship at David's Tabernacle

From the biblical accounts it appears that David appointed teams of worshipers who served in rotating shifts, day and night. Their duties consisted of praising the Lord with singing, prophesying, and playing musical instruments before the ark (1 Chron. 16:4; 25:1-31). It is reasonable to assume that many of the psalms were both written and used in this context, particularly since they were authored by David, Asaph, and others from David's worship teams, and because they frequently allude to worship in the tent in Zion.

"O Lord, open my lips, and my mouth will declare your praise," writes David. "You do not delight in sacrifice, or I would bring it; you do not take pleasure in burnt offerings" (Ps. 51:15-16). Asaph sings that the Lord "abandoned the tabernacle of Shiloh, the tent he had set up among men. . . . But he chose the tribe of Judah, Mount Zion which he loved. He built his sanctuary like the heights . . ." (Ps. 78:60, 68-69). Korah testifies, "He has set his foundation on the holy mountain; the LORD loves the gates of Zion more than all the dwellings of Jacob" (Ps. 87:1-2). The psalm goes on to sing the praises of

Zion and exult in the privilege of being born in that city. It ends, "The LORD will write in the register of the peoples: 'This one was born in Zion.' As they make music they will sing, 'All my fountains are in you'" (Ps. 87:6-7). Asaph describes the glory of the Lord radiating from the tent where the ark is resting: "From Zion, in perfect beauty, God shines forth" (Ps. 50:2). Psalm 134:1 commands all the servants of the Lord who stand in his house at night to bless him; this is apparently a reference to the worship teams that served in David's tabernacle night and day. Many of the psalms speak of praise and worship of the Lord and give instructions about performing these covenant obligations. The people of Yahweh are to clap (Ps. 47:1), lift their hands (Ps. 134:1-2), shout (Ps. 66:1), sing (Ps. 27:6), play instruments (Ps. 150:3-5), dance (Ps. 149:3), and bow and kneel before him (Ps. 95:6). Other psalms admonish the worshiper to sing a "new song" to the Lord (Pss. 96:1; 98:1; 149:1).

A number of psalms contain words spoken by the Lord himself. These probably came through various worshipers as they ministered under a prophetic anointing. Musical prophecy, both vocal and instrumental, was a feature of Davidic worship. "David . . . set apart some of the sons of Asaph . . . for the ministry of prophesying, accompanied by harps, lyres and cymbals . . ." (1 Chron. 25:1; cf. Pss. 92:1-3; 98:5).

Decline and Revival of Davidic Worship

Davidic worship was not based on ritual or ceremony but was a spontaneous response to the moving of God's Spirit. For this reason it could not be passed to succeeding generations of Israelites, as was the Mosaic sacrificial system. In periods of moral and spiritual decline in the history of Israel and Judah, Davidic praise and worship died out, and in some cases the entire sacrificial system was abandoned as well, as the nations followed their leaders into apostasy and idolatry.

However, each time a righteous king initiated a reform and return to the worship of Yahweh, it was accompanied by worship according to the pattern of the tabernacle of David. Under Asa the covenant was renewed, and Judah "took an oath to the LORD with loud acclamation, with shouting and with trumpets and horns" and sought the Lord "eagerly" (2 Chron. 15:14-15). When the child Joash was crowned king and the worship of the Lord was restored under Jehoiada the priest, "all the people of the land were rejoicing and blowing trumpets, and singers with musical instruments were leading the praises" (2 Chron. 23:13). After cleansing the temple and removing idols from Judah, Hezekiah installed the Levites in the sanctuary with their musical instruments, "in the way prescribed by David and Gad the king's seer and Nathan the prophet" (2 Chron. 29:25). Hezekiah understood David's instruction for worship to be a commandment of the Lord. The people worshiped as the singers sang, and the king ordered that the songs be those of David and Asaph (2 Chron. 29:25-30). Josiah followed the example set by Hezekiah, tearing down pagan altars and leading a great national cleansing and reform in Judah. A result of the reform was a revival of worship in which the descendants of Asaph were set in place as leaders "prescribed by David, Asaph, Heman and Jeduthun," members of David's original worship team (2 Chron. 35:15).

Zerubbabel returned to Judah from the captivity in Babylon to rebuild the temple of the Lord. In Ezra 3:10-13 it is written that a celebration of worship ensued after the foundation was laid in which the Levites and sons of Asaph praised the Lord with trumpets, cymbals, shouting, and singing, "as prescribed by David, king of Israel" (v. 10). Nehemiah led the returned captives in rebuilding the walls of Jerusalem and in a national purging and return to the covenant. At the dedication of the wall the Levites were instructed to sing and give thanks and to use David's musical instruments according to the commandments of David and Solomon (Neh. 12:27-46). "In the days of David and Asaph, there had been directors for the singers and for the songs of praise and thanksgiving to God" (v. 46).

Davidic Worship and the New Covenant

A significant feature of the worship in David's tabernacle was that it was conducted directly in front of the ark, where the presence of the Lord resided. Under the Mosaic system, the ark was kept in the inner recesses of the tabernacle and was seen only by the high priest and then only once each year. David was careful to comply with the stipulation that only the Levites could carry the ark (1 Chron. 15:2), but he did not put it out of the sight of the people. The worship that took place directly before the ark pre-figured New Testament worship, in which all Christians are members of the priesthood (1 Pet. 2:9) and have direct access to God's presence (Heb. 4:16). This is particularly significant in view of James's interpretation of the tabernacle of David as the church. Commenting on the salvation of Gentiles under Paul's ministry, James explains to the apostles gathered in Jerusalem,

> "Brothers, listen to me. Simon [Peter] has described to us how God at first showed his concern by taking from the Gentiles a people for himself. The words of the prophets are in agreement with this, as it is written:
>
> 'After this I will return
>   and rebuild David's fallen tent.
> Its ruins I will rebuild,
> And I will restore it,
> That the remnant of men may seek the Lord,
> And all the Gentiles who bear my name,'
>   says the Lord, who does these things that
>   have been known for ages.
>
> It is my judgment, therefore, that we should not make it difficult for the Gentiles who are turning to God" (Acts 15:13-19).

David prophesied this very thing in the Psalms when he wrote, "All the nations you have made will come and worship before you, O Lord; and they will bring glory to your name" (Ps. 86:9). "All kings will bow down to him and all nations will serve him. . . . All nations will be blessed through him, and they will call him blessed" (Ps. 72:11, 17). The author of Hebrews concurs when he writes to the church, "You have come to Mount Zion, to the heavenly Jerusalem, the city of the living God . . . to thousands . . . in joyful assembly, to the church of the firstborn, whose names are written in heaven . . . to Jesus the mediator of a new covenant . . . (Heb. 12:22-24).

Davidic Worship and the Church

In Christian worship, the Psalms have been normative, along with the instructions given by the Lord through David for the kind of worship he desires. Paul instructs the church to sing (Eph. 5:18-19), to lift their hands (1 Tim. 2:8), and to rejoice (Phil. 3:1; 4:4). He tells the Roman Christians that their whole bodies are to be offered to the Lord as a service of worship (Rom. 12:1-2). God's people are to sing "in the Spirit" (1 Cor. 14:15; Col. 3:16), a possible reference to the "new song" commanded by David. This practice is carried on in a number of modern churches as a musical interlude, sometimes called the *selah,* in which the congregation engages in free-flowing vocal and instrumental praise to the Lord. *Selah* is thought to be related to the verb *salal,* used in Psalm 68:4 for the "lifting up" of a song. It is usually interpreted to mean a musical interruption or pause in the worship pattern.

The tabernacle of David, like the temple, is a foreshadowing of the worship of the church of Jesus Christ. It provides a model of God's people entering his gates with thanksgiving, coming into the court of the king through praise, offering anointed sacrifices with their entire beings, night and day. "Through Jesus, therefore, let us continually offer to God a sacrifice of praise—the fruit of lips that confess his name" (Heb. 13:15).

Janice E. Leonard

159 • FEATURES OF DAVIDIC WORSHIP

During the period of the tabernacle of David, regular psalmic worship was offered at the tent on Zion that housed the ark of the covenant. (The Mosaic sanctuary with its sacrifices remained at Gibeon.) There are no biblical rubrics for this worship, as there are for the sacrificial cult. The structure of the Zion festivals and the worshiper's acts must be inferred from the relevant Psalms and historical accounts, such as 1 Chronicles 16. These materials reflect a festival celebrating the Lord's ascension as King and the renewal of the covenant.

The Pilgrimage. Going up to Zion for the festivals was a joyous time for the families of the land. As the worshipers approached the sanctuary, they might have sung the "Psalms of Ascent" (Pss. 120–134), until at last they stood in Jerusalem, "where the tribes go up . . . to praise the name of the LORD" (Ps. 122:4).

The Call to Worship. The trumpet summoned the people for the festival; the lyres and harps of the sanctuary orchestra began to play as the choirs moved into place and took up their song (Ps. 81:1-3).

The Procession. Worshipers had previously gone out on a search for the ark (Ps. 132:6-7), a reenactment of the time when it was first brought to Jerusalem. The cry went forth: "Arise, O LORD, and

come to your resting place, you and the ark of your might" (Ps. 132:8; cf. Ps. 68:1; Num. 10:35). At this, the appointed Levites begin to carry the ark back to the sanctuary. Their procession was led by dignitaries from the tribes of Israel (Ps. 68:27); it included singers and instrumentalists and young women dancing and playing tambourines (Pss. 68:24-25; 149:3; 150:4).

The Ascent. As the procession mounted the sacred hill, the people acclaimed Yahweh as their "great King," with clapping, the trumpet signal of a king's coronation, and triumphant shouting (Ps. 47:1-5). In joyful psalms, the choir celebrated his dominion over all peoples (Ps. 47:6-9).

The Entrance. As the ark reached the gates of the sacred area, an antiphonal liturgy of entrance occurred, beginning with a hymn of praise (Ps. 24:1-2). The question went forth: "Who may ascend the hill of the LORD?" The answer came from the priests guarding the entrance: "He who has clean hands and a pure heart. . . ." Those in the procession affirmed that they met the qualifications (Ps. 24:3-5) and appealed for the doors to be opened so the ark, symbol of the "King of glory," could come in (Ps. 24:7). A dialogue followed, ending with the doorkeeper's question, "Who is this King of glory?" and the answer, "The LORD Almighty [*Yahveh tzeva'ot*], he is the King of glory" (Ps. 24:8-10).

The Praise of the King. Throughout the festival, the choirs were singing hymns of praise to the Lord similar to those used when the ark had been brought to Zion (Pss. 96; 105; 106; cf. 1 Chron. 16). A favorite may have been the responsive Psalm 136: "Confess to Yahweh, that he is good; for his covenant love is forever" (v. 1, AUTHOR'S TRANSLATION).

Preparation for the Appearance of the Lord. The festival was to reach its climax at that point when the Lord "appeared" in the midst of his people: "From Zion, in perfect beauty, God shines forth" (Ps. 50:2), perhaps through the liturgical recitation of the covenant commandments (Exod. 20:1-17). In preparation for this high moment, the worship intensified into prophetic song by both choirs and orchestra, occasionally breaking out into the *selah* or general lifting up of praise at the announcement of the Lord's coming (Ps. 150:6) or the proclamation of his victories (Pss. 46; 48). One prophetic voice may have come forth, reminding the worshipers of the seriousness with which the Lord regarded their covenant vows and that the disobedient were not to "recite my laws or take my covenant on your lips" (Ps. 50:16).

Renewal of the Covenant. At the proper moment, another prophetic voice was heard, inviting the people to respond with the recitation of the covenant laws: "I am the LORD your God, who brought you up out of Egypt. Open wide your mouth and I will fill it" (Ps. 81:10). Perhaps lifting their hands in oath, the congregation reaffirmed the covenant with the words they had memorized and taught their children (Deut. 6:6-7).

Conclusion. The entire festival was a celebration of the Lord's presence with his people, enthroned in their worship and governing their life as a people bound to him. Aspects of this Davidic worship continued to govern the cult of Judah even after the temple replaced David's simple tent as the home of the ark. Although it is sometimes claimed that the ark remained within the Most Holy Place, which could be entered only once a year by the high priest, this is probably not a correct picture of actual practice. Apparently the ark was carried out of the sanctuary on occasion until a few decades before the destruction of the temple and the Babylonian exile. At that time, King Josiah ordered the Levites not to carry it anymore (2 Chron. 35:3), an instruction that would have been unnecessary had they not been doing so all along.

Richard C. Leonard

THIRTEEN

The Temple of Solomon

The temple or "house of Yahweh," was the central sanctuary of the worship of the Lord during the period of the kingdoms of Israel and Judah. Through the sacrificial and festive worship of the temple, the community of Israel expressed its covenant loyalty to God and was reminded of God's faithfulness and acts of deliverance.

160 • PURPOSE OF THE TEMPLE

The temple as the focal point of Israelite worship served as a protection against idolatry. It stood for the covenant between the Lord and Israel and was the place where God might be approached in celebration and propitiation.

The outstanding feature of the Solomonic temple is that there was no idol in it, only the mercy seat over the ark and the cherubim overshadowing the mercy seat, declaring to the world that idols are unnecessary to define the presence of God or his sanctity. Because the lightless room could only be reached through a specific ritual, at a specified annual time, for the purpose of making reconciliation for the people, the "house of Yahweh" in Jerusalem was not considered a cosmic house of God but emphasized the way of salvation to the penitent and assured to them the grace of God for their joy and blessing (1 Kings 8:27-30). God was not localized or in any sense conveyed by an image, either Egyptian, Babylonian, or Canaanite, nor bound to any other form such as the ark. The temple, therefore, was not necessary because of God's nature; he had no need of it (Acts 7:48-49). It was an accommodation to the limitations and needs of his people (1 Kings 8:27-30).

That contemporary peoples had temples is not sufficient grounds to justify the temple of Yahweh in Jerusalem. Though David saw this lack as a problem (2 Sam. 7:2), it was not the reason for which David sought to build God's house. A sufficient cause, among others, is that found in Deuteronomy 12, where the temple was to be a protective memorial for believing Israel, designed to turn their hearts away from the idols of their Palestinian contemporaries and provide them with an incentive (thus protective) not to practice the iniquities of the Canaanites, and with a memorial to the person of their God, who had delivered them from slavery in Egypt to freedom in the land of Canaan.

In addition to the practical good of centralized worship, a central cultic house was important to the covenant structure of Yahweh with Israel. The loyalty of Israel to Yahweh her God was expressed in the sacrifices and offerings that were presented at the temple. The high places of the various tribes divided the people and were disruptive of their loyalty to God; they diverted from him his rightful due as their Creator and Lord, and for this reason the high places were roundly condemned. The temple thus became an affirmation by Israel of the covenant. The temple was needed to express clearly Israel's attachment to the covenant. That David was not allowed to build the temple does not mean that Yahweh would not dwell in one, but rather that the time was not propitious (cf. 2 Sam. 7:5-7, 11; Deut. 12:11).

For Israel the temple was to be the place where, particularly in three annual festivals, they were to rejoice before their God and remember his great blessings to them (Deut. 12:12). David was the recipient of centuries of this outlook and came to realize the need for this central sanctuary for unity among the people. Thus Israel's temple in Jerusalem was from the first to differ from those of their contemporaries. Only the place God would choose was to be the center of their worship, where his judgments were to be sought, and where they were to remember particularly their deliverances (Deut. 26:1-3).

An Artistic Re-creation of the Temple of Solomon with the Prayer Altar, the Molton Sea, and the Priests' Chambers

The selection of the place of dwelling for the name of Yahweh occurred during the peculiar happenings of David's numbering the people (2 Sam. 24:1; 1 Chron. 21). On the threshing floor of Araunah the Jebusite, David was commanded to set up an altar of propitiation to God to stay the plague. This was declared to be the house, that is, the temple, of God and the place of the (sole) altar of the people Israel (1 Chron. 22:1). It became the place of obedience and propitiation for Israel.

This sanctuary symbolized the hearing ear of God (1 Kings 8:27-29), the resort of the stranger (1 Kings 8:41-43), and the house of prayer for all people (Isa. 56:7), to the end that all nations of the earth should fear God (1 Kings 8:43). In the New Testament it symbolized the body of Christ (John 2:18-21) as the obedient servant of God for propitiating God's wrath on the sinner. Further, the temple as God's dwelling place symbolizes the Christian as the dwelling place of God (1 Cor. 3:16).

In the early days of the church, Stephen, slain for his faith, was evidently going to declare that the people were putting the temple above God, forgetting that he did not really need a temple building in the sense of rooms of stone and wood (Acts 7:44-50; cf. Acts 17:24-25) but that he desired the believing heart of flesh (Ezek. 36:26-27) on which he could impress his law, that is, his nature, which would result in obedience and holiness of life. Thus the temple is mediatorial in all ages, justifying Stephen's position.

161 ✦ FURNISHINGS OF THE TEMPLE

The furnishings of the sanctuary proper and its surrounding courts all contributed to the grandeur of the worship of the Lord. The sanctuary proper, including the Holy of Holies, contained the ark of the covenant, the lampstands the altar of incense, and the table of shewbread. The great altar of sacrifice stood in the court, outside the sanctuary, together with the bronze sea.

The Sanctuary Furnishings

The ark, with its mercy seat, from the tabernacle was placed at the back of the Holy of Holies, under the cherubim, which were made of olive wood (1 Kings 6:23-27) and were gold plated. These were ten cubits high, and their wings extended to ten cubits, half the width of the room. They functioned symbolically as guardians of the way to God, solemnizing the heart of the worshiper in this approach to God. Their faces were turned toward the dividing partition. They were composite figures well known to the people of that day, requiring no description of their form. They may have been similar to the four-faced cherubim of Ezekiel and were usually represented with hands and feet, therefore having a basically human body.

In the Holy Place, before the door to the Holy of Holies, was placed the altar of incense (1 Kings 6:20; 7:48; cf. Exod. 30:1-10), probably new and made of cedar, since it was overlaid with gold. Presumably the table for the shewbread was also new, overlaid with gold, and placed on the right side of the room as in the tabernacle (cf. Exod. 40:22). In this room were the ten candlesticks (or lampstands, RSV), five on the right side and five on the left, all of gold, with their oil cups and ornamentation, to give light in the Holy Place (1 Kings 7:49).

Before the temple, on the platform surrounding the temple, stood the two brass pillars, Jachin and Boaz; Jachin means "sustainer," stressing the positive side of God's character, and Boaz means "smiter," giving the negative aspect of the character of Yahweh as keeper of Israel.

It is questionable that these pillars were for incense burning, since their height would make it difficult to reach their tops to replenish the incense. They were approximately four cubits in diameter and eighteen cubits high (1 Kings 7:15) for the shaft, with chapters (capitals, RSV) five cubits high on each. The chronicler (2 Chron. 3:15) gives the total height of both pillars as 35 cubits, apparently just the shaft length. The additional cubit of length most likely was a separate, cast base similar to some that have been found. The capitals are described as "in the shape of lilies" (1 Kings 7:19) and having a bowl-shaped member (1 Kings 7:42; cf. 7:20, belly); lily petals were below, four cubits broad (1 Kings 7:19), probably set downward as examples from this period show. Second Kings 25:17 states them to be three cubits high, but this refers to the chain network; it would appear that this measurement refers

An Artistic Conception of the Golden Lampstand (based on Exodus 25:32-35)

to the upper portion of the capital, leaving two cubits for the height of the lily decoration.

The bowls (1 Kings 7:41) had a network (checker work, 1 Kings 7:17) of chains supporting two rows of pomegranates. The chains were seven in number (1 Kings 7:17) and were divided, that is, four chains draped down from the center point at the top and three strands set around the bowl with the pomegranates attached to the bottom strand, fastened one below the other.

Furnishings in the Temple Courts

The prominent feature of the court was the molten sea (1 Kings 7:23), ten cubits in diameter, 30 cubits in circumference, and five cubits high—thus bowl shaped, with sides about as thick as the hand, and containing two thousand "baths" (1 Kings 7:24-26; 2 Chron. 4:5 gives the number as three thousand "baths"). The figures are possible if one assumes (Ezek. 41:8) the use of the great cubit (royal cubit). On this basis the capacity would have been about ten thousand gallons, using the usual formula for spherical volume. In Chronicles, another method of computation seems to have been used, the volume of a cylinder, which in this case turns out to be three thousand baths. Thus the problem is one of method by which the writers viewed the shape of the sea, not an essential contradiction in the text. The sea was located in the altar court to the southeast (2 Chron. 4:10).

The rim was finished off with the petal (lily) work familiar from the pillar capitals. It also had knops (1 Kings 7:24), or knobs, under the brim in two rows of ten per cubit. The sea stood on a base composed of twelve oxen in sets of three, one set toward each of the compass points (1 Kings 7:25). These corresponded to the twelve tribes of Israel bearing the sanctifying witness of God.

The wheeled stands for movable lavers (1 Kings 7:27ff., RSV) were ten in number, formed of boxes four cubits square and three cubits high, the sides made up of divided panels and having ornamental work. The boxes were worked onto short columns (undersetters, 1 Kings 7:30, KJV), to which axles were attached for wheels one and one-half cubits in diameter. The wheels were like chariot wheels, six-spoked as archaeological remains show. As indicated in 1 Kings 7:34, the undersetters extended upward to form the corners of the boxes. The plates of 1 Kings 7:30 were parts of the sides of the box.

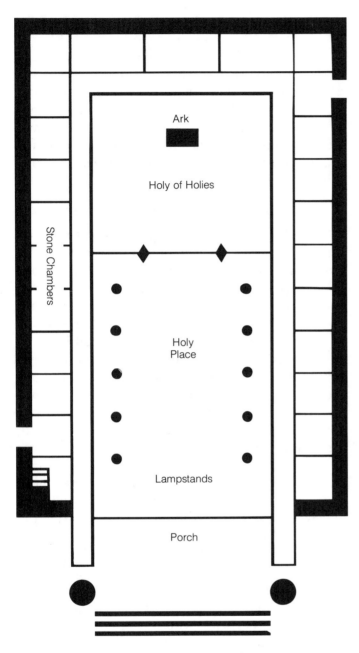

Ark

Holy of Holies

Stone Chambers

Holy Place

Lampstands

Porch

The Floor Plan of Solomon's Temple

The focal point in the court was the great brass altar (2 Chron. 4:1). It was twenty cubits square and ten cubits high. Its transportation from the Jordan required its sides to be of panel construction with corner pieces and a grate through which the ashes could fall; some method for removing these also was provided, either by the removal of the grating or through the side panels. Ezekiel's description (Ezek. 43:13ff.) does not shed much light on the Solomonic altar because too many events occurred between.

Other implements are listed (1 Kings 7:38ff.; 2 Chron. 4:6, 19ff.). There were basins for water and basins to catch the blood of sacrifices, tongs, picks, snuffers, spoons of one sort or another with which to ladle and handle the meat offerings, as well as flat implements such as cake turners for cooking the cake offerings. Likewise the incense containers for the priests are listed.

— The Courts Surrounding the Temple —

Little is said in Kings or Chronicles concerning the courts surrounding the temple building. First Kings 6:36 lists an inner court, which, due to the slope of the site, was the upper court (Jer. 36:10, RSV). The latter was formed by an enclosing wall of three courses of cut stone and a row of cedar beams to tie it together (cf. 2 Chron. 4:9, court of the priests). With the temple on a base of six cubits, the whole presented a terraced scene exposing the temple building for an easy view of its imposing character. The great court, or outer court (1 Kings 7:9, 12), enclosed both the temple and the palace works of Solomon.

The outer court was accessed through gates; though they are not specifically listed, the door leaves for them are enumerated (2 Chron. 4:9). From the outer court, the inner court was also accessed by gates to which the lay person had access (Jer. 36:10). Ezekiel 44:1 mentions the east gate, and because of the departure and return of the glory of God from this gate, it was the principal gate to the outer court of the temple, probably the gate of 2 Chronicles 4:9. Between the temple court (inner) and Solomon's palace, there was access from the palace court to the inner court through a gate, presumably in the south wall of the inner court, the gate of the guard (2 Kings

Into the stands at the top were fitted lavers containing the water for washing the sacrificial animals (2 Chron. 4:6), for the great laver (sea) was for the ablutions of the priests. These lavers held about forty baths, or two hundred gallons of water. They could be moved about as the washings required. Normally they were distributed five on the north side and five on the south side of the court before the temple. In addition there were ten tables (2 Chron. 4:8) for the flaying of the sacrifices brought by the people. These were placed in the same court as the lavers, probably five on each side.

11:19). A north gate also existed, known as Sur (2 Kings 11:6).

Harold G. Stigers[7]

162 ✦ FEATURES OF TEMPLE WORSHIP

The temple emphasized the presence of God in the midst of Israel. Worship was characterized by sacred symbols, sacred rituals, and a sacred ministry. This model had a great impact on the development of liturgical worship in the ancient church.

The temple emphasized the presence of God in the midst of Israel. For example, God spoke to Moses, saying, "Then have them make a sanctuary for me, and I will dwell among them" (Exod. 25:8; 2 Chron. 6:7; ratification of god's covenant with Israel at Mount Sinai, Exod. 24). Also the temple was seen as an expression of the antithesis between Israel and the surrounding culture. Worship set the Israelites apart from the worship conducted by the pagans and accented their relationship with Yahweh (Deut. 12). Thus, the tabernacle and the temple became the visible and tangible signs of Israel's relationship to God.

A second feature of the temple was its symbolic character. It was characterized by a sacred sense of space, sacred rituals, and sacred ministers. A striking feature of these sacred symbols is that they were ordained by God. In the account of David's giving Solomon the plans for the temple, the writer explicitly says that "he gave him the plans of all that the Spirit had put in his mind for the courts of the temple of the LORD" (1 Chron. 28:12). All this was in writing, David said because "the hand of the LORD [was] upon me, and he gave me understanding in all the details of the plan" (1 Chron. 28:19). The implication is that the pattern of the temple itself was a symbolic communication of the relationship Israel sustained with God (Exod. 25:9).

The temple was characterized by a symbolic use of space. The arrangement of the outer court, the inner court, and the Most Holy Place communicates the distance between the worshiper and God, who dwells in the Most Holy Place. All the pieces of furniture, such as the altar, the laver, the golden lampstands, the table with the bread of the presence, the altar of incense, and the ark, were laden with symbolic meaning as they depicted an encounter with God. Nothing in the temple furniture or layout was randomly selected or haphazardly placed.

Furthermore, the temple was characterized by a number of sacred rituals. In addition to the general rules for making a sacrifice (presentation of the victim, placing hands on the victim, slaying the victim, sprinkling the blood, and burning the sacrifice), there were sacrifices for various occasions, such as the burnt offering (the daily offering of a lamb, entirely consumed to indicate complete consecration to God), the fellowship offering (a voluntary offering symbolizing communion and fellowship between persons and God), and the sin offering (offered for sins of commission). The important feature of these sacrifices is that they are visible and tangible expressions of the relationship of God's people with himself. They grow out of the act of ratification at Sinai, and they anticipate the sacrifice of Christ (Heb. 10).

Finally, the temple was characterized by a sacred ministry. These ministers of the sacred ritual represented the entire nation. They were the mediators between Israel and God. Only the Levites could act as priests. They were called by God and consecrated to his service in an elaborate ceremony (Exod. 29), they wore garments fitting to their service (Exod. 28:40-43; 39:1-31), and they were given stringent requirements for holy living (Lev. 21:1–22:10).

In the New Testament the temple is fulfilled in Jesus Christ (Mark 14:58; 15:29, 38; John 2:19-21), and the church, his body, becomes the temple, the dwelling place of God (1 Cor. 3:16-17; 6:19; 2 Cor. 6:16; Eph. 2:21-22). Nevertheless, the sense that there is a physical side to spiritual life and activity—a sense that came from the temple—continued in New Testament worship. New Testament Christians rejected the nonphysical spirituality of the Gnostics and continued to express their spirituality through physical means. For that reason the sense of sacred place (church buildings), sacred rituals (the Eucharist), and a sacred ministry (ordained persons) all have a vital connection with the impact made by temple worship on the development of Christian worship.

Robert E. Webber[8]

163 ✦ FAMILY WORSHIP IN THE TEMPLE

Family worship at the temple included the rite of circumcision and various sacrifices and offerings for tithe, personal vows, sin, and sickness.

From time to time every family visited the temple in Jerusalem. Eight days after a baby boy was born he was circumcised to mark his membership in Israel. Then a month or two later the baby's mother went to the temple to offer sacrifice (Lev. 12; cf. Luke 2:22-24).

Animals were sacrificed in the lambing and calving season. The first lamb or calf born to every ewe or cow was presented as a sacrifice (Exod. 22:30). Similarly at the beginning of the harvest season a basket of the firstfruits was offered, and at the end of it a tenth of all the harvest, the tithe, was given to the priests as God's representatives (Num. 18:21-32). Deuteronomy 26:5-15 gives a typical prayer for use on such occasions.

Sometimes a person would decide to offer a sacrifice for more personal reasons. In a crisis vows could be made and sealed with a sacrifice (Gen. 28:18-22; 1 Sam. 1:10-11). Then when the prayer was answered, a second sacrifice was customarily offered (Gen. 35:3, 14; 1 Sam. 1:24-25). Serious sin or serious sickness were also occasions for sacrifice (Lev. 4-5; 13; 15).

All the animals offered in sacrifice had to be unblemished. Only the best were good enough for God, and wild animals, which cost the worshiper nothing, were unacceptable. With the obligation to bring tithes and firstlings, worship in Old Testament times could be extremely expensive.

It was also dramatic. The worshiper brought the animal into the temple court. Standing there before the priest he placed one hand on its head, thereby identifying himself with the animal, and confessed his sin or explained the reason for offering the sacrifice. Then the worshiper killed the animal and cut it up for the priest to burn on the great bronze altar. Some sacrifices (burnt offerings) involved the whole animal being burnt on the altar. In others some of the meat was set aside for the priests, and in others the worshiper and his family shared. But in every case the worshiper killed the animal from his own flock with his own hands. These sacrifices expressed in a vivid and tangible way the cost of sin and the worshiper's responsibility. The animal represented the worshiper, dying that he might live. As the worshiper killed the animal, he recalled that sin would have caused his own death, had God not provided an escape through animal sacrifice.

164 ✦ FESTAL WORSHIP IN THE TEMPLE

Three national festivals were celebrated yearly in the temple: Passover, the Feast of Weeks, and the Feast of Booths.

Three times a year all adult men went to the temple to celebrate the national festivals (Exod. 23:17; Deut. 16:16): Passover (in April), the Feast of Weeks (in May), and the Feast of Booths (in October). When possible the whole family accompanied the men. But if they lived a long way from Jerusalem, they would only go up for one of the festivals (1 Sam. 1:3; Luke 2:41).

These festivals were tremendous occasions. Hundreds of thousands of people converged on Jerusalem. They would stay with relatives or camp in tents outside the city. The temple courts would be thronged with worshipers. The temple choirs sang psalms appropriate for the festival, while the priests and Levites offered hundreds, and at Passover thousands, of animals in sacrifice. The festivals were marked by colorful processions led by leaders of the tribes, accompanied by festive dance and the beat of tambourincs (Ps. 68:24-27). The victory shout and the sound of the trumpet proclaimed the Lord's presence with his people, amid the singing of his praises (Ps. 47:5-7).

Joy was the keynote of the major festivals, for the worshipers celebrated the deliverance of Israel from Egypt. At Passover each family ate roasted lamb and bitter herbs to reenact the last meal their forefathers ate before leaving Egypt (Exod. 12). At the Feast of Booths they built shelters of tree branches and lived in them for a week, as a reminder that the Israelites camped in tents during the forty years of wandering in the wilderness (Lev. 23:39-43). These great festivals served as reminders of how God had delivered them from slavery in Egypt and had given them the land of Canaan as he had promised to Abraham.

Each of these festivals lasted a week, but one day of the year was totally different: the Day of Atonement, when everyone fasted and mourned his sins. On this day the high priest confessed the nation's sins as he pressed his hand on the head of a goat. Then the goat was led away into the wilderness, symbolizing the removal of sin from the people (Lev. 16).

Walter Elwell[9]

The Synagogue

After the dispersion of the Jews at the time of the Exile, places of assembly rose up to maintain Hebrew culture and to serve as centers for education and for the social and religious life of the Jews. These institutions came to be designated by the Greek word synagogue.

165 • ORIGIN OF THE SYNAGOGUE

The history of the synagogue as an institution among the Jews is difficult to trace to its source. Its origins seem to lie outside Palestine and apart from that sector of Jewish life which governed the nation and shaped the Old Testament. By the time of the New Testament, the synagogue had become established as the central institution of local Jewish life.

Roots in the Exile

The word *synagogue* is derived from the term for any gathering of people for religious or secular purposes. It is derived from the common verb meaning "to gather," "to gather together," "to bring together" (Matt. 2:4 "assembling"; Mark 6:30; Luke 12:1; John 8:2). The nominal form is used for any type of area or location where things or people gather or are gathered.

The removal of the Levitical and other priestly officers from Jerusalem deprived the temple of its necessary complement of attendants. The prohibition of journeys to Jerusalem and the loss of revenue must have rendered the unified cult center inoperative. The collapse of the old religious state meant a great increase in personal, rather than official, religious functions—a trend seen in the great prophetic voices, Isaiah and Jeremiah, even before the final collapse, and a theme renewed in Daniel. The necessity of preserving the Torah, the five books of Moses, not merely as the central religious document, but also as the only communication of Yahweh to his people, motivated corporate Torah study. All that can be surely stated is that the synagogue arose as a corporate Torah study, with all the legal and binding relationships such a community would form among alien and displaced Jews. The later literature always connects the origin of the synagogue with the period of Babylonian captivity and return under Ezra and Nehemiah. The terminology used for the great gathering and restatement of the Torah under Ezra is variant and uncertain, showing that new institutions were in formation.

The scholarly treatment of the problem has tended to fall under the influence of two opposing schools of thought. The traditional one that Moses founded the synagogue is as old as the Targums (Aramaic translations of the Torah) and cited by Josephus (*Apion* II xvii. 75). It has been popular at various times in recent centuries. The second thesis, that the synagogue was of societal origin and appeared during the Exile, was proposed by the Italian humanist Carlo Sigonio (1524–1584). His views wreaked havoc among the more conservative Jews and Christians of the time but were finally dominant in the treatment by the Dutch theologian Campegius Vitringa (1659–1722). Many other theories have been proposed, some locating the synagogue among the legal/political institutions of Israel rather than the religious. On the other hand, some very modern views would tend to see it as the focus of town life in what was really a nation of villages. This view is supported by the excavation of ancient synagogue sites.

Worship in the synagogue was very different from that in the temple, in that it had no priestly rituals and supported no sacrosanct priesthood. Instead a new order of religious leaders—rabbis—arose to serve the synagogue. It may be that the synagogue was only one type of worship arrangement known at the time and that it was the one that survived the Roman destruction of the great temple. It is even highly probable that one or more synagogues existed within the temple compound in Jerusalem, and it may have been there that Jesus was found sitting among the lawyers at the age of twelve (Luke 2:46). It is also clear from the later traditions that the basic unit of the synagogue was ten men who gathered for prayer. This is similar to Old Testament congregations.

The Intertestamental Period

The vast growth of the synagogue and its appearance throughout the Diaspora is noted in many documents from the time between the Old Testament and the New Testament. Both Philo and Josephus regularly mention the synagogue, as do the earliest rabbinical sources. The dominant language of its services became Aramaic as the Persian empire waxed and waned and the central autonomy of Israelite kingship faded into the past. In the new religious rituals, the chanting of the prayers and the reading of the biblical text became the central functions of the service. The officers of the new religious communities were given new titles, and soon after Alexander's conquest they were pronounced in Greek to the degree that centuries later they were transliterated into consonantal script and introduced into the Hebrew of the Mishnah and Talmud. This was the formative period that saw the final supremacy of the synagogue. It was the customary center of the Jewish community and house of worship throughout the known world in Jesus' time.

The New Testament Period

The term *sunagōgē* is used in the Gospels over thirty times, while an even greater frequency appears in Acts. It is assumed in both the Talmudic literature and in the New Testament that the synagogue leadership was the valid leadership and executive of Judaism, whether it was in Jerusalem or in Corinth. A few inscriptions have been located from synagogues of this era that are distinctive in that they are in Greek uncials (capital letters), written in the Hellenistic style. The most extensive is the Theodotus inscription, found on Mount Ophel not far from the ancient temple precinct. It specifically states that the purpose of the building on which it was a marker was for the "reading of the law" and that it was to serve as a hostel. The concept is Hebraic but the form is Greek, even to the titles of the officials mentioned. Other inscriptions from the Galilee area list Old Testament characters or indicate

the donors but in epigraphic Greek. It is this cosmopolitanism and appeal to the common conscience which marks the synagogal success. The Gospel narratives mention a number of small towns in Galilee and the synagogues where Jesus taught (Matt. 4:23; 9:35; Luke 4:16, 33). An additional group of synagogues in this area has been excavated. They are small buildings with porches and columns, often with stone seats and an outer portico. They must have been used as law courts, schools, libraries, and marketplaces as well as for the Sabbath service. It is also clear that the Jewish males took part in the service. The most important legacy of the first-century synagogue was the form and organization of the apostolic church.

The Diaspora Synagogues

The growth of popular religious organizations in Palestine was paralleled by similar establishments among the Jews of the Dispersion. Large halls were built in Dura Europus and various parts of Egypt, and the worship of the Jews from the Diaspora, mentioned in Acts 2:9-11, was presumably in synagogues in all those widely scattered places. In all, some fifty synagogues have been located within Palestine, a few more in Syria, and perhaps another ten in the neighboring lands of the eastern Mediterranean. There must have been hundreds of others by the end of the first century A.D. By that time the original Greek term had come to mean exclusively a Jewish house of worship. These communities of the Diaspora were displaced but in many cases had attained considerable wealth, and their synagogues are richly carved and well appointed with the crafts of their time.

166 • SYNAGOGUE ARCHITECTURE

Architecture of the synagogue reflected its function as a place where the Jewish community gathered for prayer, study of the Law, and other activities. The synagogue often borrowed architectural features from the prevailing Greco-Roman culture.

Architecture

The architecture of the early Middle Eastern synagogues was similar to that which prevailed throughout the Hellenistic and later Roman ages. The synagogue grounds were surrounded by a low wall within which the synagogue met. Documents from

Turkey and other countries of the early medieval period show that often the congregation met outdoors, although at other times in private rooms. Usually the synagogue was divided in some fashion into a sector for men and a separate and lesser room for the women. In the earliest Palestinian synagogues, such as that at Masada and those at Capernaum, Chorazin, and Kefr Bir'im, stone seats in the form of a double tier ran the length of three walls. Such buildings had either a separate balcony for women or some separation down the center. In the Roman age many of these buildings were of a type of Corinthian Greek design with freestanding columns in the front portico, and columns arranged in rows within the sanctuary to support the vaulted ceilings.

Location

In accordance with certain Talmudic instructions that must have been in the oral lore of Judaism, all the synagogues were built in such a fashion that the congregations could face Jerusalem. The common practice was to erect the building on a small hill or prominence, sometimes near water but always in such a fashion that the back wall, which faced the door, was toward Jerusalem. The temple in Jerusalem represented the priestly element and ritual in Judaism, so the elaborate ceremonial architecture of the later synagogues was unnecessary until after the destruction of the temple in A.D. 70. Whether the local synagogues were built as models or miniatures of the great temple or conceived as centers for the rituals is debated. By the first century the style of construction was set and the synagogue was located in the center of the market square.

Structure

By the first century A.D. the basilica type of building, with its massive and ornamented facade, became the standard synagogue form. However, the extent of symbolism and the expanse was limited by the economic ability of the congregation. There is no clear-cut evolution of synagogal architecture, and each community of the Diaspora seems to have built structures best suited to its situation. The widespread use of the half-square, half-round columns and the elaborate shell niches, both associated with Roman buildings, demonstrates how deeply Greco-Roman civilization had altered the Jewish mind. In or about the middle of the blank wall opposite the entrance doors was the location of the niche or

A Palestinian Synagogue of the First and Second Century Restored
No first-century edifice has remained, but the appearance was probably much like a second-century building.

© U.A.N.T.

chamber in which the sacred rolls of the Torah were kept. Such cabinets or chests set in the east wall were often ornamented and decorated with hangings and embellishments of considerable value. One of the most interesting appointments of the early synagogues was the *gᵉnizah,* a place either in a cellar or pit or in an old attic high in the wall, where the worn and frayed parchment scrolls were placed. Since they bore the divine name of God they could not be desecrated or destroyed, so their contents were interred. Ancient scrolls of inestimable value have been discovered in *gᵉnizot* from a number of synagogues. In the center, and later front, of the hall was the *bēma,* an upraised platform on which the scrolls were placed for reading; the *bēma* was also used for the sermon, which was a sort of explanation of the text.

Furniture and Decoration

The furniture of the ancient synagogue was utilitarian and connected with the service. The Torah ark was frequently carved or encrusted with some type of decoration and covered with magnificent hangings and covers, called *parohet,* and often richly ornamented with silver and gold embroideries. The *bema,* or lecterns, might be carved and inlaid, and often the great seven-branched candelabra, or *mᵉnorah,* was also richly decorated. Many smaller articles, lampstands, ritual implements for the holy days such as *Yom Kippur* and the pilgrimages of *Pesaḥ, Shavuʿot,* and *Sukkot,* were present in the synagogue. The decoration of the synagogues was a subject of much debate and alteration of tastes. The earliest ones often show a strangely exotic degree of profusion in Hellenistic and Roman motifs. The ancient congregations at Capernaum and Chorazin decorated their edifices with stone lions, elaborate bands of designs using plant motifs, and epigraphic inscriptions in uncial Greek. They carved many similar natural motifs on the furniture; pomegranates, grapes, and similar fruit and vegetables are seen. This type of symbolism was developed from the Old Testament as the temple was to have such ornamentation in the same fashion as the wilderness tabernacle. However, strict prohibition against the portrayal of the human form was also in evidence. One decorative feature that survived the ages in the synagogue was the use of mosaic tiles. Numerous elaborate natural figures, including the signs of the zodiac and small animals, are found. The ancient synagogue at Beit Alpha is especially noted

for these fine mosaics. Few synagogue frescoes have survived from antiquity, but those from Dura Europus and elsewhere show artistic affinities to the sculpting of the mosaics, as does Christian art of the period. Again, the scenes are of the various festivals, with some few architectural constructs and what may be patriarchal stories in smaller registers. The motifs of the sun, the wheel, the candle, the plant, the fruit, and the various Greek running figures, such as the arrow, the egg, and the dart are all found in the synagogue.

167 ◆ RELIGIOUS AND EDUCATIONAL USE OF THE SYNAGOGUE

The synagogue preserved and passed down the heritage of the Hebrew Bible and developed as an educational institution for the transmission of Jewish rabbinic tradition.

In the Old Testament it is impossible to separate religion from education. No ancient society subscribed to the modern notion of the "secular." The Jewish community as a whole was responsible for the education of children and youth, which took place in the synagogue. The later instruction of youth in the Bible and the Talmud was carried on in the *yᵉshivot,* the special schools for prerabbinical studies. In the earlier periods such usage of the sanctuary was frowned on, but as the Hebrew language and learning began to fade from daily life, the preservation of the ancient heritage became a sacred mission, and the synagogue was used for this purpose. Since the primary responsibility of the adult Jew in the corporate synagogue service was to read, reading the unpointed Hebrew text of the Torah was the goal of synagogue education. The earliest lessons were undoubtedly in the form of memorizations of biblical passages, followed by simple readings such as the familiar *Shᵉmaʿ* (Deut. 6:4-5). The advanced students read the lessons from the great synagogue scrolls, guided by the commonplace synagogue official known as the *ḥazzan.* It was in these simple schools that the elaborate oral tradition that grew up around the Torah began to take form. Unfortunately, hardly any evidence has been derived from archaeology of the shape or substance of these studies, except for some Egyptian papyri that may be fragments of school texts.

168 • OFFICERS OF THE SYNAGOGUE

Like any religious institution, the synagogue developed various leadership functions. Over the centuries the roles of the synagogue officers have altered as the needs of the Jewish community have changed. The most important development has been the emergence of the office of rabbi.

In the Old Testament the authority of the Jewish community was vested in the convention, or council, of "elders," *ziqnei,* "elders of . . ." (Gen. 50:7). The ritual and ceremonial administration was under the direction of the Levitical priesthood, assisted by a number of groups of professional aids such as singers and other musicians. These officials represented a special and privileged class in the community. After the collapse of the monarchy and its attendant feudalism and the rise of an entrepreneurial class in the period of Hellenism, the offices of the synagogue were open to a broader representation of members of the community. The increased democratization led to wider participation and a common religious interest. Without this change Judaism would never have survived the Hellenistic age and would have followed the other archaic religious traditions into oblivion. The synagogue had about five offices; however, some were probably voluntary and carried no stipend or salary.

President of the Synagogue

The chief executive of the synagogue was called in Hebrew *ro'sh hakkᵉneset,* and in Greek, *archisunagōgos,* "president of the synagogue." This official was known also among pagan associations, but by the first century the term was more commonly applied to the Jewish officials, and by the fifth century exclusively so. The title has also been found on epigraphic inscriptions. The president was responsible not merely for the upkeep and operation of the house, but also for the order and sanctity of the service (Luke 13:14). Three individuals in the New Testament are so designated: Jairus (Mark 5:22; Luke 8:41); Crispus (Acts 18:8); and Sosthenes (Acts 18:17). The interesting fact that two of these are Gentile names indicates the degree of syncretism Hellenistic Judaism permitted. The *archisunagōgos* had the responsibility of selecting the Torah reading and may have read it himself in the congregation. At first the evidence indicates that this was an elective office, later becoming hereditary, and finally perfunctory. The plural, *archisunagōgoi,* which appears in Acts 13:15, has been the center of some debate, but a text from Apamaea in Syria contains a listing of three such officials and uses the plural term. A similar difficulty has arisen concerning the simpler term "leader of the synagogue," which appears only in Luke 8:41. This term is rare but has been located in contemporary inscriptions as an alternate and less proper form of *archisunagōgos.* Since the terms were still in a state of flux and as yet not fixed in the literary language, it is to be expected that such variants would be found.

Servant of the Synagogue

The second functionary in the synagogue was the *ḥazzan hakkᵉneset,* "servant of the synagogue" (*hupēretēs,* "attendant," Luke 4:20), a term later used of ministers of the gospel (Luke 1:2; Acts 26:16). The duties of the *ḥazzan* undoubtedly varied but included at various times cleaning the premises, removing and replacing the scrolls, and perhaps overseeing the teaching of the children. He also carried out the corporal punishments of the council (Matt. 10:17; 23:34; Mark 13:9). In later times the *ḥazzan* became the chief singer of the service and the term is now used for the "cantor." The title and its etymologies have had a wide expansion. However, it is now accepted that the term was originally an Assyrianism in late Jewish Aramaic, derived from Akkadian *ḥazunu(m),* meaning "superintendent" or "overseer." Although the title was sometimes used for the sexton, it was usually applied to one of the high officers of the synagogue. The fact that the *ḥazzan* handled the sacred scrolls while in the synagogue points to the importance of the office. As with all offices of the ancient Israelite religious community, the *ḥazzan* was functional. No doubt the functions varied from town to rural communities and from great to humble congregations, but the importance of the office grew with time. As the festivals and ceremonies developed along separate lines in Diaspora Judaism, so did the officers of the synagogue. The result is that a bewildering array of functions and honors are assigned to the *ḥazzan* in the literature of the rabbis.

Leader of the Prayers

The third officer of the ancient synagogue was the "leader of the prayers," literally "messenger of the congregation" (*shᵉliᵃḥ zibbur*). This individual was chosen as representative of the New Testament congregation, in whose place he responded to the liturgical prayers. Some scholars have assumed that he fulfilled the role of priest in this delegated responsibility, but it is clear that he was not sacrosanct and acted as a layman. In the New Testament period, the function could be assigned to any adult male in the congregation who was of good standing. It may be in this capacity that Jesus read the passage from Isaiah 61 in the synagogue at Nazareth (Luke 4:17-28). In later tradition the *sheliaḥ zibbur* lost this spontaneous quality and was a regularly employed person of the congregation. Some believe that in the absence of any person willing to act as the *sheliaḥ zibbur,* the chief officers might act in this capacity themselves. Undoubtedly this practice led to the merging of the office of *sheliaḥ zibbur* with the permanent one of *ḥazzan* so that the distinction between them became obliterated and the two terms interchanged.

Other Officers

Translator. A number of less certain officers are found in records and discourses on the synagogue. Some of these must have existed in Roman times and been absorbed into the later offices of the congregation. One of these was the Hebrew *metorgaman,* "interpreter" or "translator," a person who was apparently chosen from the congregation to interpret the text of the Scripture from Hebrew into Aramaic for the purpose of the lesson. This practice may be involved in the phrase "which being interpreted is," found six times in the New Testament (Matt. 1:23; Mark 5:41; 15:22, 34; John 1:41; Acts 4:36). The *metorgaman* played a very important part in the synagogue service in areas such as Galilee where Judaism of the Hebraic period had no tradition. A similar sort of personage must have functioned in lands of the Diaspora where Greek and Latin were spoken because the inscriptions on such synagogue buildings are usually in those languages and rarely in Hebrew. It was the notion of a Targumic translation for use in the synagogue that led to the formation of the Septuagint, or Greek version of the Old Testament.

Herald of the *Shema*. The reading of the *sheliaḥ zibbur* and the interpretation of the *metorgaman* were preceded by the public proclamation of the *Shema* prayer. This was stated by a special officer, the "herald of the *Shema*." This officer probably read the *Shema* prayers as found in Deuteronomy 6:4-9, followed by passages from Deuteronomy 11:13-21 and Numbers 15:37-41, after which the congregation answered "Amen." Such public prayer was always led by an officer and was referred to by a terminology different from that of private prayer. There is some evidence that the public praying of the *Shema* was read from a scroll and that other passages, such as Exodus 20, may have been included. Some scholars have interpreted the action of the reading of the Decalogue as the promulgation of God's imperial decree, his law. Thus they would associate this herald of the *Shema* with the notion of the "herald" (*kērux*) of the gospel mentioned in 1 Timothy 2:7; 2 Timothy 1:11; and 2 Peter 2:5. This accords with the scriptural use of terms of royalty and the court to describe the reign of God. The literature of Judaism of all the ages makes clear that, in the Jewish mind, the synagogue was the kingly court of God; the most sacred place and the utmost reverence were afforded the Torah. It was in light of this devotion that all the offices of the congregation derived their place and authority. From the *archisunagōgos* to the herald, all were servants of the Torah.

Collector. Of the later administrative offices, the most important was the "collector" or "almoner," whose task it was to collect and distribute funds for the poor. The public giving of alms was a feature of the Jewish religious community. It is mentioned in the rabbinic literature and frequently in the New Testament (Matt. 6:2-4). The Gospels and other contemporary sources indicate that while the temple in Jerusalem was supported by the royal establishment and received its revenue from special taxes, the synagogues were voluntary, and freewill offerings were commonplace. There is no doubt that the collector or almoner of the synagogue who ministered to the poor was the model for the deacon (Phil. 1:1; 1 Tim. 3:8, 10, 12-13).

The Rabbinic Office

The actual origin of the rabbinic office is lost in history. The term *rabbi* is of great antiquity and can be traced to Akkadian usage. In the biblical context it means "teacher," or "master," and was at no time a priestly or ordained office. Any layman learned in the Torah and Jewish law could be called "rabbi." In the tradition of Babylonian Judaism, the term was pronounced "rav." After the destruction of the temple and its officialdom, some attempt appears to have been made to continue the priestly offices, but as the majority of Jews moved in succeeding generations to the area of Galilee, the office of rabbi came to take their place as the ordained leadership in the community.

William White[10]

169 ✦ ELEMENTS OF SYNAGOGUE WORSHIP

Synagogue worship consisted of three main elements: praise, prayer, and instruction. The earliest Christians, who were Jews, would have been familiar with this pattern, which in Christian worship gave shape to what is called the service of the Word.

Jewish scholars have helped us form a picture of the essential pattern of synagogue worship, although it must be confessed that there are some debatable matters. For the period before the destruction of the temple in A.D. 70, the New Testament is a valuable source (especially Luke 4:15-21). Very few precise details are given in any contemporary document. The general picture, however, is tolerably clear. There are three main elements: praise, prayer, and instruction.

Praise

It is the note of corporate praise that opens the service, and this is in accord with the principle laid down in the Talmud: "Man should always first utter

---

THE STRUCTURE OF THE EIGHTEEN BENEDICTIONS

The *T*fillah*, which follows the *Sh*ma'*, constitutes the petitionary prayer par excellence of Jewish synagogue worship. These prayers originated in the first century or earlier. By the second century they were more highly developed and consisted of nineteen prayers.

The structure and content of the *T*fillah* in its full form can be summarized in the following outline:

A. Three Opening Benedictions	1. Thou art God 2. Thou art mighty 3. Thou art holy	Praise of God
	Therefore we ask:	
	4. Understanding 5. Repentance 6. Forgiveness	Spiritual blessings
	7. Personal freedom 8. Health 9. Well-being 10. Reunification of the scattered	Material blessings
B. Thirteen Immediate Petitions	11. Integral justice 12. Punishment of enemies 13. Reward of the just 14. The new Jerusalem 15. The Messiah 16. Hearing of prayers	Social blessings
	Therefore:	
C. Three Final Benedictions	17. Restore worship in Jerusalem 18. Accept our gratitude 19. Grant us peace	Thanksgiving to God

Source: Carmine Di Sante, *Jewish Prayer: The Origins of Christian Liturgy* (New York: Paulist Press, 1985), 87.

praises, and then pray." The adoption of this procedure may underlie the order of 1 Corinthians 14:26, which suggests that, at the head of the list of Christian corporate worship at Corinth, "a hymn" of praise should be sung.

The "ruler" summons the "minister" (Luke 4:20) to invite someone from the congregation to commence the service with this "call to worship." He begins with the cry "Bless ye the Lord, the One who is to be blessed," and the people respond with the benediction "Blessed be the Lord . . . for ever," in the spirit of Nehemiah 9:5. At the outset, then, the worshipers are invited to think of God and to acknowledge his greatness and blessing.

Prayers

Prayers in Jewish worship fall into two types. The first group comprise two lovely utterances: the *Yotzer,* which means "He who forms," takes up the theme of God as Creator of all things, and the *'Ahᵃvah,* which means "love," is concerned both to recall God's love for his people and to pledge their obligation to love him in return. It ends, "Blessed art thou, O Lord, who has chosen thy people Israel in love." Immediately following these prayers comes the *Shᵉma',* which is both a confession of faith and a glad benediction. The title for the *Shᵉma'* derives from its opening word. ("Hear" in Deut. 6:4; "Hear, O Israel: the LORD our God, the LORD is one.") As soon as the congregation comes to the word *one*—for the *Shᵉma'* is recited antiphonally—the leader adds the glad ejaculation "Blessed be the name of the glory of his kingdom for ever and ever." The term *one,* emphasizing the unity of God, has always been the central Jewish confession. It is given, therefore, a special prominence in the liturgy. The great Rabbi Akiba (c. 50–132), influential in the formation of Jewish rabbinic tradition, died with this Hebrew word for "one" (*'eḥad*) upon his lips. In its full form the *Shᵉma'* consists of Deuteronomy 6:4-9, 11:13-21, and Numbers 15:37-41.

The second division of united prayer comes next. The way for this division is prepared by the reciting of the prayer known as "true and firm" ("is this the word—the *Shᵉma'*—to us forever"), with its reminder that God's promises are sure and dependable to his people. At this point, the "minister" summons a member of the assembly to lead in the "prayer proper," that is, the "Eighteen Benedictions," or blessings. The man so appointed steps forward in front of the ark and, with his face turned toward the ark, leads the united intercessions of the company, who reply with "Amen." These "Eighteen Blessings" cover a wide range of themes. They are partly an expression of praise, partly petitions for spiritual and material benefits and partly supplication for those in need (exiles, judges and counselors, and the chosen people). We may catch the tone of these prayers by considering the last one: "Grant peace upon Israel thy people and upon thy city, and upon thy inheritance, and bless us all together [literally, "as one"]. Blessed art thou O Lord, the maker of peace." It seems permissible to believe that these precise words were on the lips of Jesus as he entered the synagogue, according to his custom, for worship in his day.

Instruction

Once the prayers were said, the service assumed a form that has given the synagogue its distinctive ethos. Indeed, the Jews themselves called it "the house of instruction," for there is nothing more in keeping with Jewish worship than the emphasis placed on Scripture reading and exposition. Instruction was given by these two means. First, the Law and the Prophets were read by members of the congregation, who came up and shared the task (according to the length of the portions involved). As the ancient Bible language of Hebrew was not understood by all present, someone would translate the Scripture lessons into the vernacular, usually Aramaic. Then the homily, or address, based on the passages read, was delivered by a person in the assembly who was considered suitable. This person was invited to deliver the "sermon"—as proved the case both at Nazareth (Luke 4:14-30) and at Antioch (Acts 13:14-42). The service concluded with a blessing and the congregational "Amen."

There were modifications of this basic pattern, depending on the season of the year and the day of the week. (Market days, Monday and Thursday, had shorter Scripture lections!) But the ingredients that provide the staple diet of synagogue worship—praise, prayer, and instruction—are found in every case.

These same elements are discovered in the New Testament patterns of worship, along with some distinctively Christian innovations. The evidence supports the thesis that Christian worship, as a distinctive, indigenous practice, arose from the fusion, in the crucible of Christian experience, of the synagogue and the upper room.

Ralph P. Martin[11]

170 ✦ ORDER OF FIRST-CENTURY SYNAGOGUE WORSHIP

Our knowledge of worship of the synagogue in the first century of the Common Era (C.E.) is limited by a lack of source material. It seems clear, however, that readings from the Law and the Prophets, the recitation of the Shᵉma', and the prayers or benedictions formed the order of the service.

Apart from a few scattered references in the New Testament, Philo, and Josephus, most of our knowledge of early synagogue worship comes from the Mishnah, which does not date before 200 C.E. Although some traditions in the Mishnah may go back to the first century, the Mishnah represents only one form of Judaism (Pharasaic), in contrast to the diversity within Judaism reported by Philo, Josephus, the Dead Sea Scrolls, and the New Testament. Further, the first Jewish prayer books did not appear until the ninth century (for example, *Seder Rav Amram Gaon,* which represents Babylonian Jewish usage); therefore, even the earliest complete texts of the majority of Jewish liturgical prayers are relatively late.

The Place of Worship

First-century Jewish sources call the place of worship *synagōgē* ("place of gathering") and *proseuchē* ("place of prayer"). Philo and Josephus both witness to the function of these communal buildings as places where the Law was read. Detailed archaeological evidence for the synagogue dates only from the third century C.E. Some synagogues may have contained mosaics and walls painted with biblical scenes.

Reading

First-century synagogue worship probably involved readings from the Torah and prophets, the *Shᵉma',* the *tᵉfillah,* and the so-called priestly blessing (Num. 6:24-26).

Scripture Reading. The reading of Scripture is the most widely attested activity of first-century synagogue services (Luke 4:16-27; Acts 13:15, 27; Acts 15:21). Attempts to discern a lectionary cycle for Sabbath and festival day services have been unsuccessful. The New Testament and Mishnah witness to the custom that any (male) member of the congregation could be invited to read from the Law or Prophets and to expound on the reading (Luke 4:16-27).

Shᵉma'. The *Shᵉma'* (Deut. 6:4-9; 11:13-21; Num. 15:37-41) may also have been recited, as a creedal confession rather than as a reading *per se.*

Tᵉfillah, or Prayer. Later sources refer to the praying of a prayer consisting of a number of sections, each ending with a *bᵉrakhah,* or blessing. By the end of the first century C.E., the number of these sections was standardized: seven on the Sabbath and eighteen on weekdays. This prayer is known as the *tᵉfillah,* or "Prayer"; *Shᵉmoneh 'Esreh,* or "the Eighteen [Benedictions]"; and *'Amidah,* or "the Standing [Prayer]." This omnibus prayer covered the spectrum of God's blessings on Israel. While the subject of each portion of the *tᵉfillah* may have been relatively fixed from at least the second century, the actual wording of each was left to the individual.

Although later Jewish prayer consisted almost entirely of blessings ("Blessed are you . . .") there is evidence that some first-century Jewish prayer also consisted of "thanksgiving" (which can also be translated "confession" or "acknowledgment"). Contemporary liturgical scholarship has sought the origins of Christian prayers of thanksgiving (particularly the eucharistic prayer) within this diversity of first-century Jewish prayer forms.

The Leadership of Worship

The archaeological evidence for the leadership of synagogues in late antiquity suggests that women as well as men could have the title *archisunagōgos,* or "ruler of the synagogue," a title that also appears in the New Testament. Therefore it is possible that in some places in the Greco-Roman world women led some portions of synagogue worship. However, the leadership of synagogue worship would not necessarily have been limited to this individual.

Grant Sperry-White

171 ✦ SYNAGOGUE WORSHIP SPACE

The synagogue space in which Jews worshiped was treated as sacred space. Worshipers gathered around the symbols that spoke of God's redeeming and revealing activity among them.

Synagogue worship was organized around two foci. The first focus of the synagogue was the ark. Everyone, including the rabbi, who sat at the back, looked toward the ark. The original ark was the most holy symbol of the covenant and the only object ever admitted in the Holy of Holies of the temple. The ark, a kind of wooden casket, was understood to be a throne where God, the sole object of the worship of Israel, was present. The ark of the synagogue was an echo of the primitive ark of the tabernacle. It was linked to the ancient ark by the presence of the scrolls of the Torah, the Word of God. Before the ark was the veil, which protected it,

and the *menorah*, the seven-branched candlestand. In this way Israel preserved its memory of the tabernacle and of God's presence with Israel for the furniture pointed beyond itself to the ultimate site of the Holy of Holies, Jerusalem.

The second focus of the synagogue was the *bēma*, the place from which the Torah was read and the prayers were said. It was a platform that was raised in the center of the synagogue space so all the people could hear. The seats were on the side of the building so that the congregation gathered around the leader and his teaching.

Here then, in the very architecture of the building and in the manner in which the people assembled, was a profound symbol of the meaning of synagogue worship. God who was present in the past was made present through the symbols of his presence. And God's presence was also anticipated in the future, for every congregation faced Jerusalem in expectation of the gathering of the Jews there in the city of the Great King.

Robert E. Webber

The Relationship of Worship and Architecture in the Synagogue

172 ✦ THE *SHᵉMAʿ*

The Shᵉmaʿ represents the creedal affirmation of Jewish synagogue worship. It is comprised of three passages from the Pentateuch. The first of these is the most important; Jesus quoted it in response to a scribe who asked him which commandment was the greatest in the Law (Mark 12:28). The second and third portions may be shortened. The Shᵉmaʿ is recited in the opening part of synagogue worship. This section gives a translation of the text of the Shᵉmaʿ.

Deuteronomy 6:4-9—The Obligations of God's Worshipers

Hear, O Israel: The LORD our God, the LORD is one. Love the LORD your God with all your heart and with all your soul and with all your strength. These commandments that I give you today are to be upon your hearts. Impress them on your children. Talk about them when you sit at home and when you walk along the road, when you lie down and when you get up. Tie them as symbols on your hands and bind them on your foreheads. Write them on the doorframes of your houses and on your gates.

Deuteronomy 11:13-21— Consequences of Obedience and Disobedience

So if you faithfully obey the commands I am giving you today—to love the LORD your God and to serve him with all your heart and with all your soul—then I will send rain on your land in its season, both autumn and spring rains, so that you may gather in your grain, new wine, and oil. I will provide grass in the fields for your cattle, and you will eat and be satisfied.

Be careful, or you will be enticed to turn away and worship other gods and bow down to them. Then the LORD's anger will burn against you, and he will shut the heavens so that it will not rain and the ground will yield no produce, and you will soon perish from the good land the LORD is giving you. Fix these words of mine in your hearts and minds; tie them as symbols on your hands and bind them on your foreheads. Teach them to your children, talking about them when you sit at home and when you walk along the road, when you lie down and when you get up. Write them on the doorframes of your houses and on your gates, so that your days and the days of your children may be many in the land that the LORD swore to give your forefathers, as many as the days that the heavens are above the earth."

Numbers 15:37-41—Make Tassels to Be Constant Reminders of the Commandments

The LORD said to Moses, "Speak to the Israelites and say to them: 'Throughout the generations to come you are to make tassels on the corners of your garments, with a blue cord on each tassel. You will have these tassels to look at and so you will remember all the commands of the LORD, that you may obey them and not prostitute yourselves by going after the lusts of your own hearts and eyes. Then you will remember to obey all my commands and will be consecrated to your God. I am the LORD your God, who brought you out of Egypt to be your God. I am the LORD your God.'"

173 • THE *B*^E*RAKHAH* OR BLESSING

The b^e*rakhah, blessing or benediction, is the chief form of prayer in Jewish worship. The New Testament provides numerous examples of the use of this form of prayer by Jesus and the apostles.*

The *b*^e*rakhah* (translated in the Christian Scriptures as *eucharistia* [thanksgiving] or *eulogia* [blessing] and in the Latin Bible as *benedictio* [blessing] or *gratiarum actio* [thanksgiving]) was and is the chief form of prayer in Jewish liturgy and spirituality. It is the chief form of prayer because it determines the meaning and context of all prayer, as well as the dynamic movement and horizon of all liturgy and all the feasts. The *b*^e*rakhah* consists in an attitude and formula of wonder, praise, thanksgiving, and acknowledgment of the unmerited divine benevolence that provides for God's children and gladdens them with the fruits of the earth and every kind of blessing. In the course of time the mark of the *b*^e*rakhah* came to be the set, standardized words with which every prayer began and ended: "Blessed be you, Lord, our God." At times, the passive form ("Blessed be you . . .") might be replaced by the active form: "I bless you. . . ."

The New Testament tells us of many *b*^e*rakhot,* some explicit, others—the majority—implicit. Among the best known is the one in which Jesus thanks the Father for having chosen "babes" as the recipients of his revelation:

> I praise you, Father, Lord of heaven and earth, because you have hidden these things from the wise and learned, and revealed them to little children. Yes, Father, for this was your good pleasure. All things have been committed to me by my Father. No one knows the Son except the Father, and no one knows the Father except the Son and those to whom the Son chooses to reveal him. (Matt. 11:25-27; cf. Luke 10:21-22)

The most famous of the implicit *b*^e*rakhot* is the one to which all the synoptic evangelists refer in the account of "the institution of the Eucharist":

> While they were eating, Jesus took bread, gave thanks and broke it, and gave it to his disciples, saying, "Take it; this is my body." Then he took the cup, and gave thanks and offered it to them, and they all drank from it. "This is my blood of the covenant, which is poured out for many," he said to them. (Mark 14:22-24)

Another testimony to Jesus' use of the *b*^e*rakhah* form is in Mark 6:41, where the influence of the Eucharist is undeniable: "Taking the five loaves and the two fish and looking up to heaven, he gave thanks and broke the loaves . . ." (a similar passage occurs again in Mark 8:6-7). Other references to blessings are in Mark 10:16, where Jesus took the children in his arms and "blessed them," that is, said a *b*e*rakhah* over them, and in John, where Jesus utters a *b*e*rakhah* to the Father for the raising of Lazarus: "Jesus looked up and said, 'Father, I thank you that you have heard me. I knew that you always hear me . . .'" (John 11:41-42).

Other New Testament writings besides the Gospels present many other pieces of evidence. Colossians 3:17 serves as an example: "And whatever [*pan*] you do, whether in word or deed, do it all [*panta*] in the name of the Lord Jesus, giving thanks to God the Father through him." According to the rabbinical tradition, the devout Jew ought to recite over one hundred *b*e*rakhot* daily. We cannot fail to see the same sensibility at work in Paul's exhortation to "do everything" to the accompaniment of thanksgiving. In all things (*panta*), nothing excluded, Christians, like Jews, should utter a *b*e*rakhah*. The only difference is that Christians are to do this "in the name of the Lord Jesus" or "through him," that is, with the same intention and the same fullness of commitment he had.

Ephesians 5 is also meaningful: "Be filled with the Spirit. Speak to one another with psalms, hymns and spiritual songs. Sing and make music in your heart to the Lord, always giving thanks [*eucharistountes pantote huper pantōn*] to God the Father for everything, in the name of our Lord Jesus Christ" (Eph. 5:18-20). Christians should offer *b*e*rakhot* at all times (*pantote*) and for everything (*huper pantōn*).

The Pauline letters not only show the importance of the *b*e*rakhah;* they also tell us the motives that give rise to it. These can be summed up under two headings: the existence of the new Christian communities and, above all, the event that is Jesus, now acknowledged and proclaimed as Messiah and Son of God. If Christians ought to utter a *b*e*rakhah* in every situation and every event, then certainly this response is called for in face of the two main events of early Christianity: the multiplication of communities by the hundreds and the experience of the dead and risen Jesus (1 Cor. 1:4-9; Col. 1:3-5; Eph. 1:3-14).

174 ⬥ The Our Father (Lord's Prayer) in Light of Jewish B*e*rekhah

Jesus gave his disciples a model to follow in the Lord's Prayer. In this prayer, Jesus brings to a clear focus many expressions and elements already present in first-century Jewish synagogue worship.

The Our Father, of which we have two versions (Luke 11:2-4; Matt. 6:9-13), also reflects to an important degree the liturgy of the synagogue. Contrary to the claims of apologetes who like to emphasize the radical originality of the Our Father, a careful analysis shows that this prayer has deep roots in Judaism.

This statement applies first to the very structure of the Our Father. This reflects the ideal structure of Jewish prayer, as seen, for example, in biblical prayers such as that of David (1 Chron. 29:10-20); an opening *b*e*rakhah,* or petitions, and a final, summarizing *b*e*rakhah.* For this reason it is improbable that the Lord's Prayer ended with the words "but deliver us from evil." The ending in some codices of Matthew's gospel would seem closer to the original: "For yours is the kingdom and the power and the glory forever. Amen."

When we turn from the structure to an analysis of the several parts of the Our Father, the connections with Jewish prayer become even clearer.

Our Father

The description of God as a "father" recurs in Jewish prayer. The practice is attested first in the Bible itself. In Deuteronomy 32:6 and Isaiah 63:16, for example, God is called the father of Israel and Israelites are called his children. The name is attested above all, however, in the Jewish liturgy.

In the *'Amidah,* or Eighteen Benedictions, for example, the title occurs twice: "Cause us to return, O our Father, unto thy Torah; draw us near, O our King, unto they service . . ." (fifth benediction); "Forgive us, O our Father, for we have sinned; pardon us, O our King, for we have transgressed" (sixth benediction). We also find it in the second benediction before the *Sh*e*ma':* "O our Father, our King, for our fathers' sake, who trusted in thee, and whom thou didst teach the statutes of life, be also gracious unto us and teach us. O our Father, ever compassionate, have mercy on us."

The name "Father" is also widely used in the liturgy of the celebrations of the new year and of Yom

Kippur (Day of Atonement), where the phrases "Father of mercy" and "O our Father" occur with some frequency. "Father" emphasizes the trust of the people in the mercy of God, while the plural "our" underscores the solidarity of the community that is gathered for prayer.

If these similarities are taken seriously, then the opposition theologians and exegetes like to see between the Jewish conception of God and that of Jesus becomes at least questionable. Although Jesus and the early Christians addressed God as *'Abba'*, the difference between *'ab* (father) and *'abba'* (papa) should not be exaggerated. It may be true that the use of *'abba'* is predominantly Christian, but it should not be contrasted with the use of *'ab; 'abba'* represents at most a nuance of feeling.

Who Art in Heaven

This expression likewise occurs frequently in the Jewish liturgy. It occurs in the morning service: "Thou are the Lord our God in heaven and on earth." In the treatise, *'Avot,* the oldest and most important in the Mishnah, one passage reads: "Be courageous and do the will of your Father who is in heaven" (*'Avot.* 5, 23). The words are obviously meant to be metaphorical, not geographical. They express God's transcendence, his "otherness" in relation to human beings. If the word *Father* expresses God's closeness to humanity, the expression "who is in heaven" reminds us of the irreducible difference between him and us.

Hallowed Be Thy Name

The expression immediately reminds us of the *qaddish,* one of the oldest Jewish prayers, used at the end of the reading and study of the Torah and, later, in the synagogue service. "Magnified and sanctified be his great Name in the world which he hath created according to his will." The expression also occurs in the *qᵉdushah,* the third benediction of the *tᵉfillah:* "We will sanctify thy Name in the world even as they sanctify it in the highest heaven."

The parallel between these texts of the Jewish liturgy and the Our Father becomes even more startling in light of the meaning of the words "sanctify the name of God." The teachers ask: "How can human beings sanctify the name of God?" They answer: "By their words but above all by their lives." Those who are faithful to God's will and prefer it to

their own "sanctify his Name." The true "sanctification of the Name" (*qiddush hashshem*) consists in the gift of one's life; it consists in martyrdom.

We can now understand better what Jesus is referring to when he says "hallowed be thy name"; the words express his conception of God, but above all they express the gift of his life, which is "sacrificed" for all (Matt. 26:24; Luke 22:19). By his death on the cross in obedience to the Father's will, Jesus "sanctified the Name." The same thread runs through history from Jesus dying on the cross to the thousands of Jews who called on God and glorified him as they entered the gas chambers; they as well as Jesus "sanctified the Name."

Thy Kingdom Come

These words are likewise to be found in the *qaddish:* "May he establish his kingdom during your life and during your days and during the life of all the house of Israel." This is clearly a kingdom to be established not in some metahistorical realm but in our present history. The kingdom of God is to become a reality in this world and not just in the next. When Jesus calls for the coming of the kingdom of God he is thinking of a humanized world in which human beings can live in fruitful peace as brothers and sisters.

Thy Will Be Done

These words also occur in 1 Maccabees: "It is better for us to die in battle than to see the misfortunes of our nation and of the sanctuary. But as his will in heaven may be, so he will do" (1 Macc. 3:59-60). The same attitude of abandonment to God's will finds expression in the prayer which Jews utter as they feel death drawing near: "May it be thy will to send me a perfect healing. Yet if my death be fully determined by thee, I will in love to accept it at thy hand."

Give Us This Day Our Daily Bread

The preceding invocations focused on God; this and the following invocations focus on human needs. The petition for "bread" is part of the ninth benediction of the *tᵉfillah:* "Bless this year unto us, O Lord our God, together with every kind of the produce thereof, for our welfare; give a blessing upon the face of the earth. Oh satisfy us with thy goodness, and bless our year like other good years. Blessed art thou, O Lord, who blesses the years."

Some commentators liked to see in this Jewish

blessing an allusion to the manna in the wilderness. Not without reason, some fathers of the church liked to see in the "daily bread" of the Our Father an allusion to the Eucharist. Thus the Our Father is linked to the Jewish liturgy not only textually but even hermeneutically. The allusion to the manna may also shed light on the difficult Greek adjective *epiousion* (translated in Matt. 6:11 as "daily bread"); just as the Israelites were to gather the manna "as much as he needed" (Exod. 16:21) because any surplus gathered "was full of maggots and began to smell" (Exod. 16:20), so the bread we ask of God is bread that is enough for each day and frees us of any worry about the future and any hoarding. The same thought is expressed in Proverbs 30:8: "Give me neither poverty nor riches, but give me only my daily bread."

Forgive Us Our Debts As We Forgive Our Debtors

The idea of forgiveness finds expression in the sixth benediction of the *t^efillah:* "Forgive us, O our Father, for we have sinned; pardon us, O our King, for we have transgressed; for thou dost pardon and forgive. Blessed art thou, O Lord, who are gracious, and dost abundantly forgive." Even the thought in "as we forgive our debtors" has its origin in the synagogue and the Old Testament. We find it in the Yom Kippur liturgy and the Old Testament apocryphal book of Sirach: "Forgive your neighbor the wrong he has done, and then your sins will be pardoned when you pray" (28:2, RSV). The same doctrine is found in the majority of the rabbis, who teach that "if you forgive your neighbor, the One will forgive you; but if you do not forgive your neighbor, no one will have mercy on you" (Midrash *Tanhuma Genesi*).

Lead Us Not into Temptation But Deliver Us from Evil

This idea of deliverance (redemption) is found in the seventh benediction of the *t^efillah:* "Look upon our affliction and plead our cause, and redeem us speedily for thy Name's sake; for thou art a mighty Redeemer. Blessed art thou, O Lord, the Redeemer of Israel." There is an even closer resemblance in the Talmud, b. Ber. 50b: "Do not abandon me to the power of sin or to the power of guilt or to the power of temptation or to the power of shame." The Talmud was composed centuries after Christ, but many of its materials go back to a far distant period, even prior to the time of Christ.

Jesus called on the same God as did his Jewish brothers and sisters and used the same turns of phrase they did. His originality consisted in bringing to fulfillment what the biblical and liturgical texts proclaimed and expressed: "Do not think that I have come to abolish the Law or the Prophets; I have not come to abolish them but to fulfill them" (Matt. 5:17). The prayer Jesus gave us is not opposed to the prayers of the Jews but brings them to fulfillment.

Carmine Di Sante[12]

175 ✦ Bibliography: Links Between Jewish and Christian Worship

Beckwith, Roger T. *Daily and Weekly Worship: Jewish and Christian.* Bramcote, Notts.: Grove Books, 1987. This excellent introduction to Jewish worship, and the transition from Jewish worship to Christian worship, treats the Christian ministry of the Word, the origin of the Sunday Eucharist, the origin of the Eucharist prayer and of Sunday evening services, and other topics.

Bradshaw, Paul F., and Lawrence A. Hoffman, eds. *The Making of Jewish and Christian Worship.* Notre Dame: University of Notre Dame Press, 1991. The first part of this scholarly volume probes the origins of Jewish and Christian liturgy. It includes chapters on principles for interpreting early Christian liturgical evidence and for the use of archaeological sources. The second part deals with the evolution of Christian and Jewish worship. The theme of the book is that the reconstruction of yesterday's liturgical practice has an impact on today's worship and spirituality.

Di Sante, Carmine. *Jewish Prayer: The Origins of the Christian Liturgy.* Mahwah, N.J.: Paulist Press, 1991. This well-written work probes the sources of Jewish liturgy, the structure of Jewish worship, the private and communal phases of Jewish prayer, and the celebration of the feasts. The book is especially valuable in developing the impact of Jewish liturgy on Christian worship.

Dugmore, C. W. *The Influence of the Synagogue upon the Divine Office.* Philadelphia: Fortress Press, 1964. This work traces in some detail the impact of synagogue worship on the growth of Christian liturgy.

Fisher, Eugene J., ed. *The Jewish Roots of the Christian Liturgy*. Mahwah, N.J.: Paulist Press, 1990. In a semischolarly introduction to issues related to Jewish and Christian worship, the author discusses matters such as the beginnings of Christian liturgy in Judaism, the rabbinic concept of *Shekhinah* and Matthew 18:20, the Jewish sabbath, the Christian Sunday, and anti-Jewish elements in Christian liturgy. For those seeking more understanding of the roots of Christian worship in Jewish liturgical practice, this is an excellent introduction.

Petuchowski, Jacob P., and Michael Brocke. *The Lord's Prayer and Jewish Liturgy*. New York: Seabury Press, 1978. This work explores the connections between Jewish worship and the Lord's Prayer. The emphasis is on synagogue worship and the features of the Lord's Prayer which reflect that worship.

Werner, Eric. *The Sacred Bridge: Liturgical Parallels in Synagogue and Early Church*. New York: Schocken Books, 1970. This discussion of Jewish liturgy at the time of primitive Christianity considers the relation between Christian and Jewish worship in music, Scripture lessons, psalms, hymns, liturgical acclamations, doxologies, and other acts of worship.

The Church as an Institution of Worship

Christian worship is not an activity of isolated individuals but a function of the corporate life of the church. The place and shape of worship in the New Testament can best be understood against the background of the life of the church as a whole. The church, which offers worship to almighty God and to his Christ, is and has always been a human organization. While from a spiritual standpoint the church bears the unique stamp of its Lord, it may also be described in terms that compare it with other human institutions.

176 ♦ CHARACTERISTICS OF THE CHURCH

The church is the assembly of the "saints," or holy ones, a people called out of the world by God. The early church was an urban movement. It held a world view which differed from that of the prevailing culture, yet it came to include people of all social classes in its radical fellowship.

Terms for the Church

The most common word for the church in the New Testament is *ekklēsia,* or "assembly." It is a derivative of the verb *kaleō,* "call," in the sense of those who are "called out." The word was a general word for assemblies, but as used by the apostles it also has a theological significance. The church is the body of those who are called out from the "world," or surrounding culture, but primarily from traditional Judaism, which the New Testament theologians considered to be unfaithful to the genuine thrust of the Lord's covenant. Paul spoke of the new covenant community as the "Israel of God" (Gal. 6:16); he asserted that not all those who are descended from Israel are really Israelites (Rom. 9:6). Unlike the earthly Jerusalem and its religious institutions, which are in bondage, the church is the "Jerusalem above" (Gal. 4:26, NASB), an image developed as the "heavenly Jerusalem" in the epistle to the Hebrews (Heb. 12:22) and in the Revelation to John (Rev. 21:2). Although today such ideas might sound anti-Semitic, they were given expression by Jews, at

least one of whom defended his Jewish credentials to the hilt (Phil. 3:4-6).

The disciples of Jesus were first called Christians (*Christianoi*) in Antioch (Acts 11:26). By its opponents, the Christian movement was known as the "Nazarene sect" (Acts 24:5). Other designations were "the Way" (*hē hodos,* Acts 9:2; 19:9, 23; 22:4), "the way of God" (Acts 18:26), and "the way of truth" ("genuine way," 2 Pet. 2:2). New Testament writers frequently refer to the church as "the brothers" (*adelphoi,* Acts 15:36, 40; 16:2; 18:18; Rom. 12:1; 1 Cor. 16:11; 1 Tim. 4:6; 1 John 3:14; 3 John 5; Rev. 12:10). This term was borrowed from Jewish usage, as early Christian preaching illustrates (Acts 3:22; 7:37). In his letters to local churches, Paul addresses the assembly collectively as "the saints," or holy ones (*hoi hagioi*), in the sense of those who belong to the holy God. It is not only the righteous behavior of Christians that makes them "saints," but the fact that as God's own people they share in that special aura of sanctity and mystery associated with the Lord's presence, which is bound up in the Hebrew concept of holiness (*qodesh*). The author of Hebrews refers to the church as a worshiping body, using the term "festal gathering" (*panēguris,* Heb. 12:22, RSV).

Images, Concepts

The New Testament offers a panorama of images for the church that, while not sociological categories, nevertheless shed light on the way the institutional church was perceived by its spokesmen. This imagery is drawn from a wide spectrum of human experience. In a favorite metaphor of the apostle Paul, the church is a *body,* specifically the body of Christ, the continuing embodiment of his Spirit (1 Cor. 12:13; Eph. 4:4). From agricultural life come the images of the church as a *flock* protected by its Shepherd (Acts 20:28; 1 Pet. 5:2-3), as the *branches* nourished by the vine (John 15:1-5), or as the olive tree (Rom. 11:16-21). In an analogy to urban life, the new covenant community is compared to a *city,* specifically Jerusalem (Gal. 4:26; Heb. 12:22; 13:14; Rev. 21:2). Domestic life contributes the description of the church as a *household* of faith (Gal. 6:10; Eph. 2:19) and the *family* of God, in which he is Father, as well as the arresting image of the church as the *bride* of the Lamb (Rev. 19:7; 21:2; cf. 2 Cor. 11:2). Israel's religious heritage suggests the portrayal of the church as a *temple* of the Holy Spirit (1 Cor. 3:16-17; 2 Cor. 6:16). In cosmic perspective, the church is a *new creation* (2 Cor. 5:17). The covenantal foundation of Israel's faith stands behind the image of the *kingdom* of God (Rom. 14:17; 1 Cor. 4:20; Col. 4:11; 2 Thess. 1:5); though this expression has wider applications, it certainly includes the church. The covenant is also the framework for speaking of the Lord as Father, Shepherd, and Creator of his new people.

Evident in this pictorial language is the attempt to grasp a reality that can only be conveyed symbolically. There is a mystery and depth to the church as the community of the new covenant responding to the Spirit of Christ that flat sociological categories and theories of ecclesiastical polity cannot capture.

Social Character

When viewed as a social organization, the church of the first century exhibits certain traits that stand out as especially noteworthy. This discussion, while not a complete sociological analysis, treats some of these social characteristics.

An Urban Movement. Christianity began as an urban movement, spreading from city to city and only later infiltrating the rural areas. The history of the missionary expansion of the church is a narrative of activities carried out in an urban setting, and many books of the New Testament bear the names of prominent cities of the Greco-Roman world, some of which were quite large even by modern standards: Ephesus, Corinth, Rome. One factor accounting for this was the presence of Jewish congregations in these cities; usually a church was started as the result of the preaching of the apostles in synagogues of the Diaspora (Acts 13:14; 14:1; 17:17; 18:4). Paul, for one, was conscious of his urban heritage; being from Tarsus in Asia Minor, home of a major university, he termed himself "a citizen of no ordinary city" (Acts 21:39). He was also a Roman citizen (Acts 16:37; 22:25-26), which signified a relation to the city-state of Rome in an era before the modern nation-state had made its appearance.

A Countercultural Movement. Wherever it went, the church was a countercultural movement, espousing a world view at odds with prevailing outlooks. In the Gentile environment, steeped in both Hellenistic philosophy and polytheistic fertility religions, Christianity proclaimed a God who was known not through speculation or mystical ritual but through his action in history to deal with the problem of human sin (Acts 17:30-31). Such a message did not fit the presuppositions of many hearers, for whom sin was not the burning issue. Within the Jewish milieu, the church's proclamation of Jesus as the fulfillment of Israel's covenant faith called into question the entire religious system, of which Jerusalem was the center. In their advocacy of the lordship of Christ, the apostles faced open hostility, mob action, and even imprisonment (Acts 5:17-18; 12:3-4). James, the brother of John, met death at the hand of Herod Agrippa I (Acts 12:1-2). Stephen, one of the seven appointed to administer the common life of the Jerusalem congregation, was the first witness to die for his faith, being stoned by a mob stirred up by members of the Synagogue of the Freedmen (Acts 6:9-12). When Christian evangelists got into trouble with local authorities in other parts of the Roman Empire, it was not for their beliefs, but because of the civil unrest that ensued as the result of hostility toward their activities on the part of either Jews (at Damascus, Acts 9:23-25; 2 Cor. 11:32; at Corinth, Acts 18:12-13) or pagans (at Philippi, Acts 16:16-23; at Ephesus, Acts 19:29-31). Roman officialdom regarded the Christians as a Jewish sectarian movement; the Acts of the Apostles (Acts 18:14-17) records that Gallio, the Roman administrator at Corinth, refused to intervene in what he considered an internal religious dispute.

An Inclusive Organization. The infant church's constituency included people from a broad spectrum of economic classes. In the early days following the resurrection of Jesus, the believers established a community of property, placing their funds at the apostles' disposal to meet the needs of the congregation (Acts 2:45; 4:34-37). Evidently this practice was not continued, but for a time at least the Jerusalem church operated a common food service for its membership (Acts 6:1). Such policies may have been intended to demonstrate the new values of the kingdom of God, where distinctions of wealth have no place. The Jerusalem congregation included both Aramaic- and Greek-speaking Jews (Acts 6:1). Expanding from Jerusalem, the church continued to be a cross section of Greco-Roman society. All Christians were not poor, uneducated, or disenfranchised, as Paul's comments show; though there were "not many mighty, not many noble," there were some (1 Cor. 1:26, NASB). The church's assemblies were frequented by the affluent as well as the poor (James 2:2-4), and a special responsibility for liberal giving is laid on those able to do so (Rom. 12:8; 1 Tim. 6:17-18). As Paul's letter to Philemon shows, the congregation included both slaves and their masters (cf. Eph. 6:5-9; 1 Tim. 6:1). Widows with limited income (Acts 6:1; 1 Tim. 5:9-10) worshiped alongside successful businesswomen such as Lydia (Acts 16:14-15). Some members were tradesmen such as Aquila and his wife Priscilla, who, like Paul, worked in leather goods (Acts 18:2-3). Jewish priests (Acts 6:7) and synagogue officials (Acts 18:8, 17) became Christians, along with Roman officers such as Cornelius (Acts 10), government officials (Acts 8:27-39), prison administrators (Acts 16:27-34), a former companion of Herod the Tetrarch (Acts 13:1), and even members of Caesar's household (Phil. 4:22).

A Radical Fellowship. The first-century church did not crusade against social inequities or attempt to right the wrongs of its society. Its proclamation of the gospel was a radical enough stand as it was and had economic implications of its own, especially in relation to the industry connected with idolatrous worship (Acts 19:23-27). But while there was no outward thrust to call into question social conventions such as slavery or the often inferior status of women, within its own fellowship the church manifested a radical restructuring of traditional relationships. In Christ, Paul asserted, there is neither Jew nor Gentile, slave nor free, male nor female, but all are one (Gal. 3:28). This indifference to cultural labels at the spiritual level had its impact at the social level as well. For example, women played a greater role in the leadership of the church than in the synagogue, functioning as prophets (Acts 21:8-9; 1 Cor. 11:5), praying in the assembly (1 Cor. 11:5), and giving private instruction in the principles of the faith (Acts 18:26). But this openness to new patterns was balanced by deference to traditional expectations; women were not to take authority, at least in Paul's practice (1 Tim. 2:12), or to interrupt the assembly with questions (1 Cor. 14:34-35). The husband was viewed as head of the wife, yet the husband was also under the headship of Christ (1 Cor. 11:3), so that the Christian marriage relationship was one of mutual respect, submission, and interdependence (Eph. 5:21-28; 1 Cor. 11:8-12). Even an unbelieving husband was "sanctified," set apart as the Lord's, through his wife, and *vice versa* (1 Cor. 7:14). Fathers were not to act toward their children in an overbearing manner (Eph. 6:4), as cultural expectations permitted.

Perhaps the most radical step, given the Jewish origins of the church, was the breaking down of the distinction between Jew and Gentile, so vigorously pursued by the sect of the Pharisees. Inclusion of Gentiles in the covenant was the "mystery" of which Paul considered himself a steward (Eph. 3:1-8) and was a cornerstone of his teaching. Peter had taken the lead in this breakthrough (Acts 10–11; Gal. 2:8), which occasioned considerable debate within the apostolic church (Acts 15:1-29; Gal. 1–2); the issue was resolved, to the apparent satisfaction of most parties, in a decision that Gentiles coming to Christ need not become Jews also, as long as they adhered to certain basic principles.

177 • ORGANIZATION AND DISCIPLINE OF THE WORSHIPING COMMUNITY

The organization of the church was relatively fluid throughout the New Testament period. Various offices are mentioned, but their duties and interrelationships are not always clearly defined. General patterns emerge, however, permitting some description of the leadership and discipline of the church as an institution.

Leadership

The apostles maintained a general supervisory function, although their chief task was the proclamation of the gospel in an itinerant ministry. (The word *apostolos* indicates one sent out on a mission.) Apostleship was not limited to the disciples of Jesus, but also included men such as Barnabas, Apollos, James, and Paul. The criteria for apostleship are never directly set forth, though Acts 1:21-22 indicates that an apostle should have been a witness to the events leading to Jesus' resurrection. Paul claims a right to the title by virtue of having seen the risen Christ (1 Cor. 9:1; 15:8), and indicates that James had a similar experience (1 Cor. 15:7). Miracles are also among the "things that mark an apostle" (2 Cor. 12:12). The New Testament does not set out a standard procedure for becoming an apostle; to fill the vacancy left by Judas's defection, the Jerusalem congregation prayed and then drew lots between two qualified candidates (Acts 1:24-26). Paul refers to having been appointed (1 Tim. 2:7). Besides apostles, there were prophets and evangelists (Eph. 4:11; 2 Tim. 4:5) who also apparently functioned in a wider ministry.

In the local congregations, a group of elders had general oversight, so the terms "elder" (*presbuteros*) and "overseer" (*episkopos*) seem to refer to the same office. There are no set procedures for the selection of elders, though in new congregations they were appointed by the apostles (Acts 14:23). Paul, nearing the end of his career, instructs Titus to appoint them in Crete (Titus 1:5) and lays out certain spiritual, personal, and administrative qualifications (1 Tim. 3:1-7; Titus 1:6-9). Similar qualifications (1 Tim. 3:8-12) apply to the deacon (*diakonos*), a word that simply means "server." The seven men chosen to administer the food service by the Jerusalem congregation (Acts 6:2-5) are often regarded as the first "deacons," but the examples of Stephen and Philip show that they were preachers and not simply managers. Although the word is rare in the New Testament, pastors also served in the local assemblies; the pastor was a "shepherd," and therefore a teacher of the congregation (1 Tim. 4:11; 6:2), and it may be that the terms *pastor* and *teacher* are synonymous (Eph. 4:11). New Testament congregations do not seem to have had pastors in the modern sense of a full-time leader paid to manage the church's operations and conduct its worship. In addition to the above offices, members of the local body performed a variety of leadership functions according to their endowment by the Holy Spirit, such as administration, teaching, or the exercise of various vocal gifts (Rom. 12:6-8; 1 Cor. 12:7-10). The Christians of a city seem to have formed one congregation, though because they met in homes the assemblies were dispersed throughout the city; the elders and overseers apparently coordinated the activities of the church throughout an entire urban area.

Central Organization

The churches of the New Testament were connected in a loose affiliation of individual congregations, with the apostles serving as the principal links between them; Paul and Barnabas were acting in this capacity in collecting offerings for the relief of the church in Jerusalem (Acts 11:29-30; 1 Cor. 16:1-3). There was no formal, centralized organization, although Acts 15 recounts that the apostles and some elders met in informal council to resolve the issue of the standing of Gentiles in the church. The larger or older congregations may have been influential in the church at large. Certainly the church at Antioch played a key role in the direction of the missionary effort (Acts 13:1-3; 14:26). As the original congregation, the Jerusalem church was prominent in the earliest days, but its influence waned as the Christian movement expanded into the Mediterranean world.

Decision Making

Little is said in the New Testament about the decision-making process in Christian leadership. The Acts of the Apostles attributes major decisions about the direction of benevolent or missionary activity to the Holy Spirit (Acts 11:28; 13:2; 16:7-10) and suggests that apostolic decisions were arrived at by consensus, under the principle "it seemed good to the Holy Spirit and to us" (Acts 15:28). In the council of Acts 15, it is James, brother of Jesus, who formulates the prevailing opinion (Acts 15:13, 19). James was evidently the leader of the Jerusalem congregation (Gal. 2:12), although nothing is said of his being a disciple of Jesus before the Resurrection. A certain leadership role seems to have fallen to members of Jesus' family in the Judean church; another brother, Jude, is also one of the New Testament authors.

Discipline

According to Matthew (the only Gospel writer to use the word *church*), Jesus laid down procedures to be followed when a member of the community committed an offense, particularly against another disciple. If the matter could not be resolved between individuals, a small group was to be convened, and only as a last resort was the matter to come before the assembly. The penalty for continuing in the offense was exclusion from the life of the community (Matt. 18:15-18). In general, this relatively unstructured pattern is the picture of church discipline we find in Acts and the Epistles. Although the apostles possessed a formidable moral authority—evident, for example, in the results of Peter's confrontation of the duplicitous Ananias and Sapphira (Acts 5:1-11)—they do not seem to have habitually functioned as judges over the church. Paul said he would "hand . . . over to Satan" a man in Corinth who persisted in an incestuous relationship (1 Cor. 5:5), but as he was not personally present this was a measure taken in the spiritual realm. His preference was to handle disciplinary matters by exhortation and persuasion; in dealing with problems in the Corinthian church, he suggests he might "come to [them] with a whip" (1 Cor. 4:21), but exactly what he meant by this is not clear. In the case of disputes between Christians, Paul affirms that it is better to be wronged than to enter into litigation in the civil courts; a "wise man" in the assembly should be able to decide between two "brothers" (1 Cor. 6:1-7). He urges believers to break their associations with Christians whose behavioral witness is inconsistent with their profession (1 Cor. 5:11-13).

178 • PUBLIC ACTIVITIES OF THE WORSHIPING COMMUNITY

Although the church had no legitimate status in the Roman world, it was able to evangelize and expand by means of public proclamation or preaching, especially through the medium of the synagogue.

Preaching

The early church could not conduct public worship on the scale to which North American Christians are accustomed. Especially in the Jewish homeland, the church's situation was similar to that of today's believers in Muslim countries, where any public expression of Christian faith is considered highly provocative and even illegal. The cultural pluralism of Greek-speaking areas afforded a less restrictive atmosphere, but because it lacked buildings of its own the infant church was largely limited to gathering in private homes. Nevertheless, unbelievers did attend the Christian assemblies (1 Cor. 14:23).

The unbeliever's first exposure to the gospel, however, was more likely to come from the preaching of the apostles or evangelists of the faith. Preaching (*kērugma*) was a public activity intended to evangelize people who had never heard the message of the new covenant and of the lordship of Christ; the word means "announcement" or "heralding." Thus preaching in the New Testament church was distinguished from teaching (*didachē*), the exposition of scriptural truths in the gathering of believers. Preaching was an opportunistic activity; that is, it occurred whenever a suitable occasion arose. The healings and deliverances performed by the apostles were significant openings for evangelism (Acts 3; 9:36-43; 19:11-20). The apostles used the synagogue service as a platform for the proclamation of Jesus as the Christ, reaching through this medium not only Jews but Gentiles who frequented the synagogue, known as "God-fearers" (*phoboumenoi*) in New Testament terminology (Acts 10:2, 22; 13:16, 26; *cf.* 18:7). Meeting opposition in the synagogue at Ephesus, Paul expounded the faith through a series of public meetings in a rented lecture hall (Acts 19:8-10), and the Acropolis at Athens offered him a forum for public debate with Greek intellectuals (Acts 17:16-34).

Apologetic Literature

The production of literature defending the Christian gospel became important in the second century through the work of spokesmen such as Justin Martyr (c. 100-165). Some New Testament literature is already of this "apologetic" type, particularly the two-volume work by the physician Luke, consisting of his Gospel and the Acts of the Apostles. The work is written for the public as well as for the church and is dedicated to a man named Theophilus (Luke 1:3; Acts 1:1), who may have underwritten its publication. In this work, Luke shows how the church emerged from its Jewish matrix to become a recognized entity within the Greco-Roman world; his story of the church begins in Jerusalem and ends in Rome. While not concealing the Hebraic element in the Christian heritage, Luke takes pains to record the increasing Gentile involvement in the expanding movement, stresses Paul's Roman citizenship at critical points, and portrays certain government officials as knowledgeable of the Christian way, or at least not hostile to it (Acts 18:12-17; 19:35-41; 23:16-31; 24:22-26).

Public Obligations

In social services, the church was predominantly concerned with its own constituency. However, the admonition to "do good to all men" suggests an outreach not limited to "those who are of the household of the faith" (Gal. 6:10, NASB). Christians were expected to pay their taxes and to honor civil authority as given by God for the maintenance of order (Rom. 13:1-7). Whatever the situation in later centuries, in the New Testament period most opposition to the Christian movement came from Jewish rather than Roman authorities, and in fact the policies of the state were usually helpful in enabling the church to continue its activities.

179 • INTERNAL LIFE OF THE WORSHIPING COMMUNITY

A glimpse of the church's life in the earliest stages is provided in Acts 2:42, which states that the Christians "devoted themselves to the apostles' teaching and to the fellowship, to the breaking of bread and to prayer." These categories in general continue to characterize the church's activities throughout the New Testament period.

Instruction

Teaching, as mentioned above, is not the same as the public proclamation of the lordship of Christ, but is instruction in the theological, historical, and practical foundations of Christian faith (Heb. 6:1-2). The apostles were teachers of the Word (Acts 5:42; 15:35; 1 Tim. 2:7) as well as preachers, and one of the qualities of an overseer was the ability to teach (1 Tim. 6:2; 2 Tim. 2:24). Pastors were teachers also, but teaching was a general activity open to any qualified member of the assembly (Rom. 12:7; Col. 3:16; James 3:1). Women were instructors of other women (Titus 2:3-4) but in deference to custom were not generally given a role in the instruction of men (1 Tim. 2:12).

An important function in the church was the creation of materials for instruction. Some have suggested that collections of Old Testament passages

concerning the appearance of the Christ were circulated in the early church and that the apostolic preaching recorded in the New Testament draws on material from these manuals. The teachings of Jesus seem to have been gathered into collections, along with the narrative of his ministry and passion, in an oral stage. The passing of the first eyewitnesses and the linguistic transition from Aramaic to Greek necessitated the writing down of this material as an aid to instruction in the church; the Gospels of the New Testament were the result. In an age before printing, the publication of books required the services of professional copyists. Although most Jewish men could write, the ability to produce a readable scroll was a specialized skill. The church had its scribes, such as Tertius, who wrote down Paul's letter to the Romans (Rom. 16:22); Paul's own handwriting was not equal to this task (Gal. 6:11).

Communications

As it grew, the church developed an effective system of internal communication through the travels of the apostles and their coworkers and through an extensive correspondence of which the New Testament Epistles are doubtless but a small portion. Except for government business, there were few reliable public mail or courier services; therefore, a letter or any other personal shipment (such as Paul's cloak and scrolls, which he asked Titus to bring to him, 2 Tim. 4:13) had to be carried by someone who could be trusted to see that it moved toward its destination. For such couriers, a network of accommodations existed in the various cities through the hospitality of members of the congregations (Rom. 12:13; 1 Tim. 3:2), public accommodations of the time being usable only as a last resort.

Worship

The assembly usually met in private homes for worship and instruction (Acts 2:46; 16:40; 18:7; Philem. 1:2). It appears that, in commemoration of the Resurrection, the congregation assembled on the "Lord's Day," the first day of the week (Acts 20:7; 1 Cor. 16:2). Christian worship focused on the Lord's Supper (1 Cor. 10:16-17; 11:20-29) and included singing of hymns (Eph. 5:19), prayer (1 Cor. 11:4-5), vocal thanksgiving (Eph. 5:20; Heb. 13:15), and instruction (1 Cor. 14:26; Col. 3:16). Worship in Corinth, and probably elsewhere, included both singing and thanksgiving in tongues, with interpretation, and prophecy (1 Cor. 11:4-5; 14:1-33). The

New Testament does not specify who is to officiate in worship or to administer the Lord's Supper, although prophets clearly had a role in corporate worship (1 Cor. 14:23-33).

Mutual Assistance

A notable feature of early church life was the way members of the community were expected to care for one another's needs. The Epistles contain repeated exhortations to this end: to contribute to the needs of the "saints" (Rom. 12:13), to bear one another's burdens (Gal. 6:2), to do good especially to fellow believers (Gal. 6:10), to share, as a sacrifice pleasing to God (Heb. 13:16). Jesus had taught his followers the importance of serving his "brothers" (Matt. 25:40) or "little ones" (Matt. 10:42), meaning one's fellow disciples, and had set the example of service in acts such as washing the disciples' feet (John 13:1-15). In following his model, the New Testament church directed its benevolence toward two groups in particular: widows and orphans, who had meager resources of their own (Acts 6:1-6; 1 Tim. 5:3-11; James 1:27) and the congregation in Jerusalem, beset with persecution and famine (Acts 11:29-30; 1 Cor. 16:1-2; 2 Cor. 8:1-5).

180 • EXTERNAL AND INTERNAL PROBLEMS OF THE WORSHIPING COMMUNITY

Like any human organization, the church of the New Testament confronted problems and challenges, some from external pressures and some from within.

External Pressures

The major challenge from without was that of resistance to the gospel and even persecution by its opponents. In dealing with opposition, the church had to rely on the merciful intervention of its Lord, an intervention that resulted in some remarkable turns of events, such as Peter's release from prison to the amazement of the fearful church (Acts 12:6-17) and the transformation of Saul, ardent persecutor of the Way, into an even more zealous apostle of the risen Christ (Acts 9:1-31). The church's principal weapon against external hostility was the development of its unique worldview, which enabled it to see the powers coming against it as doomed to eventual defeat at the revelation of the judgments of God. The present culture and its values are passing away (1 Cor. 7:31; 1 John 2:17); at the day of the Lord, the old order of things will be replaced by "new heavens and a new earth," figurative language for the just order of the new covenant (2 Pet. 3:13; Rev. 21:1). As events unfold, human secrets will be disclosed and brought to judgment (Rom. 2:16; 1 Cor. 4:5; cf. Luke 12:2). This sense of ongoing and impending judgment was rooted in Jesus' own teaching; it is present, for example, in his parables of the workers in the vineyard (Matt. 21:33-43) and the marriage feast (Matt. 22:1-14) and his statements suggesting that the persecutors of the church (Matt. 23:34-35; 24:9) will themselves be overthrown within a generation (Matt. 16:28; 23:36; 24:34). From the perspective of the early church, the kingdom of God had already appeared in Jesus (Mark 1:14-15) and the judgment had already begun to occur in people's response to him (John 3:17-21; Rom. 1:18); the Resurrection and the coming of the Holy Spirit had made evident the arrival of the new order of the "last days" (Acts 2:16-21). Armed with these convictions, spokespersons for the Christian movement were able to withstand opposition and to maintain their witness in the face of a hostile environment.

Internal Problems

A challenge from within the church organization was false or incomplete teaching. A certain group in the Judean church had difficulty with the concept of Gentiles entering the covenant and taught the new congregations of Asia Minor that it was necessary for them to become circumcised converts to Judaism (Acts 15:1). To deal with this it was necessary to convene a council of church leaders; Paul also addressed the issue of "another gospel" in his letter to the Christians of Galatia. False teachers of various kinds are mentioned in several places in the New Testament (Acts 20:29-30; 2 Tim. 4:3-4; 2 Pet. 2:1-3; Jude 4; Rev. 2:14, 20). The nature of their doctrines is not always clear, but they are accused of advocating licentiousness (Jude 4), idolatry (Rev. 12:14), "Jewish myths and commandments of men" (Titus 1:14, NASB; cf. 2 Tim. 4:4), and ascetic self-abasement accompanied by the observance of holy days and dietary practices (Col. 2:16-23). John calls these teachers "antichrists" who deny that Jesus is the Christ (1 John 2:18-22) and who negate the Incarnation (1 John 4:2-3; 2 John 7). Some see many of these teachings as evidence of an incipient Gnosticism, a philosophy that held that the material realm is evil and only the spirit is good therefore the word of

God only appeared to be incarnate in Jesus Christ. Portions of John, 1 John, and Paul's letter to the Colossians are thought to be responding to this notion, which became a more serious threat after the first century. In addition to aberrant doctrine, failure to understand the Christian faith and its ordinances in their true depth was a problem within the church's constituency (2 Tim. 3:7; Heb. 5:12; 1 Cor. 11:18-34) and even among some of its leaders, such as Apollos (Acts 18:24-26).

Like every human organization, the institutional church of the New Testament had to deal with human weakness in many forms. Immorality was a problem that had to be repeatedly confronted, notably in Paul's Corinthian correspondence. Economic inequalities within the membership created tensions (Acts 6:1; James 2:2-6), which the leadership sought to address through benevolence programs and the establishment of the serving ministry, or diaconate. The leadership itself was not always united; Paul had a personal confrontation with Peter over the Gentile issue (Gal. 2:11-14) and broke with Barnabas over John Mark's role in the missionary team (Acts 15:36-39). Overbearing leaders sometimes gained control in local groups, refusing to cooperate with the eldership (3 John 9-10).

Conclusion

Far from idealizing the institutional church, the New Testament presents a true-to-life picture of a social group struggling with the strains and stresses that inevitably accompany a rapidly growing organization. Such honesty highlights the church's dependence not on human authority but on that of Christ, to whom all authority has been given and who, by the Spirit, must supremely direct and enable the church's witness (Matt. 28:18-20).

Richard C. Leonard

181 • THE HOUSE CHURCH AND ITS WORSHIP

At the local level, the New Testament church was a house church; Christians met for worship in small groups in the homes of those members who might be wealthier or have larger houses. In a larger city, the church might meet in a number of house churches. In the New Testament, the word church *may refer to the universal church, the church in a particular city, or the individual house church, which was part of the larger congregation.*

The Universal Church and the Local Church

In the New Testament, the Greek word *ekklēsia* (usually translated "church") is used primarily in two ways: (1) to describe a meeting or an assembly and (2) to designate the people who participate in such assembling together—whether they are actually assembled or not. The New Testament contains a few places that speak of a secular Greek assembly (Acts 19:32, 41); everywhere else speaks of a Christian assembly. Sometimes the word *ekklēsia* is used to designate the actual meeting together of Christians. This is certainly what Paul intended in 1 Corinthians 14:19, 28, and 35, in which the expression *en ekklēsia* must mean "in a meeting" and not "in the church." To translate this phrase "in the church" (as is done in most modern English versions) is misleading, for most readers will think it means "in the church building." The New Testament never names the place of assembly a "church." Aside from the few instances in which the word clearly means the actual meeting together of believers, *ekklēsia* most often is used as a descriptor for the believers who constitute a local church (such as the church in Corinth, the church in Philippi, and the church in Colossae) or all the believers (past, present, and future) who constitute the universal church, the complete body of Christ.

When reading the New Testament, Christians need to be aware of the various ways the word *ekklēsia* ("church") is used. On the most basic level, the *ekklēsia* is an organized local entity—comprised of all the believers in any given locality, under one pluralistic eldership. On another level, the *ekklēsia* is the universal church whose constituents are all the believers who have ever been, are now existing, and will ever be. The word *ekklēsia* was used by the New Testament writers with these various aspects of meaning, though at times it is not possible to differentiate one from the other. Nevertheless, students of the New Testament could avoid some confusion if they used discrimination in their exegesis of the text. Some interpreters have taught that the smallest unit of the church is the local church, but the New Testament writers sometimes used the word *church* to indicate a small home gathering. Other interpreters confuse the local church with the universal church. But some things in the New Testament are addressed to a local church that do not necessarily apply to the whole church, and some great things are spoken of the universal church that could never be attained by any particular locality. The things Paul said about the church in his epistle to the Ephesians (which was written as an encyclical for several churches and not just for the church in Ephesus) could never be attained by a local church. For example, a local church could not attain to the fullness of the stature of Christ.

There is much to be said about how interpreters have confused the local church with the universal church, but this article is devoted to clearing up the confusion about what constitutes the smallest unit of the church—the local church or what could be called the house church, or home gathering.

The New Testament seems to present the fact that a particular local church (that is, a church comprising all the believers in a given locality under one eldership) could and did have *ekklēsiai*—"meetings" or "assemblies" carried on in homes of the local Christians. Thus, the smallest unit to comprise a

"church" was one of these home meetings. However, there is no indication in the New Testament that each of these home meetings had its own eldership or was a distinct entity separate from the other gatherings in the same locality. According to Acts 14:23 and Titus 1:5, elders were appointed for every local church (compare the expressions "appointed elders for them in each church" and "appoint elders in every town")—not for every house church. Nevertheless, it appears that every local church of some size had several such *ekklēsiai* ("meetings") going on within that locality.

The church in Jerusalem must have had several home meetings (Acts 2:46; 5:42; 8:3; 12:5, 12), as did the church in Rome (Rom. 16:3-5, 14-16). A small local church may have had only one home gathering, as was probably the case with the church at Colossae (Philem. 2), but this would have been impossible for large local churches like those in Jerusalem, Rome, and Ephesus, in which there must

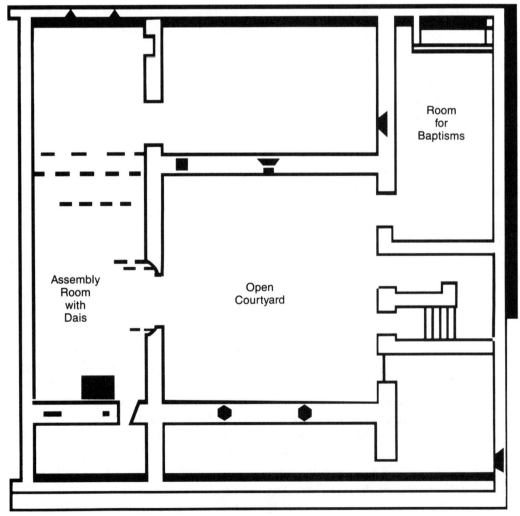

House Church Floor Plan

have been several "house churches" (1 Cor. 16:19-20, written from Ephesus). This is confirmed by an examination of the passages that deal with the issue of the house church as cited above.

——— The House Church in Rome ———

In the last chapter of his epistle to the Romans, Paul asked the believers in Rome to greet Priscilla and Aquila and the church that met in their home (Rom. 16:3-5). The entire church in Rome could not have met in Priscilla and Aquila's home, for the written from church was much too large to have assembled in a single home. Rather, the church in their home must have been one of several such "house churches" in Rome.

Elements of Worship in the Jerusalem Worship

Apostolic Teaching
Breaking of Bread (the Agape Feast)
Prayer
Fellowship
Signs and Wonders
Community
Praise
Joy
Growth

Paul's epistle to the Romans was addressed to all the "saints" in Rome (Rom. 1:7), not to "the church in Rome." At the time of writing, Paul had not been to Rome, nor had any other apostle. From Romans 15:23, we know that the church had already been in existence for many years. The church was probably started there by Jewish Romans who had been converted during their visit to Jerusalem during Pentecost (Acts 2:10) and had then returned to Rome. Since the church had not been started by an apostle, it could have been that there were no "ordained" elders in the church at Rome and there were several gatherings of believers in various parts of Rome and its suburbs. Paul knew some of the saints in Rome (whom he addressed by name in the last chapter) and thus addressed an epistle to all the saints in that locality, instead of to the church in that locality, which was his usual practice (1 Cor. 1:1; 2 Cor. 1:1; 1 Thess. 1:1; 2 Thess. 1:1). Nonetheless, "all the saints in Rome" would comprise "the church in Rome" (cf. Phil. 1:1, in which Paul addressed his epistle to all the saints in Philippi).

In the final chapter of Romans, Paul asked all the saints in Rome (which equals the "local" church in Rome) to greet the church in Priscilla and Aquila's house. Later in the chapter, Paul asks the church to greet Asyncritus, Phlegon, Hermas, Patrobas, Hermes, and the brothers with them; and then again he asks the church to greet Philologus, Julia, Nereus, his sister Olympas, and all the saints with them (Rom. 16:14-15). Evidently, Paul was identifying two other groups of believers who must have met together. And perhaps Paul was referring to two more groups in Romans 16:10-11, which in the Greek could mean either the ones of Aristobulus' and Narcissus' _household_ or the ones of their _fellowship_. It seems that the church in Rome, like the churches in Jerusalem and Ephesus, had several home _ekklēsiai_.

The Epistle to the Romans was written around A.D. 58. The Neronian persecution began around A.D. 64. Secular historians such as Tacitus say that a vast multitude (_ingens multitudo_) of Christians were tortured and killed during this persecution (_Annals_, 15.44). Seutonius said that the rapid increase of the Christians in Rome had made them unpopular. (_Nero_ 16) Indeed, at the time Paul wrote the Epistle to the Romans he said their faith was known throughout the world (Rom. 1:8), which indicates that the church in Rome had already made an impact on the Mediterranean world. When Paul came to Rome three years later (A.D. 61), he came to a city that already had a large church. The entire church could not have met in Aquila and Priscilla's home—they would have had only a modest-sized dwelling, for they were tent makers. Besides, Paul greeted over twenty-five individuals by name in chapter 16—and he had not yet even been to Rome.

Thus, nearly every commentary states that there must have been several _ekklēsiai_ in Rome—that is, several home churches all unified as the one local church in Rome. For example, the _Bible Knowledge Commentary_ says, "The Christians in Rome apparently worshipped in numerous homes such as Priscilla's and Aquila's. . . . Other churches in homes are mentioned in Colossians 4:15 and Philemon 2" (John F. Walvoord and Roy B. Zuck, eds. _The Bible Knowledge Commentary_ [Wheaton: Victor Books, 1985], New Testament edition, p. 499). The _New Bible Commentary: Revised_ says, "Groups of Christians met in houses of prominent believers or in other available rooms (cf. Matt. 26:6; Acts 12:12; 1 Cor. 16:19; Col. 4:15; Philem. 2). This [the church in Priscilla and Aquila's house] is the first of five groups of believers in Paul's list, but the only one referred to definitely as a church (see Rom. 16:5, 10-11, 14-15)" (D. Guthrie et al., eds., *The New Bible Commentary: Revised* [Grand Rapids: Wm. B. Eerdmans Publishing Co., 1970], p. 1046). *The New Layman's Bible Commentary* says, "They [Priscilla and Aquila] opened their home for Christian meetings. The church here mentioned was obviously only a part of the total number of Christians in Rome. Verses 14ff. seem to refer to two other household churches in Rome. Apparently there were at least three churches there, and probably more." The *Wycliffe Bible Commentary* says, "Household churches are probably also to be found in [Romans] 16:10-11, 14-15. If this is true, then the mention of five household churches makes one realize that Christians in Rome were members of smaller groups rather than of one large assembly" (Charles Pfeiffer and Everett F. Harrison, eds., *The Wycliffe Bible Commentary* [Chicago: Moody Press, 1962], p. 1225). Unfortunately, none of these commentaries explain what it means for several "churches" to be in Rome. Each house church could not have been a separate entity with a separate church government; rather, each house church must have been simply one home meeting of some of the saints in the one local church at Rome.

——— The House Church in Ephesus ———

In 1 Corinthians 16:19-20 Aquila and Priscilla are again mentioned as having a church meeting in their house. According to Romans, their house church had been in Rome. Many scholars think Aquila and Priscilla left Rome around A.D. 49, at the time of Claudius's edict expelling Jews from Rome. They could have already been Christians at this time. According to Acts 18, they joined Paul in Corinth (where they all worked together in their craft of making tents) and then went on with him to Ephesus, during the time the church in Ephesus was first established (around A.D. 51). Paul continued with his second missionary journey, while Aquila and Priscilla remained in Ephesus. No doubt the church there first met in their home. Paul returned to Ephesus a few years later and remained there for two years (around A.D. 53-54). During this time, Paul's proclamation of the gospel went out from Ephesus (as a center) to all of Asia Minor (Acts 19:8-10). As this was going on, the church in Ephesus grew (Acts 19:18-20).

Elements of Worship in Corinthian Worship

Opening and closing benedictions (1 Cor. 1:3; 16:23)
Doxology and acclamation (1 Cor. 15:57)
Liturgical prayer (2 Cor. 1:3)
Spontaneous prayer (1 Cor. 14:14ff.)
Hymns, psalms, and spiritual songs (1 Cor. 14:2; Eph. 5:19; Col. 3:16)
Praise, singing, and thanksgiving (1 Cor. 14:15)
Responsive amens (1 Cor. 14:16)
Physical prostration (1 Cor. 14:25)
Holy kisses (1 Cor. 16:20; 2 Cor. 13:12)
Public reading of Paul's letters (Col. 4:16; 1 Thess. 5:27)
Prophecy, revelation, and discernment (1 Cor. 14:6; 12:10)
Tongues and interpreters (1 Cor. 14:23)
Instruction, preaching, and edification (1 Cor. 1:17; 14:26; 15:14)
Healing (1 Cor. 12:9, 28, 30)
Breaking of bread (Rom. 16:16; 1 Cor. 11:20ff.; 1 Thess. 5:26; 1 Peter 5:14)
Baptism (1 Cor. 1:14)
Use of Maranatha, an Aramaic liturgical form (1 Cor. 16:22)
Collection (1 Cor. 16:1)
Liturgical Prayer (2 Cor. 1:3-4)
Creed (1 Cor. 15:3-5)

During these years Paul wrote to the Corinthians, sending greetings from the churches in Asia, from Aquila and Priscilla, and the church in their house, and from all the brothers (1 Cor. 16:19-20). In giving this kind of greeting, it seems that Paul was sending greetings from (1) all the churches in Asia Minor, (2) the church in Ephesus (equivalent to "all the brothers"), and (3) those believers who gathered with Aquila and Priscilla in their home. It would be hard to imagine that all the saints in Ephesus met at Aquila and Priscilla's home. The church probably began that way, but as it grew, so did the number of home meetings. From other portions of the New Testament (specifically 1 Timothy, which was written around A.D. 65 by Paul to Timothy while Timothy was leading the church in Ephesus), we discover that there must have been several home meetings in Ephesus because there were so many saints there (First Timothy 5:6 reveals that there must have been a large number of saints in Ephesus—young men, young women, older men, widows, and so forth). Several saints must have hosted an *ekklēsia,* or meeting, in their home. (Aquila and Priscilla left Ephesus around A.D. 56/57 and returned to Rome, where again they hosted a church in their home. Others in

Ephesus would have had to open their homes.) But each such *ekklēsia* did not have its own eldership; rather, all of the church in Ephesus was under one eldership—headed by Timothy, Paul's coworker.

The House Church in Colossae

Colossians 4:15-16 speaks of a church existing in the home of one called Nymphas. In his final remarks to the church in Colossae, Paul asked the saints in Colossae to send his greetings to (1) the brothers in Laodicea, (2) Nymphas in particular, and (3) the church in Nymphas's house. According to the structure of Colossians 4:15, it seems evident that the first greeting included all the believers in Laodicea (a neighboring church to Colossae), who would comprise the entire church in Laodicea (called "the church of the Laodiceans" in Col. 4:16), and that the second and third greetings were to a specific individual (Nymphas) in the church in Laodicea and a church meeting in Nymphas's house. This church meeting in Nymphas's house would probably be one of several home meetings—all part of the one local church in Laodicea.

A textual problem in this passage could have some effect on its interpretation. Some manuscripts read "his house"; others read "her house"; still others read "their house." Because it cannot be determined from the Greek text whether Nymphas was male or female, various scribes used different pronouns before *house*. It is far more likely that the pronoun *her* was changed to *his* than vice versa. But other manuscripts read "their house." Some scholars say "their" refers to "the brothers" at Laodicea. But that does not make sense if we understand that "the brothers in Laodicea" is equal to the church in Laodicea. How could the church in Laodicea have the church in their house? Other scholars indicate that the Greek word for "their" (*autōn*) refers to the ones with Nymphas—that is, the members of this household (see Alford's *Greek Testament* [Chicago: Moody Press, 1958], esp. vols. 3–4). Whether the reading was "her house" or "their house," a particular group of believers within the church of Laodicea met there. Their meeting could legitimately be called an *ekklēsia,* an assembling together.

In Philemon 1–2 we read about a church in a particular home. Paul wrote a short epistle to Philemon, an elder of the church in Colossae, on behalf of Onesimus, Philemon's runaway slave converted by Paul to Christ. In his introduction to this short epistle, Paul sends his greetings to Philemon, Apphia,

Archippus, and the church in Philemon's house. It is important to note that Paul did not send greetings to all the saints in Colossae and then to the church in Philemon's house (as is the pattern in 1 Cor. 16:19-20 and Col. 4:15); he sent greetings to Philemon and to the church in his house. Therefore, we can assume that the entire church in Colossae met at Philemon's house.

Worship in the House Churches

When the church first began in Jerusalem, the believers met in homes for fellowship and worship. Acts 2:42-47 tells us that the early Christians met in homes to hear the apostles' teachings and to celebrate Communion (which is called "the breaking of bread"). During such gatherings the Christians often shared meals with others in what was called a love feast (2 Pet. 2:13; Jude 12). At these meetings, the Christians recited Scripture, sang hymns and psalms, and joyfully praised the Lord (Eph. 5:18-20; Col. 3:16-17). Christians also gathered together in homes to pray (Acts 12:12) and read the Word.

Small groups of believers met in homes for worship quite regularly; and in a city where there were several such *ekklēsiai,* all the believers would gather together for special occasions. Scripture tells us that all the believers would come together to hear an epistle from the apostles read aloud (Acts 15:30; Col. 4:16), and we can surmise from the New Testament record that all the Christians in a city met together once a week on Sunday, which was called the Lord's Day. First Corinthians provides several insights about how the early Christians worshiped together when all the believers in one city met together. We know that 1 Corinthians pertains to this larger gathering because in 11:20 Paul spoke of all the believers coming together in one place and in 16:2 he spoke of the whole church coming together in one place.

Paul used this epistle to correct the Corinthians' behavior in the celebration of the Lord's Supper (1 Cor. 11:17-34) and in the exercising of spiritual gifts during church meetings (1 Cor. 14). Paul's adjustments reveal his perceptions of a model Christian meeting, and his perceptions were probably developed from actual experience in other church meetings. Paul urged the Corinthians to celebrate the Lord's Supper together in a manner that reflected Jesus' institution of that meal. They were to remember the Lord and his death for them, and they were to partake of the bread and wine with all seriousness. At the same time they were to be conscious of the fact that they were members of the same body of Christ—joined to one another, even as they were joined to Christ.

According to Paul's presentation in chapter 14, this "body consciousness" should be evident in the way the believers worshiped together. One's personal experience and liberty should not hinder the coordination of the body in worshiping God corporately. Thus, when the believers exercised their spiritual gifts—whether prophesying, speaking in tongues, providing interpretations of the tongues, or teaching—it was to be done in good order and for the edification of the congregation, not for personal edification. When all the church assembled together to worship God, it was to be a display of spiritual unity.

Philip Comfort

182 • THE CHRISTIAN GATHERING IN CITY CHURCH AND HOUSE CHURCH

Early Christian gatherings for worship included assemblies for the Lord's Supper, for the sharing of spiritual gifts, and for the baptism of new believers. The discussion of these assemblies in the New Testament, especially the writings of Paul, is clarified when we understand that some of these descriptions apply to the gathering of the citywide church, while others refer to the setting of the local house church.

The Corinthian correspondence is our main source for understanding what went on at a Christian gathering. The data, however, is fragmentary mostly because Paul did not need to describe the details of the assembly to his readers. Rather, he had to deal with problems. Nor does Paul anywhere tell us clearly about assembly activities specific to the house churches as different from those of local churches. Barring any information that would allow us to distinguish between the two assemblies, we must suppose that the two types of assemblies basically functioned the same way. Except for activities related to the size of the assembly and the availability of the full range of gifted persons, the house church, we must assume, did the same things as the local church.

The two most important descriptions of the Christian assembly, those in 1 Corinthians 11:17-34 and 1 Corinthians 14, both describe citywide meetings. Dealing with the Lord's Supper, Paul begins, "When you come together in the same place"

(1 Cor. 11:20, AUTHOR'S TRANSLATION). Speaking of the exercises of tongues and prophecy, Paul explicitly refers to the whole church (*bē ekklēsia holē*) coming together in the same place (1 Cor. 14:23). In both references, however, Paul has a specific reason for dealing with the city church. For the Lord's Supper, Paul wants to deal with the problem of rich and poor coming together, a situation virtually inevitable for a citywide assembly, and one less likely to occur in the house church. For the tongues and prophecy assembly, Paul wants to picture an outsider's reaction to the two forms of activity. Again such a situation would be more likely to occur at the large gathering of the local church than in the privacy of a house church. Because Paul thus describes the Lord's Supper and the celebration of the gifts at the level of the local church, we cannot immediately conclude that those types of celebrations occurred only on that level.

The Lord's Supper. On the contrary, the details of Paul's description of the Lord's Supper, especially when contrasted with later descriptions of the ritualized Eucharist, strongly suggest the individual household as the normal environment. Paul describes a full meal. His expression for celebrating the Lord's Supper is *kuriakon deipnon phagein.* The Greek word *deipnon* indicates a main meal, usually in the evening (cf. Luke 14:12; John 13:4; 21:20). The word describing participating in this supper is the normal word for "eating" (*phagein*). In contrast, Justin, writing about a century later, describes participating in the now ritualized Eucharist as "sharing."

The entire focus of Paul is on the manner of eating, and specifically how the Christians relate to each other in this eating. He is concerned about who goes hungry and who fills up. Later descriptions of Eucharist focus almost entirely on the manner in which an official is "to conduct the Eucharist" (*eucharistein, Didachē* 9-10; Justin, *Apology* I, 67). Paul is completely silent about any regular presider or official at this event. In contrast, the *Didachē* (late first century) speaks of prophets offering Eucharist (10:7), and Justin refers to "the president" (*ho proestōs*) as the one who prays over the bread and wine.

Even the action with the bread and wine recalls a family meal in a Jewish home. Breaking and distributing bread was a normal way of beginning a meal in a Jewish home of the time, just as sharing a cup of wine was the usual way of ending a meal. For each gesture, special blessings were said. In effect it becomes difficult to visualize how such a meal could have taken place with a group as large as "the whole church." Even supposing a very large dining room and a very generous host, we are faced with logistic problems most people are willing to face only on special occasions.

Once the Lord's Supper became a stylized meal, with a chip of bread and a sip of wine, a weekly gathering of a large group became feasible. Justin does, in fact, speak of a ritualized weekly eucharistic gathering, a blessing and a sharing of bread and wine without any accompanying meal "on the Day of the Sun." By Justin's time, the Eucharist had been separated from the supper.

A weekly "Lord's Supper" or "breaking of bread," however, appears much earlier. Acts speaks of Paul at Troas gathering on the first day of the week "to break bread" (20:7). Other early texts speak of Christians celebrating on this day. If there was a weekly Lord's Supper, then, it most likely was in the individual household church. Special occasions would have called for a gathering of the whole church for this celebration, such as Paul directly addresses in 1 Corinthians 11.

Nevertheless, a real tendency toward larger gatherings for the Lord's Supper appears in Paul's interpretation of the meaning of this action:

> Is not the cup of thanksgiving for which we give thanks a participation [*koinōnia*] in the blood of Christ? And is not the bread that we break a participation [*koinōnia*] in the body of Christ? Because there is one loaf, we, who are many, are one body, for we all partake of the one loaf. (1 Cor. 10:16-17)

Paul sees this action as an activity and a realization of the unity of the body of Christ. Paul draws up this picture by the contrast between "the many" and "the one." The more included in "the many," the more dramatic becomes the realization of "the one." It is to the whole Corinthian church that Paul addresses the words "Now you are the body of Christ" (1 Cor. 12:27). It would seem, therefore, he has in mind the whole Corinthian church as involved in the blessing of the cup and the breaking of the bread.

Sharing the Gifts. Paul's other major reference to the Christian gathering describes the activity of sharing the gifts of the Spirit:

> When you come together, everyone has a hymn, or a word of instruction, a revelation, a tongue or an interpretation. All of these must be done for the strengthening of the church. (1 Cor. 14:26)

Paul then gives precise instructions regarding tongues and prophecy along with their corresponding gifts of interpretation and discernment (14:26-33, 37-40).

The reference to "a hymn" (Greek *psalmos*) may allude to the Christian use of the Jewish psalter, or it may indicate the development of Christian compositions. Colossians 3:16 speaks of "psalms, hymns, and spiritual songs" by which Christians taught and admonished each other as well as praised God. Christian poetic compositions have in fact been identified in the New Testament, such as those in Philippians 2:6-22 or Colossians 1:15-20.

The "instruction" must have included stories about Jesus as well as the development of a Christian code of morality, whereas "a revelation" probably involved apocalyptic type predictions of things to come as well as the dramatic presentation of "a word of the Lord" (cf. 1 Cor. 7:12, 25).

The number of Old Testament citations in the letters of Paul give us a clue to the importance of Scripture in the Pauline churches. Scriptural interpretation was probably the province of "the teacher" (cf. the example of Apollos, Acts 18:24). Full-blown scriptural homilies can be identified in Paul's very letters, for example 1 Corinthians 1:18—2:16 or Romans 4:1-25. Composed prior to the letters in which they are found, these homilies most likely were delivered to church assemblies as exercises of Paul's gift of teaching.

A "tongue" and its "interpretation" formed part of the prayers of the community. Whether in the ecstatic form of "tongues" or in the communicable form of intelligent speech, prayer must have occupied a large part of the Christian gathering. Paul's letters echo "blessings" (2 Cor. 1:3-7) and "doxologies" (Rom. 7:25; 16:25-27; 1 Cor. 15:57), as well as the Aramaic acclamations that stemmed from the earliest Christians (Gal. 1:5; 1 Cor. 16:22; Rom. 8:15).

In 1 Corinthians 14 Paul dwells on the exercise of both "tongues" and "prophecy" during the Christian assembly. We get the impression from Paul's emphasis that "tongues" and "prophecy" occupied an important place in the Corinthian assembly. The rules for order apply in a particular way to the citywide assembly, "Two or three prophets should speak, and the others should weigh carefully what is said" (14:29). The private house church need hardly worry about such an abundance of prophets.

On the other hand, his instructions about prophecy in 1 Corinthians 11:2-16 might concern primarily the exercise of this gift in the private house church. His comments on the citywide gathering begin explicitly only at 11:17. In the preceding verses Paul deals with both men and women prophesying, in apparent and baffling contradiction to his later prohibition against women speaking in church (14:33-36). The more drastic resolution to this contradiction is to see 14:33-36 as a later addition to the letter. An alternative could be to see the earlier instruction about women prophets as dealing with activities in the private house church.

Whether in the private house church or the citywide gathering, the orientation of the assembly was praising God while teaching or admonishing one another. Building up the body was the goal of this gathering and the norm of its functions. The interaction among believers reflected the interaction between God and the believer. The family language of kinship that described the bonds among believers paralleled the family language describing the love of God for his people and the love of a father for his children (Rom. 8:14, 16, 19, 21; 9:8, 26; 1 Cor. 8:6; Phil. 2:15; Gal. 3:26–4:8).

The Christian gatherings under Paul may not have even looked like a religion to an outsider. The Christians had no shrines, temples, cult statues, priests, or sacrifices. For Christians, Paul writes, the community is the temple:

> Don't you know that you yourselves are God's temple of God [*naos theou*] and that God's Spirit lives in you? . . . God's temple is sacred, and you are that temple. (1 Cor. 3:16-17)

One's whole life makes up worship and sacrifice:

> Therefore, I urge you, brothers, in view of God's mercy, to offer your bodies as living sacrifices [*thusian*], holy [*hagian*] and pleasing to God, as your spiritual worship [*latreian*]. Do not conform any longer to the pattern of this world, but be transformed by the renewing of your mind. Then you

> will be able to test what God's will is—his good, pleasing and perfect will. (Rom. 12:1-2)

The Christian gathering as a sharing of gifts, as an exercise in mutual "edification," was for Paul, then, an act of worship. Sacred space was not an issue. The assembly was its own sanctuary. Hence even the family dining room was an appropriate place for church.

Were these "sharing the gift" assemblies distinct from the "Lord's Supper" assemblies? Paul treats them separately in his discussion of the needed reforms, and he never speaks about a transition from one type of activity to the other. The principal argument for seeing two separate assemblies for the two types of church activities rests on another issue, namely, the degree in which the Lord's supper excluded outsiders. We must first examine this issue.

Exclusiveness at the Assemblies? Paul makes mention of the presence of outsiders at the "gifts assemblies," at least those involving tongues and prophecies:

> So if the whole church comes together and everyone speaks in tongues, and some who do not understand or some unbelievers come in, will they not say that you are out of your mind? But if an unbeliever or someone who does not understand comes in while everybody is prophesying, he will be convinced by all that he is a sinner and will be judged by all. . . . So he will fall down and worship God, exclaiming, "God is really among you!" (1 Cor. 14:23-25)

Would Paul or the Corinthians have wanted outsiders at the Lord's Supper, where the solidarity or "body" of Christians appeared to be the objective of the service and the norm of its conduct? The only exclusion Paul associates with the Lord's Supper is an exclusion of idolatry:

> You cannot drink the cup of the Lord and the cup of demons too; you cannot have a part in both the Lord's table and the table of demons. (1 Cor. 10:21)

Dealing with meals in general, Paul speaks also of excluding a member of the community as a means of correcting immorality:

> . . . you must not associate with anyone who calls himself a brother but is sexually immoral, greedy, an

idolater or a slanderer, a drunkard or a swindler. With such a man do not even eat. (1 Cor. 5:11)

Qualifying these instructions immediately before and immediately afterwards, however, Paul points out that he is not intending this discipline for outsiders (5:10, 12).

As we have seen, the Pauline church did not exclude the outsider from its meetings (1 Cor. 14:23). General social relationships like those involving meals with non-Christians may have posed some serious difficulties but were accepted as normal (1 Cor. 10:23-33). Erastos, the city treasurer of Corinth, would certainly have had to resign his position were he unable to associate in a whole range of meals and other activities with his pagan peers.

One or Two Assemblies? If the argument concerning outsiders does not demand our seeing two assemblies for the Lord's Supper and for the sharing of the gifts, do we have any indication of both activities occurring in one assembly? While Paul does not explicitly relate the two activities, his parallel use of words in dealing with the two does in fact suggest their close connection. The term "to gather," *sunerchesthai,* is used for the Lord's Supper (1 Cor. 11:17-18, 20, 33-34) and for the sharing of the gifts (1 Cor. 14:23, 26). Forcefully disagreeing with the Corinthians, Paul writes,

> When you gather in the same place, it is not to eat the Lord's Supper, because each of you rushes to take your own supper. (1 Cor. 11:20, AUTHOR'S TRANSLATION)

The strength of Paul's rebuke depends on the presupposition on the part of the Corinthians, namely, when they did gather *epi to auto* (in the same place), it was their intention to eat the Lord's Supper. Paul, however, tells the same group,

> When you come together, everyone has a hymn, or a word of instruction, a revelation, a tongue or an interpretation. All of these must be done for the strengthening of the church. (1 Cor. 14:26)

It is the theme of "the body" (*to sōma*) that particularly links the Lord's Supper with the sharing of the gifts. The whole discussion of the organic unity of the diverse gifts centers around Paul's identification of the assembly as "the body of Christ" (12:12-30,

esp. 12:27). The "body of Christ" is in fact the gathering of Christians, who all "have been watered by the same Spirit" and thus have been incorporated by baptism into this body (12:13), who then as gifted with diverse powers and roles need each other and care for each other (12:21, 25).

Paul earlier roots the establishment of the "one body" with participating in the Lord's Supper. Christians are one body because they partake of the one bread (10:17).

If Paul then appeals to the unity of the body as the guiding idea for the proper sharing of gifts, it seems likely that he expected the sharing of the gifts and the Lord's Supper to go together. If the two types of activities went together at the same gathering, most likely the sharings of prophecy, teachings, tongues, and other services of the Word followed that of the Lord's Supper. The hint we have of this comes from those who arrived late and had nothing to eat (1 Cor. 11:21, 33). If the meal followed the "Word service," as is often supposed, then these people would be late for everything. Paul wants the Corinthians to wait before starting, that is, before beginning to eat the Lord's Supper (1 Cor. 11:21, 33).

Baptismal Assemblies. Along with the Lord's Supper, baptism appears in Paul's writings as one of the official actions of church. In the opening chapters of 1 Corinthians, Paul refers several times to baptism (1:13-17), mentioning how he personally baptized Crispus and Gaius along with the house of Stephanas (1:14-16), but that his mission was to preach, not to baptize (1:17). He was worried about factions arising among the Corinthians from an overemphasis on the person administering baptism (1:13).

Christian baptism is specifically a baptism "into Christ" (Gal. 3:27; Rom. 6:3), which, Paul explains, is a baptism "into his death." It is a way of being "buried with Christ" (Rom. 6:3; Col. 2:12). For Paul baptism is likewise a baptism "into one body," an incorporation into that diverse and organic unity that is the church with all the gifts of its members, "Jew or Greek, slave or free." Christians are baptized "in the Spirit," for baptism is being "given the one Spirit to drink" (1 Cor. 12:13).

The comparisons made between baptism and entering the tomb of Christ suggest immersion under water. This does not sound like the activity that could take place at a house church or even at the meeting of the city church at a house. The house *impluvium*—the small pool in the courtyard—would be only a few feet deep. Furthermore, an assembly of this sort might not be the appropriate place for the nudity generally involved in baptism.

To my knowledge the earliest indications we have of a setting for Christian baptism come from Justin, some one hundred years after Paul. Writing about the practice in Rome, Justin mentions the preliminary instructions and communal prayers and fasting.

> Then they are led by us to where there is water, and they are reborn in the same manner of regeneration by which we ourselves have been reborn. For they are then given washing in the water in the name of God the father and master of all, of our saviour Jesus Christ, and of the Holy Spirit.

This place "where there is water" may be the public bath, over which, according to Justin, the church of Rome assembled.

When the *Didachē* allows for different kinds of water in which to baptize and specifically describes pouring water on the head of the new Christian, it does not indicate any place where this is to happen. Baptism by pouring, however, could allow baptism to take place in church. By the third century, rooms would be designed in churches specifically for baptisms, such as that in the church of Dura-Europos.

Vincent Branick[13]

SIXTEEN

Leadership in Biblical Worship

Biblical worship is both an individual and a corporate offering of praise to the Lord; it is both spontaneous and organized. It is a declaration of God's greatness and a celebration of the covenant relationship between God and his people. It is an act of obedience to the Deity who has ordained certain ways by which his sovereignty is to be acknowledged. In order for worship to be organized as a corporate expression, there must be leadership—leadership that is acknowledged by and representative of the worshiping community, leadership that is able to assemble the resources for worship and to bring to a focus the people's motivation to express their devotion to the Most High. In the Hebrew Scriptures, representatives of four major "offices," or functions, within the community served as leaders of worship. These roles were those of family head or elder, prophet, priest, and king. In the New Testament, Jesus Christ summed up all of these roles.

183 • FAMILY HEADS AS WORSHIP LEADERS IN THE OLD TESTAMENT

The patriarchs of Israel and the leaders or elders of the Israelite tribes are portrayed often in Scripture as taking the lead in their family or community worship of the Lord.

The Hebrew Patriarchs

The Hebrew patriarchs—Abraham, Isaac, and Jacob—led worship as the heads of their families, bowing down to the Lord and offering sacrifices to him. Abraham built altars to the Lord and "called upon his name" because of his promises of the land and a multitude of descendants (Gen. 12:7-8). Likewise, Jacob, at the Lord's command, built an altar at Bethel (Gen. 35:1-3). He had wrestled with the messenger of the Lord at Penuel and prevailed (Gen. 32:22-32) yet bore in his body the marks of that nocturnal struggle even to the end of his life, when he "worshiped as he leaned on the top of his staff" (Heb. 11:21). Job, who might have been a contemporary of the patriarchs, offered sacrifices on behalf of his family (Job 1:5), and prayer on behalf of his friends, that their offerings might be acceptable to God by virtue of his intercession (Job 42:7-9).

Tribal Leaders

Family and tribal leaders, or the elders of the community, held responsibility for the worship of their people throughout the history of Israel. Emblematic of this responsibility is the repetitious accounting of twelve identical offerings brought by the leaders of the Israelite tribes at the consecration of the Mosaic tabernacle (Num. 7). The tribal leaders saw to it that their clans and families were represented at major events in the place of worship, "where the tribes go up" (Ps. 122:4). The Passover, though a festival of the entire community, was family by family (Exod. 12:21). The same was true for the Feast of Booths or Tabernacles; each home erected a shelter and lived in it for the duration of the festival (Lev. 23:42; Neh. 8:14-16). It was also the responsibility of family heads to arrange for participation in these festivals and to preside over the family's observance.

Psalm 68 pictures a festival procession into the sanctuary led by dignitaries from the tribes of Israel (Ps. 68:24-27). The "assembly of the people" and "the council of the elders" were settings in which the Lord and his wonders were extolled (Ps. 107:32). The prophet Joel called for the elders to take the lead as the people gathered at the house of the Lord in penitent, solemn assembly (Joel 1:14).

184 • PROPHETIC LEADERSHIP IN OLD TESTAMENT WORSHIP

A careful survey of scriptural evidence discloses that the worship of the Lord is most significantly influenced, and often expressly led, by persons functioning in a prophetic role (as opposed to a priestly role). Prophets served as mediators of the covenant; they were closely associated with the sanctuary and vitally concerned with the integrity of worship; they functioned as directors and musicians.

—— Prophets As Covenant Mediators ——

The prophets of Israel, as God's spokesmen (the probable meaning of the Hebrew term *navi'*), were mediators of the covenant and advocates of the covenant tradition. They called on the people to return to their loyalty to Yahweh, and they proclaimed the judgment of the Lord on an unfaithful people when the provisions of the covenant had been violated through idolatry and injustice. Since the enactment, renewal, and celebration of the covenant were a worship form, the prophets fulfilled a function as leaders in worship.

Moses, Israel's prophet *par excellence,* mediated the Sinai covenant (Exod. 19:1–24:8), which had a worship structure incorporating the appearance of the Lord, the review of his historic act of deliverance of his people, the proclamation of his Word or covenant stipulations, the people's pledge to obey the terms of the covenant, the giving of offerings to the Lord, and the eating of a covenant meal. Moses also presided at a renewal of the covenant, which had a similar structure, just prior to Israel's entrance into Canaan. The entire book of Deuteronomy is devoted to a description of this ceremony in the form of a farewell address by Moses. Of special note here is the liturgical pronouncement of the covenant sanctions: blessing if the covenant is kept, curse if it is violated (Deut. 27–29). The people were summoned to choose the way of obedience that leads to life (Deut. 30:15-20), and witnesses to the agreement were invoked (Deut. 4:26; 30:19). The ceremony concluded with two songs, the first of which returnd to the theme of the judgment inherent in the curse of the covenant (Deut. 32:1-43).

Joshua, though not called a prophet, inherited the mantle of Moses as the spokesman of the Lord's covenant and presided over the curse liturgy for which Moses had given directions in his farewell address (Josh. 8:30-35). After the conquest of the land of Canaan, he officiated at another ceremony of renewal of the covenant at Shechem (Josh. 24:1-28). This ceremony recapitulated the same treaty-covenant structure familiar from earlier examples: the recitation of the relationship between God and people, the summons to choose between the Lord and other gods, the pledge of the people to serve Yahweh, the invocation of witnesses, and the presentation of the terms of the covenant, its "words," or statutes.

—— Prophets and the Sanctuary ——

Samuel, who was to become Israel's prophetic leader, was brought up in the sanctuary and "was ministering before the LORD" (1 Sam. 2:18); later his presence was required to "bless the sacrifice" of the feasts of the people (1 Sam. 9:12-13). Bands of prophets were apparently attached to the high places, or local sanctuaries; Saul, after being anointed king by Samuel, also encountered such a group and prophesied with them (1 Sam. 10:1-13).

The prophetic association with the sanctuary continued into the period of the Israelite kingdoms; evidently the festal gatherings of the people provided an audience for the prophet's utterances, which were usually in the form of poetic compositions. Amos prophesied at the "sanctuary of the king" at Bethel and was ordered by the officiating priest, Amaziah, to return to his own country, Judah, and prophesy there instead (Amos 7:10-17). Isaiah received his prophetic vocation while attending a festival at the temple in Jerusalem (Isa. 6). He apparently was close to the king, a respected adviser to the royal house (Isa. 7:1-17; 37:1–38:22). It has been suggested that Isaiah served as the nation's "poet laureate," composing liturgical materials for public worship; the famous prophecy of the "child" who is to take the government upon his shoulder, reigning "on David's throne and over his kingdom" (Isa. 9:1-7), may have been an oracle for the coronation of a Judean king such as Hezekiah. Jeremiah delivered his indictment of the people's violation of the covenant while standing "at the gate of the LORD's house," addressing the Judeans who came there to worship (Jer. 7:1-2).

The integrity of the worship of the Lord was itself a major concern of the prophets of Israel, all the way from Samuel, who insisted that "to obey is better than sacrifice" (1 Sam. 15:22), to Malachi, who proclaimed that the "messenger of the covenant" would come to his temple, refining the priesthood so they might "bring offerings in righteousness" (Mal. 3:1-4). Elijah officiated at a sacrifice that demonstrated to the people, who had been enticed to worship the Canaanite god Ba'al, that Yahweh, "he is God" (1 Kings 18:36-39, RSV). The prophet Amaziah encouraged Asa, king of Judah, to undertake a restoration of the sanctuary, accompanied by the renewal of the covenant oath (2 Chron. 15:1-15). During the reign of Josiah, king of Judah, the prophetess Huldah was consulted in connection with the rediscovery of the Book of the Law by the priests; she declared the Lord's judgment against the temple as a consequence of the violation of the covenant (2 Kings 22:12-20).

Amos declared, in the Lord's name, "I hate, I despise your religious feasts; I cannot stand your assemblies" (Amos 5:21) because they mask injustice and the violation of the Lord's covenant with his people. similarly, Isaiah declared that the appointed feasts had become a burden to the Lord (Isa. 1:14) because of the dissolution of the wealthy and their indifference to the plight of the poor, their fellow members of the covenant community.

Jeremiah and Ezekiel, prophets of the early exilic period, were both of priestly families (Jer. 1:1; Ezek. 1:3), and each in his own way was concerned with the integrity of worship. Jeremiah believed that trust in religious institutions, without an inward bond to the Lord, was deceptive (Jer. 7:3-11). Instead, he proclaimed the coming of a "new covenant" written on the heart (Jer. 31:31-34). Ezekiel was more institutionally oriented; his passion was the restoration of the ruined temple, filled once again with the glory of the Lord (Ezek. 40–43), a source of life and healing (Ezek. 47:1-12). In the postexilic period, the prophet Haggai urged Zerubbabel the governor and Joshua the high priest to rebuild the house of the Lord (Hag. 1:1-11).

Prophetic Musicians in Worship

In ancient Israel, prophecy and music were closely associated. (A hint of this association, found in other cultures as well, appears in our English word _music,_ which betrays its derivation from the ancient Greek concept of the muse, the spirit that inspires poets and musicians.) During the Exodus, Miriam the prophetess, sister of Moses and Aaron, took tambourine in hand and led the women in song and dance, celebrating the Lord's triumph over the Egyptian pursuers (Exod. 15:20-21). As we have seen, Moses concluded his farewell address, an extended reenactment of the covenant ceremony, with a song of judgment and warning. The prophetess Deborah (Judg. 4:4) composed a song celebrating Israel's victory over a Canaanite army (Judg. 5:1-31). The prophets that Saul encountered coming down from the high place were prophesying to the accompaniment of musical instruments (1 Sam. 10:5).

The prophets of the period of the Israelite kingdoms continued the same alignment between spoken word and music. Second Kings 3:15 records that Elisha called for a "minstrel" (_meʾnaggen,_ a player on a stringed instrument) in order to prophesy to the kings of Israel, Judah, and Edom, assembled for battle against Moab. The prophets who produced the prophetic books of the Hebrew Bible composed lyric oracles, which they probably sang to their hearers—at least to their disciples, if not always to the public. Isaiah's "song of the vineyard" (Isa. 5:1-7) expresses the Lord's disappointment with his unfaithful people. Another song in Isaiah 26:1-6, celebrating the Lord's deliverance of those who trust in him, perhaps was composed as part of a liturgy of entrance into the sanctuary (Isa. 26:2). Jeremiah composed a chant of lament upon the death of King Josiah (2 Chron. 35:25), and his book of Lamentations is a song. Most of the material in the prophetic books is, in fact, poetic song, and some material in the later Prophets, now preserved in prose form, was probably originally written as song. Indeed, prophecy was so closely associated with music that Ezekiel complained that to the public he was simply a musical entertainer (Ezek. 33:32).

It is David the king, however, whose name is most closely linked with prophetic song and musical leadership in the liturgy of the sanctuary. In connection with his bringing the ark of the covenant up to Zion, David instructed the Levites to provide singers and musicians to celebrate the event (1 Chron. 15:16-24). Once the ark had been placed in its tent, he appointed Asaph as chief musician in charge of continual thanksgiving and praise before the ark (1 Chron. 16:1-7). The Levites were priests, but later we learn that David had appointed them to "prophesy"—to give thanks and praise to the Lord (1 Chron. 25:1-7). The description of their activity suggests that these musicians led in a spontaneous and overwhelming outpouring of worship, especially on high occasions such as the dedication of the temple of Solomon (2 Chron. 5:11-14).

David is associated with about half the Psalms, for which he is called a "prophet" in the New Testament (Acts 2:29-31). Many of the Psalms must have originated in the prophetic worship he instituted before the ark on Zion during the period prior to the erection of the temple, when the Mosaic sanctuary with its priestly sacrifices remained at Gibeon (1 Chron. 21:29). This explains the prophetic voice in which God himself speaks in a number of the Psalms (e.g., Pss. 2; 46; 50; 81–82; 89; 91; 95; 105; 108; 110; 132), many of which are attributed to David or to the Levitical musicians.

Certain of the sanctuary musicians were appointed to direct the performance of the music (1 Chron. 15:21), and the superscriptions to fifty-five of the Psalms refer to the choirmaster, or "director" (*menatztzeʾḥ*), often with instructions for performance (Pss. 4–6; 8–9; 12; 22; 45–46; 52–62; 67; 69; 75–77; 80–81; 84; 88). Of these Psalms, thirty-nine are associated with David, nine with the sons of Korah, and five with Asaph. (A similar designation appears in Hab. 3:19.) The director of music evidently played an important leadership role in the worship of the sanctuary from the time of David onward, as the vocal and instrumental praise of the Lord assumed greater importance. The book of Chronicles especially highlights the prominence of the prophetic sanctuary musicians as leaders of corporate worship. A well-known example of their activity occurs in the account of the invasion of Judah during the reign of Jehoshaphat, when Jahaziel, a Levitical musician, prophesied encouragement and victory to the beleaguered king and nation. The musicians then went before the army into battle, praising the Lord in full vesture, and led in celebration of the ensuing victory (2 Chron. 20:14-30). In the restoration of worship after the Exile, Ezra made a point of recruiting more than two hundred Levites for the service of the sanctuary (Ezra 8:18-20).

In Israelite worship, prophetic and musical activity offered virtually the only outlet for leadership in worship on the part of women. The prophetesses Miriam, Deborah, and Huldah have been mentioned. The enumeration of members of the assembly who returned to Jerusalem after the Exile includes 245 male and female singers (Neh. 7:67). Moses expressed the desire that all the Lord's people might be prophets (Num. 11:29). Indeed, in Psalm 105 the Lord calls all the covenant descendants of Abraham "my prophets" (Ps. 105:8-15). *The spirit of prophecy, then, is the rightful heritage of all who are bound to the Lord in covenant.*

185 • The Priest as Worship Leader in the Old Testament

In the directives of Moses, priests were specially commissioned for the role of representing the people before the Lord and thus occupied a central position in the worship life of the covenant people.

The Role of the Priest

The proper role of the priest in worship was to officiate in sacrifice and offering in order to propitiate the Deity on behalf of the worshiper. Whereas the prophet was the spokesman of the Lord, the priest represented the people before God. The prophet was privy to the counsels of God in virtue of the word that came to him by the Spirit (Amos 3:7-8; Isa. 61:1; Ezek. 6:1; 2 Pet. 1:21). The Word of the Lord burned like a fire within him (Jer. 20:9). With the priest, access to the Deity was by a careful process of consecration (Lev. 8–9), wherein enough of the overpowering holiness of the Lord was communicated to him so that he could safely approach the divine and awesome presence; otherwise he would risk being struck down in wrath as a trespasser in forbidden territory.

The priest's consecration rendered him "holy to his God" (Lev. 21:7, NASB), that is, set apart from the ordinary or the profane. For this reason, special conditions were placed on his life-style. He was not to defile himself by contact with a corpse, except that of a close family member (Lev. 21:1-4), nor cut his beard nor shave his head (Lev. 21:5), nor marry a woman who had been a prostitute or was divorced (Lev. 21:7). The priest who served at the altar needed to be free of physical defects and deformities (Lev. 21:16-21). He was not to drink wine during his time of ministering before the Lord (Lev. 10:9-10).

As one thus set apart, the priest could "draw near" (*biqriv*) to the Lord officiate in sacrifice, and place the offerings on the altar. His vocation was to minister (*sheret*) before Yahweh, performing the service (*ʿavodah*) of the house of the Lord, whether it was the service of the altar or the service of song and prayer. But the priest's activity could extend beyond the performance of sanctuary rites. Indeed, because the number of members of the priestly families of the tribe of Levi was far greater than that required for the service of the house of God, many had to reside in outlying areas far from the sanctuary, making a living from agriculture and from the tithes of local residents (Deut. 14:28-29; Neh. 10:37).

As we have seen, a number of the prophets were of priestly descent. The Levitical priests functioned also as teachers, instructing the people in the traditions of the Lord's covenant (Deut. 17:9-11; 24:8). They were the recognized custodians (Jer. 18:18; Ezek. 7:26) of the Law of God, or _Torah,_ a word that actually means "teaching" or "instruction." When the people were without a "teaching priest," the worship of the Lord lapsed into a state of decay (2 Chron. 15:3). Ezra the priest was "a teacher well versed in the Law of Moses" (Ezra 7:6), whose desire was to teach the Law to Israel. In fact, the Persian ruler Artaxerxes commissioned him for this very task (Ezra 7:25). The priesthood preserved the covenant traditions in both oral and written form and probably was responsible specifically for transmitting the historical and instructional material found in the Pentateuch. Ezra also produced the history of the Chronicler (i.e., Chronicles, Ezra, and Nehemiah), which could have been based on archival records deposited at the sanctuary, as well as on the books of Samuel and Kings.

The High Priest

A special aura surrounded the high priest. He might marry only a virgin from a priestly family (Lev. 21:10-14). A person accused of manslaughter was safe from the avenger in a designated city of refuge, provided he did not leave the city until the death of the high priest in office at the time (Num. 35:25-28). It was the role of the high priest to enter the Most Holy Place, or inner sanctuary, on the Day of Atonement with fire from the altar, incense, and blood from the sacrifices (Lev. 16). The high priest also had the sacred lot, by means of which he executed a decision in difficult cases of judgment (Exod. 28:30; Neh. 7:65).

The high priests periodically worked with Judean kings in programs for the reform and restoration of worship. For example, during the interregnum of Athaliah, the priests concealed the young Joash, heir to the Davidic throne, in the temple; Jehoiada the high priest played a key role in the _coup d'e'tat_ that restored the Davidic monarchy and in the religious restoration that followed (2 Kings 11). When the temple was being repaired early in the reign of Josiah, Hilkiah the high priest found the neglected Book of the Law in the temple and brought it to the attention of the king. The discovery led to a renewal of the covenant and the restoration of temple worship (2 Kings 22:1–23:25). In the postexilic period, the prophet Zechariah saw a vision of Joshua the high priest and Zerubbabel the governor, who was in the Davidic line, as "the two who are anointed to serve the Lord of all the earth" (Zech. 4:14). Encouraged also by the prophet Haggai (Hag. 2:4), Joshua and Zerubbabel worked together to rebuild the house of God (Hag. 1:14). Ezra, priest and scribe of the Law, led the people in an extended act of confession, the renewal of the covenant, and a pledge to support the service of the house of God (Neh. 8–10).

186 ✦ THE ROLE OF THE KING IN OLD TESTAMENT WORSHIP

Despite the predominant function of the king as a military leader, the Bible records many occasions when the kings of Israel and Judah fulfilled a significant role in the leadership of the nation's worship.

The King as Warrior

In the ancient world, kings were primarily military leaders, commanding their armies in warfare (Gen. 14:8–9:2; Josh. 12; 1 Sam. 11:1; 2 Sam. 8:1-6; Job 15:24; Prov. 30:29-31). The kings of Israel and Judah were no exceptions; their major preoccupation was the defense of their nation or the conquest of neighboring kingdoms. Their association with warfare, as well as their lack of priestly status, normally precluded their involvement in the leadership of worship. Saul, fresh from victory over the Philistines, felt the wrath of Samuel because he had offered a burnt offering himself when Samuel's arrival at Gilgal was delayed (1 Sam. 13:8-14). David was told not to build the temple because he was a man of war who had shed much blood (1 Chron. 22:8; 28:3). Uzziah was successful in warfare and strengthened Judah's defenses; when he presumed to burn incense to the Lord in the temple, however, he was opposed by the priests and became leprous (2 Chron. 26:16-21).

——— The King as Covenant Mediator ———

The religious problem of the Israelite monarchies was that, in terms of the covenant, Yahweh himself was king. Indeed, the covenant structure of Israelite worship was modeled after that of the ancient Near Eastern treaty between a "great king" and his vassals, a pattern that placed the Lord in the position of the king. Worship focused on the kingship of Yahweh, as in the "enthronement psalms" (Pss. 29; 47; 93; 95-99). The ark itself was a visible symbol of Yahweh's kingship. Moreover, the treaty-covenant structure also placed his worshipers in the position not of slaves but of vassals or subkings—a "kingdom of priests," among whom the earthly king was one worshiper among many, subject like all others to the covenant laws. Thus the covenant theology of divine kingship acted as a corrective to any spiritual pretense on the part of the ruler and served as a platform on which the prophets, especially, might stand in rebuking and correcting an errant monarch. Thus, Elijah could throw back in Ahab's face the epithet "troubler of Israel" (1 Kings 18:17-18); and Isaiah could accuse Ahaz of trying the patience of God (Isa. 7:13).

The theological "problem" with the preeminent kingship of Yahweh was partially resolved in Judah by the theological solution of royal sonship, in which the earthly ruler was seen as the adopted son of Yahweh, and as his vice regent in government. In Psalm 2, for example, the king speaks prophetically, repeating the Lord's decree of adoption: "You are my Son; today I have become your Father" (Ps. 2:7). Possibly such materials were composed for the coronation ceremonies, when the Lord would declare, "I have installed my King on Zion, my holy hill" (Ps. 2:6). Psalms 72, 101, and 110 also may relate to the same occasion, as might other passages, such as Isaiah's oracle, "to us a son is given, and the government will be on his shoulders" (Isa. 9:6). The identification of king and priest is clear in the prophetic declaration, "You are a priest forever, in the order of Melchizedek" (Ps. 110:4). Here the psalmist relates the Judean monarch to the Canaanite Melchizedek, who had ruled at the same site in Jerusalem as "king of Salem" and "priest of God Most High" (*'El 'elyon*) and to whom Abraham had offered a tithe (Gen. 14:18-20).

As the anointed representative of the Lord, the Judean king was seen by Old Testament writers as a mediator of the covenant between the Lord and his people. The prophet Nathan announced a special covenant relationship between the Lord and the dynasty of David (2 Sam. 7:5-17), proclaiming that his house and kingdom would endure before the Lord. This covenant, however, was made with David as "ruler over my people Israel" (2 Sam. 7:8). David understood "that the Lord had established him as king over Israel and had exalted his kingdom for the sake of his people Israel" (2 Sam. 5:12). Thus the Davidic covenant was a localized manifestation of the basic covenant between Yahweh and his worshipers, with the king serving in the role of mediator. This role was most adequately filled by David himself, but the theology of the Davidic covenant continued to undergird the Judean monarchy and was foundational to the work of the major Judean prophets in their vision of the maintenance and restoration of the covenant (cf. Isa. 9:6-7; Jer. 30:8-9; 33:14-26; Ezek. 34:23-24; 37:24-28) so that the postexilic prophet Zechariah could proclaim that "the house of David will be like God, like the Angel of the LORD going before them" (Zech. 12:8).

Accordingly, despite the restrictions placed on the king as an officiant in sacrifice, the biblical history records occasions when the Judean king legitimately exercised personal leadership in the worship of the Lord. David is most remarkable for his intimate devotion to Yahweh, expressed in his dancing before the ark (2 Sam. 6:14) as it was being brought, at his direction, to Zion, or in his composition of worship materials as the "sweet psalmist of Israel" (2 Sam. 23:1, NASB). David instituted and organized the Levitical, prophetic worship of the "tent of David" and had the vision for the erection of the house of the Lord (2 Sam. 7:2; 1 Chron. 22). It was left to Solomon, his son, to carry out the actual construction of the temple (1 Kings 5–7; 2 Chron. 2–4). As a priestly king, Solomon personally officiated at the dedication of the sanctuary (1 Kings 8:12-21; 2 Chron. 5), offering extended prayer (1 Kings 8:22-61; 2 Chron. 6) and sacrifices (1 Kings 8:62-66; 2 Chron. 7:1-11).

——— Kings as Reformers of Worship ———

Later kings functioned as organizers or reformers of worship and played a secondary role as officiants. Asa carried through a reform instigated by prophecy, and led the people in a renewal of the covenant (2 Chron. 15:8-15). Faced with an enemy invasion, Jehoshaphat led the people in penitential worship and instructed the Levitical musicians to lead the army into battle singing praise to the Lord (2 Chron. 20:18-21). Hezekiah, the first king since the time of David to receive the biblical historian's unqualified commendation (2 Kings 18:1-6), purged the worship of Yahweh of some of its Ba'alistic accretions. Later in the history of Judah, Josiah led the people in a renewal of the covenant, reading aloud the Mosaic Law and covenant (2 Kings 23:1-3). He also purified Israelite worship of its pagan and occult flavor and reinstituted the celebration of the Passover (2 Kings 23:21-23). Sadly, the reforming kings of Judah were in the minority. Most Judean rulers did little to protect the integrity of the covenant of Yahweh. The situation was even worse in the northern kingdom of Israel, where Jeroboam I and Ahab with his consort Jezebel took the lead in the falsification and perversion of worship.

187 ✦ WORSHIP LEADERSHIP IN THE NEW TESTAMENT

The emergent New Testament church did not have the same clearly defined offices of leadership as did the worship of Israel. However, the functions of family head, prophet, priest, and king are summed up in Christ, who through the Spirit leads the church, the community of the new covenant, in its worship of almighty God.

—— Family Heads, Elders, and Worship ——

The Christian movement expanded largely through the conversion of heads of families, who, in turn, led their entire households in baptism into the faith of Christ. Unlike the rampant individualism of the modern Western world, Jewish and Greco-Roman cultures of the New Testament era made commonplace the conversion of whole families, such as those of Cornelius (Acts 10:24-48) and the jailer at Philippi (Acts 16:27-34). Following their Old Testament counterparts, family heads made provision for the worship needs of their households; that the New Testament church met in private homes no doubt encouraged this responsibility. In the Gospels Jesus set the example for this type of leadership. As the head of the new family of the kingdom of God, he arranged for the Passover meal with his disciples (Matt. 26:17-19) and presided over the celebration. He had observed this pattern from his youth, when Jesus' extended family had seen to it that he was included in their annual pilgrimage to Jerusalem for the Feast of Passover (Luke 2:41-42).

It is often assumed that the organization of the early Christian churches was patterned after that of the synagogue, which had an officer (_ro'sh hakkᵉneset_) who presided over its exercises (Mark 5:22; Luke 8:41; Acts 18:17), an "attendant" (_ḥazzan_) who handled the sacred scrolls (Luke 4:16-20), and a "messenger" (_shᵉliᵃḥ_) who represented the congregation in leading the liturgical responses of the prayer service. Although it seems reasonable to infer that the elders of the local Christian assembly presided over its acts of worship in similar fashion, what concrete evidence exists comes from the second century (the _Didachē,_ or _Teaching of the Twelve Apostles,_ and the _Apology_ of Justin Martyr), in which we find a president of the congregation who officiated at the Lord's Supper. In the New Testament church, both theologically and practically, it was Christ himself who was the leader of the family, "head over everything for the church, which is his body" (Eph. 1:22-23). Jesus told his disciples, "One is your Father, He who is in heaven. And do not be called leaders; for One is your Leader, that is, Christ" (Matt. 23:9-10 NASB).

The New Testament offers few specific details concerning the function of the elders of the church in leading worship. They were to visit the sick in order to anoint them with oil and pray with them (James 5:14), but this was not corporate worship. The silence of the New Testament concerning the role of elders in leading worship, however, is magnificently broken in the portrayal of the twenty-four elders in the book of Revelation. These elders are archetypal worshipers, falling down before the throne of God and the Lamb (Rev. 4:10; 5:8, 14; 11:16; 19:4), casting their crowns before him (Rev. 4:10), extolling the Lord God in majestic anthem (Rev. 4:11; 5:9-10), and crying out "Amen, Hallelujah!" (Rev. 19:4). Because their number signifies the twelve tribes of the old covenant and the twelve apostles of the new, it is reasonable to conclude that these elders represented the true Israel of God, the faithful covenant community of all believers in the Lord Jesus. This, according to the view taken here, is not an eschatological image but a picture of the worshiping church as a present-day reality—the New Jerusalem, in which the Lord God and the Lamb dwell in the midst of the covenant people (Rev. 21:3). These elders are not so much leaders as _responders_ to the glory of God. Yet their actions express an important truth of Christian leadership, laid down by Jesus himself: a leader is one who _serves_ and by his serving sets the example for others (Mark 9:35; Luke 22:25-27; John 13:12-15). The most effective leader of worship leads by personal example.

Prophecy and Worship in the New Testament

The early Christian church, by virtue of its social status within a hostile culture (whether Jewish or pagan), was not able to conduct large-scale public worship. Sacrifice, of course, was no longer needed after the crucifixion of the Lamb of God. But the festive celebration of the new covenant, as described in the book of Revelation, would have appealed to the apostolic church, had it been possible to observe it; this is also clear from Paul's declaration that "every knee should bow . . . and every tongue confess" (Phil. 2:10-11) the lordship of Christ.

It is not surprising, then, that prophets played a role in shaping early Christian worship, as they had in the worship of Old Testament Israel. Paul urged believers to pursue the spiritual manifestations (*pneumatika*), especially the practice of prophecy (1 Cor. 14:1), and laid down some general rules for their use in worship. Prophecy, he wrote, is of special value in convicting both the "ungifted" and the unbeliever of the presence of God in the assembly, so that he might "fall down and worship God" (1 Cor. 14:24-25).

The exact role of a prophet as a leader in worship is not described in the New Testament (this is also true for other ecclesiastical functions), but something of the practice of the New Testament church may be reflected in the *Didachē,* where instructions are given for thanksgiving after receiving the Lord's Supper; the officiant is told to "allow the prophets to give thanks as much as they will" (chapter 10), and the comment is made that "the prophets are your high priests" (chapter 13).

As in Israelite worship, the exercise of the prophetic vocation made it possible for women to play a significant role in worship in the new covenant community. In the account of Jesus' infancy we hear of the prophetess Anna, who "never left the temple but worshiped night and day" (Luke 2:36-38). Philip the evangelist had seven unmarried daughters, all of whom were prophetesses (Acts 21:9). Paul indicated that it was perfectly proper for a woman to pray or prophesy in the assembly, provided her head was covered (1 Cor. 11:5; evidently, her long hair was considered appropriate covering, 1 Cor. 11:15). Paul echoed Moses' desire that all the Lord's people be

prophets (1 Cor. 14:5). It is correct to conclude that the Spirit of Christ is prophetic (Luke 4:18-19) and rests on the entire community of those endued with power as his witnesses (Acts 1:8).

Priesthood in the New Testament

The Acts of the Apostles reports that many of the Jewish priests became Christians in the earliest days of the Jerusalem church (Acts 6:7). The New Testament church, however, had no office corresponding to that of the priest in Israelite religion. In part, this was because it did not conduct sacrificial rites. A more basic reason, however, can be found in the underlying idea of the people of God. As far back as the giving of the Law, the Lord had called all Israel to be "a kingdom of priests and a holy nation" (Exod. 19:6), to enter into his awesome presence—a vocation the people refused to accept, preferring that Moses alone draw near to the Lord (Exod. 20:19; Deut. 5:23-27). In the crucifixion of Christ, however, the veil hiding the inner sanctuary had been stripped away (Matt. 27:51; Rev. 11:19), revealing both the emptiness of the old institutions and the fullness of the glory of the covenant God, to whom all believers, regardless of genealogy or ethnic background, have access through Christ (Eph. 2:18). Thus all Christians have been called to a "royal priesthood" (1 Pet. 2:9), a ministry not of an earthly altar, but of proclaiming the excellencies of God and his deliverance—the true sacrifice of praise and thanksgiving (Heb. 13:15). Jesus Christ, the "great high priest" (Heb. 4:14), has already offered himself as the only efficacious sacrifice (Heb. 7:26-27).

The Kingship of Christ

Perhaps because of the social position of the early Christians, earthly kings played no part in the leadership of New Testament worship (contrary to popular imagination, the magi who worship the Christ child are not called kings in the biblical text [Matt. 2:1-12]). But the role of the Davidic king as mediator of the covenant is integral to the New Testament's proclamation of Jesus as the Christ (Greek *Christos,* "anointed one," equivalent to Hebrew *Mashiaḥ,* a kingly title). In the New Testament, the concept of kingship is transferred to the spiritual plane; as crucified King (John 19:14-22), Christ disarmed the enemies of his people in spiritual warfare (Col. 2:13-15). The Lamb that was slain now has received power, dominion, and worship (Rev. 5:11-14). As the faithful witness and the Word of the covenant, the King of kings and Lord of lords has taken up the sword as the head of the armies of heaven (Rev. 19:11-16). Jesus is the priest-king "like Melchizedek" (Heb. 7:15), and the "mediator of a new covenant" (Heb. 9:15; 12:24). In the New Testament, as it was for David, the role of the king as a fighting man and his role as covenant mediator are combined into one and applied to Christ in the sphere of worship.

Further, as members of Christ, all believers are "kings and priests" (Rev. 1:6, KJV) who reign with him on the earth (Rev. 5:10). According to Paul, by grace we "reign in life through the one man, Jesus Christ" (Rom. 5:17). "You have become kings," he tells the Corinthians (1 Cor. 4:8). And to the Roman Christians he declares that God "will soon crush Satan under your feet" (Rom. 16:20). As with the offices of prophet and priest, the office of king is also applied theologically to all members of the new covenant community.

───── Christ Fulfills All Roles ─────

In the New Testament, all the Old Testament roles of worship leadership are incorporated in Jesus Christ. Christ is "head of the church" (Eph. 5:23), the new family of the kingdom of God, which by his death he has created "from every tribe and language and people and nation" (Rev. 5:9). As Spirit-endowed preacher of the kingdom of God, he is also prophet, a new Moses, teaching the people "as one who had authority, and not as their teachers of the law" (Matt. 7:29). He is the great High Priest who offers the only efficacious sacrifice for the remission of sins and so removes the barrier to covenant with God (Heb. 9:11-15). In his resurrection he is exalted to the right hand of the Father as both Lord and Christ (Acts 2:32-36) and governs as "the firstborn from the dead, and the ruler of the kings of the earth" (Rev. 1:5). As head of the family and mediator of the covenant, he officiates as host of the new covenant meal, the Lord's Supper (Mark 14:23-25), which, in the history of the church, has been the fundamental and most distinctive act of Christian worship.

The preeminence of the living Christ in the worship of the early church explains why the New Testament says so little concerning the role of ecclesiastical functionaries in the conduct of worship. Christ himself directs the worship of the church through the Holy Spirit. Thus, New Testament worship appears to be free-flowing and spontaneous. Spirit-filled believers offer "psalms, hymns and spiritual songs" (Eph. 5:19). They come offering up "to God a sacrifice of praise—the fruit of lips that confess his name" (Heb. 13:15). In their assemblies, "everyone has a hymn, or a word of instruction, a revelation, a tongue or an interpretation" (1 Cor. 14:26); Paul's strictures concerning decency and order in worship do not cancel its basic thrust of response to the Spirit of Christ. Elders, overseers, and other church functionaries have no clearly designated role as worship leaders, with the possible exception of the prophets. Nor do the New Testament writings provide any instruction concerning who is to administer the Lord's Supper; even the Pastoral Epistles are silent on this subject. The specialized functions and liturgical offices found in the later church are not present in the New Testament but belong to the postbiblical period.

Richard C. Leonard

188 ✦ Bishops, Elders, and Deacons

In the formative years of the church its ministry exhibited amazing variety and adaptability. Emerging at Pentecost as a Jewish sect, the church naturally modeled its ministry in part on patterns borrowed from the synagogue. But the Spirit of Christ also fashioned new functions and channels of ministry through which the grace of God might be communicated. The principal "orders" of ministry that arose were those of the elder (bishop) and the deacon.

From the early chapters of Acts it is evident that at the first the apostles directed the life of the infant church. Presently they were joined in their ministry by evangelists and prophets who assisted them in spreading the gospel far and wide. As new communities of Christians sprang up in Judea, Samaria, and throughout the Gentile world, the need emerged for official structures of ministry to direct the affairs of local churches. The New Testament generally employs three terms to designate the two official orders of ministry that were established: _elder, bishop,_ and _deacon._ Alongside these orders existed a constellation of other local and itinerant ministries.

Elder-Bishops

There is no record to indicate when the office of elder, or presbyter (*presbuteros*), was instituted. Elders are found early in the Christian communities of Judea (Acts 11:30), while Paul and Barnabas appointed elders in charge of the congregations they established on their first missionary journey (Acts 14:23). This office was borrowed, though modified, from the Jewish synagogue, where a company of elders ruled the religious and civil life of the community. Primarily custodians of the Mosaic Law, these Jewish elders taught and interpreted its precepts and administered discipline to its offenders.

The New Testament also designates Christian elders by the name *episkopos* ("bishop," or "overseer"). Although sometimes disputed, the evidence strongly points to this identification. In Acts 20:17 Paul summons the elders of the church at Ephesus, while in verse 28 he calls these same men "overseers" (bishops). In Philippians 1:1 Paul extends formal greetings to all the Christians at Philippi, along with their bishops and deacons, but he takes no notice of elders. This omission is inexplicable unless overseers (bishops) and elders were the same. In 1 Timothy 3:1-13 Paul sets forth the qualifications of overseers. Yet he specifically mentions elders in 1 Timothy 5, where he ascribes to them the same functions of ruling and teaching that in the earlier passage are attributed to bishops (cf. 1 Tim. 3:4-5; 5:17). In Titus 1:5-6, after commanding Titus to appoint elders in all the churches in Crete, Paul counsels him to restrict his choice to men who are "blameless." He then qualifies this requirement by adding, "Since an overseer is entrusted with God's work, he must be blameless," a pointless argument if the two terms do not designate the same office (v. 7).

"Elder" and "bishop," then, are synonymous, but whereas "elder" indicates the great dignity surrounding this office, "bishop" signifies its function of rule or oversight. In the New Testament oversight is especially related to the figure of the shepherd, who feeds and cares for his flock. It is therefore natural that pastoral language is interwoven with the use of the terms *overseer* and *bishop* (Acts 20:28; cf. John 21:15-17). In their pastoral oversight of congregational life, elders reflect Christ's own office as the Shepherd and Bishop of souls (1 Pet. 2:25; cf. John 10:11-16; Heb. 13:20; 1 Pet. 5:4).

The comprehensive character of their office involved elders in a wide variety of duties. They engaged in the ministry of preaching and teaching the Word (1 Tim. 5:17). Moreover, there is no New Testament basis for distinguishing between "teaching" and "ruling" elders, as if they formed two separate classes. Elders also guarded the churches against false doctrine (Titus 1:9), rendered pastoral service (James 5:14), and administered ecclesiastical discipline. Their participation in the Jerusalem council along with the apostles (Acts 15:1-6) indicates that their authority, though essentially local, extended to the whole church. They are charged not to rule in lordly fashion, nor for financial gain, but they are to exercise their authority with humility (1 Pet. 5:1-5). It is likely that they conducted worship, although anyone in the congregation possessing a suitable gift of the Spirit might participate in the service (1 Cor. 14:26-33). Nothing is said in the New Testament about sacramental duties, but since the sacraments were closely tied both to the ministry of the Word and to worship (Matt. 28:19; Acts 2:41-42; 8:35-38; 20:7; 1 Cor. 11:17-22), it is possible that elders were largely responsible for their administration. Clement of Rome, writing near the end of the first century, says specifically that they officiated at the Eucharist. Local churches apparently appointed their own elders, who were then ordained by other elders in a solemn ceremony of laying on of hands (1 Tim. 4:14). Presumably the elders of the apostolic church were the equivalent of pastors today (although it appears that each local congregation had not one but a plurality of elders, who shared in the exercise of the responsibilities of the office). It is especially notable that the apostles Peter and John both refer to themselves by this title (1 Pet. 5:1; 2 John 1; 3 John 1).

Deacons

Forming a secondary order of ministry were the deacons (Phil. 1:1; 1 Tim. 3:8-13.). Not copied from any Jewish or Gentile prototype, the office of deacon (*diakonos*) was a wholly new creation of the Christian church. Its origin is frequently traced to the "seven," who were appointed to administer the distribution of welfare in the Jerusalem church (Acts 6:1-6). Nowhere are the seven called "deacons," although the word *diakonia* is used in this passage to contrast their ministry of serving tables with the apostles' ministry of the Word. Moreover, two of their number, Stephen and Philip, soon distinguished themselves as highly gifted preachers (Acts 6:8-10; 8:4-8; 21:8). While there is no evidence to link the seven with the deacons of Philippians and 1 Timothy, their appointment may have provided the basic pattern for the later office.

The specific functions of the deacons are clouded by nearly as much uncertainty as their origin, and their duties must be inferred from the nature of their qualifications. They were required to be of serious mind and character, honest in speech, temperate, and free from greed for money; they were to "hold the mystery of the faith with a clear conscience" (1 Tim. 3:8-9 RSV). This list of qualifications, together with the natural associations of the word _diakonia,_ meaning "service," suggests that household visitation and administration of local benevolence funds were among their responsibilities. At a later date this was certainly so. It is further known that in the post-apostolic church deacons served as personal assistants to the bishops in conducting worship, especially at the Eucharist, and in managing church affairs. It is possible from 1 Timothy 3:11 to infer that women also held this office, and Romans 16:1 describes Phoebe as a _diakonos_ of the church at Cenchrea. The masculine form of the noun may signify that it is a common noun, meaning "servant," and not an official title. In any event, deaconesses do not appear to have been common until the third century. The New Testament nowhere indicates the manner in which the deacons were appointed to office, but as in the case of the seven, they may have been chosen by the local congregation and ordained by the laying on of hands.

In view of New Testament evidence, there seems to be no reasonable doubt that the apostolic church had only two official orders of local ministry: presbyter-bishop and deacon. The ministry exercised by these orders assumed three forms: Word, rule, and service. To this threefold ministry the body of Christ, equipped and empowered by his indwelling Spirit, is unceasingly summoned by its living Head.

Richard A. Bodey[14]

189 • WOMEN IN WORSHIP LEADERSHIP IN BIBLICAL TIMES

Women appear at critical times in the life of their worship communities. Acting as prayer leaders, prophetesses, sages, or apostles, they perform deeds that embody the spirit and life of their community. To read their stories is to discover how this people experienced God and lived in fidelity to that relationship. Their communities remembered them and retold their stories, giving them honored place in the community's oral and written memory. Their leadership continues to be handed on to renew life and spirit in communities faithful to their tradition. The importance of women in the worship life of biblical times may be seen in the stories of Miriam, Huldah, and the woman who anointed Jesus, as well as in the biblical personification of wisdom as a woman.

Miriam, Leader of Thanksgiving and Worship

In Exodus 20:15-21, at a sanctuary in the wilderness, Miriam leads the people of Israel in a celebration of the miraculous act that formed them. They had been slaves in Egypt and no people at all. Now, at Yahweh's hand, they had come through the deathly waters of the sea to life as a united people.

Miriam takes up the timbrel, a tambourinelike percussion instrument, and begins a dance and song of thanksgiving and victory. The women follow her, dancing and chanting, "Sing to Yahweh, gloriously triumphant! Horse and rider is cast into the sea!" Her shout becomes their refrain. Her movements and instrument imitate the actions and sounds of Yahweh in the winds and the sea, parting the waters and swallowing the Egyptians. She plays the part of the victorious divine warrior, Yahweh, the One who has saved Israel, the One who is alone among the gods, "magnificent in holiness," making known his presence in Israel's midst.

Such dramatic thanksgiving feasts became the very hallmark of Israel's covenant life with Yahweh. Miriam's song was like the psalms families later sang at Passover in homes and villages, like those that priests and all the people sang when they gathered for great pilgrimage feasts in the courts of the temple. In the ritual sharing of song, food, and life, young Israel, weary of what seemed to be an endless journey in harsh lands and battling unwelcoming peoples, remembered and renewed the covenant with Yahweh and their bonds as a people.

In a speech indicting the people for their faithlessness, Micah the prophet remembers Miriam, with Moses and Aaron, as a leader of the wilderness community, and associates her leadership with divine commissioning (Mic. 6:2-5). Like Moses and Aaron before the days of the temple and priesthood in Israel, Miriam served as leader of the community at prayer, expressing their faith that Yahweh had saved them and continued to be with them.

Huldah, Prophet and Interpreter of Yahweh's Word

Later in Israel's story, kings came to rule and represent Yahweh's leadership among them. They became the leaders of worship, calling all Israel together to renew the covenant by reciting, singing, and dancing Yahweh's deeds. In establishing their rule, Israel's kings made alliances with neighboring rulers, sometimes through marriage and sometimes by taking in foreign "gods" and customs. Solomon and kings following him established heavy taxes and large armies to support cities and temples. Gradually they rendered the rural villagers poor, subject to the international economy of the great city Jerusalem. It was then that prophets emerged, in court and village, to recall covenant relationships among the people and with Yahweh and to call those in power, even kings, to reform and fidelity.

When Josiah was king of Judah, his ministers found a book that told of the covenant in the temple. Was this book true to Yahweh? What did it mean for Josiah and the people? Josiah sent his ministers to Huldah, who, by her credentials, was probably a prophet active in his court and well known among the people.

Huldah spoke with authority. The book was true for Judah that very day. The people had turned to other gods and forsaken Yahweh. Yahweh's anger would blaze against them. And it did, as Josiah burned the sanctuaries of Judah and tried to purify the Jerusalem temple and center Israel's worship there among a reunited people.

Josiah heard Yahweh's word through Huldah and, in heartfelt repentance, acted to restore relationships among people and with Yahweh. The word of Yahweh was alive; Huldah had proclaimed Yahweh's deeds and called king and people to reform, renewing the covenant in their relationships. Yahweh honored Josiah's courageous leadership, and although the king died in battle at the hand of an Egyptian king, his eyes did not witness the sad march to Babylon, as Huldah had also foretold.

Woman Wisdom, Rebuilding the House of Israel

Wisdom had always been a part of Israel's experience of Yahweh. The wise were regarded as Yahweh's messengers, showing by their lives and teaching the Yahweh-fearing way to live as member of family, clan, and covenant people. In "winged word," (proverbial sayings that were easy to remember) sages captured the experience of Israel's faith in action. These proverbs provided models, or morals and cues for action, rooted in the past to renew and shape life in the present.

As Israel returned from exile without the strong national leadership of king and temple, wisdom in daily work—making families and rebuilding homes and villages—was needed more than ever. Israel had lost land and people. Women assumed a larger share in generating family life and managing households and fields. Their wisdom in refashioning home life, households, and communities came to be recognized as the word and work of Yahweh among them. Perhaps in recognition of women's importance and increased contribution to Israel's life, this wisdom was even embodied and personified in the female figure of woman Wisdom.

Wisdom was she who, begotten and "given birth" from Yahweh, played before him in the creation of the world and took special delight in human deeds and relationships (Prov. 8:22-31). She spoke with the voice of Yahweh, calling from the gates of the city into the home. She called to all who would listen. Her word was to forsake foolish, foreign, and unfaithful alliances, to come to her table and feast on her food and wine, and there to be filled with her wisdom and knowledge, the fear of the Lord, which characterized the covenant way of old.

Inviting people to find Yahweh in daily experience; in faithful human relationships between husband and wife, children and parents; in family life and public service, she was rebuilding the house of Israel. Wisdom again became the pattern of life, recognized among the people as the "order" in creation itself. Later wisdom writings identified her with Torah (Sirach, 190 B.C.). In the earlier poems of Proverbs 1–9 and Proverbs 31:10-31, Wisdom and her counterpart of the faithful wife, speaks in the very "I am" voice of Yahweh and is hymned by husband, family, and people for bearing the very life-giving qualities of Yahweh, the qualities women and men needed to reclaim their life as family and people. In this way woman Wisdom embodied the very life of Israel and came to prominence in the rebuilding of Israel as a godly people.

——— Mary, the Anointing Woman ———

The community for which Mark wrote understood themselves as Jews who were called to become a new community, bearing "good news" intended to include Gentiles and to reach the whole world as well. The gospel proclamation of Mark's community is a narrative of the great trial of Jesus and the disciples. Their story is one of struggle to accept a suffering Messiah and to accept their own suffering as the way of discipleship and life in the new community of Jesus, the Christ.

After Rome destroyed the temple and Jerusalem, these Christians were no longer welcome in the synagogues as the Jews struggled to unite and survive. Following Jesus meant leaving family members and official Judaism, the family of their faith. It meant enduring betrayal as Jesus had, welcoming strangers and Gentiles as Jesus did, and finding in this struggling community of believers new family and kin.

During Jesus' trial the Jewish high priest had asked, "Are you the Christ, the Son of the Blessed One?" Jesus had acknowledged his identity with God and had confessed, "I am" (Mark 14:61-62). In the same way, disciples faced questioning by members of their own community and betrayal and suffering as they followed Jesus.

The story of this trial begins with a scene in which Jesus was at the table among friends (Mark 14:3-10). An unidentified woman came carrying an alabaster jar of expensive aromatic perfume. She broke the jar and began to pour the perfume on his head. In Israel of old, such an outpouring of oil on the head was an act of anointing, the deed by which a prophet recognized and proclaimed a new king for Israel. It was the act by which the Spirit was outpoured, filling God's servant, the king. When the woman's action was criticized by some at the table, Jesus defended her, identified her deed with preparation for his burial, and solemnly announced that wherever the Good News was proclaimed throughout the world, what she had done would be told in her memory (Mark 14:9).

The anointing woman's deed was questioned by some who were at the table, members of her own community. Those at the table were divided. As the author tells it, Jesus himself interpreted her deed.

Her anointing embodies both recognition and proclamation. She is the disciple, the one who recognizes this suffering servant-king, the One sent by God, and bears this as good news to others. Jesus continues to be present in the community in its telling of the gospel and in the kinship of his suffering. By her deed the woman shows who an apostle is and what an apostle does.

In John's Gospel and for John's community, Jesus is the one in whom God dwells fully in human flesh and who makes life, the life of self-giving love that is God's, known. In John's Gospel, as Jesus' public ministry is ending and the "hour" of his glory begins, a woman anoints Jesus at the table (John 12:1-11). The woman is identified as Mary, the sister of Martha and Lazarus, a family "loved" by Jesus (John 11:5). Jesus has raised Lazarus in "the village of Mary and her sister Martha," and as his "hour" is beginning, Jesus is the honored guest at their table again. Martha is serving the meal, and Lazarus is among those at the table. Mary anoints Jesus' feet with a pound of perfume of genuine aromatic nard, then dries his feet with her hair. The whole house is filled with the ointment's fragrance, the perfume of her deed.

The extravagance, faithfulness, and hospitality of her deed are contrasted with the response of Judas, who questions her action and suggests that the ointment ought rather to be sold and the profit given to the poor. He is keeper of the common purse, and we are told that he used to help himself to what was deposited there (John 12:6). Jesus himself answers Judas and defends Mary's action, relating it to the death to which he is about to give himself.

Mary's deed is cast in eucharistic overtones. The anointing and then drying calls attention to her act. Jesus himself is soon to perform a similar act. In the Gospel of John the account of the Eucharist is supplanted by Jesus' washing of the disciples' feet (John 13:1-20). He tells them this is an example for them of the love they are to have for one another. It is the act of one laying down his life for his friends, as he does in his death and resurrection. This is the service of love by which others will recognize them as his disciples.

This action by Jesus helps to interpret further Mary's service to him and puts it in even greater contrast with Judas's self-serving attitude. Jesus concludes his discussion of washing the feet of the disciples with the solemn assurance that what he has done they must do: "Now that you know these things, you will be blessed if you do them" (John 13:17).

Beatitude, blessing, and discipleship are bound with doing as Jesus does. The anointing woman, Mary, gives herself bodily in a simple act of love that foreshadows Jesus' own self-giving. That the fragrance of the ointment filled the whole house suggests that her deed carries the possibility of bringing others to "come and see" and to recognize Jesus for themselves. Her deed of loving service speaks louder than words. She embodies the meaning of discipleship and, in so doing, bears life for her community.

─────────── **Conclusion** ───────────

Examining the deeds of these women in the context of their community's life and ministry shows them to be leaders of faith in groups that struggled to live their faith. Miriam, Huldah, woman Wisdom, and Mary, by their deeds even more than by their words, manifest God's life and love and what relationship with God means. Thankful prayer, prophetic proclamation, home-building wisdom, and public service in the face of criticism are the daily ways these women lived their faith and led others to it. While their acts were in some cases questioned, the written record of their deeds tells us that in their communities their service was beloved, public, and indeed divinely commissioned and inspired, if not officially recognized or appreciated. Their faith continues to invite men and women to communities that bear the good news of God's love to the world.

Susan E. Hames

190 ◆ BIBLIOGRAPHY: WOMEN IN WORSHIP LEADERSHIP

Brown, Raymond. *The Community of the Beloved Disciple: The Life, Loves and Hates of an Individual Church in New Testament Times*. New York: Paulist Press, 1979. Brown examines the Johannine gospel and letters, showing how conflicts among disciples of different (Hellenic, Samaritan and Jewish) cultural backgrounds, between men and women leaders, and between this community and the apostolic churches express and shape discipleship in this "beloved" community of Christians.

Brueggeman, Walter. *Israel's Praise*. Philadelphia: Forcress Press, 1989. Brueggeman shows how Israel's psalms and worship emerged from, expressed, and shaped its world view and way of life as a people of God and how they also become a critical and prophetic challenge to Israel's leaders when they abuse nature and oppress human beings.

──────. *The Prophetic Imagination*. Philadelphia: Forcress Press, 1978. Drawing on Hebrew prophets, this study articulates the critical vision and action that religious people must bring to society and religion today: to denounce social patterns and relationships which demean God, nature, human beings, and communities and to announce and embrace God's desire and compassion, which include all.

Camp, Claudia. "Female Voice, Written Word: Women and Authority in Hebrew Scripture" in Paula Cooey, Sharon Farmer, and Mary Ellen Ross (eds.), *Embodied Love: Sensuality and Relationship As Feminist Values*. San Francisco: Harper and Row, 1989. This essay examines the stories of Huldah, Esther, and the woman Wisdom, showing how they are authorized, recognized, and remembered by their own communities as God's spokespersons. In crisis moments they each embody God's word and will, bringing life and good to their people.

──────. *Wisdom and the Feminine in the Book of Proverbs*. Detroit: Almond Press, 1985. How does a female figure come to personify the divine in Israel? The author examines the social, historical, literary, and religious experiences which give rise to the woman Wisdom who speaks for God in postexilic Israel. This study is suggestive for understanding later Christian interpretations of Jesus as well.

Procter-Smith, Marjorie. *In Her Own Rite: Creating Women's Liturgical Traditions*. Nashville: Abingdon Press, 1990. According to this author, women's emerging ritual and spirituality, as exemplified by the bold spirit of the woman who anointed Jesus, are characterized by imaging God from women's experiences; by honoring nature, human bodies, and senses; and by attending to the languages of gesture, space, movement, and place. This study challenges contemporary liturgical renewal in Christian churches to incorporate these same values.

Schneiders, Sandra M. *Women and the Word*. New York: Paulist Press, 1986. In brief essay form, Schneiders examines two central, critical problems for women's spirituality: the gender of God and the maleness of Jesus. She asserts that reclaiming the many and varied names and images for God in the Hebrew and Christian Scriptures and the critique of patriarchal religion and society by Jesus and the prophets are necessary to allow God to be God for women and men today.

Winter, Miriam Therese. *Woman Prayer, Woman Song: Resources for Ritual—(1989); Woman Word: A Feminist Lectionary and Psalter—Women of the New Testament (1990); Woman Wisdom: A Feminist Lectionary and Psalter—Women of the Hebrew Scriptures, Part I (1991); WomanWitness: A Feminist Lectionary and Psalter—Women of the Hebrew Scriptures, Part II (1992) (New York: Crossroad).* These four volumes are beautifully illustrated by Meinrad Craighead and are intended for use in all denominations. They name biblical women and retell their stories in ways that help ordinary readers to focus on their own. With questions for reflection, and suggestions for services and prayers, they are rich ritual resources for celebrating the experiences of both biblical and contemporary women.

PART THREE

Festivals in Biblical Worship

SEVENTEEN

The Meaning of Feasts in the Biblical Tradition

The feasts of Israelite and Jewish worship, like those in other religious traditions, were occasions on which worshipers might transcend the shortcomings of ordinary life. The festivals served as "windows" into a higher order of hope and positive values. In Israel the agricultural feasts took on added meaning as celebrations of the Lord's historic acts of blessing and deliverance and as tokens of the covenant.

191 • AN INTRODUCTION TO JEWISH FEASTS

A feast is a sign of the divine in history. Israel celebrated three kinds of feasts: pilgrimage feasts, solemn or repentance feasts, and lesser feasts not mandated by the Torah. All of these commemorated God's action in the life and history of the community.

Like all peoples and all religions, Israel introduces rhythms into the cycle of time by means of recurring feasts. These include feasts in the full and proper sense, the "pilgrimage feasts" (*pesah, shavu'ot,* and *sukkot*), the solemn, that is, sober or austere feasts (*ro'sh hashshanah* and *yom kippur*), and the lesser feasts (*hanukkah* and *purim*).

The differences between the three kinds of feasts are in their degree of theological density or weight. The pilgrimage feasts (the only ones that merit the appelation *hag,* "feast") celebrate and actualize the great three-fold saving event in Israel's history: the Exodus, the Mosaic covenant, and the entrance into the Promised Land. They are therefore the most important of all the feasts; they are called "pilgrimage" (*regalim*) feasts because in biblical times they were marked by a great influx of visitors to the temple in Jerusalem, the Holy City.

The "austere" feasts celebrate not the divine event but the human outcome of freedom's failure; they recall the infidelity of human beings in response to God's faithfulness, and they are days of great repentance and profound conversion. They are "austere" because the prevailing mood is not joy but a critical facing up to self and to God.

The lesser feasts are so called because they are not commanded by the Torah and are concerned with secondary events of Jewish history. Though enriched with a variety of elements, chiefly folkloristic and popular, they cannot be put on the same level as the first two types that provide the structure of the Jewish liturgical year.

A feast is a sign of the divine initiative in history; it is a "word" that rescues history from its failures and allows us to glimpse luminous meaning through, and beyond, the absurdity and monotony of historical time. Some authors make a richly meaningful suggestion regarding the origin of the word *feast:* they say it derives from *phainomai,* a Greek verb meaning "to show oneself" or "to appear," for a feast allows a new horizon of values and meanings to manifest itself, without which life and hope would become impossible. Jewish feasts have the same function as feasts everywhere, but they have a different, more explicit and radical meaning in light of the religious experience this people has had of the God of the Exodus and the covenant.

192 • THE PURPOSE OF JEWISH FEASTS

A feast celebrates the positive character of existence. In the face of evil and pain, feasts proclaim the goodness of creation and the freedom to enjoy the world because God made it.

A feast is a statement that the world is a good place because human beings can enjoy it and because God made it. Unwittingly, and prior to any reflection on the point, the celebrants of a feast relate their activity to independent but interrelated poles: human beings, the world, and God—human beings as subjects who are good, the world as an object that is good, and the divinity as the foundation of the two goodnesses. A feast brings out the fact that the world is good and human beings can dwell in it as their native place *because* it is willed by and founded on the sacred. Here is the heart and secret of every feast; in the celebration of a feast we reappropriate, beyond and despite appearance, the positive character of existence as a space filled with fruition and making.

Feasts as Rejection of the Negative

As an interpretation of meaning, a feast can be seen as having three moments or phases. First, it is a rejection of negativity and death. The lives of individuals and groups are marked by pain and privation, poverty and injustices, violence and absurdity. Instead of displaying the original harmony, life seems to be under a constant threat that frustrates all efforts and undertakings. Instead of being drawn by a beneficent *telos* (purpose), it seems driven by a maleficent demon that has donned the hands and eyes of *thanatos,* or death. A feast represents a suspension of this entire order of things, a profession of faith that this world, in its present form, is not the true world (*kosmos*) but is negation (*chaos*) or counterfeit; it is not a home for human beings but an unrewarding wilderness. A feast challenges the primacy of evil and its claim to be ultimate reality; it is a rebellion against evil's perverse power and its claim to have the final say; it is a sign—that turns into a certainty—that evil can be dethroned and overcome. Therefore feasts are the greatest wealth of a people, especially the poorest among them, for feasts with their myths and rites preserve in concentrated form the most fruitful seeds of hope and struggle that human history contains. As long as people are able to celebrate feasts, they will also be capable of life and commitment.

Feasts as Rejoicing and Sharing

Second, a feast asserts the quality of life and defines its positive side. But what is this "quality" that a feast expresses, not conceptually but in a concrete, corporeal way? Many terms are used to describe this quality, but one seems especially important: *you.* "You shall rejoice in your feast" (Deut. 16:14 NASB). But the rejoicing here is something other than what is usually understood by the term in our affluent societies. The passage in Deuteronomy continues: ". . . you and your son and your daughter and your male and female servants and the Levite and the stranger and the orphan and the widow who are in your towns." Rabbi Elie Munk comments on this passage as follows:

> People should eat meat and drink wine, because it is these things especially that contribute to their gladness. But when we eat and drink, it is our duty to provide the necessities for the foreigner, the widow, and the orphan, that is, for all who are in need. Those who double-lock their doors and eat only with their own families, without helping the unfortunate, will not experience the joy of the *mitzvah* but "only the satisfaction given by their meal." This is why the prophet Hosea [Hos. 9:4 RSV] says: "They shall not please him with their sacrifices. Their bread shall be like mourners' bread; all who eat of it shall be defiled; for their bread shall be for their hunger only." (E. Munk, *Le monde des prières* [1970], 295)

This passage summarizes the two basic aspects of the joy a feast proclaims and bestows: the enjoyment of things ("eating and drinking") and fraternal sharing ("providing the necessities for the foreigner"). Instead of understanding joy in a purely psychological or pseudospiritual way, a feast emphasizes its corporeal element and its necessary connection with the fruits of the earth; instead of making this joy something self-centered, a feast asserts its comprehensive and nonexclusive character. True joy is born of two encounters: with the fruits of the earth and with our brothers and sisters. Where one of these two is missing, a feast changes from being an end to being a means; it ceases to be an expression of life and becomes a means of obtaining satisfaction. The joy proper to feast is in reality the plenitude of being that is in harmony with the things of this world and with this world's inhabitants; it is the fruit produced by a recovered Eden, in which the original Adam and Eve, representatives of men and women of every age, live reconciled with each other, with the garden, and with God.

Feasts As Affirmation of a Higher Order

The third and most important aspect of a feast is that it is an assertion of that which is the ontological foundation of the goodness and meaning of the human person. Are the rebellion against the power of evil and the proclamation of the victory of the positive over the negative simply an expression of impotent and deceptive desire, or are they an echo of the truth that conquers falsehood and triumphs over self-deception? A feast reveals its full depth when understood as the assertion of the second alternative: human life has meaning, beyond all its historical failures and despite all its privations, not because it is subjectively given meaning by each individual, but because it is objectively founded by and on the sacred.

A feast thus asserts the existence of meaning and at the same time sets the conditions for the attainment of this meaning, meaning that grows and flourishes because it is located within a different horizon—the horizon of the divine, the sacred—which transcends that of the profane. By means of its mythical narratives and reactualizing rites, a feast calls to mind and makes present again this foundational root; by returning to this root, human behavior overcomes fragmentation, conquering *chaos* and recovering *kosmos,* that is, order, strength, motivation, the human ideal. A feast indeed abolishes the established order (we need think only of the violations of standard norms that are to be seen in every feast), but it does so not for the sake of libertinism and chaos but in obedience to a higher order that is closer and more faithful to the divine intention. A feast overturns the world and re-creates it according to the divine model.

193 • THE CHARACTER OF JEWISH FEASTS

The three major Jewish feasts are associated with three annual harvests; historically each involved the return of a portion of the harvest to the Lord. These offerings symbolized the reasons for the feast itself: God is the source of the fruits of the earth; God's gifts of produce are for the sustenance and comfort of the people; and because God gives freely, the worshipers must do the same, sharing their benefits with the needy.

The three principal Jewish feasts (Passover, Pentecost, and Booths) had an agricultural origin, and their meaning as such did not differ greatly from the meaning of "feast" as just described. The three feasts were connected with the most important harvests in the three productive seasons of the year, and they expressed the deep joy of a people that was led and nourished by its God. Passover celebrated the barley harvest in the spring, Pentecost the wheat harvest in the summer, and Booths the fruit harvest in the fall. In keeping with an almost universally known and attested religious custom, the heart of each feast consisted in the offering of part of the harvest to the divinity. The book of Deuteronomy makes explicit reference to this practice in the cases of Pentecost and Booths, two feasts that, unlike Passover, which has been reread and historicized to a greater degree, allow us to glimpse their original agricultural basis:

> Celebrate the Feast of Weeks [Pentecost] to the LORD your God by giving a freewill offering in proportion to the blessings the LORD your God has given you. . . . Celebrate the Feast of Tabernacles for seven days after you have gathered the produce of your threshing floor and your winepress. . . . No man should appear before the LORD empty-handed: Each of you must bring a gift in proportion to the way the LORD your God has blessed you. (Deut. 16:10, 13, 16-17)

What is the meaning of such an offering, which is both the expression and the basis of feasts and their joy? To offer God the produce of the earth is not an act of self-deprivation (renouncing something in order to give it to God) but is an act of self-definition and acknowledgment that the fruits of the earth belong to the Lord and that human beings may use them only as his beneficiaries. This simple action sums up in a symbolic way three basic concepts and attitudes: (1) the produce gathered belongs to God, who is its master and owner; (2) the produce is given as a gift to meet the needs of and to comfort humans; and (3) the fruits of the earth are to be enjoyed not according to the logic of possession and hoarding but according to the divine intention that brings them into existence.

When Israel offered to the Lord part of its harvests in the three important seasons of the year, it was reaffirming this pattern of conviction and choice. Israel professed its belief that the "bread" and "wine" of the Promised Land were not the result of the people's efforts or of magical practices, but were due to the creative good will of God; and Israel renewed its commitment to share these things with others. This accounts for the biblical insistence that on these festival days no one should be in want but all should have and fully enjoy: "Be joyful at your Feast—you, your sons and daughters, your menservants and maidservants, and the Levites, the aliens, the fatherless and the widows who live in your towns" (Deut. 16:14). This emphasis on feeding the poor reflects a theological rather than a sociological concern: God intends the fruits of the earth for the enjoyment of all; if the poor as well as the rich enjoy them, God's reign is being brought to pass, and his will is being fulfilled in a concrete way.

Sharing the fruits of the earth is not simply an imperative of social ethics, but is the very heart of the theological directive: "Love the LORD your God with all your heart and with all your soul and with all your strength" (Deut. 6:5); here, to "love the LORD" means to obey his will by accepting and doing it within history.

The sacrifice of animals, which had a privileged place in the worship offered in the Jerusalem temple, had at bottom the same twofold meaning as the offering of firstfruits: it was an acknowledgment of God's lordship over the animal world and a readiness to take nourishment from that world in a spirit of sharing and not of hoarding, that is, as gifts intended for all and not as a privilege of a few.

Israel derived the three agricultural feasts from the surrounding Semitic world. However, it did not make them its own in a purely passive way; it turned them into original creations by enriching them with its own specific spiritual outlook. The name usually given to this process of reinterpretation is "historicization." By this is meant that the focus of the feast was shifted from events of the natural world to special historical events: the deliverance from Egypt in the Feast of Passover, the gift of the Torah in the Feast of Pentecost, and the enjoyment of the Torah's fruits in the Feast of Booths.

It is true that Israel "historicized" the agricultural feasts. It is necessary, however, to understand this process correctly: the process took the form not of contrasting the new with the old or ignoring the old, but of further explaining the original meaning and reaching down to its root.

The central event of Jewish history is the Exodus from slavery in Egypt, a single action with three stages: departure from Egypt, gift of the Torah (or covenant), and entrance into the Promised Land. Israel was liberated from slavery and brought into the "good and spacious land" of Canaan, but the entrance was neither automatic nor taken for granted, for between departure and entrance was Mount Sinai, the place of covenant where the Torah was offered and accepted. Here is the epicenter and secret of all Jewish history and Jewish originality: the discovery that the land, their own land, would produce "milk and honey" in abundance (Exod. 3:8, 17; Num. 13:27; Deut. 6:3; 11:9), not spontaneously, however, but only if and to the extent that Israel would be faithful to the covenant. This connection between the fertility of the soil and obedience to the Torah is clearly expressed in Leviticus 26:3-6, which is bewildering because the fruits of which it speaks are not the fruits of some special world but the normal produce of the trees of any part of our world. Yet if these fruits are truly to bring joy to all and become a sign of communion instead of destruction, a precise, divine condition must be met: they must be cultivated and eaten according to the logic of the covenant, that is, Jews must acknowledge them to be gifts and must consent to their universal destination.

This "historicity" is peculiar to the Jewish situation, but clearly it does not contradict the meaning of "feast"; rather, it further clarifies that meaning by getting to the root of one of its fundamental aspects. When early human beings offered God part of their seasonal produce, they were recognizing his fatherhood and accepting the produce as his gift. Israel accepted this logic but had a better grasp of its dynamic and its requirement. It realized that if the fruits of the earth are truly to be a gift and a blessing, it is not enough simply to accept them; rather they must be shared through a way of life based on justice and responsibility. Justice and the fruitfulness of the land are partners in an "indissoluble marriage" in which the two shed light on one another. Israel's originality lies in its having transcended a purely "natural" view of nature and having connected the abundance of the land's fruits with its own free choices.

Carmine Di Sante[15]

EIGHTEEN

Festivals of Israel

Observance of the sacred seasons and Jewish religious festivals constituted a significant aspect of the Hebrew religion. These holy days and sacred seasons were decreed by God as his gifts to Israel. God purposed to preserve by them a remembrance of such sacred events as their divine election and deliverance (the Passover celebration), their sojourn in the wilderness (Feast of Tabernacles), their constant dependence on him for all temporal blessings and prosperity (Pentecost), their preservation from Persia (Feast of Purim), and their need of cleansing and forgiveness (Day of Atonement). Many other spiritual lessons and blessings were also to be derived from the numerous festivals and holy days such as the Sabbath, new moons, Year of Jubilee, and the like. Hence, the sacred seasons were based in large measure on particular significant historical events related to the national or religious life of Israel. Furthermore, like the temple and the Scriptures, the national religious festivals were important bonds of spiritual and national unity for the Hebrew people.

194 • SABBATH AND SABBATICAL SEASONS

The word sabbath means a time of rest. In Israelite and Jewish religion, times of rest are the weekly Sabbath, the monthly new moon, the sabbatical year, the Year of Jubilee, and special festal Sabbaths. Sabbaths were times of release from the economic bondage of heavy work or constant indebtedness; they were declarations that the needs of the people were supplied not by their labor but by the Lord.

———— Weekly Sabbath ————

In addition to the annual festivals, the celebration of the weekly Sabbath (*shabbat*) and the sabbatical feast days are also called "holy convocations" (*miqra'ei qodesh*) in Leviticus 23:2-4 (NASB). During the wilderness wanderings a holy convocation was a religious assembly of all males at the tabernacle. After Hebrew settlement in Palestine, however, the universal command to appear at the sanctuary had reference only in regard to the three festival pilgrimages in which all males were to attend the Feasts of Passover, Pentecost, and Tabernacles at Jerusalem (Exod. 23:14-17; Deut. 16:16). The holy convocation commanded for the weekly Sabbath was to be observed where the people lived.

Origin. The Creation narrative in Genesis concludes with an account of the hallowing of the seventh day by God, who rested from all his creative activity on that day. Although the term *Sabbath* does not occur in this account, its verbal root, *shabat,* meaning "he rested or ceased," is used (Gen. 2:3). The Decalogue, in Exodus 20:8-11, ties Sabbath observance to the fact that God rested on this day after six days of creative work. Although there is no distinct mention of the observance in Genesis, some scholars hold that Moses treats it as an institution already familiar to the Hebrews. The words, "Remember the Sabbath day by keeping it holy" (Exod. 20:8) point to this conclusion. Furthermore, a seven-day period is referred to in Genesis (cf. Gen 1:1–2:3; 7:4-10; 8:10-12; 29:27-28).

The first definite mention of the Sabbath as a religious institution is found in Exodus 16:21-30 in connection with the giving of manna. God commanded Israel in the wilderness to begin observing the seventh day as a Sabbath of rest from all labor by gathering a double portion of manna on the sixth day. That the day was already known to them is supported by the Lord's rebuke to those who disobeyed: "How long will you refuse to keep my commands and my instructions?" (Exod. 16:28). A short time later the observance was enjoined as the fourth commandment at Sinai (Exod. 20:8-11).

Modern critical scholars assign the origin of the

Sabbath to two different sources, which on the surface appear to disagree. Exodus 20:11, it is argued, makes the Sabbath a memorial of God's rest upon the completion of Creation, whereas Deuteronomy 5:15 states that the Sabbath is a memorial of the deliverance of Israel from Egypt. However, this view ignores the context of Deuteronomy. The Sabbath was to be a perpetual covenant between God and Israel as his gift of refreshing rest; as such it served as a memorial of his rest from creative activity and was not specifically a memorial of the Exodus. The reference to the Exodus event in Deuteronomy expressly reminds Israel that out of gratitude for their freedom and rest after a long period of servile labor, they ought also to allow rest for their servants, who were now slaves as the Israelites had been in Egypt (cf. Exod. 5:14-15). Thus both passages connect the Sabbath with rest.

Some scholars have drawn parallels between the Babylonian *shabbatu* and the Hebrew Sabbath, but no such relationship can be drawn from available evidence. Furthermore, Ezekiel 20:12, 20 indicates that the Sabbaths were signs God gave to Israel to distinguish her from other nations.

Character and Observance. The Sabbath was to be observed by abstaining from all physical labor done by man or beast. But the Sabbath was not intended for selfish use in idleness; it was a divinely given opportunity, in freedom from one's secular labors, to strengthen and refresh the whole person, physically and spiritually. The Sabbath had a benevolent design and was intended as a blessing, not a burden, to humankind (cf. Deut. 5:14-15; Isa. 58:13-14; Mark 2:27). Sabbath legislation is found in several Old Testament passages (Exod. 16:23-30; 20:8-11; 31:12-17; Lev. 19:3, 30; Num. 15:32-36; Deut. 5:12-15).

Monthly New Moon

The first day of each month was designated as *ro'sh ḥodesh,* "the first or head of the month," or simply as *ḥodesh,* "new moon" (Num. 10:10; 1 Sam. 20:5). Unlike the new moon of the seventh month, which was the first day of the civil new year and was celebrated with a great festival, the regular monthly new moons were subordinate feast days celebrated with additional burnt offerings (Num. 28:11-15), the blowing of trumpets (Num. 10:10; Ps. 81:3), family feasts (1 Sam. 20:5), spiritual edification (2 Kings 4:23), and family sacrifices (1 Sam. 20:6). As on all sabbatical feast days, servile work ceased, except

the necessary preparation of food (cf. Exod. 12:16). The new moon and Sabbath are closely related in several passages (Isa. 1:13; Ezek. 46:1; Hos. 2:11; Amos 8:5).

The moon occupied an important place in the life of the Hebrews, since it was the guide to their calendar, which was based on the lunar month or period of the moon's circuit. Because of this, and the importance of the uniform celebration of the various periodic religious festivals by Jews everywhere, it was extremely important to determine the exact time of the appearance of the new moon. Thus the appearance of the smallest crescent signified the beginning of a new month and was announced with the blowing of the *shofar,* or ram's horn.

Sabbatical Year

The *shenat shabbaton,* "year of rest," or sabbatical year, like the weekly Sabbath, was designed by God with a benevolent purpose in view. Every seventh year debts were to be cancelled and the land was to lie fallow, the uncultivated increase to be left to the poor Israelites.

Observance. According to 2 Chronicles 36:21, observance of the sabbatical year had been neglected for about five hundred years, the seventy-year captivity allowing the land to enjoy its neglected Sabbaths, "for as long as it lay desolate it kept Sabbath, to fulfill three-score and ten years" (2 Chron. 36:21, ASV). After the captivity, the people under Nehemiah bound themselves to the faithful observance of the seventh year, covenanting that "we would forego the seventh year, and the exaction of every debt" (Neh. 10:31, ASV). Its observance continued during the intertestamental period (1 Macc. 6:48-53) and later (Josephus [*Antiquities*] xiv. 10.6).

Purpose. (1) The sabbatical year was rest for the land (Lev. 25:1-7). After the land had been sown and harvested for six successive years it was "to rest," or remain fallow, on the seventh year. This included the vineyards and olive yards (Exod. 23:10). This provision ensured greater productivity for the soil by the periodic interruption of the incessant sowing, plowing, and reaping. (2) The sabbatical year was to provide food for the poor. During this year, that which grew of itself in the fields, vineyards, and olive yards was not to be harvested but left so that "the poor among your people may get food from it, and the wild animals may eat what they leave" (Exod. 23:10-11). Leviticus 25:6-7 includes the owner, his or her servant, the sojourner, cattle, and beasts, as well as the poor of Exodus 23:11, as those eligible to consume the natural produce of the sabbatical year. (3) Debts were to be cancelled in the sabbatical year (Deut. 15:1-6). Each creditor was to cancel the debts of another Israelite at the end of every seven years, for it was called also "the year of release" (Deut. 15:9; 31:10, RSV). This did not apply to a foreigner, from whom the debt could be collected (Deut. 15:3). The release occurred so that absolute poverty and permanent indebtedness would not exist among the Israelites. In addition, they were not to disregard the needs of their poorer brothers and sisters by refusing to lend merely because the year of release was near (Deut. 15:7-11). (4) In the sabbatical year the Law was to be read for the instruction of the people at the Feast of Tabernacles (Deut. 31:10-13). (5) Not only during the sabbatical year, but also at the close of any six-year period, those Israelites who, because of poverty, had made themselves bond servants to their brethren were to be released (Deut. 15:12-18). In this case the year of release would be ascertained from the first year of indenture. The legislation respecting the sabbatical year was confined to the Israelites in the Holy Land and went into effect upon their arrival there (Lev. 25:2).

Year of Jubilee

Seven sabbatical cycles of years (that is, forty-nine) terminated in the Year of Jubilee (*Sheʿnat Hayyovel*), literally, "the year of the ram's horn." Thus, the arrival of the fiftieth year was designated by sounding the ram's horn (*yovel*) (Lev. 25:8-17). The fiftieth year is called "the year of liberty" (*Sheʿnat haddeʿror*) (Ezek. 46:17; cf. Jer. 34:8, 15, 17) on the basis of Leviticus 25:10: "Consecrate the fiftieth year and proclaim liberty throughout the land. . . . It shall be a jubilee for you" (Lev. 25:10).

Nature of the Celebration. According to Leviticus 25:9, the Year of Jubilee was announced by the sounding of rams' horns throughout the land on the tenth day of the seventh month, which was also the great Day of Atonement. The Year of Jubilee was not, as some have thought, the forty-ninth year, and thus simply a seventh sabbatical year, but was, as Leviticus 25:10 states, the fiftieth year, thus providing two successive sabbatical years in which the land would have rest. Certain regulations were issued to take effect during the Year of Jubilee. (1) The Year of Jubilee was to be a rest for the land. As in the preceding sabbatical year, the land was to remain uncultivated and the people were to eat of the natural increase (Lev. 25:11-12). To compensate for this, God promised: "I will send you such a blessing in the sixth year that the land will yield enough for three years" (Lev. 25:21). In addition, other sources of provision were available, such as hunting, fishing, flocks, herds, bees, and the like. (2) Hereditary lands and property were to be restored to the original family, without compensation, in the Year of Jubilee (Lev. 25:23-34). In this manner all the land and its improvements would eventually be restored to the original holders to whom God had given it, for he said, "The land must not be sold permanently, because the land is mine" (Lev. 25:23). This regulation did not apply to a house within a walled city, which stood in no relation to a family's land inheritance (Lev. 25:29-30). (3) Freedom of bond servants was to be effected in the Year of Jubilee. Every Israelite who had because of poverty subjected himself or herself to bondage was to be set free (Lev. 25:39-43).

Purpose. These regulations and provisions for the Year of Jubilee had several divine purposes. (1) It was to contribute to the abolishment of poverty by enabling the unfortunate and victims of circumstances to begin anew. (2) It would discourage excessive, permanent accumulations of wealth and property and the consequent deprivation of an Israelite of his or her inheritance in the land. "Woe to you who add house to house and join field to field" (Isa. 5:8; cf. Mic. 2:2). (3) It preserved families and tribes inasmuch as it returned freed bond servants to their own blood relations and families, and thus slavery, in any permanent sense, would not exist in Israel.

Special Festival Sabbaths

In addition to the weekly Sabbath and the monthly new moon, there were seven annual feast days that were also classed as Sabbaths. They were the first and last days of the Feast of Unleavened Bread (Lev. 23:7-8), the Day of Pentecost (Lev. 23:21), the Feast of Trumpets (Lev. 23:24-25), the Day of Atonement (Lev. 23:32), and the first and last days of the Feast of Tabernacles (Lev. 23:34-36). There was one major distinction between these festival Sabbaths and the weekly Sabbath and Day of Atonement: all work was strictly forbidden on weekly Sabbaths and the Day of Atonement, whereas rest only from "servile" labor was required on the festival Sabbaths.

195 ✦ FEAST OF PASSOVER AND FEAST OF UNLEAVENED BREAD

The Feast of Passover commemorated the Lord's deliverance of Israel in Exodus. The Feast of Unleavened Bread, which followed it, kept alive the memory of the affliction of the Israelites and their haste in departing from the land of bondage.

The Passover (*Pesaḥ*) was the first of three annual pilgrimage festivals and was celebrated on the fourteenth day of the Jewish month, Nisan (postexilic name; formerly Abib [Exod. 13:14], approximately modern Western April). The celebration, commonly known as the Feast of Unleavened Bread, continued for the next week, ending on the twenty-first day of the month. Nisan marked the beginning of the religious or sacred new year (Exod. 12:2). The Hebrew term *pesaḥ* is derived from a root meaning "to pass (or spring) over," and signifies the passing over (sparing) of the houses of Israel when the firstborn of Egypt were slain (Exod. 12). The Passover itself refers only to the paschal supper on the evening of 14 Nisan, whereas the following week-long period is called the Feast of Unleavened Bread (Exod. 12; 13:1-20; Lev. 23:5-8; Num. 28:16-25; Deut. 16:1-8).

Institution and Celebration

The purpose for the institution of the Feast of Passover was to commemorate the deliverance of Israel from Egyptian bondage and the sparing of Israel's firstborn when God smote the firstborn of Egypt. A few days prior to the feast itself, the head of each family set apart a lamb without blemish. On the evening of 14 Nisan the lamb was slain and some of its blood sprinkled on the doorposts and lintel of the house in which they ate the Passover as a seal against the coming judgment on Egypt. The lamb was then roasted whole and eaten with unleavened bread and bitter herbs. If the family was too small to consume a lamb, then a neighboring family could share it. Any portion remaining was to be burned the next morning. Each was to eat in haste with loins girded, shoes on the feet, and staff in hand.

Later Observance

After the establishment of the priesthood and tabernacle, the celebration of the Passover differed in some particulars from the Egyptian Passover: (a) the Passover lamb was to be slain at the sanctuary rather than at home (Deut. 16:5-6); (b) the blood was sprinkled on the altar instead of on the doorposts; (c) besides the family sacrifice for the Passover meal, there were public and national sacrifices offered each of the seven days of the Feast of Unleavened Bread (Num. 28:16-24); (d) the meaning of the Passover was recited at the feast each year (Exod. 12:24-27); (e) the singing of the *Hallel* (Pss. 113–118) during the meal was instituted; and (f) a second Passover on the fourteenth day of the second month was to be kept by those who were ceremonially unclean or away on a journey at the time of its regular celebration on 14 Nisan (Num. 9:9-12).

The Passover was one of the three feasts in which all males were required to come to the sanctuary. They were not to appear empty-handed, but were to bring offerings as the Lord had prospered them (Exod. 23:14-17; Deut. 16:16-17). It was unlawful to eat leavened food after midday of 14 Nisan, and all

Modern Symbol of Passover

labor, with few exceptions, ceased. According to Josephus (*Wars* vi. 9.3), each lamb was to serve ten to twenty persons, no ceremonially unclean men or women being admitted to the feast. After appropriate blessings a first cup of wine was served, followed by the eating of a portion of the bitter herbs. Before the lamb and unleavened bread were eaten, a second cup of wine was provided at which time the son, in compliance with Exodus 12:26, asked the father the meaning and significance of the Passover Feast. An account of the Egyptian bondage and deliverance was recited in reply. The first portion of the *Hallel* (Pss. 113–114) was then sung and the paschal supper eaten, followed by third and fourth cups of wine and the second part of the *Hallel* (Pss. 115–118).

———— Feast of Unleavened Bread ————

Both the Passover and the Feast of Unleavened Bread, which immediately followed, commemorated the Exodus, the former in remembrance of God's "passing over" the Israelites when he slew the firstborn of Egypt and the latter to keep alive the memory of their affliction and God's bringing them out in haste from Egypt ("bread of affliction," Deut. 16:3). The first and last days of this feast were Sabbaths in which no servile work could be done, except the necessary preparation of food. The Passover season also marked the beginning of the grain harvest in Palestine. On the second day of the Feast of Unleavened Bread (15 Nisan), a sheaf of the firstfruits of the barley harvest was presented as a wave offering (Lev. 23:9-11). The ceremony came to be called "the omer ceremony" from the Hebrew word for sheaf, *'omer.*

196 • FEAST OF PENTECOST

Pentecost, which means "fifty," is celebrated fifty days after Passover. It is the only one of the three pilgrimage feasts which did not commemorate a specific event in Israel's history. Eventually it came to be associated with the giving of the Law at Mount Sinai.

Pentecost, which is the Greek word for "fiftieth," is called in Hebrew *Ḥag Shavu'ot,* that is, "the Feast of Weeks" (Exod. 34:22; Lev. 23:15-22). Its name derived from the fact that it was celebrated seven weeks after the Passover, on the fiftieth day (Lev. 23:15-16; Deut. 16:9-10). It is also called the "Feast of Harvest" (Exod. 23:16) and the "Day of Firstfruits" (Num. 28:26).

Pentecost was a one-day festival in which all males were to appear at the sanctuary and a Sabbath in which all servile labor was suspended. The central feature of the day was the offering of two loaves of bread for the people from the firstfruits of the wheat harvest (Lev. 23:17). As the omer ceremony signified the onset of the harvest season, the presentation of the two loaves indicated its close. It was a day of thanksgiving, in which freewill offerings were made (Deut. 16:10), of rejoicing before the Lord, and of special consideration shown to the Levite, sojourner, orphan, and widow (Deut. 16:10-12). The festival day signified the dedication of the harvest to God as the provider of all blessings.

The Old Testament does not specifically give any historical significance for the day, Pentecost being the only one of the three great agricultural feasts that does not commemorate some event in Jewish history. Later tradition, on the basis of Exodus 19:1, taught that the giving of the Law at Sinai was fifty days after the Exodus and Passover, and as a result *Shavu'ot* has also become known as the Torah festival. The book of Ruth, which describes the harvest season, is read at Pentecost. The significance of the day for the New Testament is set forth in Acts 2, when Pentecost marked the beginning of the church.

197 • FEAST OF TABERNACLES

The Feast of Tabernacles came at the end of the harvest and was the outstanding feast of rejoicing in the year. During its seven days the people lived in booths to recall the time Israel spent in the wilderness.

The Feast of Tabernacles (*Ḥag Hassukkot*), the third of the pilgrimage feasts, was celebrated for seven days from 15 to 21 Tishri, the seventh month, approximating our October. It was followed by an eighth day of holy convocation with appropriate sacrifices (Lev. 23:33-36; Num. 29:12-38; Deut. 16:13-15). It was also called the "Feast of Ingathering" (Exod. 23:16) for the autumn harvest of the fruits and olives, with the ingathering of the threshing floor and the winepress, which occurred at this time (Lev. 23:39; Deut. 16:13). It was the outstanding feast of rejoicing in the year, in which the Israelites, during the seven-day period, lived in booths or huts made of boughs in commemoration of their wilderness wanderings when their fathers dwelt in temporary shelters. According to Nehemiah 8:14-18, the booths were made of olive, myrtle, palm, and other branches, and were built on roofs of houses, in courtyards, in the court of the temple, and in the broad places of the city streets. Sacrifices were more numerous during this feast than at any other, consisting of the offering of 189 animals during the seven-day period.

When the feast coincided with a sabbatical year, the Law was read publicly to the entire congregation at the sanctuary (Deut. 31:10-13). As Josephus and the Talmud indicate, new ceremonies were gradually added to the festival, chief of which was the *simḥat bet hashsho'evah,* "the festival of the drawing of water." In this ceremony a golden pitcher was filled from the pool of Siloam and returned to the priest at the temple amid the joyful shouts of the celebrants, after which the water was poured into a basin at the altar (cf. John 7:37-38). At night the streets and temple court were illuminated by innumerable torches carried by the singing, dancing pilgrims. The booths were dismantled on the last day, and the eighth day was observed as a Sabbath of holy convocation. The feast is mentioned by Zechariah as a joyous celebration in the millennium (Zech. 14:16).

198 ✦ ROSH HASHANAH AND THE FEAST OF TRUMPETS

Ro'sh Hashshanah (literally, "head of the year") the Hebrew new year, ushered in the Feast of Trumpets with the blowing of the ram's horn. It was the first of the high holy feast days and looked forward to the solemn Day of Atonement which occurred ten days later.

The new moon of the seventh month (1 Tishri) constituted the beginning of the civil new year and was designated as *Ro'sh Hashshanah,* "the first of the year," or *yom t^eru'ah,* "day of sounding [the trumpet]." Leviticus 23:23-25 and Numbers 29:1-6 are the only Old Testament references to Rosh Hashanah, the regulations, prayers, and customs of which fill volumes today in the Jewish rabbinic literature. The blowing of the *shofar,* or ram's horn, occupied a significant place on several other occasions, such as the monthly new moon and the Year of Jubilee, but especially so at the beginning of the new year, hence its name—Feast of Trumpets. The Hebrew calendar actually began with Nisan in the spring (Exod. 12:2), but the end of the seventh

month, Tishri, usually marked the beginning of the rainy season in Palestine when the year's work of plowing and planting began. Tishri was the beginning of the economic and civil year. Business transactions, sabbatical years, and Jubilee Years were all determined from the first of the seventh month. Later, Judaism associated many important events with Rosh Hashanah, including the creation of the world and humankind; the births of Abraham, Isaac, Jacob, and Samuel; and the day of Joseph's release from prison (Ben M. Edidin, *Jewish Holidays and Festivals* [New York: Hebrew Publishing Co., 1940], 53-54).

The day was observed as a sabbatical feast day with special sacrifices. It also pointed to the solemn Day of Atonement ten days later. Rosh Hashanah (new year) and Yom Kippur (Day of Atonement) constitute what are called "high holy days" in Judaism. Rosh Hashanah has come to be considered a day of judgment for one's deeds of the previous year. It is a day for examining one's life, prayer, and repentance. On this day, in Jewish thought, God judges all humans for their deeds and decides who shall live or die, prosper or suffer adversity.

199 ✦ DAY OF ATONEMENT

The Day of Atonement was a time for fasting and cleansing from sin. Traditionally, the high priest made atonement on this day for the sins of the priests, the people, and the sanctuary.

The annual Day of Atonement *(Yom Hakkippurim)* is set forth in Leviticus 16:1-34 as the day for the supreme act of national atonement for sin. It took place on the tenth day of the seventh month, Tishri, and fasting was commanded from the evening of 9 Tishri until the evening of 10 Tishri, in keeping with the unusual sanctity of the day. On this day an atonement was effected for the people, the priesthood, and even for the sanctuary because it "is among them in the midst of their uncleanliness" (Lev. 16:16).

─────── **The Ritual** ───────

This was divided into two acts, one performed on behalf of the priesthood, and one on behalf of the nation Israel. The high priest, who had moved a

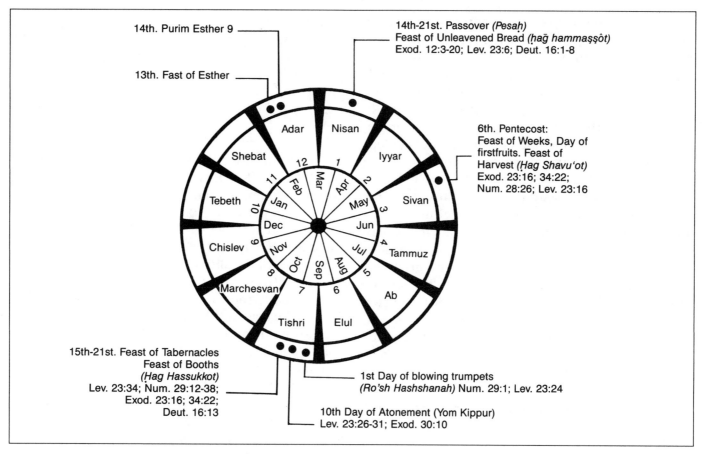

14th. Purim Esther 9

13th. Fast of Esther

14th.-21st. Passover _(Pesaḥ)_
Feast of Unleavened Bread _(ḥaḡ hammaṣṣôt)_
Exod. 12:3-20; Lev. 23:6; Deut. 16:1-8

6th. Pentecost:
Feast of Weeks, Day of
firstfruits. Feast of
Harvest _(Hag Shavu'ot)_
Exod. 23:16; 34:22;
Num. 28:26; Lev. 23:16

15th.-21st. Feast of Tabernacles
Feast of Booths
(Hag Hassukkot)
Lev. 23:34; Num. 29:12-38;
Exod. 23:16; 34:22;
Deut. 16:13

1st Day of blowing trumpets
(Ro'sh Hashshanah) Num. 29:1; Lev. 23:24

10th Day of Atonement (Yom Kippur)
Lev. 23:26-31; Exod. 30:10

Circle of Jewish calendar
(adapted from The Illustrated Bible Dictionary _(T) vol. 1, 504)_

week before this day from his own dwelling to the sanctuary, arose on the Day of Atonement, and having bathed and laid aside his regular high priestly attire, dressed himself in holy, white linen garments, and brought forward a young bullock or a sin offering for himself and for his house. The other priests, who on other occasions served in the sanctuary, on this day took their place with the sinful congregation for whom atonement was to be made (Lev. 16:17). The high priest slaughtered the sin offering for himself and entered the Holy of Holies with a censer of incense, so that a cloud of fragrance might fill the room and cover the ark in order that the priest should not die. Then he returned with the blood of the sin offering and sprinkled it seven times before the mercy seat for the symbolic cleansing of the Holy of Holies, defiled by its presence among the sinful people. Having made atonement for himself, he returned to the court of the sanctuary.

The high priest next presented the two goats, secured as the sin offering for the people, to the Lord at the door of the tabernacle and cast lots over them, one lot marked for Yahweh, and the other for Azazel (Lev. 16:8, RSV). The goat on which the lot had fallen for the Lord was slain, and the high priest repeated the ritual of sprinkling the blood as before. In addition, he cleansed the Holy Place by a sevenfold sprinkling and, finally, cleansed the altar of burnt offering.

The Goat for Azazel

In the second stage of the ceremony the live goat, the goat for Azazel, which had been left standing at the altar, was brought forward. The high priest, laying hands on it, confessed over it all the sins of the people, after which it was sent into an uninhabited wilderness, bearing the iniquity of the nation.

The precise significance of this part of the ceremony is determined by the meaning attached to the expression "for Azazel" ("for the scapegoat" [Lev. 16:8, KJV]). Basically, there are four interpretations. (1) A specific location would have been problematic for a people on the move, as was true for the Israelites at this time in their history. (2) Azazel was a *person,* either Satan or an evil spirit. But the name Azazel occurs nowhere else in Scripture, which is unlikely if he were so important a person to divide the sin offering with God, which the suggestion in itself has an offensive connotation. Moreover, demon worship is condemned in the Law in Leviticus 17:7-9. (3) Azazel was an *abstract noun* meaning "dismissal" or "complete removal." (4) The name Azazel most likely designates the goat itself. This view was held by Josephus, Symmachus, Aquila, Theodotion, Martin Luther, Andrew Bonar, the Septuagint, the Latin Vulgate, the King James Version ("scapegoat"), and others. Hence the goat was called in the Hebrew *Azazel,* meaning "the removing goat": "[Aaron] shall cast lots upon the two goats, one lot for the LORD and the other lot for Azazel" (Lev. 16:8, RSV), *for the removing goat*—i.e., for the goat as the remover of sins. Both goats were called an atonement and both were presented to the Lord. Therefore, both goats were looked on as *one offering.* Since it was physically impossible to depict two ideas with one goat, two were needed as a single sin offering. The first goat by its death symbolized atonement for sins; the other, by confessing over it the sins of Israel and sending it away, symbolized complete removal of the sins (cf. Lev. 14:4-7).

200 • POSTEXILIC FESTIVALS

With the exception of Purim, postexilic feasts are not presented in the Old Testament. For the most part, they developed in the intertestamental period and are mentioned primarily in the books of the Old Testament Apocrypha.

Feast of Purim

This feast was instituted by Mordecai to commemorate the preservation of the Jews of Persia from destruction through the plot of Haman, as recorded in the book of Esther. The term *purim,* which means "lots," was applied to the festival because Haman had cast lots to ascertain which day he would carry out the decree to massacre the Jews. The festival was to last for two days, 14-15 Adar, with "feasting and joy and giving presents of food to one another and gifts to the poor" (Esther 9:20-22). The feast has always been popular with the Jews as Josephus attests (*Antiquities* xi. 6.13), its celebration continuing down to the present time. Later generations began

to observe only one day (14 Adar). The preceding day (13 Adar) is known as the fast of Esther in commemoration of Esther's fast before seeking audience with the king on behalf of the Jews (Esther 4:15-16). Services at the synagogue on Purim include the reading of the book of Esther.

Feast of Dedication

The Feast of Dedication (*Hanukkah,* "dedication"), also called the Feast of Lights, is a significant, although extrabiblical, feast originating during the Maccabean period in commemoration of the purification of the temple and restoration of the altar by Judas Maccabeus in 164 B.C. (1 Macc. 4:36-61). The dedication of the altar was observed eight days from 25 Kislev (December) and was ordained to be observed yearly thereafter. According to 2 Maccabees 10:6-7, the feast was likened to the Feast of Tabernacles and celebrated by the carrying of boughs, palms, and branches, with the singing of psalms. Josephus called the feast "Lights," for he writes: "We celebrate this festival, and call it Lights. I suppose the reason was, because this liberty [that is, restored political and religious freedom] beyond our hopes appeared to us" (*Antiquities* xii. 7.7). The use of lights during Hanukkah celebrations has always played a significant part, especially in the homes, synagogues, and streets of Palestine. The feast is mentioned in connection with Jesus' ministry in John 10:22-23.

Subordinate Extrabiblical Jewish Sacred Seasons

The seventh day of Sukkot (Tabernacles), 21 Tishri, came to be known as *hoshi'ah-na',* "Great Hosanna" or "great help." The eighth day is now called *sh^emini 'atzeret,* "eighth day of solemn assembly," a holy convocation in which prayers for the homeland are offered. The following day (23 Tishri) is *Simhat Torah,* "Feast of the Law," a day of rejoicing and celebration marking the close of the yearly cycle of reading the Torah in the synagogues. The "fifteenth day of Shebat," or *hamishah 'asar bish^evat,* marks the beginning of spring in Palestine and is celebrated by the planting of trees (*cf.* Lev. 19:23; Deut. 20:19). *Hag b^e'omer* is celebrated on the thirty-third day of the "omer" season (18 Iyar) to commemorate the attempt by the Jews to regain their independence under Simon bar Kokheba (A.D. 132-135).

Fasts include, beside the fast of Esther (*ta'anit*

'*Ester*), *'ªsarah bᵉtevet*, "a fast in remembrance of the beginning of the siege of Jerusalem by Babylonia" (2 Kings 25:1; Jer. 39:1); *shiv'ah 'asar bᵉtammuz*, "seventeenth of Tammuz," in token of the day the city was entered by the invaders (Jer. 39:2; 52:6-7); *tish'ah bᵉ'av*, "ninth of Ab," to lament the day of the destruction of the city and temple (2 Kings 25:8-9; Jer. 52:12-13); and the fast of Gedaliah (3 Tishri) to mourn the murder of the governor Gedaliah in 586 B.C.

Hobart E. Freeman[16]

201 • SOLEMN ASSEMBLY

In ancient Israel, the solemn assembly was a special occasion solemnizing the completion of a feast, or a penitential assembly of the people under threat of national disaster. It was marked by cessation from work and fasting or prayer.

The solemn assembly was the gathering and sanctifying of the community of Israel for a solemn occasion. It was used in the technical sense as the eighth day of the Feast of Booths (Lev. 23:36; Num. 29:35; Neh. 8:18) and the seventh day of Passover (Deut. 16:8). In both instances, the people were instructed to "do no work" on this day, for they were in a state of ritual holiness. At the dedication of the temple, Solomon proclaimed a solemn assembly on the eighth day, "for they had celebrated the dedication of the altar for seven days and the festival for seven days more" (2 Chron. 7:9). For a quite different purpose, Jehu ordered the people to "call an assembly in honor of Baal" (2 Kings 10:20). He used the occasion to complete his purge of Baal worshipers from the land of Israel by massacring those who had gathered.

In contrast to the above mentioned feast days, the solemn assembly was also convened for special days of fasting. When a locust plague threatened the land, Joel exhorted Israel to "declare a holy fast; call a sacred assembly. Summon the elders and all who live in the land to the house of the LORD your God, and cry out to the LORD" (Joel 1:14; cf. 2:15).

Amos and Isaiah discredited these solemn assemblies sanction (Isa. 1:13; Amos 5:21), because the people did not do justice in the land. As Isaiah charged, "even if you offer many prayers . . . your hands are full of blood" (Isa. 1:15).

Although not mentioned in connection with the worship of the New Testament church, the concept of the solemn assembly has been retained in Christian tradition, especially in the Ash Wednesday service of the liturgical churches. Some nonliturgical churches, particularly among Southern Baptists, are restoring the solemn assembly as a weekend emphasis on church renewal.

William B. Coker[17]

NINETEEN

Biblical Foundations of Christian Festivals

Christians, like the Jews, have developed a calendar of feasts to celebrate God's great acts of salvation. These feasts are organized especially around the birth of Christ (Advent, Christmas, and Epiphany) and around his death and resurrection and the coming of the Holy Spirit (Lent, Holy Week, Easter, and Pentecost). Increasingly, churches are recovering these feasts as principal acts of worship in recognition of their relationship to the biblical events of salvation.

202 • BACKGROUND TO THE CHRISTIAN FESTIVALS

Emerging from its Judaic background, the Christian church did not continue the observance of the festivals of Israelite worship but developed a liturgical calendar of its own, based principally on major events in the life of Christ.

The Pentateuch mandates the observance of three annual feasts (Exod. 23:14-27; Lev. 23; Deut. 16:1-7): Passover, the Feast of Weeks or Pentecost, and the Feast of Ingathering, also called the Feast of Tabernacles. Jesus and the earliest Christians were familiar with this Mosaic calendar, and the New Testament records occasions when they took part in these festivals. Jesus cleansed the temple during a Passover observance (John 2:13-17), taught in the temple during the Feast of Tabernacles (John 7:14-39), and instituted the Lord's Supper during the Passover (Matt. 26:17-30). It was on the day of Pentecost that the apostles, together in Jerusalem, were filled with the Holy Spirit and first preached Jesus as the Christ (Acts 2:1). Paul, on what was to be his final trip to Jerusalem, expressed the desire to be there by Pentecost (Acts 20:16). The Jewish Sabbath was not a festival but a day of rest and of assembling in the synagogue for the study of the Scriptures. The Gospels record Jesus' participation in the Sabbath service at the beginning of his ministry (Luke 4:16). Later, however, his attitude toward the Sabbath often drew the ire of the Pharisees, for he opposed their rigorous prohibition of all forms of "work" when it would prevent doing good to people, especially healing the sick.

As the church expanded out of the orbit of Judaism, the Jewish festivals were virtually laid aside. The church could not continue their sacrificial aspects, for Christ himself had offered the only efficacious blood sacrifice (Heb. 9:11-14; 10:1-10) and in his death and resurrection had cancelled the decrees of the ceremonial law (Col. 2:13-14). The New Testament draws on the vocabulary and symbolism of the Israelite feasts and of the Sabbath to interpret God's action in Christ. The Lord's Supper, as the covenant meal of the Christian *ekklēsia,* partly absorbed the significance of the Passover; however, it was not an annual festival but, apparently, a weekly observance. The Jewish Sabbath was supplanted by the Christian worship on the Lord's Day.

The New Testament records no liturgical calendar and gives no directives for observing annual feasts. The apostle Paul expresses an indifference to the observance of special days; whether a believer keeps them should be a matter of personal conviction, for the purpose of glorifying and thanking the Lord (Rom. 14:5-6). Historically, however, the Christian church has found a special value in the annual festivals as encouragements to the believer's identification with God's action of deliverance in Jesus Christ. Within some segments of the evangelical church, there is a growing desire to return to aspects of the biblical festival calendar; some churches and groups, for example, have begun to observe an annual "Feast of Tabernacles," a time of heightened celebration of the glory and presence of the Lord.

The following is an introduction to the Lord's Day and to the major feasts of the church. Omitted in this survey are days that have no scriptural foundation, such as saints' days, events peculiar to one denominational tradition (e.g., Reformation Day or Aldersgate Sunday), or the events of the civil or popular calendar that may be celebrated in churches (e.g., Mother's Day and Thanksgiving).

Richard C. Leonard

203 • THE LORD'S DAY (SUNDAY)

From New Testament times, the church met for worship on the first day of the week, the day of Jesus' resurrection. The Lord's Day has absorbed some features of the Jewish Sabbath but also differs in important respects. It is a day that incorporates within it all the festivals of the Christian year.

Terminology

The first day of the week quite early became the regular day on which the church assembled for worship in place of the Jewish Sabbath (Acts 20:7; 1 Cor. 16:2). There is no New Testament injunction to observe this day, but the second-century *Didachē,* or *Teaching of the Twelve Apostles,* directs the church to "assemble and give thanks" on the Lord's Day (*Didachē* 14). The title "the Lord's Day" is found in the New Testament only in Revelation 1:10, where John states that he was in the Spirit "on the Lord's Day" when he received his commission to write the revelation of Jesus Christ. The expression "Day of the Lord" in the Old Testament generally describes an impending time of judgment, although in some contexts it might refer to a festival known as "Yahweh's Day," perhaps a celebration of his enthronement and possibly the new year festival (cf. Amos 5:18). In early Christian writings, "the Lord's Day" designates Sunday, the first day of the week, observed from apostolic times as a day of Christian worship. The English name *Sunday* is a holdover from the original pagan dedication of this day to the sun god; in the Romance languages, in contrast, the meaning of "Lord's Day" is better represented by names such as *domingo* or *dimanche,* from the Latin *Dominus,* "Lord."

Origin of the Lord's Day

A popular belief is that the Lord's Day originated in the Jewish Sabbath, which Jesus himself, or his apostles, changed from the seventh to the first day of the week. This belief has persisted, although there is no scriptural teaching that the Sabbath has been transferred from one day to another. The origin of the Christian Sunday is more complicated, for the transition from the Sabbath to the Lord's Day was a gradual one. Since the transition took place while Christianity was emerging from its Jewish background, it was inevitable that Judaism should contribute a great deal to a Christian institution such as the weekly day of assembly and worship. At this time, also, the church was entering into conflict with pagan cults, which, especially in later centuries, made their influence felt in the formation of Christian institutions. The Christian day of worship was bound to embrace elements that would distinguish it from both the Jewish day of assembly and the pagan observances.

The Sabbath and the Lord's Day

The Sabbath held a distinctive place in the life of the Jewish community. During the time of the Exile in Babylon, when the Judeans were cut off from their festival worship in Jerusalem, the Sabbath began to emerge as an institution that held the people together. It has been said that it was not the Jews who kept the Sabbath but the Sabbath that kept the Jews. Even after the restoration of the temple, the Sabbath continued to grow in importance; the local religious rites of the Jews came to center around this day, especially outside Palestine, and all the more so with the destruction of Herod's temple in A.D. 70.

It was natural that many of the traditions of the Sabbath should be incorporated into the life of the early church; Jews, who had been accustomed to observe the Sabbath by resting from their ordinary labors and by prayer and study in the synagogue, would have found it difficult not to maintain these customs as Christians. At first, Jewish Christians apparently observed both the seventh and the first days of the week. Later, when the Christian movement became more Gentile in its constituency, and when its distinction from Judaism became more apparent, the majority of Christians observed only the first day of the week. However, they transferred to it many of the features of the earlier institution, which had occupied such an important place in the heritage they had received from Judaism. To an extent, therefore, the character of the Jewish Sabbath was imitated in the Christian Sunday. Like the Sabbath, it was regarded as a day of joy and festivity, and fasting on it was forbidden. As the Sabbath opened and closed with appropriate celebrations, the first Christians also met early in the morning on the Lord's Day and again in the evening to worship and share a meal together.

To the Jew, the Sabbath was a memorial of the Creation of the world and of the preservation of the Lord's people. It was a weekly reminder of God's rest after the six days of Creation and also of Israel's deliverance from Egyptian slavery (Gen. 2:3; Exod. 20:11; Deut. 5:15). The most prominent feature of the Sabbath, even before it became a day of assembly, was the cessation of all kinds of work. Although this feature of the Jewish sacred day was the last to be carried over into the Christian Sunday, there are indications as early as the beginning of the third century that Christians abstained from work on the Lord's Day. The fact that the Lord's Day became a weekly day of worship and rest for Christians, as opposed to a monthly or annual observance, can be explained only by analogy with the Jewish Sabbath.

Christian Distinctives of the Lord's Day

Although it borrowed important features from the Sabbath, the Lord's Day was from the beginning a distinctively Christian institution. It was observed on the first day of the week because it was on this day that Jesus rose from the dead. All four Gospels indicate that the Resurrection was discovered early in the morning on the first day of the week (Matt. 28:1; Mark 16:2; Luke 24:1; John 20:1). Six of the eight appearances of Christ to his followers after the Resurrection took place on the first day: to Mary Magdalene (John 20:1-18), to the women bringing spices to anoint Jesus' body (Matt. 28:7-10), to two disciples on the Emmaus road (Luke 24:13-33), to Simon Peter (Luke 24:34), to the ten disciples when Thomas was absent (John 20:19-23; cf. Luke 24:36-49), and possibly (although the text uses the phrase "after eight days") to the eleven disciples when Thomas was present (John 20:24-29). These appearances of Christ on the first day were sufficient to set it apart as a day of particular significance. If the crucifixion of Jesus took place on the sixth day of the week (Friday), as is traditionally held, then the day

of Pentecost that year was also on the first day of the week, since it falls fifty days after Passover (which would have coincided with the Sabbath). If so, the outpouring of the Holy Spirit on the apostles also occurred on the Lord's Day (Acts 2:1-4).

The resurrection of Jesus, which verified that he was the Christ, the Son of God, was denied by the church's Jewish opponents. Since the Resurrection was foundational to the Christian movement, it is understandable that Christians—even those who were Jews by descent—would view a separate day of worship as something demanded by the contrast between Christianity and Judaism. In assembling on the first day of the week, the church continuously proclaimed the central fact of the gospel. In his first *Apology* (I. 67)—a defense of the church addressed to the Roman Emperor—Justin Martyr (*c.* 100–165) explains that the church chose this day for worship because it was both the first day of Creation and the day of the resurrection of Christ. Thus the Lord's Day contrasts with the Sabbath in a second respect closely related to the Resurrection. Whereas the Sabbath, or seventh day, marked God's resting from his creative activity (Gen. 2:1-2), the Lord's Day is a day of "new creation." By worshiping on the first day of the week, the Christian church is making a statement about the new beginning God has made in Jesus Christ and the people of the new covenant (2 Cor. 5:17; Rev. 21:1-5).

When questioned about his authority, Jesus quoted a psalm: "The stone the builders rejected has become the Stone; the Lord has done this, and it is marvelous in our eyes" (cf. Matt. 21:42; Ps. 118:22-23). Peter, in his address before the Jewish Sanhedrin, quoted part of the same passage and applied it to the resurrection of Christ (Acts 4:11). Athanasius, in the fourth century, added the following verse and applied it to the day of Resurrection: "This is the day the Lord has made; let us rejoice and be glad in it."

Henry Waterman[18]

204 • ADVENT

The historic starting point of the Christian year is the commemoration of the death and resurrection of Jesus, the Christian "Pascha," or Passover. However, for most Christians, the Christian seasons begin with Advent, a time of preparation for the celebration of Christ's coming.

The Christian cycle of time, with festal days that celebrate God's saving work in Jesus Christ

The season of Advent (from Latin _adventus,_ "coming") begins four Sundays before Christmas in Western churches and is considered the beginning of the ecclesiastical year. The season was not observed before the sixth century. Advent, like Lent, has been regarded as a penitential season, a time of preparation for the glorious manifestation of the Lord. Biblical themes stressed during Advent include the many Old Testament prophecies of the coming of the Messiah and of the Lord's impending judgment against sin. Thus, Advent celebrates the anticipation of both the "first coming" of Christ at his incarnation and his "coming again" as judge of the world (Acts 17:31) and vindicator of his faithful witnesses (Rev. 6:9). Amid divergent eschatologies, Christian worshipers unite during Advent as they focus on the prophetic cry: "See, your king comes to you" (Zech. 9:9; Matt. 21:5).

205 • CHRISTMAS

As the celebration of the birth of the Savior, Christmas calls attention to the mystery of the Incarnation, the vulnerable participation involvement of God in the human scene.

The New Testament offers no directive to celebrate the birth of Christ. The account of his birth is included in only two of the four Gospels, though references to it occur also in Galatians 4:4 and Revelation 12:1-5. Scripture gives no indication of the time of year when Jesus was born, although some have suggested that the evidence points to early autumn. The traditional 25 December date originated in a Roman winter festival, the _Natalis Solis Invicti,_ a festival of the sun after the winter solstice, when the days in the northern hemisphere begin to lengthen. Despite the objections of many early Christian theologians to the confusion of Christ with the sun god, Christians had begun to celebrate the birth of Jesus on this day by the fourth century.

The infancy narratives of Matthew and Luke easily lend themselves to the pageantry of the birth of Christ. In Matthew's account the Lord's messenger, appearing to Joseph in a dream, explains the meaning of the name _Jesus_ to be given to the child: "He will save his people from their sins" (Matt. 1:21). The marvel of the Virgin Birth heralded by angelic visitants taken together with the consternation of Mary and Joseph, whose contracted marriage had not been consummated at the time of conception, evoke the full range of human emotion. The perspective of Luke is especially gripping; his dramatic narrative (Luke 2:1-20) couches the oppressed of all times who, like Joseph and Mary, must pay tax and tribute to an occupying power, or who too often find "no room in the inn." The announcement of the birth of Christ the Lord to humble shepherds strikes a responsive chord in all who struggle in a world that exalts wealth and position; its promises echo Mary's earlier song magnifying the Lord, who "has brought down rulers from their thrones but has lifted up the humble" (Luke 1:52). The hymn of the heavenly host, "Glory to God in the highest, and on earth peace to men of his favor" (AUTHOR'S TRANSLATION), expresses the Christian's response of exultation in the Lord's covenant blessing of peace, made available to all by his grace in Christ. Moreover, the "good news of great joy" is not for the Jewish people alone but for all people on whom God's favor rests, Jews and Gentiles alike. Luke 2:10 proclaims the inclusion of the Gentiles in the plan of God.

Like the shepherds returning from the manger of the Christ child, the Christian worshiper glorifies God for what he or she has seen and heard, in the realization that through all this "the Word became flesh and lived for awhile among us. We have seen his glory" (John 1:14) in the incarnate mystery of Immanuel, "God with us" (Matt. 1:23). There is an unexplainable wonder and gripping power in the New Testament's proclamation that the eternal Son, through whom all things were made (Heb. 1:2), should lay aside his glory and empty himself, "taking the form of a bond-servant, and being made in the likeness of men" (Phil. 2:6-7, NASB).

206 ✦ EPIPHANY AND AFTER

The Epiphany, or manifestation, of Christ is a celebration of his revelation to the peoples of the world. The Epiphany season follows Christmas and extends to the beginning of Lent.

Epiphany

The name *Epiphany* comes from a Greek word meaning "manifestation" or "appearance." This festival originated in the third century as a celebration of Jesus' baptism (Matt. 3:13-17) and retains this character in the Eastern church. In the West, however, from the fourth century, it has commemorated the revelation of Jesus Christ to the Gentiles, represented in Scripture by the "wise men," or magi, who made a long journey to see the "King of the Jews" (Matt. 2:1-12). Although many churches incorporate the visit of the magi into their Christmas pageantry,

The five-pointed star is an early church symbol of the manifestation of Christ to the world

the journey took place some time after the birth of Jesus, perhaps months later. In the traditional Western calendar Epiphany falls on January 6. The magi, as known from other historical sources, were a class of Persian priests and astrologers, which harmonizes with the account of their following a new star to Bethlehem. The Bible does not say there were three of them; the number is inferred from their threefold gifts to the infant Jesus—gold, frankincense, and myrrh. Neither does the gospel story indicate that they were kings who rode on camels. This idea comes from Isaiah 60:1-6, a passage that proclaims a theophany, or appearance of the Lord's glory, over Israel: "Nations will come to your light, and kings to the brightness of your dawn. . . ." Camels are mentioned later in connection with the bringing of gifts of gold and frankincense (cf. Ps. 72:10-11). The giving of gifts at Christmas is sometimes related to the gifts of the magi, but the practice actually originated in pagan customs associated with festivals such as the Roman *Saturnalia*. Although some have seen a symbolic significance in the gifts of the magi (cf. the carol "We Three Kings"), this is not developed in Scripture.

In the imagery of Epiphany, the magi represent the Gentiles, to whom the Savior is now revealed. They are, in fact, the first people said to "worship" (bow down to) Christ. The union of Jew and Gentile in the new covenant of Christ is the great mystery celebrated by the apostle Paul and of which he called himself the steward (Eph. 3:1-7). Although the meaning of Jesus Christ and his embodiment of the new covenant, the kingdom of God, cannot be fully understood apart from the background of the faith of Israel, neither can it be understood apart from its universal significance for people of all cultures and ethnic groups. Epiphany is a useful vehicle by which the church may remind itself of this truth and of its mandate for worldwide evangelization (Matt. 28:18-20).

Transfiguration: The Concluding Feast of Epiphany

The Feast of the Transfiguration of Christ originated in the Eastern church, where it was adopted widely before A.D. 1000. It became general in the West by the fifteenth century; the customary date of 6 August was chosen because of a victory over the Turks on that date in 1456. Many churches now commemorate the Transfiguration on the final Sunday of the Epiphany season (the Sunday preceding Lent). This practice places the Transfiguration where it belongs in the sequence of events in Jesus' life: between his baptism and earlier ministry and the time when he "resolutely set out for Jerusalem" (Luke 9:51) where his passion and death would occur. The Transfiguration has always received more attention in the Eastern church, which emphasizes in its worship the eternal glory of Christ, whereas the Western church tends to focus on the Crucifixion and Resurrection.

The account of the Transfiguration occurs in all three synoptic Gospels (Matt. 17:1-8; Mark 9:2-8; Luke 9:28-36). Having taken his three closest disciples up a mountain, Jesus began to pray and "was transfigured before them. His face shone like the sun, and his clothes became as white as the light" (Matt. 17:2). Moses and Elijah appeared, conversing with Jesus; as the awestruck disciples watched, a cloud of glory formed about the scene, and a voice said, "This is my Son, whom I love; with him I am well pleased. Listen to him!" (Matt. 17:5). The disciples fell prostrate in fear, but when Jesus touched them and told them not to be afraid, they looked up and saw him alone.

The Transfiguration seems to be a preview of the Resurrection, as a verification of Jesus' identity as the Messiah. It took place about a week after Peter's confession of Jesus as "the Christ, the Son of the living God" (Matt. 16:16), which is reinforced by the voice from the cloud. What was confirmed to the disciples in the Transfiguration was to be affirmed by them as the focal point of their public preaching after the Resurrection: that God has made Jesus "both Lord and Christ" (Acts 2:36). Peter, recalling the event in his second epistle, emphasized the declaration of Jesus' sonship of God (2 Pet. 1:16-18). John's vision of the living Christ at the opening of the Revelation (Rev. 1:13-18) contains many similarities to the Transfiguration event, including Jesus' words, "Do not be afraid" (Rev. 1:12-18). According to Luke, the glorified Moses and Elijah were speaking with Jesus about "his departure, which he was about to bring to fulfillment at Jerusalem" (Luke 9:31), a reference to the events of his resurrection and ascension.

The presence of Moses and Elijah is of special importance, for they were the two major symbolic figures of Israel's prophetic faith. As the last two verses of the Hebrew prophetic canon make clear (Mal. 4:4-5), together they framed the history of the covenant given at Mr. Sinai; it was through Moses that the covenant was established, and Elijah was to restore the covenant bonds lest the curse of its violation take effect. Their appearance with Jesus in his transfigured glory is an affirmation that the gospel of Jesus Christ, however much it may have seemed anathema to the established Judaism of the first century, arose out of the very heart and essence of the covenant faith of Israel. On the way down the mountain, in response to the disciples' questions, Jesus clearly identified John the Baptist as Elijah. However, John had been unsuccessful in his task of restoring the covenant, for he had been persecuted just as Jesus would be (Matt. 17:9-12). By implication, then, the covenant curse must take effect after all, just as Jesus had predicted before the Transfiguration in his declaration that some standing there would not die before they saw the Son of man coming in judgment (Matt. 16:27-28).

Despite the evident theological significance of the Transfiguration, it remains a mysterious event, a theophany, or revelation of realities beyond the scope of rational analysis. The disciples, stricken with terror—the *mysterium tremendum* of the numinous—did not know how to respond to it (Mark 9:5-6). The Transfiguration is a fleeting window into the glorified realm of the Spirit, in which Jesus appeared not as an ordinary man but in his true "form" as the

Logos, the bearer of the holiness of the eternal God. It is an anticipation of the truth Paul was later to enunciate when he said that, although we once regarded Jesus from a human point of view, we do so no longer (2 Cor. 5:16). The transfiguration of Christ, together with his resurrection, embodies the promise of a corresponding transformation for those who are his. The same Greek word used for Jesus' transfiguration is used by Paul for the transformation of the life of the believer (Rom. 12:2; 2 Cor. 3:18), and John promises that "we shall be like him, for we shall see him as he is" (1 John 3:2).

207 • LENT

The season of Lent, which begins on Ash Wednesday, has traditionally been a penitential season, a time of preparation for the commemoration of the events of Jesus' passion, death, and resurrection.

Ash Wednesday

In the Bible, ashes applied to the body are sometimes a sign of mourning or repentance (2 Sam. 13:19; Est. 4:1; Job 42:6; Dan. 9:3-5). "Dust and ashes" are symbolic of humiliation or abasement (Gen. 18:27; Job 30:19). However, the use of ashes is not mandated for any annual observance. The medieval practice of marking the forehead of the worshiper with ashes, as a gesture of penitence at the beginning of Lent, was dropped by the Reformers; however, even some Protestant churches are now restoring the imposition of ashes because of its symbolic significance. For many nonliturgical churches, Ash Wednesday may be the occasion of the first of a series of Lenten services.

Lent

The Christian observance of Lent may have originated as a period of fasting for candidates for baptism at Easter; the period varied in length and could be as short as one or two days. Mention of a general forty-day period of fasting occurs in the fourth-century Canons of Nicaea, but the Western church did not settle on the present scheme until the seventh century, when the beginning of Lent was moved back to Ash Wednesday so that Sundays (which could not be fast days) would not be counted in the forty days. (The Eastern church still spreads the season over eight or nine weeks.) The association of Lent with Jesus' forty days of testing in the wilderness (Matt. 4:2; Luke 4:2) is acknowledged by liturgical historians to be an afterthought that did not affect the development of the season. The name "Lent" comes from an Anglo-Saxon word meaning "spring," the "lengthening" of days with the approach of the vernal equinox.

Lent offers the opportunity for the observance of certain biblical disciplines. In Israelite religion, fasting or "humbling the soul" was directed for the Day of Atonement (Lev. 23:27, 29). It was an act of mourning (Josh. 7:6; 1 Sam. 31:13; 2 Sam. 1:12) or penitence (1 Kings 21:27; Joel 1:14) and was also practiced by prophets seeking direction from the Lord in crisis situations (Moses, Deut. 9:18 and Elijah, 1 Kings 19:8; both forty days). Jesus assumed his followers would occasionally fast (Matt. 6:16-18), though he did not command it, and his disciples did not fast, as did the Pharisees, while he was with them (Luke 5:33-35). In recent years the liturgical churches have moderated the strict fasting formerly associated with Lent, and evangelical Christians have never consistently observed it. Fasting as a means of seeking direction from the Lord is often practiced in charismatic churches but not in association with any liturgical season. Most Protestant communions that observe Lent have done so with emphasis on additional times of worship or special disciplines of devotion and on self-denial in order to redirect funds toward worthwhile causes. While the Christian life-style of self-denial should characterize the walk of the believer throughout the year and not just during one season, the discipline practiced during Lent has particular value in leading the church to a deeper experience of Christ's passion in preparation for the more joyous experience of Easter.

208 • HOLY WEEK

In the Western church, Holy Week is not a separate season but a part of Lent. In the Eastern church, Holy Week is a season to itself. Holy Week commemorates the final events that led to the death of Jesus.

The Passion of Christ

The term *passion,* from the Latin *passus,* refers to the suffering of Jesus leading up to his crucifixion. This suffering was not only physical, but also spiritual in that Jesus was rejected by those unfaithful to the covenant. The Gospels record his agony in prayer in Gethsemane prior to his arrest; Luke writes graphically of his sweat falling to the ground "like drops of blood" (Luke 22:44) as he wrestled in the spirit with the issue of his own death. The "cup" he was asking the Father to remove from him was not simply physical pain but the just and deadly penalty for violation of the covenant—a curse he was to bear on the cross (Gal. 3:10) in order to cancel the sanctions of the old covenant and introduce the life of the new. It is perhaps this struggle in Gethsemane that the author of Hebrews has in mind when he writes, "During the days of Jesus' life on earth, he offered up prayers and petitions with loud cries and tears to the one who could save him from death, and he was heard because of his reverent submission" (Heb. 5:7). The spiritual warfare of the passion was won in the Garden, and the victory was ratified on the cross.

Thus Jesus bore both the physical agony of the cross and the accompanying spiritual agony of misunderstanding and rejection. The Judean crowds cried out, "Crucify him!" and demanded the release of Barabbas the insurrectionist instead of Jesus. They took from the vacillating Pilate the responsibility for Jesus' death: "Let his blood be on us and on our children!" (Matt. 27:25). Roman soldiers mocked and abused Jesus as "King of the Jews" (Matt. 27:27-31), while the Jewish authorities insisted, "We have no king but Caesar" (John 19:15). In the end Jesus' own disciples deserted him at his arrest (Matt. 26:56), and even the intrepid Peter denied knowing him, just as Jesus had said he would (Matt. 26:34).

It was through Jesus' suffering that the Resurrection and exaltation were to come. On the Emmaus road the risen Christ would explain to his disciples that his suffering was a necessary preamble to his entrance into glory (Luke 24:26; cf. Heb. 2:10). Peter, also, would explain to the crowd gathered at Pentecost that, because they had crucified Jesus, "therefore God has made this Jesus . . . both Lord and Christ" (Acts 2:36). Paul would assure believers that they also would be glorified with Christ, provided they suffer with him (Rom. 8:17-18). The New Testament Epistles in several places refer to the suffering of Christians after the example of Christ (1 Pet. 4:1, 12-13), but this suffering is never physical suffering alone. It is suffering brought about through persecution by those opposed to the gospel, a suffering that is only anticipatory of the greater judgment and suffering to come upon those who persist in their disobedience to the gospel (1 Pet. 4:17).

The drama of the passion has provided a basis for the worship of Christians since the early centuries of the church, giving rise to many traditional observances in both the Eastern and Western churches. The events of Christ's passion, especially the Crucifixion and entombment, have been the subject of the work of famous painters and sculptors down to modern times (Cimabue, Mantegna, Grünewald, Michelangelo, Tintoretto, Rubens, Rembrandt, James Ensor, Georges Rouault, Graham Sutherland). The faithful have been drawn to dramatic reenactments of the passion (for example, the Oberammergau Passion Play of Bavaria, the Black Hills Passion Play), and composers have created sweeping choral and orchestral settings of the Gospel narratives (Schütz, Bach, Penderecki) African-American spirituals have cast the story in very moving and personal terms.

Palm Sunday

Traditional features of Christian worship associated with Palm Sunday are the procession in commemoration of Jesus' entry into Jerusalem and the blessing of palm branches. The special observance of Palm Sunday is known to have occurred in Jerusalem as early as the fourth century and in the Western church by the seventh or eighth century. At different times some symbol of Christ has been carried in procession: the Gospel book, a crucifix, the elements of the Eucharist, or even a carved figure seated on a donkey. Jesus' entry into Jerusalem and his subsequent cleansing of the temple are visual images that have stirred the imagination of Christian worshipers through the centuries as they have taken part in the reenactment of the events joining in procession, waving palm leaves, and singing hosannas.

The story is recorded in all four Gospels (Matt. 21:1-17; Mark 11:1-18; Luke 19:28-48; John 12:12-19), though some details differ from one account to the next. Jesus enters the city riding on a young donkey, which both Matthew and John relate to Zechariah's prophecy of the king coming in humility (Zech. 9:9); Matthew takes the Hebrew poetic parallelism, donkey and colt or foal, to indicate _two_ animals. Whether one animal or two, the conveyance is covered with the garments of Jesus' followers, who also spread them in the road before him along with tree branches (John alone calls them "palm branches," John 12:13).

As Jesus enters the city in this procession, the participants acclaim him by various titles: "the Son of David" (Matt. 21:9), "the King" (Luke 19:38, NASB), and "the King of Israel" (John 12:13). The cry *Hosanna!* ("Save!" or "Deliver!") is recorded by Matthew, Mark, and John, whereas Luke records an alternate hymn, "Peace in heaven and glory in the highest!" (Luke 19:38). Notice that "hosanna" in Hebrew (*hoshi'ah-na'*) is related to the name of Jesus (*Yeshu^a'*), as both are derived from the Hebrew root denoting deliverance or salvation. Foundational to all the accounts is the cry and acclamation of Psalm 118:

> O LORD, save us;
> O LORD, grant us success.
> Blessed is he who comes in the name of
>   the LORD.
> From the house of the LORD we bless you.
>   (Ps. 118:25-26)

It is often said that the people of Jerusalem welcomed Jesus as King and deliverer, only to turn against him later in the week with the cry, "We have no king but Caesar" (John 19:15). However, a close reading of the Gospels discloses that it is Jesus' disciples, going before and after him, who acclaim him in a royal manner, and not the crowds. Luke records that the Pharisees complain about Jesus' disciples, to which Jesus replies, "If they keep quiet, the stones will cry out" (Luke 19:40).

According to Matthew and Luke, Jesus proceeds immediately to drive the traders from the temple area, quoting Isaiah 56:7 and Jeremiah 7:11. In Mark's account, Jesus inspects the temple, returning to cleanse it the next day (Mark 11:15-17); John, in contrast to the synoptic writers, places this event at the very beginning of Jesus' ministry in connection with a Passover feast (John 2:13-22).

In the symbolism of Palm Sunday we see the coming of the sovereign Lord to his people, together with his judgment on religious institutions that have ceased to serve his purposes. As the Great King of the covenant, the Lord is the deliverer or Savior of his people; when he appears, the worshiper cries, "Come and save us" (Ps. 80:1-3). Several of the psalms celebrate the Lord's entry into the Holy City and sanctuary to assume his dominion (Pss. 24:7-10; 47:6-9; 50:3). But the Great King comes also to judge (Pss. 96:11-13; 98:8-9). The Davidic rulers of Judah, as the earthly vice-regents of Yahweh, were custodians of Solomon's temple, and several of them acted with zeal as restorers and reformers of the worship on Zion (Asa, 1 Kings 15:11-15; the younger Joash, 2 Kings 12:2-16; Hezekiah, 2 Kings 18:3-6; 2 Chron. 29—31; Josiah, 2 Kings 22—23). After the Babylonian captivity, the faithful longed for "the messenger of the covenant" who would purify the Jewish worship (Mal. 3:1-3). All this forms the background for Jesus' action as he enters Jerusalem, acclaimed with a royal title, and proceeds to a symbolic act of judgment on the central religious institution of the Judean community—a judgment to be fulfilled in the temple's destruction within a generation. The Palm Sunday procession is a proclamation that the King has come to reclaim his dominion and restore the true worship of the covenant. Thus the accolades of Palm Sunday are bound to the accusations that follow in the courtyard of the temple.

There is an additional note, however, in the action that fulfills the prophecy of Zechariah and in the cleansing of the temple. Riding into the city on a humble donkey, Jesus confirms that his kingship is not the overbearing and pompous rule of an earthly monarch. Furthermore, as the agent of the sovereign Lord, the one anointed to "preach good news to the poor" (Luke 4:18) takes on the religious establishment that controls the Judean economy through the commerce associated with temple worship. In the ancient world, temples functioned as banks, being considered safe repositories for funds; the Jerusalem temple drew revenue from all parts of the Jewish Diaspora for the maintenance of its operations. Within the temple precincts were concessions that sold animals for sacrifice, and currency exchanges where worshipers traded their Roman coins (which could not be used to buy sacrifices) for special temple coinage. Both of these businesses were highly profitable to the concessionaires, at the expense of the ordinary worshiper. But economic injustice has no place within the covenant community (Deut. 15:4; Isa. 3:13-15; Amos 2:6-7). It was Jesus who had declared, "Blessed are you who are poor, for yours is the kingdom of God" (Luke 6:20), and his cleansing of the temple further demonstrates his identification with the disadvantaged. As a perceived threat to the economic establishment, this act may have been a significant "political" cause of his later arrest and execution.

The Great Triduum ("Three Great Days")

In the ancient church Christians observed the Holy Week services of Thursday, Friday, and Saturday night (the great "Paschal Vigil") as one continuous service reenacting the final events of Christ's life and death preceding the Resurrection. The entries for Maundy Thursday, Good Friday, and Easter present the biblical background for these feasts. (For details concerning the worship of the "three great days," see Volume 5, _Resources for Services of One Christian Year._)

Maundy Thursday

The special commemoration of Christ's institution of the Lord's Supper, or Eucharist, is attested as early as the fourth century. The English name _Maundy Thursday_ comes from the Latin _mandatum novum,_ "a new commandment," in Jesus' words to his disciples as he washed their feet on the night of the Last Supper: "A new command I give you: Love one another" (John 13:34). In the Eastern church the day is known as "Holy Thursday." As part of the movement for renewal of historic liturgy in the twentieth century, many churches have returned to a fuller reenactment of the events of Maundy Thursday. These ceremonies include the "_agapē_ meal," or Christian love feast (its practice in the early church is suggested by Paul's correctives in 1 Cor. 11:20-22); the rite of foot washing, symbolic of the "new commandment" (John 13:1-15); the Lord's Supper itself; and the reenactment of the journey from the upper room to the Mount of Olives and the Garden (Mark 14:26). Even many nonliturgical churches observe the Lord's Supper in the evening on Maundy Thursday.

Probably no other act of Christian worship has been known by more terms and understood in more ways than the Lord's Supper; this is due in large part to the New Testament's own richness of imagery and terminology surrounding the commemoration of Jesus' action in the upper room. The Lord's Supper is an _ordinance of Christ;_ Jesus commanded his followers to repeat his action with the words "Do this in remembrance of me" (Luke 22:19). It is the _covenant meal;_ Jesus' words, "This is my blood of the covenant" (Mark 14:24), speak of the sacrifice that enacts the restored relationship between the Lord and his people. The Lord's Supper is a _communion_ or participation (_koinōnia_) in the life of Christ, as represented by the bread and the cup (1 Cor. 10:16-17), a communion not just of the individual worshiper but of the corporate church. The action of the Lord's Supper is a _proclamation of Christ's victory_ over sin, a dramatic re-presentation of the redeeming event of Christ's death (1 Cor. 11:26). The Lord's Supper is the _Eucharist,_ the "giving of thanks" to the Lord for his gifts of life and salvation, as Jesus gave thanks over the bread and the cup (Mark 14:22-23). Finally, it is a _sacramental act,_ in the sense of an outward symbol or spiritual window through which a deeper reality may be grasped. Because of the wealth of its testimony to the gospel, the Lord's Supper became the central and distinctive act of Christian worship.

Good Friday

The English name _Good Friday_ may be derived from the expression "God's Friday," designating the day observed as the anniversary of Christ's crucifixion, the decisive event in the plan of God for the redemption of his people. However, as Massey H. Shepherd has commented, the name _Good_ Friday "helps in some way to remind us of the primitive Christian celebration of this day as one of victorious conquest by Christ over sin and death" (_The Oxford American Prayer Book Commentary_ [1950], 156). The Greek church knows the day as "Great Friday."

Historically, the day has been one of fasting, abstinence, and penance. Customary Latin rites have included the "veneration of the cross," in which worshipers kiss the crucifix, and the Tenebrae service in the evening, which incorporates the gradual extinction of lights and candles in the church, the service concluding in complete darkness, symbolic of Christ's death and descent into hades. Another observance associated with the passion of Christ is the "stations of the cross," a series of devotional acts based on fourteen events from Christ's condemnation to death and his entombment; the "stations" are represented along the _Via Dolorosa_ in Jerusalem, which annually attracts pilgrims from the Christian world, and in the naves of many liturgical churches. Traditionally, the elements of the Mass are not consecrated on Good Friday nor on the following Saturday. Protestant churches, however, may observe the Lord's Supper on this day, and a common practice in North America has been for a group of churches in a community to unite in a three-hour service beginning at noon, devotionally rehearsing the events of the day of Jesus' crucifixion.

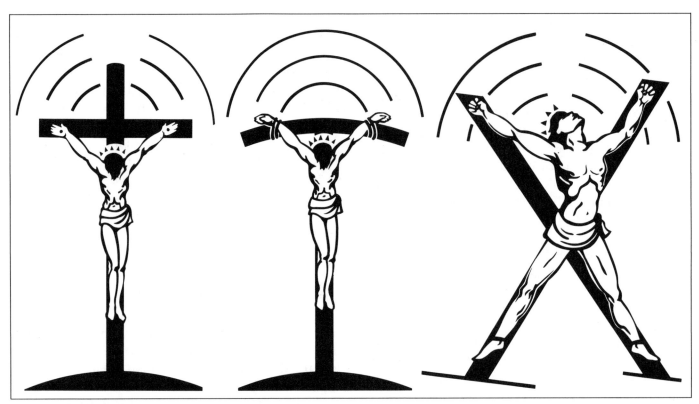

Three possible configurations of the cross.

The Gospels narrate in detail the events of Jesus' trial before the Jewish council, his arraignment before Pilate, his rejection by the multitude, his abuse by the soldiers, the carrying of the cross to Golgotha, his crucifixion between two criminals, his words from the cross, his death, and his entombment. In the Gospel records the day of Jesus' death occupies a disproportionate amount of a three-year ministry. Indeed, in Mark, it accounts for almost a tenth of the narrative. The Crucifixion, together with the Resurrection, was central in the proclamation of the early Christian preachers. This is clear from the sermons in Acts (Acts 2:23; 3:14-15; 7:52; 8:32-35; 10:39; 13:27-29); Paul, for one, determined to make it the focus of his message (1 Cor. 2:2).

The Gospels' stress on the events of Christ's passion and death reflects their origin in the expansion of the early preaching of the church. But whereas the sermons and correspondence of the apostles interpret Jesus' death through theological statements, the Gospels do so through narrative and dialogue. Developing the account of the Crucifixion in a fairly straightforward way, they allow the reader and hearer to experience the event through the record of even the smallest details. It is this quality of the

Gospel narratives that gives them their value in worship. Listening to their story, the believer becomes a participant in the drama through which the Father brings about the achievement of his purposes: the judgment of sin and the creation of the people of the new covenant.

Certain details of the Crucifixion account merit brief discussion. The cross itself (Greek *stauros*) may not have been the familiar shape of the Latin cross, but rather a vertical stake without a cross-arm (several references in the New Testament mention Christ's death on a "tree" [Acts 5:30; Gal. 3:13; 1 Pet. 2:24]). Crucifixion was a method of execution favored by Roman authorities for acts of rebellion. As a warning against other would-be disturbers of the peace, it was a form of public torture, in which the victim usually died a slow and agonizing death, as periods of unconsciousness alternated with periods of intense pain. However, Jesus' death on the cross occurred more quickly than usual. The Jewish authorities did not want those who had been executed to remain on the cross over the Passover Sabbath, so they requested that their legs be broken; this would hasten their death by suffocation, since they would not be able to push themselves up in order to breathe. Coming to Jesus, Pilate's soldiers were amazed to discover that he had already died (John 19:31-33; Matt. 27:50; Mark 15:37).

Of special note are the utterances of Jesus while on the cross. These have traditionally formed part of the basis for Christian worship on Good Friday, as well as a foundation for choral works on the "seven last words of Christ" (Schütz, Haydn, Dubois, or Stainer's _The Crucifixion_). Of these utterances, three are of special importance for the theological understanding of the Crucifixion. Jesus cries out, in Aramaic, "My God, my God, why have you forsaken me?" (Mark 15:34). Interpreters sometimes take these words to mean that the Father has "turned his back" on the Son so that he might bear the divine wrath, the penalty for mankind's sin, in utter abandonment. The words, however, are the first line of Psalm 22. Since the Scriptures at that time were not divided into chapter and verse numbers (these came much later), a section of the Bible was identified by its first line. The Gospels probably intend to tell us that Jesus recited the entire psalm, which ends on a note of praise and victory (Ps. 22:22-31). In the Christian proclamation the Cross is a defeat, not for Christ, but for the spiritual enemies of the people of God (Col. 2:8-15; _cf._ 1 Cor. 2:6-8). On the cross, Jesus willingly _gave his life_ "a ransom for many" (Mark 10:45); he "laid down his life" to take it up again (John 10:17). Thus Jesus' death is seen as his deliberate choice, as he calls out, "Father, into your hands I commit my spirit" (Luke 23:46), again a quotation from the Psalms (Ps. 31:5). Jesus died on the cross, but the cross did not kill him. He had already yielded up his life in the spiritual struggle of Gethsemane; the cross put the "It is finished" (John 19:30) to the decision he had already made.

At the moment of Jesus' death, according to Matthew and Mark, "the curtain of the temple was torn in two from top to bottom" (Matt. 27:51; Mark 15:38); Matthew adds that an earthquake occurred, releasing from their tombs "the bodies of many holy people who had died" (Matt. 27:51-53). The Gospels of Luke and John do not record these phenomena, but John in his Revelation tells of a great earthquake when two witnesses are slain and then raised (Rev. 11:11-13) and the dead are judged or rewarded" (Rev. 11:18), and the heavenly temple is opened and the ark of God's covenant revealed (Rev. 11:19). Without prejudicing their historical accuracy, these phenomena in the Gospels are perhaps best taken as word pictures on a par with the symbolic events in the drama of the book of Revelation—images through which the Christian community is expressing its understanding of the meaning of Jesus' crucifixion. His death "tore the veil" from the sanctuary, revealing the true and "heavenly" presence of the covenant God in the midst of his faithful saints. Earthquake and darkness (Matt. 27:45; Mark 15:33; Luke 23:44) are biblical images of divine judgment (Ps. 97:2-5); judgment occurs at the Cross, or rather the Cross exposes the judgment already made according to whether a person rejects or confesses Jesus as the Son of God (John 3:18-21). Significantly, a Roman centurion standing guard at the cross makes exactly this confession at the moment of Jesus' death: "Surely he was the Son of God!" (Matt. 27:54; Mark 15:39; cf. Luke 23:47).

209 • EASTER (PASCHA) TO PENTECOST

The celebrations of the Easter season have always been the most joyous festivals of the church year, for they focus on the event that vindicates Jesus as Lord and Messiah and that offers the promise of life for those who belong to him. "But Christ has indeed been raised from the dead, the firstfruits of those who have fallen asleep" (1 Cor. 15:20). The Easter or Paschal season includes Ascension Day and concludes with Pentecost.

Easter Day

The festival of the resurrection of Christ has been called "the greatest and oldest feast of the Christian Church" (_Oxford Dictionary of the Christian Church_ [New York: Oxford University Press, 1957], 432). There is no instruction in the New Testament regarding an annual festival of Jesus' resurrection; every Lord's Day, and indeed every gathering of his body, was a celebration of the presence of the risen Christ. Some exegetes, however, point to Paul's words in 1 Corinthians 5:7-8 as an indication that such an annual celebration of the Resurrection did occur among the early Christians: "For Christ, our Passover lamb, has been sacrificed. Therefore let us keep the Festival. . . ." In time, traditional rites developed for celebrating the resurrection of Christ, such as the "Paschal Vigil" in which catechumens (new converts preparing for church membership) kept watch in fasting and devotion from the day before (Holy Saturday) into the early hours of Easter Day,

The butterfly is an ancient symbol of the Resurrection.

when they were baptized and received the Eucharist. The Eastern church still observes the night vigil preceding an early morning Easter service, and it has been restored to Catholic and many Protestant churches as a result of the twentieth-century liturgical revival. The popular "sunrise service" followed by an Easter breakfast is a modern Protestant variation on this theme. These services are intended to commemorate the discovery of the Resurrection by Jesus' followers "on the first day of the week, very early in the morning" (Luke 24:1).

The English name *Easter,* according to the early eighth-century church historian Bede, is derived from the name of the Anglo-Saxon spring goddess Eostre—a name that probably goes back to the fertility goddess Ishtar, or Astarte, the Ashtoreth worshiped by the Israelites during periods of apostasy (1 Sam. 7:3-4; 1 Kings 11:33). In many languages the name of Easter is a derivation of the Hebrew *Pesaḥ,* "Passover" (as in Latin *Pascha,* French *Pâques*). Today, many students of liturgy argue for a return to the original name, Pascha, to avoid the pagan terms and concepts originally associated with the name Easter.

The date of Easter, like that of the Jewish Passover, moves each year and governs that portion of the liturgical calendar which moves with it (from the beginning of Lent through Pentecost). But whereas Passover moves with the procession of the lunar cycle of twenty-eight days, which defines the Jewish month, the date of Easter depends on the "Paschal full moon" and can fall in the Western church any Sunday from 21 March through 25 April. The early medieval church was marked by the "Paschal controversies," bitter disputes over the method of determining the date of the Easter celebration.

The Gospels do not narrate the actual resurrection of Christ, but rather its *discovery* by Jesus' disciples and his subsequent appearances to them. Thus the Resurrection retains that aura of mystery, or sense of the numinous, as an extraordinary manifestation of the power of God which cannot be encompassed by the grasp of the rational mind. To narrate the event itself would be to divest it of its gripping quality, just as artistic representations of it are unsuccessful (Grünewald's and Blake's being among the better examples). In the Gospels, one encounters the Resurrection through the eyes of its first beholders, in their startling discovery of the empty tomb and the angelic witnesses and in Jesus' own sudden appearances to them in the garden, in the street, behind closed doors, on the road to Emmaus, at the supper table, and later beside the Lake of Tiberias. Each of the Gospels tells a different story of events in the days after Christ was raised from the dead. Yet, for any who would doubt the Resurrection, the variety in the Gospel narratives only adds to their credibility. It works against any accusation of the collusion of witnesses, and shows that the wonder and excitement of the day of Resurrection was still a vivid memory in the various Christian communities out of which the Gospels emerged decades after the event.

One thing on which all the Gospels agree is that it was *women* who were the first witnesses to the Resurrection, chiefly Miriam of Migdal or Mary Magdalene (Matt. 28:1-10; Mark 16:1-8; Luke 24:1-10; John 20:1-18). According to Luke, the disciples were reluctant to believe their word (Luke 24:11), and John admits the disciples were slow to understand the Scripture that proclaimed Christ must rise from the dead (John 20:9). Sometimes the witnesses to the Resurrection did not recognize Jesus until he spoke a familiar word (calling Mary by name, John 20:16, 26; greeting his disciples, "Peace be with you," John 20:19) or performed a familiar gesture (blessing and breaking the bread, Luke 24:30-31). Thomas, who insisted he would not believe Jesus was alive until he could feel his wounds, never had to do this; it was enough for Jesus to speak, and he knew him as "My Lord and my God!" (John 20:24-28).

The Resurrection, together with the Crucifixion, formed the cornerstone of the apostolic message; an apostle had to be one who could be "a witness with us of his resurrection" (Acts 1:22). Whereas the Crucifixion effected "for all time one sacrifice for sins" (Heb. 10:12), the Resurrection verified that Jesus was "both Lord and Christ" (Acts 2:36), the Servant appointed to restore the covenant (Acts 3:20-26), the "judge of the living and the dead" (Acts 10:42), whether Jew or Gentile (Acts 17:31). Thus the earliest Christian creedal statements—like that of Paul, who "delivered to you as of first importance what [he] also received"—may have consisted largely of a listing of appearances of the risen Christ (1 Cor. 15:3-8 NASB).

Early Christian worship was therefore a celebration of the Resurrection. In Paul's interpretation, the Lord's Supper itself, though a commemoration of the new covenant in the symbols of Jesus' body and blood, was not focused on his death so much as on his coming (1 Cor. 11:26) and, in fact, on his presence with his people through the _koinōnia,_ or participation, in the life of his body (cf. 1 Cor. 10:16-17). The evidence of the life of the Spirit in Christian worship (1 Cor. 12–14; Eph. 5:18-20) is the witness to the Resurrection, since "the Lord is the Spirit" (2 Cor. 3:17). It is not by accident that Paul, writing to the Corinthians, moves directly from his discussion of the Resurrection—"Christ has been raised from the dead. . . . thanks be to God! He gives us the victory"—to instructions for the church's assembly on the first day of the week (1 Cor. 15:12–16:2). The apostle John also testifies to the centrality of the Resurrection in worship; the majestic anthems of the Revelation, which must reflect the hymnody familiar to his readers, are centered in the ascription of honor and dominion to the Lord God and to Jesus the Lamb, "the firstborn from the dead" (Rev. 1:5) who declares, "I am the First and the Last. I am the Living One; I was dead, and behold I am alive for ever and ever!" (Rev. 1:17-18). In the worship of the church, the new Jerusalem, the Lord dwells among his people, so that "there will be no more death" (Rev. 21:3-4).

Ascension

In the New Testament, the ascension of Christ marks the close of his appearances to the disciples following the Resurrection. The full account of the Ascension is given by Luke at the beginning of the Acts of the Apostles. After being raised from the dead, Jesus "after his suffering, showed himself to these men and gave many convincing proofs that he was alive. He appeared to them over a period of forty days and spoke about the kingdom of God" (Acts 1:3). At the end of this period, Jesus gathered his disciples together and promised they would soon be baptized with the Holy Spirit, receiving power to be his witnesses first in Jerusalem, then throughout Judea and Samaria, and then into other regions. Having said these things, "he was taken up before their very eyes, and a cloud hid him from their sight." Immediately, two angelic messengers appeared, telling the disciples that Jesus "will come back in the same way you have seen him go into heaven" (Acts 1:4-11). Luke presents an abbreviated version of the story at the end of his Gospel (Luke 24:50-51) which establishes Bethany, on the Mount of Olives, as the setting and indicates that Jesus was parted from the disciples as he was blessing them. The longer ending of Mark's Gospel links the Ascension to Jesus' commission to "go into all the world and preach the good news to all creation" (Mark 16:15), declaring that after Jesus had spoken to his disciples, "he was taken up into heaven and he sat at the right hand of God" (Mark 16:19).

The Resurrection establishes Jesus' victory over death and his identity as the Messiah, the Son of God. The Ascension further establishes his kingship and authority over all things, as the one "taken up in glory" (1 Tim. 3:16), exalted by the Lord God to share his throne (Rev. 3:21) and to govern at his right hand (Acts 2:33; 1 Pet. 3:22). Having "gone through the heavens" (Heb. 4:14), Jesus continues to minister as High Priest, interceding for his people before God (Heb. 7:25-26). From his exalted throne he pours out the Holy Spirit, empowering his church for witness (Acts 2:33). In ascending into heaven, he sums up or "fills" all things and gives leadership gifts for the building up of his body and the equipping of Christians for service to God (Eph. 4:7-13). Thus the Ascension speaks of Christ's present and ongoing work as "head over everything for the church" (Eph. 1:22). To the first disciples, the Ascension also spoke of Jesus' return in judgment on the unfaithful, his coming "in like manner" in the clouds, which are a biblical symbol of the Lord's dealing with violators of the covenant (Matt. 24:30).

The special observance of Ascension Day is recorded beginning with the latter part of the fourth century; rites associated with the day have included processions symbolic of the kingly authority of Christ. Since the Ascension occurred forty days after the Resurrection, Ascension Day falls on the sixth Thursday after Easter. Many churches, however, now observe it on the following Sunday.

Pentecost

The festival of Pentecost brings the Paschal season to a close. The name *Pentecost* is the Greek name for the Israelite Feast of Weeks (*Shavu'ot*); it means "fiftieth," referring to the celebration of this festival fifty days after Passover. It was on this feast day that the apostles, after Jesus' resurrection, were all "filled with the Holy Spirit and began to speak in other tongues" (Acts 2:4), and it was on this occasion that they first openly proclaimed the resurrection and Messiahship of Jesus Christ, baptizing thousands of new converts. The Christian commemoration of Pentecost is attested in Jerusalem from the late fourth century. Pentecost was, like Easter, a day for baptisms, and the traditional English name *Whitsunday* is an allusion to the white robes worn by baptismal candidates.

In ancient Israel, the firstfruits of the grain harvest were presented at the Feast of Weeks (Deut. 16:9-10), which was also known as the "Feast of the Harvest" (Exod. 23:16) or "day of firstfruits" (Num. 28:26). At the offering of firstfruits, the worshiper was to recite the story of how the Lord had delivered Israel from Egypt and brought them into the plenteous land of Canaan. The agricultural symbolism of the festival remained predominant until the destruction of Herod's temple, when the emphasis shifted to commemoration of the giving of the Torah. The symbolism of the "day of firstfruits" is important for understanding the meaning of the first Christian Pentecost.

Jesus had spoken several times to his disciples about the coming of the Holy Spirit: at the Feast of Tabernacles (John 7:37-39), on the night of his arrest (John 16:7-15), and in his appearances after the Resurrection (Acts 1:4-5). Jesus referred to the Spirit as "the gift my Father promised," and at the time of his ascension he equated the coming of the Holy Spirit with the power to be his witnesses (Acts 1:8). Acting as spokesman for the apostles, Peter on the day of Pentecost announced that Jesus, having "received from the Father the promised Holy Spirit," had now

conveyed it to his church as well. The phenomenon of speaking in other tongues is the evidence that Jesus lives, exalted at the right hand of God, from which he "has poured out what you now see and hear" (Acts 2:33). According to Mark's Gospel, speaking with "new tongues" was to be one of the signs that would accompany those who believe and preach the gospel of Christ (Mark 16:17).

The Pentecost event, therefore, is a sign that a new epoch has begun. What Jesus promised has now been realized. The "last days" spoken of by the prophet Joel have arrived (Acts 2:16-18). Just as the Israelite, presenting his firstfruits, stands in the Promised Land, so the Christian, filled with the Holy Spirit, now stands in the completion of what was promised. For Israel, the possession of the land was the blessing that fulfilled the covenant. For the Christian community, baptized by the Spirit into one body (1 Cor. 12:13), the life of the Holy Spirit is the restoration of the covenant: it is the kingdom of God (Rom. 14:17), the "new creation" (2 Cor. 5:17) of life energized by the risen Christ (Rom. 8:9-11), the "eternal life" of those who have the Son (John 4:14).

As the Holy Spirit is the "firstfruits" in Christian believers of what is to come (Rom. 8:23), so the apostolic church saw itself corporately as the firstfruits of a greater harvest. James wrotes that the church had been brought forth by the Word as "firstfruits of all he created" (James 1:18). In the Revelation, John pictures the apostolic church as the 144 thousand, or twelve times twelve times a thousand, the true Israel of whatever tribal or cultural or linguistic background, "purchased from among men and offered as firstfruits to God and the Lamb" (Rev. 14:4). Because it marks the first gathering of believers to testify to the Resurrection (Acts 2:1), the beginning of the process of world evangelization (Acts 2:41), and the initiation of the church's characteristic corporate life (Acts 2:42-47), Pentecost has rightly been called the "birthday of the church."

The Pentecost event stands at a strategic point in the basic plan of the scriptural drama: it is the typological reversal of the damage done at the tower of Babel. At Babel, people were determined to build a monument to themselves, a culture without regard for God; as a result, they were scattered over the earth, unable to communicate (Gen. 11:1-9). In Pentecost, the language barrier is swept aside, as people "from every nation under heaven" hear the apostles "declaring the wonders of God" in languages they can understand (Acts 2:5-11).

Pentecost, then, has the possibility for a rich symbolism in Christian worship. Churches that emerged in the early twentieth century around the revival of the practice of tongues and the other New Testament spiritual gifts—the "pentecostal" churches—have received their designation from this festival. Pentecost has also been important in the modern ecumenical movement as an occasion for celebrating the worldwide unity of the church. Historically, it has been a day for the baptism of new believers and was considered a festival second in importance only to Easter. Although its potential in the church's worship life today seems to be largely untapped, many churches are beginning to recover the significance of Pentecost as a major day of festive celebration.

210 • Season After Pentecost

The liturgical calendar, which sequentially presents events in the life of Christ, ends with Pentecost. The season between Pentecost and Advent is called the "season after Pentecost" in most Christian traditions. Although it does not feature any major festivals of the Christian year, many lesser feasts and fasts fall in this period. Two of these, standing at the beginning and end of the season, are Trinity Sunday and the Festival of Christ the King.

Trinity Sunday

Beginning in the Middle Ages, the first Sunday after Pentecost began to be designated in honor of the Holy Trinity as a kind of capstone to the portion of the liturgical year that celebrates the major events of the Christian revelation. The observance of Trinity Sunday became especially popular in England, and the Anglican community has traditionally observed only a brief Pentecost season, followed by a long Trinity season lasting until Advent. Although the "season after Pentecost" has more recently been restored, the Festival of the Trinity continues as part of the liturgical calendar. It is the only major observance of the Christian year dedicated to a doctrine, rather than to an event.

Christ the King

The feast of Christ the King was initiated by Pope Pius XI in 1925 and assigned to the last Sunday of October. Subsequently, it has been moved to the last Sunday of the season after Pentecost (the Sunday before Advent). In its position at the end of the liturgical year, this festival proclaims the goal toward which human history moves: the universal reign of Jesus Christ. The Festival of Christ the King has its foundation in the biblical vision of God's purpose, "to be put into effect when the times will have reached their fulfillment—to bring all things in heaven and on earth together under one head, even Christ" (Eph. 1:10). In some denominations "Kingdomtide" is an alternate name for the greater part of the season after Pentecost.

World Communion Sunday

Nonliturgical churches have traditionally limited their observance of festivals to major events such as Christmas, Holy Week, and Easter. Those churches that follow the seasons of the liturgical year usually celebrate the Eucharist or Holy Communion each week. In other Protestant denominations the Lord's Supper is generally observed periodically (a common practice being the first Sunday of each month). World Communion Sunday developed in the twentieth century as a device to encourage nonliturgical churches of all types to celebrate the Lord's Supper on the same day at least once annually. While the day is not part of the traditional calendar, it has special value for many churches as a reminder of the local congregation's oneness with the "catholic," or universal, church. The New Testament holds the unity of the church, in faithfulness to the purposes of God, in high esteem. Jesus prayed for such unity among his own in all eras, as a reflection of his own unity with the Father (John 17:20-22), and Paul proclaimed "one Lord, one faith, one baptism" (Eph. 4:5). In relationship to the Lord's Supper, he declared that "we who are many, are one body, for we all partake of the one loaf" (1 Cor. 10:17). World Communion Sunday is a reflection of this truth.

Richard C. Leonard

211 • Bibliography: Festivals in Biblical Worship

Bubsbazer, Victor. _The Gospel in the Feasts of Israel._ Fort Washington, Pa.: Christian Literature Crusade, 1954. This popular treatment examines each of the feasts of Israel for its gospel associations.

Stallings, Joseph. *Rediscovering Passover: A Complete Guide for Christians*. San Jose, Calif.: Resource Publications, 1988. Written in nontechnical language, this book introduces the reader to the basic biblical and historical material on the Passover, as well as its liturgical form. Emphasis is placed on the Christian understanding of the Passover.

Yee, Gale A. *Jewish Feasts and the Gospel of John*. Wilmington, Del.: Michael Glazier, 1989. This is an excellent presentation of the Sabbath, Passover, Tabernacles, and the Feast of Dedication in the Gospel of John.

Zimmerman, Martha. *Celebrate the Feasts*. Minneapolis: Bethany House Publishers, 1981. This work is a popular Christian exploration of the feasts of Israel and their meaning for Christians. It contains specific directions for the celebration of the feasts.

PART FOUR

Music and the Arts in Biblical Worship

◦ TWENTY ◦

Biblical Philosophy of the Worship Arts

Throughout the history of the Christian church, worship has made use of the fine arts as vehicles for bringing glory to God and for augmenting the worshiper's awareness of the presence of God. In considering the biblical foundations for Christian worship, therefore, it is appropriate to give attention to the biblical perspective on the arts.

212 • THE WORSHIP ARTS IN BIBLICAL PERSPECTIVE

The biblical doctrine of Creation has important implications for the use of the fine arts in worship, as does the doctrine of the Incarnation. The scriptural view of humankind as created in God's image, the concept of inspiration, and the biblical understanding of the covenant also contribute their perspective on the fine arts. The arts are uniquely capable of expressing the nonrational element in the worship experience.

——— Renewal of Interest in the Arts ———

Art, as a human activity, is a reflection of the activity of the Creator. Worship is a response to the Creator's revelation of himself. It is understandable that throughout history, and in all cultures and religious traditions, worship and the arts have been allied. The closeness of this alliance, however, has varied from era to era and community to community. In the centuries following the demise of the Roman Empire it was Christendom that supplied the framework holding European civilization together; during the Middle Ages, the arts were placed almost completely at the disposal of the church. The Renaissance was marked by a recovery of the principles and preoccupations of classic, pre-Christian art, and in the following centuries much of the church (the Protestant wing in particular) reacted to the secularization of the fine arts by virtually turning its back on them, concentrating on the spoken word and the life of piety. As a result, art became separated

from faith, and worship often became a barren and colorless affair.

More recently, Christian churches have begun to move back toward the appropriation of the arts in the service of God, especially in worship. But unless renewed appreciation for the fine arts is grounded in a clear understanding of their foundation and function within the biblical perspective, the church faces two dangers. The first is that this recovery of the arts is likely to be a passing phenomenon, soon abandoned for the next stimulating trend. The second is that artistic activity within the Christian community will become art for its own sake, inadequately anchored in the principles of the gospel, as has often been the case in the past. The biblical perspective offers an approach to the philosophy of the fine arts as vehicles for the worship of God.

Richard C. Leonard

——— Art and the Creation ———

A biblical philosophy of the arts may take its departure from the scriptural understanding of the creative activity of God. In the biblical perspective, the Creation is the result of the initiative of God in bringing order out of chaos, "dividing" light from darkness, the land from the waters (Gen. 1:3-8). The Genesis account of Creation proceeds from the appearance of basic energy ("light") to formless substance ("the waters"), to the separation of the heavens and earth, then to *terra firma* with its vegetation, followed by aquatic animal life, and ending with the appearance of land animals and, finally, humankind. The created universe is coherent and planned, exhibiting the design of its Maker: "the heavens declare the glory of God" (Ps. 19:1).

By producing new forms, new artifacts, new expressions that communicate truth in fresh ways, artists function as "creators," in finite measure, to the glory of the infinite Creator. Essentially, the work of the artist is to bring about new patterns of significance by reshaping the gifts given by God in creation. This means, above all, producing images and patterns of order, beauty, and meaning. Many of the greatest works of art in the world—the Sistine Chapel, Dürer's *Praying Hands,* Bach's B-minor Mass, Dante's *Divine Comedy*—do precisely this, and elevate those who contemplate them.

Human art, however, is subject to the condition in which the human race exists, and that entails creativity within the condition of fallenness. Consequently, to communicate truth in art may mean producing accurate images of our sin, our dysfunction, our brokenness. The literary art of the Bible does not compromise on this score; it portrays humans as they are, warts and all. Similarly, Scripture vividly portrays human doubt and human protest against evil in the world. Art, then, may serve a positive function even when it shows us what is wrong in the world, and by implication points to what is right. Because of its power, however, art can also be turned to purposes that foster and justify evil when it becomes pornography or the glorification of violence or propaganda.

The creative impulse, then, is one of the greatest natural gifts of God to humanity, and has everything to do with being created in the image of God. His power can be turned to the greatest possible good when, as heirs of Adam, human beings name their world in order to offer it back up to God in praise and adoration.

Larry Nyberg

— Art and the Celebration of Creation —

Artistic activity can be a celebration of God's creation, drawing on motifs and patterns found in the created order. The description of the decorative work of Solomon's temple (1 Kings 6–7) contains examples of such borrowing. The interior walls, of cedar overlaid with gold, were engraved with gourds, open flowers, palm trees, and cherubim. In the inner sanctuary stood two cherubim, carved from olive wood and covered with gold; here was placed the ark of the covenant, which had been made along with the Mosaic tabernacle (Exod. 25:10-22) and also had two cherubim of hammered gold on its cover. The lampstands were probably similar to that of the tabernacle, which was of hammered gold with cups shaped like almond blossoms (Exod. 25:31-36). Similar designs were found on the doors to the inner and outer sanctuaries, and the linen veil of the inner sanctuary, like that of the tabernacle, had cherubim worked into it (2 Chron. 3:14). Framing the great outer door of the temple were two freestanding columns; the Bible does not ascribe any function to them, so we must assume they were purely decorative, adding to the august dignity of the house of the Lord. Their bronze capitals were "in the shape of lilies" (1 Kings 7:19), set over pomegranates, and festooned with chainwork. Next to the temple stood the bronze "sea," a water reservoir set upon four rows of three oxen, each facing one of the cardinal directions; under the edge of the sea, which was "like the rim of a cup, like a lily blossom" (1 Kings 7:26), was a border of gourds. The lavers, where the priests washed, stood on frames decorated with lions, oxen, and cherubim. The vestments of the high priest, as described in the directions for the construction of the tabernacle, which preceded the temple (Exod. 28), included the breastpiece decorated with twelve precious gems and the robe with a hem of golden bells alternating with blue, purple, and scarlet pomegranates.

In this way the visual imagery of the Solomonic sanctuary replicated motifs from the created order of plant and animal life. But these motifs are not actually flowers, lions, trees, or pomegranates but representations of them: blossoms engraved in *gold,* bulls cast in *bronze,* pomegranates colored *blue.* In other words, art is *artificial,* the result of the application of a humanly conceived design and human skills to materials found in the "natural" state.

Of special interest are the cherubim in the inner sanctuary, or "Holy of Holies," and on the ark of the covenant. The Bible does not describe the appearance of these symbols. Their function, however, was to represent the throne of the Lord of Hosts, *Yahveh tzᵉva'ot,* the name of the Lord as Israel's King and leader in battle; in several places he is referred to as dwelling "above" or "between the cherubim" (Exod. 25:22; 1 Sam. 4:4; Pss. 80:1; 99:1; Isa. 37:16). Archaeology has revealed that the thrones of ancient rulers, such as the Assyrian kings of Nineveh, were often flanked by guardian figures in the form of a winged creature with the head of a man and a body with features of the lion and the ox. This composite motif resembles the four "living creatures" of Ezekiel's vision and the Revelation to John, and we note that there were actually _four_ cherubim in the temple in addition to those carved on the walls and doors. If the biblical cherubim resembled the "living creatures," we see in them a masterful artistic transformation of imagery found in animate life, centrally placed within the symbolism of the house of God.

Biblical worship thus may incorporate artistic motifs drawn from a creation God pronounced to be "very good" (Gen. 1:31; the Hebrew word can have the sense of "beautiful"). The appropriate use of such imagery can be an affirmation of the supreme authority of God the Creator, in the conviction that "the earth is the LORD's and everything in it" (Ps. 24:1). On the other hand, when the motivation to glorify the Lord is lacking, such usage can be a worship and glorification of "the creature rather than the Creator" (Rom. 1:25, NASB). This is why the bronze serpent, a work of art created by Moses at the Lord's command (Num. 21:8-9), eventually had to be destroyed in a reform of King Hezekiah (2 Kings 18:4), in the same manner as all idols and images originating in polytheistic worship outside God's covenant.

Art and the Incarnation

Most attempts to shape a Christian philosophy of the arts have centered around the doctrine of the Incarnation. The biblical proclamation that "the Word became flesh and made his dwelling among us" (John 1:14) is viewed as an affirmation that humanity, along with the physical world in which people live, is made sacred in virtue of God's participation within it. Christ's emptying of himself, to be "made in human likeness" (Phil. 2:7) and to be subject to the conditions of human existence in an imperfect world, is understood to provide a basis for the Christian's approach to the work even of non-Christian artists. One may see in Christ, as "the image of the invisible God" (Col. 1:15), the supreme artistic expression of the Creator; God's action in Christ to recreate the world through redemption may be understood as a basis for the artistic work of recreation. The idea that in Christ God has become

one with his creation, in order to redeem it for _recreation_ through human artistic activity, is a theological interpretation of biblical data. Consequently, the fuller articulation of an incarnation-based philosophy of the arts has not been the work of biblical expositors but of aesthetic theorists and theologians working with the materials of historic Christian theology.

The Image of God and the Arts

In both ancient mythological religions and modern evolutionary philosophy, humankind is an accidental appearance on the earth. In ancient Mesopotamian myths, for example, the creation of man is a by-product of the cosmic struggle between competing deities. The evolutionary philosophy that underlies the modern view of man is not far removed from that of ancient mythology, for it sees the origin of humankind as the result of the operation of blind, impersonal forces of time and chance. By contrast, the Bible represents humankind as the deliberate creation of God, who made humans, male and female, in his own image (Gen. 1:27).

The concept of humankind as created in God's image has several implications for human artistic activity. First, it suggests that there is no need to fashion an artistic image of the deity; humankind is already that representation—the handiwork of the Creator who has provided his own visual reminder of his presence in, and ownership of, the earth. As an ancient king would erect an image of himself at the boundaries of his territory to signify the extent of his kingdom, so God has placed humankind on the earth as a sign of his dominion. The scriptural prohibition of any kind of molten or sculpted image of Yahweh, which stands at the head of the laws of the covenant (Exod. 20:4; 34:17), gives statutory expression to this principle.

Second, as the representative of the Creator, humankind is charged with the management of the earth and the life that fills it (Gen. 1:28-30; 2:15). Human beings fulfill this role in exercising their capacity for making. To use J.R.R. Tolkien's word, they become _sub-creators;_ as sub-creators, "we make in our measure and in our derivative mode because we are made: and not only made, but made in the image and likeness of a Maker ("On Fairie Stories," in _Tree and Leaf_ [Boston: Houghton Mifflin, 1964], pp. 54-55). To create a work of art, as a reflection of God's creative activity, is to bring together seemingly unrelated elements into a new design that does not occur in nature.

Third, as beings made in the image of God, people find their deepest selves through worship, the expression of communion and covenant with their Maker. The artistic effort should not be motivated by "self-expression" in worship but by the desire to glorify the Lord and express longing for him.

Inspiration in the Fine Arts

The Bible recognizes general revelation, the idea that God can be known in some measure to all people through his creation; indeed, Paul asserts that this general revelation renders people without excuse for failing to acknowledge God or give thanks to him (Rom. 1:18-21). The understanding of God's specific character and historic purposes, however, can be known only by revelation at his initiative; it cannot be known in the first instance by visual or auditory perception or by the imagination of human intellect (Isa. 64:4; 1 Cor. 2:9) but must be revealed "through the Spirit," the breath or life of God directly impacting the soul.

In Scripture, activity associated with the fine arts is connected with divine inspiration. In the case of visual arts, Bezalel, the chief artisan of the Mosaic tabernacle, is introduced as a man "filled with the Spirit of God" (Exod. 31:1-3). The association of the Spirit of God with musical activity is more pronounced. Samuel, having anointed Saul king, tells him that he will encounter a band of prophets coming down from the sanctuary, prophesying to the accompaniment of musical instruments; the Spirit of God will come upon him, and he himself will prophesy, being "changed into a different person" (1 Sam. 10:5-6). Prophetic activity is carried out under the direction and impulse of the Spirit of God, and in the Bible, prophecy and music are closely allied. David appointed the Levitical musicians to "prophesy" in the praise and thanksgiving of worship before the ark (1 Chron. 25:1-7). Elisha called for a player on the lyre in order to prophesy to the kings of Israel, Judah, and Edom (2 Kings 3:13-15). The prophetic books of Scripture are filled with song, and the public regarded Ezekiel more as a musician than as a prophet, to his consternation (Ezek. 33:32). In early Christian worship, constant thanksgiving with "psalms, hymns and spiritual songs" is a direct result of being "filled with the Spirit" (Eph. 5:18-20). Rejoicing, whether in music, spoken praise, or choreography, can be at the impulse of the Holy Spirit. The gospel records that Jesus was "full of joy through the Holy Spirit" when the seventy reported the results of their preaching of the kingdom of God; the Greek word can indicate leaping or dancing (Luke 10:21).

Of paramount importance is the Spirit's direction in literary activity; the doctrine of the inspiration of Scripture is well developed and needs no elaboration here. The role of the Spirit of God in the formation of prophetic literature is, of course, especially evident; prophecy took shape as "men spoke from God as they were carried along by the Holy Spirit" (2 Pet. 1:21). A hint of the impulse of the Spirit in psalmic poetry may be seen in the poet's words, "My heart is stirred by a noble theme. . . . my tongue is the pen of a skillful writer" (Ps. 45:1). In a similar vein, the young man Elihu claims a spiritual impetus for his poetic contribution to the debate between Job and his friends (Job 32:6-22). Some of the great word pictures of Scripture are presented in the context of the special movement of the Spirit upon the author. Ezekiel's spectacular vision of the four living creatures supporting the throne of the glorious Lord was the occasion of the Spirit's coming upon him (Ezek. 1:1–2:2), and John the Revelator was "in the Spirit on the Lord's day" (Rev. 1:10, NASB) when he was granted the vision of the radiant, living Son of man.

In scriptural perspective, therefore, one may speak of an inspired work of art, particularly one that is rendered in the service of God. Of course, not all visual, musical, choreographic, or literary materials, even if used in a worship context, are inspired in the biblical sense; while they may have been executed with great skill, they may not have the stamp of the Spirit of God as vehicles of the holy. Further, an artistic creation may indeed be "inspired" but not with the Spirit of God; in the spiritual warfare of the unseen realm, so real to biblical people but a closed book for modern rationalistic minds, other dark powers make their influence known through the work of practitioners of the fine arts. The Christian worshiper uses a biblically informed discretion in judging any artistic creation to be "inspired."

Worship Arts and the Covenant

As the framework of God's relationship with his people, the biblical covenant finds expression in the worship arts. Worship celebrates the distinctive themes of the covenant: the kingship of the Lord; his leadership and protection in warfare; his covenant promises and the story of his great deeds of deliverance; his laws and precepts, in the observance of which the worshiper maintains his place in the covenant; and his judgments against violation of the relationship, as expressed in prophetic psalm or song uttered during the assemblies of the people.

The covenant is corporate; it is a relationship between the Lord and the entire _worshiping community_. In revealing his covenant name to Moses, Yahweh related it to his involvement in the history of a people, the ancestors of Israel: "The LORD, the God of your fathers—the God of Abraham, the God of Isaac and the God of Jacob" (Exod. 3:14-15). Although the covenant is promised, mediated, and renewed through individual leaders—patriarchs, prophets, kings—it is made with _all the people,_ a people consecrated to the Lord: "The LORD your God has chosen you out of all the peoples on the face of the earth to be his people, his treasured possession" (Deut. 7:6). In the prayer and hymnody of covenant worship, the speaker represents the entire community, not himself as an individual. This accounts for the prominent place given to the king, as the nation's representative, in the prayer and praise of the Psalms and in the erection and dedication of the temple. It accounts for the role of the prophet as intercessor for the people in the face of impending judgment (Amos 7:1-6). It also accounts for the fact that so much of the biblical literature is really _anonymous,_ though often included in books associated with the names of prominent figures. Although more than half of the Psalms are related in their superscriptions to David, Asaph, or other musicians, many psalms have no superscription. Of the prophetic books, one that eloquently proclaims the Lord's purification of covenant worship is anonymous: "Malachi" simply means "my messenger" in Hebrew. Only later, in the Hellenistic period, did Hebrew thought come to see the arts and literature in terms of individual authorship. In the well-known passage beginning, "Let us now praise famous men" (Sir. 44:1), Jesus ben Sirach celebrates the achievement of "those who composed musical tunes, and set forth verses in writing" (Sir. 44:5). But the visual art of the early Christian movement, and most of its hymnody, are anonymous. From the biblical standpoint, individual creativity is not important, especially in the worship arts. Here the Christian artist is

not making a statement of personal religious experience or calling attention to himself but is seeking to sum up the corporate experience of the church. When he or she expresses a personal faith, it is faith as practiced within the context of the community of faith.

The Numinous Aspect of the Arts

The biblical conception of God as holy has profound significance for the philosophy of the worship arts. The biblical worshiper encounters the Lord as the Holy One. The basic connotation of holiness (Hebrew _qodesh_) is not the goodness or righteousness of Yahweh but the fact that he is encountered as one "set apart," sacred or sacrosanct, unlike that which is experienced in the ordinary events of life. There is, in other words, a _numinous_ aspect to the encounter with the Lord, a quality of mystery, dread, and fascination in his presence, which calls forth a spontaneous and intuitive response of worship. The rational mind cannot encompass his being, nor can human language adequately bear the majesty of his presence. Worship, like theology, must express itself through transforms of the experience of the holy, symbols that point beyond themselves to the reality reason alone cannot grasp.

It is here that the fine arts make their essential and distinctive contribution to the worship of Almighty God. Whether visual, auditory, literary, choreographic, or liturgical, art forms can augment the worshiper's sensitivity to the sacred in a way that common verbal communication cannot. Language, as a means of communication, depends on the premise that a symbol used by one speaker will be intelligible to another and therefore involves a rational process that issues in some kind of linear, conventional ordering of phonemes and thought units. Art forms, as well, require the application of rational processes in their creation and appreciation, but as a means of communication they operate at another level, touching the intuitive faculties of the human psyche. Art may be a window into unseen realities. The _Last Supper_ fresco of Leonardo da Vinci is more of a humanistic _tour de force_ of Renaissance technique than a vehicle for grasping the passion of Christ. By contrast, the roughly contemporaneous _Last Supper_ of Tintoretto, its scene shading from the table of Christ and the disciples into the heavenly host, is a numinous window into the eternal truth "This is my body"; and the *Isenheim Altarpiece* of Grünewald, with its massive, distorted depiction of the crucified Christ, conveys with compelling force the weight of sin and suffering borne by the Savior.

The Bible is full of artistic creations, symbols fashioned or enacted by worshipers as expressions of that which cannot be encompassed by ordinary speech: the tabernacle and the temple, with their furnishings; the vesture of the priests; the ark of the covenant and its cherubim; the symbolic acts of liturgy and sacrifice; sacred gesture such as bowing down and lifting hands and festival processions; the many word symbols of covenant liturgy, hymn and psalm, prophetic song and vision, parable and preaching. The colors used in the Mosaic tabernacle and its priestly vesture are sometimes interpreted as prophetic, standing for some theological truth or concept; in fact, their "meaning" is to serve as artistic expressions of the numinous quality of the house of God. As an art form, even unintelligible speech, or speaking in tongues, conveys such a meaning in relationship to the presence of the holy and is not an ecstatic or emotional activity as some nonpractitioners suppose. The most numinous of the arts is music, which speaks most directly to the intuitive capacities of the worshiper, bearing a sense of majesty, wonder, mystery, and delight, and bringing a release of the soul even without recourse to words. It is well to recall, in this connection, how much of the Bible is poetry and song. God is not an idea but a reality encountered at the deepest level of being; from this perspective, art is not only permitted in biblical worship, it is mandatory.

213 • THE VISUAL ARTS IN WORSHIP

As worship arts, the visual arts include architecture, sculpture, painting, mosaic, and the crafting of artifacts. These arts create durable objects that may be seen and handled. Although of lesser importance in the biblical perspective than some other art forms, the visual arts may serve as effective windows into the holy.

Static Nature of the Visual Arts

With the exception of architecture and its associated furnishings, the visual arts are given lesser importance in biblical worship than are other art forms. The reason for this may be found in the character of Yahweh. The Bible associates his name with a Hebrew phrase meaning "I will be who I will be," and makes clear that he is known by his people through their experience with him in the ongoing events of redemptive history. In other words, Yahweh is not known *statically,* as a reality to be grasped only at one moment of time; no static image can represent him. Rather, he represents himself *dynamically,* as one known through his actions and deeds of deliverance.

The visual arts tend to have a static character; that is, objects of visual art may exist in their entirety at one moment. Moreover, they do not require the participation of a community in order to exist; a temple or a painting does not cease to be when no one is looking at it. On the other hand, literature (especially in its oral stage), music, and liturgy are dynamic arts. They must be presented over a period of time, and they require the participation of the community in order to exist. These dynamic arts can more adequately reflect the character of God as he has revealed himself within the biblical tradition, in the context of his covenant and of the unfolding of his historical purposes. Further, though all the fine arts tend to be the creations of gifted individuals, the need for individual design and execution is greater for a material object than for a work of music, literature, or drama, which can be modified by those who recite or perform it. The visual arts, however much they may assume traditional forms and may be intended to express the identity and faith of the artist's community, are still prone to be personal expressions, stand-alone creations representing the work of an individual.

Nevertheless, since worship depends on symbolism, the visual arts play a role in the worship of the covenant people. The fashioning of effective symbols requires the skilled hand of the artisan. There is the ever-present danger that the symbol can be misunderstood—the dilemma of Jeroboam, whose bull images of Yahweh's throne (1 Kings 12:28) were too easily taken for Baalistic motifs. Ancient Israel always faced, and often yielded to, the temptation to compromise the historical faith of Yahwehism by combining it with the cyclical, mythological rites of popular fertility cults, with their associated idolatry. Also, it is an easy step to magnify the symbol over the reality it represents. The indispensable function of symbols as windows into the holy, however, requires that the biblical worshiper employ them, taking the risks involved and trusting in the integrity of the covenant faith and its precepts to protect him or her from apostasy.

Architecture: The Temple

The great visual symbol of biblical worship is the temple. Both the Solomonic and the Herodian temples were architectural monuments, neither of them destined to survive the centuries (although the foundation stones of the temple enclosure remain as the *Qotel Hamma‘ravi,* or Western Wall, in Jerusalem). The temple of Herod was still under construction during the time of Jesus' ministry and was completed only a few years before its destruction by the armies of Rome in A.D. 70, as Jesus had predicted (Mark 13:1-2). The decorative motifs of Solomon's temple, of which we have a good biblical description, disclose the link between the created order and human artifice. On a larger scale, the temple was really an architectural microcosm of the whole of creation, of "heaven and earth." In it, the worshiper

Architecture of the temple

encountered God enthroned in the heavens (Ps. 123:1), establishing the earth (Ps. 96:10) and preserving its creatures (Ps. 36:6-7), defeating the enemies of his people (Ps. 76:2-3), and blessing the land as the source of the river of life (Ps. 46:4; Ezek. 47:9).

Israel's theologians understood, of course, that the sanctuary, however magnificent as a work of art, was inadequate as a bearer of the sacred (1 Kings 8:27; cf. Isa. 66:1). Moses did not invent the design of the tabernacle but was told by Yahweh to make it according to the pattern he would reveal (Exod. 25:9); in the New Testament, we encounter the concept of the heavenly sanctuary, of which the earthly one is but a copy (Heb. 8–9; cf. 2 Cor. 5:1; Rev. 11:19). No holy place of human construction may contain the presence of the holy; in Jesus' words to the woman of Samaria, "neither on this mountain [Gerizim] nor in Jerusalem" (John 4:21) may people worship the Father in the authenticity of spiritual worship. Nevertheless, the Israelite temple, as a work of art and beauty, is the background for the New Testament symbolism of the worshiping church, the New Jerusalem, the tabernacle in which God dwells among his people (Rev. 21:1-3).

Artistic Craftsmanship

To execute a work of art requires craftsmanship; in the biblical perspective, craftsmanship itself is an art form, employing the skills of the artisan in the creation of useful objects. A corollary of the dynamic conception of Yahweh as Creator of a coherent universe and the doer of "mighty works" in his historic deeds of deliverance is the ability to find beauty in that which is utilitarian, that which functions properly and accomplishes useful work, as well as in that which is decorative. This is especially true of the implements of worship. Only this can account for the prominence given to the skilled craftsmen Bezalel and Oholiab in the instructions for the creation of the tabernacle (Exod. 31:1-11). When viewed with an eye to visual appeal, the artifacts of the Mosaic sanctuary are mostly functional rather than "beautiful" in the aesthetic sense. They are described in terms of how they are to fit together for assembly, disassembly, and transport during the travels of the people; this is their "beauty."

Scripture places a high value on skillful work: "Do you see a man skilled in his work? He will serve before kings; he will not serve before obscure men" (Prov. 22:29). Such was true of Huram-abi (also called Hiram), the chief craftsman of Solomon's temple. He was sent to Solomon by Hiram, the king of Tyre, who furnished the materials for the sanctuary, and though Phoenician he was half Israelite (2 Chron. 2:13-14). The application of training and skill to the worship arts is also seen, for example, in the work of David's musician Asaph and his associates (1 Chron. 25:1-7). The apostle Paul gave voice to the foundational biblical philosophy of artistic craftsmanship when he placed it within a wider context: "Whatever you do, whether in word or deed, do it all in the name of the Lord Jesus, giving thanks to God the Father through him" (Col. 3:17).

——— Painting, Sculpture, and Mosaic ———

Painting as an art form was practiced in ancient cultures, though most of what has survived for the appreciation of the modern student has been limited to decorated pottery or frescoes on the walls of tombs. The sculpture and statuary of Hellenistic civilization are well known and played a major role in the recovery of the principals of classical art during the Renaissance. Sculpture in stone was an important art in Semitic cultures of the ancient Near East, as attested by the numerous cultic images, palace bas-reliefs, commemorative obelisks, and the like that have come to light through archaeological research. Mosaic, or inlaid multicolored tile, came into use at a later period than these other arts, beginning with Hellenistic floor designs and becoming increasingly important until well into the Christian era.

The Bible does not discuss these visual arts, except to condemn and ridicule the sculpted images of the polytheistic religions (Ps. 115:4-8; Isa. 44:12-19; 46:1-2; cf. Acts 17:16; 19:23-26). In the centuries following the New Testament period, Christian theologians held a negative view of the visual arts, rejecting them as sensual and unspiritual. Here, as with so much else, the postapostolic church departed from the biblical perspective, influenced by Hellenistic philosophy, which created an unscriptural dichotomy between the spiritual and the material. Paul had decried such asceticism, calling it "hollow and deceptive philosophy" (Col. 2:8) and asking, "Why do you submit to regulations, 'Do not handle, Do not taste, Do not touch?'" (Col. 2:20-21 RSV).

Despite the strictures of theologians, the visual arts flourished in the early church; the ordinary worshiper at this period had a more sure instinct than the theologian for what was biblical. The walls of the Roman catacombs, or burial chambers, are adorned with scenes and characters from the Bible, including events in the ministry of Jesus, and with Christian symbolism. The same is true of sculpture on early Christian sarcophagi, or stone coffins. A favorite theme, for example, was that of Jonah and the great fish, a symbol of the Resurrection (Matt. 12:40); it appears on the tomb alleged to have been Peter's, in Rome. The loaves and fish of Christ's feeding of the multitude (John 6:1-14) occur, in fresco, as a symbol of the Eucharist. Furthermore, the catacomb paintings provide a pictorial record of the early church, depicting men and women with arms lifted in prayer. As the church emerged from its subversive status and began to erect buildings for worship, the art of mosaic took up many of the same themes. The pointillistic, two-dimensional technique of mosaic gives it a special quality as a vehicle for the expression of the numinous. It was to reach its peak of development centuries later in the majestic *Christos Pantokratōr* ("Christ, Ruler of All") mosaics above the apses of many basilicas in the Mediterranean world; in them we view an awesome, powerful, living Christ, his right hand raised in the gesture of blessing, in his left the gospel book.

214 ✦ MUSIC AS A WORSHIP ART

Music plays an integral part in biblical worship. As one of the arts most accessible to the ordinary worshiper, it became important in the expression of the faith of the corporate community.

——— The Importance of Music in Worship ———

Although the Mosaic directives for sacrifice and offering do not mention music, it became important in the worship of the Jerusalem sanctuary. Musicians accompanied the ark of the covenant when it was brought up to Zion (1 Chron. 15:16-24), and David established professional guilds of singers and instrumentalists to continue the celebrative worship of Yahweh there (1 Chron. 16:4-7; 25:1-7). Thus, music eventually also came to attend the sacrificial rites when they were transferred to Zion with the dedication of the temple (2 Chron. 5:11-14; Ps. 30). The Psalms reflect this dual role of music in worship; while it accompanied the offerings, it was itself considered by its performers to be the payment of a vow or a sacrifice of praise and thanksgiving (Pss. 22:25;

27:6; 50:14, 23; 65:1), sometimes to the denigration of the animal sacrifices (Pss. 40:6; 50:8-13; 51:15-17).

Music was closely associated with prophecy; the Israelite prophets were musicians (1 Sam. 10:5; Ezek. 33:32) who created songs, laments, and other poetic compositions (2 Chron. 35:25; Isa. 5:1-7; 26:1-6). Music in the sanctuary was also considered prophecy (1 Chron. 25:2), and the Psalms often serve as the vehicle for the prophetic word (Pss. 2; 50; 81–82; 91; 95; 110). The people of Israel and Judah were noted for their "songs of Zion," even in exile (Ps. 137:3-4).

In the New Testament, the apostle Paul views the musical expression of thanksgiving as the outflow of being filled with the Holy Spirit and the word (Eph. 5:18-20; Col. 3:16). Luke includes several early Christian hymns in his narrative of the birth and infancy of Jesus (Luke 1–2). The importance of music for the new covenant celebration of God's victory in Christ is evident from its place in the worship of the Revelation to John: the chorus frames the dramatic unfolding of divine judgments with majestic hymns and doxologies that, more powerfully than prosaic spoken words, convey the grandeur of the Creator and the Son.

Exactly how biblical music sounded and how it was performed are matters still subject to musicological research. Music in Scripture is viewed as a functional activity, each type of music having its particular use in the life of the people of the Lord. As a utilitarian enterprise, music was not an art intended to highlight the skill of the virtuoso performer or call attention to the creative composer. Musical modalities were traditional forms, each appropriate for particular occasions. Musical skill was admired, as was the craftsmanship of the artisan, but all was subordinate to the purpose of the event the music accompanied. People did not attend "concerts" just for the purpose of hearing music.

—— Music As a Corporate Expression ——

Music was also a corporate expression of worship; even when led and performed by professionals, it belonged to the whole celebrating community. It appears that some of the Psalms were sung responsively, not only by the Levitical priests but also by the lay Israelite worshipers present at the festivals, and even perhaps by Gentile worshipers of the Lord, of whom there were many in the ranks of David's soldiers. Thus, Psalm 124 begins with a line

sung by the leader, followed by the invitation for "all Israel" to join in the psalm. In Psalm 115:9-11, three groups of worshipers are identified: Israel, the priests or "house of Aaron," and "you who fear the LORD" (NASB), perhaps the Gentile worshipers; all three are called to trust in the Lord and to give the response, "He is their help and shield." The same three groups are invited to respond, "His [covenant] love endures forever" in Psalm 118:1-4 and to praise the Lord in Psalm 135:19-20.

Antiphonal music expressed this involvement of the congregation by surrounding it with song. In Psalm 24 the liturgy at the entrance to the sanctuary is sung by two groups, those entering and those guarding the doors, who answer one another. The hymn of the seraphs in Isaiah's vision (Isa. 6:3) is sung antiphonally, as "they were calling to one another"; this probably reflects the practice of the sanctuary choirs. At the dedication of the rebuilt wall of Jerusalem, Nehemiah appointed two choirs with trumpeters, which processed in opposite directions around the city, encircling it with praise, until they met in the sanctuary (Neh. 12:27-43). This use of the double choir was perpetuated in the great basilicas and cathedrals of the Christian church, providing an early version of stereophonic sound. The opening worship of the Revelation uses antiphonal choirs to portray an ever-widening circle of praise; the hymn of the four living creatures is joined by the twenty-four elders, then by thousands of angels, then by every living creature (Rev. 4:8–5:14). From all this we see that the musical arts, as used in biblical worship, are not esoteric skills but vehicles through which all worshipers may express their adoration and praise to the God of the covenant.

215 ◆ MOVEMENT ARTS IN WORSHIP

Worship and liturgy not only involve the use of the fine arts but may themselves be understood as art forms within the broader category of dance and other movement arts. These arts contribute to the worshiper's awareness of something "happening" in the corporate celebration of the people of God.

Biblical worship always involves orchestrated movements, whether of gesture (bowing, kneeling, lifting hands), procession and pageantry, festive dance, coordinated movements of worshiper and priest involved in offering sacrifice, or the order for the administration of the Lord's Supper. Even the verbal worship of antiphonal statement and response may be understood in this way, so that all worship becomes a form of choreography.

There is an ebb and flow in worship, times of solemnity alternating with times of abandon, as the congregation responds to the presence of the holy. Effective worship builds to a climax or central event. In ancient Israel it was the theophany or appearance of the Lord, the manifestation of his glory or "heaviness" in the sanctuary: "From Zion, perfect in beauty, God shines forth" (Ps. 50:2). This occurred not through spontaneous eruptions of the overwhelming presence of the Lord—how could these be timed to coincide with important festivals?—but probably through the solemn recitation of the laws of the covenant. There are indications in the Psalms that this took place (Pss. 50:16; 81:10), and many of the covenant laws, including the Decalogue (Exod. 20:1-17), are arranged in metrical groupings that render them appropriate for recitation in worship (Exod. 22:18-22; 23:1-9; 34:11-26; Lev. 18:7-18; Deut. 27:15-26). For the Christian worshiper, the Lord's Supper is the climactic event of worship, when the risen Lord is revealed in the corporate action of distributing and receiving the symbols of his life and of his sacrifice, which has activated the new covenant. Failure to understand liturgy as an art form, requiring skill and insight in its choreography, results in "meetings" that are flat and unsatisfying because nothing happens.

The movement arts, in particular, contribute to the sense of something happening in worship. Processional pageantry, the movement of choirs and other leaders and worshipers into or around the worship area, contributes to the sense of the glory of the Lord filling the sanctuary, especially if banners or other visually effective symbols are included. The use of the various biblical gestures of worship involves the whole person—not just the mind and the voice—in submission to the majesty of God; such gestures are therefore an important statement about the philosophy of worship. Dancing before the Lord makes a similar statement and serves also as a powerful symbol of the worshiper's abandon before the holy, as the creature forgets self in the presence of the Creator. Orchestrated dancing by specially trained groups supplies an element missing from spontaneous, individual dancing; the coordinated movement of many worshipers expresses the corporate nature of covenant worship,

in which the individual is part of a larger community that has entered into a common bond in the Lord. The expression of praise and adoration by solo dancers is an effective testimony, as the example of David reminds us; to reflect the biblical philosophy of the worship arts; however, it must always be balanced by worship activities involving the entire assembly.

216 ✦ THE LITERARY ARTS

By far the most important of the fine arts in Israel and the early church was the field of literature. The Bible itself is the result of the sensitivity of literary artists to the Spirit of God. Each of the many forms of biblical literature contributes to our understanding of the philosophy of the worship arts.

Literature: Israel's Enduring Monument

Archaeological excavations reveal that the material culture of ancient Israel was less advanced than that of the Canaanite city-states it displaced. Coming from a seminomadic state as a nation of tent dwellers, the Israelite tribes had no significant tradition of architectural, artistic, or technological innovation, although the nation had artisans such as Bezalel and Oholiab. Even the great temple of Solomon was actually designed and erected by a foreign contractor and reflects Phoenician models; it stood for less than four centuries. Israel left no monumental works of sculpture, art, or architecture to be placed alongside the cultural remains of other ancient civilizations that have survived to our day. The monument of Israel is a literary one: the Bible. It was in the various forms of the literary arts that Israel, including the Israel of the new covenant, excelled.

The literature of the Scriptures is the testimony to a community's faith. The names of individual authors may be attached to it, and it may bear the distinctive imprint of a personality such as David, Jeremiah, or the apostle Paul. Nevertheless, as literature it is never the artistic creation of an individual for the purpose of self-expression or recognition. In ancient cultures the ability to write was a specialized skill, whereas the art of recitation from memory was widely practiced. Most of the Bible existed first in oral form and depended for its survival on a circle of people who memorized it, recited it, and handed it down to successive generations. Isaiah gives us a glimpse of this practice in his remark, "Bind up the testimony, seal the teaching among my disciples" (Isa. 8:16 NASB). Eventually some major crisis in the circle of tradition, such as the insecurities of the period of the fall and exile of Judah, would provide the impetus for writing the material down. Even in New Testament times the teachings of Jesus and the stories of his acts seem to have circulated orally until the passing of the apostles and the linguistic transition from Aramaic to Greek made it desirable to produce written Gospels for the instruction of the church. In the Gospels we read of "the scribes and Pharisees" (Matt. 5:20, RSV); the scribes were men who had memorized the Mosaic law and the traditions associated with it and who served as a kind of walking concordance or reference Bible for the Pharisaic teachers. The practice of memorizing large portions of the Scripture and the rabbinic traditions continues in Judaism to this day. These procedures of oral transmission in a circle of dedicated people highlight the point that, from the biblical perspective, literature as a form of art belongs to the covenant community as a whole and not to the individual authors who serve as its spokespersons.

——— Forms of Biblical Literature ———

The important forms of literature preserved in Scripture can be listed briefly, in order to convey something of the fullness of this form of artistic activity as practiced in the life of the people of the covenant.

History. Historical literature, including chronicle and genealogy, grows out of covenant worship, in which the worshiper confesses his faith by telling the story of God's dealings with his people. But the narrative and saga of the Hebrew Bible is remarkable in that, while written from a pronounced theological perspective, it often presents a realistic, nonidealized portrait of human leaders such as Abraham, Moses, Samuel, David, and those who followed. The Gospels and the Acts continue the same tradition, portraying Jesus in an authoritative yet convincing manner and his apostles as down-to-earth and familiarly human types. Biblical history shows that God deals with people as he finds them, in whatever circumstance or state of personal growth. God's openness to people as they are allows the worshiper to come before him honestly, not boasting in his or her own worth but confident of the grace of God as manifested in his great redeeming acts.

Law. Covenant structure also yields the laws or instructions governing the community's relation to the Great King. The Mosaic Torah contains laws in both the absolute form ("Thou shalt, thou shalt not . . .") and the conditional form ("If this happens, then . . . , but if this happens, then . . ."); the absolute form especially is well adapted to recitation in worship acts of covenant renewal. Jesus' principles of the kingdom of God are sometimes similarly cast in metrical form, as in the Beatitudes and other parts of the Sermon on the Mount (Matt. 5–7). The nature of Israelite "law" is often misunderstood; as Torah, it is really "instruction" rather than law in the modern sense of legally binding statutes and belongs in the context of worship rather than that of jurisprudence.

Prophetic Indictment. Equally dependent on the covenant foundation is the basic form of prophetic utterance, the judgment speech (or covenant lawsuit), in which the spokespersons of the Lord utter the consequences of the people's unfaithfulness to their agreement with him. These indictments, as well as other kinds of prophetic address, are almost always given in poetic and musical form, evidencing considerable artistic reflection on the part of the prophets as they opened themselves to the word of the Lord. The same artistic skill is evident in the Revelation, where John uses a dramatic idiom to amplify the effects of the ruptured covenant.

Poetry. Since a great part of the Bible is poetry, the principles of poetic composition apply to many of the biblical literary forms. As to metrical structure, biblical poetry does not scan in some recurring pattern of metric "feet," nor does it use rhyme. Instead, it generally employs a rhythm of stressed syllables, with a variable number of intervening unstressed syllables. Such a structure is well adapted to chanting or singing, in a style similar to what we know as the "recitative" in seventeenth-century oratorios such as Handel's *Messiah;* most of the poetic material in Scripture was probably originally sung.

The most distinctive feature of biblical poetry, however, is the principle of *parallelism* of ideas. That is, the second line in a couplet repeats the same idea, using different words (synonymous parallelism); or it may present the contrasting or opposite idea (antithetic parallelism); or it may take the idea of the first line and develop some aspect of its thought (synthetic parallelism). Parallelism in one form or another appears throughout the Bible in poetic or semipoetic sections such as the Genesis account of Creation, the oracles of the prophets, the Psalms, the Proverbs, and the Sermon on the Mount.

Both the stressed metrical structure and the parallelism of ideas of biblical poetry can be translated into other languages without destroying their character; they are what makes the Bible sound like the Bible in any language. Philosophically speaking, the proper use and appreciation of literature constructed in this way require close attention to the words being used and the images and associations they bear, not only from an intellectual standpoint, but also from that of a word artist. The cadence of biblical poetry and hymnody, or even of metrically grouped teachings and commandments, adds to worship a sense of awe and solemnity, lifting it above the plane of the merely prosaic.

Proverb and Wisdom. The biblical proverb, or wise saying, is part of an international tradition of wisdom Israel shared with other cultures of the ancient Near East. Biblical wisdom, however, takes on a distinctive coloration because of the character and sovereignty of Yahweh. The temptation to exalt human wisdom is always tempered by the realization that "there is no wisdom, no insight, no plan that can succeed against the LORD" (Prov. 21:30). Biblical wisdom is therefore practical; it is not the exploration of the esoteric but the consideration of how to live in "the fear of the LORD" (Prov. 9:10). Even the books of Ecclesiastes and Job, which probe the deeper issues of human suffering, eventually come up against the sovereignty of God as the only "answer" to life's ultimate quest. This literature, too, is thus brought within the orbit of worship, which celebrates the sovereignty of the God of the covenant.

Dialogue. The biblical concept of "truth" is not the modern idea of absolute, scientifically verifiable fact; in Hebraic culture "truth" is created by speaking it, and the most powerful speaker creates the prevailing truth, hence the importance of dialogue as a way of approaching the truth. The best example of this principle is the dialogue of Job, in which Job, his three friends, and Elihu approach the problem of justifying God's seemingly unjust ways from a variety of angles; if they cannot solve the problem, they can at least talk it to death. However, as the book brings out at the end, the supreme biblical dialogue

is always with God, who listens but whose word establishes the final truth. Men and women of the Bible are not afraid to argue with God, to plead with him to change his mind, especially about the execution of his judgments, as we note from the examples of Abraham (Gen. 18:22-33), Moses (Exod. 32:7-14), Amos (Amos 7:1-6), and even Jesus in the garden (Matt. 26:36-44). God expects such a dialogue from his partners in the covenant, and this principle undergirds the teaching of Jesus and the apostles about the importance of prayer.

Parable. Although the parable was an ancient literary form, Jesus brought it to its highest level of artistic development in his parables of the kingdom of God. In these stories, Christ used familiar characters and situations from common life—a farmer sowing seed, a rebellious son, a corrupt judge, a woman who loses a coin, a servant forgiven a great debt, a merchant who discovers a priceless pearl—to illustrate the value of God's kingdom and the consequences for those who refuse it. A parable is not an allegory, in which every detail stands for some hidden truth; the meaning of Jesus' parables was quite clear and was offensive to the religious establishment of the time (Luke 20:19). To make its point, the parable depends on the human capacity to imagine and to make a transference of imagery from an ordinary sphere of activity to another, more significant sphere of concern. This must take place in the words and motions of worship, which is therefore highly parabolic.

Drama. In drama there is a movement from problem to resolution presented in dialogue and action involving complementary and contrasting characters. Biblical history as a whole is a great drama; the problem is the rebellion of humankind, and the resolution is the appearance of the New Jerusalem in which the Lord dwells in the midst of his faithful people. The drama has its ebb and flow, with a hint of the ultimate resolution appearing already in the Lord's covenant with Abraham. Scripture embraces a more specifically dramatic idiom in several places, particularly at the very culmination in the Revelation to John.

A feature of biblical drama wherever it appears is dynamic imagery in the form of word pictures that convey the sense of movement and energy in the situation. The description of Solomon's bride (Song of Sol. 4), the four living creatures supporting God's throne, the sun darkened and the moon turned blood red, fire or stars falling from heaven, the rending of the temple veil, the beasts from the sea and the land, the Word of God with the sword, a city coming down from heaven—these are images intended to propel and intensify the drama. As literary symbols they are powerful and gripping. Reduced to visual form, as though literal, they lose their compelling power and become merely grotesque or even trite. Biblical drama builds with word pictures; the cross of Christ itself is such a word picture, an instrument of execution transferred through preaching (not visual representation) into a symbol of victory and the renewal of the covenant. Biblical worship is the enactment of the imaged resolution to the great drama of Scripture. The loaf and the cup of the Eucharist are powerful not as visual symbols, but as dramatic symbols, an acted-out word picture of the presence of the living Christ with his people. Perhaps more than any other literary form, drama brings the worshiper into the realm of the numinous and that communion with the holy that fulfills the chief end and aim of humankind: to glorify God and to enjoy him forever.

Richard C. Leonard

TWENTY-ONE

Music in Israelite Worship

Song and instrumentation played a vital part in biblical worship. In ancient times, as today, music was an important way of approaching the mystery of God and of expressing the joy of being in God's presence.

217 • THE PROBLEM OF BIBLICAL MUSICOLOGY

Music is gone as soon as it is made; especially where music is not recorded in some fashion, a piece of music can be reconstructed only if there are people who remember it and how to perform it. Because of the cultural and linguistic differences between our civilization and that of the ancient Israelites, it is difficult to recover the exact sound and use of biblical music in its historical context.

Words about music are secondary to music itself. This is the dilemma of the historian, whose obligation it is to bring enlightenment and perspective to music making. He is successful only if his work finally draws the reader to music itself and if he avoids the temptation of allowing word impressions to replace the musical ones.

Music is the most abstract of the arts. Its components—pitch, duration, texture, rhythm, color, and ultimately form—speak their own language. The composing experience, which brings these together in a satisfying wholeness, is to be matched in the listening experience, which then must comprehend this wholeness. Hence, the final meaningfulness of music lies in the aural experience. Other experiences are merely adjuncts or glosses on the acoustical event.

All of this is true whether one is dealing with music for its own sake, a comparatively recent phenomenon in Western culture, or music that is inseparable from function as in the case of music in the Bible. In either instance, the primary problem is the hearing and understanding of inherent musical sound as it occurs in its cultural contexts. Furthermore, music is gone as soon as it is made. It is a temporal art; its sounds do not coexist as the parts of a painting do;

they succeed each other chronorhythmically. Their recapture or repetition does not guarantee entire faithfulness to the original. One cannot return to a performance of a concerto or a folk song the way he can to a painting or an artifact. The advent of electronic media has only partially solved this problem. A very important element, the performer, is still missing, and total fidelity to the original sound is unattainable even with the most sophisticated equipment.

The historian's problem is further complicated when the primary data—the music itself—is partly or completely missing, and the secondary data—the historical contexts—are removed by vast cultural and linguistic distances. The success with which these barriers are overcome determines how accurately deductions can be made as to what the music of another culture in another time might have been, what its instrumentations were, and what its formulae and functions entailed.

Many recent archaeological discoveries, coupled with heightened musicological skills and insights, have clarified much of what was previously obscure or romanticized. Still, the primary task in the field of biblical music is to be assumed by the scholar whose insights into biblical history are coupled with a mastery of the languages of biblical contexts. The role of the musicologist is to be taken only when judgments are to be made in the presence of musical data that surface one way or another. While the first two sections of the present article depend to a great extent on the outstanding research of scholars such as Eric Werner, Abraham Idelsohn, and Egon Wellesz, it assumes a theological and biblical perspective different from theirs.

218 • MUSIC IN ISRAELITE COMMUNITIES

In Israelite life music was central to all that the people did. It is found not only in their worship, but also in their work, in their personal recreation, and in their military activities.

Genesis 4:21 mentions Jubal as the protomusician. The distance, both stylistic and chronological, between him and the later music making of the Jewish community can only be a matter of speculation. The real importance of Jubal is in the attention given to music making this far back in sacred history, and further, that such attention is focused on its natural appearance along with other human and cultural activities. Jubal's brother, Jabal, was a cattle breeder; his half-brother Tubal-Cain, the first smith. This is important, for music is first described in a functionally neutral sense. Jubal is the "father of all who play the harp and flute." His music making is not religiously caused or primarily associated with worship, nor is it necessarily an activity that, by contrast, bears only the association of any number of so-called secular activities. Even though Yahweh was to be worshiped in his sanctuary, the earth and all its fullness was also his; and as human habitat, of which humanity was to be the steward, the world was to be an arena for praise. Accordingly, the use of music is as much an integral part of the gathering of harvest as the worship in the sanctuary. The uniqueness is that while harvest songs are sung, they are sung to the Lord of the harvest; while battle songs are sung, Yahweh is to win the battle.

Thus if there is one consistent stand concerning music in the Old Testament, it is that it is inseparable from all of life. Although in its earliest stages or as related to certain activities, it may have been little more than noise making, music accompanied work, worship, merrymaking, and military activities (Gen. 31:27; Exod. 32:17-18; Num. 21:17; Judg. 11:34-35; Isa. 16:10; Jer. 48:33). Instances of music making are connected with specific acts of God: the collapse of the walls of Jericho (Josh. 6:4-20), the enthronement of kings (1 Kings 1:39-40; 2 Kings 11:14; 2 Chron. 13:14; 20:28), music for the court (2 Sam. 19:35; Eccles. 2:8) and feasting (Isa. 5:12; 24:8-9), as well as for the restoration of prophetic gifts (2 Kings 3:15) and the soothing of personality disturbances (1 Sam. 16:14-23). These latter two instances superficially seem to belong to the psychomusical realm, or the blatantly magical. Along with the narrative in Joshua 6:4-20, in which the combination of trumpet sounds with people shouting precede the felling of Jericho's walls, an immediate relation is seen by some biblical scholars between music and magic. It cannot be denied that this relationship is assumed in the myths and legends of the religious systems surrounding Judaism. Nor can it be denied that music and magic are linked in religious systems of primitive cultures everywhere. Furthermore, the more sophisticated Greek ethos, which granted intrinsic power to activities in the created order, still has overtones in much of today's thinking regarding musical values.

In the earliest parts of Scripture, however, the created order is to be subject to human dominion, and it is good. Humankind is to be sovereign over it and not the reverse; the goodness of creation is a reflection of God's handiwork, but it is a goodness not in the sense of inherently causing good; otherwise it would be sovereign and the cultural mandate would be irrelevant. In addition, the fact that creation has been ravished by Satan does not mean that it has become intrinsically bad in the sense of causing immorality. Ultimately, the Judeo-Christian perspective maintains that humankind is wrong within itself and that until persons are made right they will place the blame for their condition outside themselves. Hence, they will assume that created things or activities have power over them and their activity, as is often the case with music. Consequently, the parallels that are drawn, in comparative religious studies, between Israelite religion and its contemporary systems are in fundamental error because fundamental perspectives are overlooked.

219 • MUSIC IN THE TEMPLE

Music in the temple was made for the worship of God. More than 10 percent of the people serving in temple ministries were musicians. Their music occupied a central place in the worship of God's people.

The idea of special creative skills in cultic worship occurs long before the advent of professional musicians. In the building of the tabernacle of Moses, artisans were chosen to "make artistic designs" and were given the Holy Spirit to do so (Exod. 35:30–36:2). The ability to devise these works is interestingly related to intelligence, knowledge, and finally craftsmanship. Although the mention of music is minimal in the matter of worship in the tabernacle,

Exodus 28:34-35 describes a golden bell attached to the lower hem of Aaron's robe, which sounds as he goes into the Holy Place.

The trained musicians who eventually appear around the time of David and Solomon mark a distinctive change in the history of biblical music. Before this time much of the music was made by women. Miriam led a group of women in singing and dancing that followed the song of Moses and the children of Israel, celebrating the overthrow of the Egyptians (Exod. 15:1-21); women sang, danced, and played for the conquering David (1 Sam. 18:6-7); Jephthah's daughter met her father with timbrels and dance upon his return from battle (Judg. 11:34).

With the professionalization of music in the royal courts, and more especially in temple worship, music making was restricted to men. This is not to say that in the nonprofessional realm women ceased making music; this continued as before. In the accounts in Chronicles that give the statistics of the temple ministries, 4,000 of the 38,000 Levites chosen by David for temple service were musicians (1 Chron. 15:16, NASB; 23:5). These were "the singers, with instruments of music, harps, lyres, loud-sounding cymbals, to raise sounds of joy." In 1 Chronicles 25:6-7, the number of musicians is listed as 288, divided into twenty-four orders of twelve each. The descriptions of the musical activities that occur thereafter give the impression of an awesome spectacle. This rich array parallels the existence of professional guilds of musicians in the neighboring kingdoms of Egypt and Assyria.

The transition from an unsettled, nomadic life to one of a centralized monarchy provided an opportunity for training and the regulation of a musical system that would serve the needs of the royal court and the worship in the temple. No efforts, it seems, were spared in the full realization of this. The importation of musical instruments and musical systems was no doubt carried out. The normal cultural intercourse during Israel's sojourn was formalized in the monarchy. The *Midrash* alludes to a tradition in which King Solomon's Egyptian wife included 1,000 musical instruments in her dowry. More concrete archaeological evidence makes clear that the instruments of the ancient world were similar from culture to culture. This implies a similarity of musical systems, although it does not rule out the possibility of indigenous change.

There have been many highly romanticized and exaggerated speculations about a never-to-be-repeated musical situation in the temple. These have distorted a true contextual sense of what might have happened, and since there is no precise knowledge of the full musical style, one must remain content with the central concept of a solemn yet exuberant mode of worship. Moreover, it is important to remember that though these musical activities were quantitatively and qualitatively professional, the matter of functionality mentioned earlier still prevailed. The central importance in temple ritual was sacrifice. All else served this centrality. The system of daily sacrifices, morning and evening, was carefully regulated. The liturgical activities were complex and cumulative. The *Mishnah* gives the number of instruments in the temple during the Common Era as follows: *nevel,* minimum two, maximum six; *kinnor,* minimum nine, maximum limitless; cymbal, one only; *ḥalil,* minimum two, maximum twelve.

The choir consisted of a minimum of twelve adult male singers, the maximum limitless. The singers served between the ages of thirty and fifty, with a five-year training period preceding this. The lack of mention of a large percussion group as well as the absence of a corps of dancers might indicate an attempt to evade a similarity to pagan forms of worship, although this is only conjecture. It must be balanced with those occasions in which dance is mentioned as a legitimate way of praise elsewhere in the Old Testament (2 Sam. 6:14; Pss. 149:3; 150:4).

Although a good part of the musical performance must have been left to the trained singers and players, the congregation was also musically involved. There is record in the first century of three forms of public singing of the Scriptures, including the Psalms, each based on the response principle. (a) First form—the leader intoned the first half verse repeated by the congregation. The leader then sang each succeeding half line, but the congregation responded with the same first half line. This became a refrain throughout the entire song. (b) Second form—the leader sang a half line at a time, and the congregation immediately repeated what had just been sung. (c) Third form—the leader sang the whole first line. The congregation answered with the second line of the verse. This was true responsorial singing.

220 • MUSIC IN THE SYNAGOGUE

Synagogue worship expanded and developed the use of the voice. No musical instruments were used in synagogue worship.

Not long after the destruction of the temple, instrumental music fell into disuse and for some reason was never revived. Vocal tradition and practice, however, continued and became the central musical feature of synagogue worship.

In contrast to the temple with its system of sacrifice, the synagogue was primarily for public worship and instruction as well as for secular assemblage. It was and is, in Werner's terms, a "layman's institution," in which the Torah, its study and interpretation, readings from the Scriptures, and devotional prayers took the place of the sacrificial ceremonies of the temple. There was only one temple but numerous synagogues. The Talmud states that there were 394 synagogues in Jerusalem alone at the time of the destruction of the temple. The number of synagogues, contrasted to the unique singularity of the temple, is explained not only "theologically," in that there was but one place for sacrifice and there were many places for instruction, but it was also logistical. The Dispersion, over a vast geographical spread, deprived the Jew of temple worship. The synagogue helped fill this need for corporate solidarity and for communion with God. It is within the framework of synagogue worship, however, that the vocal elements of temple worship were most likely perpetuated. The intonations of the Psalms and the Pentateuch and perhaps the recitation of prayers were all a part of this perpetuity. Furthermore, these intonations or cantillations, mentioned as far back as the first century, were cast into a system of modes or formulae, one for each of the books of the Bible intended to be publicly read. These are the Pentateuch, the Prophets, Esther, Lamentations, Ruth, Ecclesiastes, Song of Solomon, Psalms, and in some communities, Job. Little is known about when the transition from declamatory to musical reading was first evidenced except that the Psalms were sung in temple worship. Idelsohn and Werner both believe that the chanting of Scripture, in one form or another, went back perhaps as far as Ezra (fifth century B.C.), and that its eventual complexity and organization was the result of hundreds of years of crystallization.

221 • STYLE OF ISRAELITE MUSIC

It is difficult to determine the style of biblical music. Recent studies and discoveries, however, are resulting in an improved picture and expanded understanding of music in ancient Israel.

The crucial task in determining matters of style is one of identifying relationships that are found in available music and that can be shown also to have been present in music that is not available. Through a combination of linguistics, history of culture, and comparative musicology, discoveries have been made that make this possible to a considerable extent. Excavations have produced ancient instruments from Ur, Kara-Tepe, Mesopotamia, and Egypt, as well as from Israel. Liturgies, in whole or in part, from Sumer, Akkad, Egypt, and Ugarit, have been reconstructed. Finally, comparative musicology has endeavored to examine the most ancient melodic elements of the Near East and to set forth criteria for their age and locale.

As a result of all these efforts, certain distinguishing characteristics of Semitic oriental music may be identified (Abraham Z. Idelsohn, _Jewish Music in Its Historical Development_ [New York: Schocken Books, 1967]): (a) modality—this is not to be confused with the later Western use of the term. A mode comprises a number of motives within a certain scale, each of which has different functions. The resulting composition is an arrangement and combination of these motives; (b) ornamentation—the modes and their motive partials are, within the arrangement of the modality, subject to ornamentation and decoration, often very florid and extended. To a large extent this depends on the skill and training of the singer, whose object it is to keep within the perimeters of the mode itself, while at the same time enhancing its basic profile with ornaments. The contour of such ornamentation is basically step-wise; skips of more than a third are rare. Thus the style is eminently vocal; (c) rhythm—all music is rhythmic in the sense that its sequence of tones is subject to virtually infinite temporal variations. Metrical music is that which is subject to regularly recurring, equally divided measures. Within each of these, rhythmic development takes place. Semitic music lacks regularly recurring meters. Nonetheless it is freely and richly rhythmic; its rhythmic structure is as complex as its ornamentation. In fact, it may be said that rhythm is to meter what ornamentation is to scale; (d) scale—the general nature of melody is diatonic, although this is mixed with a certain feeling for quarter tones, a distinctive which is foreign to most music to which we are accustomed; (e) monophony—Jewish music is unharmonized and depends for its beauty on elaborate ornamentation of the melody alone. Occasionally, in group singing, intervals of fourths or fifths appear, more out of limitation in vocal range than because of an inherent harmonic vocabulary. However, it probably is true that the natural acoustical compatibility of these intervals allows for departure from the unison and therefore gives room for speculation as to the relation of this kind of primitive harmony to the development of harmonic procedures. When vocal music was instrumentally accompanied, heterophony (a way of embellishing the basic melodic line with concurrent decoration) was often employed;

(f) improvisation—the performer and composer were the same person. The modal formulae were elaborated upon, as discussed above in connection with modality and ornamentation. A combination of long training and inherent ability were necessary to accomplish this.

For several centuries, musicians sensed an essential identity between archetypes of Christian chant and Hebraic counterparts but were unable to substantiate this until recently. The French musicologist Amadé Gastou established the first concrete evidence and support of this. Then Idelsohn was able to establish the essential identity of certain melodic archetypes in the Yemenite tradition with the earliest Gregorian chant. The significance of this is that the Yemenites had left Palestine during the beginnings of Christianity and have remained isolated from contact with the church ever since.

Harold M. Best and David K. Huttar[19]

Music in New Testament Worship

Although the New Testament Scriptures do not treat music and musical instrumentation extensively, they contain important references to music in primitive Christianity. On the basis of these references we may develop a general outline of the use of music in early Christian worship.

222 • MUSIC MAKING IN THE NEW TESTAMENT

Although the New Testament says little about music making, it is clear that the worship life of the early church was characterized by the use of psalms and other forms of song.

Superficially the New Testament appears almost to disregard music. Outside of the book of Revelation, in which music is a part of a rich eschatological drama, not more than a dozen passages in the entire canon shed light on music making. Of these, five mention music only metaphorically (Matt. 6:2; 11:17; Luke 7:32; 1 Cor. 13:1; 14:7-8). The remaining cast important light, especially when seen in broader context—that of the rich heritage of temple and synagogue worship known and practiced by the early Christians.

There are four passages in the Gospels, two of which are parallel. Matthew 26:30 and Mark 14:26 mention the use of a hymn by Christ and his disciples at the conclusion of the Last Supper. Although there is debate as to the exact nature of the Last Supper with regard to its full content and relation to Jewish traditions and practices, as well as the attendant possibilities of adaptation and change by Jesus himself, it is probably true that the words and music that were used were traditional. This is the only specific mention in the New Testament of Jesus himself singing, although it is highly likely that when he read in the synagogue (Luke 4:16-20) he chanted the lesson in the accustomed manner. The other two passages in the Gospels mention instrumental music and dance: the mourning for the death of a girl

(Matt. 9:23) and the merriment upon the return of the Prodigal Son of Jesus' parable (Luke 15:25). Finally, when Paul and Silas were jailed for their activities, they spent some of the time singing (Acts 16:25). It can be readily seen that in all these examples nothing is said about how the music was performed or how extensive was the musical activity. Nevertheless the basic concept present in the Old Testament still remains: music accompanied the varied activities of the Jewish community.

Instructions for music making are found in the Epistles, embedded in the general instructions and principles that were set forth for the various churches. All but one are given by Paul. They are conceptual rather than literally musical. In 1 Corinthians 14:15 Paul seems to be calling for a balance between ecstasy and discipline in music making (as well as praying) by asking that singing be done with the mind (or understanding) as well as in the spirit. He asks also that singing (as well as teaching, revelations, and speaking in tongues) be done for edification (1 Cor. 14:26). Two other passages (Eph 5:19; Col. 3:16) are somewhat similar. The Ephesians are encouraged to address one another in psalms, hymns, and spiritual songs as a sign of being filled with the Spirit. The Colossians are encouraged to do the same as a sign of being indwelt by the word of Christ (Col. 3:16). The apostle James insists that cheerfulness should lead to singing (James 5:13).Though Paul brings three terms together with particular force *(psalms, hymns, spiritual songs)* it is almost impossible to determine any musical or textual difference among them. The safest conclusion would be that *Psalms* are those of the Old Testament, although not without the possibility of Christian additions. *Hymns,* or songs of praise, would perhaps be those newly composed texts directed to Christ. *Songs* (the most inclusive of the types, comprising all kinds of songs, secular or sacred, accompanied or unaccompanied) are distinguished by the adjective *spiritual,* which seems to set these apart from all other songs as inspired by the Spirit and perhaps composed spontaneously.

223 • SUPERNATURAL AND ESCHATOLOGICAL REFERENCES TO MUSIC

References to music occur in New Testament texts that are concerned with the raising of the dead or with the Lord's return.

The bulk of supernatural and eschatological references to music have to do with the trumpet sound of the Lord at the raising of the dead (1 Cor. 15:52; 1 Thess. 4:16) or the gathering of the elect (Matt. 24:31). They are extensions of the many associations of musical sounds accompanying specific acts of God that appear throughout the Old Testament. The ultimate instances of this are found throughout Revelation, in which the final, cumulative acts in history are announced by trumpet sounds and where singing seems to be a part of the eternal round of praise to be rendered to God. If any light can be gathered from these eschatological passages it would be that the literary style of the utterances (as well as other poetic utterances in the Epistles) would give a clue to the style of the composed and spontaneous texts that were actually sung by the new church.

In addition to the foregoing, a few passages mention music in a metaphorical way, such as 1 Corinthians 13:1, in which lovelessness is equated with sounding brass or tinkling cymbals (KJV). This passage has caused some critics to draw the conclusion that there is some prejudice against instrumental music in Paul's thinking, if not in the church itself. This seems a bit flimsy in view of Paul's directness and outspokenness in cases where he felt a vital principle was at stake. The Corinthian passage is too oblique to be considered this way.

224 • TEMPLE AND SYNAGOGUE WORSHIP IN EARLY CHRISTIANITY

The musical culture of Jewish worship was carried over into the church by the Jewish converts to Christianity. In this regard, there was no radical break from Judaism that resulted in new forms of Christian music.

The New Testament Christians did not consider Christianity antithetical to Judaism but as its fulfillment. Jesus Christ was the ultimate conclusion to the Law and to the Prophets, whose essential truth he came to fulfill. Hence, it is not surprising to find that the followers of Christ frequented the temple and synagogues not occasionally but "every day" (Acts 2:46; 9:2, 20). Their purpose, in addition to worship, was obviously to complete the fulfillment of Christ, with regard to the forms of worship indigenous to these places, by the exposition and debating that issued from the centrality of Christ and his opposition to the gospel synagogue, however, forced the Christians to worship and speak of Jesus elsewhere, and for some time the home, the open air, or any other available place became the forum for worship and witness.

The change of locale, however, did not preempt the influences of the musical and liturgical activities to which the Jewish Christians had long been accustomed. The entire vocabulary of such activities is familiar to the New Testament. The Old Testament was still the only Scripture from which one could teach. Certainly the prayers were not forgotten. To quote Oesterley: "Nobody, in reading the pre-Christian forms of prayer in the Jewish liturgy and the prayers of the early church, can fail to notice the similarity of atmosphere of each, or to recognize that both proceed from the same mold. Even when one perceives, as often happens, variety in the latter form, the *genus* is unmistakable" (W. O. E. Oesterley, *The Jewish Background of the Christian Liturgy* [Oxford: Clarendon Press, 1925], p. 125).

Musicological research has clarified the similarity of early Gregorian chant and Jewish music. The significance of this is heightened not only in light of the similarities in prayer forms just mentioned but in the matter of the cantillation of Scripture, in which a common ground is again struck between Judaism and Christianity. Whatever else the church eventually developed on her own, liturgically, scripturally, and musically, these early bonds cannot be denied. The chief strata of liturgical music in church and synagogue, as Eric Werner identifies them, are (a) the scriptural lesson; (b) the vast field of psalmody (not only the singing of psalms but of any text sung in the fashion of psalms); (c) the litany, or congregational prayers of supplication and intercession; and (d) the chanted prayer of priest or precentor. These together form the primary areas of liturgical music to this day (Eric Werner, *The Sacred Bridge* [New York: Schocken Books, 1970]).

225 • THE PHILOSOPHY OF MUSIC IN THE NEW TESTAMENT

The philosophy of music in the New Testament is broadly conceived. It is shaped particularly by Paul's worldview, which did not accept the Greek ethos of the arts nor regard them as having intrinsic powers but focused rather on human responsibility. Such a view permitted Paul to encourage the extensive use of music in worship.

If one were to take the position that only those things that Scripture specifically allows are allowable and those that Scripture does not specifically mention are prohibited, then the perimeters of musical practice in the New Testament would be severely limited. There are two basic reasons why this cannot be the case and why the "philosophy" of church music in the New Testament is, in fact, exceedingly broad.

First, the Old Testament was still considered the scriptural authority for the early church (2 Tim. 3:16-17). Hence its broad principles and practices were normative, though now Christ-centered. Second, by maintaining the perspectives on righteousness, faith, and lawfulness inherent in God's revelation throughout the Old Testament, the writers of the New Testament are careful to maintain these by extension. Hence Paul's conclusion in Romans 14 that nothing is impure in itself is an extension and a further filling out of the concept of the goodness of creation found early in Genesis. To Paul, the ultimate right was to avoid the offense of one's own conscience or that of one's neighbor by the superiority of quality of life over categories of creation. The Judeo-Christian worldview is unique in that it refuses to locate moral causation in the created order. Rather, it places moral responsibility squarely within the human heart. For this reason the Greek ethos, which ultimately says that both the creative and the created orders have an inherent

power and which implicitly allows humankind to locate virtue or its opposite in the created order, is *by principle* out of place in the Judeo-Christian worldview. Therefore, what the New Testament leaves *unsaid* about music, among other things, has a healthy quality.

If such a view were an integral part of Paul's worldview he would have insisted on the use of music as a powerful source in the overwhelming task of witness and persuasion the church took upon itself. Instead, people were to be persuaded alone by the words and actions of people and ultimately of the Holy Spirit. The gospel was to be preached as the "power of God for salvation" (Rom. 1:16, RSV). It seems obvious that Paul intended to keep clear of anything that, to the presuppositions of the unsaved, would have a power of its own and by virtue of this tincture the primary, essential power of the gospel.

Second, the church is instructed to use music, to address itself (one another) in psalms, hymns, and spiritual songs. If there are omissions concerning instrumental music or dance, they need not necessarily be construed as wrong. The primitive church was transient, temporarily quartered in homes, ships, beaches, and public squares. It often was hidden away from those who tried to stamp it out. It had no time for anything but the most simple musical devices and activities in its own worship.

More important, certain types of music might have been avoided, not because of an intrinsic wrongness, but by the strong associations in the minds of some that were brought from pre-Christian experiences. However, the governing radically Christian principle was that whatever was to be avoided was to be avoided because it would offend a weak conscience, not because it was intrinsically empowered to change behavior. The distinction therefore between the pagan concept of the empowerment of things and the Christian concept of discernment among things, none of which are impure *in themselves* (Rom. 14:14) and are not empowered, overrides any opinion which states that the early church set a standard in music that was rigid, unchangeable, and limited. The range of musical practice is rather to be construed as broadly as possible because it is based on a principle that speaks to a total way of life, including music.

Harold M. Best and David K. Huttar[20]

TWENTY THREE

Musical Instruments in Scripture

The Bible frequently mentions musical instruments in association with the praise of the Lord. Percussion, wind, and string instruments each had their place in the worship of the people of God.

226 • Scriptural References to Instruments

In Scripture, musical instruments serve a purpose within and for the life of the covenant community; their function was not a matter of individual self-expression, as is often the case today.

Musical instruments in general are designated by the term *kelim* (instruments for singing, Amos 6:5; 1 Chron. 16:42; the instruments of David, 2 Chron. 29:26; Neh. 12:36). The fact that this Hebrew term also denotes utensils and implements of various types, such as kitchenware, weapons, and "things" generally, including the "baggage" by which Saul was hiding when Samuel came to anoint him (1 Sam. 10:22), underscores the utilitarian nature of musical instruments in the biblical perspective. Music, along with all the worship arts, was not a means of individual self-expression but an activity that performed a specific function within the life of the covenant people.

Several passages in Scripture provide brief lists of instruments used in the worship of the Lord (1 Sam. 10:5; 2 Sam. 6:5; 1 Chron. 13:8; 15:16, 28; Pss. 81:2-3; 92:3; 150:3-5). In addition, lists of instruments occur in connection with banquets (Isa. 5:12), the wicked person's celebration of prosperity (Job 21:12), the foreign worship of images (Dan. 3:5, 7, 10, 15), and the destruction of the unfaithful city that had persecuted the saints (Rev. 18:22). The apostle Paul lists several instruments metaphorically in his discussion of speaking in tongues (1 Cor. 14:7-8).

Because ancient instruments differed from those in common use in Western culture, a correct under-

standing of the types of instruments signified by the various biblical terms is a task for musicologic research. An important tool in this research is archaeological evidence, in the form of actual instruments preserved in tombs or reproductions of them in coins, monuments, seals, manuscripts, and the like. The instruments used in biblical times fall into the same general classes with which we are familiar: percussion, wind, and stringed instruments. Instruments of all three classes were used in the praise of the Lord. Many of these instruments were also used for other purposes, such as warfare, family celebrations, and mourning. Some instruments had erotic associations or connections with fertility cults, and their use in the worship of the sanctuary was avoided.

227 • Percussion Instruments

Percussion instruments are those that make their sound when struck or shaken; biblical percussion instruments include cymbals, the sistrum, bells, the gong, and the tambourine.

——— Cymbals ———

The usual Hebrew word for cymbals is *m^{e}tziltayim* (1 Chron. 15:16; 16:42; 25:1; 2 Chron. 5:13), a dual form indicating a pair of instruments struck together. Another form is *tziltz^{e}lim*, which may be onomatopoeic, that is, an attempt to represent the clashing sound made by the instrument in its name. This word is used in Psalm 150:5, which refers to two types of cymbals, literally "cymbals of sound" and "cymbals of shout"; these expressions are usually translated "loud cymbals" and "high sounding

Flat, round cymbals were popular in many parts of the ancient world. Some were made of silver, but most, like these pictured above, were of heavy bronze. Egyptians made a smaller style sometimes called "finger cymbals," or castanets.

cymbals," although their exact meanings are uncertain. According to 1 Chronicles 15:19, the cymbals of the sanctuary were made of bronze; there they joined the wind and stringed instruments in concerted praise to the Lord. Paul mentions the cymbal, *kumbalon,* in a metaphor, comparing to it the exercise of vocal gifts where love is lacking (1 Cor. 13:1).

The Sistrum

This instrument, not well known in Western culture, was widely used in antiquity, being common, for example, in Egypt. It consisted of a small frame with metallic pieces loosely attached, which made a rattling sound when shaken. The term *mᵉnaʿanᵉʿim* in 2 Samuel 6:5 seems to indicate such an instrument or perhaps another type of shaken instrument, such as beads in a gourd. The translation "castanets" (NASB) is questionable.

The Tambourine

Although large drums were used in ancient times, especially by the military, in Scripture the drum family is represented only by the timbrel or tambourine (Hebrew *tof*). Again, the name may be onomatopoeic; the instrument consisted of membranes of

animal skins stretched over a cylindrical frame, which made a "tof" sound when beaten by hand. The modern tambourine has discs that produce the jingling sound we now associate with the instrument; the biblical timbrel may have had these discs also, but unlike the tambourine of today it always had the membrane. It was a small hand-held drum usually played by women and was used in dance (Exod. 15:20; 1 Sam. 18:6; cf. Ps. 68:25); however, Isaiah mentions it in the context of warfare (Isa. 30:32), and it also accompanied prophetic activity (1 Sam. 10:5). The timbrel was not used within the sanctuary, since women could not perform Levitical functions; its use may also have been forbidden there due to its connection with fertility rites. The instrument designated as *sumponyah* in Daniel 3:5 may be a drum of some type, if the word is related to the Greek *tumpanon;* in any case, the translation "bagpipes" (NASB, RSV) is incorrect.

Bells

Bells are not mentioned in the Bible as musical instruments. However, bells were attached to the hem of the high priest's robe (Exod. 28:33-34). They probably did not have clappers but made their sound by striking one another or the simulated pomegranates with which they were interspersed. The Bible does not explain the purpose of these bells; some have suggested a magical function of warding off evil spirits, attested in other cultures, but their biblical usage may have been purely decorative.

The Gong

Paul refers metaphorically to the gong, or "brass" (*chalkos,* 1 Cor. 13:1). Gongs were used in pagan temples of the ancient world, as in oriental temples today, but were not used in the worship of Israel.

228 ◆ WIND INSTRUMENTS

Wind instruments are of three general classes: those that use lip vibrations in creating the sound (trumpets and horns); those that use a vibrating reed or reeds (the clarinet and oboe); and those in which the vibrations are created by wind directed across the opening of an air column (flutes, whistles, and pipe organs). The latter two kinds may be classified together as "pipes." Scripture mentions several varieties of wind instruments.

Horns

The biblical horn is literally a horn (*qeren*, 1 Chron. 25:5), usually a hollowed ram's horn with a mouth hole, although horns of certain wild animals were sometimes used. Many English translations create confusion by calling them "trumpets." The ram's horn is usually called the *shofar* (Exod. 19:16; Josh. 6:4, 9, 13; 1 Chron. 15:28; Pss. 81:3; 98:6). Another term is *yovel* (Exod. 19:13; Josh. 6:5). The two words seem to be interchangeable and are sometimes found paired (Josh. 6:4, 6). The ram's horn could play only a restricted number of pitches and was more a signaling instrument than a musical one. As such, it had an important function in warfare as well as in worship. In the sanctuary it was used to announce the various sacrifices and festive days and to proclaim the Year of Jubilee (Lev. 25:9), which takes its name from that of the instrument, *yovel*. The *shofar* was the one instrument carried over into the worship of the synagogue, which did not continue the sanctuary tradition of instrumental music, using vocal music only. Musicologists have attempted to reconstruct some of the patterns of horn signaling used in the ancient synagogue.

Trumpets

The biblical trumpet (*ḥᵃtzotzᵉrah*), made originally of silver (Num. 10:2), is shown on ancient coins as a straight tube, similar to the later heraldic trumpet but shorter and with a larger bore. Unlike the modern concert trumpet, it had no valves and could therefore play only a limited number of notes. The silver trumpets were used in pairs, and large numbers of them might be employed at one time. The uses of the trumpet were virtually identical to those of the ram's horn: to sound the alarm in warfare; to herald the festivals, sacrifices, and offerings (Num. 10:8-10; 2 Chron. 13:12, 14; 29:27); and generally to join the other instruments in praise of the Lord (Ps. 98:6). Both the ram's horn (1 Kings 1:39; 2 Kings 9:13) and the trumpet (2 Kings 11:14) were sounded to herald the coronation of a king, and this motif is appropriate in their use for the worship of Yahweh, the Great King of Israel (Ps. 47:5). The instructions for the so-called Feast of Trumpets (Lev. 23:23-25) do not specifically mention trumpets but a "memorial of shout" (*tᵉru'ah*) or sounding.

Pipes

The instrument known as the *ḥalil* is mentioned a number of times in the Bible. The name is related to a word meaning "pierced," indicating that the instrument had fingering holes. Thus, unlike the horn or trumpet, it was able to play a melodic line, as was its New Testament equivalent, the *aulos* (1 Cor. 14:7). Although the *ḥalil* or *aulos* is usually called a "flute" in English versions, archaeological evidence suggests that it had a reed mouthpiece and was therefore a primitive form of clarinet; illustrations show musicians playing two pipes simultaneously, a difficult feat unless each had a reed. Jeremiah refers to the "wailing" or "moaning" sound of the instrument (Jer. 48:36). The *ḥalil* was played for occasions of rejoicing, as at the coronation of Solomon (1 Kings 1:40), or by worshipers as they marched to the festivals on Zion (Isa. 30:29). Jesus refers to the use of the *aulos* to accompany dancing (Luke 7:32) and in the customary rites of mourning for the dead (Matt. 9:23). The *ḥalil* had a limited function in the sanctuary; the superscription of Psalm 5 directs the use of the *naḥilah*, a related word, in performance. Another instrument, called the *'ugav* (Gen. 4:21; Ps. 150:4), may have been a form of pipe, though this is not certain; it was also used for rejoicing (Job 21:12) and mourning (Job 30:31). However, it seems to have had erotic associations and was not played in worship. The *mashroqi* mentioned in Daniel 3 in connection with Nebuchadnezzar's worship may have been a type of flute.

229 • STRINGED INSTRUMENTS

Several sorts of stringed instruments are mentioned in the Bible. The harp and the lyre, especially, were prominent in the music of the sanctuary.

Ancient stringed instruments were plucked, not bowed like the instruments of the violin family that are the mainstays of the classic orchestra in Western culture (the translation "viol" is inaccurate). The superscriptions of the Psalms, in the instructions for performance, refer to stringed instruments under the general term *nᵉginot* (Pss. 4; 54–55; 61; 67; 76); the noun is derived from the verb *nagan*, to "pluck" or "play." Another general term for strings is *minnim* (Pss. 45:8; 150:4). Two principal kinds were used in worship: the harp and the lyre.

The lyre was a popular musical instrument born in the shepherd's field and in the courts of Israel. The musician tuned the lyre by tightening the strings. As the strings were plucked, the sound was amplified by the sound box at the base of the instrument.

The Harp

An important instrument in Israelite worship was the *nevel,* evidently a type of harp. Several psalms refer to its use in the orchestra of the sanctuary (Pss. 57:8; 81:2; 92:3; 150:3). The strings of the harp are strung across a curved neck, like an archer's bow, or across a frame consisting of two members at right angles. Ancient Egyptian harps that have been preserved typically have ten or twelve strings; the Psalms refer to the *nevel 'asor,* or "harp of ten [strings]" (Pss. 33:2; 144:9) or simply *'asor,* "instrument of ten [strings]." As the harp lacks a fingerboard, each string is restricted to one pitch. The *kithara* of the New Testament was probably a harp, although it might have been a lyre. Paul refers to its ability to produce distinct pitches (1 Cor. 14:7); John portrays the elders worshiping with the harp (Rev. 5:8), and the music of harps figures in his depiction of the worship of the New Jerusalem (Rev. 14:2; 15:2).

The Lyre

The lyre (*kinnor*) is mentioned more frequently than the harp and seems to have been a more popular instrument in common life as well as in the worship of Yahweh. The strings of the lyre are stretched across a frame from a bar supported by two necks.

The lyre had a fingerboard, so the pitches of the strings could be changed. The Psalms frequently refer to this instrument (Pss. 43:4; 71:22; 98:5; 137:2, RSV; 147:7, RSV; 149:3, RSV), and it appears elsewhere in Scripture (Gen. 4:21; Job 30:31 RSV; Isa. 5:12; Ezek. 26:13 RSV). The superscriptions of Psalms 6 and 12 direct their performance with instruments "upon the *sheminit,*" perhaps an eight-stringed lyre. The *kinnor* is frequently mentioned together with the *nevel* (1 Kings 10:12; Pss. 57:8; 81:2; 150:3). Rabbinic tradition indicates that nine or more lyres were always used in the worship of the sanctuary. The lyre was David's instrument (the translation "harp" is incorrect), and with it he soothed Saul's mental depression (1 Sam. 16:16, 23, RSV). Together with the harp and other instruments, the lyre was associated with the activities of prophetic bands that frequented the sanctuaries (1 Sam. 10:5); when the central sanctuary was established, its musicians, led by Jeduthun, prophesied to the accompaniment of the lyre (*kinnor,* 1 Chron. 25:3, RSV). The prophets of Israel were musicians who customarily uttered or sang their oracles, apparently with stringed instruments; Elisha called for a string player or "minstrel" (*menaggen*) when the king asked him to prophesy (2 Kings 3:15, RSV).

Other Stringed Instruments

The *shalishim* of 1 Samuel 18:6 were instruments played by women to welcome Saul and David returning from battle against the Philistines. The name of the instrument is related to the Hebrew word for "three," so it may have been a three-stringed lute with a long neck of the type pictured in Egyptian tomb paintings being played by a young woman. However, it could also have been a percussion instrument such as a triangle. The *pesanterin* in Nebuchadnezzar's orchestra (Dan. 3), sometimes translated "harp" or "psaltery," was more likely an early type of dulcimer, in which the strings were stretched over a frame and struck with a rod. In this respect it would have been a precursor of the piano, but it was not an Israelite instrument. The *sabbekha* in the same orchestra was probably another stringed instrument used in Babylon, possibly a seven-stringed lyre; the King James Version translation "sackbut" (an early type of trombone) is incorrect. None of these instruments were used in the worship of the Lord.

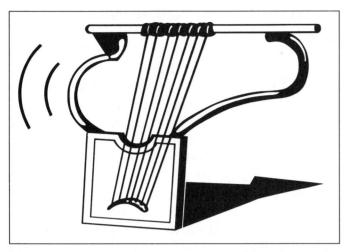

The origin of the lute is uncertain, although wooden lutes became common in Egypt. They were played much like a guitar. The type pictured here was one of the first stringed instruments developed in Egypt. This style was balanced on one shoulder with the long neck sticking out behind the musician. The pegs were to hold the strings tight, and not for tuning.

230 • THE SANCTUARY ORCHESTRA

The sanctuary orchestra accompanied the singers and served to call the people to the worship of Yahweh.

The sanctuary orchestra contributed to the celebrative character of Israel's covenant worship. Horns, trumpets, cymbals, harps, and lyres were used when the ark was brought up to Mount Zion (1 Chron. 13:8; 15:28), and David promptly established permanent Levitical orders whose duty it was to play the various instruments used in the continuing worship on that site (1 Chron. 15:16-24; 16:4-7; 25:1-7). The sanctuary instruments were not primarily solo instruments but were used orchestrally in the praise of Yahweh; they sounded simultaneously to call the assembly to worship (Ps. 98:6). This appears to have been the custom in pagan cults as well, as the instruments summoning the people to bow down to the gold image of Nebuchadnezzar (Dan. 3:4-6) seem to be playing together. However, orchestral "parts" as we know them did not exist. The stringed instruments and pipes, if used, probably played the modalities (or tune ele-

ments) being used in the psalm being sung, with perhaps distinctive patterns of ornamentation; the horns, trumpets, and cymbals were primarily for the purpose of adding to the festive joy through the multiplication of sound. The *selah* of the Psalms may have been an instrumental interlude or a general "lifting up" of sound by both singers and instrumentalists.

231 • SYMBOLISM OF INSTRUMENTATION

Each of the instruments used in Israel had its function in the life of the people, as described. Their customary uses also gave them symbolic significance, especially in the New Testament, which rarely mentions their actual use in music.

The clanging gong of the pagan temples, together with the clashing cymbal, suggest to the apostle Paul the outwardly impressive but inwardly empty life without true *agapē* love (1 Cor. 13:1). The trumpet (Greek *salpingx;* verb *salpizō,* "sound a trumpet") conveys a varied symbolism. As the instrument used to signal the sacrificial offerings, it provided Jesus with an image of the ostentatious worshiper who announces his gift with much fanfare (Matt. 6:2). As an instrument used in warfare, it symbolizes for John the Revelator the judgments to be poured out against those who are unfaithful to the covenant. As the instrument that heralded the ascension of a king, it symbolizes for Paul the inauguration of the dominion of Christ in the new life of the resurrection (1 Cor. 15:52). For John, the harp or lyre, so closely associated with the worship of the sanctuary, is emblematic of the church's triumphant worship in the presence of God. The symbolic use of instruments has its antecedents in the Old Testament; in a remarkable passage that suggests a role for instruments in spiritual warfare, Isaiah portrays the defeat of the Assyrian enemy of the Lord's people in these words: "Every stroke the LORD lays on them with his punishing rod will be to the music of tambourines and harps" (Isa. 30:32).

Richard C. Leonard

Psalms in Biblical Worship

=====================

The Psalms contain in miniature the whole of God's covenantal dealings with his people in a form that speaks directly from heart to heart. Because they are poems of worship, they have been called "the prayer book of the Bible." Within the framework of doxology, which is built into the structure of the collection itself, the Psalms praise, give thanks, petition, curse, and tell stories, employing a variety of structures and techniques along the way. In every period of the life of both Israel and the church, the Psalms have been employed in worship and regarded as indispensable.

=====================

232 • THE IMPORTANCE OF THE PSALMS

The book of Psalms is one of the most important sections of the Bible and is frequently quoted in the New Testament. The Psalms were used in the worship of the Israelite sanctuary, and church and synagogue have continued this usage. The book of Psalms provides a comprehensive picture of the covenant faith of Israel.

The book of Psalms, or "Praises" (Hebrew *t*ᵉ*hillim*), is one of the major portions of the Holy Scripture. In the Hebrew Bible, it stands at the beginning of the third division of the canon, the "Writings" (*K*ᵉ*tuvim*), after the Law (*Torah)* and the Prophets. The three Old Testament books most often quoted in the New Testament are Deuteronomy (from the Law), Isaiah (from the Prophets), and the Psalms, for the apostles saw the Psalms as prophetic of Christ. In this they were following the lead of Jesus himself, who, in appearing to his disciples after the Resurrection, had reminded them; "Everything must be fulfilled that is written about me in the Law of Moses, the Prophets and the Psalms" (Luke 24:44).

The Psalms are invaluable as a source for our knowledge of the worship of ancient Israel. The Pentateuch lays out the procedures to be followed in the sacrificial cult and in the observance of the various festivals. The Mosaic directives, however, focus on the priests and their responsibilities or on the external obligations of the lay worshiper. The Psalms most clearly reveal the faithful Israelite's "heart for God," the devotion of the loyal covenant partner of the Lord. They express the religious experience, not of those who officiated in sacrificial rites, but of those who appeared before the Lord to bring the tribute of praise or the offering of prayer and song as a personal and deeply felt response to Yahweh's covenant love. These things hold true although the Psalms were performed by the sanctuary's professional musicians, the Levitical singers, and although the majority of them seem to speak with the voice of the Davidic king as representative of the covenant community.

The Psalms were used in the worship of the Israelite sanctuary in Jerusalem, as an offering of song alongside the offering of sacrifices. In fact, many of them probably originated in the worship of the tent (or tabernacle) of David, the sanctuary established on Mount Zion when David brought the ark of the covenant up from Kiriath-Jearim (2 Sam. 6; 1 Chron. 13:13). When the temple of Solomon was erected and the sacrificial rituals were moved from Gibeon to Jerusalem, the Psalms passed into the worship of the temple. With the rise of the synagogue, the Psalms eventually took their place alongside the recitations of the Torah and the Prophets in the weekly and festal worship of the Jewish community. Jesus and the early Christians worshiped with psalms (Matt. 26:30; Acts 16:25; 1 Cor. 14:26; Eph. 5:19). The church in every age has made extensive use of the psalmody of Israel: in the historic chant of the liturgical churches, in the psalters of the Reformation congregations, in the responsive readings of modern Protestant denominations, and in the Scripture songs of charismatic and other contemporary worship.

The book of Psalms offers a panorama of the religious life of the people of God. If we had no other biblical sources, we could reconstruct a fairly accurate picture of the faith and history of Israel from the Psalms alone. Taken as a whole, the Psalter provides the resource for a comprehensive biblical theology, with a special stress on the covenant. The different types of psalms bear a relationship to the elements of the ceremony of covenant making and covenant renewal, so that "the Psalter served broadly as a cultic instrument for the maintenance of a proper covenantal relationship with Yahweh" (M. G. Kline, *The Structure of Biblical Authority* [Grand Rapids: Wm. B. Eerdmans Publishing Co., 1972], p. 63). Finally, the Psalms are poetry and hymnody of great beauty and expressive power and can be appreciated for their literary value as well as for their application to theology and worship.

233 ◆ Authorship and Origin of the Psalms

Although they bear the stamp of gifted poets such as David, the Psalms are conventional worship texts, adapted to the needs of the community as a whole. The prophetic voice that often speaks in the Psalms reflects their development through the work of the Levitical musicians of the sanctuary.

The book of Psalms is customarily associated with the name of David, though less than half of the Psalms (seventy-three) bear his name in their superscription or introductory note; of these, fourteen are related by their superscription to events in the life of David. Other names that appear are those of Asaph (twelve), the sons of Korah (twelve), Solomon (two), Heman (one), Ethan (one), and Moses (one). A third of the Psalms have no such attribution.

The meaning of the expression *leDavid* in the superscription has occasioned much debate; some exegetes are of the opinion that it does not mean "by David" but "for David," that is, for the use of the Davidic ruler, whether for David himself or for one of his descendants on the Judean throne. In any case, several things are clear. First, the Davidic psalms have a poetic quality that seems to reflect the personal faith and creativity of a gifted individual such as David; moreover, these songs typically portray a worshiper involved in a struggle with powerful enemies, a situation that fits the circumstances of David's career. Second, the sanctuary on Zion was established and maintained under the personal sponsorship of the royal house of David; its worship expressed, especially, the situation of the king as leader of the covenant community and the viewpoint of the prophetic architects of Davidic theology. Third, despite what has just been said, the language of the Psalms is generalized to fit the attitude and condition of any worshiper who, in covenant with the Lord, feels the pressures of others against his or her commitment and is moved to express that commitment in prayer and song. Fourth, the Psalms were not offered spontaneously by individual worshipers but were presented by the appointed musicians of the sanctuary in behalf of the king and of the entire community (although it is possible that the congregation joined in responses or other portions of the Psalms).

In sum, even if many of the Psalms did originate in specific events in David's life, through their subsequent use in the sanctuary they have been adapted to the needs of the general worshiper and of the covenant people as a whole. Thus the psalmist's description of his distress, for example, often fits many types of situations, as in Psalm 22:

> I am poured out like water,
>   and all my bones are out of joint;
> My heart has turned to wax;
>   it is melted away within me.
> My strength is dried up like a potsherd,
>   and my tongue sticks to the roof of my
>   mouth;
>   you lay me in the dust of death.
> Dogs have surrounded me;
>   a band of evil men has encircled me,
>   they have pierced my hands and my feet.
> I can count all my bones. (Ps. 22:14-17)

The church has understood this psalm as prophetic of the suffering of Christ; as used by the Israelite worshiper, however, its language could well describe warfare, persecution, illness, old age, or a feeling of abandonment by God. This universal quality of expression has given the Psalms their continuing appeal in the worship of the church. Like the hymns of a church hymnal, the Psalms are conventional worship texts. In such texts, individual authorship is unimportant, for the aim is to express the corporate faith of the gathered community.

It is often said that the Psalms are the voice of the worshiper calling out to God, rather than the word of God directed to his people. In actuality, the Psalms are a dialogue, for God speaks in them as well. Frequently we hear the prophetic word in the Psalms declaring the word of the Lord to the community or its representative for judgment or for encouragement:

The LORD will keep you from all harm—
    he will watch over your life.
the LORD will watch over your coming and going
    both now and forevermore. (Ps. 121:7-8)

Where your fathers tested and tried me,
    though they had seen what I did.
For forty years I was angry with that generation;
    I said, "They are a people whose hearts go astray,
    and they have not known my ways."
So I declared on oath in my anger,
    "They shall never enter my rest." (Ps. 95:9-11)

Such utterances occur in perhaps a tenth of the Psalms and are a clue to the origin of psalmic worship in the cult of Zion during the Davidic era. Prophecy and music were closely associated in ancient Israel; the prophets were musicians, and the sanctuary musicians, at least, seem to have been prophets. When the ark of the covenant was brought to David's tent on Zion, he appointed Levitical musicians "to prophesy with lyres, harps, and cymbals" (1 Chron. 25:1, NASB); regular animal sacrifices were not offered here at this time, but these priests "prophesied in giving thanks and praising the LORD" (1 Chron. 25:3, NASB). The origin of most Israelite psalmody with the Levitical prophet-musicians of the sanctuary would explain why the Psalms so seldom refer to the sacrificial cult of the Zadokite priesthood.

This is not to say that all the Psalms stem from the Davidic period; some of them, for example, obviously reflect the circumstances of later centuries, including the destruction of the temple and the exile in Babylon (Pss. 74; 137). However, the tendency of scholarship during the past century to assign a late, postexilic date to a large proportion of the Psalms does not do justice to that remarkable burst of insight and creativity that occurred during the era when the institutions of Israel's covenant worship were being established in Jerusalem.

234 • STRUCTURE OF THE BOOK OF PSALMS

The Psalms are organized in five books. The general organization of the book of Psalms reflects the growth of the collection in several stages. The superscriptions of many psalms contain information relevant to their collection, as well as their performance.

— Divisions within the Book of Psalms —

The present book of Psalms is divided into five books, probably intended to correspond to the five books of the Pentateuch, or law of Moses. The divisions are: Book I, Psalms 1–41; Book II, Psalms 42–72; Book III, Psalms 73–89; Book IV, Psalms 90–106; and Book V, Psalms 107–150. Each of the first four books ends with a doxology, and Psalm 150 serves as the doxology to the entire collection. The first psalm, which describes the righteous worshiper who delights in the law of the Lord, serves as an introduction to the Psalms.

Several subgroups occur within the Psalms that may be remnants of earlier collections. Psalms 2–72 make up "the prayers of David son of Jesse" (Ps. 72:20); the two psalms that frame this collection are psalms for the coronation of the Davidic ruler. (Psalms of David also appear in other parts of the Psalter.) Within the "prayers of David" are another subgroup (Pss. 42–49) related to the sons of Korah. Other obvious subgroups include a collection of psalms of Asaph (Pss. 73–83), the "Songs of Ascents," evidently for the use of pilgrims going up to Zion for the annual festivals (Pss. 120–134), and the "Egyptian Hallel" (Pss. 113–118), a group of psalms used during the Passover celebration, four of which end with "Hallelujah!"

The number of 150 psalms may be an imitation of the 153 pericopes (sections to be read in the synagogue) of the Torah. To make up this number, some psalms or sections of psalms are repeated. Psalm 53 repeats Psalm 14; Psalm 29:1-2 is found also as Psalm 96:7-9; Psalm 70:1-5 is a duplicate of Psalm 40:13-17. Psalm 108 consists of Psalms 57:7-11 and 60:5-12, while Psalm 135 is made up entirely of portions of several other psalms. Psalms 9 10 and Psalms 42–43 are each one psalm, artificially divided. Much psalmlike material is found in other parts of the Old Testament, especially in the prophetic books and in the New Testament (Luke 1–2).

Superscriptions

About half the Psalms have the introductory note, or superscription. The superscription may indicate the collection to which the psalm belongs and often gives directions to the choirmaster for performance, such as the instrumentation to be used and possibly the names of well-known tunes or modes to which the psalm is to be sung. Fourteen of the superscriptions relate the psalm to events in the life of David. Most authorities hold that the superscriptions were prefixed to the Psalms only at a late stage in the organization of the collection, but it is impossible to be certain one way or the other. In printed Hebrew texts, the superscription is verse 1, so that in the case of many psalms the verse numbers in the Hebrew differ from those in the English translations. (This discussion cites the English verse numbers.)

Certain terms in the superscriptions refer to various types of psalms. Many are called a "song" (*shir*), or a "psalm" (*mizmor*), a term that probably indicates a song performed to the accompaniment of a stringed instrument. The title *shir hamma‘alot* in Psalms 120–134 means literally "song of the goings up," often translated "Song of Ascents"; because the expression "go up" often means to go up to Jerusalem, this title probably indicates psalms used by pilgrims to the annual festivals. The designation *maskil* (Pss. 32; 42; 52; 78) may mean "skillful psalm" or "contemplative psalm," while the term *mikhtam* (Pss. 56; 60) may indicate a psalm of expiation. A few psalms are called prayers (*tefillah*, Pss. 86; 90). Occasionally a psalm is designated by more than one of these terms (Pss. 75; 88; 92). Interestingly, only Psalm 145 is called *tehillah,* "psalm of praise," the Hebrew title of the book of Psalms.

235 • POETIC AND MUSICAL FEATURES OF THE PSALMS

The Psalms are first of all poetic song. As such, they incorporate many of the features of poetry and music, including picturesque language, a principle of the correspondence of lines, metrical patterns, and instructions for performance.

Metaphorical Language

Psalmic poetry shares with other biblical poetry, and indeed with that of all cultures and eras, the use of picturesque and metaphorical language. "The LORD God is a sun and shield" (Ps. 84:11); "He makes the clouds his chariot and rides on the wings of the wind" (Ps. 104:3). The worshiper's enemies are "bulls" or "dogs" (Ps. 22:12, 16); they are "lions, . . . those who breathe forth fire, . . . whose teeth are spears and arrows" (Ps. 57:4, NASB). Celebrating Israel's deliverance in the Exodus from Egypt, the psalmist addresses natural features as though they were persons:

> Why was it, O sea, that you fled,
> O Jordan, that you turned back,
> you mountains, that you skipped like rams,
> you hills, like lambs? (Ps. 114:5-6)

Pictorial comparisons occur frequently. The wicked are "like chaff that the wind blows away" (Ps. 1:4); they are venomous and dangerous, "like that of a cobra that stopped its ears, that will not heed the tune of the charmer" (Ps. 58:4-5). The rule of the righteous king is "like showers watering the earth" (Ps. 72:6). Children, given by the Lord, are "like arrows in the hands of a warrior" (Ps. 127:4). The unity of family and community is celebrated in a beautiful image of the priestly anointing:

> It is like the precious oil upon the head,
> running down upon the beard,
> upon the beard of Aaron,
> running down on the collar of his robes! (Ps. 133:2 RSV)

Parallelism

Poetry generally employs some principle of correspondence for successive lines; in conventional English poetry, for example, lines are usually matched through rhyme. Biblical poetry does not use rhyme, but rather uses parallelism or the correspondence of ideas. There are three main types of parallelism: antithetic, synonymous, and synthetic. In two lines of antithetic parallelism, the second states a concept that is the opposite to that stated in the first:

> For evil men will be cut off,
> but those who hope in the LORD will inherit the land. (Ps. 37:9)

This contrasting parallelism, very common in the book of Proverbs, is not used much in Psalms. The psalmists prefer synonymous parallelism, in which the second line of a couplet restates the idea presented in the first, using different words:

It is good to give thanks to the LORD,
And to sing praise to Thy name, O Most High. (Ps. 92:1, NASB)

"It is good" is not paralleled in the second line, but "to give thanks" (the Hebrew verb actually means "to confess") equates with "to sing praise," and "thy name, O Most High" corresponds to "the LORD." The frequent use of synonymous parallelism in the Psalms helps us to understand theological terms in their fuller sense:

Lovingkindness and truth have met together;
Righteousness and peace have kissed each other.
    (Ps. 85:10, NASB)

Obviously, in the psalmist's thinking, "lovingkindness" (*ḥesed,* "covenant love") must be understood to include "righteousness," while "peace" (salvation or wholeness) must incorporate "truth" (*'emet,* "reliability").

A third form of parallelism in the Psalms is called synthetic parallelism because the successive lines correspond through development or synthesis:

Blessed is the man who does not walk in the
        counsel of the wicked
    or stand in the way of sinners
        or sit in the seat of mockers.
But his delight is in the law of the LORD,
    and on his law he meditates day and night.
He is like a tree planted by streams of water,
    which yields its fruit in season,
    and whose leaf does not wither.
Whatever he does prospers. (Ps. 1:1-3)

Here the psalmist develops a picture of the righteous worshiper through successive clauses that build on the ideas previously presented.

Refrains in the Psalms

An additional poetic feature of the Psalms is the use of the refrain, a recurring phrase that marks off the stanzas of a psalm. The four central stanzas of Psalm 107 each conclude with the same refrain:

Let them confess to Yahweh because of his
        covenant love,
    And for his mighty acts in people's behalf! (Ps.
    107:8; repeated in verses 15, 21, and 31,
    AUTHOR'S TRANSLATION)

Other examples include Psalms 42–43, actually one psalm linked by the same refrain (Pss. 42:5, 11; 43:5), Psalm 46 (verses 7, 11), Psalm 57 (verses 5, 11), and Psalm 67 (verses 3, 5).

Acrostic Psalms

Several psalms (Pss. 34; 111–112; 145) are constructed as acrostics; that is, each couplet begins with the successive letters of the Hebrew alphabet. The skill of the psalmists is evident in the fact that this artificial device (included in the category "learned psalmography" by the great psalm scholar Sigmund Mowinckel) in no way detracts from the beauty and flow of the psalm:

I will bless [*'avarakhah*] Yahweh at all times;
Ever his praise will be in my mouth.
In Yahweh [*beYahveh*] shall boast my soul;
Shall hear the humble, and shall rejoice.
Magnify [*gaddelu*] the Lord with me,
And let us exalt his name in unity. (Ps.
    34:1-3, AUTHOR'S TRANSLATION)

The apotheosis of the acrostic psalm is Psalm 119. This psalm has twenty-two stanzas of eight verses each; in the first stanza, every verse begins with the first letter of the Hebrew alphabet; in the second, every verse begins with the second letter, and so on for 176 verses, the longest chapter in the Bible.

Metrical Patterns

Like all poetry, psalmic poetry has a metrical structure. Meter refers to the rhythm of successive syllables. Conventional English poetry uses metric "feet" in various patterns, such as iambic pentameter: "A *little learn*ing *is* a *dan*gerous *thing*" (Alexander Pope). Biblical poetry employs instead a pattern of stressed syllables, with an intervening variable number of unstressed syllables and no fixed rhythmic "beat." Therefore, it can be translated into English without losing its Hebraic poetic character:

By the *word* of the LORD the *heav*ens were
    made,
And by the *breath* of his *mouth all* their *host.*
    (Ps. 33:6, NASB)

Here, each line contains four stressed syllables, a common metric pattern in the Psalms. The use of stressed syllables rather than metric feet renders the Psalms especially suitable for chanting or recitative-style musical performance. When the Psalms are set to music using conventional Western tunes with regular bar lines and a fixed beat, it is necessary to paraphrase them. Consider Psalm 100:1-2:

> Shout joyfully to the LORD, all the earth.
> Serve the LORD with gladness;
> Come before him with joyful singing.
> (Ps. 100:1-2 NASB)

Compare the following paraphrase to the "original" verses:

> All people that on earth do dwell,
> Sing to the Lord with cheerful voice.
> Him serve with mirth, his praise forth tell;
> Come ye before him and rejoice. (William Kethe)

Such paraphrases have produced great hymnody and occupy an important place in historic Christian worship. However, they disguise the Hebraic character of the biblical Psalms. While the contemporary Scripture song tends to retain more of the original word order, often avoiding rhyme, it too is usually sung to a tune with regular bar lines and so lacks the chantlike quality of psalmic poetry.

——— Antiphonal Psalmody ———

Some of the psalms are antiphonal or responsive in form, evidently intended to be sung by two or more groups of singers. The recurring phrase, "his love endures forever," which forms the second half of all twenty-six couplets in Psalm 136, was perhaps sung by a choir responding to the statement of the first half verse. Psalm 24 is a dialogue between two groups of singers, one seeking entrance to the sanctuary, perhaps bearing the ark of the covenant in procession, and another standing guard at the gate:

> *Choir I:*
> Lift up your heads, O you gates;
> lift them up, you ancient doors,
> that the King of glory may come in
> *Choir II:*
> Who is he, this King of glory?
> *Choir I:*
> *Yahveh tzᵉva'ot* [The LORD Almighty]—
> He is the King of glory. (Ps. 24:9-10)

Three choirs seem to be involved in the liturgical dialogue of Psalm 118; they are "Israel," the gathered covenant community; "the house of Aaron," or the priests; and "those who fear the LORD," perhaps

Gentile worshipers of Yahweh. All three groups are invited in turn to give the response, "his love endures forever" (Ps. 118:2-4; cf. Pss. 115:9-11; 135:19-20). Both Psalms 124 and 129 begin with a leader inviting the assembly to join in the psalm:

> "Had it not been the LORD who was on our side,"
> Let Israel now say,
> "Had it not been the LORD who was on our side,
> When men rose up against us,
> Then they would have swallowed us alive . . ."
> (Ps. 124:1-3 NASB)

——— Directions for Performance ———

The superscriptions of some of the psalms are apparently addressed to the "director" or "choirmaster" (the meaning of the Hebrew word is uncertain). These instructions occasionally indicate the instrumentation to be used, such as stringed instruments (Pss. 4; 55; 67), the eight-stringed lyre (Ps. 12), or the clarinet or flute (Ps. 5). Many of the psalms mention instruments in their vow of praise or invitation to worship (Pss. 43:4; 57:8; 81:2-3; 92:3; 150:3-5). Although the translations are often obscure, some of the superscriptions appear to designate tunes or modes upon which the psalm is to be performed (*'Ayyelet hashshahar,* "The Doe of the Morning," Ps. 22; *Shoshannim,* "Lilies," Pss. 45; 69; *Yonat 'elem rᵉhoqim,* "The Dove on Distant Oaks," Ps. 56; *'Al tashhet,* "Do Not Destroy," Pss. 57–59; 75). It is regrettable that today we have little concrete knowledge of how psalmic music actually sounded, although some of the oldest liturgical chants of the church have been shown to have features in common with Yemenite Jewish music, which in turn may have been preserved with little change from biblical times.

——— *The Selah* ———

The term *selah,* occurring seventy-one times in the text of thirty-nine psalms, evidently derives from the verb *salal,* to "lift up" a song. It is most often interpreted to indicate an instrumental interlude; however, it could designate a point where free-flowing vocal and instrumental praise occurred, perhaps using a familiar refrain such as, "Give thanks to the LORD, for he is good; his love endures forever" (Ps. 118:1).

236 • CLASSIFICATION OF THE PSALMS

Students of the Psalms have attempted to categorize them by content, literary type, and cultic usage. Though each of these methods has its value, an approach to the Psalms through the concept of the covenant correlates both the general theological stance of the Psalter and the variety exhibited by the individual psalms.

Classification by Content

A traditional method of classifying the Psalms has been by content or subject matter; this method has great appeal when the chief aim of the student is to apply biblical teaching to the support of Christian doctrine and the practice of personal faith. Psalms of praise speak of the character and attributes of God: his creative activity (Pss. 8; 33; 104), his eternity (Ps. 90), his infinity (Ps. 139), his dominion and judgment (Pss. 96–97), his holiness and justice (Ps. 99), his mercy (Ps. 103), his word of revelation of his precepts (Pss. 19; 119). Historical psalms rehearse the saving events of Israel's sacred history (Pss. 78; 105; 136). Penitential psalms (Pss. 6; 32; 38; 51; 69; 102; 130) express the sinfulness of the worshiper before the Lord. Psalms of imprecation, or cursing of enemies (Pss. 35; 69; 109; 137), have been something of an embarrassment to expositors; Wesley, for example, considered them unworthy of Christian usage. Messianic psalms, celebrating the Lord's "anointed," are seen as prophetic of Christ (Pss. 2; 22; 40; 89; 110; 132). Some interpreters have identified social psalms, dealing with the nature, ethical obligation, and destiny of humanity, but the examples of this kind overlap all the others. In focusing on the didactic content of the Psalms, it is easy to lose sight of their purpose, for the Psalms are not intended to be doctrinal expositions but to be acts of worship, facilitating the believer's approach to the living God.

Classification by Literary Type

Classification by type focuses on the literary form or structure, rather than doctrinal content, of the Psalms. Hymns of praise (Pss. 29; 33; 65–67; 100; 103; 113; 117; 124; 136) begin with an invitation to praise the Lord, followed by the reasons for doing so. Sometimes the invitation becomes a complete psalm (Pss. 148; 150); in other instances, the hymn specifically celebrates Yahweh's role as Creator (Pss. 8; 104; 148) or as King and Judge (Pss. 47; 96; 98–99) or exalts his law (Pss. 19; 119). The hymn of praise may take an individual form, in which the worshiper states his intention to praise the Lord and then testifies to what the Lord has done for him (Pss. 30; 34; 92; 116; 138). While the community hymn may be "descriptive praise" (Pss. 29; 113), extolling Yahweh's enduring qualities, usually both corporate and individual hymns are "narrative praise" or "confessing praise," recounting his acts of creation and redemption.

Psalms of lament also fall into both the community and individual categories. The community lament (Pss. 44; 74; 79–80; 83) begins with an introductory petition for the Lord to hear and deliver his people and may include a description of their distress (usually invasion by enemies) and a reminder of the Lord's past deeds in behalf of his people and the acknowledgment of the Lord's answer to prayer. The individual lament, the most numerous type in the Psalter (about fifty examples, including Pss. 9–10; 13; 22–23; 27; 31; 36; 42–43; 55; 57; 63; 69; 73; 86; 109; 130), has a similar format: the worshiper's address to the Lord; complaint concerning some distress (usually illness or oppression by the wicked); petition for relief; acknowledgment of the Lord's answer and a promise to bring him praise. However, these psalms may have different emphases. In some, trust and confidence predominate (Pss. 23; 27). Others offer the worshiper's confession of sin, removing barriers to the Lord's answer to prayer (Pss. 32; 38; 51; 130). Some (the "psalms of imprecation") stress the condemnation of the psalmist's oppressors (see Claus Westermann, _The Psalms: Structure, Content, and Message_ [Minneapolis: Augsburg Publishing House, 1980]).

In addition, the Psalter includes alphabetical or acrostic psalms (Pss. 34; 111–112; 119; 145), wisdom poems similar to material in Proverbs (Pss. 37; 127), and liturgies (Pss. 24; 68; 118), or psalms that appear to combine song with visible actions of worship. These categories represent clearly distinguishable psalmic forms and are useful when studying the book of Psalms from the literary standpoint.

Classification by Cultic Usage

Like the chants, hymns, anthems, Scripture songs, and choruses of Christian worship, the Psalms must have been used on specific occasions in the liturgy of the Israelite sanctuary. The literary form of the Psalms, and the ideas they express, may suggest the kinds of occasions on which they were sung. The chief exponent of this approach has been the Norwegian scholar Sigmund Mowinckel (*The Psalms in Israel's Worship,* 2 vols. [New York: Abingdon Press, 1962]). In general, Mowinckel's scheme corresponds to the categories as defined by literary type, but he associates them with specific observances and rites, both joyful festivals and times of penitence.

Mowinckel views the individual psalms of lament as appropriate for various cultic acts mandated in the ritual laws of the Pentateuch, such as offerings to atone for unintentional sin (Lev. 4) or ceremonies that certify the cleansing of leprosy (Lev. 14). Recovery from illness in general warranted a visit to the sanctuary, and Mowinckel suggests that the "enemies" in these psalms of lament are people who had caused the speaker's illness through the practice of sorcery. The communal laments would have been used on days of penitence or fasting, which were proclaimed in response to national disasters such as defeat in warfare, epidemics, drought, or famine. Hymns of narrative praise would be suitable for public acts of thanksgiving after victory in battle or following a bountiful harvest (Pss. 65; 67) or for the individual's presentation of an offering vowed as an act of thanksgiving for benefits received (Lev. 7:11-18). There are psalms exalting Zion as the sanctuary of God (Pss. 48; 84; 87; 122), perhaps used by pilgrims to the annual festivals. Other categories include special psalms for the king's accession to the throne (Pss. 2; 72; 110) and for an annual festival celebrating Yahweh's enthronement as King (Pss. 47; 93; 95-99), including the procession of the ark to Zion (Pss. 24; 68; 132).

Although not all his suggestions have gained wide acceptance, Mowinckel's views have exerted considerable influence on subsequent attempts to categorize the Psalms. One difficulty with classification by usage in the various cultic observances of Israel is that it is largely conjectural and may involve circular reasoning. By linking many psalms to a hypothetical annual festival of the enthronement of Yahweh, for instance, the exegete may develop a full picture of this festival, which in turn governs the interpretation of the Psalms. Moreover, the content of a psalm may not always be a clue to its cultic usage. Conventional texts are sometimes associated with particular festivals by tradition, rather than by internal features. There is no particular reason why Isaac Watts's hymn "Joy to the World" should be used only during Advent and Christmas (it is actually a paraphrase of Psalm 98). The superscription of Psalm 30 refers to it as a song for the dedication of the temple, although nothing in the psalm would suggest this application. Finally, when biblical worship, in all its aspects, is understood as the renewal and celebration of the covenant between the Lord and his people, there is less need to relate the different types of psalms to specific acts and festivals; they may also be seen as expressions of the various elements of covenant structure.

— Classification by Covenant Structure —

The structure of the Lord's covenant with Israel has been compared to that of the ancient treaty between an overlord and his vassal king. In these agreements the overlord, or "great king," grants a territory to a client king, his vassal or "servant," with a promise of protection. In return, the servant king pledges his loyalty to the overlord, to the exclusion of other allegiances, and agrees to pay tribute as required. In form, the treaty may include a historical prologue, or statement of the previous relationship, in which the overlord reminds the vassal of what he has done for him; the stipulations or "words" of the agreement, the servant king's obligations to the great king; an act of ratification of the pact; a pronouncement of the benefits to the vassal if he maintains the terms of the treaty; and a declaration of the sanctions, or punishments, that will follow if the client violates the agreement.

This treaty structure is evident in the covenant of Mount Sinai and in its renewal in Moses' final address in Deuteronomy, where Yahweh is in the place of the "great King" and all Israel is the vassal or servant. It is also evident in the prophetic books, where the prophets, as spokespersons for the covenant, often indict the community for its failure to keep the agreement and articulate the enactment of the sanctions or judgments. But the same covenant structure underlies the Psalms, where the speaker stands in the place of the servant king, representing the faithful congregation. Although all aspects of the covenant pattern are represented in the Psalms, the definitive features are the servant's vow of allegiance to the overlord and an appeal to the Great King to honor the treaty he has granted by delivering the servant from their mutual enemies.

When the background of treaty-covenant structure is borne in mind as the foundation for Israel's worship in the sanctuary of Yahweh, many recurrent features of the Psalms fall into place, and the specialized Psalm categories are seen to reflect the different movements of covenant enactment. The enthronement psalms set the stage in their portrayal of Yahweh as the Great King. Psalms that rehearse the course of redemptive history (Pss. 78; 105–106; 135–136), along with the psalms of confessional praise, reflect the historical prologue of the treaty-covenant and are recited as acts of covenant reaffirmation. Psalms in praise of the law of the Lord reflect the congregation's renewed submission to the stipulations of the covenant. The psalms of praise and the worshiper's vow of praise in the psalms of lament are part of the fulfillment of Israel's obligation of tribute to the Great King (M. G. Kline, *The Structure of Biblical Authority* [Grand Rapids: Wm. B. Eerdmans Publishing Co., 1972], p. 63). The speaker's repeated pledge of loyalty in the psalms of lament is an act of covenant ratification, and the picture he draws of his enemies shows that he will have nothing to do with authorities who oppose his covenant overlord. His prayer for vindication and salvation is based on the Great King's guarantee of protection, which from his perspective is the whole purpose and benefit of the covenant. The invective against the ungodly in the psalms of imprecation invokes the covenant sanction of curse upon the apostate; in contrast, the worshiper (or a sanctuary prophet) often recites the blessings and benefits he has received, not so much in virtue of *his* obedience to the agreement, but through *Yahweh's* faithfulness.

In essence, there are only two basic categories of psalms: psalms of petition and psalms of celebration. Both are based on the covenant. In the first category, the servant pledges his commitment to the Great King and appeals to him in turn to honor the agreement. In the second category, the worshiper (or the congregation) exalts the Lord as the Great King and declares his faithfulness or develops some aspect of the covenant ceremony.

237 • THE COVENANT IN THE PSALMS OF PETITION

The covenant between the Lord and his people, represented especially by the Davidic king, is the governing theological concept in psalmic worship. The covenant is the basis for the worshiper's appeal to the Lord, and covenant terminology supplies themes and motifs that are prominent especially in the psalms of petition.

The Davidic Kingship

The covenant is an agreement granted by Yahweh, as the Great King, to his servant people, represented in the Psalms especially by the Davidic ruler. The traditional identification of half the Psalms with David, as well as the obvious association of many of the Psalms with the king as military leader and spokesman for the community, underscore the association of the Psalter with the Judean royal house. The Jerusalem sanctuary, with its priesthood and musicians, was established by David and Solomon and continued under the patronage of the royal house of Judah. A theology of the Lord's special choice and anointing of David and his dynasty, first enunciated by the prophet Nathan (2 Sam. 7:7-17), seems to have been developed in association with the worship on Zion. Thus many of the Psalms appear to be for the use of the king (or in his behalf), as the covenant partner or vassal of the Lord, the "great King."

> He gives his king great victories,
>   he shows [covenant love] to his anointed,
>   to David and his descendants forever. (Ps. 18:50)

> But the king will rejoice in God;
>   all who swear by God's name will praise him,
>   while the mouths of liars will be silenced. (Ps. 63:11)

The Psalms reflect the king's involvement in warfare. They represent him engaged in a bitter struggle against dangerous enemies, the opponents of Yahweh's covenant, calling out to the Lord for deliverance and vindication in behalf of the righteous. Several psalms celebrate the Lord's covenant with David to establish his dynasty in Zion (Pss. 89; 110; 132). There are special psalms associated with the coronation of the Davidic ruler (Pss. 2; 72), and even a nonreligious poem celebrating the royal marriage (Ps. 45).

In all this, however, the king stands before the Lord in behalf of the community. He speaks as the representative worshiper, and what he says to the Lord is generalized to express the need and the devotion of all the faithful. The same principle applies to the Lord's words to the king in the Psalms; they declare his faithfulness and deliverance to all worshipers. Biblical culture did not think of personality in the individualistic way to which we in the West are accustomed; the Hebraic mind worked with an understanding of "corporate personality," in which the individual's view of himself or herself was bound up in his or her solidarity with the leader of the community. (Christ's atonement for the sin of others and his impartation of new life to those who are "in Christ" can be fully understood only in light of this Hebraic sense of corporate identity.) For these reasons it is not always appropriate to distinguish between the "individual" and the "community" psalms.

Yahweh's Covenant Love

The Psalms in several places refer to the covenant granted by the Lord as the foundation for Israel's hope of deliverance from distress, the basis for the doctrine of the enduring rule of the Davidic dynasty, and the formulation of the worshiping community's obligation to its God:

> He provided redemption for his people;
>   he ordained his covenant forever—
> holy and awesome is his name. (Ps. 111:9)

> You said, "I have made a covenant with my
>   chosen one,
>   I have sworn to David my servant,
> I will establish your line forever
>   and make your throne firm through all
>   generations." (Ps. 89:3-4)

> He took note of their distress
>   when he heard their cry;
> for their sake he remembered his covenant
>   and out of his great [covenant love] he relented.
>   (Ps. 106:44-45)

> But from everlasting to everlasting the LORD'S
>   [covenant] love is with those who fear him,
>   and his righteousness with their children's
>   children—
> with those who keep his covenant
>   and remember to obey his precepts. (Ps.
>   103:17-18)

Although the community of Israel has bound itself to God by covenant (Ps. 50:5) and is pledged to abide by its precepts, in the psalmist's eyes it is chiefly the Lord who, having initially granted the covenant, upholds it by his grace. Frequently the Psalms speak of his "faithfulness" (*'emunah*) and his "righteousness" (*tzedaqah*); these qualities are not indiscriminately displayed attributes of God but more specifically express his active intervention in

the life of his people to maintain the covenant. Virtually synonymous with these terms, and used more frequently (more than 120 times in 53 psalms), is the word *hesed,* often translated "loving-kindness," "love," "steadfast love," or "mercy." Again, Yahweh's *hesed* is not his impartial benevolence to all creation but specifically his love and mercy to his own people, out of loyalty to the covenant. Only those who have obligated themselves in treaty with the Great King have the right to appeal to him on the basis of his *hesed;* the best translation is therefore "covenant love."

In a treaty relationship, the servant-king may appeal to the overlord for protection from enemies on the basis of the great king's good offices in granting the agreement and his loyalty to his word. In the same manner, it is in virtue of the Lord's covenant love to his servants that the worshiper may plead with him for help and salvation:

> Remember not the sins of my youth and my
>   rebellious ways;
>   according to your [covenant love]
>   remember me,
> for you are good, O LORD (Ps. 25:7)

> Rise up and help us;
>   redeem us because of your [covenant
>   love]. (Ps. 44:26)

> In your [covenant love], silence my
>   enemies;
>   destroy all my foes,
> for I am your servant. (Ps. 143:12)

In many respects "covenant love" is the key word or concept in the book of Psalms; it pervades all that is said to, or about, Yahweh, whether the word *hesed* is present or not. In its praise of the Lord, Israel joyfully celebrates his covenant love:

> It is good to [confess to] the LORD
>   and make music to your name, O Most High,
> to proclaim your [covenant love] in the morning
>   and your faithfulness at night. (Ps. 92:1-2)

The most oft-repeated thanksgiving in the Psalter (Pss. 106:1; 107:1; 118:1, 29; 136:1-26; cf. 1 Chron. 16:34; 2 Chron. 20:21) praises Yahweh for his loyalty to the covenant:

Confess to Yahweh, that he is good,
For his covenant love is forever. (AUTHOR'S TRANSLATION)

Yet in times of distress the Psalms express the community's anguish with a shocking candor. The speaker may even take the Lord to task for seemingly failing to honor his obligation to defend his partner:

> You sold your people for a pittance,
> gaining nothing from their sale.
> You have made us a reproach to our neighbors,
> the scorn and derision of those around us. . . .
> All this happened to us, though we had not
> forgotten you
> or been false to your covenant. (Ps. 44:12-13, 17)
>
> You have renounced the covenant with your servant
> and have defiled his crown in the dust. (Ps. 89:39)

Such language reveals the extent to which the concept of the treaty could be taken in Israel's understanding of its relationship with Yahweh.

The Righteous and the Wicked

The Faithful and the Ungodly Contrasted. The theme of the opposition between the faithful worshiper and his ungodly enemies, which surfaces repeatedly in the book of Psalms, is an integral part of the covenant pattern of psalmic worship. This motif predominates in the first part of the Psalter, the "prayers of David," and extends into the remainder of the collection as well; in its various forms, it is present in fully half of the Psalms. On the whole, the Psalms do not present a picture of a people worshiping in complacent unity, but rather reflect an intense struggle for dominance between rival groups within the nation. Some have taken this as evidence for a late origin for the Psalms, reflecting the period when the Jews dwelt alongside other cultural groups in the context of larger empires. However, this is essentially the same situation as that depicted in the preexilic prophetic books, in which Israel's covenant with Yahweh is viewed as being in constant jeopardy due to spiritual indifference and the encroachments of false religious influences.

The contrast between the faithful and the ungodly is set forth at the very beginning of the Psalter, in the introductory psalm:

> Therefore the wicked will not stand in the
> judgment,
> nor sinners in the assembly of the
> righteous.

> For the LORD watches over the way of the
> righteous,
> but the way of the wicked will perish.
> (Ps. 1:5-6)

The Psalms exclude from the sanctuary of the Lord those who have made a covenant, lifting the hand in oath, with divinities other than Yahweh, the true God:

> Who shall ascend to the hill of the LORD?
> And who shall stand in his holy place?
> He who has clean hands and a pure heart,
> who does not lift up his soul to what is
> false,
> and does not swear deceitfully. (Ps. 24:3-4,
> RSV)

The Worshiper's Pledge of Loyalty. Frequently, the speaker affirms his loyalty to Yahweh in terms reminiscent of the vassal's response ratifying the treaty offered by the great king. Thus, the psalmist often pledges himself to the Lord with expressions such as "You are my God" (Pss. 63:1; 118:28; 140:6; 143:10), "You are my [Yahweh]" (Ps. 16:2), or "You are my King" (Ps. 44:4; cf. Ps. 74:12). This pledge is in contrast to the attitude of his adversaries, those outside the covenant. Typical of this response is Psalm 31:

> I hate those who cling to worthless idols;
> I trust in the LORD. . . .
> They conspire against me
> and plot to take my life.
> But I trust in you, O LORD;
> I say, "You are my God."
> My times are in your hands;
> Deliver me from my enemies and from those
> who pursue me.
> Let your face shine on your servant;
> Save me in your [covenant love]. (Ps. 31:6,
> 13-16)

The Enemies and Their Fate. The psalmist's enemies appear in many guises. They may be people bringing false accusation (Ps. 109:2-5) or who ridicule the worshiper's submission to the Lord (Ps. 69:7-12); the prosperous whose wealth renders them arrogant and indifferent to spiritual matters (Ps. 73:3); former friends and fellow worshipers who have turned against the speaker (Ps. 55:12-14); rebels within the community (Ps. 86:14), potential assassins (Pss. 56:6; 59:3), or foreign invaders (Ps.

79:1-4). The common thread is that they are a menace to the worshiper and stand outside the covenant with Yahweh. More than thirty psalms include a description of these enemies:

> Do I not hate those who hate you, O LORD,
> and abhor those who rise up against you?
> I have nothing but hatred for them;
> I count them my enemies. (Ps. 139:21-22)

> An oracle is within my heart concerning the
> sinfulness of the wicked:
> There is no fear of God before his eyes. (Ps.
> 36:1)

> His mouth is full of curses and lies and threats;
> trouble and evil are under his tongue.
> He lies in wait near the villages;
> from ambush he murders the innocent,
> watching in secret for his victims. (Ps.
> 10:7-8)

> The wicked draw the sword and bend the bow
> to bring down the poor and needy,
> to slay those whose ways are upright. (Ps.
> 37:14)

Against the ungodly the worshiper often feels inadequate; his enemies seem to be the wealthy, the privileged, and the powerful:

> Therefore pride is their necklace;
> they clothe themselves with violence.
> From their callous hearts comes iniquity;
> the evil consents of their minds knows no
> limits.
> They scoff, and speak with malice;
> in their arrogance they threaten oppression.
> Their mouths lay claim to heaven,
> and their tongues take possession of the earth.
> (Ps. 73:6-9)

Because of Yahweh's faithfulness, however, the fate of the worshiper's enemies is sealed. Although the psalmist's situation may appear desperate from the perspective of ordinary life, when he enters the place of worship he receives a new insight:

> When I tried to understand all this,
> it was oppressive to me
> till I entered the sanctuary of God;
> then I understood their final destiny.

> Surely you place them on slippery ground;
> you cast them down to ruin. (Ps. 73:16-18)

> The sorrows of those will increase who run
> after other gods.
> I will not pour out their libations of blood
> or take up their names on my lips. (Ps.
> 16:4)

The imprecatory psalms, or psalms of cursing, are an important part of the psalmic portrayal of the defeat of the enemies. Like the curses of the ancient treaty, they invoke the sanctions against those who, as opponents of Yahweh and his servant, have broken the bonds of covenant faithfulness. Psalm 109 is the epitome of these psalms of cursing:

> When he is tried, let him be found guilty,
> and may his prayers condemn him.
> May his days be few;
> may another take his place of leadership.
> May his children be fatherless
> and his wife a widow. . . .
> May a creditor seize all he has;
> may strangers plunder the fruit of his
> labor. . . . .
> For he never thought of [acting according to
> covenant love],
> but hounded to death the poor and the needy
> and the brokenhearted. . . .
> May this be the LORD's payment to my accusers,
> to those who speak evil of me. (Ps. 109:7-9, 11,
> 16, 20)

———— The Lord's Deliverance ————

The Appeal of the Worshiper. The Psalms echo with the worshiper's appeal to the Lord for deliverance from his enemies and for vindication of his determination to remain faithful to the covenant. Repeatedly the speaker cries out, "Hear my cry!" or "Save me!" or "Rescue me!"

> Do not turn me over to the desire of my foes,
> for false witnesses rise up against me,
> breathing out violence. (Ps. 27:12)

> Vindicate me, O God, and plead my [case]
> against an ungodly nation;
> rescue me from deceitful and wicked men.
> (Ps. 43:1)

> Rescue me and deliver me in your
> righteousness;
> turn your ear to me and save me. (Ps. 71:2)

Deliver me and rescue me from the hand of
[aliens],
whose mouths are full of lies,
whose right hands are deceitful. (Ps.
144:11)

The Lord's Answer; the Worshiper's Vow. The psalmist's petition never goes unanswered. Even the most intense and anguished portrayals of the worshiper's plight also include some recognition that the Lord has heard the speaker's prayer. The psalmist celebrates the Lord's answer, his victory, his faithfulness to the covenant. Closely associated with the proclamation of Yahweh's deliverance is the worshiper's vow of thanksgiving and praise; he promises to make the Lord's saving deeds known to the worshiping congregation.

For he has not despised or disdained the suffering
of the afflicted one;
he has not hidden his face from him
but has listened to his cry for help.
From you comes the theme of my praise in the
great assembly;
before those who fear you I will fulfill my
vows. (Ps. 22:24-25)

I will not die but live,
and will proclaim what the LORD has done.
The LORD has chastened me severely,
but he has not given me over to death.
Open for me the gates of righteousness;
I will enter and give thanks to the LORD. (Ps.
118:17-19)

As a response to Yahweh's faithfulness to the covenant, the speaker promises to perform the vow of praise (Pss. 65:1; 116:14), to give thanks or render thank offerings (Pss. 30:12; 35:18; 56:12; 116:17), to declare the Lord's righteousness (Ps. 35:28), to sing praise, sometimes to instrumental accompaniment (Pss. 30:12; 43:4; 61:8; 69:30; 71:22), or simply to praise the Lord (Pss. 22:22; 63:3; 71:23). The worshiper, while still pleading for the Lord's help, may offer the vow as an "incentive" for the Lord to save him:

O Lord, how long will you look on?
Rescue my life from their ravages,
my precious life from these lions.
I will give you thanks in the great assembly;
among throngs of people I will praise
you. (Ps. 35:17-18)

The worshiper's act of praise is his covenant obligation to Yahweh; it is part of the tribute the servant brings to the Great King. The worshiper does not hesitate to remind the Lord that he will not receive his tribute unless he rescues his vassal:

No one remembers you when he is dead.
Who praises you from the grave? (Ps. 6:5)

Is your [covenant love] declared in the grave,
your faithfulness in Destruction? (Ps.
88:11)

Entire psalms may be given over to the celebration of Yahweh's deeds of redemption, whether in the past or yet to come (Pss. 27; 30; 46; 76; 118; 124). Occasionally, the voice of the sanctuary prophet heralds the Lord's protection and deliverance to the faithful:

"Because he loves me," says the LORD, "I will
rescue him;
I will protect him, for he acknowledges my
name.
He will call upon me, and I will answer him;
I will be with him in trouble,
I will deliver him and honor him." (Ps.
91:14-15)

The LORD will keep you from all harm—
He will watch over your life;
the LORD will watch over your coming and going
both now and forevermore. (Ps. 121:7-8)

Such utterances are a reminder that it is in the sanctuary that the Lord hears the plea of the afflicted (Ps. 18:6), and it is in the sanctuary that he reveals and enacts his deliverance (Pss. 73:17; 76:2-3). The Psalms, however realistically they may portray the life situation of the worshiper, do so not in the context of that original situation—the street, the marketplace, the sickbed, the battlefield—but in the midst of the assembly gathered in the presence of the Lord. They are a cultic reenactment of problems and difficulties encountered in remaining faithful to the Lord, so that the good news of his covenant love may be applied to them in the setting of the worshiping congregation.

238 • THE COVENANT IN THE PSALMS OF CELEBRATION

Whereas in the psalms of petition the focus is often on the worshiper and his needs, in the psalms of celebration the emphasis is on the dominion and authority of the Great King, the grantor and guarantor of the covenant.

———— Enthronement Psalms ————

Of all acclamations in the Psalms, perhaps the most joyful is the cry, "Yahweh has become King!" (Pss. 93:1; 96:10; 97:1; 99:1). The psalms of the Lord's enthronement set the scene for the renewal of the covenant in the invitation to worship him as the Great King:

> Come, let us sing for joy to the LORD;
>   let us shout aloud to the Rock of our salvation.
> Let us come before him with thanksgiving
>   and extol him with music and song.
> For the LORD is the great God,
>   the great King above all gods. (Ps. 95:1-3)

Although Israel understands its special role as the covenant partners of Yahweh (Ps. 147:19-20), it also understands that Yahweh's dominion is universal:

> Say among the nations, "The LORD reigns . . ."
> He comes to judge the earth.
> He will judge the world in righteousness
>   and the peoples in his truth. (Ps. 96:10, 13)

In ancient treaties, the great king is often compared to a shepherd; the shepherd-sheep image is therefore covenant language. The Psalms speak of Yahweh as the "Shepherd of Israel" (Ps. 80:1; cf. Ps. 23:1) and of his people as sheep:

> Come, let us bown down in worship,
>   let us kneel before the LORD our Maker;
> for he is our God
>   and we are the people of his pasture, the
>   flock under his care. (Ps. 95:6-7; cf. Ps.
>   100:3)

The declaration "he is our God" is an affirmation of covenant ratification, reminiscent of the covenant formulary as found in the prophetic books: "I will be their God, and they will be my people" (Jer. 31:33).

Related to the psalms of enthronement are those that depict Yahweh's ascent of Zion to take up his rule. The language of these psalms may hark back to the time when David first had the ark of the covenant brought up to Jerusalem, or it may reveal an ongoing reenactment of that event in a procession of the ark:

> Your procession has come into view, O God,
>   the procession of my God and King into the
>   sanctuary. (Ps. 68:24)

> Lift up your heads, O you gates;
>   lift them up, you ancient doors,
>   that the King of glory may come in. (Ps.
>   24:9)

> God has ascended amid shouts of joy,
>   the LORD amid the sounding of trumpets.
> Sing praises to God, sing praises;
>   sing praises to our King, sing praises. . . .
> God reigns over the nations;
>   God is seated on his holy throne.
>   (Ps. 47:5-6, 8)

———— Hymns of Praise ————

The hymn of praise is the offering of tribute to the Lord, the fulfillment of a covenant obligation and the worshiper's vow of praise:

> I will sacrifice a [sacrifice of confession] to you
>   and call on the name of the LORD.
> I will fulfill my vows to the LORD
>   in the presence of all his people,
> in the courts of the house of the LORD—
>   in your midst, O Jerusalem,
> Praise the LORD. (Ps. 116:17-19)

The joyful cry "Hallelujah! ("Praise the LORD," or "Praise Yah," a shortened form of the name Yahweh) occurs in sixteen psalms. It introduces and concludes several of the hymns of praise:

> Praise Yah!
> Praise, O servants of Yahweh,
> Praise the name of Yahweh.
> Blessed be the name of Yahweh
> From this time forth and forever. (Ps. 113:1-2,
>   AUTHOR'S TRANSLATION)

The concept of "name" or reputation is important in treaty terminology, for the treaty stands upon the name of the great king who grants it. Thus Yahweh declares his name, together with his act of deliverance in the Exodus, at the beginning of the Sinai covenant (Exod. 20:2). In the psalms of praise, worshipers often "bless the name" of Yahweh (Pss. 96:2; 100:4; 103:1; 145:1, all NASB).

Like the enthronement psalm, the hymn of praise may be universal in scope, inviting Gentile worshipers as well as those of Israel to participate in the act of tribute:

> Praise the LORD, all you nations;
>   extol him, all you peoples.
> For great is his [covenant love] toward us,
>   and the faithfulness of the LORD
>   endures forever.
> Praise the LORD. (Ps. 117:1-2)

Hymns of praise may celebrate different aspects of the Lord's activity in maintaining the covenant. Some of them emphasize his act of creation, as a demonstration of his power, which holds at bay those who may threaten his covenant partners:

> By the word of the LORD were the heavens made,
>   their starry host by the breath of his mouth.
> He gathers the waters of the sea into jars;
>   he puts the deep into storehouses.
> Let all the earth fear the LORD;
>   let all the people of the world revere him.
>   (Ps. 33:6-8)

In other psalms, Yahweh's power is made known through his actions in history to save his people:

> Shout with joy to God, all the earth!
> Sing the glory of his name;
>   make his praise glorious! . . .
> He turned the sea into dry land,
>   they passed through the waters on foot—
>   come, let us rejoice in him.
> He rules forever by his power,
>   his eyes watch on the nations—
>   let not the rebellious rise up against him.
>   (Ps. 66:1-2, 6-7)

The psalm of praise may also extol the laws of the covenant. The massive acrostic, Psalm 119, has been called "a great doxology of God's word" (Claus Westermann, _The Psalms: Structure, Content, and Message_ [Minneapolis: Augsburg Publishing House, 1980], p. 117). In Psalm 19 the hymn of praise combines the "creation" theme with that of the Law:

> The heavens declare the glory of God;
> The skies proclaim the work of his hands. . . .
> The statutes of the LORD are trustworthy, making
>   wise the simple. (Ps. 19:1, 7)

Many interpreters consider this psalm to be two separate compositions that were joined together at a late date in the formation of the Psalter. In their view, psalms that celebrate the Law or Torah must have originated only after the Law came to be revered, at times, to excess. But if the proclamation of the stipulations or "word" of the covenant between Yahweh and his people was part of the ongoing festal worship of the Israelite sanctuary—as evidence suggests—it is to be expected that some psalms would especially celebrate that "word" or law, even from an early period. The link between Yahweh as Creator and Yahweh as Lawgiver is integral to his role as the Great King.

Almost all psalms of praise and psalms of enthronement begin with an invitation to worship the Lord: to bless his name; to "sing to the LORD a new song" (Pss. 96:1; 98:1; 149:1); to raise a shout (Pss. 47:1; 66:1; 95:1; 100:1); to clap the hands (Ps. 47:1); to fall prostrate or kneel before the Lord (Ps. 95:6); to enter his presence joyfully with thanksgiving and praise (Ps. 100:4); to celebrate with dancing and music (Ps. 149:3). The invitation may be extended to occupy the entire hymn, as in Psalms 148–150. In the Psalter's concluding doxology, every line save the last begins with the imperative, "Praise!" (_Halᵉlu!_), and the last ends with "Hallelujah!" These psalms represent a heightened recognition of the homage due the Great King from his partners in the covenant.

Psalms of the Sanctuary

As the site of the annual festivals, where the covenant with the Lord was renewed, Jerusalem was the place "where the tribes go up" (Ps. 122:4). The sanctuary on Mount Zion was especially esteemed in the eyes of the faithful of Israel and Judah. The house of the Lord was the place where Yahweh's faithfulness in protecting his servants was revealed:

> In Judah God is known,
> His name is great in Israel.
> His tabernacle is in Salem,
> His dwelling place in Zion.
> There he broke the flashing arrows,
> The shield, the sword, and the weapons of war.
>   (76:1-2, AUTHOR'S TRANSLATION)

Thus, psalms of Zion developed; they exalted the city of the sanctuary and spoke of Yahweh's love for it:

> The LORD loves the gates of Zion
>   more than all the dwellings of
>   Jacob.
> Glorious things are said of you,
>   O city of God. (Ps. 87:2-3)

In the perspective of the worshiper of Yahweh, it seemed that Zion, "the city of the Great King" (Ps. 48:2), would be established forever as a stronghold and defense for his people (Pss. 46; 48). The psalmic portrayal of Zion became the basis for the New Testament picture of the worshiping church as the New Jerusalem, the refuge of the saints of God (Gal. 4:26; Heb. 12:22-23; Rev. 21:2).

——— Psalms of Historical Recital ———

Ancient treaties are prefaced by a narrative of the previous relationship between the overlord and his vassal, usually reciting the benefits the great king has conferred on the servant, such as his elevation to a place of authority, the granting of territory, or protection from invasion. Biblical covenants begin with a similar "historical prologue":

> "I am the LORD your God, who brought you out of Egypt, out of the land of slavery." (Exod. 20:2)

> "I took you from the pasture and from following the flock to be ruler over my people Israel. I have been with you wherever you have gone, and I have cut off all your enemies from before you. . . ." (2 Sam. 7:8-9)

The historical recital forms part of the act of covenant renewal, and may be greatly extended, as in Moses' renewal of the covenant prior to Israel's entrance into Canaan (Deut. 1–4). The historical psalms represent a development from this element in the covenant structure.

> They wandered from nation to nation,
>   from one kingdom to another.
> He allowed no one to oppress them;
>   for their sake he rebuked kings:
> "Do not touch my anointed ones;
>   do my prophets no harm." . . .
> He brought out his people with rejoicing,
>   his chosen ones with shouts of joy;
> he gave them the lands of the nations,
>   and they fell heir to what others had toiled for—

> that they might keep his precepts
>   and observe his laws.
> Praise the LORD. (Ps. 105:13-15, 43-45)

In the faith of the prophetic psalmists of the sanctuary, the covenant was not to be taken for granted; its effectiveness was dependent on the continued obedience of the worshiping community—an obedience that had been all too often compromised:

> Today, if you hear his voice,
>   do not harden your hearts as you did at Meribah,
>   as you did that day at Massah in the desert,
> where your fathers tested and tried me,
>   though they had seen what I did. (Ps. 95:7-8)

Thus the recitation of covenant history may take the form of the confession of Israel's sin and rebellion:

> Thus he brought them to the border of his holy
>   land,
>   to the hill country his right hand had taken.
> He drove out nations before them
>   and he allotted their lands to them as an
>   inheritance;
>   he settled the tribes of Israel in their homes.
> But they put God to the test and rebelled against
>   the Most High;
>   they did not keep his statutes.
> Like their fathers they were disloyal and
>   faithless,
>   as unreliable as a faulty bow.
> They angered him with their high places;
>   they aroused his jealousy with their idols.
>   (Ps. 78:54-58; cf. Ps. 106)

The psalms of historical recital are a reminder not only of Yahweh's choice of his people and his deeds of deliverance, but also of the servant's constant temptation to fall away from a commitment to the Great King.

——————— Festal Liturgies ———————

A proviso of treaties between the great king and the servant king is the requirement to present tribute at stated intervals. In the same way, Yahweh in his covenant required Israel to appear before him in the three great annual festivals (Exod. 23:14-17; Lev. 23; Deut. 16:1-17). The festivals were a heightened time of celebration of the covenant relationship between God and his people. It is not surprising that some of the Psalms mirror the liturgical actions that took place on these days or on other occasions when worshipers assembled at the sanctuary.

In Psalm 118 we encounter what appears to be a liturgy celebrating a victory in battle, evidently conducted during one of the sacrificial festivals (Ps. 118:27). Several voices speak in this psalm. It opens with the invitation to all Israel (the lay worshipers), the priests, and even "those who fear the LORD," perhaps Gentile members of the community, to respond in turn with the antiphon, "his love endures forever" (Ps. 118:1-4). The king, or the sanctuary singers in his behalf, then describes the dangerous situation the army encountered on the battlefield, how he appealed to Yahweh his overlord for help, and how the valiant hand of the Lord brought deliverance (Ps. 118:5-18). A "ritual of entrance" follows, in which the worshiper asks to be admitted to the sanctuary to give thanks and is told, "This is the gate of the LORD through which the righteous may enter" (Ps. 118:19-21). The next movement in the liturgy features rejoicing by the community at the king's victory, followed by what may be a responsive section in which several voices are heard: the congregation, the priests, and perhaps the king.

> This is the day that the LORD has made;
>   let us rejoice and be glad in it.
> O LORD, save us;
>   O LORD, grant us success.
> Blessed is he who comes in the name of the
>   LORD.
>   From the house of the LORD we bless you.
>   (Ps. 118:24-26)

The worshipers then call for the festival sacrifice to be offered (Ps. 118:27). The ceremony concludes with the pledge ratifying the covenant, "You are my God, and I confess you" (Ps. 118:28, AUTHOR'S TRANSLATION), followed by a repeat of the opening doxology (Ps. 118:29).

The psalms that relate to Yahweh's ascent of Mount Zion to be enthroned as King are also liturgies. In Psalm 68 we see the ark of the covenant setting out on its journey to the sanctuary, to the traditional acclamation, "May God arise, may his enemies be scattered" (Ps. 68:1; cf. Num. 10:35), the procession up to Zion with singers, musicians, and dancers (Ps. 68:24-27), and finally Yahweh enthroned "in the skies," above the cherubim in the sanctuary (Ps. 68:34-35). The "entrance liturgy" as the ark is brought through the sanctuary gates is preserved in Psalm 24. It is impossible to know how much of this language is literal and how much is symbolic imagery; what in earlier times may have actually been performed may have been recalled in a later era only through song.

Finally, the Psalms contain evidence of the reenactment of the original covenant of Sinai in the sanctuary of Zion, through the "appearance" of the Lord and the declaration of the covenant commandments. Psalm 81 opens with the invitation to assemble with rejoicing on the "day of our Feast" (Ps. 81:1-5); Yahweh then speaks through the prophetic word, reminding the congregation that he rescued them from oppression in Egypt (Ps. 81:5-7). The basic covenant obligation is then set forth, the requirement to give exclusive allegiance to Yahweh:

> You shall have no foreign god among you;
>   you shall not bow down to an alien
>   god.
> I am the LORD your God,
>   who brought you up out of Egypt. . . .
>   (Ps. 81:9-10)

These words introduce the Decalogue, the "word" of the Sinai covenant, which the congregation is then invited to recite: "Open wide your mouth and I will fill it" (Ps. 81:10).

Something similar occurs in Psalm 50. Here Yahweh "appears" in his sanctuary, in imagery reminiscent of that of Mount Sinai:

> From Zion perfect in beauty,
>   God shines forth.
> Our God comes and will not be silent;
>   a fire devours before him,
>   and around him a tempest rages.
> He summons the heavens above,
>   and the earth, that he may judge his people:
> "Gather to me my consecrated ones,
>   who made a covenant with me by
>   sacrifice."
> And the heavens proclaim his righteousness,
>   for God himself is judge. _Selah._ (Ps. 50:2-6)

The stage is set for the judgment of the community on the basis of its obedience to the covenant obligations—a judgment proclaimed in prophetic word through the remainder of the psalm. Again, we hear the opening of the covenant act of Sinai: "I am God, your God" (Ps. 50:7; in this portion of the Psalter, "God" is often substituted for "Yahweh"). And again we learn of the liturgical recitation of the covenant commandments:

> But to the wicked, God says:
> "What right have you to recite my laws
>   or take my covenant on your lips?" (Ps. 50:16)

The indictment that follows (Ps. 50:17-21) mirrors the covenant stipulations as set forth in the laws of Sinai; it has the character of the "covenant lawsuit," a form of address often found in the prophetic books.

Psalms such as these show that the covenant between the Lord and Israel was not an antiquarian document, cold tablets of stone shut up in a darkened sanctuary. It was a living instrument in the mouth of the spokespersons of the Lord, governing the relationship he had so graciously granted his servants and giving form and order to their worship in his presence.

Richard C. Leonard

Hymns in New Testament Worship

A number of hymns may be identified in the literature of the New Testament. These hymns express the developing convictions of the Christian church, particularly the Christological confession that sets God the Son alongside God the Father, resulting in the praise of Jesus Christ.

239 ♦ CHRISTOLOGICAL PSALMS

Early Christian hymnody was influenced by the tradition of psalm singing in the temple. The hymns of the New Testament church served both a doxological and an apologetic function.

Introduction

In a useful series of essays titled "Modern Issues in Biblical Studies," published in *Expository Times* a generation ago, one notable contribution was "The Evidence in the New Testament for Early Creeds, Catechisms and Liturgy" (*Expository Times* 71 [1960]: pp. 359-363). Professor G. W. H. Lampe's far-ranging essay was prescient in several ways. For instance, it accurately pinpointed the direction in which liturgical and ecumenical studies were moving as, in the following decades, they have sought to build on a firm biblical base in such controversial practices as baptism, the Eucharist, and the role of Mary, the Lord's mother. Lampe's survey also paid tribute to the gains accruing to New Testament study from an application of the principles of form criticism. More recent interest in the tradition history and the redaction criticism of the New Testament liturgical passages has produced a spate of articles and books on the setting of the New Testament churches at worship. A valiant attempt has been made—with some measure of success—to press back behind the canonical New Testament documents to the pulsating life of the worship congregations in which these pieces of literature first took shape.

The aim of this study is to take up one aspect of recent research that stands at the meeting point of New Testament academic study and the liturgical interest that is shared not only by professional liturgiologists but equally by ministers and by all who have a concern for a more adequate expression of the church's praise of God. The center of our interest is the age-old practice of singing hymns.

What kind of precedent is there for that part of our worship in which all the participants are directly involved? Geoffrey Wainwright's comment (in *Doxology: The Praise of God in Worship, Doctrine, and Life,* [New York: Oxford University Press, 1980], p. 200) expresses a judgment that can hardly be disputed:

Singing is the most genuinely popular element in Christian worship. Familiar words and music, whether it be repeated response to biddings in a litany or the well-known phrases of a hymn, unite the whole assembly.

The concern posed by the following discussion asks two questions: (1) Granted the church meetings in New Testament times included the use of religious song, can we trace a line of development from one "type" of hymn to other specimens? and (2) What was the "catalyst" that led to the creation of new forms of hymns in the New Testament period, specifically the hymn directed to the praise of Jesus Christ as exalted Lord and ruler of creation?

The Earliest Christian Hymnody

We may begin with the earliest report we have of Christian hymns (1 Cor. 14:26): "everyone has a hymn." Paul's word (*psalmos*) has an unusual connotation, since it could be misunderstood by Greek-speaking people as a special form of musical composition, and yet it would be familiar to readers of the Septuagint who would recognize it as the heading given to many psalms. The suggestion, recently made by Martin Hengel ("Hymn and Christology," *Studia Biblica,* 3 [1978], pp. 173-197), is that *psalmos* would be understood in its non-Greek, therefore Jewish, background. If Paul's term is deliberately chosen, it would indicate a contribution to Corinthian worship in religious song, which was based on the Hebrew Psalter.

The origin of the church on its Jewish side made it inevitable that the first followers of the risen Jesus, themselves Jews by birth and tradition, would wish to express their devotion in a way to which they were accustomed. But did the synagogue pattern of worship include the use of religious song? The evidence is difficult to interpret, and it is safest to conclude that psalm singing was confined to the temple and its choirs, while the Palestinian synagogues adopted a severely didactic form of worship based on a sequence of prayers, Scripture lections, homily, and confession of Israel's faith.

This distinction may well have held for Palestinian Judaism or at least for Judaism in its orthodox center at Jerusalem. But clearly the practices of sectarian groups at Qumran, and among the Therapeutae according to Philo, did include a celebration in song shared by all the community members. In the world of the Jewish Dispersion, the Hellenistic synagogues were more open to this type of worship. It may be, as Hengel suggests, that the excluding of hymns from the orthodox synagogues was a response to the use of hymns among groups the Pharisees judged to be heretical.

The evidence of the Lucan canticles (Luke 1:46-55, the *Magnificat;* Luke 1:68-79, the *Benedictus;* Luke 2:14, the *Gloria in Excelsis;* Luke 2:29-32, the *Nunc Dimittis*), certain hymnic fragments in the book of Revelation (Rev. 15:3-4), and the early scenes recorded of the Jerusalem church, support the conclusion that messianic psalms were being sung in the Jewish-Christian circles that treasured these compositions. The purport of these compositions was partly celebratory but chiefly apologetic and formed part of the theodicy by which the early Christians sought to justify their conviction that God was sovereign in their affairs despite the suffering and opposition they were called on to endure (Acts 4:24-31). The theme of the fulfillment of Old Testament prophecy in their day linked these messianic pietists with the Qumran covenanters, with the obvious difference that the Jewish messianists held firmly to the belief that the promised Messiah had come and that his name was Jesus of Nazareth. His sufferings had issued in a triumphant vindication by God (Acts 2:32), attested by Davidic oracles and by their own experience as witnesses. And now Jesus of Nazareth was exalted as head of a messianic community in which alone salvation was offered as a present reality (Acts 2:37-42; 4:10-12).

The Theme of Christ's Victory

From the early speeches in Acts we may conclude that the leading theme of both their proclamation and worship relating to the understanding of Jesus' mission was his rejection and vindication, and to illustrate this nexus the proof text appealed to was Psalm 118:

> The stone the builders cast aside
> Is now the building's strength and pride. (Ps. 118:22, MOFFATT)

The continuance of the theme of victory in Psalm 118:26 apparently found its way into early liturgies as an acclamation heralding the triumphant return of the Messiah, based on his entry into the Holy City (Mark 11:9 and parallels), but soon the text came to be associated with his Parousia in glory. The evidence for the latter idea is the Aramaic prayer call *marana tha,* "our Lord, come!" found in 1 Corinthians 16:22 and *Didachē* 10:6. The division of the letters in the original term *maranatha* so as to yield the translation just given is all but conclusively proved by some recent discoveries from Qumran's Cave 4 (dated in the Middle Aramaic period). A fresh look at 1 Corinthians 16:22 by J. A. Fitzmeyer in light of Qumran material recently published not only establishes that the Aramaic watchword means "our Lord, come!" but "gives evidence of a veneration of Jesus by early Jewish Christians as the 'Lord,' as a figure associated with Yahweh of the Old Testament, even as one on the same level with him, without saying explicitly that he is divine" (J. A. Fitzmeyer, *To Advance the Gospel: New Testament*

Studies [New York: Crossroad, 1981], p. 229). Thus the contention that the earliest believers invoked the risen Jesus as Lord and awaited his return in glorious power rests on a firm linguistic basis.

Yet it was not appropriate to relate his glory to his pretemporal existence (his "preexistence") or his future lordship at the end of the age. The earliest Christology had a vision of the Easter triumph of the crucified Jesus and its immediate afterglow in his being exalted to the Father's presence, whence the blessedness of the new age of messianic salvation flowed down to those men and women who in turn were caught up to share his present reign.

Thus one specimen of "religious song" was patterned on the Old Testament Psalter and expressed conscious tribute to the messianic types already available for the fulfillment of Israel's hope for a coming savior. He was hailed as Jesus of Nazareth, who, after the humiliation of rejection and death, was now raised to his Father's presence where he enjoyed the divine glory (Acts 7:56). He will come again from his seat at the right hand of God to consummate God's purposes (for Israel); and in the meanwhile—and it may be as a prelude to his advent—he was invoked to "come" and visit his people who "broke bread" as a sign of their joyful participation in the new age of the messianic banquets soon to be spread and shared (based on Isa. 25). Such examples of psalms applied to Christ may well be accurately called "messianic" tributes, or "Christ psalms."

240 • THE SETTING OF HYMNS IN THE GRECO-ROMAN WORLD

Singing hymns to deity was an established practice in the Greco-Roman world long before the emergence of Christianity. Christian hymns differed from pagan hymnody, however, in celebrating a redemptive historical event; they have a "prophetic" quality.

With Stephen and those who followed him, the early Christian mission reached out to offer its message to those who lived in Greco-Roman society. In that world the singing of hymns to the deities of contemporary religious cults was already an established practice. The use of hymns in corporate and private worship in that culture went back a long way, but it reached its high point at a time when the finest and most sensitive spirits in late classical civilization

were becoming conscious of their need of "salvation." The immediate occasion was the onset of pessimism and despair caused partly by Greek science, which offered a naturalistic explanation of the universe, and partly by Eastern astrology, which placed a vast distance between human beings and the gods Homer and Hesiod had described. A valiant attempt to relate the traditional deities to human life was made as an answer to belief in impersonal fate or chance or iron necessity. These terms imply that human life is at the mercy of cosmic forces alien to humans.

New Testament examples of hymnic prayer are quite different, as they center on the basic idea of "remembering" construed in a dynamic way (drawn from Old Testament worship, which celebrated Yahweh's mighty acts) and carried over into the new Israel and its worship. The events of the "new Exodus" were similarly rehearsed and recalled in a dramatic retelling. At this point we are touching on the shift in an understanding of New Testament canticles that focus on Christ's saving achievement. Unlike the earlier species of "messianic psalms," these hymns seem to have been newly created as spontaneous utterances of gifted, Spirit-filled members of the community (1 Cor. 14:15; Eph. 5:18-20; Col.3:16-17), who may be further identified as prophets. If this title is accurate, it suggests that their role was one of instruction and exhortation (*paraklēsis*), according to 1 Corinthians 14:3. Their ministry was intended to build up the congregations and to do so in one specific regard, namely to ward off erroneous teaching by a positive statement, at services of worship, of how the faith was to be understood and applied with particular reference to Christ's redeeming mission.

We find several extensive pericopes in Paul where, on lexical, stylistic, and contextual grounds, we may well suspect that he has taken over and set into the flow of his epistolary correspondence these preformed liturgical passages. The more obvious examples in the Pauline corpus are Philippians 2:6-11, Colossians 1:15-20, and 1 Timothy 3:16, though the list can be considerably enlarged. Extending the survey to include, along with Paul, the rest of the New Testament, M. Hengel speaks of "a dozen Christological texts originating within a fifty to sixty year period (A.D. 40–100)." After that terminal point at the close of the century there are several well-known references to *carmina Christi* or "Hymns to Christ" in Pliny, the Letters of Ignatius, and the Odes of Solomon (an early Christian "hymnbook"). Interestingly, by the time of Justin, at the mid-second century, the flow of such compositions has apparently been checked.

241 • THE SIGNIFICANCE OF HYMNS TO CHRIST

New Testament hymns to Christ celebrate what he did before Creation, his mission of incarnation and reconciliation, and his present exalted position as Lord of the universe. In so doing, they counter heretical ideas that were influencing some segments of the early church.

The Reason for Christological Hymns

The teasing question asks what purpose was served by these Christological hymns. The examples we may point to in Paul's writing suggest that they were well known in the various churches, or why would Paul have taken them over, sometimes with slight—if important—adaptation? They were clearly fresh creations and not simply a reworking of ancient Jewish or messianic texts, though their imagery and idiom have identifiable echoes drawn from the biblical literature. They were also more extensive in length and scope than either the messianic psalms or the fragments of creedal statement that can be spotted very obviously in Paul's pastoral discussions in such places as Romans 10:9-10, 1 Corinthians 12:3, and Colossians 2:6; these are all variations on the creedal "Jesus is Lord" motif.

Hymns As a Response to Gnostic Ideas

What was the "catalyst" for the creation of the more elaborate "hymns to Christ"? The delicate issue is to ascertain why this hymnic praise to Christ took the shape it evidently did, namely in celebration of what Christ was and did before Creation and in his mission of incarnation and reconciliation that led to a universal acknowledgment that he is now installed as Lord of all worlds and ruler of every agency, heavenly, human, and demonic.

The reason may be traced to a serious threat to the Pauline *kērugma* associated with a religious attitude known generically as *gnōsis*. As early as the situation in 1 Corinthians, a rival understanding of the Christian message arose, partly drawn from the prevailing Greco-Roman religious scene and partly as

an attempt to turn the church into a Hellenistic conventicle. The fullest example is seen in the crisis that prompted the writing of Colossians and perhaps the Pastorals and Ephesians. Gnostic teachers offered a teaching that quickly challenged the apostolic message as Paul had delivered it and imposed their presence on the churches of the Pauline mission. The tenets of this "alternative gospel" are seen in features such as these: (1) a denial of the lordship of Christ as the sole intermediary between God and the world; (2) the insidious relaxing of the moral fiber, which led Christians to be indifferent to bodily lusts and sins; and (3) the uncertainty that underlay the meaning of life, since the star gods still held sway and needed to be placated. At this point we uncover an important fact: the main specimens of New Testament hymns address the various situations in which the presence of Gnostic ideas has been suspected and form the polemical counterthrust to deviant teaching in the areas of doctrine and morals.

These threats form a network of ideas and practices that are built on a single notion, namely a dualism that separated God from the world. In Gnostic thought, God is pure spirit who, by definition, is both untouched by matter and has no direct dealings with the material order. The Creation of the universe was relegated to the work of an inferior deity, sometimes linked with the God of the Old Testament. The interstellar space between the high God and the world was thought to be populated with a system of emanations or *aeons* in a connected series and stretching from God to the point at which contact with matter, which was regarded as evil, was just possible. In the Colossian teaching that threatened the church in the Lycus valley, Christ was evidently given a role as one *aeon* in a hierarchy and treated as himself part of the network spun off from the emanating power of the high God.

The "fullness" (*plērōma*) of aeons that filled the region between heaven and earth was somehow thought to contain "elemental spirits," which in turn the Colossians needed to venerate (Col. 2:8, 18). Nor was there any assurance that a person's destiny was secure since the regimen of "decrees" (*dogmata,* Col. 2:20-21) imposed an ascetic way of life, which, being essentially negative, gave no certainty of salvation and inspired no confidence that these astral deities had been successfully overcome. Life's mystery remained to haunt the devotee, and he or she was virtually imprisoned in a mesh of superstition, fear, and uncertainty with no way to break the iron grip of astrological control and cultic taboos. What was needed—as we learn from contemporary tributes of praise offered to deities in the mystery religions—was fellowship with a mighty god or goddess who would lift his or her adherents out of this imprisoning circle and give assurance of salvation and new life. Not surprisingly, the delivering deity was hailed as "lord" (*kurios)* and "savior" (*sōter).*

Paul's use of the traditional hymns directed to Christ exactly met the need of his congregations. The ruling idea in such Christological tributes as survive is a portrayal of the odyssey of Christ. His course is surveyed from his life in the Father's presence, where he functions as God's *alter ego* or "image," to include his descent and humiliation in obedience and on to his exaltation in heaven, where he receives the accolade of a title and a new dignity as ruler of all (*cosmokratōr).* The imagery is one of descent/ascent, which replaces the Judaic model of rejection/vindication current in the earlier Christianity.

But the real point of distinction has more to do with an exploration of the *cosmological role* attributed to the person of Christ. There is a double way in which that adjective came to be applied. First, his preexistence and pretemporal activity in creation were made the frontispiece of the hymns. The existence of Christ is taken back to speak of a relationship with God he enjoyed "in the beginning." Whether the raw materials of this idea derive from wisdom speculation or from the idea of a heavenly man or from an idealized picture of Adam cannot be ascertained; what matters is that, as a direct response to the threatening charge that Christ was part of an angelic hierarchy and so linked more with the creation than the Creator, the early church in its outreach to Gentiles came quickly to trace back his being to the very life of God himself. This was done not in a developed way nor, at this stage, as a piece of theologizing, but by attributing to the cosmic Christ an active share in the glory of God (Phil. 2:6) and a role in the creating of the world (Col. 1:15; cf. John 1:1-3). His *protological significance* was seen as a necessary part of his true being, since only if he existed with God and as God in the beginning (John 1:1) was he able to be linked with creation not as part of it but as its maker and ground plan. And only on the assumption of his preexistent relationship with God could these confessional texts meaningfully speak of Christ's "being sent" (Rom. 8:3, 32;

Gal. 4:4) or alternatively of his "choosing" to accept the humility of incarnation and obedience (2 Cor. 8:9; Phil. 2:6-8).

Second, at the conclusion of his earthly life, he took his place in God's presence by receiving universal homage and the acclamation of cosmic spirit powers that confessed his lordship and so were forced to abandon their title to control over human destiny. This *eschatological dimension,* heralding the dawn of a new age already glimpsed as a present reality—since "Jesus Christ is Lord"—would be important to assure believers that their lives were safe under the protection of the reigning Christ. The church that sang the text of Philippians 2:6-11 knew itself to be living in that new world where, all external appearances to the contrary, the astral powers were defeated and Christ, the sole ruler of all the worlds, was truly Lord. His lordship offered the living assurance they needed to face their contemporary world with its many "gods" and "lords" (1 Cor. 8:5-6) and to rebut the false ideas, both theological and practical, that their lives were the playthings of fate or chance or in the grip of iron determinism. The enthronement of Jesus Christ "to the glory of God the Father" (Phil. 2:11) gave confidence that God had brought victory out of defeat, installed his son as world ruler, and now wore the face of Jesus Christ, whose characteristic name for God was "Father" (note that the hymn of Philippians 2 ends with this word, as though to betoken a restoration of men and women in God's family).

Conclusion

We have seen clear signs of Christian hymns that are in transition. The idioms and concepts the hymns use vary with a changing cultural scene so that Judaic messianic canticles no longer served the needs of Pauline churches in Hellenistic society; new forms needed to be created, while there was still a reluctance to cut ties with the past. The Aramaic *maranatha* persisted even in a Greek-speaking environment like Corinth. So, we may say, modern hymns should express a cultural sensitivity to modern needs, without rejecting the best of our heritage.

The use of hymns as weapons of warfare is seen already in the New Testament period. Paul exploits traditional hymns (if we are correct in seeing pre-Pauline examples in Phil. 2:6-11 and Col. 1:15-20), yet he suitably adapts the hymnic material to bring out emphases he felt were in danger of being neglected or denied. He can add phrases like "death on a cross" (Phil. 2:8) and "the church" (Col. 1:18) to underscore the atonement wrought at the Cross (against any idea of automatic cosmic reconciliation). Repeatedly in church history the hymnbook has kept the people of God on course and faithful to their apostolic deposit of faith.

The genius of the Christian hymn on its New Testament side is the *carmen Christi,* the worship in song offered to the exalted Lord (Rev. 5:9-12). Admittedly there remains a tension the New Testament writers are apparently content to live with. They are too unflinching in their monotheism to accord any veneration to God's creation, even where the angels are proposed as mediators (Col. 2:18). The finale of Philippians 2:6-11 ensures that the confession "Jesus Christ is Lord" is made "to the glory of God the Father." The throne of Revelation 5:13 is occupied by both God and "the Lamb." Yet as Christ's saving achievement in bringing the world back to God implies that he has done what God alone can do, it was a natural step for a functional Christology to take on a Trinitarian formulation. And that implies, too, that the first Christians made *in worship* the decisive step of setting the exalted Christ on a par with God as the recipient of their praise. Hymnody and Christology thus merged in the worship of the one Lord. And, from the controversy to the modern Christology debate, the litmus test remains:

That the Maker should become man and should even go to death for the love of man—that astonishing thing evoked *rapturous praise* from believers.

Ralph P. Martin[21]

TWENTY-SIX

Dance and Banners in Worship

Recent years have seen a resurgence of the practice of "dancing before the Lord" as a form of worship. The activity known as "dancing in the Spirit" has long been a part of Pentecostal worship, and with the growth of charismatic churches dancing began to be encouraged as a response to the scriptural invitation to praise the Lord in this manner. More recently, the worship of God through ballet, folk, interpretive, and other forms of dance has found expression in church bodies across the Christian spectrum. The following is a discussion of the scriptural basis for worship dance.

242 • DANCE IN THE OLD TESTAMENT

Dance is a regular feature of Israel's festive worship and is viewed as an act of obedience to the Lord, for his praise and glory.

References to dancing abound in the Old Testament. Actual accounts of dancing reflect thoughtful, deliberate acts of offering praise to God. Several obvious references to dancing occur in the English versions of the Bible. Psalm 150:4 commands us to praise God in dance (Hebrew *maḥol*). In this same verse we find justification for using organs and stringed instruments. The word *'ugav,* translated "organ" (KJV) or "pipe" (NASB), is used only four times in the Bible, whereas there are many references to dance. If one cannot use Psalm 150 to advocate deliberately dancing before God, perhaps the church should also remove organs and other musical instruments from its corporate worship. The fact is that the musical instruments listed in Psalm 150, including organs or pipes, are not mentioned at all in the New Testament. Thus, if dance is forbidden because it is an Old Testament phenomenon, the use of musical instruments, being in the same category, should be forbidden as well. Psalm 150 advocates dancing, along with the use of instruments, as an act of obedience in regular corporate worship, rather than out of a spontaneous response prompted by extraordinary events.

The Hebrew Old Testament uses a number of words for dancing. These include: *gil,* "circle in joy, dance"; *maḥol* and the related term *mᵉḥolah,* "dancing"; *pazaz,* "leap"; *raqad,* "dance, skip about"; *ḥagag,* "celebrate, dance"; *'alatz,* "rejoice, exult, leap"; *karar,* "whirl, rotate." Although the word *gil* actually indicates twirling, rotating, or dancing in a circle, it is usually translated "rejoice" in the English versions. The psalmist uses this word in the phrase, "Let the earth rejoice" (Ps. 97:1, NASB). If even the earth as it spins on its axis is obeying the Old Testament command in this New Testament era, God's redeemed creation should also honor the Creator by spinning in worship.

The verb *ḥul* can mean travailing in childbirth, which involves a twisting or writhing motion, or "to dance in a circle of joy." The translators of the King James Version of the Bible chose the first usage for Psalm 96:9: "O worship the Lord in the beauty of holiness; fear before him, all the earth," and the New American Standard Bible renders the verse, "tremble before Him." The context of Psalm 96:9 clearly requires the second usage; the verse should read, "O worship the Lord in the beauty of holiness; dance with joy before him, all the earth." The psalmist is inviting the people of the whole earth to come before God in holy worship, demonstrating their joy through dance.

A final Old Testament term to be considered here is *samaḥ.* The word appears 150 times in the Old Testament as "rejoice." According to *Nelson's Expository Dictionary of the Old Testament* (Merrill F. Unger and William White, Jr., eds. [Nashville: Thomas Nelson, 1980]), *samaḥ* "usually refers to a spontaneous emotion of extreme happiness which is expressed in some visible and/or external manner. . . . The emotion represented in the verb . . . is sometimes accompanied by dancing, singing and playing musical instruments."

Some teachers contend that since dancing was performed outdoors in the worship of Israel, it is not proper to engage in it within the church building. Old Testament believers worshiped outside because only the priests had access to the tabernacle and temple. Now, however, the veil of the temple has been torn from top to bottom, and all Christians are members of the kingdom of priests who can worship "inside" the Holy of Holies, offering the incense of praise and worship to God. Worshiping indoors would have been physically impossible in ancient Israel, since the community numbered some three million and could not have been accommodated in any building. (In addition, the climate in the eastern Mediterranean region makes it possible for many activities to take place outdoors that, in colder and wetter climates, are not usually convenient.) Many churches are now building edifices that accommodate the growing crowds, with areas specifically designed for praise and dance. As a biblical basis for doing so, they cite Psalm 150: "Praise God in his sanctuary; . . . Praise him with tambourine and dancing" (Ps. 150:1, 4).

243 ✦ DANCE IN THE NEW TESTAMENT

Although dance is not commanded in the New Testament as in the Hebrew Scriptures, the New Testament confirms its use and place in Christian worship.

Church leaders who oppose dancing in worship frequently say dancing is not mentioned in the New Testament. Such a statement reflects little understanding of the Greek text. Greek scholar Spiros Zodhiates explains that the word *chairō,* frequently translated "rejoice," "may also be related to the Hebrew word meaning a young sheep or lamb, indicating the skipping or frisking of a lamb for joy" (S. Zodhiates, The *Hebrew-Greek Key Study Bible* [Grand Rapids: Baker, 1985]). Jesus called his people sheep and lambs, and this picture of rejoicing fits with the imagery inherent in *chairō.* Paul uses this word in its imperative form in his letter to the Philippians when he writes, "Rejoice in the Lord always. I will say it again: Rejoice!" (Phil. 4:4). In Kittel's *Theological Dictionary of the New Testament* (Vol. 9 [Grand Rapids: Wm. B. Eerdmans Publishing Co.,

1974], pp. 362-363), *chairō,* which occurs 28 times in the New Testament, is related to the Hebrew words *samaḥ, gil,* and *'alatz,* discussed earlier. Understanding its Old Testament background, Paul uses the term in commanding the church to participate in a full expression of praise and joy, in the same way the psalmists instructed God's people in the Old Testament.

Some other Greek words for dancing are *skirtaō* (used three times), "leap with joy"; *hallomai* (used once), "leap"; *choros* (used once), indicating circle dancing; and *agalliaō* (used ten times), "leap." These terms are used to describe dancing that occurred on some forty-three different occasions as recorded in the New Testament. William Morrice

An artistic conception of biblical dancers

discusses the word *skirtaō* in Luke 6:23, in which Jesus instructs his disciples to rejoice, or leap for joy, when they are persecuted. He writes, "in the present instance . . . the 'dancing for joy' is to be done on that day when persecution takes place in anticipation of the reward in heaven" (W. Morrice, *Joy in the New Testament* [Greenwood, S.C.: Attic Press, 1982]). The church of the present day is battling opposition and being persecuted by spiritual forces that array themselves against it; therefore, this is the very day in which Jesus taught that Christians are to respond by dancing for joy.

Another significant New Testament use of a word for dancing is found in Luke 15:25, when the Prodigal Son of Jesus' parable returns home. The text indicates that music and dancing were considered appropriate by the father on this occasion. The

Greek word used here is _choros,_ from which the modern word "choir" is derived, and it literally means "circle dancing." The choir's original role was to dance in a circle, a practice being restored in some modern churches. One purpose of the parable of the Prodigal Son is to picture the great joy experienced by the heavenly Father when a sinner is restored to fellowship with him. This parable strongly suggests that _choros,_ or circle dancing, takes place in heaven when a prodigal comes home to the Father. As a matter of fact, the Old Testament presents the same picture; Zephaniah says of the Lord, "He will rejoice [_gil,_ "spin around under the influence of violent emotion"] over you with singing" (Zeph. 3:17).

244 ◆ BIBLICAL DANCE AND CONTEMPORARY WORSHIP

Despite objections, the Scriptures offer a solid foundation for the continuation of dance in the worship of today's church.

Opponents to dance in the church have sometimes objected that dancing is a worldly entertainment and should be avoided by Christians. However, a human being's inherent rhythm, demonstrated unequivocally by the natural response of a small child to music, is a gift of God, and dance therefore belongs to our nature. If the world has taken it over, it must also be admitted that it has invaded the area of music and songwriting as well, but the church continues to make use of both of these in the worship of the Lord. The church should not abdicate its leadership in the use of dance, leaving the only expression of this joyous activity to the corruption of the world. Whatever the enemy has done to make dance a worldly form of amusement does not invalidate the teaching of the Bible on this subject.

Not everyone in the church will dance. Some have argued that the use of dance in worship will put undue pressure on all worshipers to do so and may serve to exclude persons who are not physically able to join in this activity. The logic in this argument is faulty. The church does not cease to sing when the mute are present, nor does it disallow musical instruments and choirs because not everyone can play or sing. Certainly it does not ban the lifting of hands in praise for the sake of arthritics who may be in the congregation, or the reading of Scripture for the sake of not excluding the blind, or kneeling because the handicapped may be present. Dancing

is one of a multitude of ways in which believers can bless God, and it should be made available to church congregations so that they are free to make the choice to dance.

Some say that if dancing is done before the Lord it should take place only in an individual's private worship. This argument, if carried to its logical conclusion, would do away with public prayer and the congregational singing of hymns directed to God.

Others object to the wearing of special clothing by dancers or the decoration of their tambourines with streamers, assuming that the dancers are attempting to please their audiences. One could as easily say that a minister who wears a nice suit or a clerical robe is doing the same. Dance attire is part of a worshiper's preparation for worship; not all clothing is suitable for the purpose. Special gowns for worship dance usually ensure modesty and allow for freedom of movement. When dancers wear uniform dress they draw attention to the corporate group rather than to themselves individually.

Should dancing be prohibited in the church because some Christians may be offended by it? While dancing is now accepted by a growing number of churches, obedience should never be determined by a majority vote. Should Christians cease lifting their hands to the Lord because people in some churches are offended by the practice? Should they stop playing musical instruments because a major denomination does not allow it? Must Pentecostals and charismatics no longer speak in tongues because it offends fundamentalists? The Bible instructs us to employ the high praises of God (Ps. 149:6) and not to seek the lowest common denominator of praise in order to avoid offending people.

Those Christians who object to worship dance may be reverting to the first-century heresy known as Gnosticism, in which the spirit is thought to be entirely good, while matter is viewed as totally evil. This unbiblical dualism resulted in the teaching that the human body, which is matter, is evil, and that salvation is the escape from the body. Many who embraced this teaching in the first century either treated the body in an ascetic, harsh way, or paradoxically, they practiced the error of licentiousness. Both 1 John and the letter to the Colossians are written to correct this error. Unfortunately, many well-meaning Christians are still being influenced by Gnosticism. They insist that dancing stirs carnal rather than spiritual responses because it involves body movements. If the body is the expression of the spirit, then its movements *should* be used in worship to glorify God, as the Bible advocates, since both body and spirit belong to God (1 Cor. 6:19-20).

Some Christians have said that the promotion of dance as a worship form implies immaturity and lack of desire for unity on the part of its advocates. It should be remembered in this connection that the Christian's maturity is based on attaining to "the whole measure of the fullness of Christ" (Eph. 4:13). Maturity is measured by a person's likeness to Christ and unity by "the faith," the biblical revelation of truth. Being mature and promoting unity do not imply being forced into a nonscriptural position on the issue of praise in order to please all other believers and to satisfy their objections. Rather, both unity and maturity are products of a total commitment to the life-style of Jesus, which was a determined allegiance to Scripture and its patterns of response to God in the face of every human, rational, and religious objection to God's revelation.

Does one who dances before the Lord violate Paul's injunction to the Romans against causing a brother to stumble (Rom. 14:13, 21)? No more so than when a worshiper plays an instrument, kneels, claps his or her hands, or engages in any other worship practice that might cause offense to another Christian. Obedience to the truth always causes offense; the gospel itself is an offense (1 Cor. 1:23; Gal. 5:11) but should not be abandoned on that account.

When God asks for a response from his people that requires liberty in praise, the acceptance of the limitation of other believers might satisfy them but could at the same time offend the Lord. Idolatry is the intrusion of any other object between the Christian and God in worship—even if the intruder is the desire for the approval of humans. When a local church relates boldly and unashamedly to God in its praise and worship, God will shine his glory upon it, bringing the greatest possible benefit to other believers as well as to the unconverted.

Wally Odum, Tom Gulbronson, and David Baird

245 • BANNERS IN WORSHIP

A banner is a standard or ensign that serves as a focal point for a community or a rallying point in warfare. Such symbols appear in the Bible chiefly in a military context. Analysis of the function of banners in the Bible, however, reveals their applicability to worship as well.

—— Banners in the Old Testament ——

Although banners and standards originated in Egypt and countries like Babylonia, Assyria, and Persia to the East, they also made their way into Palestine during Old Testament times. The children of Israel carried such standards on their march through the deserts to the Promised Land. Thereafter, standards or banners (depending on how one conceives of them) must have been quite common on the biblical scene because of the rather frequent use of such designations in the Scriptures.

The development of ensigns and standards no doubt took place in a military context. In the countries surrounding Israel, including Rome, standards

This Assyrian military banner depicts the figure of Ashur or Ninurta as the god of war. Similar banners or standards may have been used by Israel in procession, particularly in war, and possibly in worship.

were carried by the various divisions of the army or were attached to the masts of fighting ships. The early standards were not banners or flags made of fabric but figures, emblems, or images of animals and birds, or of the gods, made of wood or metal, brightly painted and fastened at the end of a long pole or staff.

The eagle was a common emblem on a banner in all countries. Some of the ensigns or standards were connected with the religion of the country and could be found at temples or other places of worship. The exact nature of the standards of Israel (Num. 2) is not known, but their presence at the camp causes scholars to believe that the wandering in the desert was understood as a military expedition. Later, standards and banners were used for other purposes, such as communication.

The purpose of standards has evoked debate among Bible scholars. Were they simply symbolic identification marks, for example, of a regiment of the army? Or is a deeper meaning and purpose to be seen? Such banners or standards certainly served as marks of identification, but they also represented the ideals and aspirations of the people bearing them, and were used as a means of arousing the emotions and devotion to a cause, person, or nation. Images and inscriptions carried at the head of a group, or mounted on an elevation, caused the people to "rally around the flag" in unified effort. Through human history, loyalty to movements or causes has been encouraged through the use of powerful symbols, slogans, or songs that help to create a common identity for those in the movement. Banners and standards have served this purpose. Since worship is the declaration of loyalty to the Great King, one can readily see the application of banners in a worship setting.

In the Old Testament, three different Hebrew words are used to designate a standard or banner. Often they seem to be synonymous, but broader usage allows one to make certain distinctions between them. _Degel_ is used for the standard or ensign of Israel encamped in the desert. "The Israelites are to set up their tents by divisions, each man in his own camp under his own standard" (Num. 1:52). "The Israelites are to camp around the Tent of Meeting some distance from it, each man under his standard [_degel_] with the banners [_ot_] of his family" (Num. 2:2). The standard of Judah was on the east side of the camp, Reuben's on the south, Ephraim's on the west, and that of Dan on the north. "So the Israelites did everything the LORD commanded Moses; that is the way they encamped under their standards, and that is the way they set out, each with his clan and family" (Num. 2:34). It appears from this that _degel_ designates a larger group or division of people organized around a central goal, and no doubt the "armies of Israel" marched in this fashion to the Promised Land. In Psalm 20:5, _degel_ becomes a battle flag: "We will shout for joy when you are victorious and will lift up our banners in the name of our God." In Song of Solomon 2:4, however, it is used in a beautiful figure of love: "He has taken me to the banquet hall, and his _banner_ over me is love."

The word _nes_ is translated "ensign" or "standard" in the English Bible, but it refers more specifically to a rallying point for the people. It marks the center of attraction on which people should pin their hopes. Generally, such a signal was raised on some special occasion, always on a high elevation and very conspicuous. After Amelek's defeat, Moses called the altar of thanksgiving _Yahveh nissi,_ "[Yahweh] is my banner" (Exod. 17:15). Messiah himself becomes such a standard and a rallying point of nations (Isa. 49:22). The banner was raised to assemble the soldiers of an army at the sound of trumpets (Isa. 13:2; 18:3). As in Isaiah 30:17, a banner was set up on a hill to communicate an urgent message. The banner tells the people to flee from the country to the cities for safety (Jer. 4:67). When the army left a banner on a hill unattended, it was a sign of defeat (Isa. 31:9). Under this type of standard may be included the fiery serpent of bronze raised on a pole, which was to be the rallying point of salvation for the people (Num. 21:8-9).

The third term, _'ot,_ is used less frequently than _degel_ and _nes_ and generally refers to lesser banners, such as signals and signs. In Numbers 2:2, as we have seen, it is issued to identify the smaller family within the entire division, the latter being described by _degel._ In Psalm 74:4 (RSV) it is used to speak of enemy forces setting up "their own signs [or banners] for signs."

Roland de Vaux has questioned whether the terms translated "banner" or "standard" really refer to signs or flags. The word _degel,_ he suggests, means a division of the army itself. The word _nes_ refers to a pole or mast raised on a hill, as a signal to rally against the enemy (in a manner similar to Moses' upraised arms in the battle against Amalek). In de Vaux's view, these standards or ensigns were religious symbols, and the ark of the covenant played a similar role. The main argument for the use of banners and flags in Israelite warfare is that other ancient Near Eastern armies used them (Roland de Vaux, _Ancient Israel: His Life and Institutions_ [London: Darton, Longman & Todd; New York: McGraw-Hill, 1961], pp. 226-227).

Banners in the New Testament

The New Testament does not speak of banners and ensigns in the same sense as the Old Testament. Luke designates the figurehead of the Alexandrian ship "Castor and Pollux," with the term *parasēmos,* meaning "distinguished, marked," and not with the expected word *sēmeion,* "sign" (Acts 28:11). A connecting link between the Testaments might be the Septuagint's translation of '*ot* in Numbers 2:2 by the term *sēmeion,* which brings to mind the numerous occurrences of *sēmeion* in the New Testament in the general sense of "sign, mark, signal": "Teacher, we want to see a miraculous *sign* from you" (Matt. 12:38); "at that time the *sign* of the Son of Man will appear in the sky" (Matt. 24:30); "This will be a *sign* to you" (Luke 2:12); "no *sign* shall be given to it but the *sign* of Jonah" (Luke 11:29, NASB). It is significant that the Septuagint seems to support de Vaux's view; in Numbers 2:2, *degel* is translated by the word *tagma,* which in Greek literature is generally a military term meaning a detachment or division of soldiers.

The most significant occurrence of a banner in Scripture, however, is found in the portrayal of the triumphant Christ in the Revelation to John. Here, as the Word of God, Christ appears at the head of the armies of heaven, executing the judgments of the Almighty (Rev. 19:14-15). "On his robe and on his thigh he has this name written: KING OF KINGS AND LORD OF LORDS" (Rev. 19:16). No banner is mentioned, but the robe itself, evoking the image of a flowing, richly colored royal mantle, performs the function of a banner with its proclamation of Jesus' dominion over all authorities. The victorious church, the company of those who have "overcome" the pressures of a hostile culture and false religious system, rallies to its banner and to its Lord. The imagery of this entire passage is reminiscent of Psalm 149, which speaks of those who take "the high praises of God . . . in their mouth, and a two-edged sword in their hand, to execute vengeance on the nations, . . . to execute on them the judgment written" (Ps. 149:6-7, 9, NASB).

Thus the robe of the King of kings forms the link between the banners or standards of warfare mentioned elsewhere in Scripture and the banner as associated with worship. Unlike the poles or ensigns of military usage, this garment is a piece of fabric similar to the flags or banners we now associate with the pageantry of Christian celebration. Worship—the ascription of dominion to Christ—and warfare—the defeat of his enemies—here become one and the same. It is this understanding of worship as spiritual warfare that gives banners their place and value in the context of worship.

Lorman M. Peterson[22]

PART FIVE

The Biblical Foundations of Christian Worship

TWENTY-SEVEN

Charismatic Aspects of Worship

Worship in the Pentecostal and charismatic churches has been characterized by certain features that distinguish it from the worship of other Christian communities. These distinctive aspects of charismatic worship are, in greater or lesser degree, related to the "baptism" or "filling" of the Holy Spirit, which these churches have sought to recover in its scriptural dimension. Openness to the manifestation of New Testament spiritual gifts in the setting of corporate worship has resulted in gatherings marked by speaking or singing in tongues, prophecy, and other vocal gifts; laying on of hands and anointing with oil, especially for healing; and acts of "spiritual warfare" and deliverance ministry. Since apostolic times many of these phenomena had formed part of the religious expression of isolated groups of believers, even though for long periods they had all but vanished from the larger body of organized Christianity.

The Pentecostal revival of the early twentieth century marked a turning point in recovery of these New Testament phenomena. Today's Pentecostal churches are, strictly speaking, those affiliated with groups that emerged from this revival. In the 1960s, practices traditionally associated with Pentecostal churches began to be taken up by worshipers in the so-called mainline denominations, Catholic and Protestant. This was the origin of the "charismatic" movement, which has resulted in a proliferation of nondenominational or loosely related churches that may be generally termed "charismatic." Although viewed with suspicion by some theologians and denominational leaders, the recovery of an emphasis on the work of the Holy Spirit has brought about a renewal movement affecting almost all Christian groups.

The chief feature of charismatic worship has been a free-flowing celebrative style focusing on the praise of the Lord through contemporary choruses, accompanied by certain biblical acts of worship such as lifting the hands or clapping. As this style of worship is now being adopted in other evangelical churches, and indeed in liturgical and even "mainstream" Protestant churches, it becomes increasingly difficult to define it as exclusively "charismatic."

246 • SPIRIT BAPTISM IN THE NEW TESTAMENT

Foundational to many aspects of charismatic worship is the concept of the baptism in the Holy Spirit. Even where prophecy and speaking or singing in tongues are not regularly practiced as part of worship, the expectancy and vitality of celebration are influenced by the understanding of Spirit baptism.

As it is described in the New Testament, the baptism in the Holy Spirit inevitably results in an outpouring of praise to the Lord on the part of the one baptized. The first recorded instance of such a baptism is in Acts 2:1-5. The disciples of Jesus, 120 in number, including his mother and brothers, waited in an upper room in Jerusalem for the gift of power Jesus had promised to send them. When it came, accompanied by a sound like wind and tongues of fire that rested on each person, the meeting erupted into spontaneous praise. The believers began to glorify the Lord, speaking in languages unknown to themselves but understood by the foreign Jews who were gathered in Jerusalem to celebrate the Feast of Pentecost.

Explaining the phenomenon to Jerusalem's amazed citizenry, Peter quoted from the prophecy of Joel: The outpouring of the Spirit on Jesus' followers was a fulfillment of God's promise and an indication that the "last days" had arrived (Acts 2:14-30; Joel 2:28-32). Peter went on to say that this glorious baptism was a gift from Jesus Christ, whom the Jews had recently crucified, certain proof that God had raised him up to sit on the throne of David as King forever. Moreover, the gift was available to them all and to their households and descendants and to all whom the Lord calls (Acts 2:38-39).

With the baptism in the Holy Spirit came an infusion of joy. Not only did the disciples continue to offer praise and thanksgiving, but three thousand new converts joined in the chorus (Acts 2:44-47), and it spread to the streets of the city (3:8-9).

In addition, this baptism conferred on its recipients the ability to perform signs and wonders (2:43). Jesus had said this would happen when he appeared to the disciples after his resurrection. Those who believe, he told them, will be accompanied by such signs, which include the ministries of healing and deliverance from demonic powers, speaking in tongues, and protection from physical harm (Mark 16:17-18).

The second recorded occurrence of the baptism of the Holy Spirit is in the account of Peter's ministry to the household of Cornelius, a Gentile. Instructed by the Lord in a vision, and not fully understanding the significance of what he was undertaking, Peter answered the summons of this God-fearing Roman centurion and preached Jesus to the group of friends and relatives who had congregated in his home. To the utter astonishment of Peter and the Jews who had accompanied him, the Holy Spirit fell upon the entire group, who began to speak with tongues, or languages they did not understand, and to praise God (Acts 10:44-47). This phenomenon is alternately described as the Spirit "falling upon" Cornelius and those in his house (10:44), the gift of the Spirit being "poured out" on them (10:45), as their having "received" the Holy Spirit (10:47), and as the baptism in the Holy Spirit (11:16).

In the case of Cornelius, the Holy Spirit baptism occurred simultaneously with conversion. This was not the usual pattern, however. A company of Samaritans, who had already been converted and baptized in water when Peter and John were sent to them, received the baptism of the Holy Spirit after the apostles laid hands on them (Acts 8:14-17).

When Paul discovered "disciples" in Ephesus he asked specifically if they had yet received the Holy Spirit; their answer indicated they may have been followers of John the Baptist (Acts 19:1-4). These Ephesians were told about Jesus and baptized in water in his name; subsequently, Paul laid hands on them and they began to speak in tongues and prophesy (Acts 19:5-7). It is not said that they extolled or magnified God, but Paul later explains to the Corinthians that speaking in tongues is synonymous with thanksgiving or praise. In giving regulations for the use of the various spiritual gifts, he explains that interpretation should take place when a person speaks in tongues before the church so that the congregation will be able to say the "Amen" to this thanksgiving. The person speaking in tongues gives thanks well, he continues, but what he is saying must be interpreted so that it can be shared by the whole community of believers.

The revival that Philip brought to Samaria was accompanied by healings and deliverance, but not, apparently, with the baptism in the Holy Spirit. When the Jerusalem apostles heard about the many Samaritans who were being converted, they sent Peter and John to pray for them to receive the Holy Spirit. A former sorcerer named Simon saw that "the Spirit was given at the laying on of the apostles' hands" (Acts 8:18) and tried to purchase their power with money. Obviously, the baptism in the Spirit was producing results which Simon could see; it was not confined to the spirit of these believers but manifested itself in some visible phenomenon. One can reasonably assume that the Samaritans, like the Ephesians, were speaking in tongues when Peter and John laid their hands on them.

Based upon the scriptural accounts of those who were baptized with the Holy Spirit, traditional Pentecostals teach that speaking in tongues is the initial evidence of this experience. Other gifts and fruits will eventually surface in the life of the person so baptized, but the phenomenon of speaking in an unknown tongue always occurs and confirms that the Spirit has, indeed, fallen upon him. All Spirit-filled believers are to speak in tongues as a part of their personal prayer life, although not all will speak before the entire church during worship. Charismatic churches, on the other hand, usually teach that the gift of tongues is only one of several manifestations that may accompany Spirit baptism.

Janice E. Leonard

247 • USE OF THE VOCAL GIFTS IN CORPORATE WORSHIP

Speaking with tongues, interpretation of tongues, prophecy, the word of knowledge, and the word of wisdom are among those accompaniments to the baptism in the Holy Spirit that are used in the setting of corporate worship.

The New Testament contains several lists of spiritual gifts, or gifts that accompany the baptism in the Holy Spirit; they are sometimes called *charismata,* "gifts" or "graces" (Rom. 12:6; 1 Cor. 12:4) and sometimes identified as *pneumatika,* "spiritual gifts" (1 Cor. 12:1; 14:1). Paul wanted worshipers to seek the *pneumatika,* especially to prophesy (1 Cor. 14:1). Tongues, he explains, are a sign to unbelievers. A "sign" in the Bible often carries the connotation of "offense," just as Simeon prophesied over the infant Jesus in the temple that he would be "a sign to be opposed" or "spoken against" (Luke 2:34). Tongues, however, edify or build up worshipers (1 Cor. 14:4) as they speak to God in mysteries (things revealed) in the Spirit (14:2).

——— Prophecy ———

The biblical prophet (Hebrew *navi',* Greek *prophētēs*) is a spokesman for the Lord. In the Old Testament, the prophet is concerned primarily with maintaining the covenant; in the New Testament the prophet's purpose is to mediate instruction, exhortation, and comfort to the body of believers (1 Cor. 14:3).

When Luke records how the Holy Spirit fell upon the Ephesian believers, he mentions that they not only spoke in tongues but also prophesied (Acts 19:6). Although speaking in tongues appears to be strictly a New Testament phenomenon, prophesying under the anointing and influence of the Holy Spirit was a regular occurrence in the worship that took place before the ark of the covenant in David's tabernacle in Zion. This Davidic worship has been called New Testament worship before its time since it took place directly before the ark in the presence of God, without animal sacrifices. It was probably in this setting that many of the psalms were written, and it is partly from them that information can be gleaned about worship in Zion. Both the account in 1 Chronicles 16:4-7 and the Psalms reveal that vocal and instrumental praise music was its primary characteristic; Psalms and 2 Samuel add dancing and shouting (2 Sam. 6:14-15; Pss. 66:1; 149:3). The Psalms speak of standing (134:1), lifting the hands (134:1-2), clapping (47:1), and bowing and kneeling (95:6), and 1 Chronicles specifically mentions prophecy on musical instruments (25:1).

The New Testament does not refer to prophecy being given musically, but since believers were familiar with the Old Testament practice, and Paul mentions singing in tongues (1 Cor. 14:13-15), it is likely that prophecy as a New Testament spiritual gift is meant to be given to the accompaniment of music. A case can be made for musical prophecy from Paul's instructions to the Colossians to teach and admonish one another in "psalms, hymns and spiritual songs" (Col. 3:16) and to the Ephesians to "speak to one another with psalms, hymns and spiritual songs . . . . giving thanks" (Eph. 5:19-20). Musical prophecy, then, is for the giving of thanks as well as for edification.

Some Pentecostal churches teach that if tongues are accompanied by interpretation, these are equivalent to prophecy, since both are supernatural utterances and both constitute thanksgivings. However, while the Bible does not say that tongues are ever used for any other purpose, prophecy does have functions other than the giving of thanks, which include instruction and revelation. In his instructions concerning spiritual gifts, Paul writes to the Corinthian church that they should pursue prophecy (1 Cor. 14:1), which, he reasoned, would serve to convict any unbeliever who might visit the worship service, as he hears "the secrets of his heart . . . laid bare" (14:24-25).

Prophecy also has its aspect of predicting events to come. Through a revelation of the Holy Spirit, the prophet Agabus informed the believers at Antioch that a famine would occur (Acts 11:28). In a later prophecy, he warned that Paul would be bound and delivered over to the Gentiles in Jerusalem (21:10). This incident may provide the biblical background for the practice of "personal prophecy" that is common in Pentecostal and charismatic circles, in which a prophet reveals to another believer information concerning some future event, blessing in that person's life, or insight into a present difficulty.

Tongues and Interpretation

In Pentecostal and charismatic churches, speaking in tongues is often used as a part of the "liturgy." Contrary to what is often believed by those not familiar with the practice, tongues are not an ecstatic or emotional utterance but are under the control of the worshiper (1 Cor. 14:27-32), who exercises the gift as an act of obedience to the biblical injunction to continually be filled with the Spirit (Eph. 5:18). It is common practice in Pentecostal or charismatic churches for one person to speak in tongues while the congregation listens and then for another person to interpret the message, according to Paul's instructions (1 Cor. 14:27-29). The New Testament seems to indicate that the interpretation should always take the form of a thanksgiving to God. Paul writes:

> For this reason anyone who speaks in a tongue should pray that he may interpret what he says. . . . If you are praising God with your spirit, how can one who finds himself among those who do not understand say "Amen" to your thanksgiving, since he does not know what you are saying? You may be giving thanks well enough, but the other man is not edified. (1 Cor. 14:13, 16-17)

The New Song

Charismatic congregations frequently sing in tongues, as Paul suggests (1 Cor. 14:15); such singing usually follows immediately after the congregation sings in the known language. In this expression, worshipers weave their individual melodies through the final chord of the congregational song just ended, or even a chord progression, singing personal praises to the Lord either in tongues or in the known language. This does not occur randomly, but for congregations accustomed to this practice, at fairly predictable points in the flow of the "liturgy." It is variously known as singing a "new song" to the Lord (Pss. 40:3, 96:1, 98:1, 149:1), the "song of the LORD" (2 Chron. 29:27, KJV), "sing[ing] with my spirit" (1 Cor. 14:15), or the *selah,* a term found in many of the psalms which may indicate a musical interlude or "lifting up" of praise. Sometimes a solo voice, generally the worship leader, will lead out in such "prophetic song," and musicians will occasionally "prophesy" on their instruments, in solo or ensemble.

An especially vibrant and powerful worship segment of the "song of the LORD" is sometimes referred to as the "high praises of God" (Ps. 149:6 NASB). This spontaneous chorus of praise, usually supported by instrumental accompaniment, corresponds to John's description of the voice of the Lord as he stands in the midst of the seven churches (Rev. 1:12-15) speaking with a voice "like the sound of rushing waters." Ezekiel described the voice of God in the same way (Ezek. 1:24; 43:2). In the Scripture, water is frequently used as a metaphor for the Holy Spirit. Speaking in the context of worship, at the Feast of Tabernacles, Jesus described the flow of the Holy Spirit as a spring of water erupting from within the deepest part of the believer (John 7:37-39).

Ezekiel sees a vision of the life or Spirit of God flowing from his sanctuary in an ever-deepening river that brings healing to all it touches (Ezek. 47:1-12). John the Revelator sees the same river in his vision of the church as the city of God; the "water of life" issues from the throne of God in the midst of the city and flows through the center of its street (Rev. 22:1-2). Peter alludes to this metaphor of water when he tells the curious crowds gathered in Jerusalem for the celebration of Pentecost that the outburst of praise by the disciples is the fulfillment of the Lord's promise through the prophet to "pour out" his Spirit (Acts 2:16-17).

Charismatics view the vocal and instrumental praise song that wells up and flows from God's people as the voice of the Spirit of God in their midst, evidence of his life being released in the sanctuary and flowing out to bless the nations. Taken seriously is Jesus' statement to the woman of Samaria that the Lord seeks out worshipers who will worship him "in spirit," i.e., with energy and vitality, and "in truth," or according to the principles of the Word ("Your word is truth," John 17:17).

Word of Wisdom and Word of Knowledge

In addition to speaking in tongues and prophecy, Paul teaches about two other vocal gifts that are exercised in the context of worship. They were prophesied in the Old Testament as endowments of the Messiah, the righteous Branch that would come from the stem of Jesse, the Messiah Christians understand to be Jesus Christ. Isaiah wrote, "The Spirit of the LORD will rest on him—the Spirit of wisdom and . . . the Spirit of knowledge and of the fear of the LORD" (Isa. 11:2). Proverbs equates "the fear of the

LORD" with "wisdom" (9:10) and also with "knowledge" (1:7).

In the New Testament these gifts that accompany the resting of the Spirit of God on a believer are known as "the word of wisdom" and "the word of knowledge"; Paul mentions them in 1 Corinthians 12:8. Their source is Christ, who distributes them to his body through the Spirit. As generally understood, the word of wisdom is the supernatural ability to understand and to speak concerning the direction either the church or an individual should take in a given situation. Paul exercised this gift when he advised the ship captain not to continue his journey toward Phoenix, but to winter in Fair Havens. "Men," he told the officials in charge, "I can see that our voyage is going to be disastrous and bring great loss to ship and cargo, and to our own lives also" (Acts 27:10). Later, after the captain had ignored Paul's warning, as the ship was breaking apart on rocks and the sailors were attempting to escape in the lifeboat, Paul again gave a word of wisdom. To the centurion and soldiers in charge of the prisoners he said, "Unless these men stay with the ship, you cannot be saved" (27:31).

The word of knowledge, on the other hand, is information given to a believer about some work God is doing in a specific setting; for example, a person with that gift might tell the congregation that the Lord is at that moment healing someone with heart disease or cancer or another infirmity. In the story referred to above, Paul operates in the word of knowledge as well as the word of wisdom when he assures the frightened sailors that they will all arrive at land in safety and only the ship will be lost (Acts 27:34). Another biblical example of a word of knowledge is God's revelation to Peter that Ananias and Sapphira were lying about the amount of money they had received for the land they sold (Acts 5:1-10).

Teaching and Exhorting

While the gifts of teaching and of exhorting can be exercised outside the context of worship, they are also frequently used within that setting. Both are "horizontal" activities that operate from believer to believer, instead of being a worship activity which focuses "vertically," toward God himself. To be considered as having a relationship to the baptism of the Holy Spirit, these functions must be performed under his power and anointing, in the same manner as prophesy or speaking in tongues. Strictly speaking, although they are a part of the order of service, they are not worship-oriented.

Conclusion

The exercise of those gifts particularly associated with worship, such as speaking in and interpreting tongues, prophecy, healings, working of miracles, and the gifts of wisdom and knowledge, is intended both to edify the believer and the church (1 Cor. 14:26) and to bring glory to God (Col. 3:16-17). The practice of the vocal gifts is not intended to elevate or call attention to the practitioners. According to Peter, the church exists for the primary purpose of exhibiting and proclaiming the surpassing worth of the One who has brought it into existence as the people of God, calling it from darkness into the kingdom of light (1 Pet. 2:10).

248 • OTHER SPIRITUAL GIFTS ASSOCIATED WITH WORSHIP

Although not acts of worship as such, the exercise of other spiritual gifts such as healing or the working of miracles may occur in the setting of corporate worship. Worship also aids in the cultivation of the fruit of the Spirit in the Christian's life.

Miracles and Healings

In the Acts of the Apostles, believers who perform miracles and healings are said to be full of the Holy Spirit; the implication is that the ability to do such things is a direct result of Spirit baptism. Paul includes these abilities in the "spiritual gifts" (1 Cor. 14:1), that is, gifts that draw upon the power given a believer when the Holy Spirit comes upon the worshiper. Stephen (Acts 6:5, 8), Philip (8:7), Paul (19:12), and all the apostles (2:43) cast out demons, healed illnesses, and did mighty works too numerous to mention. Frequently these demonstrations of the power of the Spirit resulted in conversions, and for this reason miracles, and especially healings, are thought by some Christians to be intended for use in evangelizing unbelievers.

However effective they may be for that purpose, the Bible also gives instructions concerning the healing of Christians. The sick person is to call for the elders of the church to anoint him with oil and pray for him, with the result that he is both healed and forgiven. This text seems to link sickness with sin, since the instruction is followed by the admonition "Therefore confess your sins to each other and pray for each other, so that you may be healed" (James 5:13-16).

Miracles and healings often take place in the course of everyday life and are not specifically related to worship. However, because they bring glory to God (Matt. 9:1-8; John 11:4) they are valid activities for inclusion in the worship of the church.

Other Gifts and Fruit of the Spirit

Other gifts of the Holy Spirit include such things as faith, discernment of spirits, serving, giving, leading, showing mercy, helps, and administrations (Rom. 12:6-8; 1 Cor. 12:8-10). All of these can operate within the context of the body of Christ, although they are not usually observable in the worship itself.

Paul describes the fruit (*karpos*), or inevitable result of the working of the Holy Spirit in the life of the believer, as being love, joy, peace, patience, kindness, goodness, faithfulness, gentleness, and self-control (Gal. 5:22). While all believers receive the Holy Spirit at conversion, the Scripture seems to teach that a subsequent baptism in the Holy Spirit produces both the fruit of the Spirit and his gifts in an increased abundance. For this reason, Christians are exhorted to be continually filled with God's Spirit (Eph. 5:19; Col. 3:16).

Janice E. Leonard

249 ◆ LAYING ON OF HANDS

The Christian church has practiced the laying on of hands in the context of worship since apostolic times. In the New Testament, three purposes are associated with this act: healing, the impartation of the Holy Spirit, and commissioning for service.

The practice of the laying on of hands for blessing or consecration is of ancient origin. Jacob blessed the children of Joseph by laying his hands upon their heads (Gen. 48:14, 18). Worshipers in Israel laid their hands upon the head of their atonement sacrifices before offering them (Lev. 1:4). The "sons of Israel" laid their hands on the Levites in presenting them to the Lord (Num. 8:10, NASB). Like the sprinkling of blood, the laying on of hands constitutes an identification between the two participants in the ritual. Jacob claimed Joseph's two sons as his own, including them in the family inheritance. The Israelite worshiper recognized that the slain animal was taking on itself the judgment belonging to the

one who sacrificed it, and the sons of Israel presented the Levites to the Lord as a substitute for themselves and their children.

In the New Testament, the laying on of hands also indicates identification and confers blessing. Accordingly, it is regularly practiced in Christian churches. This practice is carried on in three principal areas: healing of the sick, impartation of the Holy Spirit, and various practices of commissioning.

Healing

Although most Christians pray for healing, the Pentecostal movement has always maintained it as a major emphasis. The "full gospel," say Pentecostals, includes healing as one of its components; their common practice is to pray for healing with the laying on of hands, frequently anointing the sufferer with oil according to James 5:14.

The biblical foundation for this ritual is drawn from several New Testament accounts. Jesus himself often laid hands on people for healing. Luke writes: "The people brought to Jesus all who had various kinds of sickness, and laying his hands on each one, he healed them" (Luke 4:40). Mark records a number of instances in which Jesus used his hands in healing the sick and raising the dead: he took both Peter's feverish mother-in-law (1:31) and Jairus's dead daughter (5:41) by the hand, took the hand of a demonized boy and lifted him up (9:27), reached out his hand to touch a leper (1:41), put his fingers into the ears of a deaf-mute (7:33), and laid his hands on a number of sick people in his hometown (6:5). Apparently Jesus' own spiritual vitality was transferred to those in need through the physical touch of his hands.

After his ascension, Jesus' healing ministry was carried on through his church, as the book of Acts records. Peter took a lame beggar by the hand, and he was healed (3:7); he raised Tabitha from the dead, lifting her by the hand (9:40-41); handkerchiefs and aprons that had come into contact with Paul's body were used to heal the sick (19:12); Paul laid hands on Publius's father and he was made well (28:7-8). Before his ascension Jesus had given all believers the authority to lay hands on the sick for their healing. "In my name," he said, "[those who believe] will place their hands on sick people, and they will get well" (Mark 16:17-18).

In view of the scriptural precedents and Jesus' clear statement, "full gospel" Christians affirm that laying on of hands for healing should be a regular practice in the church. They see no biblical reason why the body of Christ should not continue to provide healing in his name in this way for all time to come.

Impartation of the Holy Spirit

A number of Bible passages connect the laying on of hands with the gift of the Holy Spirit. Most of these occur in the Acts of the Apostles. After Philip had proclaimed the gospel and baptized a group of Samaritans, Peter and John, who had come down from Jerusalem, "placed their hands on them, and they received the Holy Spirit" (8:17). Some three days after Saul of Tarsus had recognized Jesus as Lord, Ananias went to him and, "placing his hands on Saul," declared both his healing from temporary blindness and his being filled with the Holy Spirit (9:17). Many years later Saul, now known as Paul, ministered in a similar fashion to a number of disciples in Ephesus. They came to faith in Jesus, were baptized in his name, and subsequently received the Holy Spirit "when Paul placed his hands on them" (19:6).

The Bible records a few instances in which the Holy Spirit was given without the laying on of hands. These include the initial outpouring of the Spirit on the day of Pentecost (Acts 2:4) and the occasion on which Peter preached to the household of Cornelius (10:44). In the first case, the 120 believers on whom the Spirit fell were the first to receive this gift; there was no one available to lay hands on them. In the latter instance, Peter himself was taken by surprise when the Holy Spirit fell on Cornelius and his family and friends who were Gentiles; he had apparently not intended to pray for them to receive the gift. In both cases, God acted sovereignly to bestow his Spirit without the use of a human intermediary.

An important concern for Catholic charismatics is the relationship between the laying on of hands in the sacrament of confirmation and the baptism of the Holy Spirit. The church teaches that the Spirit is conferred on believers for their strengthening and outward witness when the bishop lays his hands on them in confirmation. For this reason, Roman Catholics sometimes refer to confirmation as "the Pentecostal sacrament." However, Catholic charismatic believers also recognize and practice the laying on of hands by laypersons of all denominations for the baptism of the Holy Spirit. These two apparently conflicting doctrines have been reconciled in a number of ways. Some Catholics view the charismatic laying on of hands as a prayer for the confirmand that he or she will have "full docility" to the grace received in the sacrament. Others regard the baptism in the Spirit as the release of the power of the Spirit already given at confirmation, in which a person experiences "the effects of confirmation." Still others believe that the Holy Spirit is offered at confirmation but must be accepted personally by the confirmand. This latter view moves the emphasis away from a sacramental understanding of the laying on of hands as an objective medium of Spirit baptism to an offer of the Spirit that can be received subsequently.

Clearly, there is a need in the church at large for a better understanding of the relationship between the laying on of hands and the gift of the Holy Spirit. The writer of Hebrews refers to the laying on of hands as an elementary doctrine that the church should already have mastered (6:12); the context of this passage indicates that he is talking about the impartation of the Holy Spirit. Without having clarified its understanding of this doctrine, then, the church cannot very well go on to maturity as the writer admonishes it to do (6:1).

Commissioning

Most Christian bodies practice the laying on of hands for commissioning (ordaining, appointing). In its first move toward organization, the infant church chose seven men to serve tables; in preparing them for this responsibility the apostles laid their hands on them and prayed (Acts 6:5-6). Several years later, prophets and teachers in the church at Antioch set aside Paul and Barnabas to be missionaries by fasting, praying, and laying hands on them (Acts 13:1-3). During one of their journeys, Paul and Barnabas appointed (literally "chose by stretching out the hand") elders in a number of churches (Acts 14:23).

Paul's references to Timothy's being consecrated for ministry through the laying on of hands have prompted churches of various denominations to continue the practice when ordaining ministers. Paul says that a body of elders laid hands on Timothy (1 Tim. 4:14) and indicates that he himself was a part of that group (2 Tim. 1:6). In both of these passages Paul says that the gift for ministry was given to Timothy through the process of laying on of hands.

In all three situations in which the Bible mentions

the laying on of hands, impartation of some grace is the result; a closer examination will reveal that this grace always involves the Spirit of Christ. In the case of healing, there is a transfer of energy or life, which is the Spirit; in the baptism of the Holy Spirit, the connection is explicit; and in commissioning, a gift of the Spirit is given.

J. Rodman Williams[23]

250 ✦ ANOINTING WITH OIL

As used in the church today, the term anointing *refers to a special grace given to a believer by the Lord through the Holy Spirit. The practice of anointing a person with olive oil symbolizes this spiritual endowment. It also pictures the power of Jesus to heal, which was conferred on him by the Spirit at his baptism.*

In the ancient world, olive oil served a variety of purposes. It was burned in lampstands, was used on the body as a healing agent and cosmetic, and was an ingredient in breads and other food items. In Israel, olive oil was applied to the tabernacle furnishings and to the ears, thumbs, and great toes of the priests in setting them apart for the special use of the Lord (Num. 35:25; Ps. 133:2). Kings and prophets were also anointed with oil when they undertook their sacred callings: the king as God's vice-regent and mediator of the covenant and the prophet as guardian of the covenant and spokesman for the Lord. For this reason, these men are often referred to as "the Lord's anointed" (*mashiah*, "oily," 1 Sam. 16:6; 24:6, 10; 2 Sam. 23:1; Ps. 2:2).

Many Christian congregations anoint with oil in conjunction with prayers for healing. The New Testament basis for this practice is found in the letter of James, in which he gives specific instructions to afflicted believers to have the church elders anoint them with oil and pray for them; confession of sin is also a requirement in this case. In obedience to these instructions, many charismatic and Pentecostal pastors routinely maintain a supply of olive oil at the church altar, available to be applied to those who ask for prayer for some physical infirmity.

This practice also has foundation in the understanding that Jesus is called "the Christ" (*Christos*, Acts 4:26), which is the Greek equivalent for the Hebrew "messiah" (*mashiah*). Peter refers to Jesus as the Servant whom God has anointed (Acts 4:27). When a sick person is anointed with oil, then, the healing power which Jesus Christ manifested in his ministry is being imparted to him. If anointing oil is associated with Jesus Christ, it follows that it will also be used as a symbol of the holy breath, or Spirit (Hebrew *ruah*; Greek *pneuma*) of Christ. Indeed, Jesus' anointing, which was foretold by Isaiah (61:1) and fulfilled at his baptism in the Jordan river, was an anointing of the Spirit rather than of oil. Its purpose was not healing but commissioning (Luke 4:18).

Paul tells the Corinthian church that God has anointed him and sealed him, giving the Holy Spirit in his heart as a pledge (2 Cor. 1:21). John writes to an anonymous first-century church, "You have an anointing from the Holy One" (1 John 2:20). That this is an endowment of knowledge is made clear in verse 27:

> As for you, the anointing you received from him remains in you, and you do not need anyone to teach you. But as his anointing teaches you about all things and as that anointing is real, not counterfeit—just as it has taught you, remain in Him.

Pentecostal and charismatic Christians use the term *anointing* to mean empowerment or blessing conferred by Christ through the medium of the Holy Spirit. Pastors, teachers, musicians, and other Christian workers actively seek a special anointing of the Holy Spirit for effectiveness in their ministries. While oil is used frequently in prayer for healing, it is not as commonly used in requests for blessing or power in service. On occasion a missionary or other worker will be anointed with oil when the church commissions him or her; in most cases, however, oil itself is not used but an anointing of the Spirit is petitioned.

Janice E. Leonard

251 ✦ SLAIN IN THE SPIRIT (FALLING UNDER THE POWER)

The experience of being "slain in the Spirit" often accompanies worship in Pentecostal and charismatic churches. It is attested in the history of Christian revival movements, and a certain basis for it may be found in the Scriptures.

The expression *slain in the spirit* is a relatively modern expression, denoting a religious phenomenon in which an individual falls down, the cause being attributed to the Holy Spirit. This experience is also known in Pentecostal and charismatic churches as "falling under the power." Although the nomenclature may not have been in place for very long, it is generally recognized that the phenomenon (or something closely related to it) has occurred throughout the history of the church.

John Wesley's journal tells of people who "were struck to the ground and lay there groaning" during his preaching. Similar phenomena occurred during the New England Great Awakening of 1740–1743; they are attested in the writings of Jonathan Edwards and also accompanied George Whitefield's preaching. Charles G. Finney's autobiography recounts episodes in which people could not move or speak, in one instance for sixteen hours. In the 1800–1801 revival at the University of Georgia, students who attended camp meetings "lay for hours in the straw prepared for those 'smitten of the Lord,' or they started suddenly to flee away and fell prostrate as if shot down by a sniper" (E. Merton Coulter, *College Life in the Old South* [New York, 1928], 194-195, as quoted in Vinson Synan, *The Holiness-Pentecostal Movement in the United States* [Grand Rapids: Wm. B. Eerdmans Publishing Co., 1971], 25). The preaching ministry of nineteenth-century Methodist circuit-rider Peter Cartwright was characterized by the same kinds of response.

On April 9, 1906, while conducting prayer services in a private home, W. J. Seymour, the apostle of the Azusa Street revival in Los Angeles, fell upon the floor, along with seven other people, and began speaking in tongues. This was to become a common occurrence in the meetings on Azusa Street, in which falling under the power resulted in speaking in other tongues. A similar phenomenon took place when hecklers came into the meetings intending to break them up; on the way down the aisle they are reported to have fallen on the floor, unable to rise. The Azusa Street Revival is generally regarded as instrumental in the birth of the modern Pentecostal movement.

During the 1960s and 1970s, being slain in the Spirit took place regularly in Pentecostal and charismatic meetings. As an example, during a revival at the Oak Cliff Assembly of God Church in Dallas, Texas, conducted by evangelist Marvin Schmidt, young people filling the church aisles in a "victory march" suddenly fell to the floor like dominoes. In another service during the same revival, two unchurched children, who had come for a children's club and were taken into the revival meeting instead, fell to the floor, raised their hands, and began speaking in tongues when the evangelist stretched out his hands in their direction.

More commonly, falling under the power is a liturgical practice, which takes place at a certain point in Pentecostal or charismatic worship services, usually at the time when people are called forward for prayer for healing and other needs. As the minister lays hands on them and prays, the worshipers often fall backward to the floor. Specified assistants, such as church elders, stand behind those being prayed for, to catch them as they fall and prevent physical injury; usually a female assistant is present to cover the legs of any women wearing skirts, for modesty's sake. After several minutes of lying with eyes closed and sometimes speaking in tongues, the worshipers return to their seats. Probably a majority of charismatic churches do not regularly include this practice in their worship.

A number of Scripture texts are enlisted to support the legitimacy of the phenomenon, although the Bible offers no support for it as an experience to be expected in the normal life of the believer. Ezekiel (1:28) and John the Revelator (Rev. 1:17) both fell on their faces in the presence of the Lord. Jesus' disciples "fell facedown" at the voice of God (Matt. 17:6), and the guards at the garden tomb "shook and became like dead men" at the appearance of the angel of the Lord (Matt. 28:1-4). Both of the Matthean texts may simply describe a reaction to fear.

Two important texts that appear to support the experience of falling under the power of the Spirit are John 18:1-6 and Acts 9:4; 22:7; 26:14. Neither of these occurrences are placed within the context of worship. In the first, the officers from the chief priests and Pharisees who have come to arrest Jesus fall backward to the ground at his word. In the latter, Saul falls at the sound of the Lord's voice and the great light which accompanies it at his conversion on the Damascus road. This event closely parallels the modern experience of being slain in the Spirit, but there is no intimation that it is normative for all Christians. In fact, it is the uniqueness of the occurrence that prompts Luke to record it three times.

Thus, the phenomenon of falling down under the power of God is enigmatic. Although there seems to be no direct biblical support for it as a normal Christian practice, the fact cannot be questioned that Christians have experienced it throughout history and that those who undergo it attribute the experience to God.

Patrick H. Alexander[24]

252 ✦ DELIVERANCE FROM DEMONS

While not regularly practiced in all segments of the charismatic and Pentecostal community, deliverance ministry is prominently featured within some circles. Most leaders within the movement acknowledge its validity as a legitimate continuation of the ministry of Jesus and the apostles.

The rise of the charismatic movement in the 1960s engendered a corresponding increase in the practice of casting out demons. Attuned as they are to supernatural realities, charismatics take seriously the presence and influence of demonic powers in the lives of both Christians and unbelievers. It is not difficult to locate biblical support for the casting out of demons. Jesus himself is reported to have cast evil spirits out of a great number of people as he went about healing the sick. This is one of the specific areas of ministry he delegated to his disciples (Matt. 10:1, 7-8) and to all believers (Mark 16:17), along with preaching the good news, healing the sick, and raising the dead.

In some biblical narratives the presence of a demon is related to physical illness (Mark 1:23-26; Luke 9:38-42; 13:32), while in others it results in bizarre behavior, violence, divination, and the like (Matt. 8:28-32; Luke 4:33-34; Acts 16:16). In accordance with these precedents, charismatics often view intractable behavior patterns, incurable illnesses, social evils, and other problems as having their origin in demonic activity. The key to curing the difficulty is commanding the demon, by the authority of Jesus Christ, to depart from the afflicted person, group, or social system, using the New Testament accounts as a pattern.

Deliverance can and often does take place in the context of public worship. Sometimes entire services or conferences are specifically convened to deal with demonic activity and engage in spiritual warfare, and within the Pentecostal/charismatic community a significant number of ministries have arisen that specialize in deliverance. (The term *exorcism* is rarely used to describe this activity.)

A typical deliverance service will begin with praise and worship, after which those persons with severe problems are invited to approach the altar for prayer. The minister or another Christian worker may ask the nature of the problem or might receive a supernatural revelation about it through a word of knowledge. Sometimes the demon will be asked to identify himself. The minister then lays hands on the head of the afflicted person and commands the demon to come out in the name of Jesus. It is not uncommon for the person being delivered to cough or even vomit up a phlegmlike substance or to fall on the floor, at which point the demon is said to have departed.

Although most Pentecostals and charismatics accept the validity of deliverance ministry, not all of them practice it on a regular basis or in the same way. Some believe that Christians may be subject to demonic influence and need deliverance; others vehemently deny that anyone who has the Holy Spirit can be oppressed by other spirits. There is a stated reluctance in many circles to accord prominence to Satan by calling attention to him and his hordes. Many charismatics prefer to engage in spiritual warfare through worship, which lifts up the person of Jesus Christ instead.

253 ✦ WORSHIP AS SPIRITUAL WARFARE

Only recently, in its expanded awareness of entrenched spiritual evil, has the Christian church begun to recover the scriptural understanding of warfare in the realm of the spirit. The Bible clearly reveals the spiritual nature of the struggle against sin and the opposition of demonic powers to the gospel of Christ. As the celebration of the Lord's dominion and victory, worship is a major weapon in the arsenal of spiritual warfare.

Spiritual Opposition to God in Scripture

The presence of evil in the created order is a given in Scripture. No explanation is offered for either its origin or its place in a world created and governed by a good, righteous, and all-powerful God; nevertheless, from the opening pages of the Bible, evil exists. And from the beginning of history, the Lord gives the job of overcoming evil to human beings. To a jealous and vengeful Cain he says: "But if you do not do what is right, sin is crouching at your door; it desires to have you, but you must master it" (Gen. 4:7).

The person of Satan appears both in the Chronicles and in the story of Job. In the first case he is in an adversary relationship with Israel and moves David to disobey God by numbering the people (1 Chron. 21:1), an act that brings punishment on the entire nation. In the Job narrative, Satan is portrayed as a spirit being who talks God into letting him bring tragedy into the life of the most righteous man on earth (Job 1:6–2:7). It is commonly taught that the serpent who tempts Eve in the garden of Eden is really Satan, although the Genesis account does not make such a connection. John does refer to the devil as "that old serpent" in his Revelation and links him to the person of Satan, whom he also calls a dragon (12:9; 20:2). In Zechariah's vision, Satan stands ready to accuse Joshua the high priest, who is before the angel of the Lord (Zech. 3:1). Indeed, his very name means "adversary" or "accuser," and John refers to him as "the accuser of our brothers" (Rev. 12:10). Satan tempts Jesus to commit sin (Matt. 4:10), enters into Judas Iscariot and inspires him to betray Jesus (Luke 22:3), desires to possess Peter (Luke 22:31), and is said to have entered the heart of Ananias and led him to lie to the Holy Spirit (Acts 5:3).

John is obviously referring to Satan when he talks about the "prince of this world" (John 12:31; 14:30; 16:11), as is Paul when he refers to the "ruler of the kingdom of the air" (Eph. 2:2). At the conversion of Saul, the Lord describes Satan as the ruler of the kingdom of darkness to which human beings belong until God removes them from his control and places them in the kingdom of light (Acts 26:18). Peter says that Satan roams like a lion looking for people he can destroy (1 Pet. 5:8). He is wily (Eph. 6:11) and a deceiver (Rev. 20:10), always seeks an advantage (2 Cor. 2:11), and can appear as an angel of light (2 Cor. 11:14).

In addition to the devil or Satan, Scripture reveals the existence of an unnumbered host of devils or demons who inhabit human beings, bringing with them various infirmities and bondages. Demons apparently require a body to dwell in if they are to function (Matt. 8:31; Mark 5:12). Paul writes to the Corinthians that demon spirits are the reality behind the idols worshiped by the heathen (1 Cor. 10:19-21).

What emerges from all this is the picture of an evil spirit called "the devil" or "Satan" who opposes God and desires to destroy his people and who reigns over a kingdom composed of God's enemies. In some cases, at least, he is behind the propagation of evil in the world. This is the adversary whom Christians are told to conquer. Working with, and perhaps for, this major evil personality are lesser evil spirits called devils or demons.

Spiritual Warfare in Israel

For Israel, the enemy was a company of hostile neighboring nations that periodically threatened to overrun it. These were not spirits but very physical fighting men who came against Israel with swords, spears, and bows. However, behind these pagan peoples were spiritual forces associated with the practice of idolatry, fertility rites, child sacrifice, and other abominations. The Lord made it clear that it was not because of Israel's righteousness that the Lord gave them victory but because the nations with whom they struggled were Yahweh's own enemies. As his covenant people, Israel joined the Lord in fighting these wicked nations and driving them out of the Promised Land.

In that sense, then, Israel's battles constituted spiritual warfare and were often won with spiritual weapons. An example is the attack that Joshua led against the city of Jericho. The Lord gave Joshua the battle plan, which consisted of a series of seven processions around the city, with the Levites bearing the ark of the Lord and the priests blowing trumpets. On the seventh day Israel paraded around Jericho seven times, the priests blew the trumpets, the people gave a great shout, which brought down the walls, and Israel walked in and took over the city without opposition (Josh. 6:8-20). There are numerous indications in the narrative that this is a covenant-related assault. In the first place, it is carried out over a period of seven days, with seven processions on the seventh day. Seven is the number that signifies the covenant relationship in general and God's covenant with Israel in particular. In the second place, the ark of the Lord, which symbolizes his presence, goes with the procession. As the great King of the covenant, Yahweh is, in effect, leading the armies of Israel into battle against his enemies. The blowing of trumpets and the final shout are declarations of victory; Israel is acclaiming the power and authority of its King, which constitutes praise.

Jehoshaphat's war with the nations of Ammon, Moab, and Mt. Seir is also a covenant conflict and is won with spiritual weapons. Upon hearing that he is about to be attacked, the king goes before the Lord and appeals to him for deliverance on the basis of the covenant. "O LORD, God of our fathers," he prays, "Did you not drive out the inhabitants of this land before your people Israel and give it forever to the descendants of Abraham your friend?" (2 Chron. 20:6-7). Yahweh responds through a prophet who tells King Jehoshaphat and his frightened subjects that they will not have to fight in the battle but need only go out against the enemy the following day and watch the Lord give them victory. Jehoshaphat puts the army in array, appointing singers to go ahead of the fighting men to praise the Lord for his covenant love. As soon as the singers begin to magnify the Lord, he causes the enemy nations to start killing one another until all are destroyed. Jehoshaphat and his army return home in triumph and joy, carrying their weapons of warfare: psalteries, harps, and trumpets. The fear of God falls on the surrounding nations, and Israel enjoys a period of peace.

Isaiah describes the judgment that the Lord will bring upon Assyria because they have pillaged his covenant people. Once again the victory will be wrought through the praises of Israel. Isaiah writes:

> The LORD will cause men to hear his majestic voice
>   and will make them see his arm coming down
> with raging anger and consuming fire,
>   with cloudburst, thunderstorm and hail.
> The voice of the LORD will shatter Assyria;
>   with his scepter he will strike them down.
> Every stroke the LORD lays on them with his
>   punishing rod
> will be to *the music of tambourines and harps,*
>   as he fights them in battle with the blows of his
>   arm. (Isa. 30:30-32; italics added)

In all of these accounts, Israel does battle and the Lord brings judgment on the powers of evil through musical praise. The war is being fought in the supernatural realm as it is carried out on the earth.

Two of the psalms specifically refer to praise as the means by which God brings victory and deliverance. David sings of the praise of children, which puts to silence the enemy and the avenger (Ps. 8:2). Psalm 149 contains a graphic description of the effect of the praise of God's people on his enemies:

> Praise the LORD!
> Sing to the LORD a new song,
> And His praise in the congregation of the godly
>   ones.
> Let Israel be glad in his Maker;
> Let the sons of Zion rejoice in their King.
> Let them praise His name with dancing:
> Let them sing praises to Him with timbrel and
>   lyre.
> For the Lord takes pleasure in His people;
> He will beautify the afflicted ones with salvation.
> Let the godly ones exult in glory;
> Let them sing for joy on their beds.
> Let the high praises of God be in their mouth,
> And a two-edged sword in their hand,
> To execute vengeance on the nations,
> And punishment on the peoples;
> To bind their kings with chains,
> And their nobles with fetters of iron;
> To execute on them the judgment written;
> This is an honor for all His godly ones.
> Praise the LORD! (Ps. 149:1-9, NASB)

The high praises of God in the mouth of the worshiper and the two-edged sword in hand (see Eph. 6:17; Rev. 1:16) effectively bind the rulers of wickedness, rendering them powerless. In this way the believer participates in the reign of the Lord over the earth. It is through his praising God with song and dancing that the powers of evil are brought into subjection.

The "prayers of David son of Jesse" (Pss. 2–72), and many other psalms, are primarily concerned with the struggle between the Lord's faithful worshiper and the wicked. In these psalms the enemy is not just any difficult person but is specifically one who opposes the person speaking, who is usually the king. Since Israel's king, and David in particular, was the representative of its covenant with Yahweh, opposition to him was tantamount to an assault on the Lord. Thus, the one who troubled the king became an enemy of Yahweh. Typical of these psalms is the idea that praise and victory are inextricably linked. David understood praise as a throne God's people build for their King, from which Yahweh reigns over the nations and brings salvation. In crying to the Lord for protection and deliverance, he sings, "Yet Thou art holy, O Thou who art enthroned ["sits upon," *yashav*] upon the praises of Israel" (Ps. 22:3, NASB).

Spiritual Warfare in the New Testament

For the New Testament believer, the enemy is not so much wicked persons as ungodly systems and the demonic powers behind them. When Jesus calls down curses on the scribes and Pharisees (Matt. 23:13-36), he is denouncing the Judean religious establishment which has rejected him. However, when individuals from within that system came to him, he received them. Indeed, the battle between Yahweh and the wicked has now become a contest between Jesus and Satan, who is described as a predatory beast who goes about looking for ways to destroy God's people and his plan of salvation for them. Paul describes it as a power struggle between two opposing kingdoms (Col. 1:13), and John uses the metaphor of light and darkness in picturing their conflict (John 1:4-5; 3:19-21).

The ministry of Jesus and his disciples dealt a blow to Satan even before the Crucifixion sealed his doom. The Lord spent a great deal of time during his brief ministry in delivering demon-possessed people and healing their afflictions. On more than one occasion he sent his disciples out to do the same. When the seventy had returned from preaching the Good News of the kingdom and exulted to Jesus that even the demons were subject to them in his name, the Lord replied, "I saw Satan fall like lightning from heaven" (Luke 10:18).

As he approached the moment of betrayal, Jesus warned his disciples that "the prince of this world is coming"; but, he added, "he has no hold on me" (John 14:30). This was probably a reference to Jesus' spiritual struggle in Gethsemane, during which he engaged in a battle so intense that it caused him to sweat drops of blood. Jesus' response to this attack was to fall on his face before God and pray until the victory was effected and he could go forth in assurance and submission to the Cross.

John quotes Jesus, just before the crucifixion, as he predicts the imminent casting out of Satan. "Now is the time for judgment on this world; now the prince of this world will be driven out" (John 12:31). Christians understand, therefore, that Satan's defeat is already accomplished through the death and resurrection of Jesus Christ. John confirms this in the Revelation when he says of Michael and his angels (who seem to be synonymous with "our brothers" in verse 10) that they overcame Satan "by the blood of the Lamb and by the word of their testimony; they did not love their lives so much as to shrink from death" (Rev. 12:7, 11).

In his instructions to the disciples just prior to his ascension, Jesus promised all baptized believers power over evil spirits and their effects (Mark 16:16-18). Christians do not need to fear a defeated Satan or any of his forces. Jesus made a public show of their humiliation in his death and resurrection (Col. 2:15). It is important to remember, however, that God's people are not fighting human beings who may be under Satan's control but the demonic forces that enslave them (Eph. 6:12). "The weapons that we fight with are not the weapons of the world. On the contrary, they have divine power to demolish strongholds. We demolish arguments and every pretension that sets itself up against the knowledge of God" (2 Cor. 10:4-5). The name of Jesus, invoked in worship and praise, establishes God's sovereignty over Satan and renders him powerless.

Janice E. Leonard

254 • SPEAKING IN TONGUES

Speaking in tongues is not a natural gift or talent for languages but a gift from God, a supernatural endowment. Tongues are not ecstatic utterance but an activity under the control of the speaker, offered in obedience to the prompting of the Spirit.

Introduction

The *pneumatika,* "spiritual gifts," are "supernatural" manifestations of the Holy Spirit. They are not "natural" talents. They are supernatural inasmuch as the operation of any and all of them is contingent upon the divine initiative. Miracle working, except it be a manifestation of divine initiative and power, is mere chicanery; the word of wisdom is simply human perspicacity; the word of knowledge is but the product of human intellectual effort. This distinction must be kept in the foreground of our discussion if we are to understand the nature of these supernatural manifestations of God's Spirit.

Supernatural Nature of Tongues

Stated negatively, tongues are not to be confused with a natural facility for mastering foreign languages. The "gift of tongues" is not a shortcut to the mastery of a foreign language. "As the Spirit give utterance" indicates that the vocabulary, syntax, and thought content expressed in "tongues-speech" are in the mind of the Holy Spirit and not in the mind of the individual speaking. Neither is the manifestation of interpretation of tongues a native ability to translate foreign languages. Much less is prophesying a natural talent for preaching the gospel in a persuasive manner. It is not a manifestation of mere human fluency of speech. It is rather an "intuitive" knowledge of the divine counsels supernaturally revealed and spontaneously uttered for the "edification and exhortation and consolation" (1 Cor. 14:3, NASB) of the assembled worshipers.

The supernatural nature of these gifts is verified by at least three lines of reasoning. First, the Holy Spirit is directly referred to nine times in 1 Corinthians 12:1-11 in relation to his manifestations: (1) "by the Spirit of God," verse 3; (2) "by the Holy Spirit," verse 3; (3) "the same Spirit," verse 4; (4) "the manifestation of the Spirit," verse 7; (5) "through the Spirit," verse 8; (6) "the same Spirit," verse 8; (7) "in the same Spirit," verse 9; (8) "in the one Spirit," verse 9; and (9) "the one and the same Spirit," verse 11.

Second, a glance at the context in chapters 12–14 reaffirms the Spirit's authorship of these charismatic enablements. In this context, the gifts of the Spirit are discussed in relation to the unity of Christ's body, the church, chapter 12—observe the parallelism between one Spirit, many gifts, and one body, many members; the preeminence of love (chapter 13); and the use of the gifts of the Spirit in Christian worship, especially tongues and prophesying (chapter 14). In this context, the supernatural nature of these manifestations is reiterated in the definition appended to one of these gifts, "faith." It is not saving faith but wonder-working faith "that can move mountains" (1 Cor. 13:2).

Third, the supernatural nature of these gifts is emphasized by the use of the term *pneumatika*, "spiritual gifts" (1 Cor. 14:1).

Tongues Not a Psychological Abnormality

A recognition of the supernatural origin of these gifts is necessary for a proper understanding of their true nature and function. Of all these spiritual manifestations, tongues are the most frequently misunderstood and misrepresented. The commonplace assumption that biblical *glossolalia* are the result of pathological emotional states simply ignores the fact that they are a supernatural manifestation of the Holy Spirit. To ascribe them to the abnormal working of a damaged psyche is to impugn the veracity of the biblical records, to say nothing of the integrity of multiplied thousands of tongues-speaking Christians whose emotional health is equal, if not superior, to that of their critics. Perhaps even worse than that, it is closer to blasphemy than to heresy to thus project the neurosis of a neurotic age into the Deity. It is an unwarranted assumption to say that the tongues at Corinth are "the gift of men, who rapt in an ecstasy and no longer quite master of their own reason and consciousness, pour forth their glowing spiritual emotions in strange utterances, rugged, dark, disconnected, quite unfitted to instruct or to influence the minds of others" (J. H. Thayer, *A Greek-English Lexicon of the New Testament* [New York: American Book Company, 1889], 188). Were this true, then the self-control counsel by Paul—"if there is no interpreter, the speaker should keep quiet in the church and speak to himself and God" (1 Cor. 14:28)—would be impossible.

On the contrary, the tongues-speaker is in complete control of all his faculties at all times. His "mind is unfruitful" (1 Cor. 14:14) because he does not understand the words he utters in the Spirit, not because he has lost control of himself. The Holy Spirit never violates the integrity of one's personality. He exercises no coercion save the coercion of love: "If you love me," said Jesus, "you will obey what I command" (John 14:15). The fallacy in the interpretation quoted above is its uncritical correlation of the "gifts" of the Holy Spirit with the psychic phenomena encountered in pagan religions or in spiritism, the inspiration of which is demonic.

Always and everywhere, the Bible distinguishes between the activity of the Holy Spirit and the activity of demonic spirits. The attempt to link biblical *glossolalia* with the cataleptic trance states of mediums or other pagan devotees of demonic spirits reflects unfavorably upon Paul's spiritual discernment. It implies that he could not distinguish one from the other. Certainly Paul's counsel to regulate the Spirit's gifts of tongues and prophecy at Corinth indicates that he did not regard them as spurious. Paul never "regulated" demonic manifestations; he exorcised the "spirits" behind them (Acts 16:16ff.). Yet the attempt to correlate biblical tongues with the psychic counterfeits is repeatedly made. The following is another such example: "There is no doubt about the thing referred to, namely, the broken speech of persons in religious ecstasy. The phenomenon, as found in Hellenistic religion, is described especially by E. Rhode. . . and Reitzenstein" (F. W. Arndt and W. F. Gingrich, *A Greek-English Lexicon of the New Testament* [Chicago: University of Chicago Press, 1957], 161). Behind this glib assumption is the erroneous *a priori* that superficial correlation proves mutual causation.

Tongues As Languages

The tongues of Pentecost were recognizable dialects or languages. They were not the incoherent ravings of men in a trance state. Neither were they kin to the maudlin mouthing of intoxicated men. When the wiseacres of that day tried to shrug it off as such, Peter was at pains to rebut their haughty rationalization, saying, "these men are not drunk, as you suppose" (Acts 2:15).

On the day of Pentecost, they spoke dialects known to many of their auditors "as the Spirit enabled them." Luke ascribed these utterances to the direct agency of the Holy Spirit. In Corinth, they spoke "families of languages" (*genēai glōssōn*) as a manifestation of the Holy Spirit. In both cases, the Holy Spirit is the one with whom the languages originated. If there was any difference in the nature or expression of the respective utterances, this difference originated with the Holy Spirit, not with the person uttering the language.

Paul further identified the languages at Corinth as the "tongues [languages] of men and of angels" (1 Cor. 13:1). They were the vehicle for expressing the praise and worship of men who, in full possession of all their faculties, had discovered that there are levels of communication with God that transcend the finite limitations of the merely rational. They are not, therefore, subrational; they are suprarational.

There is, furthermore, continuity in biblical *glossolalia.* There is no difference in kind in the various references to this phenomenon in Scripture. In commenting on the Pentecostal manifestation, A. T. Robertson wrote:

The gift of tongues came also on the house of Cornelius at Caesarea (Acts 10:44-47), the disciples of John at Ephesus (Acts 19:6), the disciples at Corinth (1 Cor. 14:1-33). It is possible that the gift appeared also at Samaria (Acts 8:18). . . . The experience is identical in all four instances and they are . . . for adoration and wonder and worship (*Word Pictures in the New Testament,* [Nashville: Broadman Press, 1932], vol. III, p. 22).

Henry Alford affirmed with equal candor that the tongues are "one and the same throughout" (*The Greek Testament,* 5th ed. [1865], vol. 2, 15, 122). In our own day, there is an increasing number of testimonies by Christians who have spoken known languages "in the Spirit." On one occasion I was participating in a healing service in a church on the west coast of the United States. As I prayed in tongues, an Armenian Baptist woman listened to my "tongue" and identified it as prayer in Russian. Again, while I was praying with a small group for the healing of a missionary who speaks Spanish fluently, the missionary identified my "tongue" as a Spanish dialect. The vocabulary was clearly identified, but the inflections were strange to her. On another occasion, while praying for the healing of the little daughter of a Japanese Buddhist woman, I spoke a "tongue" she later identified to mutual friends as Japanese. Still more recently, in a ministry service in my own church, an Armenian man for whom I prayed identified two foreign languages spoken in prayer. One was a dialect spoken by the Indian colonial troops of the British Empire, which he had heard as a young man in the seaport cities of the Orient. The second language he described as Kurdish, a language he himself speaks. Most recently of all, in fact just a few weeks ago, the phenomenon was repeated again. While praying with a young man acquainted with both Spanish and Portuguese, I prayed in a language identified by the young man as Portuguese. When asked what was said, he replied: "You told God my need in high Portuguese." Needless to say, all of these languages are unknown to me and consequently were spoken "as the Spirit himself gave utterance."

On another occasion, I identified the last sentence of a song sung "in the Spirit" as biblical Greek, although the man singing knew no Greek. A Norwegian woman received the baptism in the Holy Spirit at a service in my church. The next day she prayed in tongues in the presence of some Italian friends who identified the "tongue" she was speaking as Italian, a language in which she is not conversant. In charismatic services in my church, other languages have been identified on several occasions. It is also significant to note that each participant in these services prays in a distinctive and clearly recognizable tongue. Vocabulary, inflexions, intonations are all distinctive and clearly distinguishable. Such experiences lead the present writer not only to affirm Dr. Robertson's words—"The experience is identical in all four instances" referred to in Scripture—but to add: the experience is identical with the biblical prototype whenever Spirit-filled Christians pray in tongues "as the Spirit gives them utterance."

Howard M. Ervin[25]

255 ◆ BIBLIOGRAPHY: CHARISMATIC ASPECTS OF WORSHIP

Agrimson, Elmo G. *Gifts of the Spirit in the Body of Christ*. Minneapolis: Augsburg Publishing House, 1974. This collection of essays is written from a Lutheran perspective. Of special note are Duane Priebe, "Charismatic Gifts and Their Existence in St. Paul"; Arnold Buttlinger, "Baptized in Water and the Spirit," which discusses the link between baptism and the receipt of the Spirit and *charismata,* and implications for liturgy; and Elmo Agrimson, "The Congregation and the Gifts," which advocates use of the charismatic gifts according to New Testament practice.

Bruner, Frederick D. *A Theology of the Holy Spirit*. Grand Rapids: Wm. B. Eerdmans Publishing Co., 1974. This volume is called "an essay in case-study theology of the missionary movement known as Pentecostal." Of particular interest is the chapter on "The Gifts of the Spirit"; the writer deals with such topics as the gift of the Spirit and spiritual gifts, the nonsuspension of gifts, the Pentecostal meeting as the locus of gifts, and the place of music, prayer, and the ministry of the congregation in the practice of the gifts. He divides the spiritual gifts into "remarkable" (sign gifts) and "nonremarkable." Also valuable is the chapter on the baptism of the Holy Spirit in the Acts of the Apostles.

Ervin, Howard M. *These Are Not Drunken As Ye Suppose*. Plainfield, N.J.: Logos, 1968. This volume is a scholarly presentation of New Testament material concerning all aspects of the baptism in the Holy Spirit by a Baptist author, one of the earlier writers of the contemporary charismatic movement. The author presents a successive topical/textual analysis of all aspects of the baptism in the Holy Spirit.

Gee, Donald. *Concerning Spiritual Gifts*. Pasadena: Regal Books, 1980. This collection of Bible studies on the subject of spiritual gifts first appeared in the 1920s and is now accepted as good source material for understanding earlier classical Pentecostal thought on the baptism of the Holy Spirit and spiritual gifts. For similar treatments from the Assemblies of God perspective, see G. R. Carlson, *Spiritual Dynamics* (Springfield, Mo.: Gospel Publishing House, 1963) and Harold Horton, *The Gifts of the Spirit* (Springfield, Mo.: Gospel Publishing House, 1938).

Green, Michael. *I Believe in the Holy Spirit*. Grand Rapids: Wm. B. Eerdmans Publishing Co., 1975. Written in apologetic style by an Anglican writer, this is an exegetical study in topical format, oriented to issues of practice in the church. Treatment of the New Testament text is combined with observations on the contemporary scene. The author sees Spirit baptism as taking place at sacramental baptism, with the "fullness" of Spirit baptism as a secondary and continued action. An annotated bibliography is included.

Hamilton, Michael P., ed. *The Charismatic Movement*. Grand Rapids: Wm. B. Eerdmans Publishing Co., 1975. This work is a collection of studies of charismatic phenomena in the church, including the following: James Logan, "Charismatic Revival and the Bible," discussing the relationship of Holy Spirit baptism to water baptism; Krister Stendahl, "New Testament Evidence," an analysis of scriptural *glossolalia;* G. H. Williams and Edith Waldvogel, "History of Speaking in Tongues and Related Gifts"; and Josephine M. Ford, "The Charismatic Gifts in Worship," discussing tongues, prophetic utterances, evangelization and teaching, and healing.

Koenig, John. *Charismata: God's Gifts to God's People*. Philadelphia: Westminster Press, 1978. An appeal for a biblically honest theology of gifts by a historical-critical scholar, this book argues for a contemporary understanding of charismatic expressions based on the experience of the New Testament church. In the author's view, the primitive community experiences renewal to service through the gifts and through the "dark side" of God's *charismata* in the joy of the cross.

McDonnell, Kilian, and George Montague. *Christian Initiation and Baptism in the Holy Spirit*. Collegeville, Minn.: Liturgical Press, 1990. Written from a Roman Catholic perspective, this work presents an analysis of Spirit baptism and spiritual gifts in the New Testament and discusses applicable post-biblical texts in the writings of Christian theologians during the following eight centuries. This book contains interesting insights on charismatic phenomena in the context of primitive Christian worship.

Montague, George. *The Spirit and His Gifts*. Mahwah, N.J.: Paulist Press, 1974. This scriptural analysis links the sacrament of baptism with the experience of the Holy Spirit and openness to *charismata*. It deals especially with the gifts of tongues, prophecy, and interpretation.

Wagner, C. Peter. *Your Spiritual Gifts Can Help Your Church Grow*. Pasadena: Regal Books, 1979. An authority on church growth analyzes 27 spiritual gifts in the New Testament in the conviction that rediscovery of the gifts is essential for church renewal and growth. The book is written for a popular audience, offering practical advice on the practice of a wide range of gifts.

Williams, J. Rodman. *Renewal Theology*. 2 vols. Grand Rapids: Zondervan Publishing House, 1990. This is a systematic theology written from a Presbyterian charismatic viewpoint. Of special interest are the chapters on the phenomena of tongues, the reception of the Holy Spirit, and the effects of the coming of the Spirit. The chapters on the gifts of the Spirit and the ninefold manifestation of the Spirit are limited to Paul's list in 1 Corinthians 12:8-10.

❧ TWENTY-EIGHT ❧

Acts of Entrance in Traditional Worship

Over the centuries, traditional acts of worship have developed in the various liturgies of the Eastern and Western churches, many of them of ancient origin. These actions fall into one or more of the movements of Christian celebration: the gathering of the community and entrance into the place of worship, the service of the Word of God, the service of the table of the Lord, and the dismissal. Chapters 28–30, while not exhaustive treatments of traditional acts of Christian worship, explore the scriptural foundation for some of the more familiar parts of the service in the Western church. The succeeding chapters further discuss the Lord's Supper, or Eucharist, and other sacred and sacramental rites of Christian worship.

Christian worship incorporates not only the central acts of celebration and the service of the Word and of the Lord's Table, but also those actions that proclaim the Lord's exalted presence in the midst of the assembly and that prepare the worshiper to receive the benefits of God's grace as administered through worship. Such "acts of entrance" stand in the tradition of biblical worship, as exemplified in the invitation of Psalm 100: "Enter his gates with thanksgiving and his courts with praise; give thanks to him and praise his name" (Ps. 100:4).

256 ◆ PROCESSIONAL

Traditional Christian worship often begins with a processional in which the officiants and other representative worshipers, such as the choir, enter the sanctuary. Processions may also occur outside the church on festive occasions. The procession is based on biblical models and is a way of proclaiming the victory and dominion of the Lord and of his Christ.

The history of religions contains abundant evidence of the use of processions in popular worship. The Old Testament alludes to processions of pagan worshipers with idols of their gods. When Isaiah says, "Bel bows down, Nebo stoops low; their idols are borne by beasts of burden" (Isa. 46:1), he is portraying a procession featuring the idols of lifeless, burdensome divinities. The same image underlies the scorn heaped on false gods in Psalm 115:7: "They have . . . feet, but they cannot walk." In contrast, Yahweh, the God of Israel, is "enthroned between the cherubim" (2 Sam. 6:2; Pss. 80:1; 99:1),

over the guardian figures on the ark of the covenant. He "rides on the heavens to help you and on the clouds in his majesty" (Deut. 33:26); he "rides the ancient skies above" (Ps. 68:33).

Nevertheless, Yahweh could go in procession *symbolically* in those processions of worshipers into the sanctuary that were a feature of festival worship of Israel. Several of the psalms refer to these processions into the house of the Lord. In Psalm 100 the worshipers are invited to "enter his gates with thanksgiving and his courts with praise" (Ps. 100:4). Psalm 24 appears to be a "liturgy of entrance" into the courts of the Lord in the form of a dialogue between the sanctuary gatekeepers and a group of worshipers in procession, possibly with the ark of the covenant. To the question "Who may ascend the hill of the LORD?" (Ps. 24:3) the leaders of the procession respond with an affirmation of their fitness to stand in the sanctuary (Ps. 24:6); they then ask that the gates be opened so that the procession may continue and "the King of glory may come in" (Ps. 24:7, 9). This dialogue underscores the double symbolism of the festal procession: it is not the worshipers only who enter the holy place, but the Lord's presence also symbolically enters the sanctuary that he might meet with his covenant people and receive their tribute of praise and worship. Psalm 68, which pictures a festal procession, underscores the point that the Lord and his people ascend the sacred hill together:

> Your procession has come into view, O God,
> the procession of my God and my King into
> the sanctuary.
> In front are the singers, after them the musicians;
> with them the are maidens playing
> tambourines. . . .
> There is the little tribe of Benjamin, leading them,
> there the great throng of Judah's princes,
> and there the princes of Zebulun and of
> Naphtali. (Ps. 68:24-25, 27)

Perhaps such processions were reenactments of the time David first had the ark brought up to the former Jebusite sanctuary in Jerusalem with great rejoicing and abandon as the king himself danced before the Lord (2 Sam. 6:12-19). In such celebrative acts Yahweh laid claim to his throne in Zion and his dominion over all the nations:

> God has ascended amid shouts of joy,
> the LORD amid the sounding of trumpets.
> Sing praises to God, sing praises;
> sing praises to our King, sing praises.
> For God is the King of all the earth;
> sing to him a psalm of praise.
> God reigns over the nations;
> God is seated on his holy throne. (Ps. 47:5-8)

Festivals, and the processions that accompanied them, were occasions of joy and abandon in the Lord; with great longing the speaker in Psalm 43, apparently describing a circumstance in which he was unable to attend the festivals, remembers how he "used to go with the multitude, leading the procession to the house of God, with shouts of joy and thanksgiving among the festive throng" (Ps. 42:4). After the Babylonian Exile, the reestablishment of Jerusalem as a fortified city where the worship of the Lord could be protected from enemies was the occasion of a procession of thanksgiving organized by the governor Nehemiah (Neh. 12).

As a small group surrounded by a hostile culture, the early church could not conduct worship on the scale of the festive gatherings familiar to the Jewish tradition. Nevertheless, the procession continued to have symbolic meaning for the New Testament writers. Jesus and his disciples had orchestrated a procession into the sanctuary at the beginning of the week, which was to climax in his death and resurrection; we must understand the purpose of this first Palm Sunday event in light of the symbolism of the Israelite processions in which the King and his servants come to establish his dominion in the place of worship. Note, for example, the cry "Blessed is the king who comes in the name of the Lord!" (Luke 19:38) and Jesus' subsequent action in token of cleansing the temple of corrupt practices.

The concept of the procession led by a victorious king appears elsewhere in the New Testament. When Paul describes the ministry gifts of the ascended Christ (Eph. 4:7-13), he evokes the image of the procession pictured in Psalm 68 (Eph. 4:8; Ps. 68:18). Paul elsewhere alludes to the processions led by victorious commanders in which enemy prisoners were often paraded in humiliation; such processions were symbolic of the believers' being taken captive by the triumphant Christ (1 Cor. 4:9; 2 Cor. 2:14). At the climax of the Revelation to John, the victorious Christ appears at the head of a procession of the armies of heaven; they follow the banner that proclaims him "KING OF KINGS AND LORD OF LORDS" (Rev. 19:11-16).

Processions have been part of traditional Christian worship from ancient times. Many churches of the Protestant Reformation discontinued or restricted their use in an effort to refocus Christian worship around the proclamation of the Word. In recent years, however, evangelical and charismatic churches have begun to recover the biblical values in the pageantry of the processional, not only in congregational worship, but also in street marches held in many communities as a public proclamation of the lordship of Christ.

257 • CALL TO WORSHIP

Worship that begins with a call to celebration, such as that in many of the psalms, follows a well-established biblical procedure for summoning the assembly into the presence of the Lord and encouraging its praise of the great King.

In ancient cultures, most people had no time-pieces, and even the sundials and water clocks available to some were not very precise. Thus, a community could assemble together for worship only when summoned by a signal or other announcement, as in Muslim cultures today. In Israel, the ram's horn and the silver trumpet were used to call the people to festal assembly (Lev. 23:24; Num. 29:1); musical instruments in general were sounded to call the community together (Ps. 81:2-3; cf. the use of instruments to call the people to the worship of Nebuchadnezzar's image, Dan. 3:10).

In the Psalms, the invitation to worship is frequently verbalized, often including the mention of music. Psalm 150 consists almost entirely of imperatives to praise the Lord with instruments and dance. Psalm 148 is devoted to an invitation addressed to all members of the created order to praise the Lord. Psalm 149 invites the people of God to rejoice in their King:

> Praise the LORD.
>   Sing to the LORD a new song,
>   his praise in the assembly of the saints.
> Let Israel rejoice in their Maker;
>   let the people of Zion be glad in their
>   King.
> Let them praise his name with dancing
>   and make music to him with tambourine
>   and harp. (Ps. 149:1-3)

Many psalms begin with the invitation to praise the Lord. Worshipers are urged to "sing to the LORD a new song" (Pss. 96; 98); to "sing the glory of his name" (Ps. 66:2). Psalm 29 begins with the invitation to "ascribe to the LORD the glory due his name; worship the LORD in the splendor of his holiness" (Ps. 29:1-2; cf. Ps. 96:7-9). Several psalms begin by urging worshipers to "shout joyfully" to the Lord (Pss. 47; 66; 88; 100) or to clap the hands (Ps. 47), while the invitation to give thanks, or "make confession" of Yahweh's redemptive acts, forms the opening of another group (Pss. 105; 106; 107; 118; 136). Other psalms begin with the summons to "bless the LORD" (Ps. 134, NASB) or to "bless his name" (Ps. 96:2, NASB); sometimes the worshiper calls on himself to "bless the LORD" (Pss. 103–104, NASB). The general imperative "praise Yah!" (*Hallᵉlu Yah!*) stands at the head of Psalms 106; 111–113; 117; 135; and 146–150.

258 ◆ SILENCE

Silence is often unrecognized as an act of worship. However, it is an important element in the biblical attitude of awe before the majesty and mystery of a holy God.

The biblical worshiper encounters God in the first instance as the Holy One, whose being cannot be encompassed by the categories of the human intellect (Isa. 55:8-9; Rom. 11:33). The communication of the presence of the holy comes intuitively, in the sense of awe and mystery before a reality that transcends the normal or mundane plane of human experience. The response of the biblical worshiper is like that of Jacob ("How awesome is this place!" Gen. 28:17), Isaiah ("Woe to me! . . . I am ruined! . . . my eyes have seen the King, the LORD Almighty," Isa. 6:5), or John the Revelator ("When I saw him, I fell at his feet as though dead," Rev. 1:17). Such a response issues from a process in the human personality that operates at a level deeper than that of rational reflection. Where this element of the numinous is missing, worship fails to approach the intensity and depth of biblical worship.

In the presence of the mystery of the being of God, silence is an appropriate act of worship. Silence is the recognition that human utterance is often presumptuous in the face of the divine self-revelation. Before the Creator, the creature must confront his or her finitude. The worshiper is as nothing before him who is all. The biblical worshiper understands that to occupy oneself with verbal products of the human mentality is an act of pride, in effect a denial of God's place as sovereign Lord (Ps. 131:1; Job 42:3). Thus, when God speaks, there is nothing for the argumentative Job to do but repent: "I am unworthy—how can I reply to you? I put my hand over my mouth" (Job 40:4). Sounds of human origin—speech, music, or other noise—can be idolatrous creations, like images of wood or stone. "But the LORD is in his holy temple; let all the earth be silent before him" (Hab. 2:20). In the sanctuary of Zion there is silence before there is praise (Ps. 65:1). As the recognition of the kingship of God, worship is the revelation of his judgments; and when his judgments are so manifested, an awesome and suspenseful silence must fall even on the saints. In the book of Revelation, at the breaking of the seventh seal releasing the outpouring of God's wrath, "there was silence in heaven for about half an hour" (Rev. 8:1).

Many churches have incorporated periods of silence into their orders of worship, usually for "silent prayer," although there is little biblical basis for such a concept. The silences of biblical worship are not for prayer, which is always vocal, but rather are for a response to the manifestation of the majesty and mystery of God, and therefore a part of his praise. Silence, used dramatically at high moments of celebration, is an aspect of worship in which there is much room for creative development according to scriptural models.

259 • INVOCATION

Although the presence of the Lord is always with the people of God, worshipers may especially focus on the divine presence through a prayer of invocation. The invocation is based on scriptural models for "calling upon the Lord" and celebrating the dwelling of God with the covenant people.

The English word *invocation* is based on a Latin expression meaning to "call toward" or "call upon." An invocation may be included in the acts of entrance, as the congregation calls upon the Lord to meet with his people and to manifest his presence in the worship to follow. Invocations are used at other points in the liturgy as well; the preacher may call upon God to assist him or her in proclaiming the Word, and at the Lord's Table the Holy Spirit may be invoked upon the people (*epiklēsis,* the Greek equivalent of "invocation").

References to invocation occur frequently in Scripture, especially in Psalms; examples are the opening of Psalm 105, "Give thanks to the LORD, call on his name; make known among the nations what he has done" (Ps. 105:1) or the worshiper's vow in Psalm 116: "To thee I shall offer a sacrifice of thanksgiving, and call upon the name of the LORD" (Ps. 116:17, NASB). The expressions "call upon the name of the LORD" (Gen. 4:26; 21:33; 26:25; Pss. 80:18; 99:6; 116:4, 13; Joel 2:32; Zeph. 3:9) and "call upon the LORD" (1 Kings 18:24; Pss. 17:6; 18:3; 53:4; 55:16; 88:9; 91:15; 145:18) are biblical synonyms for prayer and worship, indicating that the first act of the worshiper was to invoke the name of Yahweh.

From the New Testament perspective, the Lord is always present with his people. The worshiping church is the "temple" or dwelling of the Holy Spirit (Rom. 8:9; 1 Cor. 3:16; 2 Cor. 6:16; Eph. 2:21-22), the New Jerusalem in which God dwells with his partners in the new covenant (Rev. 21:1-3; cf. Heb. 12:22-23). While there is no need to "call" a God who is already present, an invocation is helpful in preparing the worshiper to receive the signs of God's action in the celebration that follows and to "recognize the body" (1 Cor. 11:29) of the Lord's faithful ones, not only in the Lord's Supper but in every corporate act of worship.

Traditional worship, especially in liturgical churches, may use invocations in the form of the *collect,* or summary prayer. A classic prayer often used as an invocation (although it is really a prayer for a purification of the worshiper's approach to God) is the following from the *The Book of Common Prayer:*

> Almighty God, to you all hearts are open, all desires known, and from you no secrets are hid: Cleanse the thoughts of our hearts by the inspiration of your Holy Spirit, that we may perfectly love you, and worthily magnify your holy name; through Christ our Lord. *Amen.*

Another traditional prayer that is more properly an invocation is the following, appropriate especially for the season of Epiphany:

> Almighty God, we invoke thee, the fountain of everlasting light, and entreat thee to send forth thy truth into our hearts, and to pour upon us the glory of thy brightness; through Christ our Lord. *Amen.*

Richard C. Leonard

260 • DOXOLOGY (*GLORIA*)

A doxology is a hymn of praise ascribing glory to God. Scripture includes many doxological expressions, and several traditional doxologies have developed through use in the historic liturgies of the church. In Christian usage, doxologies are often ascriptions of praise to the Trinity; they constitute an important element in the acts of entrance.

—— Doxologies in Scripture ——

The word *doxology* comes from the Greek *doxa,* "praise, honor, glory," and *logos,* "a speaking, a saying, a word"; hence, it means "a praising, ascription of glory." In the general sense, the term describes any act of Christian worship that is a verbal declaration of the glory and majesty of God.

Since the Bible is the literary deposit of the covenant people's experience of the glorious Lord, it is not surprising that doxologies abound in Scripture. In the Old Testament, for example, each of the first four books of the Psalter ends with a doxology (Pss. 41:13; 72:18-20; 89:52; 106:48); Psalm 150, in which the expression *praise* appears thirteen times, is the concluding doxology for the entire collection of Psalms. Other notable doxologies include that with which David began his prayer at the ascension of Solomon:

> Praise be to you, O LORD, God of our father Israel, from everlasting to everlasting. Yours, O LORD, is the greatness and the power and the glory and the majesty and the splendor, for everything in heaven and earth is yours. Yours, O LORD, is the kingdom; you are exalted as head over all. Wealth and honor come from you; you are the ruler of all things. In your hands are strength and power to exalt and give strength to all. Now, our God, we give you thanks, and praise your glorious name. (1 Chron. 29:10-13)

The opening words of David's doxology are echoed in the traditional doxology that ends the prayer Jesus gave his disciples for a model: "For yours is the kingdom and the power and the glory forever. Amen" (Matt. 6:13). Although these words do not appear in the oldest Greek manuscripts, they may have been added from liturgical usage in the ancient church, a usage that could have originated in the first century and is certainly consistent with the thrust of the Lord's Prayer.

Doxologies occur elsewhere in the New Testament, beginning with the narrative of the birth of Jesus, in which Luke records the doxology of the hosts of heaven: "Glory to God in the highest, and on earth peace to men on whom his favor rests" (Luke 2:14). The disciples praise God with a variant of this doxology during Jesus' triumphant entry into Jerusalem (Luke 19:37-38). Doxologies also occur in the Epistles; Paul's letters contain a number of spontaneous doxological outbursts (Rom. 11:36; 16:27; Eph. 3:21; 1 Tim. 1:17). The longest and most comprehensive doxology in the New Testament, and one frequently used as a benediction by pastors, is found in the brief letter of Jude:

> To him who is able to keep you from falling and to present you before his glorious presence without fault and with great joy—to the only God our Savior be glory, majesty, power, and authority, through Jesus Christ our Lord, before all ages, now and forevermore! Amen. (Jude 24-25)

In the Revelation to John, the chorus, led by the four living creatures and the twenty-four elders, inserts a number of doxologies into the drama at appropriate points. After the Lamb has taken the book of the seven seals, John hears all created beings ascribing glory to God: "To him who sits on the throne and to the Lamb be praise and honor and glory and power, for ever and ever!" (Rev. 5:13). Another doxological outburst begins in Revelation 19:1: "Hallelujah! Salvation and glory and power belong to our God. . . ."

Guy B. Funderburk[26]

Liturgical Doxologies

Several doxologies are in common use in the worship of both liturgical and nonliturgical churches. While not entirely quotations from the Scriptures, these doxologies rest on a biblical foundation.

The Doxology. In the worship of many Protestant churches a brief hymn, known familiarly as "The Doxology," consists of four short praises, beginning with "Praise God, from whom all blessings flow." This doxology is ascribed to Thomas Ken (1637–1711) and is usually sung to the tune "Old Hundredth" from the Geneva Psalter. In many churches it regularly accompanies the presentation of the offering but can be used at any appropriate point in the service, especially as one of the acts of entrance. This doxology strikes the scriptural note of universal praise to God the Father, Son, and Holy Spirit.

Gloria Patri. Another familiar doxology, known as the Gloria Patri, is typically used after a Scripture reading or the singing of a psalm or liturgical canticle:

> Glory be to the Father and to the Son and to the
> Holy Ghost;
> As it was in the beginning, is now, and ever shall
> be, world without end. *Amen.*

From an early period this doxology has been used to place the Psalms into a Christian frame of reference. It is sometimes called the "lesser doxology," in contrast to the *Gloria in Excelsis* or "greater doxology." The exact form of this doxology varied in antiquity, becoming fixed only after the fourth century as an affirmation of orthodox Trinitarianism. In its present form the Gloria Patri is based largely on the

Trinitarian formula as found in Matthew 28:19; primitive versions of it appear also in Romans 16:27, Ephesians 3:21, and 2 Peter 3:18.

Gloria in Excelsis. The Gloria in Excelsis, or "greater doxology," is an ancient Greek hymn in use since the fourth century in Eastern churches. It gradually found its way into the liturgies of the Western church, where it has generally been considered a festive hymn not sung on penitential occasions. The Gloria in Excelsis is a series of three acclamations, beginning with an antiphon based on the angelic hymn at the birth of Christ (Luke 2:14). The acclamations have been drawn from phrases used at various points in the eucharistic liturgy of the Eastern church. The first acclamation expands the theme of praise to God the Father because of the appearance of his salvation in the Messiah. The second stanza is addressed to the Son; it focuses on "the Lamb of God, who takes away the sin of the world!" (John 1:29) and on Christ in his exaltation to the right hand of the Father (Acts 2:33; 5:31). The third acclamation recalls the most primitive Christian confession of faith: "Jesus Christ is Lord!" (cf. Acts 2:23; 1 Cor. 8:6; Phil. 2:11). Recently published hymnbooks have returned to a more ancient version of the text of the Gloria in Excelsis. The full doxology appears as follows:

> Glory to God in the highest,
>   and peace to his people on earth.
> Lord God, heavenly King,
>   almighty God and Father,
>   we worship you, we give you thanks,
>   we praise you for your glory.
> Lord Jesus Christ, only Son of the Father,
>   Lord God, Lamb of God,
>   you take away the sin of the world;
>   have mercy on us;
> you are seated at the right hand of the Father;
>   receive our prayer.
> For you alone are the Holy One,

> you alone are the Lord,
> you alone are the Most High,
>   Jesus Christ,
>   with the Holy Spirit,
>   in the glory of God the Father. _Amen._

261 • Lord, Have Mercy (Kyrie)

The Kyrie Eleison, or "Lord, have mercy," is a supplication that appears in the acts of entrance in many historic liturgies. In these words, the worshipers acknowledge before a holy God their sinful state and their need of divine mercy.

The phrase "Lord, have mercy" is taken from the lips of the publican in Jesus' parable of the two men who went up to the temple to pray (Luke 18:9-14). In contrast to the self-justifying prayer of the Pharisee, the tax collector could only cry out, "God, have mercy on me, a sinner" The phrase is also used by many who begged Jesus to heal them: the blind (Matt. 9:27; 20:30-31; Mark 10:47), the lepers (Luke 17:13), a Canaanite woman whose daughter was demon-possessed (Matt. 15:22), and the father of an epileptic boy (Matt. 17:15).

The Kyrie in the liturgy usually occurs after the Gloria in Excelsis. In the early church it was considered laudatory, although in later centuries it was considered penitential and in some liturgies it followed the recitation of the commandments. The _Kyrie_ is the only part of the traditional Latin Mass that remained in the Greek language. It may be spoken or sung, and like many parts of the historic Roman rite, it has inspired powerful settings such as those of Bach's _Mass in B Minor_ or Beethoven's _Missa Solemnis._ Classically, it appears in worship in a responsive form:

> Kyrie eleison!
> _Christe eleison!_
> Kyrie eleison!
>   or
> Lord, have mercy!
> _Christ, have mercy!_
> Lord, have mercy!

TWENTY-NINE

Service of the Word

As the worship of New Testament Christians began its evolution into the historic liturgies of the church, the order of worship became differentiated into two major segments: the service of the Word and the service of the Lord's Table. Second-century sources already reveal this differentiation; recent converts to the faith were present during the time of instruction in the Scriptures and the prayers of the community but were generally dismissed before the Lord's Supper, in which only baptized and committed believers would participate. The service of the Word included the reading of Scripture, teaching by leaders of the assembly, and the prayers of the community. Gradually it came to include other acts of worship, such as creedal affirmations or confessions of sin.

262 • SCRIPTURE READING IN THE EARLY CHURCH

In the assemblies of the early church, the Scriptures were read to the congregation by a lector, or reader. This practice was modeled on that of the synagogue, wherein the Old Testament Scriptures were read aloud every Sabbath by a reader appointed from the congregation. The practice of the synagogue, in turn, had developed from the ancient concept of a literary document as something recited, rather than something read silently from a manuscript.

Reading of the Law in the Old Testament

Ancient literature in general was intended to be read aloud or recited and not to be read silently, even if written copies existed as a control. The form of ancient manuscripts suggests they were intended as guides for public reading; the very structuring of the words on written documents (all capital letters run together with no space between words) defied silent reading and required special skills of interpretation.

The poetry of the Israelite prophets was composed orally and handed down by disciples who memorized it (Isa. 8:16). Jeremiah's prophecy was read in the house of the Lord and then to the Judean royal officials, and when the king destroyed the manuscript the prophet was able to dictate it again, with additions (Jer. 36). Messages or letters, even when written down, were not properly "delivered"

until the messenger had read them to the recipient (Ezra 4:18, 23). Paul asked that his letters be shared among the local churches by being read to the congregations (Col. 4:16). Even archival material was sometimes read aloud; in the narrative of Esther, the Persian monarch, unable to sleep, had the royal chronicles read to him and thus discovered that Mordecai had never been rewarded for supplying information about a plot to assassinate the king (Est. 6:1-3).

Ancient treaties often contained a provision that the "words" or stipulations of the agreement be read periodically to those to whom the treaty had been granted. This requirement is the background for Moses' instruction that the people assemble every seven years for the reading of the Law at the Feast of Tabernacles (Deut. 31:10-11). Moses himself had read the Book of the Covenant to the Israelites at Mount Sinai (Exod. 24:7). Joshua read the Book of the Law in a ceremony at Mount Ebal (Josh. 8:34-35); in the renewal of the covenant at Shechem, Joshua's action in establishing "a statute and an ordinance," which were written "in the Book of the Law of God," suggests a public reading of the covenant stipulations (Josh. 24:25-26). Subsequent leaders, however, failed to obey the Mosaic directive; in fact, by the time of Josiah the Law had been lost and was recovered from the temple by Hilkiah the high priest. It was then read aloud by Shaphan the scribe to King Josiah (2 Kings 22:8-10), who in turn read "all the words of the Book of the Covenant" to an assembly of the people of Jerusalem in a ceremony of renewal (2 Kings 23:1-3).

Following the reestablishment of worship in Jerusalem after the Babylonian captivity, Ezra took it upon himself to read the Law to the captives returned from Babylon. Ezra was a "scribe trained in the Law," who "had set his heart to study the Law of the LORD, and to do it, and to teach the statutes and ordinances in Israel" (Ezra 7:6, 10, NRSV). After the rebuilding of the temple in Jerusalem, Ezra gathered together all the Jews to hear a reading of the Scriptures. Ezra and some trained companions "read from the book, from the Law of God, with interpretation. They gave the sense, so that the people understood the reading" (Neh. 8:8, NRSV). This indicates that the people, having been in Babylon for over 70 years, needed help in comprehending the Hebrew, as well as in understanding the meaning of the text. Thus, the reader functioned as both translator (into Aramaic) and interpreter. This event marked the beginning of a practice that took place in the temple and in synagogues.

— Scripture Reading in the Synagogue —

Even though there is no Old Testament record of the Scriptures being read in the synagogues, we know this must have become a practice from intertestamental times until the time of Jesus. The Jewish philosopher Philo, who lived at the time of Christ, described a meeting in an Essene synagogue where "one takes the books and reads them aloud, another more learned comes forward and instructs them in what they do not know" (*Quod omnis probus, liber sit*, 81–82).

The Gospel of Luke also tells about the reading of Scriptures in the synagogue. Luke 4:16-21 says that it was Jesus' custom to read the Scriptures on the Sabbath in his hometown synagogue at Nazareth. The event is described as follows:

And He came to Nazareth, where He had been brought up; and as was His custom, He entered the synagogue on the Sabbath, and stood up to read. And the book of the prophet Isaiah was handed to Him. And He opened the book and found the place where it was written, "The Spirit of the LORD is upon Me, because He anointed Me to preach the gospel to the poor. He has sent Me to proclaim release to the captives, and recovery of sight to the blind, to set free those who are downtrodden, to proclaim the favorable year of the LORD." And He closed the book, and gave it back to the attendant, and sat down; and the eyes of all in the synagogue were fixed upon Him. And He began to say to them, "Today this Scripture has been fulfilled in your hearing." (Luke 4:16-21, NASB)

The Greek expression *kata to eiōthos autō* ("according to his custom") grammatically governs the whole expression in Luke 4:16—"as was His custom, He entered the synagogue on the Sabbath and stood up to read" (NASB). Jesus was handed the scroll of Isaiah, from which he read Isaiah 61:1-2 and then proclaimed its fulfillment. Jesus selected this text because he had just been anointed with the Holy Spirit and thereby empowered for his ministry. He read the passage, then provided an explanation by way of self-fulfillment.

History tells us that the Jews first read the Law (Torah) and then the Prophets every Sabbath day in the synagogue. For example, when the apostle Paul entered the synagogue in Pisidian Antioch, it is said that Paul was given a chance to speak after "the reading from the Law and the Prophets" (Acts 13:15). Very likely, the reader of the Law would be the main teacher in the synagogue—a man trained in biblical studies. The reader of the Prophets would also have to be trained in Hebrew and in biblical interpretation. Thus, Jesus must have had this training if it was his custom to read the Prophets in his synagogue.

The important point of this brief history is that the majority of Jews never read by sight the written Hebrew Scriptures but rather received them through oral transmission by trained lectors. The lectors were those who understood the Scriptures in the original language (or in a translation such as the Septuagint); they could read the text to the congregation and could perhaps offer an interpretation. H. Lietzmann said that these readers "understood the difficult art of reading aloud at public worship with melodic and rhythmic correctness the prescribed biblical lessons out of codices written without word-division or punctuation" (*Geschichte des alten Kirche* [1911; 1961], 256; translated by E. G. Turner in *The Typology of the Early Codex* [1977], 84-85).

— Christian Reading of the Scriptures —

With respect to the oral reading of Scriptures, early Christian meetings greatly resembled the Jewish synagogue. "Public recitation of scripture which was part of Temple worship became the essential feature of synagogal worship in pre-Christian times and appears in the New Testament as a well established custom" (P. R. Ackroyd and C. F. Evans, eds., *The Cambridge History of the Bible* [Cambridge: Cambridge University Press, 1970], vol. 1, 201). In church meetings, Christians were encouraged to recite the Scriptures to one another and sing the Psalms (1 Cor. 14:26; Eph. 5:18-19; Col. 3:16). Church leaders were exhorted to read the Scriptures to their congregation (1 Tim. 4:13). Whereas the Jews would read the Law and then the Prophets, the Christians would read the Prophets (with special emphasis on messianic fulfillment) and the Gospels. Writing around A.D. 175, Justin Martyr indicated that when all the believers would assemble on the Lord's Day for worship and Communion, "the memoirs of the apostles or the writings of the prophets are read as long as time permits" (*Apology* I, 67). Melito of Sardis, speaking of a Christian meeting, said that the Scripture of the Hebrew Exodus was first read, then explained (*Cambridge History of the Bible* [1970], vol. 1, 574).

As in the synagogue, so in the early church: one person was given the task to be the reader. There are allusions and clear references to this "reader" in the New Testament. This "reader" is probably referred to in Matthew 24:15 and Mark 13:14 by way of a parenthetical expression: "let the reader understand." (The use of the singular in Greek [*ho anaginōskōn*] points to one reader—the one who read the Gospel to the congregation.) Other passages clearly point to the one who read the Scriptures aloud to an assembly of believers. In 1 Timothy 4:13, Paul urged Timothy to "devote [him]self to the public reading of Scripture." Revelation 1:3 promises a blessing to "the one who reads the words of this prophecy"—speaking specifically of each of the readers who would read the book of Revelation to each of the seven churches addressed in the book.

Some Christians who were educated and who could afford copies of the Scriptures read them in their homes. Some of the wealthier Christians had Bibles copied at their own expense and given to poorer brothers and sisters. For example, Pamphilus had Bibles copied to keep in stock for distribution to those in need (Jerome, *Against Rufinus* 1.9). And some of the writings of several early church fathers indicate that Christians were encouraged to read the Scriptures in private. Irenaeus, for one, encouraged the unrestricted use of Scripture (*Against Heresies* 5.20.2). Clement of Alexandria exhorted married couples to read the Scriptures together (*Paedagogus* 2.10.96), promoted personal study of Scripture (*Paedagogus* 3.12.87), and said that such reading should be done before the chief meal of the day (*Stromata* 7.7.49). Origen, who believed the Scriptures were accessible to all, spoke frequently of individuals reading the Scriptures at home, as well as at church (*Homily on Genesis* 2.8) and recommended that Christians read the Old Testament, Apocrypha, Psalms, Gospels, and Epistles (*Homily on Numbers* 27.10).

Although some read the Scriptures privately, the majority of early Christians never read by sight the written Scriptures but heard them read by a lector. These lectors were trained to read the texts in Greek and perhaps to provide interpretations. In the early days of the church, the reader was simply a member of the church who knew Greek well enough to read and write it. In the third century, lectors were appointed to this function but were not ordained. Hippolytus says, "The reader is appointed by the bishop's handing to him the book, for he does not have hands laid upon him" (*The Apostolic Tradition* 1.12). One such reader was Procopius (martyred in A.D. 303). Eusebius said he had rendered a great service to the church both as reader and as translator from Greek into Aramaic (*Martyrs of Palestine* 1.1). Other lectors were Pachomius and his companion Theodore, both of whom read the Scriptures to their fellow monks. After the fourth century, the lector was generally a minor church officer. According to the part of the *Apostolic Constitutions,* the reader must also be able to instruct and to explain the text. And according to Basil, in the fourth century lectors read from the Law, the Prophets, the Epistles, Acts, and the Gospels (*Apostolic Constitutions* 8.5.5).

Philip W. Comfort

263 ◆ Sermon (Homily)

The New Testament distinguishes between preaching and teaching. Preaching is the proclamation of the Messiahship of Jesus, as revealed in his ministry, death, and resurrection. Preaching, therefore, occurs not in the worship of believers but in the public forum. The worship assembly is the setting for instruction in the faith and exposition of the Word of God. Although the sermon or homily of today may be a presentation of the gospel and an appeal for commitment to Christ, it had its origin as a part of worship in the teaching activity, rather than the public preaching, of the New Testament church.

Biblical Terms for Preaching

Preaching is the proclamation of the Word of God recorded in the Bible and centered in the redemptive work of Jesus Christ. Preaching summons persons to repentance, faith, and obedience. It is God's appointed means for communicating the gospel of salvation in Christ to the unbelieving world and for strengthening the spiritual life of God's people.

Of the many New Testament terms for preaching, the most characteristic is the verb *kērussō,* "to proclaim as a herald," which occurs about sixty times (Matt. 3:1; Mark 1:14; Acts 10:42; 1 Cor. 1:23; 2 Tim. 4:2). The principal synonym is *euangelizomai,* "to announce good news, to evangelize," a common verb used more than fifty times (Luke 3:18; 4:18; Acts 5:42; Rom. 10:15; 1 Cor. 1:17). Whereas *kērussō* stresses the activity of preaching as an announcement or heralding of the action of God, *euangelizomai* accents the message that is proclaimed as one of deliverance and hope. The combination "to proclaim the gospel" is also found (Matt. 4:23; Gal. 2:2).

In view of its prominence in the New Testament, it may seem surprising that the Old Testament seldom refers to the proclamation of the prophets as "preaching." However, allowing the difference between prophetic proclamation (which is generally ascribed to a direct revelation from the Lord) and Christian preaching (which is the apostolic witness to the event of Jesus Christ), the prophets of Israel are properly regarded as the preachers of their day, the predecessors of the New Testament heralds of the gospel. The prophets proclaimed divine judgment because of the broken covenant and announced salvation to the repentant; the preacher of the early church came with a corresponding message, declaring that the covenant has been renewed in the mission, death, and resurrection of Jesus.

The Basic Content of Preaching

The synoptic Gospels summarize Jesus' public ministry as one of preaching, teaching, and healing (Matt. 4:23; Mark 1:39; Luke 4:44). His message was the good news of the kingdom of God, with its demand that people should repent and believe in the gospel (Matt. 9:35; Mark 1:14-15; Luke 4:43). By this proclamation, Jesus signified that in his ministry the sovereign power of God had invaded history to establish a new reign of righteousness in the salvation of his people. Jesus conceived of his preaching ministry as a divine commission (Mark 1:38), in fulfillment of messianic prophecy (Luke 4:18-21).

The preaching of the apostles, as reported in Acts and gleaned from scattered fragments in the Pauline epistles, seems at first glance to strike a somewhat different note. Although the apostles are still said to preach the kingdom of God (Acts 28:31), the central affirmation of their message is the identification of Jesus as Messiah, the Lord and Redeemer (Acts 2:22-36; 5:42; 11:20; 17:3; 1 Cor. 1:23-24; 2 Cor. 1:19; 4:5). This difference, however, represents not a contradiction but a progression. The kingdom of God that Jesus proclaimed achieved its triumph over the forces of evil and unleashed its creative power in the world through his own death and resurrection. In Christ, God's sovereign power acted decisively and continues to act for the salvation of his people, so that beginning with the Resurrection, to preach the kingdom is to preach Christ (cf. Acts 8:12). Jesus himself both anticipated and authorized this shift of emphasis when he commanded his disciples to be his witnesses to the ends of the earth (Acts 1:8).

The apostolic message (*kērugma*) in its essential substance can be reconstructed according to this general outline: (1) In fulfillment of Old Testament prophecy, the new age of salvation has dawned through the ministry, death, and resurrection of Jesus, now exalted as Lord and Messiah. (2) The presence of the Holy Spirit in the church testifies to Christ's present power and glory. (3) The messianic age will reach its consummation at the return of Christ in judgment. (4) God's action in Christ promises forgiveness of sins, the gift of the Holy Spirit, and eternal salvation to all who repent and believe in Jesus.

On the basis of this reconstruction the following observations can be made about the Christian message: (1) It consists of a definite body of facts. (2) It is essentially neither a doctrinal nor a philosophical system, still less an ethic, but it is a proclamation of those mighty acts in history whereby God has accomplished the salvation of his people. (3) It is centered in the person and work of Jesus Christ, especially in his cross and resurrection. (4) It is organically related to the Old Testament. (5) It imposes a forceful ethical demand on its hearers. (6) It has an eschatological dimension, looking forward to a realized fulfillment. The sermon that is inconsistent with these themes does not stand in the apostolic tradition of preaching.

Preaching and Teaching

The New Testament distinguishes between "preaching" and "teaching" (Matt. 4:23; 11:1; Eph. 4:11; 1 Tim. 2:7; 2 Tim. 1:11; 4:2-4). The publication of C. H. Dodd's *The Apostolic Preaching and Its Developments* (New York: Harper, 1937) called attention to the difference between preaching and teaching in their New Testament senses, and it became fashionable in some circles to restrict the term *preaching* to evangelistic proclamation to the unconverted. Alan Richardson, for example, wrote, "In the New Testament, preaching has nothing to do with the delivery of sermons to the converted . . . but always concerns the proclamation of the 'good tidings of God' to the non-Christian world" (*A Theological Word Book of the Bible* [New York: Macmillan, 1950], 171-172). Understood this way, preaching in the New Testament is not a worship activity, comparable to the sermon of today, but the announcement (*kērugma*) of the Christian message to the unbelieving public. Within the Christian assembly, the speaker's address might more properly be termed teaching or instruction (*didachē*), directed to already committed believers "to prepare God's people for works of service, so that the body of Christ may be built up" (Eph. 4:12). Thus, throughout the history of Christian worship, the sermon or homily has often assumed the form of extended exposition of biblical passages, doctrinal instruction, ethical exhortation, or discussion of various aspects of Christian life and experience directed to largely Christian audiences.

The New Testament contains examples of sermons in the form of instruction in the principles and practice of the life of the new covenant community, such as Jesus' Sermon on the Mount (Matt. 5–7) and the letter of James. The teaching function was an important role in the early church and one not to be taken lightly, as James himself stresses (James 3:1).

Apparently, however, it was not restricted to certain designated officers. Paul indicated that teaching is one of a number of gifts with which certain members of the congregation might be endowed (Rom. 12:7), but also noted that in the Corinthian assembly "each one . . . has a teaching" (1 Cor. 14:26, NASB). The exposition of the Scriptures during the assembly of Christian worshipers was a continuation of the practice of the synagogue; after the Babylonian exile, biblical exposition emerged as an important and regular feature of synagogue worship.

However, the distinction between preaching and teaching in the New Testament is by no means absolute. Whereas Matthew reports that Jesus went about Galilee "teaching . . . [and] preaching" (Matt. 4:23), the parallel passages employ only the word *preaching* to describe this ministry (Mark 1:39; Luke 4:44). Where Matthew and Mark represent Jesus as preaching the gospel of the kingdom (Matt. 4:17; Mark 1:14-15), Luke says, "He taught in their synagogues" (Luke 4:15). More significant still, Mark uses these two terms interchangeably (cf. Mark 1:14-15, 31, 38-39). Elsewhere in the New Testament, the apostolic testimony to Jesus is likewise described in the same reference as both "preaching" and "teaching" (Acts 5:42; 28:31; Col. 1:28).

Teaching and preaching in the New Testament are intimately related and share the same basic content: the gospel of salvation through the death and resurrection of Jesus Christ, the Son of God. Teaching is simply the extension of preaching into the regions of doctrine, apologetics, ethics, and Christian experience. Preaching includes all these elements. The difference lies in emphasis, objective, and setting. Whereas the primary thrust of preaching is evangelistic, looking to the conversion of unbelievers, teaching unfolds and applies the fullness of the gospel to the total sweep of life, challenging and enabling believers to become more mature followers of Christ. The teaching function in the context of Christian worship is the necessary extension of proclamation of the Christian message to the unconverted; it is the proclamation of "the whole purpose of God" (Acts 20:27, NASB; cf. 2 Tim. 4:2). The sermon in the context of a service of worship may be both *kērugma* and *didachē;* it may effectively appeal for conversion and commitment while instructing Christians in the teachings of Scripture and the principles of spiritual growth.

Richard A. Bodey[27]

264 ✦ Creed (Affirmation of Faith)

The historic creeds of the church have their origins in the Scriptures of the Old and New Testaments. Although the Bible contains no formal creedal statements, it contains affirmations of faith that have something of the character of the later Christian confessions. These rudimentary biblical statements were primarily acts of worship, as opposed to tests of doctrinal orthodoxy. The historic creeds have their place in traditional Christian worship, often following the sermon as a response to the proclamation of the Word of God.

Biblical Confessions of Faith

Biblical "creeds" are not precise definitions of doctrinal issues but rather acts of worship in response to God's revelation of himself through deeds of salvation and covenant faithfulness in behalf of his people. Yahweh's character as a God who reveals himself through historical events, especially through his deliverance of Israel and his granting of the covenant with his people, means that Israel typically affirms its faith by telling the story of these events. An example of this type of confession appears in Deuteronomy 26:

> Then you shall declare before the LORD your God: "My father was a wandering Aramean, and he went down to Egypt with a few people and lived there and became a great nation, powerful and numerous. But the Egyptians mistreated us and made us suffer, putting us to hard labor. Then we cried out to the LORD, the God of our fathers, and the LORD heard our voice and saw our misery, toil and oppression. So the LORD brought us out of Egypt with a mighty hand and an outstretched arm, with great terror and with miraculous signs and wonders. He has brought us to this place and gave us this land, a land flowing with milk and honey." (Deut. 26:5-9)

The fact that this affirmation of faith occurs in the setting of worship (the offering of the firstfruits) underscores its nature as an act of celebration, rather than as a theological norm.

Such confessions of faith are related to the structure of the biblical covenant, which has the form of the ancient treaty between a great king and his servant ruler. These treaties often contain a preface or prologue narrating the previous relationship between the partners and especially the deeds of the granter of the treaty in behalf of the recipient. At Mount Sinai, Yahweh begins the declaration of the covenant commandments with a brief prologue of this type, identifying himself to the people in terms of what he has done for them: "I am [Yahweh] your God, who brought you out of the land of Egypt, out of the house of slavery" (Exod. 20:2, NASB). In Israelite worship, which in its essence is the renewal of the covenant, this historical recital can become an extended narrative. This occurs in Deuteronomy 1–4, the prologue to the renewal of the covenant prior to the death of Moses. Some of the psalms (Pss. 78; 105; 106; 136) rehearse the history of Yahweh's deliverance and judgments in the same creedal fashion, and often in Psalms one hears the invitation to "give thanks," which really means to "make confession" (*hodu*) of the Lord's deeds of deliverance in faithfulness to his covenant oath: "Confess Yahweh, that he is good; for his covenant love is forever" (Ps. 136:1 AUTHOR'S TRANSLATION; cf. Ps. 100:4-5). There is a sense in which the historical narrative of the Bible as a whole, as the record of God's dealings with humankind, has this same celebrative character as a confession of faith, revealing its intrinsic association with the sphere of worship.

The familiar *Shema'* of Deuteronomy 6:4, "Hear, O Israel: The LORD our God, the LORD is one" is often called the creed of Israel, an affirmation of the distinctive monotheistic stance of biblical faith. However, it is not really a statement about the being of Yahweh but a summons to covenant loyalty, as its continuation shows: "Love the LORD your God with all your heart . . ." (Deut. 6:5). A better translation might be "Yahweh is our God, Yahweh alone!"

New Testament "creeds" have the same confessional and narrative character as the Israelite recitals. The primitive and distinctive Christian confession is "Jesus Christ is Lord" (Phil. 2:11); the context in which Paul inserts this phrase reveals its function as an act of worship as well as a Christological precept, for the apostle envisions the time when "every knee should bow, . . . and every tongue confess" the dominion of the Messiah Jesus. The affirmation that Jesus is both Lord and Christ is the heart of the apostolic proclamation, or *kērugma,* and the affirmation is grounded in a narrative of the events in which the messianic identity of Jesus has been made evident. Thus Peter, preaching on the day of Pentecost, announces that "God has made this Jesus, whom you crucified both Lord and Christ" (Acts 2:36) through the events of the Crucifixion and Resurrection (Acts 2:22-32; cf. Acts 3:14-21; 10:36-41). This early affirmation is anticipated by confessions of Jesus' messianic identity in the Gospel narratives, by disciples such as Peter (Matt. 16:16), Nathanael (John 1:49), and Thomas (John 20:28). Echoes of this early confession occur in the Epistles (1 Cor. 12:3) and in the phrase "KING OF KINGS AND LORD OF LORDS" (Rev. 19:16; cf. Rev. 17:4; 1 Tim. 6:15).

As the Lord's deliverance of Israel in the Exodus from Egypt formed the heart of the Old Testament creedal narrative, so the New Testament confession of faith centers in the narrative of the resurrection of Jesus, the pivotal act that has brought into being the "new creation" (2 Cor. 5:17), the community of the new covenant. It is the Resurrection that substantiates the confession "Jesus Christ is Lord"; the earliest Christian affirmation of faith in narrative form may have been a recital of the Resurrection appearances of Jesus, similar to that of Paul in 1 Corinthians 15:

> For what I received I passed on to you as of first importance: that Christ died for our sins according to the Scriptures, that he was buried, that he was raised on the third day according to the Scriptures, and that he appeared to Peter, and then to the Twelve. After that he appeared to more than five hundred of the brothers at the same time, most of whom are still living, though some have fallen asleep. Then he appeared to James, then to all the apostles, and last of all he appeared to me also, as to one abnormally born. (1 Cor. 15:3-8)

The witness of the New Testament is that the resurrection of Christ is the "nonnegotiable" element of Christian confession. Paul's words to the church in Rome indicate that confessing the resurrection and messiahship of Christ was part of the process of becoming "saved," or a member of the community of the new covenant; he declares "that if you confess with your mouth 'Jesus is Lord,' and believe in your heart that God raised him from the dead, you will be saved" (Rom. 10:9).

It was through the Resurrection that the new community came into being. Clustering around the confession of the lordship of the risen Christ, therefore, are other affirmations that are corollaries to the Resurrection. Thus, Paul affirms "one Lord, one faith, one baptism" (Eph. 4:5). Interestingly, the context of this phrase reveals an incipient Trinitarian creedal structure of Spirit, Lord, and Father, similar to that which was to emerge in the classic creeds of the church:

> There is one body and one Spirit—just as you were called to one hope when you were called—one Lord, one faith, one baptism; one God and Father of all, who is over all and through all and in all. (Eph. 4:4-6)

Paul records another confession, the "mystery (revelation) of godliness," in his first letter to Timothy. It takes the form of a listing of events associated with the appearance of Jesus Christ, climaxing in his exaltation:

> He appeared in a body,
>   was vindicated by the Spirit,
> was seen by angels,
>   was preached among the nations,
> was believed on in the world,
>   was taken up in glory.
>   (1 Tim. 3:16)

The letter of Jude speaks of contending "for the faith that was once for all entrusted to the saints" (Jude 3) in terms that suggest a focused and recognizable body of beliefs. The words of the author of the letter to the Hebrews similarly suggest that the "confession of our hope" (Heb. 10:23, NASB) was a definite cluster of convictions; his listing of the "elementary teachings about the Christ" (Heb. 6:1-2) may indicate something of what he had in mind.

Historic Creeds

The creedal material of the New Testament is rudimentary in form and is presented in interaction with practical issues facing the early Christian communities. The study of these materials provides insight into the process by which the tenets of Christian orthodoxy came to the surface: the Trinity, the deity and humanity of Jesus Christ, his atonement for sin, his death and resurrection, the gift of the Holy Spirit, the judgment of the world, and the catholicity and basic unity of the church. The formation of actual creeds, as tests of orthodox belief, occurred in the postapostolic period largely as a response to the spread of heterodox doctrines. Such summaries of belief began to appear in the second and third centuries with the work of theologians such as Irenaeus and Tertullian. Although a number of statements of faith were formulated by ancient councils of the church, the most important in contemporary usage is the Nicene Creed; the Apostles' Creed, which was not the work of an ecumenical council, is the other historic creed in common use in the Western church.

The Apostles' Creed. The Apostles' Creed is the oldest creed in continuous use in the church. Although its ascription to the twelve apostles is legendary, dating only from the late fourth century, most of its content dates from the middle of the second century. It was never used in the Eastern church but originated in Rome, whence it spread to other churches of Western Christendom. The "Roman Symbol," as it was originally called, was a baptismal creed, intended as a basis for the instruction of candidates for Christian initiation; it was not formulated as a comprehensive statement of Christian doctrine. The Apostles' Creed is Trinitarian in structure, an expansion of the baptismal formulary given by Jesus in the great commission (Matt. 28:18-20). The central section, confessing faith in God the Son, retains the narrative form of the creedal material found in both the Old and New Testaments.

The Apostles' Creed was a counter to the influence of Gnostic teaching, which advocated a dualistic view contrasting the pure realm of the spirit with the evil material world. Thus Gnosticism denied that the Creator God of the Old Testament was the supreme God, the Father of the Lord Jesus; it held that Christ had not been born, suffered, and died in real human flesh but had only appeared to do so; and it rejected the concept of the resurrection of the body, whether of Christ or of his followers. The Apostles' Creed refutes these precepts point by point with statements based on scriptural teaching. The exact meaning and scriptural basis for the statement "He descended into hell" has occasioned debate in recent centuries, and some churches have modified or omitted it; broadly conceived, however, the phrase may be related to the baptismal origins of the creed and the symbolic identification of the believer with Christ in his death as well as in his resurrection (Rom. 6:3-4). The full text of the Apostles' Creed, in its traditional English wording, is as follows:

> I believe in God, the Father almighty,
> maker of heaven and earth;
> And in Jesus Christ his only Son our Lord;
> who was conceived by the Holy Ghost
> born of the Virgin Mary,
> suffered under Pontius Pilate,
> was crucified, dead, and buried.
> He descended into hell.

> The third day he rose again from the dead.
> He ascended into heaven,
> and sitteth on the right hand of God the
> Father almighty.
> From thence he shall come to judge the quick
> and the dead.
> I believe in the Holy Ghost,
> the holy catholic church,
> the communion of saints,
> the forgiveness of sins,
> the resurrection of the body,
> and the life everlasting. _Amen._

The Nicene Creed. The Nicene Creed was formulated at the Council of Nicaea in A.D. 325. Whereas the Apostles' Creed was a baptismal confession, the Nicene Creed was promulgated to combat the views of Arius (c. 250-336), an Alexandrian preacher who denied the eternity of God the Son and his full deity as of "the same substance" with the Father. (Some historians, however, are of the opinion that the Nicene Creed derives ultimately from the baptismal confession of the Jerusalem church.) The creed was later revised and enlarged; although ancient sources ascribing this revision to the Council of Constantinople in A.D. 381 are of uncertain value, the creed is often termed the "Niceno-Constantinopolitan Creed." It was this larger version that came to be used in the liturgy. The Nicene Creed was the first ecumenical creed of the church, both Eastern and Western; in the Western church, the opening word of the creed was later changed from "We believe" to "I believe" (contemporary liturgical usage has restored the original wording), and in the sixth century the word meaning "and the Son" (_filioque_) was added to the clause concerning the Holy Spirit's proceeding from the Father.

The Nicene Creed was introduced into the liturgy of the Eucharist by the patriarchs of Antioch (in A.D. 473) and Constantinople (in A.D. 511); in the West, its use in the liturgy began with the Spanish Visigoths after the Third Council of Toledo (A.D. 589), and in the eleventh century it was introduced into the Roman rite under Pope Benedict VIII. In the Eastern churches, the Nicene Creed is recited just before the consecration of the Eucharist and is one of the acts of the Lord's Table or "liturgy of the faithful." In the West, it came instead to be placed after the Gospel and sermon, as a conclusion to the service of the Word.

The Nicene Creed, though longer, follows the same Trinitarian outline as the Apostles' Creed, and its central section assumes the same form of the recital of historic events associated with the incarnation, death, and resurrection of Christ. Like the Apostles' Creed, it is based on scriptural concepts, though it presses beyond biblical language, especially in its formulation of the divinity of the Son and his relationship to the Father ("God of God, Light of Light, very God of very God . . . being of one substance with the Father" [traditional wording]). As it was not set forth as a baptismal confession, the Nicene Creed omits the statement "He descended into hell." The text of the Nicene Creed, as found in many contemporary liturgies, is as follows:

> We believe in one God,
>   the Father, the Almighty,
>   maker of heaven and earth,
>   of all that is, seen and unseen.
> We believe in one Lord, Jesus Christ,
>   the only Son of God,
>   eternally begotten of the Father,
>   God from God, Light from Light,
>   true God from true God,
>   begotten, not made,
>   of one Being with the Father.
>   Through him all things were made.
>   For us and for our salvation
>   he came down from heaven;
>   by the power of the Holy Spirit
>   he became incarnate from the Virgin Mary,
>   and was made man.
>   For our sake he was crucified under Pontius
>   Pilate;
>   he suffered death and was buried.
>   On the third day he rose again
>   in accordance with the Scriptures;
>   he ascended into heaven
>   and is seated at the right hand of the Father.
>   He will come again in glory to judge the living
>   and the dead,
>   and his kingdom will have no end.
> We believe in the Holy Spirit, the Lord, the giver of
>   life,
>   who proceeds from the Father and the Son.
>   With the Father and the Son he is worshiped and
>   glorified.
>   He has spoken through the prophets.
> We believe in one holy catholic and apostolic
>   church.
> We acknowledge one Baptism for the forgiveness
>   of sins.
> We look for the resurrection of the dead,
>   and the life of the world to come. *Amen.*

The historic creeds of the church mark Christianity's transition from the Semitic culture in which the Bible took shape to the culture of Greco-Roman civilization. In the biblical perspective, "truth" is a relationship, the integrity of the covenant between God and his people. The true "word" is that which creates and maintains this living relationship. The formulation of creeds results from the adoption of another concept of "truth," that of ideas that must somehow correspond to objective facts. Here the true "word" represents agreement with a rational concept rather than an expression of personal commitment. Paul warned his disciple Timothy about getting embroiled in "quarrels about words" (1 Tim. 6:4). In formulating the creeds, the ancient church was responding to heterodox teaching. If this was a necessary step, it was also one that carried it further from a purely biblical perspective. Something was gained, and something was lost.

265 ✦ Prayers of Intercession

In the religious life of the biblical communities, as in that of the churches of today, prayer was both individual and corporate. Although the biblical worshiper always approaches the Lord as a member of a larger covenanted community, there is a distinction between prayer in general and prayer set in the context of acts of corporate worship. Because prayer is a pervasive posture and activity in the Christian life, the subject of prayer is a comprehensive one; the following discussions are confined largely to prayer as a part of the worship of the gathered community.

Prayers of intercession are petitions offered to the Lord on behalf of others: people in special personal need; those who bear particular responsibility for the welfare of others, such as leaders of church and state; the many concerns and issues affecting the church, local and universal; and the larger community of the nation and the world.

—— Intercession in Israelite Worship ——

If prayer can be broadly understood as calling on the Lord or crying out to God, the Bible contains many prayers and much material of a prayerlike nature, ranging from the appeals of the psalmists to the complaints of Moses and Jeremiah. It is striking, however, to discover that in biblical prayer the note of intercession is seldom sounded; the speaker often appeals to the Lord on his or her own behalf but rarely for other people and almost never in the context of _corporate_ prayer in the worship of the assembled community.

The book of Psalms (the first half of which is called "the prayers of David son of Jesse," Ps. 72:20) are no exception to this rule, despite their use in the worship of the gathered community. If the speaker in the Psalms is frequently the king, calling out to Yahweh as representative of the people, then the Psalms may have the effect of intercession on the nation's behalf. The intercessory form, however, is rarely used. In a few instances the speaker prays for the king (Pss. 20:1-5; 72:1-17); even here the words constitute more of a blessing than an intercession. In Psalm 122, worshipers are urged to "pray for the peace of Jerusalem" and are given the words to say (Ps. 122:6-9). When the speaker prays for the people as a whole, he does so as one of the people (Pss. 90:13-17; 144:12-15) rather than as one interceding for a third party. The psalmists know the Lord's concern for the needy, oppressed, and defenseless, but rather than intercede for them they celebrate what the Lord has already done in his providence and justice (Pss. 107; 146:7-9; 147:2-6).

The Israelite priesthood performed an intercessory function in officiating in the sanctuary worship. The priest was to "make atonement" for the worshiper in bringing his or her sacrifice before the Lord (Lev. 4–7), and the high priest performed special acts of intercession on the Day of Atonement. Although the sacrificial offerings themselves were considered the principal vehicle of intercession (Lev. 6:30), they might be accompanied by prayer calling upon the Lord to have mercy on the people. Thus Samuel interceded for Israel during a period of warfare against the Philistines; offering a lamb as a whole burnt offering, he "cried out to the LORD on Israel's behalf, and the LORD answered him" (1 Sam. 7:9). Evidently Job also was understood to have been something of a priestly intercessor; Yahweh instructs Job's friends to offer up burnt offerings for themselves and says, "My servant Job will pray for you, and I will accept his prayer and not deal with you according to your folly" (Job 42:8).

The prophets, as mediators of the covenant between the Lord and Israel, may intercede for the people, especially that the Lord's judgment may not overtake them because of their unfaithfulness. Moses is the paradigm of the prophetic intercessor, appealing to Yahweh on the basis of his promises to the Hebrew patriarchs (Exod. 32:11-13; 31-32; cf. Num. 21:7). Amos intercedes for the nation in a similar manner (Amos 7:2, 5). Jeremiah's words to the people during the last days of the kingdom of Judah highlight the customary role of prophets as intercessors on behalf of the community: "If they are prophets and have the word of the LORD, let them plead with the LORD Almighty" (Jer. 27:18). King Zedekiah himself sent to Jeremiah, asking him to intercede for the nation (Jer. 37:3). Although the prophetic intercessions are not liturgical acts in a corporate setting, the relationship of the prophets to the sanctuary and to the renewal and maintenance of Israel's covenant with Yahweh places such acts within the broader framework of worship.

In the Old Testament, the magnificent exception to the general absence of intercessory liturgical prayer is the prayer of Solomon at the dedication of the temple (2 Chron. 6:14-42). The king intercedes with the Lord on behalf of those who may sin or on behalf of the nation should it experience defeat, drought, famine, pestilence, captivity, or another consequence of the Lord's judgment. He even intercedes for the foreigner, that Yahweh might respond to his requests. The entire prayer is based on the understanding that difficulties encountered are the result of the Lord's judgment on sin and that the deepest need of all people is the application of his forgiveness and covenant love: "Hear thou from heaven thy dwelling place; and when thou hearest, forgive" (2 Chron. 6:21, RSV).

Intercession in the New Testament

The New Testament does not record any intercessory prayers as specific acts of the church's worship; there is no mention of corporate intercession, for example, in the various accounts of the Lord's Supper. However, Jesus' great prayer on the night of his arrest (John 17) is the intercession of the Lord on behalf of his disciples that they may be unified and protected from evil. While not a corporate prayer, it is a model of intercession with a liturgical stamp, and its setting on the night of the Last Supper (though John has omitted mention of the ordinance) places it in the context of early Christian worship. This prayer is often called Jesus' "high priestly prayer," a reminder that Jesus as the great High Priest (Heb. 4:14) continues to intercede for "those who come to God through him" (Heb. 7:25). There is a similar liturgical quality to Paul's prayer at the beginning of his letter to the Ephesians, which begins in the form of Jewish _bᵉrakhah_ or blessing (Eph. 1:3) and then moves into an intercessory mode (Eph. 1:15-19) as he prays that his readers will know the fullness of the Father's glory and the greatness of their calling in Christ.

Intercessory prayer is encouraged in several places in the New Testament. James calls on the person who is ill to ask the elders of the church to pray for him, both for restoration and for forgiveness of sin, and invites Christians to "pray for each other" (James 5:14-16). Paul, writing to the pastor Timothy, urges him to see that "requests, prayers, intercession and thanksgiving be made for everyone—for kings and all those in authority" (1 Tim. 2:1-2); such prayers are the response to God's desire for "all men to be saved and to come to a knowledge of the truth" (1 Tim. 2:4). In the Old Testament, an intercessor was one who stood in a special relationship of consecration to the Lord, as prophet, priest, or king. In the New Testament, all these roles are summed up in Christ and are conveyed also to his people in the community of the new covenant. Thus the church as a body is a royal priesthood (1 Pet. 2:9) and a prophetic assembly (1 Cor. 14:1, 24-25) and assumes the intercessory role in corporate worship.

— Prayers of Intercession in the Church —

The ancient church incorporated acts of general prayer and intercession into its observance of the Lord's Supper. Justin Martyr, writing in the middle of the second century, indicates that prayers "for all men everywhere" were included in the liturgy preceding the celebration of the Eucharist (*Apology* I, 65). Such prayers have continued as a regular part of Christian worship. Although for many centuries only the officiating clergy would offer prayers of intercession, the liturgical renewal movement in the traditional denominations has restored much of the ancient congregational participation. In some churches a kind of "bidding" form is used, in which the leader invites worshipers to offer spontaneous prayers for various stated needs. At other times, the act of intercession may take the form of a litany or responsive prayer, as in this example from *The Book of Common Prayer*:

Father, we pray for your holy catholic church;
 That we all may be one.
Grant that every member of the church may truly
 and humbly serve you,
 That your name may be glorified by all people.

We pray for all bishops, priests, and deacons;
 That they may be faithful ministers of your Word and sacraments.
Give us grace to do your will in all that we
 undertake;
 That our works may find favor in your sight.
Have compassion on those who suffer from any
 grief or trouble;
 That they may be delivered from their distress. . . .
We praise you for your saints who have entered into joy;
 May we also come to share in your heavenly kingdom. Let us pray for our own needs and those of others.
 [*Silence.*]

266 ✦ CONFESSION OF SIN

In traditional Christian worship, acts of confession of sin may appear in the acts of entrance, the service of the Word, or at the Lord's Table in association with the prayer of thanksgiving. In the worship of the contemporary liturgical renewal, the confession of sin usually occurs after the prayers of intercession, marking the transition into the service of the Lord's Table. Prayers of confession are not usually found in the corporate worship of evangelical and charismatic churches; confession of sin is an act that usually accompanies individual conversion to Christ and personal counseling situations, rather than the life of the gathered assembly.

The concept of "confession" in the Bible is broader than the confession of sin; it includes above all the acknowledgment of the historic saving deeds of the Lord. Confession thus has a dominant creedal element that focuses attention on God rather than on the worshiper. Biblical worship is typically not introspective, as worship tends to be in contemporary North American culture. The Hebrew word for "making confession" means to confess Yahweh: to "confess [his] name" (1 Kings 8:33) and to acknowledge his acts in behalf of his people; it is often translated "give thanks." Israel is often invited to "Confess Yahweh, that he is good; for his covenant love is forever" (Ps. 136:1, AUTHOR'S TRANSLATION). Confession is "agreement with God" in the sense of ratification of his offer of covenant.

This does not mean that the biblical worshiper is unmindful of sin in approaching the Lord. On the contrary, the majesty and dignity of the Holy One frequently evoke an acute consciousness of the worshiper's sinful estate. One thinks of the archetypical experience of Isaiah, beholding in vision the presence of the Lord of Hosts in the sanctuary, and crying, "Woe to me! . . . I am ruined! For I am a man of unclean lips, and I live among a people of unclean lips" (Isa. 6:5). The sin of which Isaiah is conscious is not in the first instance his violation of moral precepts or of the laws of God; rather, it is the deeper sin of having trespassed into forbidden territory, the creature's fleeting glimpse of the glory of his Creator: "My eyes have seen the King, the LORD Almighty." It is not humanity's meditation on itself that calls forth confession of sin but the revelation of the surpassing worth of the awesome God: "Man shall not see me and live" (Exod. 33:20, RSV). Biblical confession is always God-centered.

The sacrificial worship of the Israelite sanctuary was based on the worshiper's awareness of the distance between him or her, as a member of an all-too-often faithless and indifferent people, and Yahweh in his holiness and faithfulness to the covenant. While prayers of confession of sin are not typically part of the sacrificial worship, it is the Lord's express desire that his people "humble themselves and pray and seek my face and turn from their wicked ways" (2 Chron. 7:14).

Thus prayers of confession are found in the Davidic worship of the Psalms, which express a personal and intense relationship between the Lord and his "godly ones" or ḥᵃsidim (Pss. 50:5, NASB; 149:5 NASB), those returning his covenant love. For such worshipers, consciousness of having violated the divine commandments can become a matter of acute spiritual crisis, as given voice in David's outcry:

> Against you, you only, have I sinned
>   and done what is evil in your sight,
> so that you are proved right when you speak
>   and justified when you judge. . . .
> Do not cast me away from your presence
>   or take your Holy Spirit from me. (Ps. 51:4, 11)

The psalmists recognize the necessity of confession of sin in order to open oneself to the forgiveness of God, to restore the broken relationship:

> When I kept silent, my bones wasted away
>   through my groaning all day long.
> For day and night your hand was heavy upon me;
>   my strength was sapped as in the heat of summer.
>   _Selah_.
> Then I acknowledged my sin to you
>   and did not cover up my iniquity.

> I said, "I will confess my transgressions to the
>   LORD"—
> and you forgave the guilt of my sin. _Selah_.
> Therefore let everyone who is godly pray to you
>   while you may be found. (Ps. 32:3-6)

Although such prayers are offered in the form of an individual confession, the speaker—especially in the role of the king—represents the community as a whole. Moreover, the use of the Psalms in the celebrations of the sanctuary, through the performance of the Levitical singers and musicians, places their confessional portions, along with all else, within the orbit of corporate worship.

There are also psalms (such as Pss. 78; 106) that specifically address the corporate sin of the nation in the form of extended confessions of both Yahweh's deeds of deliverance and the people's rebellion and unfaithfulness:

> But then they would flatter him with their mouths,
>   lying to him with their tongues.
> Their hearts were not loyal to him,
>   they were not faithful to his covenant.
>   (Ps. 78:36-37)

> We have sinned even as our fathers did;
>   we have done wrong and acted wickedly.
>   (Ps. 106:6)

The psalmists are aware that the sin of the community is not hidden from the Lord; they call on him for his mercy:

> You have set our iniquities before you,
>   our secret sins in the light of your
>   presence. (Ps. 90:8)

> Do not hold against us the sins of the fathers;
>   may your mercy come quickly to meet us,
>   for we are in desperate need. (Ps. 79:8)

Similar confessions of sin are found in the utterances of individual spokespersons for the Israelite community during the Exile and the following period of restoration. Lamentations, written by Jeremiah, is a confession of national sin. The prophet Daniel prayed a prayer (Dan. 9:4-19) acknowledging that the curse of Yahweh's judgment was justified by the unfaithfulness of the people (cf. 2 Chron. 6:37). He pleaded with the Lord to turn his wrath away from Jerusalem and to restore his presence in the sanctuary. Nehemiah prayed a prayer of the same type upon learning of the distress of the remnant in Judea in the early postexilic years (Neh. 1:5-11). While not corporate prayers, these confessions may have been based on liturgical models recalled from the suspended worship of the Jerusalem sanctuary.

The early Christians were a community gathered around the joyous "good news" of the Resurrection and the restoration of the broken covenant in Jesus Christ. The church viewed itself as the "Jerusalem that is above" which was freed from the bondage of guilt under the law (Gal. 4:26); for those spiritually reborn in Christ, "therefore, there is now no condemnation" (Rom. 8:1-2). As the bride of Christ, the church is "the Holy City, the new Jerusalem" (Rev. 21:2), a "general festal gathering" (*panēguris,* Heb. 12:22 AUTHOR'S TRANSLATION). The New Testament church was a celebrative assembly in which corporate prayers of confession of sin were out of place. The church's confession was confession of Jesus Christ as the incarnate Son of God (1 John 4:15; 2 John 2:7), the anticipation of a universal confession "that Jesus Christ is Lord, to the glory of God the Father" (Phil. 2:11).

That *individual* Christians might sin, however, was readily acknowledged, and provision was made for the worshiper to confess his or her faults and be restored. Thus James urged believers to "confess your sins to each other and pray for each other so that you may be healed" (James 5:16), while John reminded the church that Jesus Christ is its Advocate with the Father, and that "if we confess our sins, he is faithful and just and will forgive us our sins and purify us from all unrighteousness" (1 John 1:9).

The recognition of persistent human failure and unfaithfulness, even within the community of those who had responded to the call of God in Christ, eventually led to the inclusion of prayers of corporate confession into Christian liturgies, often as acts of preparation for participation in the Lord's Supper or Holy Communion. An example of a contemporary prayer of general confession, based on historic models, is taken from the *Lutheran Book of Worship* (Minneapolis: Augsburg Publishing House, 1978):

Most merciful God, we confess that we are in bondage to sin and cannot free ourselves. We have sinned against you in thought, word, and deed, by what we have done and by what we have left undone. We have not loved you with our whole heart; we have not loved our neighbors as ourselves. For the sake of your Son, Jesus Christ, have mercy on us. Forgive us, renew us, and lead us, so that we may delight in your will and walk in your ways, to the glory of your holy name. *Amen.*

Richard C. Leonard

THIRTY

Service of the Lord's Table

Ancient Christian worship was based on the celebration of the Lord's Supper; the service of the Word was followed by the service of the Lord's Table. Participation in the rites of the Lord's Supper was limited to baptized believers; those still receiving instruction as new converts to the faith were dismissed following the service of the Word. The eucharistic liturgies of the historic denominations include a variety of acts of the Lord's Table deriving from ancient practice and ultimately from scriptural precedent. This discussion is confined to those major actions likely to be found in the traditional worship of many churches.

267 • THE EXCHANGE OF PEACE

Most contemporary Christian liturgies include an exchange of peace, in which worshipers greet those around them with expressions such as "The peace of the Lord be with you." The exchange is usually accompanied by physical contact such as a handclasp or, where appropriate, an embrace. This act is of ancient origin and was originally known as the "kiss of peace"; other terms for it are "passing the peace" or "sign of peace." It often takes place at the beginning of the service of the Lord's Table as an expression of the reconciliation of believers with one another through their common reconciliation with God in Christ.

In concluding his letters to local churches, the apostle Paul several times urged his readers to "greet one another with a holy kiss" (Rom. 16:16; 1 Cor. 16:20; 2 Cor. 13:12; cf. 1 Thess. 5:26). Peter likewise ended his first letter, "Greet one another with a kiss of love. Peace to all of you who are in Christ" (1 Pet. 5:14). This gesture was a sign of the reconciliation and unity that mark the lives of believers within the body of Christ; it was a symbol of the peace of the community of the new covenant. Admonitions to peaceable living appear in the Epistles, as in Paul's description of the transformed life in Romans 12 (Rom. 12:18), his remarks on dissolution of marriage with a departing unbeliever (1 Cor. 7:15), and his concluding exhortations in the second letter to the Corinthians (2 Cor. 13:11).

The New Testament concept of peace (*eirēnē*) is based on the Hebrew *shalom* and embodies not simply the absence of strife but, more importantly, the wholeness, blessing, and salvation that are the benefits of the Lord's covenant and of the *koinōnia*, or mutuality and communion, that flow from life in Christ. Peace—together with joy in the Spirit and righteousness, or faithfulness to God's covenant—forms the substance of the kingdom of God (Rom. 14:17). The worshiping community of those made new in Christ is to be the embodiment of the peace of Christ, in whom the divisive walls of human culture, tradition, and ethnicity, epitomized in the Jew-Gentile dichotomy, are broken down (Eph. 4:13-19). John declares that lack of love, or lack of commitment to the welfare of others, is inconsistent with commitment to God: "for anyone who does not love his brother, whom he has seen, cannot love God, whom he has not seen" (1 John 4:20). Such commitment finds expression in gestures and deeds of peace within the worshiping assembly.

The link between peace, symbolized in the "holy kiss" or "kiss of peace," and the Lord's Supper may be seen both in Jesus' action on the night of his arrest and in Paul's teaching on the Last Supper. In his discourse to the disciples in the Upper Room, Jesus concluded his promise of the coming of the Holy Spirit with these words: "Peace I leave with you; my peace I give you. I do not give-to you as the world gives" (John 14:27). Appearing to them after the Resurrection, perhaps during an evening meal, Jesus spoke the greeting of peace: "Peace be with you!"

(John 20:19). In celebrating the Supper of the Lord, early Christians would have recalled the association of their common meal with the declaration of the Lord's peace.

Paul, in his exposition of the Lord's Supper (1 Cor. 10:16-17; 11:17-34), views the broken bread as symbolic of common participation or *koinōnia* in the "body of Christ" (1 Cor. 10:16). By the "body" he means not the literal flesh of Jesus but the "one body" of the Spirit (Eph. 4:4), which is Christ's church. Eating the meal as an act of individual consumption, in a factious and self-centered manner, invalidates it as the Lord's Supper (1 Cor. 11:18-21). This failure to "recognize the body" therefore brings judgment—spiritual exclusion from the covenant and its blessings—upon the careless (1 Cor. 11:29). The exchange of peace at the Lord's Table is a sign of "recognizing the body," the community of faith. It is the recognition of the worshipers' awareness "that we are very members incorporate in the mystical body of thy Son, which is the blessed company of all faithful people" (as the 1928 *Book of Common Prayer* so well expressed).

The greeting, or kiss, of peace became part of the service of the Lord's Table by the middle of the second century. Justin Martyr (*Apology* I, 66) describes it thus: "We salute one another with a kiss when we have ended the prayers. Then is brought to the president of the brethren bread and a cup of water and wine." The form of the exchange of peace has been subject to variation due to cultural differences regarding appropriate forms of physical contact. Originally it was a type of kiss, a customary gesture of close relationship found frequently in the Bible (for example, Esau and Jacob, Gen. 33:4; Joseph and his brothers, Gen. 45:15; Jonathan and David, 1 Sam. 20:41; the Ephesian elders and Paul, Acts 20:37) and still observed in Eastern cultures, having no sexual overtones and being exchanged between members of the same sex. In the early church, men and women probably worshiped in separate sections of the assembly and did not kiss or embrace unrelated members of the opposite sex. The ancient Christian practice of exchanging the sign of peace fell out of common usage for many centuries but has been restored in the liturgical revival of the twentieth century.

268 • THE GREAT THANKSGIVING

The sequence of liturgical actions immediately preceding the partaking of the Lord's Supper has often been called the "great thanksgiving." These acts may include the Sanctus ("Holy, Holy, Holy"), the eucharistic prayer incorporating the invocation of the Spirit (epiklēsis), and the words of institution. The great thanksgiving may be concluded by the Lord's Prayer. The order of these components varies in the practice of different churches, and they may not all be present. The constant element is the words of delivery, which occur in almost all observances of the Lord's Supper, regardless of Christian tradition.

"Holy, Holy, Holy" (Sanctus)

The "Holy, Holy, Holy" is a hymn of praise or doxology typically found in the liturgy preceding the receiving of the Lord's Supper. From its Greek version it is sometimes called the Trisagion or "thrice holy." The text of the Sanctus, as used in most worshiping communities, is as follows:

Holy, Holy, Holy Lord, God of power and might,
Heaven and earth are full of your glory.
   Hosanna in the highest.
Blessed is he who comes in the name of the Lord.
   Hosanna in the highest.

The first part of the Sanctus is taken verbatim from the hymn of the seraphs, or "burning ones," in Isaiah's vision of the majesty of the Lord (Isa. 6:3), a vision in which he received his call as a prophet of the Lord. The hymn articulates something of the wonder and adoration of all creatures before their Creator, who is called the Lord of Hosts, or armies (*Yahveh tz²va'ot*). Because of the use of this name, associated with Yahweh's enthronement above the ark of the covenant and because of the other imagery of the vision (coals taken from the altar, the sanctuary filled with the smoke of incense, the antiphonal chanting of the seraphs reminiscent of the interplay of the priestly choirs), it is likely that the context for Isaiah's vision was his participation in an actual festal liturgy at the Jerusalem sanctuary, the "house of the LORD."

The second part of the "Holy, Holy, Holy," the Hosanna, is based on the words of Psalm 118:25-26. The Hebrew *hoshi'ah-na'* is a cry for deliverance: "Save, we beseech thee!" The psalm is a liturgy in which a blessing is pronounced on those who enter the sanctuary in the name of the Lord; it focuses especially on the entrance of the king, having been delivered in battle against his enemies (cf. Ps. 118:10-18). The acclamation was echoed in the shouts of Jesus' disciples as he first entered Jerusalem in the week of his death and resurrection (Luke 19:38). The Hosanna gives the Sanctus a christological character, reminding worshipers of the fullness of the holy God dwelling in his incarnate Son (Col. 2:9). Christ ever comes as "KING OF KINGS AND LORD OF LORDS" (Rev. 19:16) when his people gather to celebrate his victory and declare his dominion.

The "Holy, Holy, Holy" is a fitting expression of the worshiping church's awe before the mystery of the presence of God. The Sanctus and Hosanna convey an awareness of the real presence of the Lord in his sanctuary, as his people gather to celebrate their bond with him in the covenant meal. But, although the Eucharist is a sacramental act pointing through physical objects to spiritual realities, the "Holy, Holy, Holy" does not necessarily suggest to Christians that the Lord's presence is coextensive with the elements of the Lord's Supper and their architectural surroundings. In New Testament imagery the sanctuary to which the Lord comes, in which he is blessed and exalted as holy, is the assembly of his worshipers (1 Cor. 3:16-17; 2 Cor. 6:16; Eph. 2:21; Rev. 21:3).

Eucharistic Prayer

In all Christian traditions the receiving of the Lord's Supper is accompanied by prayer. The content and thrust of such prayer differ from church to church. In historic Christian worship, however, two themes have predominated: thanksgiving to God for his acts of redemption culminating in Christ's giving of himself, and the invocation of the Holy Spirit on the congregation and on the gifts of bread and wine. The eucharistic prayer is sometimes called the prayer of consecration.

Thanksgiving. The word *Eucharist* means thanksgiving and refers to Jesus' act of blessing the Father and giving thanks as he distributed to his disciples the loaf and cup of the Last Supper (Matt. 26:26-27). Jesus' giving of thanks was consistent with Jewish custom of the period. At the end of a common meal, the host would offer thanks over the "cup of blessing"; this prayer had three themes: thanksgiving for

the food and for God's providence, thanksgiving for the covenant and the redemption of the people of God, and a prayer for the reunification of the faithful in the kingdom of God. The eucharistic prayer transposes these same themes into the framework of the new covenant centering in Jesus Christ.

Both the *Didachē* and the *First Apology* of Justin Martyr attest that by the middle of the second century the practice was for the president of the assembly to give thanks over the bread and wine. In keeping with Jesus' example, the eucharistic prayer may begin with a blessing or doxology. The body of the prayer typically takes the form of a recital of God's action to redeem his people through Jesus Christ. This is seen in the eucharistic prayer quoted by Hippolytus from the early third century:

> We render thanks to you, O God, through your beloved Servant Jesus Christ, whom in the last times you sent to us as Savior and Redeemer and Messenger of your will; who is your inseparable Word, through whom you made all things, and in whom you were well pleased.
> You sent him from heaven into the Virgin's womb; and, conceived in the womb, he was made flesh and was manifested as your Son, being born of the Holy Spirit and the Virgin.
> Fulfilling your will and gaining for you a holy people, he stretched out his hands when he should suffer, that he might release from suffering those who have believed in you.
> And when he was betrayed to voluntary suffering that he might destroy death, and break the bonds of the devil, and tread down hell, and shine upon the righteous, and fix the limit, and manifest the resurrection, he took bread, and gave thanks to you . . . (Hippolytus, *The Apostolic Tradition* 4.4-9)

The same narrative form, similar to that of biblical creedal statements, is found in the eucharistic prayers of many contemporary liturgies; the recital of God's deeds of creation and of the deliverance of his people culminates in thanksgiving for the salvation made available through Jesus Christ. Such is the case in this example from the *Lutheran Book of Worship* (1978):

> Holy God, mighty Lord, gracious Father: endless is your mercy and eternal your reign.
> You have filled all creation with light and life; heaven and earth are full of your glory.

Through Abraham you promised to bless all nations.
  You rescued Israel, your chosen people.
Through the prophets you renewed your promise;
  and, at this end of all the ages, you sent your Son,
  who in words and deeds proclaimed your kingdom and was obedient to your will, even to giving
  his life.

In evangelical and charismatic churches, prayer during the administration of the Lord's Supper usually
focuses on the death of Christ in atonement for sin,
with the intent that partaking of the Supper might
be of spiritual benefit to the worshipers in reminding them of Christ's sacrifice. However, the note of
thanksgiving is often present as well, especially
thanksgiving for that salvation in Christ of which
the Lord's Supper is a symbol.

Invocation of the Spirit. The *epiklēsis,* or invocation
of the Holy Spirit, is based on Jesus' promise of the
Holy Spirit as recorded in the Gospels and in the
Acts of the Apostles. In his discourse to the disciples
at the Last Supper, Jesus affirmed that he would send
the Helper, the Spirit of truth, to guide his followers
after his departure and to glorify him (John 16:7-15).
Appearing to the disciples after his resurrection,
Jesus further declared that the Holy Spirit would
come upon the church, empowering it for witness
to the gospel (Acts 1:8).

The New Testament accounts of the institution of
the Lord's Supper do not expressly link it with the
Holy Spirit, but rather with the body of covenanted
believers; the connection with the Spirit is supplied
by the vital role of the Holy Spirit in the life of the
church as the body of Christ. The biblical history of
the apostolic church and the teaching of the New
Testament Epistles both stress the dependence of
the church on the Holy Spirit. There is "one body
and one Spirit" (Eph. 4:4); those who are Christ's
live in the resurrection by the Spirit of Christ (Rom.
8:11), having confessed his lordship by the Spirit
(1 Cor. 12:3). As Christian liturgy developed, prayers
began to be offered, invoking the Spirit's presence
both upon the elements of the Lord's Supper—the
emblems of the body—and upon the people celebrating through these gifts. An early example is the
epiklēsis from the eucharistic prayer quoted in *The
Apostolic Tradition* of Hippolytus:

And we ask that you would send your Holy Spirit
upon the offering of your holy church; that, gathering them into one, you would grant to all who partake of the holy things [to partake] for the fullness of
the Holy Spirit for the confirmation of faith in truth.
(Hippolytus, *The Apostolic Tradition* 4.13)

In traditional worship, the invocation of the Spirit
may precede or follow the words of institution. In
this example from *The Book of Common Prayer,* the
invocation comes just before the concluding doxology of the eucharistic prayer:

Sanctify them [that is, the gifts of bread and wine] by
  your Holy Spirit to be for your holy people the
  body and blood of your Son, the holy food and
  drink of new and unending life in him. Sanctify us
  also that we may faithfully receive this holy sacrament, and serve you in unity, constancy, and
  peace; and at the last day bring us with all your
  saints into the joy of your eternal kingdom.
All this we ask through your Son Jesus Christ. By
  him, and with him, and in him, in the unity of the
  Holy Spirit all honor and glory are yours, Almighty Father, now and for ever. *Amen.*

———— Words of Institution ————

The words of institution are the biblical narrative
of Jesus' institution of the Lord's Supper. Almost
universally, they have been included in the observance of the Lord's Supper in Christian worship. In
liturgical churches and others with more traditional
forms of worship, the words of institution are
printed in the service book or hymnal as part of the
great thanksgiving; in evangelical and charismatic
churches, the minister, deacon, or other officiant
may read them directly from the Bible. The words
of institution are usually quoted from Paul's account
of the Supper in 1 Corinthians 11:

For I received from the Lord what I also passed on to
you: The Lord Jesus, on the night he was betrayed,
took bread, and when he had given thanks, he broke
it and said, "This is my body, which is for you; do
this in remembrance of [him]." In the same way after
supper he took the cup, saying, "This cup is the new
covenant in my blood; do this, whenever you drink
it, in remembrance of me." For whenever you eat
this bread and drink this cup, you proclaim the
Lord's death until he comes. (1 Cor. 11:23-26)

In addition to narrating Jesus' acts of distributing the
bread and the cup, the words of institution as given

by Paul introduce several interpretive concepts. First, Jesus ordained that his followers continue to practice the ceremony, "in remembrance of [him]." The Greek word *anamnēsis* refers not merely to remembering but to "recalling" in the sense of making present once again. Understood in this way, the Lord's Supper is a sacramental action serving as a vehicle for the intensified awareness of Christ's presence with his church. The understanding of how this presence of Christ is related to the elements of the Lord's Supper differs among Christian traditions. As to what Jesus himself meant by "in remembrance," we must bear in mind that we have his words only in Greek translation. What is clear is that the observance of the Lord's Supper, under any historic theological understanding, is in obedience to the ordinance of Christ.

Jesus spoke of "the new covenant in [his] blood." The Lord's Supper is a sign of the restoration of the covenant broken by the unfaithfulness of Israel, in the "new covenant" announced by Jeremiah (Jer. 31:31-34). The concept of *covenant* in the Lord's Supper places the emphasis on the common life of the community of Christian disciples in interrelationship with one another and with the God who dwells in their midst (Exod. 25:8; Ezek. 37:27; Rev. 21:3). The cup represents the blood of the sacrifice, which enacts the covenant (Exod. 24:6-8), and the Supper as a whole is the meal that ratifies the new covenant (Exod. 24:11). Since the Lord God, in granting the covenant, stands in the place of the great King, the Lord's Supper is also a declaration of the kingdom of God.

Third, Paul interprets the Lord's Supper as a proclamation of the Lord's death in anticipation of his coming. Paul may have in mind Jesus' statement at the Last Supper that he would not partake of it again until the arrival of the kingdom (Luke 22:15-18). In the New Testament, the "coming" of Christ is anticipated as a judgment on sin and disregard for the laws of God (Acts 17:31; 1 Thess. 5:3; 2 Thess. 2:8) and also as the gathering up and transformation of his elect (Mark 13:27; 1 Cor. 15:22-23; 1 Thess. 4:16-17; 1 John 3:2). And, since the atoning death of Christ has freed from bondage to the old system all those who have united with him in his death (Rom. 6:3; Gal. 3:13; Col. 2:12-14), the proclamation of his death also looks forward to the redemption of the children of God (Rom. 8:23; Col. 3:3-4). For first-century Christians, there was an immediacy to the expectation of Christ's coming, for "in just a very little while, he who is coming will come and will not delay" (Heb. 10:37).

Robert E. Webber

269 ◆ The Lord's Prayer (Our Father)

The "Lord's Prayer" and "Our Father" are traditional names given to the set of petitions and doxologies recorded in Matthew 6:9-13 and Luke 11:2-4, which Jesus gave his disciples as a model or example for prayer. The prayer has been included in the catechisms and liturgies of most Christian traditions since the period of the apostolic fathers, usually in close association with the partaking of the Lord's Supper.

Text and Setting

The Lord's Prayer is the most widely known passage from the Bible, so familiar that it is usually known by its opening words: "Our Father." In many circles of Western Christianity it is the only part of the Scripture handed down by oral tradition, many members of the community having learned it from memory before being able to read it in the printed Bible, hymnal, or prayer book. Church bulletins usually do not need to print its words in the order of service.

Although Jesus evidently spoke the Lord's Prayer in Aramaic, the oldest sources are the Greek Gospels; the ancient Syriac (Aramaic) version appears to be a retranslation from the Greek rather than an independent Aramaic recension. The text of the prayer is given in Matthew's narrative of the Sermon on the Mount (Matt. 5–7), in which Jesus taught a large crowd on the shore of the Sea of Galilee. The version of the prayer given by Luke is not set in the same historical situation but is included in that portion sometimes known as the Perean ministry, after Jesus' departure from Galilee. The Lukan version is shorter and is incorporated into a general discourse on prayer (Luke 11:1-13).

The Lord's Prayer is really intended to be the Disciples' Prayer; the real "Lord's Prayer" of the gospel record is the prayer of Jesus on the night of his arrest (John 17). Although Jesus taught the Lord's Prayer as a model to follow, rather than a fixed liturgical recitation, apparently he himself repeated it, with variations, in teaching on different occasions. For this reason, alternate versions continued to be used devotionally in different circles of disciples, and these versions have passed into the corporate worship of the church in various localities. This probably accounts for the existence of more than one form of the prayer in the inspired Word of the Gospels.

Outline and Analysis

Analysis of the Lord's Prayer reveals a clear outline that balances petition with praise, especially when the traditional concluding doxology is taken into account.

Address. The address, or invocation, of the prayer follows, in both cases, a discourse on prayer by Jesus. The early church seems to have adopted certain liturgical phrases that combined Aramaic with Greek, as in the "Abba! Father" of Romans 8:15; the vocative "Father" was the common address for God. Although there is evidence of this familiar form of address in ancient Jewish prayer, it does not appear to have been popular within rabbinic Judaism until after the beginning of the Christian era. It is more likely that Jesus here expressed the common piety of the people, giving it the stamp of his own unique relationship with the Father. The specific sense in which God's fatherhood is interpreted has been a matter of debate. It may refer to God's creative fatherhood (Deut. 32:6), to God's special relationship with Israel (Jer. 3:4), or to God's fatherhood by virtue of redemption (Isa. 63:16). It is worth noting, however, that "father" is a title sometimes used in ancient treaties for the overlord granting a covenant to a client king, a fact that relates the address "Father" to much of the subsequent content of the prayer. The additional phrase "who is in heaven" is characteristic of the qualifying usage of both Judaism and the Gospel of Matthew; it is a reminder that the being of God transcends the efforts of people to restrict his presence within temples, religious systems, and the categories of human understanding.

First Petition: "Hallowed be your name." That is, "May your name be held in reverence." This clause refers to the giving of Yahweh's covenant name to Moses (Exod. 3:13-14) and to the requirement of the Decalogue that his name not be invoked to a purpose contrary to the covenant (Exod. 20:7). The Lord's name in the Bible is not merely his appellation but the characteristic revelation of himself to his worshipers. All the qualities he has disclosed in his covenant and in his working in history are summarized in the knowledge of his name, especially his covenant love or faithfulness to his word, since it

is by his name or reputation that the covenant stands. To defile, deface, subvert, or dishonor the divine name is to reject the sovereignty of God and abrogate his covenant. Appeals to "bless the name" of the Lord were commonplace in Jewish prayers of the time and are found in the Psalms (Pss. 96:2; 100:4; 103:1). The hallowing or sanctifying of the divine name is the recognition of its being "set apart" for the special use of God's worshipers. The petition does not restrict reverence for God's name to any designated time or space but is universal in its scope: the sovereign presence of God, invoked in his name, is to be kept holy in every area of life and throughout the cosmos.

Second Petition: "**Your kingdom come, your will be done, on earth as it is in heaven.**" Few biblical concepts are as pervasive as the kingdom, or sovereignty, of God. The term is synonymous with the covenant, for in granting his people a treaty Yahweh stands in the position of the Great King. The celebration of the Lord's dominion lies at the heart of Israelite worship and finds expression especially in the enthronement psalms (Pss. 47; 93; 95–99; *cf.* Pss. 24; 29; 68; 132). Jesus inaugurated his public ministry with his announcement of the restoration of the kingdom of God (Mark 1:14-15), and the sovereignty of God was the theme of his teaching, the source of his signs and wonders, and the reality demonstrated in his passion, death, and resurrection.

By parallelism, the petition "your kingdom come," or "may your kingdom come," is interpreted by the phrases, "may your will be done, as in heaven so upon earth." The kingdom is the application of the sovereignty of God not only in the realm of the transcendent but also in the here-and-now of human culture and personal issues of life. As this is the prayer of Jesus' disciples, the dominion of the sovereign God must begin first of all in their personal obedience; the will of God is the goal of Christian ethics and the norm of Christian behavior, and must certainly be the governing factor in their life together as a church. The teaching of Scripture on God's will must be applied and reapplied in each situation by the people of God. But since the Lord is "the Judge of all the earth" (Gen. 18:25), there are societal and cosmic dimensions to the kingdom. God's will applies to the created order, for all things owe their existence to that will and to its expression in the Word that has ordained them (Ps. 33:6; Isa.

40:21-26; John 1:1-3; Rev. 4:11). The concluding words of this petition introduce a certain eschatological dimension; what is presently the reality in heaven will also be fulfilled on earth. Although the Bible says relatively little about heaven, in this context it is viewed as the place and state where God's will is carried out perfectly in all respects; in like manner, earth, the sphere of human activity, must also in the end become fully the environment of God's will.

Third Petition: "**Give us today our daily bread.**" This request is based on a common Semitic ideal, the king's provision for the needs of his subjects. It is expressed in ancient treaties and may be seen in the Bible in such passages as Psalm 72. As supreme King, the Lord is the provider of that which sustains life (Ps. 104:15; Acts 17:25; 2 Cor. 9:10). The "daily bread" of this petition is reminiscent of the manna that sustained the Israelites in the wilderness after their deliverance from Egypt; except for the day before the Sabbath, it could be gathered only for use on the same day, and it spoiled if held for later use (Exod. 16:13-21). Jesus is teaching his disciples to pray in faith for what they need—to depend on the Lord's provision alone (Ps. 37:4-5) and not on human schemes for attaining material security, schemes that ultimately come to nothing (cf. Prov. 16:1; *passim,* Eccl. 2:11; 6:1-2). He returns to this theme in the discourse following the prayer. Moth, rust, and thieves can destroy what we so diligently lay up (Matt. 5:19); believers are not to "worry about tomorrow" but to "seek first his kingdom" (Matt. 6:33-34).

Although in context Jesus is clearly referring to God's care for the physical needs of his children, the believer's "daily bread" is also the "bread of life," or spiritual food. Jesus spoke of this particularly in his discourse following the feeding of the multitude (John 6:22-59). "Do not work for food that spoils," he said, "but for food that endures to eternal life, which the Son of Man will give you" (John 6:27). The manna of the wilderness was perishable, and those who ate it died; in contrast, Jesus declared, "I am the bread of life. . . . Whoever eats my flesh and drinks my blood has eternal life" (John 6:48, 54). Jesus here equates his death on the cross with the release of the "bread" of eternal life. In the structure of John's Gospel, however, this is also clearly a teaching concerning the Lord's Supper or Eucharist, which is missing from his narrative of the meal on the night of Jesus' arrest. The passage pointedly refers twice to Jesus' "giving thanks" (*eucharisteō,* 6:11, 23) in the feeding of the crowds. Jesus' discourse centers on the symbolism of the "living bread," as Paul's discussion of the Lord's Supper also focuses on the "one loaf" as emblematic of "one body" (1 Cor. 10:17). In early Christian art, the loaves and fish alone, without the chalice, were a symbol of the Eucharist. The comparison of the "daily bread" of the believer with the life released in Christ's death, as symbolized in the Eucharist, is the principal reason the church found the Lord's Prayer especially appropriate for use at that point in the liturgy immediately before the participation in the Lord's Supper.

Fourth Petition: "**Forgive us our debts as we also have forgiven our debtors.**" The Lukan version reads, "forgive us our sins" (Luke 11:4). In each case, God's forgiveness of an offender's wrongdoings is linked to the offender's forgiveness of those who have offended him or her. Jesus illustrated this truth in his parable of the slave, forgiven a great debt, who refused to forgive the lesser debt owed him by a fellow slave (Matt. 18:23-35). Paul took up the same theme in exhorting the Ephesians to forgive one another "just as in Christ God forgave you" (Eph. 4:32). It is ludicrous to dwell on the petty offenses of others against us when we have been forgiven a much greater offense against God. In the covenant, all are servants of the same Lord, who alone is supreme; to refuse to forgive a brother's or sister's infraction is to elevate oneself to a position of judge in rivalry with the Lord. Citizens of the kingdom are to "not judge" (Matt. 7:1) in this sense (as opposed to the appropriate judgment of recognizing evil for what it is), for "God himself is judge" (Ps. 50:6). But beyond this, there is a principle of the kingdom of God at work here, the "law of reciprocity," which applies to all forms of behavior: loving, blessing, giving, lending, showing mercy, pardoning, as well as negative actions (Luke 6:27-38). Just as when we give it is given to us, so only in forgiving can we be forgiven; forgiveness of others takes the prideful self out of the center, the very obstacle to receiving the pardon of God for our own failures and misdeeds.

Fifth Petition: "**And lead us not into temptation [trials], but deliver us from the evil one.**" The usual translation, "lead us not into temptation," obscures the true intent of Jesus' words. The Greek term *peirasmos* means "testing, trial," and refers more to pressure from outside than to inward weakness or moral failure, although of course the two concepts overlap. The testing the infant church would have undergone would be that of persecution by its enemies; the individual Christian might be tempted to yield to such pressure in both the verbal denial of his or her faith and the practical denial represented in behavior falling short of the standards of the kingdom. James, the Lord's brother, exhorted the church to rejoice in such testing, as an opportunity to develop endurance (James 1:2-3), while Paul reminded the Corinthians that they could withstand the pressures of idolatrous influence, since God in his faithfulness to the covenant "will provide a way out" (1 Cor. 10:13). The thrust of Jesus' petition is similar, but perhaps we are to understand it specifically in view of the great testing he predicted would come with those events leading to the destruction of Jerusalem and its sanctuary (Mark 13:9-13). He teaches his followers to pray for deliverance in that time, for "who stands firm to the end will be saved." To the faithful, the risen Christ promises, "I will also keep you from the hour of trial" (Rev. 3:10).

The corollary "deliver us from evil" may equally be translated "deliver us from *the evil one,*" in harmony with Jesus' later prayer for his disciples, that the Father might "protect them from the evil one" (John 17:15). The New Testament personification of evil in Satan or the devil does not exclude its personification in human authorities as well, such as the "man of lawlessness" described by Paul (2 Thess. 2:3) or the "beast from the sea" and the "beast from the land" in the Revelation. The New Testament writers are vague concerning the identity of these authorities, but their meaning must have been clear to a church that faced great danger from these figures—and the system they represented—in the latter part of the first century.

Doxology and Close: "For yours is the kingdom, and the power, and the glory forever and ever. Amen." This addition, found in no ancient version, commentator, or exegete, has evidently been added from liturgical use of the Lord's Prayer as a congregational response in worship. In both the *Didachē* from the second century and the early liturgies of the third and fourth centuries, the congregation responded antiphonally as the deacon or presbyter led the prayers. The doxology of the Lord's Prayer is similar to the blessing or *beʿrakhah* so characteristic of synagogue prayer as it was developing in the New Testament period. Whether the use of this doxology originated with Jesus himself or was a Christian adaptation of Jewish practice, the doxology is ultimately modeled on David's prayer at the coronation of Solomon (1 Chron. 29:11). As a celebration of the surpassing dominion of the great King, it well summarizes the thrust of Jesus' proclamation of the kingdom of God.

The Lord's Prayer in the Church

The pronouns of the Lord's Prayer are plural. The prayer was not formulated for singular, personal devotion; it was to be an act of corporate worship, the petition of a community or body of believers. The prayer is addressed to the Father, articulating the needs of the church and of its members in view of the emergence of the kingdom of God. At the same time, the prayer is Christocentric, its character entirely determined by the person and work of Christ in redemption; it is by his act of atonement that any or all of the petitions may be heard and granted, for he says, "no one comes to the Father except through me" (John 14:6).

The Jewish temple service, and later the service of the synagogue, was rich in liturgical material drawn from the Psalms, the Law, and other scriptural sources, much of it incorporated in prayers and responses repeated in unison or antiphonally by the congregation. Probably the early church drew on these resources in the evolution of its worship and added liturgical material of its own, some of which has been preserved in the New Testament (for example, the hymns of Luke and the Revelation to John; prayers, doxologies, and creedal statements preserved in the epistles of Paul; the doxology of Jude 24-25). The Lord's Prayer was involved in this process, evidently from an early period.

The use of the Lord's Prayer in the eucharistic liturgy can be traced back to the fourth century, although originally it did not come at the end of the great thanksgiving or prayer of consecration. Pope Gregory I (*c.* 540-604) made it the climax and the most important part of the consecration. In the early centuries, when the church was persecuted, the Lord's Prayer was considered one of the "mysteries" to be said only in the company of baptized believers. In contemporary prebaptismal rites that follow the fourth-century catechumenate pattern, the Lord's Prayer is formally "presented" to baptismal candidates shortly before their baptism. Devotional manuals from the early medieval period indicate the repetition of the Lord's Prayer at all six of the stated "hours" of prayer: matins, lauds, terce, sext, none, and vespers. The wealth of conflicting rituals led the Franciscans to condense and collate the services in the *Breviary,* and its companion the *Missal,* for Holy Communion, but the Lord's Prayer was central in both.

The Lutheran liturgy followed the custom of the Lollards and the Bohemian Brethren, precursors of the Protestant Reformation, in simply translating the prayer from the Latin into the colloquial speech. The Reformed churches that followed Calvin and the Swiss Reformation dispensed with much of the medieval liturgy but retained the Lord's Prayer in a French version. In other Reformed churches it was removed from the liturgy but placed in the catechism for the instruction of those to be confirmed. Although the Lord's Prayer has not usually been incorporated into the regular worship of evangelical and charismatic churches, which tend to view written or recited prayers with some reservation, its use is increasing today. Familiar to Christians of all traditions as a prayer given for their use and example by Christ himself, the Lord's Prayer is a unifying element in the revival of scriptural forms of worship in the contemporary scene.

William White[28]

270 • ACTS OF RECEIVING

Several traditional acts of worship accompany the receiving of the Lord's Supper. Some form of "fraction," or breaking of the bread, is found in most observances of the rite. In addition, the distribution of the Eucharist may incorporate the Agnus Dei *("Lamb of God"), the acclamation "Christ Our Passover," and a concluding prayer of thanksgiving.*

———— Fraction ————

Fraction is the liturgical term for the breaking of the bread by the officiant during the celebration of the Eucharist. The fraction may occur during the singing of the *Agnus Dei* or other hymn; in many churches, however, especially Protestant communities, the fraction occurs during the words of institution, at that point where the text mentions Jesus' breaking of the bread (Matt. 26:26; 1 Cor. 11:24).

The Lord's Supper is a dramatic re-presentation of Jesus' last meal with his disciples. The fraction is perhaps the most vivid and original action in this re-enactment; it gives visible—and even auditory, if a wafer or crisp bread is used—expression to the remembrance of the broken body of the Lord. The visual impact of the fraction is greatest when the congregation is served from a single loaf, broken apart for distribution; such a practice preserves the symbolism of the unity of the church, as articulated by Paul: "Because there is one loaf, we, who are many, are one body, for we all partake of the one loaf" (1 Cor. 10:17).

———— "Lamb of God" (*Agnus Dei*) ————

In historic Christian liturgies the hymn or prayer known as the "Lamb of God" or *Agnus Dei* is sung during the breaking of the bread and the final preparation of the elements for distribution to the people. The text of this hymn, as it occurs in contemporary liturgies, is the following:

> Lamb of God, you take away the sins of the world:
>   Have mercy on us.
> Lamb of God, you take away the sins of the world:
>   Have mercy on us.
> Lamb of God, you take away the sins of the world:
>   Grant us peace. *Amen.*

The New Testament symbolism of the lamb, as applied to Jesus Christ, is based on the sacrificial rites of Israelite worship, in which unblemished animals were offered in atonement for sin to maintain the covenant and restore communion between the Lord and his worshipers (Lev. 1–6). In addition, a lamb was eaten in the Passover meal, which celebrated the events of Israel's deliverance from Egypt; the blood of a lamb, applied to the doors of their homes, protected the Israelites from the wrath of the Lord visited upon their enemies (Exod. 12).

The writings of the apostle John especially refer to Jesus as the Lamb. The *Agnus Dei* is a quotation from the words of John the Baptist, as recorded in the fourth Gospel (John 1:29, 36); in the Revelation to John, the victorious Christ is often simply called "the Lamb" in both the dramatic narrative and its accompanying hymnody (Rev. 5:12; 7:9-10; 12:11; 13:8; 17:14; 21:22-23; 22:1-3). Peter also compares Christ to the sacrificial lamb: "For you know that it was not with perishable things such as silver or gold that you were redeemed from the empty way of life handed down to you from your forefathers, but with the precious blood of Christ, a lamb without blemish or defect" (1 Pet. 1:18-19). Paul alludes to the lamb of Passover in declaring, "For Christ, our Passover lamb, has been sacrificed. Therefore let us keep the Festival" (1 Cor 5:7-8).

The title "Lamb of God" recognizes the centrality of Jesus' sacrificial death in bringing about the reconciliation of God and his people, the restoration of the relationship violated by sin. Thus the Agnus Dei, or "Lamb of God," appropriately accompanies the distribution of the Lord's Supper in traditional worship. The Supper is a memorial of the death of Christ, through which God's forgiveness has been made available to repentant humanity and continues to be applied to the faithful who confess their sins (James 5:15; 1 John 1:9); the hymn therefore petitions the Lamb, "Have mercy on us." The Lord's Supper is also the Christian Passover, the covenant meal; since "peace," or wholeness of life, is the content of the covenant, in this hymn the worshipers petition the Lamb of God, "Grant us peace."

Christ Our Passover

In some liturgical traditions the words of Paul in 1 Corinthians 5:7-8 may be spoken or sung responsively at the distribution of the Eucharist:

> Alleluia, Christ our Passover is sacrificed for us;
> *Therefore let us keep the feast. Alleluia.*

This acclamation is not part of any specific teaching about the Lord's Supper but is found in the context of Paul's admonition to the Corinthian church to purify itself of immorality. In the New Testament, leaven, or yeast, is a symbol of false teaching and corruption (Matt. 16:6; Mark 8:15; Luke 13:21; Gal. 5:7-9). Just as the Passover bread must be free from any contamination of leaven, so the body of Christ must be free from moral permissiveness and the teaching that encourages it: "Therefore let us keep the Festival, not with the old yeast, the yeast of malice and wickedness, but with bread without yeast, the bread of sincerity and truth" (1 Cor. 5:8). In Paul's exhortation, the common life of the Christian community is analogous to the keeping of the feasts prescribed in the Mosaic Law, in particular the Feast of Passover. It is this analogy to the theme of *festival,* rather than the note of purification, that forges the link between Paul's words and the observance of

the Lord's Supper. The church's life together, including its worship centering in the Lord's Table, is a *feast* to be celebrated with great joy.

Prayer of Thanksgiving

In the early church, the congregation was dismissed by a deacon immediately following the distribution of the Lord's Supper. By the fifth century, however, an additional prayer of thanksgiving had been added before the dismissal, a practice retained in many liturgies today. The prayer of thanksgiving returns to, and sums up, the eucharistic motif with which the great thanksgiving begins, as the congregation reflects on the benefits mediated through participation in the Lord's Supper. This example is from a Lutheran service:

> We give you thanks, almighty God, that you have refreshed us through the healing power of this gift of life; and we pray that in your mercy you would strengthen us through this gift, in faith toward you and in fervent love toward one another; for the sake of Jesus Christ our Lord. *Amen.*

271 • BENEDICTION (BLESSING)

As traditional Christian worship begins with acts of entrance, it also closes with acts of dismissal, chiefly a benediction. The benediction invokes the blessing of the Lord upon the congregation and sends the worshipers forth in the strength of God.

Historic worship typically concludes with a blessing or benediction (from a Latin term meaning "pronouncement of good"), spoken over the assembly by one of the officiants in the liturgy. In the church of the early centuries, the benediction was spoken by the bishop just before the Eucharist, but by the second millenium it had become common for priests to say it at the conclusion of the service.

In Scripture, a blessing (*berakhah*) is more than the mere recitation of a formula. Words, in biblical psychology, convey the "soul," or life force, of their speaker; a powerful person utters powerful words, with a telling impact on those to whom they are directed. As the Almighty, God speaks the most powerful Word of all, through which all things have come into being and are sustained (Pss. 33:6; 107:20; John 1:3; Heb. 1:3). The word of a king (Prov. 8:4), a family patriarch (Gen. 27:34-35), a priest (Num. 6:22-27), or a prophet of the Lord (1 Sam. 3:19) is more effective, both for blessing and for curse, than the word of a person of lesser station or presence. Certain people, such as Balaam, son of Beor, were known to be especially effective in such utterances (Num. 22:6).

The blessing, or pronouncement of favor and peace, by a community leader is part of the process by which the welfare of the community is furthered and sustained. Thus Jacob blessed his sons before his death (Gen. 49:28), and Moses blessed the tribes of Israel before their entrance into Canaan (Deut. 33). Paul sometimes included benedictions in the conclusion of his epistles (Rom. 15:13; 2 Cor. 13:14; Eph. 6:23-24). The blessing of the congregation by their spiritual leader is frequently recorded in accounts of biblical worship. Aaron and Moses blessed the people as they presented their offerings in the wilderness (Lev. 9:22-23); David "blessed the people in the name of the Lord Almighty" when the ark of the covenant was brought up to Zion (2 Sam. 6:18); Solomon blessed the people during the dedication of the house of the Lord (1 Kings 8:14) and at the conclusion of the ceremony (1 Kings 8:55); the Levitical priests blessed the assembly following the renewal of the Passover observance under Hezekiah (2 Chron. 30:27). The customary posture of blessing is the lifting of the hands (Lev. 9:22); in departing from his disciples, the risen Christ lifted up his hands and blessed them (Luke 24:50).

The blessing of the worshiping congregation is the pronouncement of *the Lord's* blessing, the invocation of his name upon the people. This is exemplified in the best-known of the biblical benedictions, widely used today in Christian worship, the priestly blessing with which Moses directed Aaron and his sons to bless the people:

> The Lord bless you, and keep you;
> The Lord make his face shine on you,
> And be gracious to you;
> The Lord lift up his countenance on you,
> And give you peace. (Num. 6:24-26, NASB)

Another traditional Christian benediction, invoking the Trinity, is based in part on Paul's words in Philippians 4:7; it is cited here from a 1932 Methodist hymnal:

> May the peace of God, which passeth all understanding, keep your hearts and minds in the knowledge and love of God, and of his Son Jesus Christ our Lord; and the blessing of God Almighty, the Father, the Son, and the Holy Spirit, be among you, and remain with you always. *Amen.*

Several biblical passages often pronounced at the conclusion of traditional Protestant worship, such as Hebrews 13:20-21 or Jude 24-25, are not properly benedictions but doxologies, expressions of praise and glory to the Lord. Nevertheless, blessing in Scripture is a reciprocal act; while the Lord, through his spokespersons, may bless his people, the worshipers may also bless the Lord and give him glory (1 Chron. 29:20; Neh. 9:5; Pss. 34:1; 103:1; 134:2; 135:19-20; James 3:9).

Richard C. Leonard

THIRTY-ONE

The Lord's Supper (Eucharist)

When Jesus ate with his disciples in the upper room on the night of his arrest, he instituted the ceremony that has become the basic act of distinctively Christian worship: the Lord's Supper, known also as the Eucharist, or Holy Communion. This central Christian rite is rich in theological symbolism; as an outward action signifying a spiritual reality, it has a sacramental character (whether or not it is termed a sacrament by those who observe it). It is an ordinance of Christ, an act of worship the church performs in obedience to his express command. In the early church, the Lord's Supper usually took place in the context of a community meal.

272 • THE BREAKING OF BREAD

The most primitive term for what Christians do at the Lord's Table is "the breaking of bread" (Acts 2:42). This action in the early Christian assembly recalls how Jesus became present to his disciples in the breaking of bread at Emmaus and in other postresurrection appearances. The breaking of bread was an occasion of great joy, as the risen Jesus became present to his assembled followers.

It is agreed that the oldest celebrations of the Lord's Supper took place in the setting of an actual meal, in which the drinking of wine was not absolutely necessary as we find from Acts, which speaks only of "breaking of bread." The fact that one says "breaking of bread" and not "eating of bread"—an unusual expression to designate a meal—indicates that those present were conscious of performing at the same time an act of special significance. The connection with the blood, and in general with the death, of Christ seems here to be missing. It is an essential characteristic of this meal that, as Acts 2:46 says, "exuberant joy" (AUTHOR'S TRANSLATION) prevailed among them. This was not aroused primarily by the remembrance of the Last Supper but is explained in the first instance by the remembrance of those other occasions on which Jesus, immediately after his resurrection, appeared to the disciples while they were having a meal. According to Luke 24:36, the Eleven ate with the risen Christ on the day of Resurrection after Jesus (Luke 24:30) had also

broken bread with two disciples on the road to Emmaus shortly before.

According to Luke 24:42, as in the narrative in John 21:12ff., the meal taken with the risen Christ consisted of fish. This may to some extent account for the fact that later the symbol of the fish was associated with the Eucharist, though the symbol certainly has other roots (such as the feeding of the multitudes recorded in John 6). This symbolism also points to the connection between the early Christian celebration of the Lord's Supper and the resurrection appearances of Christ at meals.

If the first appearances of the risen Christ took place during meals, we must take into consideration the fact that the first eucharistic feasts of the community look back to the Easter meals in which the messianic meal promised by Jesus at the Last Supper was already partly anticipated. How closely the thought of the Resurrection in general was linked with the recollection of those Easter meals shared with the Christ of the appearances can be gauged from Acts 10, where Peter's address says, "God raised him from the dead on the third day and caused him to be seen. He was not seen by all the people, but by witnesses whom God had already chosen—by us who ate and drank with him after he rose from the dead" (Acts 10:40-41). Acts 1:4 refers also to the risen Christ "eating with them."

The "rejoicing" at the eucharistic meals is thus explained by the connection of this celebration with the thought of the Resurrection on the one hand,

and by the connection with the thought of the messianic meal on the other hand. The eucharistic meal of the community that is gathered in Jesus' name and at which consequently he is now effectively present in the Spirit, occupies its appointed place between Christ's resurrection meal and the expected eschatological meal. The coming of Christ into the midst of the community gathered at the meal is in anticipation of his coming to the messianic meal and looks back to the disciples' eating with the risen Christ in the days following the Resurrection. In the book of Revelation, which correlates the present service of worship and its fulfillment in the events of the last days, Christ says: "Here I am! I stand at the door and knock. If anyone hears my voice and opens the door, I will come in and eat with him, and he with me" (Rev. 3:20). That is the answer to the old eucharistic prayer: *Maranatha!* The prayer is fulfilled already in the community's celebrations of the Lord's Supper.

The emphasis laid on the presence of the risen Christ at these early meals is in keeping with the fact that the first Christians chose the day of Christ's resurrection as the day for the service of worship and conforms also with the central meaning of the prayer *Maranatha!* The term *Lord's Supper* (1 Cor. 11:20) also points this direction.

Oscar Cullmann[29]

273 • THE LORD'S SUPPER

Protestants commonly use the term Lord's Supper *for the act of worship that centers about the table of the Lord. The Lord's Supper originated with Jesus' last supper with his disciples, in the context of the Passover, and shares with the Passover the theme of the Lord's deliverance of Israel. As interpreted in the Gospels and by Paul, the Lord's Supper is symbolic of Christ's death, a memorial that places the worshiper at the Cross. It is the ratification of the covenant between the Lord and the people of God, an emblem of the communion or mutual participation of all members of the body of Christ. The Supper is a proclamation of the gospel and a symbol of faith in Christ.*

Introduction

The expression "Lord's Supper" (*kuriakon deipnon*) occurs only once in the New Testament (1 Cor. 11:20), where it refers not only to the special Christian rite of breaking the bread and drinking the cup, but also to the "love feast" that accompanied it. The expression "breaking of bread," found several times in Acts (Acts 2:42; 20:7, 11), may be another reference to the Lord's Supper; certainly it became so in the subsequent history of the church. Later names for the Supper, such as *Eucharist* or *Communion,* are not used in the technical sense in the New Testament. The former, however, is derived from Jesus' act of thanksgiving (*eucharisteō*) before offering the cup to his disciples (Mark 14:23) and the latter from 1 Corinthians 10:16, where Paul writes of the "communion" (*koinōnia*) of the body and blood of Christ.

The Lord's Supper, by whatever name, began with the Last Supper of Jesus and his friends before his death. The principal texts dealing with this subject are Matthew 26:26-29, Mark 14:22-25, Luke 22:14-20, and 1 Corinthians 11:23-26. Apart from Paul and the synoptic Gospels, the New Testament is virtually silent on the rite of the Lord's Supper, although allusions to it may be present in John 6:22-59; Acts 2:46; 20:7, 11; Hebrews 6:4; 13:10; 2 Peter 2:13; Jude 12; and Revelation 14:15-20. The early church may have felt a need to keep its central act of worship a "mystery" or secret hidden from the prying eyes of a hostile culture; the general silence of the New Testament could also mean that the Lord's Supper was well known, at least within the church, and it was unnecessary to mention it except where disorders called for clarification.

The Lord's Supper and Passover

Whether Jesus' last supper with the disciples was an actual Passover meal (and there is some question in this regard with respect to the interpretation of the Gospel accounts), his words instituting the new Christian meal were spoken in the context of the Passover celebration and may be understood accordingly. The liturgy of the Passover began as the presiding person (usually the family head) pronounced a blessing (*kiddush*) over the first cup of wine, which at Passover was always red. After he and the others present had drunk the cup, they took bitter herbs and ate them after dipping them in a fruit sauce (*haroset*). Next came the explanation of the feast as the food for the meal was brought in. The son asked his father why this night differed from other nights, and the father explained why the different foods were eaten: the Passover lamb because God passed over the house of our fathers in Egypt (Exod. 12:26-27), the unleavened bread because our fathers were redeemed from Egypt (Exod.

12:39), and the bitter herbs because the Egyptians embittered the lives of our fathers in Egypt (Exod. 1:14). After this the family or group sang the first part of the *Hallel* (Ps. 113 or Pss. 113–114). Then came the drinking of a second cup, after which the president took unleavened bread and blessed God with these words: "Blessed art thou who bringest forth bread from the earth." He then broke it and distributed it to the guests. At this point the meal proper was consumed, ending with another prayer by the president, a prayer of thanksgiving for the meal pronounced over a third cup of wine, "the cup of blessing" (cf. 1 Cor. 10:16, NASB). After supper the group sang the remainder of the *Hallel,* through Psalm 118. The liturgy concluded with a fourth cup of wine, taken to celebrate God's kingdom.

Jesus' Words of Institution

It is not possible to be certain exactly what Jesus said when, following the Passover ceremony, he singled out the bread and the cup of wine for special consideration and reinterpretation. The principal texts that relate his words do not agree in every detail and have been translated into Greek from Jesus' original expressions in a Semitic language. When all sources are woven together, the words over the bread take the following form: "Take (Matthew, Mark), eat (Matthew), this is my body (Matthew, Mark, Luke, Paul), which is given for you. Do this for my remembrance (Luke's longer text, Paul)." The saying over the cup is also recorded variously: "All of you drink from it, for (Matthew) this (Matthew, Mark, Luke, Paul) cup (Luke, Paul) is my blood of the covenant (Matthew, Mark; 'is the new covenant in my blood,' Luke, Paul), which is poured out (Matthew, Mark, Luke) for many (Matthew, Mark; 'for you,' Luke) for the remission of sins (Matthew). Do this as often as you drink it for my remembrance (Paul)." These cup words are followed immediately in Matthew and Mark by Jesus' promise not to drink again of the fruit of the vine until he drinks it new with his disciples in the kingdom of God. The same eschatological hope is found also in Paul, though worded differently, and he too places it after the cup saying. Luke, on the other hand, couples the promise not to drink of the fruit of the vine with a similar promise not to eat again of the Passover until its real meaning is fulfilled in the kingdom, and he places both these sayings before the words spoken over the bread and the cup.

Essentially, then, there seem to be two accounts that are independent of each other—that represented by Mark and that of Paul. It is difficult, and perhaps unnecessary, to know which is older, for there are "primitive" elements in each. And despite all the minor differences between the accounts, they are in substantial agreement.

Meaning of the Lord's Supper in the Synoptic Gospels

A Symbol of Christ's Death. The bread and wine of the Last Supper are a symbol of the Lord's body and blood, a symbol of his death: "This is my body given," Jesus said, "This is my blood poured out." The verb *is* need not mean "is equivalent to"; often it conveys merely the idea of *represents* or *signifies* (as in the interpretation of the parables, Matt. 13:38; cf. John 10:9, 14). It would have been almost impossible for Jesus to have equated the bread with his body and the wine with his blood, and then have asked his Jewish disciples to eat and drink. It is more likely that they viewed Jesus in the tradition of the prophets of Israel and interpreted his words and actions accordingly. As the prophets had predicted future events by symbolic and dramatic actions (1 Kings 21:11; Jer. 19:1-11; Ezek. 4:3), so Jesus broke the bread and took the cup as an acted parable to denote his impending death and to point out its meaning. Several other ideas cluster around this basic symbolism of the Last Supper.

A Substitutionary Death. The Lord interpreted his death as a substitutionary event, one of self-giving in behalf of others, universal in scope: "This is my body given *for you*"; "this is my blood poured out *for many.*" This "many" is not to be understood as a limiting expression, in the sense of "some, but not all." It is a Semitic way of contrasting the many with the one, resulting in the meaning "all" (cf. Matt. 10:28 with 1 Tim. 2:6; Rom. 5:18 with Rom. 5:19).

Ratification of the New Covenant. Jesus further interpreted his death as the means of ratifying the new covenant proclaimed by Jeremiah (Jer. 31:31-34). This may be observed in his words, "my blood of the covenant" (Mark 14:24), which are almost identical with those of Exodus 24:8, where the ratification of the old covenant with Israel is recorded. But the addition of the pronoun *my* indicates that Jesus placed his blood in contrasting position to that of the covenant-inaugurating animal sacrifice of the Old Testament and that he viewed his death as fulfilling and bringing to an end the old covenant and as the supreme sacrifice necessary to introduce the new and give it permanent validity.

A Means of Forgiveness. There are also elements in the account of the Supper that indicate that Jesus interpreted his death as the consummate act of the Servant of the Lord described in the prophecy of Isaiah. This is particularly clear in Matthew, who adds the words "for the forgiveness of sins" to the saying about Jesus' blood poured out (Matt. 26:28; cf. Isa. 53:12: "He poured out his life unto death, and was numbered with the transgressors. For he bore the sin of many, and made intercession for the transgressors").

Passover Themes: Deliverance, Messianic Anticipation. Perhaps the most obvious meanings attached to the Lord's Supper are those associated with the Passover, since apparently the Lord's Supper originated in a Passover context. In the first century, Passover was in reality a celebration of two events: it *looked back* to commemorate Israel's deliverance from the oppression of Egypt (Exod. 12:14, 17; Mishnah, *Pᵉsaḥim* 10.5), and it *looked forward* to anticipate the coming messianic kingdom (Mishnah, *Pᵉsaḥim* 10.6; *cf.* Rabbi Joshua ben Hananiah, *Mᵉkhilta,* Exod. 12:42; *Rabbah,* Exod. 15:1). Two themes are prominent in the narrative of the Last Supper. Selecting only two elements from the liturgy of the Passover—the unleavened bread and the cup after the meal—Jesus seemed to be saying, "As Israel was spared from death at the hand of the destroying angel and delivered from servitude to Pharaoh by the death of the Passover lamb and the sprinkling of its blood, so you are spared from eternal death and freed from slavery to sin by my body broken and my blood poured forth." In Jesus' action, the original meaning of the Passover has been superseded. Christ is the Paschal Lamb (1 Cor. 5:7), and by his death becomes the author of a new exodus, the Redeemer of an enslaved people. Such, at least, was the understanding of the early church, an understanding most beautifully expressed in a sermon of Melito, Bishop of Sardis (died *c.* A.D. 190):

> For this one, who was led away as a lamb, and who was sacrificed as a sheep, by himself delivered us from servitude to the world as from the land of Egypt, and released us from bondage to the devil and from the hand of Pharaoh, and sealed our souls by his own Spirit, and the members of our bodies by his own blood.

> This is the one who covered death with shame and who plunged the Devil into mourning as Moses did Pharaoh.
> This is the one who smote lawlessness, and deprived injustice of its offspring as Moses deprived Egypt.
> This is the one who delivered us from slavery into freedom, from darkness into light, from death into life, from tyranny into an eternal kingdom, and who made us a new priesthood and a special people forever.
> This is the passover of our salvation. (*Homily,* 67, 68)

The cross and the fish are ancient symbols of the Eucharist. The artistic depiction above is from a floor mosaic found in a church at Tabgha in Galilee in the fifth century A.D. This symbol is rooted in biblical teaching.

The other theme of eschatological expectancy is also present in the Lord's Supper. It is found in Jesus' promise not to eat the Passover or drink the fruit of the vine until the kingdom of God shall have arrived. This promise is not a word of despair but a note of joy. Jesus sees beyond the darkness of Calvary to that time when he would share with his disciples the messianic banquet and enjoy with them the life of the age to come (cf. Isa. 25:6-8).

Massey H. Shepherd has summarized the meanings of the Last Supper in these words: "Thus Jesus offered his disciples in the Supper a full participation in the atoning benefits of his own self-offering on the cross—deliverance from the bondage of this world, remission of sins, incorporation into the new people of God, an inner obedience of the heart to the will of God, and the joy and benediction of his presence and fellowship in the age to come."

Paul's Understanding of the Lord's Supper

The disorders at the Lord's Table in Corinth gave the apostle Paul the opportunity to provide teaching on the Lord's Supper that appears nowhere else in the New Testament. Paul's account of it is generally thought to be the earliest in the New Testament by several years. He says he "received from the Lord" (1 Cor. 11:23). This may mean that Paul learned of the events of the Last Supper and its meaning in the same way he says he had earlier received the content of the gospel: not by human teaching, but through a revelation of Jesus Christ (Gal. 1:12). More likely, however, Paul's statement should be interpreted to mean that he understood himself to be handing on in unaltered fashion that which had come to him as church tradition. The words he uses for "receive" and "deliver to" are equivalents of rabbinic terms for the normal passing down of tradition. Paul may have meant, then, that he received the story of the Last Supper and its meaning from the Lord through the apostolic witness. For the Lord was not simply a remembered historical figure but a living presence in the church, guiding the community into all truth (John 16:13) and seeing that this truth was transmitted accurately to each succeeding generation.

A Memorial Feast. "Do this in remembrance of me" (1 Cor. 11:24-25) occurs in Paul and Luke but does not appear in Mark and Matthew. Paul therefore understands that the purpose of the Lord's Supper is to commemorate the death of the Lord Jesus and that this purpose originated with the Lord himself. Here again is a parallel between this new feast and the feast of the Passover. As the Passover was basically a remembrance celebration calling to mind the mercy and greatness of God in delivering his people from Egypt (Exod. 12:14; 13:8-10), so the Lord's Supper is designed to constantly remind the church of God's greatest act, that of deliverance from sin through the death (not the teachings) of the Lord Jesus.

But the biblical idea of "remembering" is more profound than our modern conception of it. For the biblical writer it meant more than simply having an "idea" about something that happened. It also involved action, a physical response to the psychological process of recollection. When the dying thief asked the Savior to "remember" him, he meant more than "Have an idea of me in your mind"; he meant, "Act toward me in mercy. Save me!" There was, then, this closeness of relation between thought and action. Thus when the Jews celebrated the Passover, they did more than just think about what happened to their forefathers. In a sense, they reenacted that event and themselves participated in the Exodus. They became as one with their past.

There may also be this dimension to the word *remembrance* as it is used in 1 Corinthians 11. When the Christian partakes of the Lord's Supper, he or she not only has an idea in his or her mind about a past event; in a sense, the worshiper "recalls" that event in such a way that it can no longer be regarded wholly as a thing "absent" or past, but rather present, and powerfully so. Uniquely in the Lord's Supper, then, the death of Christ is made so vivid that it is as if the Christian and the worshiping body of which he or she is a part were standing beneath the cross.

A Proclamation of the Gospel. Paul also understood the Last Supper to be a proclamation: "For whenever you eat this bread and drink this cup, you proclaim the Lord's death" (1 Cor. 11:26). The verb *proclaim* found here is used elsewhere in the New Testament of heralding the gospel (1 Cor. 9:14) and of making known one's faith (Rom. 1:8). Hence, its action seems to be directed toward humankind rather than toward God. In performing the rite, the celebrant proclaims to all the Lord's death as victory. The Supper, therefore, becomes the gospel, a visible *verbum,* as Augustine said.

This idea of the Lord's Supper as gospel is helpful in understanding the Lord's presence in the Supper. In the New Testament, proclamation has the character of event. As Edouard Schweizer has said, the Word is never "merely" something spiritual intended for the intellect. Christ himself comes in the Word: "He who listens to you listens to me; he who rejects you rejects me" (Luke 10:16). In a similar way he comes in the Supper. Christ's presence is brought about not

"magically by a liturgically correct administration of the sacrament. . . . It comes to pass where the Lord's Supper is understood as gospel, whether this gospel is believed or rejected. . . . This means, therefore, that the real presence in the Lord's Supper is exactly the same as His presence in the word—nothing more, nothing less. It is an event, not an object: an encounter, not a phenomenon of nature; it is Christ's encounter with His Church, not the distribution of a substance" (E. Schweizer, *The Lord's Supper According to the New Testament* [Philadelphia: Fortress Press, 1967], 37-38).

Communion (*koinōnia*). The words of Paul in 1 Corinthians 10:16 are not easy to translate, especially the expressions "communion of the blood of Christ," and "communion of the body of Christ" (KJV). The word translated "communion" (*koinōnia*) may also be translated "fellowship," meaning a group of people bound together in a "communion" or "fellowship" by what they have in common with each other. And the preposition *of* does not exist in Greek but is an interpretation of the genitive case. It may also be interpreted to mean "brought about by" or "based on." Translated this way, Paul is saying, "The cup of blessing which we bless, is it not (does it not represent) the fellowship which is brought about by the blood of Christ? The bread which we break, is it not the fellowship brought about by the body of Christ?" The Lord's Supper, then, is understood to witness to the fact that Christians belong to a special family, which includes the Son and the Father (cf. 1 John 1:3) and is marked by unity and love. It is a communion that required the death of Christ to create and that is so close that it is as though believers were one body: "For we being many are one bread, and one body: for we are all partakers of that one bread" (1 Cor. 10:17, KJV). Perhaps, then, this was the great disorder in Corinth that prompted what little teaching there is on the Lord's Supper. The Corinthians' sin was in not "recognizing the body" (1 Cor. 11:29), that is, in failing to understand the oneness of the body of which each person was a part.

In Paul's day a fellowship meal preceded the breaking of the bread and drinking of the cup. It was not an unimportant part of the Lord's Supper, and Paul had no desire to abolish it. What he was concerned to do, however, was to correct its abuses. For instead of symbolizing the unity its name intended, the fellowship meal at Corinth had become an occasion for manifesting the opposite. The freemen despised the slave class, going ahead with the meal before the latter had opportunity to arrive (1 Cor. 11:21). The wealthy scorned the poor, feasting to the point of gluttony while the latter went hungry (1 Cor. 11:21-22). Thus eating and drinking unworthily (1 Cor. 11:27) may have meant for Paul partaking of the Lord's Supper while holding each other in contempt, neither party striving to live up to the unity that the Lord's death had brought about.

The word *koinōnia* has still another meaning. It means also "participation in." Hence, 1 Corinthians 10:16 may be translated as the Revised Standard Version does: "The cup of blessing which we bless, is it not a participation in the blood of Christ?" If this is so, then perhaps Paul understood the cup and bread to symbolize the worshiping assembly's participation in the death of Christ. Perhaps by borrowing his vocabulary from the mystery religions he showed that the Redeemer and the redeemed are so intimately bound up with each other that what happened to the Redeemer happened also to the redeemed. Thus when Christ died, the Christian died also, and partaking of the Lord's Supper symbolizes this participation in the body and blood of the Savior. Such a description of the Supper is Paul's way of stating what Christ had already said: "I am the living bread that came down from heaven. If anyone eats of this bread, he will live forever. . . . I tell you the truth, unless you eat the flesh of the Son of Man and drink his blood, you have no life in you" (John 6:51, 53).

The Lord's Supper, though of great importance to Paul, is not all-important. There are no magical qualities to it. It has no more power to communicate life and maintain it than did the spiritual food and drink provided Israel in the wilderness (1 Cor. 10:1-13). It cannot in and of itself debilitate or bring about death, despite the fact that Paul says that many who eat and drink unworthily are weak and ill and some have died (1 Cor. 11:30). Such sickness and death result from the judgment of the Lord (1 Cor. 11:32), not from any magical power of the Supper. The importance of the Supper exists solely in the person it points to and whose redemptive acts it proclaims.

The Lord's Supper in the Gospel of John

There is no specific reference to the Lord's Supper in the fourth Gospel. John describes a final meal Jesus had with his disciples (John 13) when he taught then the importance of humble service to others by himself washing their feet. But there are no bread or wine here, no words of institution. Many, however, see the Johannine Eucharist in John

6, the discourse on the bread of life. It is here that Jesus says, "My flesh is real food and my blood is real drink. Whoever eats my flesh and drinks my blood remains in me, and I in him" (John 6:55-56). [This possibility is reinforced by the reference to Jesus giving "thanks" in John 6:11, 23, using the Greek verb related to the word *eucharist*.] If this is so, it appears that for John the Lord's Supper is spiritual food (cf. John 6:63) that nourishes and strengthens the life of the Christian (cf. *Didachē* 10.4).

But perhaps John's primary aim was to discourse, not on the Lord's Supper but on the meaning of faith. Certainly this is a subject that is continually being put forward in his Gospel. What does it mean to have faith in Christ? When "I tell you the truth, he who believes has everlasting life" (John 6:47) is placed over against "Whoever eats my flesh and drinks my blood has eternal life," (John 6:54), it seems that John, in searching for the way to answer this question, has at last found the model he needs. To believe on Christ is analogous to eating him. As one would take food and eat it, so that it is assimilated into the system and becomes one's very life, so faith is a similar appropriation of Christ with the result that he is at the very center and is the energizing force of the Christian's life. In any case, this is precisely what the Lord's Supper is designed to remind us of.

When Was the Lord's Supper Observed?

One might expect that if the Lord's Supper developed out of the Passover meal it would be celebrated only once a year, on 14–15 Nisan. There is some evidence in early church history to support this idea. Epiphanius, for example, observed that the Ebionites (an early Jewish-Christian sect) celebrated the Eucharist as an annual feast, like the Passover, in memory of Christ's death (*Haereses* 30.16.1). And Christians in Asia Minor in the second century held a special Eucharist as a parallel to and at the same time as the Passover. The mention in Acts of the disciples "breaking bread" every day (Acts 2:42, 46) need not refute this idea, for these meals, which were similar to religious meals elsewhere in Judaism, may have originated in the postresurrection meals Jesus had with his followers (Luke 24:30-43; John 21:1-14; Acts 1:4; 10:41). Whereas the Lord's Supper, as described in the New Testament, was a remembrance of Christ's death, these daily meals of the Jerusalem church were times of joyful

fellowship celebrating Jesus' resurrection and his continued presence with the church.

In time, however, as the church moved out from Jerusalem and the role of Jewish influence in the development of Christian worship was reduced, the two meals were combined into one event. In Paul's discussion of the Lord's Supper, the joyful postresurrection fellowship meal has become the "love feast" element (1 Cor. 11:20-21), and the annual Passover meal has become the Eucharist element (1 Cor. 11:23-26). By this time, the Lord's Supper was apparently celebrated neither daily nor annually, but weekly, on the first day of the week, the day of the Resurrection, and possibly in the evening, like the Passover ceremony (Acts 20:7; cf. 1 Cor. 16:2; Rev. 1:10; *Didachē* 1).

How Was the Lord's Supper Observed?

The New Testament provides little information about how the Lord's Supper was observed. However, from 1 Corinthians 11:20-34, it is possible to reconstruct the following order: (1) There was a dinner or love feast, to which each worshiper brought his or her own food (1 Cor. 11:20-22), though the intent was no doubt to share the food among the participants. (2) There may have been a period of self-examination, suggested by Paul's words "a man ought to examine himself" (1 Cor. 11:28-29). However, it is impossible to tell whether the form of this examination was inward, a public confession to the church, or a corporate confession in a liturgical prayer (cf. *Didachē* 6.14; 14.1). [However, since the burden of Paul's admonition to "examine [oneself]" is that the worshiper might "recognize the Lord's body" in the Supper, rather than discover some hidden personal shortcoming, this self-examination may not have been a part of the rite at all, but simply a warning Paul inserted in his teaching on the Lord's Supper. (3) Finally, the Lord's Supper proper involved only the bread and the cup, which recalled the death of the Lord Jesus (1 Cor. 11:24-26). Acts 20:7-11 suggests that some sort of homily may have preceded these actions, forming part of the liturgy of the Supper. The New Testament contains no traces of the eucharistic prayers found in other early Christian literature (*Didachē* 9.10), nor is there evidence of the ceremony of footwashing in association with the Lord's Supper. [Also, the New Testament gives no indication as to which ecclesiastical officers customarily presided over the celebration.]

Gerald F. Hawthorne[30]

274 ✦ EUCHARIST IN SCRIPTURE

Although the New Testament offers several versions of Jesus' institution of the Lord's Supper, or Eucharist, common themes emerge. In observing the Lord's Supper, the church puts the worshiper in contact with the redemptive death of Jesus—the act that has brought the church into being as one body, the eschatological new covenant community.

Eucharist, from the Greek _eucharistia,_ from the verb "to give thanks," is properly a New Testament term. For though it finds a material equivalent in "songs of thanksgiving" (Jer. 30:19) and "sacrifice of thanksgiving" (Ps. 116:17, RSV) in the Old Testament, _eucharistia_ has no formal equivalent in Hebrew. Its intelligibility, nevertheless, remains contingent on an understanding of such Old Testament and contemporary Jewish institutions as the Passover, the prayer of thanksgiving (_todah_), and sacrifice. Its ultimate intelligibility, however, whether in the Old Testament or the New Testament, depends on grasping the essential fact that all gratitude is the child of memory, that _eucharistia_ is inseparable from _anamnēsis_ (remembrance), whether of the saving events of the Exodus or of the redemptive death of Christ on the cross "for us and for our sins."

The Lord's Supper in the Pauline Literature

From the middle of the first century we have from Paul not only the earliest record of the institution of the Lord's Supper but also its first interpretation. To commence the examination of the New Testament evidence with Paul is, therefore, to witness the interpretation of a tradition in the very act of its transmission. For, though less influential in shaping subsequent doctrinal developments than either John or the Synoptics, Paul's account in 1 Corinthians does set the pattern for all future interpretations of the tradition. Indeed, his approach to this tradition, to what he "received" and "passed on" (1 Cor. 11:23) should spare both exegetes and theologians the _cul-de-sac_ of interpreting beyond the sufferance of the text both the Johannine and the synoptic accounts.

Thus, the first statement in 1 Corinthians 11:23, "I received from the Lord what I also passed on to you," not only puts the risen Lord at the source of the tradition as its author and the abiding guarantor of its authenticity, but also obviates the debates on the "historicity" of the institution accounts themselves. To create a dichotomy between the Jesus of Nazareth and the risen Lord would be to introduce an element alien to Paul's thought and inimical to Christian faith (cf. 1 Cor. 7:10 with Mark 10:11 and parallels). Therefore, to the question "Who instituted the Eucharist?" the response has to be unequivocally "the Lord Jesus" (1 Cor. 11:23), and no "quest of the historical Jesus," old or new, can alter this fundamental datum.

Similarly, the "on the night he was betrayed" (1 Cor. 11:23) is not a reference to the Passover but a linking of the institution to the Passion. Paul regards the Passover as one key to understanding the Passion ("Christ, our Passover lamb, has been sacrificed," 1 Cor. 5:7), but nowhere does he link the feast itself to the Lord's Supper. This fact ought to alert us not to assume the existence of such a link elsewhere in the New Testament unless explicitly stated.

It is in Paul's account that Jesus' taking of the bread is followed by "when he had given thanks (_eucharistēsas_)." Of course, this is the verb whence, as early as the _Didachē_ (9.1; 10.7) and Ignatius of Antioch (_Philadelphians_ 4), the substantive _eucharistia_ came to designate what had hitherto been referred to as "the Lord's Supper" (1 Cor. 11:20).

"This is my body, which is for you" refers to the redemptive death of Christ for us, as is evident from the "for you." This fact is made explicit in 1 Corinthians 11:26: "For whenever you eat this bread and drink this cup, you proclaim the Lord's death until he comes." Furthermore, the reference to the eating and drinking applies the formulae themselves, not to the bread and wine, but to their consumption, that is, not to the elements as such but to the action of eating and drinking (see 1 Cor. 11:27).

The injunction "Do this in remembrance of me" (1 Cor. 11:24-25) is—as has often been remarked (P. Benoit, "Le récit de la céne dans Lc. xxii, 15-20. Étude de critique textuelle et littéraire," _Revue biblique,_ 48 [1939]: 357-393; reprinted in _Exégèse et Théologie,_ vol. 1 [1961])—a rubric rather than a report. But what has not sufficiently been remarked is that the reference to the whole person of Christ, the "me," is in parallel to "my body." In the common biblical acceptance of the term, *body* (*sōma*) here refers to the whole person seen as the subject of relationships (see, for example, "absent in body," 1 Cor. 5:3, RSV). Thus "body" underlines further the "for us" aspect of the passion, even as the words over the "cup" stress the covenantal aspect of the new relationship that is now in force.

Paul, unlike Mark and Matthew, identifies the cup as "the new covenant in my blood" (1 Cor. 11:25). The fact that, here at least, the reference is not directly to "my blood of the covenant" (as it is in Mark 14:24 and Matt. 26:28) should alert us to the multiplicity of possible interpretations of the Lord's Supper even within the New Testament.

The transmission of any truly living tradition is, of course, an act of interpretation, as for instance the words over the cup or the injunction to "do this . . . in remembrance [*anamnēsis*] of me (1 Cor. 11:24-25), which is more than an exhortation to perpetuate the pious memory of a departing hero. It is rather the essential element in the believer's response to the proclamation of the good news of salvation in Christ Jesus, whether in baptism (see "baptized into his death" in Rom. 6:3) or in the Eucharist.

The *anamnēsis* is what places the believer in contact with the abiding redemptive effect of the death of Christ. Thus, when Paul interprets the whole action, he describes, as it were, a full circle: the *anamnēsis* puts the believer in contact with the efficacy of the gospel proclaimed, even as the eating and drinking proclaim the saving event announced by the gospel. Paul, therefore, provides an interpretation, not just of the Lord's Supper, but also of the celebration of the rite within the community of believers down the ages.

In his interpretation of the Lord's Supper, Paul also provides the fundamental clue to this and every other sacrament: "For whenever you eat this bread and drink this cup, you proclaim the Lord's death until he comes" (1 Cor. 11:26). Every sacrament is essentially the proclamation of the redemptive work of Christ, and the Eucharist in particular is this proclamation *par excellence*. All sacraments derive their meaning and significance from the word they proclaim, even as each in its own way proclaims that same word. The sacraments are thus another mode of this proclamation, in their words no less than in their gestures and actions.

Elsewhere in the same letter to the Corinthians we find not so much another version of the institution as another interpretation of its content. In this instance, it is the interpretation that dictates the sequence in 1 Corinthians 10 of "the cup of blessing which we bless" preceding the "bread which we break" (1 Cor. 10:16, RSV). Here "participation/communion" (*koinōnia* has both senses) is the key to the significance of the action. That the "cup of blessing which we bless" is a "*koinōnia* in the blood of Christ" makes explicit the function of the "remembrance" in "Do this in remembrance of me" (1 Cor. 11:24-25). It makes explicit, that is, the function of the celebration in putting the believer in contact with the redemptive death. But it stresses an aspect of this contact precisely as "*koinōnia* in the blood of Christ," that is, in the death of Christ on the cross.

Moreover, in the following statement on the bread, it elaborates the notion further ("Because there is one loaf, we, who are many, are one body, for we all partake of the one loaf," 1 Cor. 10:17). It was this logical order of argument, and not some echo of a different tradition such as, for instance, in the *Didachē,* that dictated the cup-bread order in 1 Corinthians 10:16-17.

By introducing the reference to the "body of Christ" in the sense of the community of the redeemed (Rom. 12:5; 1 Cor. 12:27), the interpretation of the "bread we break" as a *koinōnia* in "the body of Christ" underscores two aspects of the Eucharist: it, like baptism (1 Cor. 12:12-13; Rom. 6:3-11), makes the believers beneficiaries of the redemptive act of Christ, at the same time that it incorporates them into this one body. The Eucharist is the sacrament of the church in that it brings the church into being as the body of Christ, but it can take place only as an act of the church *as* the body of Christ. These two aspects are so inextricably linked that their converse is equally true. The absence of one makes the other impossible: "When you come together, it is not the Lord's Supper you eat" (1 Cor. 11:20). Precisely as, and only insofar as, the community of believers assembles "as a church" (1 Cor. 11:18) can it celebrate the Eucharist and, celebrating it, become the body of Christ (1 Cor. 10:17). "The Lord's Supper sets us in the Body of Christ, in the presence of the Exalted One who, having passed through death, now reigns: it therefore places us under the lordship of the Kyrios" (E. Käsemann, "The Pauline Doctrine of the Lord's Supper," *Essays on New Testament Themes* [Naperville, Ill: Allenson 1964], 132).

The *Didachē* echoes this mode of understanding the eucharistic celebrations: "As this broken bread was scattered upon the mountains, but was brought together and became one, so let thy church be gathered together from the ends of the earth into thy kingdom" (*Didachē* 9.4).

The Lord's Supper in Mark and Matthew

Both in their similarity to one another and in their concordant divergence from the accounts in Luke and in Paul, these two narratives of the institution can be treated simultaneously. The setting of the event in them is unmistakably the eating of the Passover (*to pascha*) (Mark 14:12-16; Matt. 26:17-20). Therefore, whether or not the Last Supper itself was a Passover meal (see J. Jeremias, *The Eucharistic Words of Jesus* [New York: Scribner, 1966], 15-88; V. Taylor, *The Gospel According to Mark,* 2nd ed. [London: Macmillan, 1966], 664-667), there is no reason for trying to interpret that action and the blessing pronounced (*eulogēsas*) in Passover categories. But this is not true of the altogether remarkable "this is my body . . . ; this is my blood . . ." For "important though the Passover motif may otherwise be in the Christological ideas of early Christianity, for the words of institution it contributes nothing" (G. Bornkamm, "Lord's Supper and Church in Paul," in *Early Christian Experience* [London: SCM Press, 1969], 134; and see X. Léon-Dufour, *Sharing the Eucharistic Bread* [Mahwah, N.J.: Paulist Press, 1987], 189-194).

Jesus "took bread, and blessed, and broke it, and gave it to them" in Mark 14:22 (RSV); his action is made explicit in Matthew 26:26 as "to the disciples" (RSV). Mark's "take; this is my body" becomes "take, eat" in Matthew. This latter modification would have been a negligible redactional retouch did it not affect the meaning of the formula. In general, commentators are content to regard the addition as merely stylistic, setting the bread formula in parallel with that of the cup. Nevertheless, a case can be made for taking the neuter *touto* (this) in "this is my body" as referring, in what is called an *ad sensum* construction, to the taking and eating rather than to *body* (*sōma*), which is masculine. Thus, while in Mark the reference is clearly the bread, in Matthew a case can be made for taking it to be the "take, eat." If this be so, then we have even here, not one but two interpretations of the formula, where Mark's would lend itself more readily to later disputations

on the "substance" than would Matthew's. While the formula over the bread itself, either in Mark or in Matthew, does not in any way link the "body" to the death of Jesus, the meaning of *body* in Mark is, and remains, more of a crux for interpreters than in Matthew.

The cup formula, however, evinces a marked difference between the two evangelists. In Mark it is pronounced by Jesus *after* "they all drank from it" (Mark 14:23). Thus here the question of the referent can and does arise: "this is my blood of the covenant" refers to the cup, since there is no mention of "wine" as there is of "bread" in Mark 14:22. But it refers especially to the drinking, "And he took the cup . . . offered it to them . . . and they all drank from it" (Mark 14:23; see 1 Cor. 11:26, where the reference to the eating and the drinking is unequivocal). In Matthew, however, the situation is slightly adjusted by the addition of the imperative "drink from it, all of you. This is my blood" (Matt. 26:27-28).

Any understanding of the Eucharist inevitably hinges on determining what precisely the "this" (*touto*) refers to. In Mark and Matthew it is the cup formula that really interprets the action as a reference to the redemptive death: "which is poured out for many" (Mark 14:24) and, in Matthew, by "for the forgiveness of sins" (Matt. 26:28). Thus in these two gospels, as in the other accounts of the institution in the New Testament, the narrative and its content are already theologically interpreted, and no amount of exegetical ingenuity can wholly separate the "fact" from that interpretation. Therefore, each account of the Last Supper in the New Testament is a distinct eucharistic theology. [While we may accept the basic fidelity of all the Gospel accounts to the tradition of the Last Supper, Jesus' original words to his disciples on that occasion would have been in Aramaic. The various nuances of the Greek Gospels may attest to distinct views of the Eucharist in the circles in which they appeared but may not necessarily clarify Jesus' original intention.]

Luke's Account of the Lord's Supper

Of all the accounts of institution, the one in the Gospel of Luke is the most textually vexing. But whether one adopts the shorter version (Luke 22:15-19) or the longer (Luke 22:15-20), the order of cup-bread in the former and cup-bread-cup in the latter requires explanation. Descriptions of the Passover seder, of Jewish celebratory practices, and of their background in the Old Testament, are all called on to provide an explanation. Nevertheless, the mere fact of the cup preceding the bread, if surprising, need not be inexplicable. As indicated in 1 Corinthians 10:16-17, the order of cup first is dictated by Paul's interpretation of the Lord's Supper in terms of the bread rather than of the cup. Though both "the cup of blessings which we bless" and "the bread which we break" are interpreted as *koinōnia* in the blood and the body of Christ respectively, it is the bread/body that provides Paul with the image he needs in order to proceed: "Because there is *one bread,* we who are many are *one body,* for we all partake of the *one bread*" (1 Cor. 10:17, RSV). Moreover, since the reference to blood is clearly to the redemptive death, as it is elsewhere in Paul (Rom. 3:25; 5:9), the cup-bread order in 1 Corinthians 10 is dictated by the logic of expository exigence as it is not in, for example, an almost equally ancient, extra-canonical work, the *Didachē:* "And concerning the Eucharist [this is one of the earliest instances of the usage of this term], we hold Eucharist thus: First, concerning the cup, 'We give thanks to thee, our Father, for the holy vine of David thy child; to thee be glory forever.' And concerning the broken bread: 'We give thee thanks, our Father, for the life and knowledge which thou didst make known to us through Jesus thy child. To thee be glory forever'" (*Didachē* 9.1-3).

Luke's text is usually regarded as being closer to that of 1 Corinthians 11 than to Mark and Matthew. For, in addition to "do this in remembrance of me" (Luke 22:19; cf. 1 Cor. 11:24-25), it is prefaced by an explicit reference to the coming of the kingdom of God (Luke 22:16; cf. 1 Cor. 11:26). Whether it be taken as integral to the account of the institution or regarded as prefatory to it, the reference indelibly marks the account and its understanding as eschatological, that is, as belonging to the "last times" inaugurated by the coming of the Lord. The Eucharist is an act that proclaims the presence of the last times in our midst. No understanding of "the new covenant in my blood," in Luke or elsewhere, is possible without the realization that the covenant is both final and definitive (see Heb. 7:27). Thus it is that the church, in celebrating the Eucharist, has with unfailing insight coupled the Lord's Prayer and the words of the institution; "Your kingdom come . . . give us our bread" find their true meaning in the "for you" of the bread formula and in the "of the covenant" of the cup formula.

Eucharist in the Fourth Gospel

It is not an unremarked fact that the fourth Gospel has no narrative of the eucharistic institution. If at first baffling, such omission is not the least logical of the Gospel's qualities. What the prologue climax affirms, "The Word became flesh" (John 1:14), is elaborated throughout both the "book of signs" (John 1–12) and the "book of glory" (John 13–21). To have inserted an institution account in the closing chapters would have been redundant. What the fourth Gospel does, however, is more illuminating. It explains, in the discourse on the bread of life in chapter 6, the meaning of the Eucharist in terms of the prologue. This is why the "sacramental realism" of John 6:53-58 can best be understood in terms of the Word, which "became flesh" for the "life of the world." Here alone do we have the properly biblical coupling of "flesh and blood" and not, as elsewhere in the institution accounts, "body and blood."

It is at this point that one can best understand how the Eucharist is, above all else, the "mystery of faith," faith in the flesh that the Word became. If a proper understanding of John 6:52-59 is to be sought, then it is to be sought not in the abstract theological terminology of later eucharistic debates but in its collocation in the same chapter with two major themes: the banquet of wisdom and the meaning of discipleship. The proper significance of the mystery is given final expression in the Petrine confession, "Lord, to whom shall we go? You have the words of eternal life. We believe and know that you are the Holy One of God" (John 6:68-69).

Stanley B. Marrow[31]

275 • THE LORD'S SUPPER AS COVENANT MEAL

The Lord's Supper, as instituted by Jesus Christ and elaborated in the Epistles, has its roots in the ancient rite of covenant, a practice that predates Abraham. Indeed, the covenant forms the basic structure of Yahweh's relationship with Israel and is, for this reason, the underlying motif for the establishment of Christ's relationship with the new people of God.

The cutting of covenants (*karat b'rit*) appears to have been a universal practice in the ancient world. Complete covenant documents pertaining to the Hittite peoples, neighbors of the patriarch Abraham, have been excavated in the Near East, and traces of covenant rituals are to be found in ceremonies of the Native Americans of the Western hemisphere. Treaty covenants are known to have regulated relationships among the various city-states and empires of Mesopotamia. The king of a defeated army entered into such an agreement with his conqueror, who specified the terms of the pact. Usually these stipulations included a vow of total loyalty to the great king, or "lord," as the covenant initiator was called, and a payment of annual tribute.

In some cases, less powerful rulers requested a treaty with a stronger king to secure his protection from invading armies. The weaker king, the vassal or "servant," agreed to assist the great king in battle, to make no friendships with nor provide safe harbor for his lord's enemies, and to appear in the courts of the lord at specified times to pay the required tribute.

Terms of the treaty covenant were written in two copies—one for the vassal king to read periodically to his people and the other to be placed in the shrine of the major god of the territory, who acted as a witness to the agreement and also enforced it.

A treaty between two nations was not in force until it was ceremonially ratified, usually with the blood of a slain animal. After cutting the sacrifice into pieces, the parties to the agreement walked between them as an identification with the animal, making the symbolic vow "The gods do so to me and more also if I break the terms of this covenant." Then they shared a meal of the animal's flesh and drank its blood in a sealing ritual.

The covenant meal is a frequent occurrence in the Old Testament. Isaac hosted Abimelech and his commanders at a meal that verified an agreement about the use of some wells that had been dug by Abraham (Gen. 26:26-31). Likewise, Laban and Jacob ratified their nonaggression pact with a sacrificial meal (Gen. 31:43-54).

Israel's covenant with Yahweh followed the prescribed pattern of covenants between tribal leaders. The covenant meal was first eaten in Egypt, when the Hebrews accepted Yahweh as their God and prepared to follow him out of Pharaoh's clutches and into the Promised Land. At the Passover meal, all Israel ate and drank their commitment to this new relationship: "I will take you as my own people, and I will be your God" (Exod. 6:7), and they were commanded to repeat the ceremony in a recommitment to the covenant every year thereafter (Exod. 12:21-24).

At Mount Sinai the terms were written on tablets of stone, which were later deposited in the ark of the covenant under Moses' direction. As leader of Israel and covenant mediator, Moses read the covenant text to his people (Exod. 24:7) and sacrificed burnt offerings to Yahweh, sprinkling their blood on the people (Exod. 24:8) as a means of identification with the animals. Following this part of the ritual, Moses and the elders of Israel ate and drank in the Lord's presence (Exod. 24:9-11). Since the drinking of blood was prohibited for the Hebrews, wine was used as a substitute.

This practice of confirming a covenant with a sacrificial meal is the background for the words of our Lord as he sat at the Passover table with his disciples. In his death he would become the sacrifice that ratifies the covenant between God and the new covenant people. Paul identifies Christ as the Passover Lamb who makes possible the feast, or covenant meal (1 Cor. 5:8), an assertion based on the words of Jesus himself. Breaking the bread and offering it to the Twelve, he said, "Take and eat; this is my body." Lifting a cup of wine he continued, "This is my blood of the covenant, which is poured out for many for the forgiveness of sins" (Matt. 26:26-28; Mark 14:22-24). Luke records that Jesus said "This cup is the *new* covenant in my blood which is poured out for you." (Luke 22:20, emphasis added). Paul testifies to having received the same from the Lord (1 Cor. 11:23), as he writes to the Corinthian church, "In the same way, after supper he took the cup, saying, 'This cup is the new covenant in my blood'" (1 Cor. 11:25).

The concept of Jesus as the covenant sacrifice underlies his "hard saying" recorded in John's Gospel. The day following Jesus' miraculous multiplication of the loaves and fish, he initiates a discussion with his disciples on the subject of manna. Moses was not the source of that bread, he tells them, but the Lord God was. He then moves the focus of the conversation to his own role as the bread given by God which brings life to the world. "I am the bread of life," he explains. "He who comes to me will never go hungry, and he who believes in me will never be thirsty" (John 6:35). The Jews, overhearing this extraordinary statement, begin to complain, and Jesus becomes even more explicit:

I am the living bread that came down from heaven. . . . Whoever eats my flesh and drinks my blood has eternal life. . . . For my flesh is real food and my blood is real drink. Whoever eats my flesh and drinks my blood remains in me, and I in him. (John 6:51, 54-56)

"Do this in remembrance of me," Jesus instructs his disciples at the Passover table. But he does not intend the act as a sentimental or maudlin ceremony in which the disciples mourn the loss of their leader. Jesus has just informed them that the bread and wine, his body and blood, comprise the meal that ratifies the new covenant. They are to recall this truth each time they participate in the ritual. In eating the flesh of the sacrifice and drinking the blood these disciples commit themselves afresh to the covenant formula, "I will be their God, and they will be my people" (Jer. 31:33). And in so doing they become the body of the Lord, his covenant people. Paul stresses this truth in his discourse to the Corinthians concerning abuses at the Lord's Table. In committing themselves to the covenant, Christians must recognize the Lord's body if they do not wish to incur judgment (1 Cor. 11:29).

The purpose of the Lord's Supper, then, is to remember his death—not the agony in the garden or the beatings or the crown of thorns or even the nails in his hands and feet. Rather, the recalling is to be of Jesus' sacrifice, which ratifies the covenant between himself as representative man and God the Great King of the covenant.

For the amazing truth is that Jesus fulfills the symbolism of all parts of the covenant ceremony. As the Son of man, he assumes the role of the servant king who represents the people of God; he is also the covenant lord, or Great King; as the Word of God, he is the covenant text, deposited in God's temple, the church; he is the sacrifice, which is eaten and drunk, completing the covenant agreement. To be "in Christ," as Paul says (2 Cor. 5:17), is to be in the covenant he represents. It is this relationship that God's people affirm when the church eats and drinks with the Lord at his table.

Janice E. Leonard

276 • PASSOVER AND THE LORD'S SUPPER

There is an integral correspondence between the Christian Lord's Supper and the Israelite Passover. Like the Passover, the Lord's Supper is a joyful reaffirmation of the covenant. And like Passover, it recalls the Lord's great act in the deliverance of a people. But the Lord's Supper also points ahead to the ultimate destiny of Christians: freedom in the presence of God.

The Last Supper

The tradition that Paul received and put down in writing belongs to the earliest accounts of what took place the night Jesus was betrayed (1 Cor. 11:23-25). This account states that it was at night, that there was a meal, that he took bread and broke it and said, "This is my body which is [broken] for you; do this in remembrance of me." The same with the cup: "This cup is the new covenant in my blood; do this, whenever you drink it, in remembrance of me." There is no mention of Passover in Paul's account, except in a circumstantial way: the breaking of bread in a solemn manner, the drinking of the cup of wine, the reference to the covenant, and above all the paschal overtones. The synoptic account does not differ in essence from the Pauline tradition, except that it represents the Last Supper as a Passover meal (cf. Matt. 26:17; Mark 14:12; Luke 22:7).

The Memorial Meal

Remembrance is the keynote of Passover: Israel is to call to memory what God has done for his people. The whole festival is a remembrance (Exod. 12:14). Jesus followed custom but reinterpreted the Passover in terms of the messianic event: the Messiah took the role of the paschal lamb. It is therefore correct to say that the Last Supper provides Passover with a new content. Henceforth the bread and the wine of the seder become the signs of the Messiah's sacrifice on the cross. The paschal meal becomes a messianic meal.

The Last Supper and Passover

In the time of the temple, the paschal meal consisted not only of the lamb but also of the special festive sacrifice of which everyone partook (cf. 2 Chron. 35:13). Such eating of the sacrifice was a joyous occasion that gave cohesion to community life. This is to be distinguished from the sin offering that was totally burned and never consumed. For the Israelite, eating the sacrifice never meant eating his God. Participation in the body and blood of the Messiah creates a problem if the Last Supper is conceived in purely sacrificial terms. For this reason, the emphasis in the Lord's Supper must be placed as much on the covenant as on the sin offering, if not more so. The blood that sealed the covenant is not the blood poured on the altar but the blood sprinkled on the people. There is a correspondence between the Last Supper and Exodus 24:11, which records that the elders of Israel on Mount Sinai beheld God and ate and drank.

The covenant is at the core of the Passover account. On the eve of the Exodus, God revealed himself as the God of the fathers who remembered his covenant (Exod. 2:24; 3:15). On the eve of the Crucifixion, this covenant was reaffirmed by the Messiah's willingness to shed his blood. The paschal lamb is therefore not sufficient to explain the full meaning of the Last Supper; the covenant intrudes as the overarching theme.

This raises the problem of the meaning of the new covenant: in what sense is it a new covenant? The writer of Hebrews, and sometimes Paul, gives the impression of a radical break: the former commandment is set aside "because it was weak and useless" (Heb. 7:18); had the first covenant been faultless there would have been no need for a second (Heb. 8:7); "by calling this covenant, 'new' he has made the first one obsolete" (Heb. 8:13). Those who are in Christ are new creations; "the old has gone; the new has come!" (2 Cor. 5:17).

Since Marcion, a second-century theologian held to be heretical, there has persisted a tendency to separate the two Testaments and to understand the "new" in the radical sense. From Paul's exposition of Israel's destiny (Rom. 9–11), such a break becomes impossible. The Logos doctrine allows no such break; the preexistent Christ spoke already in the Old Testament (cf. 1 Pet. 1:11). The writer of Hebrews bases his argument on the premise that the preincarnate Christ was present in Israel's history. The new therefore must be understood in connection with the messianic event. The new covenant brings the old covenant to the brink of eschatological fulfillment, but the people of God are one continuum from Abel to this day. Christ as the *telos* (fulfillment) of the Law (Rom. 10:4) brings in the new era but does not change God's promises. The new covenant is called "better" than the old (Heb. 8:6) because God in Christ fulfills his promise to write his law on the believer's heart (Heb. 8:8-13).

The Lord's Supper therefore continues the Passover theme in the new messianic context: (1) It is a memorial feast of the person and work of the Messiah. The remembrance goes beyond the historical events and becomes a proclamation and confession of faith (*cf.* 1 Cor. 11:26). (2) It is an avowal of loyalty between master and disciples, expressing the cohesion and the mutual interdependence of the Christian brotherhood. (3) It reaffirms the covenant of old and seals it in the blood of the Messiah. (4) It expresses the joy of salvation and the eschatological hope of the Messiah's ultimate triumph.

The Christian Exodus

The keynote of the New Testament message is messianic fulfillment; Jesus was the One of whom Moses and the prophets had written (John 1:45). The Messiah, by his life, work, death, and resurrection, accomplished "eternal salvation" (Heb. 5:9). This the law had been unable to do, for the Law had made nothing perfect (Heb. 7:19); it only served as a schoolmaster until Christ came (Gal. 3:24). The salvation of Yahweh as demonstrated in the story of the Exodus (cf. Exod. 14:13) was thus only a foreshadowing of what was to come. All God's acts in the Old Testament point to an ultimate future. A day will come when the Lord will reveal himself as the "warrior who gives victory" (Zeph. 3:17, RSV). The difference between the redemption from Egypt and messianic salvation is not that the one is in time and the other beyond it. Biblical salvation is always rooted in time and in history; this is its most peculiar feature. Also, the distinction is not that the one is physical (or political) and the other spiritual. The distinction rather lies in the area of eschatology; messianic salvation is ultimate. The rabbis regarded redemption from Egypt as foreshadowing final redemption; the New Testament claims it an accomplished fact. Passover is the beginning of the journey the Messiah completes by reaching the goal.

"Eternal salvation" means there can be no other salvation after the messianic event, which is the ultimate salvation. The eternal covenant that God promised to the fathers (Jer. 32:40; 50:5; cf. Isa. 55:3; Ezek. 16:60) has now been established and sealed in the blood of the Messiah (Heb. 13:20). In Hebrews the dissolution of the cult, the change of the priesthood, and the removal of the Law are the consequences of the messianic event. Christ has become the living way (Heb. 10:20) to the inner sanctuary (Heb. 6:19), the new High Priest who by his sacrifice has made possible for humans to draw near into the presence of God himself (Heb. 10:20ff.).

Jesus completes what Moses began but could never accomplish ultimately. True freedom is freedom from sin. No one is truly free who is a slave to sin. Only the one whom the Son makes free is free indeed (John 8:34-36). Paul arrives at a similar conclusion; the fathers were all under the cloud, passed through the sea, were baptized into Moses, ate spiritual food and drank spiritual drink, yet they perished in the wilderness (1 Cor. 10:1-5). The Exodus had a limited goal which was not reached until a new generation grew up. It is therefore only a parable of humankind's journey to its ultimate destiny—the promised land. This journey the human cannot make on his or her own strength. The slave has to become the freedman of the Lord (1 Cor. 7:22), and the emancipation takes place at the cross of Jesus Christ. In him people become sons of God (Gal. 4:4-6) and enjoy the freedom of the children of God (Rom. 8:2-4). The Exodus from Egypt to the land of Canaan leads beyond history to the "city with foundations, whose architect and builder is God" (Heb. 11:10). Whereas the historic Exodus was limited to the experience of one people, the Christian exodus is open to the nations of the world. Humankind's ultimate destiny is the heavenly Jerusalem, the city of the freed (Gal. 4:26).

Jakob Jocz[32]

277 • THE LOVE FEAST (*AGAPĒ*)

The love feast is a meal set in the context of Christian worship, usually the Lord's Supper. It expresses the spiritual aspect of fellowship and compassion within the body of Christ.

It is generally recognized that primitive Christian worship was set in the context of a meal in the home of a member of the local congregation (see Acts 2:42-47). Here foodstuffs were brought by those who were blessed with abundance, and through their generosity shared with the poorer members of the assembly. Together they ate and worshiped the Lord. The relationship between worship, the meal shared in the Lord, and concern for the needy brothers and sisters is clearly recognized by the early church.

The Lord's Supper, originally celebrated in the context of the love feast or *agapē* meal, was distinguished from it in Pauline instruction (1 Cor. 11:17-34) and came to be observed separately. There is evidence that the *agapē* feast continued to be celebrated as a distinct event into the fourth century. It has been revived in the contemporary liturgical renewal, and many churches celebrate it in members' homes prior to the Maundy Thursday service, as a memorial of the meal in the upper room before Jesus instituted the Lord's Supper on the night of his arrest. The occasional "fellowship supper" held by many Christian congregations today bears a certain resemblance in spirit and function to the ancient love feast.

Robert E. Webber

THIRTY-TWO

Other Sacred Actions in Worship

Although the Eucharist, or Lord's Supper, has always been the most distinctive sacred or sacramental act of Christian worship, the historic church has found certain other events of worship to be especially symbolic of spiritual realities. These actions are "sacramental" in that they serve as windows into the unseen aspects of the relationship between God and the people of God. They have their foundations in the experience, the understanding, and the practice of the New Testament church; in some cases they are "ordinances" of Jesus, symbolic actions he himself performed and commended to his disciples. The rites of baptism, confirmation, foot washing, anointing with oil, ordination, and marriage all have this sacramental or symbolic quality for Christian worshipers.

278 ◆ Baptism in Scripture

Christian baptism has its origins in the various Jewish rites of ritual purification and in John's baptism of repentance. Christian baptism differs from its antecedents, however, in important respects. It is baptism in the name of Jesus, signifying a belonging to him, and is associated with the gifting of the Holy Spirit. Baptism symbolizes a participation in Christ's death and resurrection and the believer's incorporation into the new covenant people of God. The New Testament does not lay out a specified order for the rite of baptism.

Baptismal Terminology and Water Symbolism

The English word *baptism* derives from the Greek verbs *baptō* and *baptizō*. In Greek *baptō* means "dip," "dye" by dipping something into dye, and "draw [water]." The intensive form *baptizō* means "dip," or "cause to perish" by drowning or sinking (as a ship). The nouns derived from these verbs are *baptismos* ("dipping, washing") and *baptisma* ("baptism"). The usual Hebrew equivalent for *baptō* and its cognates is *taval;* both terms imply an immersion and often carry the meaning of destruction by drowning. In the context of religious purifications the Greek verbs *louō* ("wash"), *niptō* ("wash, rinse"), and *rainō* ("sprinkle") are more common than *baptō* or *baptizō*. The ambivalence expressed in the words *baptō* and *baptizō* is based on the natural symbolism of water, which holds an important place in all religious traditions. Water can refer to both the life-giving blessings of God and the evil forces opposing God's authority.

Since all forms of biological life need water to exist, water is a natural symbol of life. Water quenches thirst and renews the human body. We use water to cleanse our bodies and to purify our food and all objects related to human life. An abundant supply of water—either through rain or from springs and rivers—brings growth, fertility, and prosperity. For those who live in dry climates water is a special sign of happiness and divine favor.

Yet water can be destructive as well as life-giving. Floods destroy homes, crops, and persons. Polluted water carries infectious diseases. The formlessness and force of water in a storm at sea or in a raging river make it a fitting symbol of chaos. In a religious setting water can symbolize powers in opposition to the Creator God who imposes form and stability on creation. The ambivalence of the terminology for baptism and for water as a symbol finds expression in what the New Testament writers say about baptism.

Antecedents in Israelite and Jewish Practice

The remote antecedents of Christian baptism are to be found in Old Testament texts concerning ritual purification. Before carrying out rites in the tent of meeting (and later in the Jerusalem temple) priests washed themselves with water (Exod. 30–32; 40:2). On the Day of Atonement the high priest bathed his body before putting on the priestly garments and performing sacrifices (Lev. 16). The Pentateuch also prescribed washings as part of rites intended to end ritual uncleanness brought about through contact with unclean objects (Lev. 11:24-40; 14:1-8; 15:1-13; Num. 19:1-24). Ritual washings were so familiar to Old Testament writers that they used them in metaphors, thus endowing them with moral and spiritual dimensions (Pss. 24:4; 51:7) and in some cases eschatological overtones (Ezek. 36:25; Zech. 13:1).

Closer in time to early Christian baptism were Jewish practices that arose from or adapted the biblical rules about ritual purity. Part of the Pharisees' program for a "priestly" Israel was the observance even by nonpriests of the biblical rules for ritual purity. Ritual immersion baths from second temple times have been discovered by archaeologists at several sites in the land of Israel (Masada, Herodium, Jericho, Jerusalem, Qumran), a sign that ritual immersions were widely practiced.

The elaborate system of water channels found at Qumran indicates that ritual purification was a regular feature of life within the Essene community. The *Community Rule* (columns 2-3, 5-6) suggests that initiation into the Qumran community was accompanied by a special rite of washing that symbolized the initiate's inner life: "And when his flesh is sprinkled with purifying water, it shall be made clean by the humble submission of his soul to all the precepts of God" (3:8-9). The community lived in expectation of the coming visitation of the Lord. From the beginning of their association with the sect, the members had a strong eschatological consciousness.

Two other possible antecedents for baptism are more controversial. The "proselyte baptism" in rabbinic literature (see *b. Yebamot* 46–47) is sometimes proposed as a model. A female convert to Judaism was required to undergo a ritual immersion, and a male convert underwent both circumcision and ritual immersion before undertaking Jewish life in its fullness. But doubts about how early this ritual was used and whether it should be called a "baptism" analogous to Christian baptism render it a questionable influence.

Likewise, the rites associated with initiation into Greco-Roman mystery religions are uncertain antecedents for baptism. That Jews of Jesus' time knew about such rituals is entirely possible. But it is unlikely that such rites exercised more than a passing influence on the vocabulary and practice of baptism among the followers of John the Baptist and Jesus.

The Baptism of John

The Jewish rite most influential on early Christian baptism was the baptism of John the Baptist. John's activity was centered in the Judean wilderness by the River Jordan. Not far from Qumran, this area seems to have attracted several "baptist" sects in the first century. The Mandaean movement probably originated in this milieu, though their claims to a direct tie to John the Baptist arose late, in response to Islam. Though part of a larger "baptist" movement, John was so striking a figure as to merit the title "the Baptist/Baptizer" from both Josephus (*Antiquities* 18:116-119) and the Evangelists (Mark 1:2-11 and parallels).

Whereas most of the Jewish ritual washings were self-administered, John's baptism was administered by another. Whereas most Jewish ritual washings were repeated, John's baptism seems to have been a once-for-all-time affair. John's baptism demanded a turning around of one's life in the face of the coming kingdom of God. Several important characteristics of early Christian baptism derive from John's baptism: a water ritual, once for all time, administered by another, involving conversion and oriented toward the coming kingdom.

Two features distinguish Christian baptism from John's baptism: Christian baptism is "in Jesus' name" and involves the gift of the Spirit.

The point of contact between John's baptism and Jesus' baptism was Jesus' membership in John's movement (Mark 1:9) and the attraction of some of John's disciples to Jesus when he went on his own (John 1:35-42). That Jesus accepted baptism from John is one of the best-attested facts of his life. Yet the accounts of his baptism (Mark 1:9-11; Matt. 3:13-17; Luke 3:21-22; John 1:31-34) are more concerned with presenting that event as the manifestation of God's Son and Servant than as a model for Christian baptism. Despite the silence of the synoptic Gospels, it is possible that Jesus himself baptized (John 3:22, 26; 4:1), though this would not qualify as "Christian" baptism. [John 4:2, however, indicates that the actual baptisms were performed by Jesus' disciples] The great commission of Matthew 28:19 reflects the liturgical language of the late first-century church. Neither Jesus' own baptism by John, nor his activity as a baptizer, nor the great commission provides the one definitive link between John's baptism and Jesus' baptism. But given the common membership in the two movements, it seems that Jesus' followers would have understood baptism "in Jesus' name" and with the Holy Spirit (Mark 1:8 and parallels) as the continuation and fulfillment of John's baptism.

Meanings of Christian Baptism

Baptism in Jesus' Name. Christian baptism takes place "in Jesus' name," a formula that represents an earlier stage than the Trinitarian formula of Matthew 28:19. This Christological formula is taken for granted by Paul (Rom. 6:3; 1 Cor. 1:13, 15; Gal. 3:27) and expressed in various ways in Acts (Acts 2:38; 8:16; 10:48; 19:5). The Semitic expression underlying "in the name of" (_l^eshem_ in Hebrew, _l^eshum_ in Aramaic) allows several interpretations: with respect to, for the sake of, and with thought for. In any case, the baptized person now belongs to God through the saving event associated with Jesus. In baptism one belongs to Jesus (1 Cor. 1:10-17) and confesses him as Lord (1 Cor. 12:3; Rom. 10:9), thus putting aside all other masters. Perhaps with a deliberate allusion to slavery, Paul refers to baptism as the "seal" (2 Cor. 1:22). In baptism one is delivered from the dominion of darkness and transferred to the kingdom of God's beloved Son (Col 1:13).

Baptism and the Spirit. Christian baptism also differs from John's baptism by its association with the gift of the Holy Spirit (Mark 1:8; Acts 1:5; 11:16). Although the fullness of the Spirit is reserved for the eschaton, baptism brings the "firstfruits of the Spirit" (Rom. 8:23). The present experience of the Spirit is also described as the "down payment" or "first installment" (_arrabōn_) of what will be in the future (2 Cor. 1:22; 5:5; Eph. 1:14).

The precise relationship between water baptism and the gift of the Spirit seems to have been a problem for some early Christians. That the two belong together is affirmed by many New Testament texts (John 3:5; 1 Cor. 12:13; 2 Cor. 1:22; Titus 3:5). How they fit together is problematic mainly because of some strange texts in Acts. At Pentecost the gift of the Spirit is a consequence of water baptism (Acts 2:38). Whereas some Samaritans had been baptized in Jesus' name but had not yet received the Spirit

(Acts 8:14-17), in the Cornelius episode Gentiles first receive the Spirit and then undergo water baptism (Acts 10:44-48). Those at Ephesus who had received John's baptism need to receive the Spirit through the agency of Paul (Acts 19:1-7). Nevertheless, despite the variety in order, Luke's point in all these texts is that water baptism and the gift of the Spirit belong together.

Baptism and the Death of Christ. The most extensive and profound reflection on the meaning of baptism appears in Romans 6. There Paul joins the baptismal themes of belonging to Jesus as Lord and the first installment of the gift of the Spirit to his theology of the cross: "Don't you know that all of us who were baptized into Christ Jesus were baptized into his death? We were therefore buried with him through baptism into death in order that, just as Christ was raised from the dead through the glory of the Father, we too may live a new life" (Rom. 6:3-4). The connection between baptism and Jesus' death may have been suggested by the ambivalence of water as a symbol—both life-giving and death-dealing. Paul finds in baptism a death to the world ruled by the evil powers (sin and death) and the possibility of living a new life under the guidance of the Spirit (Rom. 8). Yet the new life is not yet fully realized; it demands conduct appropriate to one who is led by the Spirit (Rom. 12:1-8) and rejects the idea that "everything is permissible" (1 Cor. 6:12; 10:23). Thus in Romans 6 Paul specifies the point of identity between Christ and the baptized person as Jesus' death and resurrection, underlines the preliminary nature of the gift of the Spirit, and challenges his readers to "walk" appropriately as they await the fullness of God's kingdom.

The notion of baptism as passing from the dominion of sin, death, and the Law to the dominion of Jesus and the Spirit is Paul's way of talking about a motif that runs from John's baptism to Christian baptism: the forgiveness of sins (Mark 1:4; Luke 3:3; Acts 2:38; 10:43; 26:18). This motif is also the starting point for reflection on the problem of repentance after apostasy (Heb. 6:1-6; 10:26). Other New Testament baptismal motifs associated with the forgiveness of sins include baptism as "pledge of a good conscience toward God" (1 Pet. 3:21), as a means of rebirth (John 3:3, 5; 1 Pet. 1:3, 23; Titus 3:5-7), and as a washing (1 Cor. 6:11; Eph. 5:26; Titus 3:5; Heb. 10:22).

Baptism and Incorporation into the People of God.
The communal dimension of baptism and its power
to incorporate even non-Jews into the people of
God emerges from Paul's reflection on people of
faith as the true children of Abraham: "For all of you
who were baptized into Christ have clothed yourselves with Christ. . . . If you belong to Christ, then
you are Abraham's seed, and heirs according to the
promise" (Gal. 3:27, 29). In the midst of that conclusion Paul quotes an early Christian baptismal slogan:
"There is neither Jew nor Greek, slave nor free, male
nor female, for you are all one in Christ Jesus" (Gal.
3:28). Though Paul showed interest in only the first
of the three pairs, the content of the slogan corresponds to his themes of nonpartiality before God
(Rom. 2:11) and the equality of access to God's grace
in Christ (1 Cor. 10:1-6; Eph. 2:1-16).

Baptismal motifs are so prominent in 1 Peter that
it has been interpreted as a baptismal instruction or
catechesis. Whatever the validity of this interpretation, it is fair to describe the spirituality of 1 Peter as
thoroughly baptismal. A consequence of the author's reflection on baptism is his bold address to a
largely Gentile community in terms applied in Exodus 19:5-6 to Israel at Sinai: "a chosen people, a
royal priesthood, a holy nation, a people belonging
to God" (1 Pet. 2:9). What makes possible such as-
sertions is the incorporation of non-Jews into God's
people through baptism "in Jesus' name." [Baptism,
therefore, corresponds to circumcision as the sign
of the covenant between the Lord and his people.
Paul compares baptism with circumcision in Colossians 2:11-13.]

—— Order for New Testament Baptism ——

There is no explicit description of the rite of baptism in the New Testament. What can be said about
that rite must be inferred from passing comments.
This is a dangerous procedure, since one can imagine all kinds of rituals on the basis of metaphors and
other figures of speech.

With that caution in mind, it is possible to say the
following about the rite of baptism in New Testament times. The person to be baptized received a
form of instruction (1 Cor. 15:1-8, Heb. 6:1-2). As
with John's baptism, Christian baptism was administered by another (1 Cor. 1:14-17). The word *baptizō,* the imagery of baptism as a drowning (Rom.
6:1-11), and the practices associated with Jewish ritual ablutions and baths (*miqva'ot*) all indicate that
immersion was the usual method of baptizing.

*The scallop shell was an early Christian symbol
of baptism. Note the three drops of water representing baptism in the name of the Father, the
Son, and the Holy Spirit (see Matt. 28:19).*

Women may have been baptized by other women
(Rom. 16:2), though this is never made explicit.
Where there was not sufficient water available for
immersion, it was allowable to "pour water three
times on the head" (*Didachē* 7.3). The person was
baptized "in the name of"—at first that of Jesus, and
later that of the Father, Son, and Holy Spirit (Matt.
28:19; *Didachē* 7.3). There may also have been
questions directed to the congregation about the
candidate's fitness (Acts 8:37; Mark 10:14), hymns
(Col. 1:12-20; Eph. 5:14), confessions of faith (Rom.
10:9; 1 Cor. 12:13; Heb. 4:14; 1 John 4:15; 5:5), and
the imposition of hands (Acts 8:16-17; 19:6).

The premise behind most New Testament baptismal texts is that candidates were adults. It cannot be
proved (or disproved) that young children or infants
were also baptized in New Testament times. It is not
certain that texts about the baptisms of entire households (1 Cor. 1:16; Acts 2:38-39; 11:14; 16:15, 33-
34; 18:8) really include infants. Peter's promise "for
you and your children" in Acts 2:39 refers to the succeeding generation(s), not to infant baptism. Jesus'
rebuke of his disciples, "Let the little children come
to me, and do not hinder them" (Mark 10:14), had
nothing to do with baptism in New Testament times.
Whether young children or infants should be baptized raises the question about the nature of baptism. Is the essence of baptism the candidate's

confession of faith, or is it the reception and appropriation of the salvation offered "in Jesus' name?" [Or is it the sign of membership in the covenant community, corresponding to circumcision? Jewish males were circumcised at the age of eight days, not by their own volition but by that of their parents; it seems reasonable that some Christian converts might have viewed the baptism of their children as a parallel rite.]

Perhaps the strangest element in the New Testament teaching about baptism is the practice of baptism for the dead: "What will those do who are baptized for the dead? If the dead are not raised at all, why are people baptized for them?" (1 Cor. 15:29). It seems that people in Corinth had themselves baptized vicariously for dead people. Instead of criticizing this custom directly, Paul uses it to bolster his argument about the reality of resurrection. The practice was continued by the Marcionites and other heretical groups but condemned by the church at large. Paul's point was that this practice was a sign of belief in resurrection at Corinth. The magical assumptions behind it ran counter to Paul's insistence on "walk[ing] in newness of life" (Rom. 6:4 RSV), as his reflection on the wilderness generation shows: "all were baptized into Moses in the cloud and in the sea. . . . God was not pleased with most of them" (1 Cor. 10:2, 5).

Daniel J. Harrington[33]

279 ✦ CONFIRMATION IN SCRIPTURE

Confirmation is the historic rite of initiation into the full fellowship of the body of Christ. Christian initiation in the early church apparently consisted of two actions, baptism followed by imposition of hands for the gift of the Holy Spirit. The sequence of events was governed by the early disciples' personal experience of salvation in Christ and the endowment of his Spirit. Paul, reflecting theologically, brought out the underlying spiritual unity of the two rites.

——— The Issue of Confirmation ———

In general terms the question of confirmation may be described as the place of the gift of the Spirit of God in the practice of Christian initiation in the early church. But the matter requires closer definition.

The gift and presence of God's Spirit in the church is a prominent assertion and theme of the New Testament. This gift is presented as a fruit of the redemptive victory of Christ and as a foundational event that brings into existence and thereafter maintains the Christian community or church. It is a _community_ endowment establishing _this_ community with its specific identity. Apart from the original individuals who, precisely as forming the _original_ community received the Spirit directly (John 20; Acts 2), all others receive this gift only by becoming members of this community and thereby sharing in the Spirit with which it has been originally endowed. To receive the gift of the Holy Spirit is simply to become a member of this Spirit-filled community. The precise question to be faced is this: how in the actual practice and understanding of the early church was this gift received—as an effect of baptism or of a postbaptismal rite or as a somehow free gift of God later acknowledged by the community?

The New Testament material bearing on this issue has to be situated within the particular stratum of New Testament literature to which it belongs. Following this principle one may group the relevant material as follows: (1) the evidence in the Acts of the Apostles on the practice of Christian initiation in the early church; (2) the references in the Pauline letters on baptism and the gift of the Spirit; (3) material in the synoptic Gospels that reflects the early church's practice and understanding of initiation (of special significance here is the way Jesus' baptism by John is reported); and (4) references to initiation in the other documents of the New Testament.

Acts is specifically concerned with giving a picture of the life of the church in the early period. Its narrative thus bears directly on the issue under discussion and for this reason is the more hopeful document we possess for information on the early practice of Christian initiation.

Paul's main interest is not to give any description of the initiation practice with which he and the addressees of his letters are familiar, but rather to develop a deeper understanding of what this now-past event means in the present and the future for Christian faith and life. This is essentially and totally a _theological_ enterprise and _not_ an exercise in description of current ritual practice. For information on the initiation _practice_ of the early church, Acts is the primary and controlling source; for developed theological insight, Paul is the significant writer.

Initiation Practice of the Early Church

The understanding of the gift of the Spirit in the Acts of the Apostles has its determining source in the event of Pentecost. This event signifies the endowment of the community of Jesus' disciples with the promised eschatological gift of God's Spirit. Together with the resurrection and exaltation of Jesus, this event signifies the effective dawn of the messianic age and establishes the community of Jesus' disciples as the messianic community, the group that has received and now possesses the promised messianic blessings. Pentecost is thus the second event that brings the Christian church into existence and gives it its identity. The first and prior of these events is the life, death, and resurrection of Jesus Christ, which brings into existence the community of the disciples of Christ. The second is the coming of the Spirit, which establishes this already-existing community as the *Spirit-filled* community of the disciples of Christ.

It is important to note that the coming of the Spirit is a *community* gift and endowment. The question that arises, and that arose immediately, is how others could come to share in the blessings the community now possesses, including the gift of the Spirit. This is the question of the initiation practice of the early church, the system whereby new converts were admitted to membership in the community. The question arose immediately on Pentecost Sunday, according to Acts 2, in the reaction to Peter's sermon. In reply to his audience's question, "what shall we do?" (Acts 2:37), Peter answers: "Repent and be baptized, every one of you, in the name of Jesus Christ for the forgiveness of your sins. And you will receive the gift of the Holy Spirit" (Acts 2:38). The text goes on to state that on that day three thousand "were added" to the number of the community (Acts 2:41).

This passage describes, however summarily, the earliest practice of Christian initiation. A number of points arising from the text deserve notice. The words *were added* show that it is a question of new members joining an already-existing group and coming to share in their specific status and privileges. The issue that arises is what process or system of initiation the passage envisages. This process is described summarily in Acts 2:38. The text mentions explicitly the rite of immersion baptism, which is directly associated with "the name of Jesus

Christ," that is, personal adherence to or discipleship of Christ, and its effect is described as "the forgiveness of sins." There then follows the reference to the gift of the Holy Spirit: "and you will receive the gift of the Holy Spirit." The double reference to Christ and the Spirit clearly refers to and reproduces the two events that brought the community into existence and have given it its identity. This double reference, the christological and the pneumatological, continue to characterize mention of Christian initiation not only throughout the New Testament but throughout Christian history.

But how does Acts 2:38 envisage the relationship between the water rite of baptism and the gift of the Spirit? At first reading, three interpretations seem possible: the gift of the Spirit is an effect of baptism itself; the coming of the Spirit is a subsequent event in the life of the baptized person unmediated by any rite; or the Spirit is conferred by means of a subsequent rite. While most commentators assume the first interpretation as correct, with little attempt at critical examination, it needs to be stressed that, taken in itself, the text has to be left open in its meaning and can only be finally interpreted in light of how Christian initiation is presented throughout the rest of Acts. But it should be noted that the particular Greek grammatical structure here, an imperative followed by a future indicative, strongly suggests that the first interpretation can scarcely be the correct one.

It is not possible to undertake here a detailed examination of the material throughout Acts referring to Christian initiation. It must suffice to mention some factors that enable one to determine the meaning implicit in Acts 2:38 concerning the gift of the Spirit.

A number of studies have made clear that consistently throughout Acts the gift of the Spirit is *not* presented or envisaged as an effect of baptism. Commentators have generally paid too little attention to the precise concept of the Holy Spirit Acts presents. This is the classical biblical and Jewish concept of the prophetic Spirit. But this concept in itself is not intrinsically connected either with ritual washing or forgiveness of sins, the stated effect of baptism in Acts. It would be extraordinary indeed if such an intrinsic connection now suddenly appeared in early Christianity, which, for its own thought and practice, was so heavily indebted to biblical and Jewish concepts.

Further, Acts 2:38 clearly presupposes a particular

system of Christian initiation. This practice consists of baptism *and* the rite of imposition of hands for the gift of the Spirit (Acts 8:12-17; 19:1-7). Apart from Luke's obvious familiarity with this initiation ritual, it is also clear that whatever sources he was relying on (probably oral, not documentary) confirmed him in his view.

Various other data that can be gleaned from Acts concerning Christian initiation cohere with and strengthen this assessment. Moreover, material from the synoptic Gospels now also falls easily into line. This applies in particular to the narrative of Jesus' baptism by John in the Jordan. As described by the Synoptics (Matt. 3:16-17; Mark 1:9-11; Luke 3:21-22), this event is undoubtedly presented as a paradigmatic model of the initiation of the Christian convert and reflects the church's early initiation practice. It is therefore highly significant that this event also consists of immersion in water followed by the descent of the Spirit upon Jesus. "At that time Jesus came from Nazareth in Galilee and was baptized [that is, immersed] by John in the Jordan. As Jesus was coming up out of the water, he saw heaven being torn open and the Spirit descending on him like a dove" (Mark 1:9-10). Here also the coming of the Spirit is a postbaptismal event. Given the literary form within which Mark is writing, those scholars who would wish to see the gift of the Spirit as an effect intrinsic to the baptismal rite of immersion would logically have to maintain that here the dove alighted on Jesus while he was immersed *under* the water. The text of Hebrews 6:2 adds its further confirming weight to the argument advocated here concerning the practice of initiation in the early church. This text can only be understood as implying a reference to Christian initiation as consisting of two rites, baptism and imposition of hands.

The conclusion to this summary investigation of the New Testament sources concerning the initiation practice of the early church is that this consisted of *two* rites, baptism followed by imposition of hands for the gift of the Spirit (or, in later terminology, confirmation). It may seem surprising to us today that formal entry into the Christian community was thought to require two distinct rites. Under normal circumstances it seems that one would be sufficient. This, however, is to impose a modern, rationalistic approach on the more imaginative and symbolic mind of former ages. One must remember the seedbed from which early Christianity, as regards both thought and practice, derived, namely Judaism, with the biblical history that lay behind it and the actual experience of the members of the foundational Christian church.

The original community recognized and identified itself as the community of the new era, the promised messianic community inheriting and possessing the messianic blessings. In typical biblical manner, this community and its privileges are presented as coming into existence in accordance with the model or pattern of salvation history, that is, a series of separate events following one another and building on one another until eventually a climax is achieved. The foundational community experienced the culmination of this history in the events of Christ and the Spirit, the two climactic events that have brought the community into existence and that gave it its identity as the Spirit-filled community of the disciples of Jesus. In opening itself to new converts, the community reproduces and expresses in effective symbol or sacrament the salvation history it has experienced. Hence the double reference in its initiation ritual, both to Christ and to the Holy Spirit, expressed by means of the two distinct rites.

This initiation ritual, however, based as it is on the model of salvation history and the actual experience of the original community, poses a challenge to the Christian mind to discern the unity that lies behind its discrete references. This challenge, which is an invitation to a strictly *theological* enterprise, was soon recognized and addressed. Herein lies the significance of Paul on the gift of the Holy Spirit and Christian initiation.

Deepening Insight: Paul

The Holy Spirit figures prominently in the thought and writings of Paul. The Spirit is an endowment of and a vital presence in the Christian community. It is clear that the gift of the Spirit is an effect of the past, once-for-all event of Christian initiation. But it represents an abiding presence, and Paul's main interest lies not in the particular moment of the past or any description thereof but rather in illuminating the significance of this presence *now* for the life of the church and the Christian. This is the reason he shows little or no interest in any factual description of the actual event of initiation and why so little information can be gleaned from his scattered references concerning it. He was not liturgically minded. His interest was in developing a deeper understanding of what Christian faith and life mean. This is a theological enterprise in the proper sense, an effort of faith seeking understanding. It is an effort that searches earnestly for the unity underlying the discrete references of Christian faith and practice and in pursuing its tasks often finds itself embarrassed by these references and the salvation history model that has determined them.

Paul's silence concerning a postbaptismal rite is largely explained by this context. For he was familiar with what we have seen was the regular practice of the early church. His references in Acts echo much of the same general understanding of initiation found in the early church. The characteristic double reference, both to Christ and to the Spirit, occurs again and again in the Pauline texts. But Paul's effort to develop a deeper understanding of the mystery of Christian initiation leads him to develop new emphases and to bring the separate references together into a deeper unity. This is his significance and his achievement, and it is in this enterprise that the key to his thought and texts lies. His references are concerned with illuminating the existing, regular practice of the church, and they thus constitute, in the words of Rudolf Schnackenburg, "a marriage of the existing rite with the weighty thought of his theology" (*Baptism in the Thought of St. Paul* [New York: Herder & Herder, 1964], 30).

Central to this bold effort of Paul is the new concept of the Spirit of God he introduces that is to have such a profound influence in Christian theology. In early Christianity the spirit of prophecy was understood to inspire forceful preaching of the gospel and accompany that preaching with confirming signs. But Paul now retrieves the other biblical concept of the Spirit, the *life-giving* Spirit (prominent in the Prophets, see especially Ezek. 36–37). This provides him with one of the ideas he is seeking to develop, a more unified understanding of Christian faith. It enables him to connect the separate references, bringing them into harmonious unity. In particular, he is now able to unite the references to Christ and to the Spirit in the rite of initiation. To be united to Christ means also to share in the Spirit of Christ, the Spirit of God; to receive the Holy Spirit implies union with Christ. This explains why the typical Pauline expressions, to be "in Christ," and "in the Spirit," in their deepest significance blend into one another and become almost synonymous.

This achievement of theological insight enables Paul to see the power of the Spirit at work also in the process of baptism itself, both in the genesis of faith and conversion preceding the sacrament and in the union with Christ therein accomplished. He is thus able to present Christian initiation as the unity it is, and this is the main thrust and direction of his thought. But this does not at all mean that on his own initiative he would have interfered with the established and inherited practice of Christian initiation and bent it at his will to his way of thinking. Nothing in his writings suggests he was or needed to be that kind of radical innovator. His theological enterprise transcended the salvation history model he was commenting on. Consciously or unconsciously, this was his purpose and his achievement.

But it is worth noting that in his most extensive and significant reference to baptism, Romans 6:3-11, Paul makes no mention of the Holy Spirit. This latter theme, so prominent in his thought, is not introduced until chapter 8. It is difficult to see how, if in the initiation practice of the church, the gift of the Spirit was seen as an effect of baptism, he could have avoided reference to the Spirit in this passage. No doubt the structure of Romans is important here. Nevertheless, if there is an argument from silence in the Pauline writings on this issue, it surely lies here.

Conclusion

The remaining documents of the New Testament throw little further light on this question. Something of the influence of Paul is discernible in the close linking in some texts of the work of Spirit with baptism (John 3:5; Titus 3:5). Though such references are often interpreted as implying that the Spirit is given in baptism, this judgment is over hasty. Here again is the Pauline understanding of the Holy Spirit and the Spirit's role in the process of initiation. No more than in Paul himself, therefore, this close association of Christ and the Holy Spirit does not imply any denial of the existence of a special postbaptismal rite of the Spirit.

Viewing the evidence of the New Testament as a whole, therefore, one finds that Christian initiation in the early church consisted of two rites, baptism followed by imposition of hands for the gift of the Spirit. This complex ritual was derived from and determined by the perspective of biblical salvation history and the personal experience of the original disciples. Paul, introducing a new and more profound understanding of the Spirit, was able to envisage and indicate the unity underlying this complex ritual with its discrete references. We meet here for the first time the tension between these two approaches to understanding Christian faith and practice, the theological and the salvation history approaches. Both methods will continue in the church, the salvation history model being more congenial to instruction of new converts and teaching within the context of worship, the theological to the effort to achieve a more unified understanding. Both approaches are necessary; neither can be reduced to the other. When one approach tends to overdominate, false questions arise and inevitably receive false solutions. Much of the oft-referred-to "confusion" concerning the sacrament of confirmation has its source here. The legitimacy and necessity of both approaches have to be recognized and a balanced tension maintained. This is the way toward progress and understanding in this area of Christian faith and practice. It is also the way that offers the best hope for ecumenical discussion. This is perhaps the most valuable lesson the New Testament teaches us today concerning the gift of the Holy Spirit in Christian initiation.

Thomas A. Marsh[34]

280 ✦ THE RITE OF FOOT WASHING

While foot washing is not one of the traditional sacraments of the church, it is recognized as a sacramental action in many segments of the Christian faith.

Though never a major rite, the washing of the hands and feet of the priests did have a place in the Mosaic ritual (Exod. 30:17-21). It may indeed be that all ablutions of the Bible are ritual, rather than sanitary, though they rise out of assumed sanitary practices. Guests customarily were offered water and vessels for washing the feet (Gen. 18:4; 19:2; Judg. 19:21). As a special act of affection or humility, the host or hostess might even wash the feet of his or her guests (1 Sam. 25:41). A "sinful woman" spontaneously and gratefully so served the Lord (Luke 7:36-44).

At the Last Supper the Lord Jesus, taking a towel and basin during the meal (John 13:4-10), proceeded to wash the disciples' feet and wipe them. This action was not to observe a custom, for the disciples were mystified by it. There is no doubt that Jesus gave it the spiritual significance of the symbolic cleansing of the believer from the defilement of present sin, as baptism symbolized cleansing

from all guilt—the former practical and temporary, the latter complete and permanent. "A person who has had a bath needs only to wash his feet" (John 13:10). This is the main lesson here, rather than humility.

Whether foot washing is an ordinance (see John 13:14, 16) must be decided by whether it meets the three qualifications of a church ordinance: an action (1) instituted by Christ, (2) of universal application, and (3) of permanent application. A number of denominations developing out of the Anabaptist wing of the Reformation, in particular the churches of the Brethren, believe it to be an ordinance, citing, in addition to John 13, 1 Timothy 5:10. In these communities, foot washing is observed in connection with the annual or semiannual celebration of the love feast and the Lord's Supper. Liturgical churches commonly practice foot washing as part of the observance of Maundy Thursday.

Robert D. Culver

281 ✦ SACRAMENTAL ANOINTING

Anointing, as a physical action pointing to a spiritual reality, had its origins in the practical use of oil for cosmetic and therapeutic purposes. Anointing became a symbolic expression of blessing or of the setting apart of a person or object for purposes that transcend the profane or common dimension of life. The title Christ _or_ Messiah _applied to Jesus means "Anointed One."_

The Origins of Anointing

The practice of anointing, whether in the context of ritual or not, is an ancient one. It did not originate with Judaism or Christianity. Anointing with oil, especially olive oil, can be traced back to certain customs in the Near East. Sometimes the anointing took place in the context of a ritual and sometimes it did not. When anointing had a liturgical context, it often was the way a culture dealt with such life crises as suffering, sickness, and death. Religious anointing in many of these older societies was one of the many ways they attempted to give meaning to situations of human fragmentation. Often the anointing was connected with something that seemed to be out of harmony with the universe, a liminal situation. Because ancient peoples had difficulty explaining the origins of sickness, they often created myths to explain what appeared to be unnatural or even evil. Since ritual is a combination of mythic content and external activity, a rite of anointing would easily be used to express a belief in an order that transcends the limitations of sickness and death.

It would be impossible to distinguish which of these ancient rituals were directed to physical healing and which were concerned with spiritual effects. Because these cultures took a more holistic view of the person, anointings were both occasions of providing meaning in situations of human brokenness and a form of medicine to restore a person to physical health. Such anointings very easily possessed a sacramental character in that they were symbolic actions by means of which one reality existed in another. There was no clear dichotomy between material and spiritual dimensions of the rites. Although there has been considerable ambiguity regarding the proper effects of the anointings, it can be said that they at least inserted the persons anointed within the larger system of meaning in their particular communities. This more holistic perspective was as characteristic of ancient Israel as of its pagan neighbors. It is an approach that should not be considered naive. Today, anointing is again seen as a way of engaging the whole person, a way of healing the body/mind split.

Anointing in Scripture

Anointing in the Bible has both a religious and a secular purpose. In a land characterized by dry weather, it was natural that anointing with oil would have a cosmetic and therapeutic intention. The secular use of oil is clear from Ezekiel 16:9, where it is the completion of the bathing process. Isaiah 61:3 speaks of the "oil of gladness instead of mourning," which indicates a more symbolic experience of anointing. Second Samuel 14:2 makes clear that the absence of anointing is the sign of grief. There are many other instances of anointing in the Bible that operate in a religious context: anointing the heads of guests as a sign of respect (Matt. 26:7), the feet of visitors (Luke 7:46), those freed from captivity (2 Chron. 28:15), the wounded (Isa. 1:6), and the dead as part of the preparation for burial (Mark 16:1).

There are many biblical examples of anointing in a religious context, especially in the Hebrew Scriptures. To anoint a person or an object was to bless that person or thing and set it apart for religious purposes. For instance, Moses anointed the ark, the altar, and the lampstand, as well as Aaron and his sons.

Exodus 30:22-29 records the anointing of sacred furniture and vessels. For the most part only priests and kings were anointed in the Bible. Exodus 28:40-42 describes the consecration of priests, although the anointing may have been usually restricted to the high priest. Prophets were also anointed, but this practice may have been connected with the anointing of kings (1 Kings 19:16). The anointing of kings was an anointing done both by prophets and by priests, and it had the special meaning of designating the king as anointed of Yahweh (1 Sam. 10:1; 16:13; 24:6). The anointing of the king is an example of how often the civil and religious meanings of anointing blended together. The ceremony may have been civil, but the meaning was religious. Even secularly kingly anointing meant being consecrated to God's service. Through anointing the king was removed from ordinary life and was made directly responsible to God.

While the New Testament is rich in the healing ministry of Christ and his followers and in the designation of Christ as the Anointed One, there is little recorded about the practice of anointing with oil beyond those instances found in the Hebrew Scriptures. Because healing took place in the name of Christ, often no specific symbolic action was involved, although there is evidence of human gesture connected with healing situations. One anointing recorded in the New Testament, in Matthew 26:7, tells of Jesus being anointed in Bethany shortly before his death. Here anointing was a sign of honor. Anointings were also employed in conjunction with exorcisms, as in Mark 6:13, "They drove out many demons and anointed many sick people with oil and healed them." And the celebrated text of James 5 includes "Is any one of you sick? He should call the elders of the church to pray over him and anoint him with oil in the name of the Lord" (James 5:14).

The title of Jesus is the Anointed One. He comes in the line of Hebrew prophets who were sometimes recognized as charismatic persons through anointing. This signaled that their mission was under the power of the Spirit of God. Christ inserts himself in that tradition when he quotes Isaiah 61, "The Spirit of the Sovereign LORD is on me, because the LORD has anointed me" (Isa. 61:1). The Christian church has interpreted Mark 1:9-11, which depicts the baptism of Jesus by John and the descending of the Spirit on Jesus as the "messianic anointing of Jesus" by the Holy Spirit. It was only logical that the therapeutic use of oil by the Jews and the theologizing of the early church on the baptism of Jesus would lead to anointing becoming part of the sacramental activity of the church, especially in the rites of initiation, ordination, and healing.

John J. Ziegler[36]

282 • ORDINATION IN THE NEW TESTAMENT

The specific terminology of ordination is not found in the New Testament, although several occasions are described on which people were set aside for special tasks of ministry. A fuller development of the theory of ordination took place in the post–New Testament church.

Ministry Differentiation in the New Testament

The present state of scholarship demands great caution in speaking about ordination, its meaning, or its rites in the New Testament. The words *ordain* and *ordination* are not found there, and there is considerable disagreement about the extent to which this later Christian use may coincide with the categories of the New Testament and with its pattern, or varied patterns, of understanding, vocabulary, and practice.

Evidence suggests that the church had both unity and differentiation from the beginning. There is equality based on baptism, equality that nevertheless requires authority, leadership, that is structured and maintained as a unity through special ministers. Ministry rather than order or status is the predominant emphasis: a mission to be accomplished, a task to be done, rather than a class to be entered or a status to be attained. These differences should not be exaggerated; ministry may well involve position, and a mission may carry with it or may require a certain personal status, and ministers may be grouped together because of the nature of their function.

Ministry does not arise merely out of sociological pressure; its necessity is found at a deeper level in the person and mission of Jesus Christ. The entire ministry is ultimately the work of God (1 Cor. 12:6), the gift of Christ (Eph. 4:7-12) and of the Holy Spirit (1 Cor. 12:4-11; cf. Acts 20:28) in and through and for the church, the body of Christ. The most important forms of ministry can be characterized as those of leadership: preaching the gospel and founding new churches, supervising and nurturing the growth of the young churches, leading the communities as they become established. This ministry of leadership manifests itself in a variety of activities: instruction, encouragement, reproof, visitation, appointment and supervision of some ministries, and so on—all that is demanded by the task of building up the body of Christ.

Procedures for Designation of Leadership

Scholars are not agreed about the manner in which Christian positions of leadership came into being in the early church. The recent trend has been toward the view that leaders emerged or were appointed in different ways in different communities with different church orders. Is there any evidence of a rite associated with this? Rather than discuss the question simply as a New Testament issue, it is best to look at it with an eye to subsequent developments.

The New Testament mentions the laying on of hands on four main occasions that could be important for consideration of the sacrament of orders (Acts 6:6; 13:3; 1 Tim. 4:14; 2 Tim. 1:6; cf. 1 Tim. 5:22). Scholars do not agree on the background of this Christian action, whether it was borrowed from a supposed Jewish rite of ordination or was derived from more general Old Testament influences or was primarily a Christian introduction. Nor is there agreement that in these instances the function and the meaning of the gesture are the same.

In Acts 6:6 the seven are chosen in Jerusalem by the whole body of disciples for appointment by the apostles, who pray and lay their hands on them. In Acts 13:1-3 Barnabas and Saul are set apart in the church at Antioch for a mission in obedience to a command of the Holy Spirit. After fasting and prayer they (the prophets and teachers? others?) lay hands on Barnabas and Saul and send them on their mission. They are understood to be sent out by the Holy Spirit (Acts 13:4). In neither of these cases do scholars agree about the function or the meaning of this imposition of hands. The second especially may have been no more than a blessing or the acknowledgment of a mandate (cf. Acts 14:26, which may interpret this rite in saying that they were commended to the grace of God for this work). One other text from Acts makes an interesting parallel. According to Acts 14:23, Paul and Barnabas appointed elders in every church with prayer and fasting. The mention of prayer and fasting and the absence of reference to the laying on of hands are worth noting, though it could well be that the latter is assumed.

Although there is also disagreement as to the meaning of the imposition of hands in the two instances from the Pastoral Epistles (1 Tim. 4:14; 2 Tim. 1:6), perhaps there is a firmer consensus that it is part of what may be called with greater confidence an ordination rite. The choice of Timothy may have been made by prophetic utterance (1 Tim. 1:18; 4:14; cf. Acts 13:2), and the core of the rite by which he was commissioned is presented as the laying on of hands done by the body of presbyters and by Paul (1 Tim. 4:14; 2 Tim. 1:6). Probably this was done in public (cf. 2 Tim. 2:2 "in the presence of many witnesses"). In or through this rite a spiritual gift, a gift of God, has been conferred. This gift is at the service of the Word, strengthening Timothy to bear public witness to the gospel (2 Tim. 1:8-14). He is warned "do not neglect" (1 Tim. 4:14); he is to "rekindle" this gift of God that he has received, and in fact the last two chapters of 1 Timothy envisage a broad range of responsibility for the apostolate and the community. It is a power that enables him to carry out his ministry, a charisma for the office that he has received. Here we have the makings of a later, explicitly "sacramental," understanding of such a rite.

No doubt these texts, partial as they are, represent different situations of time and place. They may not simply be collated in the expectation that the ensemble will provide the ordination rite of the early church or of Paul. Scholars maintain that the pattern of ministry, its understanding, and its mode of appointment or recognition, may be more varied than has been acknowledged in the past. In addition, as has been pointed out, the precise influences that led to the Christian use of the laying on of hands are unclear, and so the meaning of this action, and in some cases its role, are also unclear. It is not evident that some such form was always and everywhere used during the New Testament period or indeed for some time after it, nor is there any probability that all these elements were present on all occasions. But neither can it be proved from the evidence of the New Testament that such a form was exceptional. Elements do undoubtedly emerge from the church of the New Testament that will influence all later generations and that will in fact endure.

Subject to all the qualifications that have been made, the following may serve as a summary of some of the points from the New Testament that will

be prominent also in the subsequent tradition. In the appointment of ministers to positions of leadership, the whole local body of the church, and yet also particular ministers or groups of ministers, have an important role. The context of worship, of prayer and fasting, is mentioned, suggesting a liturgical setting and referring the ministry and appointment to it by God. Hands are laid on the candidate by a group within the church and/or by such individuals as Paul and Timothy. What the church does through its corporate action or through its leaders is regarded as inspired by the Holy Spirit, and through the church's choice and the liturgical action, God provides for the church and gives a spiritual gift that in some way endures. This interworking of God-church-special ministers is to be noted, as is the religious form of prayer-fasting-liturgical rite that is part of it.

— Post–New Testament Developments —

During the second century, episcopacy, presbyterate, and diaconate emerge almost everywhere as the most important ministries and form what will be the universal pattern. From the letter of Clement onward, correspondences are noted between the Jewish structure of authority and the Christian. Ignatius of Antioch already presents the bishop as an image of the Father, and here and elsewhere bishop, presbyter, and deacon are related in a variety of ways to God and to Jesus Christ. These comparisons manifest the conviction that the existence and the pattern of this ministry in the church are willed by God and mediate the authority and the power of God. Between God and the church is Jesus Christ, who came from God and from whom the power and the authority of the church originated historically. In the second and third centuries a consensus may not yet have emerged as to the way the church commissions these ministers. Tertullian is the first that we know to use the Latin words *ordo-ordinare-ordinatio* as part of the Christian terminology.

Patrick McGoldrick[37]

283 • CHRISTIAN MARRIAGE

In biblical cultures, the celebration of marriage was not a religious rite but a festival of common life involving family, friends, and community. Although Scripture contains some poetry for use in marriage celebrations (Song of Songs, Psalm 45), it does not describe a marriage as a religious ceremony. However, in both the Old and New Testaments the institution _of marriage is viewed as sacramental, as a symbol of the relationship between the Lord and the covenant community._

Christ's Headship in the Marriage Covenant

The covenant of marriage is a mutual commitment not only to create a life of equal partnership, but also to nurture and sustain. When a man and a woman covenant in Christian marriage, therefore, they commit themselves mutually to create rules of behavior that will nurture and sustain the marriage resulting from their covenant. For committed Christians, those rules are found by paying careful attention to their tradition.

The letter to the Ephesians provides scriptural rules for the living out of the marriage covenant. Its writer inherits a list of household duties traditional in the time and place. He critiques the cultural assumption of inequality in this list and instructs all Christians to "submit to one another out of reverence for Christ" (Eph. 5:21). This critique challenges the absolute authority of any one Christian group over another, of husbands over wives for instance. It establishes as the basic attitude required of all Christians, even in marriage, an awe of Christ and a giving way to one another because of this.

As all Christians are to give way one to another, it is hardly surprising that a wife is to give way to her husband, "as to the Lord" (Eph. 5:22). There is a surprise, however, in the instruction given to husbands, at least for those husbands who see themselves as lord and master of their wives and who appeal to the letter to the Ephesians to support this perspective. The instruction is not that the husband is the head of the wife, which is the preferred male reading, but that "the husband is the head of the wife _as_ [that is, in the same way as] Christ is the head of the church" (Eph. 5:23). How does Christ act as head of the church? The writer answers: "[He] gave himself up for her" (Eph. 5:25). It is an echo of a self-description that Jesus offers in Mark's gospel: "The Son of Man did not come to be served, but to serve" (Mark 10:45).

The Christ-way to exercise authority is to serve. Jesus constantly pointed out to his power-hungry disciples that in his kingdom a leader is one who serves (Luke 22:26). A husband who wishes to be head over his wife, or a wife who wishes to be head over her husband, in the way that Christ is head over the church, will be head by serving, by giving himself or herself up for the other.

Christlike headship is not absolute control of another human being. It is not making decisions and passing them on to another to be carried out. It is not reducing another human being to the status of chattel. To be head as Christ is head is to serve. The Christian head is called always to be the servant of others. As Markus Barth says beautifully, the Christian husband-head becomes "the first servant of his wife" (_Ephesians: Translation and Commentary on Chapters 4–6_ [Garden City, N.Y.: Doubleday, 1974], p. 618), and she becomes his first servant. One rule of behavior for the nurturing and sustaining of the covenant of Christian marriage is the rule of mutual service.

The letter to the Ephesians embraces another rule for behavior in Christian marriage, a great Jewish and Christian commandment: "Love your neighbor as yourself" (Lev. 19:18; Mark 12:31). Husbands are instructed that they "ought to love their wives as [or, for they are] their own bodies" (Eph. 5:28), and that the husband "who loves his wife loves himself" (Eph. 5:28). We can assume the same instruction is intended also for a wife. The Torah and gospel injunction to love one's neighbor as oneself applies in Christian marriage. As all Christians are to give way to one another and to love one another so also are the spouses in a Christian marriage. The rules of Christian behavior that will respect, nurture, and sustain the covenant and the community of marriage are easy to articulate: love of one's neighbor-spouse as oneself, love that is giving way, love that is mutual service, love that is abiding.

A Christian marriage is not just a wedding ceremony to be celebrated. It is also a loving and equal partnership of life to be lived. When they covenant in marriage, Christian spouses commit themselves to explore together in their married life the religious depth of their existence and to respond to that depth in light of Christian faith.

Discipleship in Christian Marriage

One of the most central affirmations of Christian faith is the affirmation of discipleship. _Disciple_ is an ever-present New Testament word, occurring some 250 times throughout the Gospels and Acts and always implying response to a call from the Lord. By definition disciples are learners, and the disciples of Christ are learners of mystery. They gather to explore together a triple mystery: the mystery of the one God who loves them and seeks to be loved by them; the mystery of the Christ in whom this God is revealed and whom God raised from the dead (1 Cor. 15:4; Acts 2:24); the mystery of the church in which they gather and which is the body of Christ (Eph. 1:22-23; Col. 1:18, 24). Spouses in a covenant marriage are called to be disciples of these mysteries and of their implications for their married life together.

Christian marriage does not separate spouses from life. It immerses them in life and confronts them with the ultimate questions of life and of death that are the stuff of religion. There are questions of joy in love and loving and the birth of new life; of pain in illness and suffering and alienation; of grief and fear in loneliness and isolation and death; of happiness in friends and beauty and success. Marriage demands that sense be made of these competing questions and many others like them. Christian marriage demands that sense be made of them in light of the shared Christian faith of the spouses.

As they find together adequate responses to the demands their married life imposes on them, Christian spouses mutually nurture one another into Christian discipleship. They learn together and they grow together in Christian maturity. The more they mature, the more they come to realize the ongoing nature of becoming married and of becoming a covenant sign. They come to realize that, though their marriage is already a sign of the covenant between Christ and his church, it is not yet the best sign it can be and is called to be. In Christian marriage, which is a life of ongoing Christian discipleship, even more than in secular marriage, the answer to the question of when two people are married is simple: thirty, forty, even fifty years later.

Christian Marriage As Sacrament

Religions are always on the lookout for the images of God and of God's relationship to the human world. In the Jewish prophets, we find an action image, known as the prophetic symbol. Jeremiah, for instance, buys an earthen pot, dashes it to the ground before a puzzled crowd, and explains to them what it is he is doing. "This is what the LORD Almighty says: I will smash this nation and this city just as this potter's jar is smashed" (Jer. 19:11).

The prophet clarifies the radical meaning of his actions, which clarifies the radical meaning of a prophetic symbol. As Jeremiah shattered his pot, so God shatters Jerusalem. The depth, meaning, and

reality symbolized by Jeremiah is not the shattering of a cheap pot but the shattering of Jerusalem and of the covenant relationship between Yahweh and Yahweh's people. The prophetic symbol is a representative action, that is, an action that proclaims, makes explicit, and celebrates in representation some other, more fundamentally meaningful reality.

Since the idea of their special relationship to Yahweh arising out of their mutual covenant was so central to the self-understanding of the Israelites, it is easy to predict that they would search out a human reality to symbolize the covenant relationship. It is equally easy, perhaps, to predict that the reality they would choose is the mutual covenant that is marriage. The prophet Hosea was the first to act in and speak of marriage as the prophetic symbol of the covenant.

At a superficial level, the marriage of Hosea and Gomer was like many other marriages. But at a deeper level, Hosea interpreted it as a prophetic symbol, proclaiming, making humanly explicit, and celebrating in representation, the covenant union between Yahweh and Israel. As Gomer left Hosea for other lovers, so also did Israel leave Yahweh for other gods. As Hosea waited for Gomer to return to him, and as he took her back without recrimination when she did return, so also did Yahweh with Israel. Hosea's human action is a prophetic symbol, a representative image, of God's divine action, an abiding love despite every provocation. In both covenants, the human and the divine, the covenant relationship had been violated. But Hosea's action both mirrors and reveals Yahweh's abiding love. It proclaims, makes explicit, and celebrates not only Hosea's faithfulness to his marriage covenant, but also Yahweh's faithfulness to Israel.

One basic meaning about Hosea and Yahweh is clear: Each is steadfastly faithful. There is also a clear, if mysterious, meaning about marriage. Besides being a universal human institution, it is also a religious and prophetic symbol proclaiming, making explicit, and celebrating in the human world the abiding union of Yahweh and Yahweh's people. Lived into from this perspective, lived into a faith as we might say today, marriage becomes a two-tiered reality. On one level it bespeaks the mutual covenant love of this man and this woman; on another, it represents and symbolizes the covenant love of Yahweh and Yahweh's people. First articulated by the prophet Hosea, this two-tiered view of marriage becomes the Christian view of marriage that we have found in the letter to the Ephesians. Jewish prophetic symbol becomes ultimately Christian sacrament, through which the church, the body of Christ, proclaims, makes explicit, and celebrates in representation that presence and action of God which is called grace.

To say that Christian marriage is a sacrament is to say that it is a prophetic symbol, a reality that has two tiers. On one tier it proclaims and makes explicit and celebrates the intimate community of life and love between a Christian man and a Christian woman. On another deeper tier, the religious and symbolic tier, it proclaims and makes explicit and celebrates the intimate community of life and love between Yahweh and Yahweh's people and between Christ and Christ's people, the church.

Michael G. Lawler[38]

284 ✦ Reconciliation and Priesthood

Reconciliation, as a result of Christian worship and community life, is an important New Testament concept. Reconciliation is mediated through the practice of the apostolic vocation of all believers and supremely through the priesthood of Jesus Christ. Although there is no specific rite of reconciliation in the New Testament, both baptism and the Lord's Supper, or Eucharist, have sacramental implications in the process of reconciliation through communion with God in Christ.

Reconciliation is an achievement, a process, and a goal in the life of the human community. It suggests the divisions and hostilities found among nations and peoples, within societies and families, between people and their environment, and even within each person. *Priesthood,* on the other hand, is a term that has meaning only within a religious frame of reference. Usually concerned with mediation or sacrifice, the term *priesthood* can assume a variety of meanings and is sometimes used in analogous or extended senses. To associate reconciliation with priesthood is to suggest that alienation and reconciliation pertain to humanity's relationship with God and that priesthood concerns some of the most decisive events in human life.

Reconciliation and priesthood are to be understood only in light of Jesus Christ and God's work in him. In Christ, God created the human family with one purpose in view: that each person should freely accept a share in eternal life and communion with the triune God. This creative purpose established

unity and peace as a perfection proper to human life (Eph. 1:3-10).

Rather than accept God's dominion in their lives, human beings have chosen to live in ways that declare their independence from God and his life-giving purpose. This causes alienation from God and accounts for the evil and hostility found in human life (Gen. 3). These effects lead to new rejections of God in an ongoing process that enmeshes all people (Rom. 3:9; 5:12). The term *sin* can refer to the cause, state, or results of this complex condition of evil and alienation.

Given this state of affairs, reconciliation necessarily requires the overcoming of sin by means of repentance and forgiveness and ultimately by an inner transformation that eliminates the tendency to sin and alienation (Jer. 31:33; Ezek. 36:25-28; Ps. 51:10). This could be accomplished only by God's special intervention, which took place through the incarnation of Jesus Christ. Because he was fully divine and fully human, Jesus was uniquely able to mediate between and draw together God and the human family. By his suffering, death, and resurrection, Jesus reconciled us to God and made possible the forgiveness of our sins and the hope of a human life marked by justice, peace, and unity (Rom. 5:1-11; Col. 1:19-22; 2 Cor. 5:18-19).

Although there is no question as to who Jesus was or the reconciliation he accomplished, the New Testament seldom uses the terms *mediator* or *priest* in speaking of him. The principal exception is the epistle to the Hebrews, which seeks to understand Jesus and his work in light of the Israelite priesthood, especially that of Melchizedek. This epistle and the background it assumes made it inevitable that later generations would also view Jesus Christ as priest of the new dispensation and consider his work as uniquely priestly.

Jesus Christ and his work of reconciliation were unique and effective for all people and all times (1 Tim. 2:5). Even so he required the service of others to extend the fruits of his reconciliation to people in every age and place (Matt. 28:18-20; Mark 16:15-16; Luke 24:47-49; John 20:21-23). Until the work of Christ is brought to its final perfection, sin and alienation remain urgent problems in human life. Christ relies on apostles and others to call people to repentance, forgiveness, and reconciliation. Required by Christ's explicit mandate, this missionary apostolate is an essential part of the life and ministry of the church. Members of the church must confront all forms of alienation and work to remedy them by preaching forgiveness and witnessing reconciliation. Giving to the poor, making peace between adversaries, teaching and interpreting the signs of the times, caring for the sick and dying, giving hospitality to the homeless, and especially working for justice and peace are important aspects of the missionary apostolate.

These activities are important and called for on their own terms. They must also interpret the meaning of human alienation and evil and point toward the reconciliation with God in Christ that all people need and are called to share. This witness will be credible only to the degree that the church shows forth a convincing example of reconciliation in its own life.

As the reconciliation with God Jesus Christ won for us is progressively shared with more people through the ministries of the Word and forgiveness, a visible community of reconciled people is assembled, the church (Eph. 2:11-22). The church has an intimate relationship with Christ, whose life and power it shares (Acts 1:8; 2:1-4; 1 Cor. 3:16; 12:27). The church increases as the preaching of the gospel prompts its hearers to repentance, faith, and a request for baptism. In baptism their past sins are forgiven, and they begin to share in the church's reconciled life (Acts 2:22-41; Rom. 6:3-11). In this context, baptism counts as the primary sacrament of reconciliation.

The church's supreme act of worship is the Eucharist. Nourished by the Word, the assembly celebrates in sacrament the mystery of Christ's passion, death, and resurrection. From this mystery the church draws its life and unity. At the Eucharist, the church most intensely realizes itself as a reconciled community, a priestly people that offers God the sacrifice of a holy life (1 Pet. 2:5, 9). From the perspective of the church's life, the Eucharist is the sacrament of its reconciliation, its communion with God in Christ.

Every effort must be made to assure that justice and peace characterize relationships within the church. Its own integrity and the credibility of its witness and preaching are at stake. A crisis occurs when a member of the church insists on living in a way that means abandonment of the commitments undertaken in baptism and inherent in the eucharistic life of the church. This kind of failure simultaneously involves the offender's personal responsibility, alienation from the church and its

eucharistic life, and a turning away from God. The offender's position is analogous to that of one as yet unconverted and unbaptized. Reconciliation is urgently needed.

The process required to bring this about takes into account many factors, notably the nature of the offense, the disposition of the offender and the adequacy of the repentance shown, and the requirements of the church body. Reconciliation normally involves a cooperative effort by the repentant offender and an authorized minister of the church; it is another evidence of the faithful love of Christ and the church.

Walter J. Woods[39]

285 ✦ BIBLIOGRAPHY: SACRED ACTIONS IN WORSHIP

Most of the books listed here treat the sacred actions of the church throughout history. However, all have pertinent sections on the scriptural foundations for various sacramental acts.

General

Champlin, Joseph M. *Special Signs of Grace*. Collegeville, Minn.: Liturgical Press, 1986. This volume is a brief introduction to all the sacred actions of the church.

Eller, Vernard. *In Place of Sacraments*. Grand Rapids: Wm. B. Eerdmans Publishing Co., 1992. This study presents a provocative and convincing discussion of the sacraments from a free-church position.

Staples, Rob L. *Outward Sign and Inward Grace*. Kansas City, Mo.: Beacon Hill Press of Kansas City, 1991. The author approaches sacred actions from a Wesleyan point of view; his work abounds with New Testament references and scriptural interpretation.

The Eucharist (Lord's Supper)

Cabié, Robert. *The Church at Prayer*. Vol. 2, *The Eucharist*. Collegeville, Minn.: Liturgical Press, 1986. In addition to historical material, this work presents the New Testament understanding of the Lord's Table as "Supper" and speaks to the issue of the Jewish *b*ᵉ*rakhah,* or blessing prayer, as a connecting link to the church's early eucharistic prayer. In addition, the author develops a picture of the New Testament house church.

Crockett, William B. *Eucharist: Symbol of Transformation*. New York: Pueblo Publishing Co., 1989. This work deals with the Eucharist in the New Testament and addresses the tradition of the Last Supper, the relationship between Jesus' death and the Eucharist, and the link between Communion and community.

Léon-Dufour, Xavier. *Sharing the Eucharistic Bread*. Mahwah, N.J.: Paulist Press, 1987. A thorough treatment of the eucharistic assemblies of the early Christians, this book examines the various traditions concerning the final meal of Jesus.

Schmemann, Alexander. *The Eucharist*. Crestwood, N.Y.: St. Vladimir's Seminary Press, 1988. The author roots all aspects of the worship of the church in the New Testament Scriptures. Although this material is developed from an Eastern Orthodox perspective, it will prove helpful to all Christians because of its broad scope and biblical basis.

Baptism

Beasley-Murray, G. R. *Baptism in the New Testament*. Grand Rapids: Wm. B. Eerdmans Publishing Co., 1978. An exceptionally thorough study, this volume discusses all the references to baptism in the New Testament.

Kavanagh, Aidan. *The Shape of Baptism: The Rite of Christian Initiation*. New York: Pueblo Publishing Co., 1978. In this study, the author traces the history of baptism through Judaism and into the New Testament period.

Osborn, Kenan B. *The Christian Sacraments of Initiation*, Mahwah, N.J.: Paulist Press, 1987. The author deals with the New Testament evidence for baptism, confirmation, and the Eucharist as three phases of initiation.

Stevick, Daniel. *Baptismal Moments, Baptismal Meaning*. New York: Church Hymnal Corp., 1987. In a sketch of the historical development of baptism, the writer summarizes New Testament teaching on this issue.

Confirmation and Anointing with the Spirit

Austin, Gerard. *The Rite of Confirmation: Anointing with the Spirit*. New York: Pueblo Publishing Co., 1985. This work addresses the issue of initiation and the anointing of the Spirit in the New Testament. The author argues that, as Jesus was anointed with the Spirit, so are his followers.

Anointing with Oil

Ziegler, John J. *Let Them Anoint the Sick*. Collegeville, Minn.: Liturgical Press, 1987. This work contains a chapter on anointing the sick in the first four centuries, including a discussion of anointing in the New Testament period.

Marriage

Mackin, Theodore. *The Marital Sacrament*. Mahwah, N.J.: Paulist Press, 1989. In addition to discussing marriage throughout Christian history, this book contains two excellent chapters on marriage as viewed in the Hebrew Scriptures and on the New Testament sources for early Christian understandings of marriage.

Stevenson, Kenneth W. *To Join Together: The Rite of Marriage*. New York: Pueblo Publishing Co., 1987. This book discusses both the pre-Christian foundation of marriage and the early Christian practice of marriage.

Reconciliation

Dallen, James. *The Reconciling Community*. New York: Pueblo Publishing Co., 1986. This volume tackles the issues of confession, penance, and reconciliation; it begins with an excellent treatment of these questions in the New Testament and early Christian literature.

Osborne, Kenan B. *Reconciliation and Justification*. Mahwah, N.J.: Paulist Press, 1970. The first two chapters deal with Jesus himself as the primary "sacrament" of reconciliation and with his life, death, and resurrection as the source of reconciliation.

Works Cited

GENERAL NOTE: All of the previously published material in this volume has been adapted.

[1] Janice E. Leonard, *I Will Be Their God: Understanding the Covenant* (Chicago: Laudemont Press, 1992), *passim.*

[2] J. D. Crichton, "A Theology of Worship," in Cheslyn Jones, Geoffrey Wainwright, and Edward Yarnold, eds., *The Study of Liturgy* (New York: Oxford University Press, 1978), 3–29, passim.

[3] Donald L. Williams, "The Israelite Cult and Christian Worship," in James M. Efird, ed., *The Use of the Old Testament in the New and Other Essays: Studies in Honor of William Franklin Stinespring* (Durham, N.C.: Duke University Press, 1972), 110–124.

[4] Ralph P. Martin, "Worship," *International Standard Bible Encyclopedia,* vol. 4 (Grand Rapids: Wm. B. Eerdmans Publishing Co., 1988), 1117–1123.

[5] Geoffrey W. Bromiley, "Worship," *Zondervan Pictorial Encyclopedia of the Bible,* vol. 5 (Grand Rapids: Zondervan Publishing House, 1975), 984–990.

[6] Charles L. Feinberg, "Tabernacle," ibid., 572–577, 582–583.

[7] Harold C. Stigers, "Temple, Jerusalem," 624–631.

[8] Robert E. Webber, *Worship Old and New* (Grand Rapids: Zondervan Publishing House, 1982), 25–27.

[9] Walter Elwell, "Worship," *Baker Encyclopedia of the Bible* vol. 2 (Grand Rapids: Baker Book House, 1989), 2164–2166.

[10] William White, "Synagogue," *Zondervan Pictorial Encyclopedia,* vol. 5, 555–566.

[11] Ralph P. Martin, *Worship in the Early Church* (Grand Rapids: Wm. B. Eerdmans Publishing Company, 1974), 24–27.

[12] Carmine Di Sante, *Jewish Prayer: The Origins of the Christian Liturgy* (Mahwah, N.J.: Paulist Press, 1991), 13–23.

[13] Vincent Branick, *The House Church in the Writings of Paul* (Collegeville, Minn.: Liturgical Press, 1989), 96–113.

[14] Richard A. Bodey, "Ministry," *Zondervan Pictorial Encyclopedia,* vol. 4, 239–240.

[15] Di Sante, *Jewish Prayer,* 189–195.

[16] Hobart A. Freeman, "Festivals," *Wycliffe Bible Encyclopedia,* vo. 6 (Chicago: Moody Press, 1975), 599–605.

[17] William B. Coker, "Solemn Assembly," *Zondervan Pictorial Encyclopedia,* vol. 5, 469.

[18] Henry Waterman, "Lord's Day, The," ibid., vol. 3, 961–964.

[19] Harold M. Best and David Huttar, "Music; Musical Instruments," vol. 4, 311–316.

[20] Ibid., 316–319.

[21] Ralph P. Martin, "New Testament Hymns: Background and Development," *Expository Times,* vol. 94, February 1983, 132–136.

[22] Lorman M. Petersen, "Banner," *Zondervan Pictorial Encyclopedia,* vol. 1, 461–463.

[23] J. Rodman Williams, "Baptism in the Holy Spirit," *Dictionary of Pentecostal and Charismatic Movements* (Grand Rapids: Zondervan Publishing House, 1988), 535–537. Adapted.

[24] Patrick H. Alexander, "Slain in the Spirit," ibid., 789–791. Adapted.

[25] Howard M. Ervin, *Spirit Baptism* (Peabody, Mass.: Hendrickson, 1987), 101–104.

[26] Guy B. Funderburk, "Doxology," *Zondervan Pictorial Encyclopedia* vol. 2, 161–162.

[27] Richard A. Bodey, "Preacher, Preaching," ibid., vol. 4, 844–845. Adapted.

[28] William White, "Lord's Prayer, The," ibid., vol. 3, 972–977. Adapted.

[29] Oscar Cullmann, *Early Christian Worship* (London: SCM Press, 1966), 14–17.

[30] Gerald F. Hawthorne, "Lord's Supper," *Zondervan Pictorial Encyclopedia,* vol. 3, 978–983.

[31] Stanley B. Marrow, "Eucharist in Scripture," *New Dictionary of Sacramental Worship* (Collegeville, Minn.: Liturgical Press, 1990), 393–397.

[32] Jakob Jocz, "Passover," *Zondervan Pictorial Encyclopedia,* vol. 4, 605–611.

[33] Daniel J. Harrington, "Baptism in Scripture," *New Dictionary,* 83–87.

[34] Thomas A. Marsh, "Confirmation, Biblical," 254–260.

[35] Robert D. Culver, "Foot Washing," *Zondervan Pictorial Encyclopedia,* vol. 2, 588.

[36] John J. Ziegler, "Anointing," *New Dictionary,* 49–50.

[37] Patrick McGoldrick, "Orders, Sacrament of," ibid., 896–899.

[38] Michael G. Lawler, "Marriage, Sacrament of," ibid., 808–810.

[39] Walter G. Woods, "Reconciliation and Priesthood," ibid., 1034–1036.

Index